RESEARCHING SEXUAL BEHAVIOR

THE KINSEY INSTITUTE SERIES

John Bancroft, *General Editor*

Volume I
MASCULINITY/FEMININITY: *Basic Perspectives*
Edited by
June Machover Reinisch, Leonard A. Rosenblum,
and Stephanie A. Sanders

Volume II
HOMOSEXUALITY/HETEROSEXUALITY:
Concepts of Sexual Orientation
Edited by
David P. McWhirter, Stephanie A. Sanders,
and June Machover Reinisch

Volume III
ADOLESCENCE AND PUBERTY
Edited by
John Bancroft and June Machover Reinisch

Volume IV
AIDS AND SEX: *An Integrated Biomedical and Biobehavioral Approach*
Edited by
Bruce Voeller, June Machover Reinisch,
and Michael Gottlieb

Volume V
RESEARCHING SEXUAL BEHAVIOR:
Methodological Issues
Edited by
John Bancroft

RESEARCHING SEXUAL BEHAVIOR

Methodological Issues

Edited by John Bancroft

Indiana University Press
Bloomington • Indianapolis

© 1997 by The Kinsey Institute for Research in Sex,
Gender, and Reproduction
All rights reserved

No part of this book may be reproduced or utilized in
any form or by any means, electronic or mechanical,
including photocopying and recording, or by any
information storage and retrieval system, without
permission in writing from the publisher. The
Association of American University Presses' Resolution
on Permissions constitutes the only exception to this
prohibition.

The paper used in this publication meets the minimum
requirements of American National Standard for
Information Sciences—Permanence of Paper for Printed
Library Materials, ANSI Z39.48-1984.

Manufactured in the United States of America

Library of Congress Cataloging-in-Publication Data

Researching sexual behavior : methodological issues /
  edited by John Bancroft.
       p.   cm. — (The Kinsey Institute series ; v. 5)
   Papers presented at an international meeting
hosted by The Kinsey Institute for Research in Sex,
Gender, and Reproduction.
   Includes bibliographical references and index.
   ISBN 0-253-33339-3 (cl : alk paper)
   1. Sexology—Research—Congresses.   I. Bancroft,
John.   II. Kinsey Institute for Research in Sex,
Gender, and Reproduction.   III. Series.
HQ60.R47   1997
306.7'07'2—dc21   97-11417

1   2   3   4   5   02   01   00   99   98   97

Contents

Introduction and Overview   ix
JOHN BANCROFT

PART 1: Linking Research to Policy   1

DIANE DI MAURO
Sexuality Research in the United States   3

RICHARD G. PARKER
International Perspectives on Sexuality Research   9

Discussion   23

PART 2: Methodology for the Individual   35

CHARLES F. TURNER, HEATHER G. MILLER, AND SUSAN M. ROGERS
Survey Measurement of Sexual Behavior: Problems and Progress   37

ALAIN GIAMI, WITH HÉLÈNE OLOMUCKI AND JANINE DE POPLAVSKY
Surveying Sexuality and AIDS: Interviewer Attitudes and Representations   61

Discussion   78

PART 3: Methodology in Specific Contexts   85

FREYA L. SONENSTEIN, LEIGHTON KU, AND JOSEPH H. PLECK
Measuring Sexual Behavior among Teenage Males in the United States   87

JOHN PETERSON AND JOSEPH A. CATANIA
Item Nonresponse in the National AIDS Behavioral Surveys among African American and White Respondents   106

JOSEPH A. CATANIA, DIANE BINSON, JOHN PETERSON, AND JESSE CANCHOLA
The Effects of Question Wording, Interviewer Gender, and Control on Item Response by African American Respondents   110

FABIO SABOGAL, DIANE BINSON, AND JOSEPH A. CATANIA
Researching Sexual Behavior: Methodological Issues for Hispanics   114

ALEX CARBALLO-DIÉGUEZ
Sexual Research with Latino Men Who Have Sex with Men: Methodological Issues   134

LYNDA S. DOLL
Sexual Behavior Research: Studying Bisexual Men and Women
and Lesbians — 145

Discussion — 159

PART 4: Change in Behavior over Time — 183

ALFRED SPIRA
Pooling Information from Repeated Population Surveys: Its Use in
the Evaluation of the Efficacy of AIDS Prevention Campaigns — 185

FRANÇOISE DUBOIS-ARBER, B. SPENCER, AND A. JEANNIN
Methodological Problems in Trend Analysis of Sexual Behavior — 196

Discussion — 213

PART 5: Retrospective versus Daily Assessment — 225

CYNTHIA A. GRAHAM AND JOHN BANCROFT
*A Comparison of Retrospective Interview Assessment versus
Daily Ratings of Sexual Interest and Activity in Women* — 227

J. DENNIS FORTENBERRY, HEATHER CECIL, GREGORY D. ZIMET,
AND DONALD P. ORR
*Concordance between Self-Report Questionnaires and Coital Diaries
for Sexual Behaviors of Adolescent Women with Sexually
Transmitted Infections* — 237

Discussion — 250

PART 6: Participation Bias — 259

THEO G. M. SANDFORT
Sampling Male Homosexuality — 261

ANNE M. JOHNSON AND ANDREW COPAS
Assessing Participation Bias — 276

Discussion — 288

PART 7: Researching Sexual Networks — 297

STUART MICHAELS
Integrating Quantitative and Qualitative Methods in the Study of Sexuality — 299

J. RICHARD UDRY
A Research Design for Studying Romantic Partners — 309

Discussion — 320

PART 8: Researching Sexual Interactions   *339*

ULRICH CLEMENT
Coding Interactional Sexual Scripts   *341*

Discussion   *346*

PART 9: Conclusions   *353*

JOHN M. KENNEDY
Sex Surveys in the Context of Survey Research   *355*

ANKE A. EHRHARDT
Gender   *361*

BARBARA VANOSS MARÍN
Cross-Cultural Issues   *363*

PART 10: Postconference Papers   *367*

CAROL JENKINS
Qualitative Methods in Sex Research in Papua New Guinea   *369*

ANN STUEVE AND LYDIA N. O'DONNELL
*Item Nonresponse to Questions about Sex, Substance Use, and School:
Results from the Reach for Health Study of African American
and Hispanic Young Adolescents*   *376*

EDWARD O. LAUMANN AND L. PHILIP SCHUMM
Measuring Social Networks Using Samples: Is Network Analysis
Relevant to Survey Research?   *390*

JOSEPH A. CATANIA
*A Model for Investigating Respondent-Interviewer Relationships
in Sexual Surveys*   *417*

Contributors   *437*

Index   *445*

Introduction and Overview
JOHN BANCROFT

The last 10 years have seen an unprecedented surge of survey research into sexual behavior, driven predominantly by concern over human immunodeficiency virus (HIV) infection and acquired immune deficiency syndrome (AIDS) and the need to establish the frequency of behaviors which might facilitate spread of the virus. In 1989, Charles Turner and his colleagues pointed out that "in the face of the epidemic, conducting and reporting studies has assumed a higher priority than the refinement of methodology."[1] The following year Joe Catania and his colleagues[2] published a comprehensive review of the relevant methodological issues. They cited a substantial body of literature but nevertheless concluded that crucial issues remained to be resolved if research was to be effective.

Seven years and several large surveys later it is pertinent to ask whether this is still the case. There has undoubtedly been a huge international effort, with most if not all research groups tackling urgent issues before finalizing their methods. Yet there are many differences in method across the studies, and in most cases the generalizability of such methods across contrasting cultures is most uncertain. What can we learn from all this? Would these research groups use the same methods again? What would they now do differently?

From April 26 to April 28, 1996, the Kinsey Institute for Research in Sex, Gender, and Reproduction at Indiana University hosted a small international meeting to address these issues. The participants included representatives from most of the recent large-scale surveys in the United States and Europe, as well as other persons with a wide range of research experience and methodological expertise. A principal objective of the meeting was to promote discussion among these researchers. The meeting was made possible by a grant from the Ford Foundation.

The choice of the Kinsey Institute as the venue was appropriate. Whereas Alfred Kinsey's research can justifiably be criticized for its sam-

---

1. Turner, C. F., Miller, H. G., & Moses, L. E. (Eds.). (1989). *AIDS, sexual behavior, and intravenous drug use.* Washington, DC: National Academy Press.
2. Catania, J. A., Gibson, D., Chitwood, D., & Coates, T. J. (1990). Methodological problems in AIDS behavioral research: Influences on measurement error and participation bias in studies of sexual behavior. *Psychological Bulletin, 108*(3), 339–362.

pling methods, the interview method used by him and his small group of trained researchers stands up to careful scrutiny. Indeed, it is questionable whether modern survey methods for studying sexual behavior, using market researchers with usually no more than one or two days' training in asking questions about sex, can compare with Kinsey's exceptionally skillful interview technique. It is also remarkable that Kinsey was able to collect such a large amount of information from his interviewees; the Kinsey interview database remains the most comprehensive in its scope, and researchers are still using it to carry out secondary analyses.

Numerous methodological issues could have been addressed; in planning the program we could choose only a few. These, however, included key issues relating to both qualitative and quantitative research methodology, issues which not only are of crucial importance in themselves but also led to discussion of broader issues. Each contributor prepared a paper (sometimes with colleagues) which was circulated to all participants before the meeting. This procedure allowed each presentation to be limited to about 10 minutes, leaving most of the program time for discussion. The discussion was recorded and subsequently transcribed. Whereas the participants were aware of each other's work, it was the first opportunity for many of them to discuss their research face to face. Not surprisingly, the discussion adds considerable depth and breadth to the papers.

This volume is the published result of the meeting. The papers included are, in most cases, revised and expanded versions of those circulated before the meeting. Occasionally this has led to some discontinuity between the paper as printed here and the discussion which followed. The discussion has been edited, however, and in most respects stands on its own. The reader will quickly discover the extent to which the papers presented led to important issues in discussion. A few participants who did not present papers during the meeting wrote papers afterward which have been included in this volume.

We start in part 1 with overview presentations by Diane di Mauro and Richard Parker. Di Mauro, from the Social Science Research Council, writes about the Sexuality Research Assessment Project, which she directed and which was funded by the Ford Foundation. She emphasizes the extent to which sex research in the United States is fragmented, with little contact or awareness between different disciplinary groups. In addition, most sex research has been problem driven, motivated by specific concerns such as teenage pregnancy and sexually transmitted disease. As a consequence, we know much less about "normal" sexuality than we do about the problems associated with it. Her project also highlighted the importance of developing and using qualitative as well as quantitative methodologies. One major consequence of this assessment project has been establishment of the Social Science Research Council's Sexuality Research Fellowship

Program, which di Mauro now directs. It too is funded by the Ford Foundation, which is playing a crucial role at this difficult time for sex research.

Parker brings a cross-cultural perspective to the volume. HIV-related concerns outside Europe and the United States—in Africa, for example, where the epidemic is of horrendous proportions—confronted researchers with the specter of the research community's abysmal lack of knowledge about sexual conduct in many parts of the world. The story Parker tells is salutary. The first wave of enthusiasm for filling the data gap reflected the naive but prevalent assumption that to find out about high-risk sexual behavior one simply had to ask about it, using the same approach in Papua New Guinea that appeared to work in New York. The initial program of studies sponsored by the World Health Organization's Global Program on AIDS soon led to disillusionment and skepticism. Sexuality was more complex than had been realized, at least by those who had only recently started to study it. Before starting to measure sexual behavior, one needs to understand the meanings associated with it, meanings which vary considerably from culture to culture. That has led to a paradox which in some respects is captured in this volume. Outside North America and Europe, sex researchers are now grappling with fundamental questions about the meaning of sexuality which can only be addressed using qualitative methods and, as Anke Ehrhardt stresses in her concluding statement (in part 9), with a theoretical framework to guide them. This was well illustrated in a conference organized by Parker, "Reconceiving Sexuality," that was held in Rio de Janeiro a few days before our Kinsey meeting. It also will result in a volume. In North America and Europe, the recent wave of research into sexual behavior has been driven by a need to identify and measure high-risk behaviors which might influence the course of the epidemic. As Turner and colleagues pointed out in 1989, this massive research program has been implemented before the key methodological issues have been resolved, and the point that surfaces repeatedly throughout this volume, at least in the discussions, is that the key methodological issues are unlikely to be resolved without first formulating appropriate theoretical models.

The discussion in part 1 focused first on how we can train people to work effectively in this highly interdisciplinary field. It is questionable whether sexology will ever establish itself as a discipline in the conventional sense, because its coverage is simply too broad. But it will not make progress if its researchers approach sexuality with training limited by a traditional discipline. This is a challenge, and it is not unique to sexuality. We see similar needs emerging in the related area of gender studies. It also became clear in the discussion that our training as researchers did not equip us to deal effectively with policymakers, who in the majority of cases will determine whether our research is funded. The incongruence between the aims of scientific researchers and policymakers is striking and cannot be denied or ignored. This challenge led to a lively discussion about value-free or value-laden research. The participants ranged from those like Parker, who was quite clear that his research was driven by his own political agenda, and those like Colin Williams, who saw his role as a strict academic, establishing, as best he could, the truth about human sexuality "warts and all." Probably the majority of us acknowledged the extent to which our values shaped our research agendas, but whether the majority of us are clear about the extent to which this can distort our findings is another matter. As the current director of the Kinsey Institute, I am particularly sensitive to this issue. Alfred Kinsey was scrupulous about being nonjudgmental and value-free in his approach to his study of the human sexual condition. This was typical of the rhetoric of science at the time. But Kinsey's lack of explicitly stated values has allowed others to attribute values to him, usually with no grounds other than their own political expediency. Yet it doesn't take long, when reading Kinsey's writings, to see how his compassion was stirred by what he found, and his disdain for the social system which fostered the often severe repression of the "sexual nonconformist" was all too apparent. He was a friend of the underdog, but there is absolutely no reason to believe that he had a political agenda to undermine the social structure of the United States, as is often attributed to him. One wonders whether, if he had lived longer, he would have stated his own values more explicitly. All of us working in the field today should ponder on this and consider our own positions.

In part 2 we focus on the process of obtaining information from the subject, in particular the interview. Charles Turner and colleagues present the intriguing finding that people are more prepared to reveal sensitive information when interviewed by a computer than when interviewed by a person. The reasons why this should be so are not yet clear, but they will be of considerable interest. In a computerized world this appears counterintuitive; the computer seems like the obvious way to lose control over sensitive personal information. But not so, apparently. Then Alain Giami and colleagues confront us with the all-too-human interviewer, with his or her own attitudes, prejudices, and expectations, an aspect of survey research which is seldom considered. These two papers were followed by a fascinating discussion on the nature of the interaction between the interviewer and interviewee and how, in sex research, this interaction may inevitably have a sexual component to it. It was during this discussion that the first mention of a need for a theory of the interview was voiced.

In part 3 we go beyond the universal interview and consider specific groups and how they might vary in their response to interviewing, and hence need adaptations of method. Freya Sonenstein and colleagues reassure us that adolescent males, who have usually been ignored because they have been assumed to be inaccessible or unreliable, are no worse than adolescent females in their preparedness to participate in surveys. They discuss, among several important methodological aspects, the crucial issue of parental consent for this age group.

Joseph Catania, John Peterson, and their colleagues, in two papers, use data from the National AIDS Behavioral Survey, conducted in 1990–1991, to compare African Americans with white Americans. One paper focuses on nonresponse as a potential indicator of response bias. What can we learn from the questions which people decline to answer, and who declines to answer? Overall, few differences between ethnic groups were found; those that did arise involved mainly sensitive questions in the older age groups. The other paper focuses on three aspects of the interview: the gender of the interviewer, the use of enhanced questions to try to increase the reporting of sensitive information, and the effect of allowing the respondent to choose the gender of the interviewer. These researchers found no differences related to ethnicity, and any differences they did find were apparent only in the men, who showed an increased tendency to respond to enhanced questions.

Fabio Sabogal and colleagues and Alex Carballo-Diéguez consider methodological issues related to Hispanic American heterosexuals and homosexuals, respectively. Here the impact of ethnicity was clear and marked. It was also apparent that the effects of ethnicity were more marked in Hispanic Americans of lower socioeconomic status and less acculturation within the United States. Interview as well as recruitment methods obviously need to be modified for such groups if valid results are to be expected.

The final paper in part 3, by Lynda Doll, reviews the literature for studies of bisexual men and women and lesbian women. She concludes that studies of bisexuality have been overwhelmingly quantitative, often with inconsistencies of definition making cross-study comparisons difficult. Studies of lesbian women, by contrast, have been predominantly qualitative in their approach.

The discussion on these papers dealt with various methodological points but was most vigorous in debating the purposes of obtaining a "representative random sample" of bisexual men or women. The view was expressed that such samples may be obtained "for the sake of it" without the "representativeness" necessarily being meaningful. This found the survey researchers in the group on the defensive. There was also discussion of the use of large samples to identify and reinterview subsamples of specific interest. This raised the vexed issue of confidentiality and protection of the interviewee; most of the recent large surveys have destroyed any means of recontacting the subjects in order to protect them, thereby precluding any follow-up study.

In part 4, European participants Alfred Spira of France and Françoise Dubois-Arber and colleagues of Switzerland consider the fundamental issue of using survey data to measure change in behavior over time. Spira focuses mainly on controlled evaluations of behavior change, whereas Dubois-Arber considers the use of repeated surveys in the same population. Various complexities, such as the change in meaning of words or questions over time, were revealed. In the discussion that followed, two of their themes received particular attention. First, given the need for methodological improvement, it is unlikely that we would want to continue to use the same method as we learn better methods, but if we change the method we lose comparability. Turner provided a solution for this problem, at least in large surveys: continue to use the old method in a subsample while introducing a new method for the main sample. Second, is it ethical to do nothing in a control group? Is it ethical not to, if doing nothing is the only way to demonstrate efficacy? Can there be guidelines which enable the researcher to stop the controlled comparison as soon as a conclusive answer is obtainable? Once again the matter of lack of theory guiding such studies was raised.

In part 5, two papers present the use of daily diaries as a method of monitoring behavior. Cynthia Graham and John Bancroft's study involved sterilized women in Edinburgh, Scotland, and Manila, Philippines, who volunteered to take oral contraceptives in a placebo-controlled evaluation of their effects. The data Graham presented was from the baseline period. Dennis Fortenberry and colleagues' study involves adolescent females who had attended a sexually transmitted disease clinic. In both cases a comparison of daily ratings of behaviors and retrospective recall of those behaviors for the same time period are presented. Interestingly, Graham used this technique as a means of validating the retrospective method, whereas Fortenberry, who sees the diary as the only way of studying certain specific events, used the retrospective questionnaire as validation. Both have a point. In any case, it is probably fair to say that the potential value of daily diaries in sex research has not yet been realized.

Part 6 deals with the central issue of participation bias. Theo Sandfort considers this issue with respect to sampling homosexual men. Whereas it may be virtually impossible to obtain a representative sample of homosexual men, that is no reason for ignoring the sampling issue. He demonstrates, with data from several studies, that different types of samples produce very different results. This may not matter as long as one is clear about the characteristics of the sample in question and the purpose of the study and is cautious about generalizing from it. He points out that convenience samples of gay men have often led to the conclusion that gay men are much more promiscuous than in fact they typically are. He also stresses the importance of definition: surveying men who have sex with men is very different from surveying men who regard themselves as gay or homosexual. Anne Johnson and Andrew Copas, from the British survey group, consider the various factors that might influence nonparticipation; even when good representative samples are obtained there are possible ways that the nonresponders might be relevant to the main conclusions. Clearly more careful research on this critical issue is needed. The discussion that followed considered the use of payment as an inducement to participate and how the effectiveness and acceptability of such inducement might vary cross-culturally. The question of why people participate rather than refuse was also considered, leading to a discussion of the impact of the motivation of the researcher on the results, an extension of the earlier discussion on interviewer influences.

Part 7 turns to the investigation of sexual networks. Two contrasting methods are described. Stuart Michaels reports on an ongoing study in Chicago in which respondents are asked about members of their sexual networks. Richard Udry describes the remarkable Add Health survey of adolescent schoolchildren. By interviewing large numbers of children from the same schools, total networks of romantic, sexual, and other types of relationships can be identified, and he estimated that they had gathered data on about 20,000 relationships in this fashion. The first approach is called egocentric, centering on the individual. The latter approach is sociocentric, focusing on the social group or community under study (i.e., the school). Michaels's paper also described an interesting combination of quantitative and qualitative methods. He has taken specific communities within Chicago and surveyed representative samples in a quantitative manner. Then he has investigated these communities by interviewing key and influential community figures to obtain a "qualitative" description of the community which may help to interpret the quantitative data obtained. The discussion that followed revealed that several participants, while recognizing the fundamental importance of sexual networks, had difficulty grasping the methods of analyzing them. (See also Laumann and Schumm's paper in part 10.)

Part 8 contains one paper, from Ulrich Clement, on the analysis of sexual narratives or scripts. This is an interesting approach to content analysis of narrative descriptions of specific sexual interactions that allows assessment of varying dimensions of the interaction. This approach, though extremely time consuming, does offer a method for identifying different patterns of sexual interaction and their gender-specific characteristics.

Part 9 concludes the proceedings of our meeting with three summary statements by participants who were asked to consider certain aspects of the meeting as it progressed and then comment at the end. John Kennedy, commenting from the perspective of a survey researcher, is reassuringly positive about how seriously sex researchers are tackling the key methodological issues. Anke Ehrhardt considers gender and finds that it did not receive the attention it deserves at the meeting. Finally, Barbara Marín considers the impact of culture, which perhaps was considered more systematically than gender.

The postconference papers in part 10 were responses to a variety of needs identified during the meeting. Carol Jenkins, who has researched sexual behavior in Papua New Guinea, confronts us with the sobering reality of working in a multilingual, largely illiterate society. Ann Stueve and Lydia O'Donnell complement the paper of Peterson and Catania (in part 3) by reporting data on nonresponse from their study of African American and Hispanic American adolescents living in Brooklyn. They reassuringly report that nonresponse rates are not disturbingly high, though higher in boys than in girls, and their repeated testing of the same adolescents over time suggests a volatility of responding or nonresponding which may be a state-dependent characteristic of this age group; it will need to be taken into consideration when interpreting findings from such studies. Ed Laumann responded to the obvious bewilderment that many of us revealed about network analysis by preparing, with Philip Schumm, a comprehensive description of this approach. This paper is most useful, though it is noteworthy that, as yet, there are few examples of analyses of sexual networks. These authors emphasize, however, that if network analysis is to be useful, it must be part of the basic design of any study and not tacked on. Finally, Joe Catania took seriously the repeated calls for a "theory of the interview" and wrote a useful response. He comments that whereas one may criticize the seat-of-the-pants quality of much of the methodology in recent sex research, "work is continuing at a pace that is somewhat unprecedented historically."

I believe this volume illustrates Catania's point. We are grappling with very fundamental issues, some for the first time, and it is easy to say that such work should have been done before large and costly surveys were implemented. In some respects, there was research into sexual behavior prior to AIDS which has not been fully utilized by the group of new sex researchers which the epidemic has recruited. We should nevertheless learn an important lesson from these recent years. If the academic community had given the importance to the serious study of normal human sexuality that most other aspects of human behavior have received, we would have established the methodologies that we needed before being hit by the HIV/AIDS epidemic. The passing of the AIDS crisis is not in sight, but we must make sure that the unprecedented amount of research into sexual behavior that it has evoked will leave us with a vigorous and ongoing scientific study of the human sexual condition in all its aspects. Then next time—and with something as fundamental as sex there will be a next time—we will be better prepared.

Part 1.
Linking Research to Policy

Sexuality Research in the United States

DIANE DI MAURO

The Sexuality Research Assessment Project final report, *Sexuality Research in the United States* (di Mauro, 1995), was published last year. I'd like to thank many of you personally for such helpful input and feedback during the preparation of that report as I now find myself in the odd position of reporting back to you what you originally reported to me. I hope to provide you with an interesting and informative summary overview of the findings of that report and an update on what has transpired since publication—specifically the initiation of a new fellowship program at the Social Science Research Council, the Sexuality Research Fellowship Program.

The assessment report was commissioned by representatives of the U.S. donor community in recognition of the need to expand the knowledge base about human sexuality and to respond to insufficient funding for sexuality research by the private sector. Initiated in February 1993, the project had as its primary objective to provide an overview of sexuality research as it is concurrently conducted in the social and behavioral sciences, assessing the "who, what, when, and where" of research on sexuality topics and issues in various disciplines. The report highlights the important research trends, priority topic areas and issues, obstacles, and gaps in sexuality research, some of which I'll touch on in this presentation.

If I were to briefly characterize the current status of sexuality research and provide a critique of it, I would have to say that it is fragmented across many social science disciplines with little integrative or collaborative efforts evident and that much research focuses on sexuality as represented by risk behaviors. By this very definition, sexuality is negatively viewed as the source of problems and disease rather than an integral part of human development and health. The report makes a strong case that the usefulness of this research should not be limited to a problem-solving approach, even though sexuality research can provide crucial information and provide a greater understanding of such challenges as teenage pregnancy, HIV/AIDS, and sexual coercion. This problematic approach is quite evident when reviewing the published literature—for example, what we know about childhood sexuality is what the literature on child abuse tells us. What we know about adolescent sexuality is what the literature on teenage pregnancy and HIV/AIDS tells us. What we know about the sexuality of the college-age population is HIV/AIDS and coercive sexuality, such as date rape. After that, adult sexuality is barely represented in the literature. Moreover, we have very little understanding of what constitutes sexual health, what motivates sexual behavior, how sexual norms are developed and sustained, and how these evolve over time. Efforts to enact a more positive research agenda would significantly help to promote a much-needed view of sexuality not as a source of problems and risks but as a domain of well-being and human potential. With a model of sexual health and human development as the framework, research inquiries regarding public health concerns and current public debates can be more easily addressed, including such issues as sexual harassment, coercion, and appropriate educational efforts to stem HIV.

To adequately understand the current situation of sexuality research in the social and behavioral sciences—and especially the gaps and obstacles—it is necessary to address its historical context. To a large extent, the limitations of the research agenda are the result of controversies; in fact, the history of sexuality research—from the early surveys of 1892 to the present—can be aptly described as one of valleys and hills. For example, during times of public health crises, there has been sufficient support for health research linked to sexuality, yet during episodes of political conservatism an oppositional backlash has denied support for any research on the topic. One of the more telling early episodes of this history occurred in 1921, when the National Research Council formed the Committee for Research and Problems in Sex with support from the Rockefeller Foundation. The committee received approximately 1.5 million dollars between 1922 and 1947 and supported, among others, the work of Alfred Kinsey and Terman and Miles's 1936 work on sex and personality. In the face of controversy, support was abruptly cut off in the 1950s for Kinsey's work when the House Committee to Investigate Tax-Exempt Foundations warned the Rockefeller Foundation that its nonprofit 401C status was being "reevaluated." This event had a chilling and significant impact on the field from then on: a subsequent reluctance to fund sexuality research by both the private and public sectors, hesitancy to publicly promote sexuality research, lack of legitimacy given to researchers, a fragmentation of disciplines conducting research in this area, and a resulting lack of information on human sexuality. Many of the difficulties encountered today, including the uneven development of methodological design and technique, are due to controversy and the resulting lack of support for this work.

Moreover, the impact of controversy has much to do with the continuing needs and gaps in sexuality research. What is conspicuously missing in the research agenda is a developmental focus on sexuality that acknowledges the primacy of society and culture in order to understand how health crises are related to human sexuality. What we lack is an understanding of how sexual attitudes, beliefs, and values act as antecedents and contributing factors to the public health challenges we face. Research structured within a developmental framework and within the context of society and culture would incorporate a view of human sexuality throughout the life cycle, starting with infancy and early childhood and extending beyond the reproductive years. This needed approach would seek to understand exactly how societal and cultural forces "structure" sexuality by examining how sexual socialization occurs in families, schools, the media, and peer groups, determining the impact and significance of this process for the individual within his or her social network. Data broadly collected on a range of sexuality topics is sorely needed, especially on the following topics: the diversity and distribution of sexual values and behaviors within different populations, societies, and cultures; the impact of sexuality on personal and family relationships; and the specific and varied meanings of sexuality for individuals. Comprehensive data on these topics are simply not available.

I'd like now to highlight the assessment findings regarding methodology. The important methodological issues in sexuality research include design and execution issues, difficulty in operationalizing sexuality concepts, sample selection, participation and self-report bias, and the complexity of incorporating gender and cultural factors. Briefly, two of the more theoretical issues addressed in the assessment report are the need for both basic and intervention research and the importance of utilizing both qualitative and quantitative research designs as equally legitimate methods. The report makes a case for the greater use of basic research focusing on the social, physiological, and psychological aspects of human sexuality in general and sexual behaviors in particular and a greater use of qualitative research as a particularly useful tool for examining the experiential and/or subjective and for describing the social and cultural contexts of sexual experience. This is not to say that intervention or quantitative research is any less important. The positive attributes of quantitative research reside in its descriptive and analytic potential; it is greatly needed to provide useful descriptions of the epidemiological parameters of a given behavior and of the distribution of sexual behaviors and their correlates in a given population. Intervention, or applied, research is needed to inform and make effective diverse programmatic interventions targeting health issues, interventions that are attuned to community needs and incorporate appropriate evaluative processes. Without more basic or fundamental research that expands the knowledge base about sexuality, the effectiveness of such research is limited, a situation which has unfortunately been quite evident in the public health arena. Likewise, qualitative research in the form of more open-ended interviews, case studies, and other ethnographic approaches can greatly enrich sexuality research and get at data otherwise unobtainable, although well-designed, sophisticated quantitative methods continue to be much needed. In terms of integrating the two, qualitative methods can be used as important theoretical guides for pilot studies or can represent the second phase of research as a way of interpreting quantitative data in order to explore the significance or meaning of certain behaviors identified in the quantitative survey. Such an approach would require both multidisciplinary and interdisciplinary collaborative efforts of researchers versed in different methods.

I'd like to highlight two of these methodological issues—multidisciplinary collaboration and qualitative research—and address their significance for the new Sexuality Research Fellowship Program. First some background information about the program. Now beginning its second year, the SRFP provides dissertation and postdoctoral support for social and behavioral research on sexuality conducted in the United States, with funds provided by the Ford Foundation. Applications are invited on a wide range of sexuality topics and issues from many disciplines, including anthropology, demography, economics, education, ethics, history, cultural and women's studies, political science, psychology, and sociology. Applications from other fields, such as the biomedical/physical sciences, nursing, law, and clinical fields, are welcome as long as they are grounded in social science theory and methodology. The committee that selected the 1996 fellows was multidisciplinary, with two sociologists, two psychologists, one historian, one anthropologist, one demographer, and one education/women's studies representative; they selected three postdoctoral and eleven dissertation fellows. It was a very successful selection process, although it was evident how arduous multidisciplinary work can be, particularly in that it demands familiarity with another disciplinary framework and method and, at the same time, requires a willingness to consider it of equal value to one's own. On the point of methodological eligibility, the program's promotional material emphasized both traditional and innovative methodology, especially those methods that advance theory or test new methodology, including qualitative and quantitative approaches to data collection and analysis, participatory and comparative research methods, secondary analyses of existing data sets, and social-historical analyses. Six fellows are in sociology, three in anthropology, three in psychology, and two in history. In terms of research methodology, seven are utilizing qualitative methods, one is using a quantitative methodology, and two are using both qualitative and quantitative methods. The qualitative methods being utilized include archival analysis, ethnographic observation, interviews, and organizational, textual, and/or phenomenological analysis. The program's first-year achievement of helping to cultivate new generations of scholars who address the complexity and contextual nature of human sexuality is especially noteworthy; by exploring the links across disciplines, methods, and issues, the program hopes to build constituencies among sexuality researchers, strengthen existing research networks within the social sciences, and promote a more relevant and useful research dissemination.

I'd like to highlight the report's structural recommendations to revitalize and legitimize social science research on sexuality. Three categories were outlined: (1) expanding the research base by expanding the scope of existing research and supporting new research; (2) providing comprehensive training in sexuality and research methodology with specialized programs of study and training fellowships; (3) building a research constituency that will raise awareness within and outside the research community on the centrality of sexual research to strengthen existing networks and improve dissemination. Two of the more crucial and continuing gaps in sexuality research are the lack of comprehensive research training for social scientists interested in this area and the inadequate dissemination and accessibility of the research findings. On the issue of training, researchers in this area come from a variety of social science disciplines, but few have had specific training in designing, conducting, and evaluating research in sexuality. In fact, it is assumed that such research requires no specific preparation or training other than the ability to integrate questions about sexual behavior into the research design. As a result, many call themselves sexuality researchers who have had no training and little expertise in the area. Comprehensive training programs that provide formalized training opportunities in both methodology and sexuality simply do not exist—only training opportunities in the form of graduate seminars, conference workshops, and staff training at research institutes. While many of these training forums are highly regarded and well organized, they are not comprehensive in scope. Also, what is typically identified as training often consists of an overreliance on individual mentoring. Regardless of its merits and contributions, individual mentoring is not and cannot take the place of a systematic, comprehensive training program.

On the issue of dissemination, there are no adequate mechanisms or efforts to disseminate research to those who need it, namely, policymakers, social welfare advocates, health practitioners, and program personnel. In turn, the concerns and needs of these constituencies are seldom taken into consideration in the research methodology. Granted, considering these topics when designing the research can substantially complicate the work—for example, ensuring policy-relevant research, incorporating qualitative methodology, providing for adequate dissemination, and involving various constituencies, or even the subject population. The first step to adequately address these issues is to ask the difficult questions: What are the implications for methodological design and execution to integrate qualitative methods? What does it mean to bring in a community in the research design and evaluation process from beginning to end? How can dissemination occur so that the research is more useful and relevant to those in need of it? What does it methodologically mean to conduct policy-relevant research? Over the next few days we will address such questions at greater length. There is much work ahead, but support for forums such as this one which will provide an important opportunity for taking stock of methodological needs and moving forward in this field is greatly needed.

Reference

di Mauro, D. (1995). *Sexuality research in the United States: An assessment of the social and behavioral sciences.* New York: Social Science Research Council.

International Perspectives on Sexuality Research

RICHARD G. PARKER

The rapid development of sexuality research in recent years has raised the need for a thorough assessment of this field. In order even to begin to think more effectively about the key issues in contemporary sexuality research, we need some sense of the historical development of research activities and research communities—to map the major trends and tendencies that have shaped research in the past and, on the basis of this, to begin to define the kinds of issues that we would hope to address in the future. Yet, with the exception of the United States, where a systematic attempt was recently made to take an inventory of past and present research activities (see the preceding paper by di Mauro as well as di Mauro, 1995), very little has been done to review the current state of research on sexuality in the social and behavioral sciences. Indeed, for most of the world, this kind of mapping has hardly begun, and much remains to be done before we will have a clear sense about the current state of the art in sexuality and sexual behavior research.

If this general lack of clarity is apparently widespread, however, it is probably even more evident in turning from the various countries of the developed world, where the vast majority of research activity has been carried out, to the developing world, where resources and institutional support for sexuality research have always been scarcer and more precarious. While a number of important attempts have been made recently to stimulate research on sexuality in the developing world, little has been done in the way of compiling a complete picture of the range of research activities currently under way or of the kinds of theoretical issues and methodological approaches that have provided the major focus for research.[1]

While neither the resources nor the space available to me here make possible a really thorough review of international research on sexuality, as a point of departure for thinking about at least some of the dilemmas that

---

1. Indeed, it would be fair to argue that an assessment project comparable to the study carried out in the United States (di Mauro, 1995) but with a global focus and special attention to the situation in developing countries would be an urgent priority. A growing number of donors now support sexuality research internationally, but with little in the way of coordination or even systematic information about existing programs.

currently confront us I will try in this paper to provide a brief overview of key trends and tendencies that seem to have characterized recent research on sexuality, particularly in developing countries. In the first section of the paper, I will briefly review major international research initiatives that have been launched over the past 10 to 15 years. In the second section, I will draw on my own recent experiences working with a range of colleagues from diverse regions and countries in order to examine the current state of debate and discussion in what might be described as an emerging global sexuality research community. Finally, I will try to draw attention to the need for a strategic dialogue between research and policymaking communities and to suggest steps that might be taken to increase the impact sexuality research findings have on the formation of more effective social policies. While this overview will necessarily be rather open-ended, resolving fewer issues than it opens up, I hope that it will offer some sense of an important set of questions that must be taken into account in thinking about the ways in which we might seek to move forward.

Sexuality, HIV/AIDS, and Reproductive Health

Until quite recently, sexuality research in most of the developing world was very limited. Relatively superficial insights concerning sexual behavior, or at least reproductive behavior, had been gained through population studies and in the development of demography as a field of study. Two major international initiatives—the World Fertility Surveys (WFS), which were carried out between 1972 and 1984 in 42 countries with funding jointly by UNFPA and USAID, and the Demographic and Health Surveys (DHS), conducted since the early 1980s in approximately 50 sites with support from USAID—had provided information on a number of issues related to fertility, family planning, and maternal and child health (see Cleland & Ferry, 1995, chap. 9). Still, in spite of such initiatives related to population and reproductive health, when AIDS entered the international arena in the mid-1980s, one of the first things that researchers everywhere came up against was the lack of available data on sexual conduct (beyond reproductive behavior) that could be used to think about the epidemic. As AIDS became a global problem, stimulating sexuality research internationally and in the developing world in particular became a priority (see Parker, 1994). So it is, in fact, a very recent history that we are talking about. Indeed, even though international attention started to focus on HIV/AIDS in 1985 or 1986, when the first formal AIDS programs were initiated by international agencies such as the World Health Organization, it wasn't until 1988 that money was actually available to fund studies and to stimulate training and capacity-building for researchers beginning to work in this field.

In any review of the history of research on sexuality and related health issues since that time, a relatively limited number of initiatives and institutions are relevant. Clearly the World Health Organization's Global Program on AIDS (WHO/GPA) has played a key role since 1988. This program took place in two quite distinct phases (see Aggleton, 1996a, 1996b). From 1988 to 1990, through the Social and Behavioral Research Unit (WHO/GPA/SBR), an initial phase of mostly survey research was carried out on fairly small budgets with instruments that were designed to be comparable, although the true extent of such proposed comparability is obviously questionable (see Carballo, 1988; Carballo, Cleland, Caraël, & Albrecht, 1989). But in a number of areas, population-based surveys of sexual behavior and partner relations were indeed carried out (see Cleland & Ferry, 1995).[2] A series of studies on gay and bisexual behavior was conducted (see, for example, Parker, 1993, 1996; Schifter & Madrigal, 1992).[3] Studies on sex work in a number of contexts, as well as studies of injecting drug use and sexuality in relation to injecting drug users, were initiated (see, for example, Gillies & Parker, 1994).[4] All of these studies developed a survey instrument that could be translated and applied cross-culturally with (hopefully) the necessary adaptations to make it useful. And, at least in principle, such quantitative investigation was to be complemented by a range of more qualitative research designs which would serve to situate and interpret behavioral findings within specific social and cultural settings (see Parker & Carballo, 1990; Parker, Herdt, & Carballo, 1991; Scrimshaw, Carballo, Caraël, Ramos, & Parker, 1991).

In the early 1990s, WHO/GPA went through a reorganization, which led for a time to the extinction of social and behavioral research. Then, thanks to pressure from a number of progressive governments, a Social and Behavioral Studies and Support Unit (WHO/GPA/SSB) was reestablished in 1991. This unit initiated a second wave of WHO/GPA research which intentionally moved from the earlier primary emphasis on large-scale quantitative studies to a new emphasis on systematic, small-scale, qualitative studies—again, with the ultimate goal of cross-cultural comparability but with a different methodological focus and a different set of reflections about what would be necessary for comparability (see Aggleton, 1993). In

2. National surveys on partner relations and AIDS related knowledge, attitudes, beliefs, and practices were ultimately carried out in Burundi, the Central African Republic, Côte d'Ivoire, Guinea Bissau, Kenya, Lesotho, Mauritius, Singapore, Sri Lanka, Tanzania, Thailand, and Togo. Surveys were also conducted in three major urban centers: Lusaka, Zambia; Manila, Philippines; and Rio de Janeiro, Brazil.

3. Surveys on gay and bisexual behavior were conducted in Austria, Brazil, Costa Rica, Great Britain, Greece, Israel, the Netherlands, and Spain.

4. Studies on sex work were carried out in Brazil, Dominican Republic, Ghana, Great Britain, and Thailand.

particular, there were studies of the sexual cultures, meanings, and identities among young people; studies of the social acceptability of the female condom and hence of heterosexual negotiation; and most recently a new phase (which apparently will be carried on in the new UNAIDS program, which has superseded WHO/GPA) focusing on issues related to stigma and discrimination with regard to HIV/AIDS and to sexual behaviors associated with vulnerability to HIV infection (see Aggleton, 1996a, 1996b; Mane & Aggleton, 1996).[5]

At much the same time that these WHO/GPA studies were going on with an AIDS agenda as the driving force (indeed, health problems, in particular perceived health risks, have been the driving force in almost all international research on sexuality), WHO's Special Program of Research, Development, and Research Training in Human Reproduction (WHO/HRP) developed a quite differently structured global research initiative on sexual behavior. Rather than trying to work simultaneously with equivalent data-collection instruments and research designs in different countries, WHO/HRP sent out a periodic call for proposals and selected a number of projects from different countries. In this case, the focus was on issues linked to reproductive health—such as contraceptive use, sexually transmitted diseases (STDs), and so on—but also on trying to stimulate local research initiatives and the development of local research communities, rather than cross-cultural or cross-national comparison as the primary goal of research activities. Central emphasis was given to methodological innovations. At least two of the studies that I am familiar with in Brazil, for example, sought to develop methodologies for quantitative analysis of data that was collected qualitatively (see Leal, 1995; Loyola, 1994). Since WHO/HRP emphasized such innovation, many of the studies supported through this program were unusually complex and necessarily slow to develop. For the most part they are just now coming in with their research findings, and few published reports are available. But we can expect a significant increase in reporting and publication in the next two years.

At roughly the same time the WHO initiatives were undertaken, a number of important initiatives gained support through bilateral donors and development cooperation agencies of diverse sorts. Probably the largest amount of money was spent by USAID's HIV/AIDS Program through a number of evolving phases, such as the AIDSCOM Project, the AIDSTECH Project, and more recently the AIDSCAP Project. In addition, USAID has supported important initiatives related to women and AIDS through its

5. Studies supported by WHO/GPA/SSB have focused on the sexual culture of young people in Cambodia, Cameroon, Chile, Costa Rica, Papua New Guinea, Philippines, and Zimbabwe; on sexual negotiation, the empowerment of women, and the female condom in Costa Rica, Indonesia, Mexico, and Senegal; and on household and community responses to HIV/AIDS in the Dominican Republic, India, Mexico, Tanzania, and Thailand.

program with the International Center for Research on Women (ICRW) (see Gupta & Weiss, 1995).[6] In general, unlike the work carried out by WHO, which has provided direct financial support to studies by developing country researchers themselves, the bilateral work supported by agencies such as USAID has been carried out by offering a grant to a university or institution from the United States, which then develops a collaborative research project with investigators from a given developing country. Increasingly, however, USAID has provided in-country support for behavioral research on sexuality in HIV in a fair number of what are considered to be priority countries. Similar policies, focusing on providing often relatively low-level but nonetheless direct research support to developing country investigators, have been pursued by a range of smaller agencies, such as IDRC in Canada (see Chouinard & Albert, 1989), and by private donors, such as the Ford, John D. and Catherine T. MacArthur, and Rockefeller foundations in the United States. In the 1990s such agencies have come to play a key role in stimulating sexuality research in relation to both HIV/AIDS and men's and women's reproductive health.

Over the past 10 to 15 years, then, a rapidly growing range of initiatives, supported by an increasingly large number of agencies and working in a growing range of settings, have been made in research activities focusing on sexuality. What is most striking, however, is the extent to which this growing range of activities has nonetheless been driven by a relatively limited set of issues, almost exclusively linked to questions of sexual health. The driving forces for most research on sexuality have been concerns related to HIV/AIDS and other STDs, women's and men's reproductive health, contraceptive use, and related issues. An important question for the future will thus be the extent to which it will be possible to build on this base, retaining the potential of sexuality research to investigate pressing practical concerns while opening up a range of new research questions and concerns that go beyond health issues.

Reconceiving Sexuality

In the late 1980s and early 1990s, researchers from developing countries came together to form the AIDS and Reproductive Health Network (ARHN). The secretariat for the ARHN was based at the Harvard School of Public Health, but the network was global in scope and began developing a series of research activities trying to look at the linkages between HIV/AIDS and reproductive health issues. In 1991, the network organized an international Working Group on Sexual Behavior Research (WGSB),

---

6. ICRW's program on women and AIDS has supported research and intervention studies in Brazil, Guatemala, India, Jamaica, Mauritius, Papua New Guinea, South Africa, Thailand, and Zimbabwe.

which I coordinated between 1991 and 1995, when it completed its program of activities.[7] The key focus of this working group was to provide a forum for critical reflection and reevaluation of existing theoretical and methodological paradigms that had dominated the development of sexuality research in the past and to develop a number of seminars, meetings, training activities, and workshops in different geographical regions which might serve to stimulate dialogue, debate, and research, particularly in developing countries.[8]

In 1993, ARHN/WGSB organized an important conference to bring together researchers from different cultural traditions to think about the conceptual and methodological issues involved in trying to do work on sexuality cross-culturally in the rapidly changing world of the late twentieth century. Cutting across at least some of the divisions that have often complicated dialogue and exchange between feminist studies, lesbian and gay studies, HIV/AIDS and reproductive health research, the results of this meeting were published as *Conceiving Sexuality: Approaches to Sex Research in a Postmodern World* (Parker & Gagnon, 1995), and served as the key point of departure for the ARHN/WGSB's regional training efforts. In line with debates at this conference, central emphasis was placed on seeking to stimulate social science perspectives and approaches in a field that had long been dominated by biomedical perspectives and in which a necessarily pragmatic or applied focus, linked to issues such as HIV/AIDS and reproductive and sexual health, continued to determine the research agendas and funding possibilities available to most researchers (see ARHN/WGSB, 1995).

Following completion of ARHN/WGSB's activities at the end of 1995, many of these same issues have been taken up again, although with a slightly different focus, in work carried out by a number of my Brazilian colleagues and myself through the Program on Gender, Sexuality, and Health in the Institute of Social Medicine at the State University of Rio de Janeiro.[9] While ARHN/WGSB had made important headway in trying to bring together researchers from a variety of theoretical and methodological

---

7. Funding for the ARHN/WGSB's work was provided by the Ford, John D. and Catherine T. MacArthur, and Rockefeller foundations.

8. A key characteristic of sexuality research in the developing world is that it has advanced at different rates in different regions. In particular, it would appear that sexuality research initiatives have generally moved forward much more rapidly in Latin America and in Asia than in Africa, where, for a variety of reasons, stimulating research interest has proved to be more complicated.

9. Major support for initiation and development of this program was provided by the Ford Foundation. Additional support has more recently been provided by the John D. and Catherine T. MacArthur Foundation as well as the Brazilian National Research Council (CNPq).

perspectives in the social sciences and in opening up a dialogue about how best to think about sexuality cross-culturally, we nonetheless felt that the approaches, perspectives, and conceptual/methodological frameworks elaborated in the developed world, particularly in the United States and Europe, had continued to dominate thinking about these issues. Indeed, in some ways ARHN/WGSB (like similar initiatives by a number of development cooperation agencies such as IDRC) had served as a mechanism for a kind of technology transfer—bringing the third world up to speed, if you will, on current methodological and theoretical approaches but with relatively little sensitivity to needs and potential for creative innovation on the part of developing country scientists.

In an attempt to move beyond this model (with its obvious possibilities but real limitations), we thought that it would be important to try to invert that relationship—in a sense, to ask how it might change the kinds of things that we would want to look at and the ways in which we might go about looking at them, if the problems that are taken as the point of departure for thinking about sexuality are not necessarily defined in terms of the agenda of the developed countries, but, on the contrary, in terms of the developing world and of its diverse cultural traditions. To begin to explore some of these issues, in 1996 we organized a four-day conference, "Reconceiving Sexuality: International Approaches to Gender, Sexuality and Health," aimed at rethinking emerging approaches to sexuality research from this decentered perspective (see Parker & Barbosa, n.d.). While we hardly succeeded over the course of such a short meeting in reconceiving sexuality and sexuality research, we did make headway in mapping the kinds of issues that seemed to be at the cutting edge of concern cross-culturally. Precisely because the meeting brought together leading researchers from every region of the globe and from more than 20 countries in the developing world, it can thus perhaps be used as a kind of litmus stick for assessing the kinds of research activities, concerns, and perspectives that seem to be the most important focus of contemporary attention.

With this in mind, what was most evident and striking at this meeting was clearly the attempt of a growing number of researchers to find ways of reframing the current discourse of sexuality research, ways of rethinking some of the basic kinds of terminologies that have dominated much of the theoretical discussion and much of the research practice over the course of the past decade. The social construction of sexuality, for example, was transformed into the sexual construction of society by at least one participant (see Dowsett, 1996). Conceptual and methodological innovation was central, as well, with important emphasis placed both on the need to analyze more carefully the dialogical context of the in-depth interview in sexuality research (see Dowsett, 1996; Amuchastegui, 1996), as well as the possibilities and limitations involved in analyzing sexual networks as a way of thinking not only about HIV transmission but more complexly about the ways in which different societies and cultures organize their sexualities (see Bond, 1996; Preston-Whyte, 1996). And perhaps most important, the discussions at this meeting reaffirmed the absolute centrality of gender as a focus of concern in the analysis of sexuality. While many recent debates in sexuality research have focused on the need to treat gender and sexuality as distinct analytic objects, it was apparent from the discussions at this meeting that it continues to be fundamentally important to maintain an analytic tension between these domains and to more effectively address the ways in which gender identities, gender scripts, and gender power crisscross the sexual field, making it impossible to effectively analyze sexuality without adequate reference to the specificities of this interaction (see, for example, Barbosa & Uziel, 1996; Ehrhardt, 1996; Oetomo, 1996).

Clearly, the dominant paradigm, intentionally, of the people we had brought together at this meeting was basically a social constructionist framework—indeed, in many cases, almost postconstructionist, as a fair number of these researchers are struggling with the limitations of constructionist paradigms, and in diverse manners are seeking ways of moving beyond these limitations. Still, it seems to me that increasingly social science approaches and methods and a clear focus on the social dimensions of sexuality are clearly at the forefront of most of the research that is being carried out in the developing world. In spite of the continued importance of issues related to health as the key questions drawing research attention, a broadening range of applied social science perspectives has been employed in seeking to address these pressing practical concerns, and an increasingly meaningful interaction between research findings and policy formation has begun to emerge.

From Research to Policy

Indeed, the last point that I would like to stress in this brief overview of recent international research on sexuality is the growing importance of linkages between research and policy. My sense is that the potential significance of sexuality research findings for policy formation has been especially pronounced in much of the work that has been carried out internationally—for a number of reasons, the whole question of the policy implications that such work may have is perhaps more evident in the developing world than it often is in Europe and the United States. More than in the developed countries, I think, in the developing world, where resources are often especially scarce, the space for an ivory tower academia is probably a good deal more limited. If immediate policy implications are not part of the research project, there simply isn't money to fund it. Indeed, also because of scarcity, together with the vicissitudes of life experience, I suspect, most of the people who carry out this kind of work internationally wear a number of hats. They may be university researchers, but they are also likely to work in community-based organizations or in policy or program positions that virtually guarantee that the linkage between research and policy will be present and will be more constant and more necessary to address in order to even begin to think about the research that should be carried out.

Whatever the setting, there is no doubt that this passage from research findings to policy implications is rarely easy or simple to make. It seems to me that researchers, generally all of us, myself certainly included, are not very effective when we start talking about policy and when we think about the ways in which policy implications are going to be incorporated into the kind of work that we're designing and doing. In the first place, we often don't know what we mean by the word—the term *policy* gets thrown around in a variety of ways, but we often have difficulty specifying just what kind of policy, at what level, we're actually talking about. Indeed, most of the time when people use the word policy and talk about the policy implications of research, I suspect that it's a kind of vague notion that we will send our results to the policymakers and hopefully they'll do something with them. And my sense is, fairly obviously, that this is not at all an effective way to think about the policy implications of our work. We need to be more sophisticated in thinking about the different levels that exist in policy formation and the different social spaces in which research can have policy value or policy implications. In the developing world, at least, where many countries have passed through long periods, often quite recently, of authoritarian rule, military dictatorship, and so on, there's a good deal of debate, as the redemocratization process is taking place, about the relationship between the public sector, on the one hand, and civil society, on the other hand. One implication of this distinction is that there may be policy implications and effective spaces for influencing policy development that may not be involved with public policy but with the different initiatives taking place in civil society. Certainly different levels of intervention are possible—cultural intervention in a broad-based sense, through mass opinion and media dissemination of research findings—but there are also community bases in which research can flow into programming and policy activities in effective ways. In short, my argument would be that it is necessary to think more strategically about the policy impacts of the work that we do before designing and beginning the research process.

I use the term *strategically* quite intentionally here, as I am committed to a vision of social science as quite clearly *not* value-free. My view is that what we do as social scientists in general and as sexuality researchers in particular is in fact strategic—that it has strategic utility, or that it can have if we look for those possibilities. And if we think strategically about the policy implications of our work, this in turn has implications for the kinds of theoretical and methodological approaches we use, for the kinds of topics that we address, the research designs that we develop, and so on.

To make this discussion of the strategic goals of sexuality research more concrete, I would like briefly to give an example. My work in Brazil began more than 15 years ago, focusing on ethnographic description and looking primarily at the social and cultural construction of sexual meanings. By chance—historical accident or what have you—this happened to be at the very start of the HIV epidemic in Brazil. I was carrying out fieldwork in Brazil in 1982 when the first cases of AIDS were reported there. In first considering the practical implications of my own research, I looked at the extent to which sexual identity and sexual behavior were clearly disconnected in a variety of situations and contexts that might have important implications for HIV transmission (see Parker, 1987; more generally, see Daniel & Parker, 1991, 1993). Today this may seem like a fairly obvious insight, as it is almost common knowledge to all of us working in this field—but in 1983 and 1984, it was new at least to the epidemiologists who were talking about the spread of HIV infection. So it became important to package some of my ethnographic findings in ways that became meaningful for policymakers and programmers over the course of the mid-1980s in the country where I was working (see Daniel & Parker, 1991, 1993).

Initially, of course, in strategic terms, such arguments were intended to sensitize policymakers to the fact that HIV/AIDS in Brazil was unlikely to remain confined in clearly defined epidemiological risk groups such as gay men. An effective strategy for AIDS prevention would need to take account of the broader fluidity of sexual desire and practice in Brazilian culture. By the late 1980s, however, many policymakers in Brazil, at least, on the basis of our research findings, had almost gone to the opposite extreme and had concluded that HIV must not in fact be a significant problem for men who have sex with men. Since patterns of sexual desire and identity in Brazilian culture are so fluid, since people appear often to have sex across the traditional heterosexual/bisexual/homosexual boundaries, and since the epidemic is spreading rapidly through heterosexual transmission, they had concluded that the key focus ought to be entirely on prevention for the so-called general population. By that time, then, it became strategic to reconstruct what we had as social researchers deconstructed—to focus on the differential vulnerabilities of different sexual communities within the wider Brazilian population.

In the late 1980s and early 1990s, my colleagues and I started developing quantitative work specifically on homosexual and bisexual men and on the ways in which their behaviors were changing (or not) in response to the epidemic. Over the course now of seven or eight years, we have continued a series of ongoing surveys focusing on such changes over time (see Parker & Terto, Jr., 1997). We chose that particular methodology quite consciously—again, strategically—knowing that our key goal was to work through the media and, via the media, to try to create pressure on policy-makers and to convince them not to take the question of men who have sex with men completely off the agenda of AIDS programming and policy-making. At least in part, we probably succeeded in making this point, or least contributing to a revision of program thinking, so that by the mid-1990s there are now a number of fairly well-established programs working for AIDS prevention among men who have sex with men. These programs exist in a variety of settings and are supported by the National AIDS Program and private donors.

In recent years, we have changed tack once again. Although we continue doing that quantitative work which is really intended to interface with the media and to disseminate research findings in a particular way for a strategic result, we have started working much more in terms of life histories, looking at the impact of seropositivity in relation to the lives of men who do sero-convert (see Terto, Jr., 1996; Parker & Terto, Jr., 1997). This also has a strategic goal. What we have found is that over the past three or four years, because of an increasing emphasis on AIDS prevention at the expense of care and treatment programs in the developing world, people who are seropositive have often been written off, so to speak, in AIDS program activities. There is thus a need to bring attention back to the specificities, the concerns and needs of those people and of their sexual realities, which continue to exist, of course. For more than a decade, in one way or another, our research has thus been guided not merely by theoretical concerns or purely academic preoccupations but by strategic goals that we hope to accomplish as researchers. For me, at least, this is necessarily the point of departure for thinking concretely about the policy implications of the work that we do.

Conclusion

In spite of its necessarily incomplete and open-ended quality, this brief review has tried to draw attention to issues that seem most important in contemporary international research on sexuality and to suggest their implications for thinking about the development of sexuality research in the future. In particular, it is important to highlight the growing range of international research initiatives and prospective donors—but also to problematize the fact that such initiatives have largely been linked (and will continue to be linked in the future) to specific health-related issues that necessarily condition the kinds of questions that they have been able to raise, as well as the findings that they have reached. On the basis of a number of recent events, such as the international meetings described in this paper, it is clear that a growing community of social science researchers focusing on sexuality has begun to emerge and to push for expanding the boundaries of existing perspectives, while at the same time preserving a fundamental relationship between research and practice, as well as a dialogue aimed at guaranteeing the impact of research findings on the formation of social policies. While not without their problems, in general such trends bode well for the future of sexuality research internationally. The challenge that most clearly confronts us today is how best to build upon such a foundation in seeking to develop a truly global research community.

References

Aggleton, P. (1993). *Sexual behavior research and HIV/AIDS.* Paper presented at the VIII International Conference on AIDS in Africa, Marrakech.
Aggleton, P. (1996a). Global priorities for HIV/AIDS intervention research. *International Journal of STD & AIDS, 7* (Suppl. 2).
Aggleton, P. (1996b, April). *(Is there) method in the madness?: Methodology and interpretation in socio-sexual research on HIV and AIDS.* Paper presented at the Conference on Reconceiving Sexuality: International Perspectives on Gender, Sexuality and Health, Rio de Janeiro, Brazil.
Amuchastegui, A. (1996, April). *The interview as dialogue: Negotiation of meanings of virginity and sexual initiation in Mexico.* Paper presented at the Conference on Reconceiving Sexuality: International Perspectives on Gender, Sexuality and Health, Rio de Janeiro, Brazil.
ARHN/WGSB. (1995). *Gender, sexuality and health: Building a new agenda for sexuality research in response to AIDS and reproductive health.* Rio de Janeiro: Center for Research and Study in Collective Health (CEPESC).
Barbosa, R. M., & Uziel, A. P. (1996, April). *Gender and power: Sexual negotiation in the time of AIDS.* Paper presented at the Conference on Reconceiving Sexuality: International Perspectives on Gender, Sexuality and Health, Rio de Janeiro, Brazil.
Bond, K. (1996, April). *Friends and lovers: Social and sexual networks of urban migrants in northern Thailand.* Paper presented at the Conference on Reconceiving Sexuality: International Perspectives on Gender, Sexuality and Health, Rio de Janeiro, Brazil.
Carballo, M. (1988). International agenda for AIDS behavioral research. In R. Kulstad (Ed.), *AIDS 1988: AAAS symposia papers* (pp. 271–273). Washington, DC: American Association for the Advancement of Science.
Carballo, M., Cleland, J., Caraël, M., & Albrecht, G. (1989). A cross-national study of patterns of sexual behavior. *Journal of Sex Research, 26,* 287–299.
Chouinard, A., & Albert, J. (Eds.). (1989). *Human sexuality: Research perspectives in a world facing AIDS.* Ottawa: International Development Research Centre.
Cleland, J., & Ferry, B. (Eds.). (1995). *Sexual behaviour and AIDS in the developing world.* London: Taylor & Francis.
Daniel, H., & Parker, R. (1991). *AIDS: A terceira epidemia.* São Paulo: Iglu Editora.
Daniel, H., & Parker, R. (1993). *Sexuality, politics and AIDS in Brazil.* London: Falmer Press.

di Mauro, D. (1995). *Sexuality research in the United States: An assessment of the social and behavioral sciences.* New York: Social Science Research Council.

Dowsett, G. (1996, April). *Bodyplay: Corporeality in a discursive silence.* Paper presented at the Conference on Reconceiving Sexuality: International Perspectives on Gender, Sexuality and Health, Rio de Janeiro, Brazil.

Ehrhardt, A. (1996, April). *Differences in sexual behavior within the context of gender scripts.* Paper presented at the Conference on Reconceiving Sexuality: International Perspectives on Gender, Sexuality and Health, Rio de Janeiro, Brazil.

Gillies, P. A., & Parker, R. G. (1994). Cross-cultural perspectives on sexual behaviour and prostitution. *Health Transition Review, 4* (Suppl.), 257–271.

Gupta, G. R., & Weiss, E. (1995). Women's lives and sex: Implications for AIDS prevention. In R. G. Parker & J. H. Gagnon (Eds.), *Conceiving sexuality: Approaches to sex research in a postmodern world* (pp. 259–270). London and New York: Routledge.

Leal, O. (Ed.). (1995). *Corpo e significado: Ensaios de antropologia social.* Porto Alegre: Editora da Universidade.

Loyola, A. (Ed.). (1994). *Aids e sexualidade.* Rio de Janeiro: Relume-Dumará Editores.

Mane, P., & Aggleton, P. (1996, April). *Cross-national perspectives on gender and power.* Paper presented at the Conference on Reconceiving Sexuality: International Perspectives on Gender, Sexuality and Health, Rio de Janeiro, Brazil.

Oetomo, D. (1996, April). *Constructing and challenging masculinity in Indonesia: Gender categories and sexualities in a changing society.* Paper presented at the Conference on Reconceiving Sexuality: International Perspectives on Gender, Sexuality and Health, Rio de Janeiro, Brazil.

Parker, R. G. (1987). Acquired immunodeficiency syndrome in urban Brazil. *Medical Anthropology Quarterly, n.s., 1*(2), 155–175.

Parker, R. G. (1994). Sexual cultures, HIV transmission, and AIDS prevention. *AIDS 1994, 8* (Suppl. 1), S309–S314.

Parker, R. G. (1996). Bisexuality and HIV/AIDS in Brazil. In P. Aggleton (Ed.), *Bisexuality and AIDS: International perspectives* (pp. 148–160). London: Taylor & Francis.

Parker, R. G., & Carballo, M. (1990). Qualitative research on homosexual and bisexual behavior relevant to HIV/AIDS. *Journal of Sex Research, 27,* 497–525.

Parker, R. G., Herdt, G., & Carballo, M. (1991). Sexual culture, HIV transmission, and AIDS research. *Journal of Sex Research, 28,* 77–98.

Parker, R. G., & Barbosa, R. M. (Eds.). (n.d.). *Reconceiving sexuality: Gender, sexuality and health in a postmodern world.* Forthcoming.

Parker, R. G., & Gagnon, J. H. (Eds.). (1995). *Conceiving sexuality: Approaches to sex research in a postmodern world.* New York and London: Routledge.

Parker, R. G., & Terto, V., Jr. (1997). *Entre Homens: Homosexualidade e AIDS no Brasil.* Rio de Janeiro: ABIA/IMS-UERJ/Relume-Dumará Editores.

Preston-Whyte, E. (1996, April). *Sexual networks, race, gender and prostitution: Cross-cultural perspectives from South Africa.* Paper presented at the Conference on Reconceiving Sexuality: International Perspectives on Gender, Sexuality and Health, Rio de Janeiro, Brazil.

Schifter, J., & Madrigal, J. (1992). *Hombres que Aman Hombres.* San José, Costa Rica: ILEP-SIDA.

Scrimshaw, S., Carballo, M., Caraël, M., Ramos, L., & Parker, R. (1991). *Rapid anthropological approaches for studying AIDS related beliefs, attitudes and behaviors.* Geneva: World Health Organization.

Terto, Jr., V. (1996, April). *Male homosexuality and seropositivity: The construction of social identities in Brazil.* Paper presented at the Conference on Reconceiving Sexuality: International Perspectives on Gender, Sexuality and Health, Rio de Janeiro, Brazil.

Discussion

Ed Laumann: To address one of Diane's issues, how do we train people to do this sort of work? This is the biggest challenge because particular methodologies for studying sexuality turn out to be associated with very distinctive ways of interpreting results. For the last seven or eight years, we have been running a sex and gender faculty seminar at the University of Chicago that includes people with backgrounds ranging from medicine and biopsychology to sociology, anthropology, and history. It has been a fascinating experience because we are always surprising each other by reporting findings or views that are wholly unknown or ignored by one or another of the disciplines represented. How do you train people to have sufficient exposure and sensitivity to the necessary medical and biological issues as well as to survey design or qualitative fieldwork? Each methodology is so embedded in particular disciplines, yet the discourse that arises around the methodology reflects presumptions about what we're trying to study. I would certainly like to see this group consider this since so many of us are drawn from very different backgrounds. How can we begin to design meaningful training programs that expose people to the range of relevant issues?

Charles Turner: Yes, I'd like to echo what Ed just said; in thinking about a broad-based training program, it's important to represent different disciplinary viewpoints and get those who teach the different perspectives to talk to each other. We're constantly batting each other on the head trying to do qualitative and quantitative research in an interactive mode—trying to figure out how one's own particular social construction of reality might be reconstructed, and so forth. I particularly liked the idea of the sexual construction of the social world mentioned by Richard. I've heard the other phrase often, but it's quite clear, society's organized around sex.

John Bancroft: Can we see social constructs as sound bites suitable for the media? Do we need to conceptualize what we're talking about in ways which are easily conveyed to the public through the media?

Richard Parker: What concerns me is that we often exercise very little control over our interaction with the media and that's a dangerous thing. Certainly, Ed Laumann and Stuart Michaels and others who are involved in research here in the States have a lot more experience dealing with the media than I do. We need to learn much more about the media to be able to work more effectively with them; to be used less for their purposes and to use them more effectively for our own purposes. My sense is that in most of the countries in the world, developed and developing, the power of the media in terms of motivating public opinion is immense. You can interact directly with policymakers, but if the understanding that results is contradicted by the media, you've lost everything. So there's a need to think much more clearly about how we're working with the media, what the media are and how the media work.

Anne Johnson: On the issue of dissemination, from a media point of view it may be very difficult to sell research exactly along the lines that it is presented in the scientific press. If you want to disseminate through the media, you have to find something that is sufficiently interesting to journalists, sufficiently different to make a good story, while also including a message that you personally want to get across. We were lucky that the Wellcome Trust gave us training in media dissemination and organized press conferences. We were taught to write our press releases so that there was something interesting in them for the press. In our case, one thing that really gets the British going is social class. There was a small increased odds of having more sexual partners in those from a higher social class. That was really what got the tabloid press going. But in a way, that was a better headline for us than many others might have been. There are useful ways of working with the press, but you can't expect everybody to be interested in the lower confidence limits of your odds ratios. But hearing you talking about dissemination made me think "I have to go back home and organize seminars with the Department of Health and the Health Educational Authority about our work." I don't think we have addressed some of the issues. It isn't sufficient to publish scientific papers because policymakers have so little time to read them.

Stuart Michaels: First, I would like to comment on the issues we deal with as researchers in getting funding, since this is also a very political process. I think this discussion reflects what so many of us have been through, especially in the era of AIDS, and how that's influenced the research that we've been able to get funding for. Diane developed this theme and I think it is especially important. Too often external pressure to do with getting funding and support has shaped the research that we've done and made it into a narrow study of sexual problems and risk behavior, thereby contorting the notions of sexuality that inform the research. One of the problems with trying to get support for broader studies that include the positive aspects of sexuality that Diane correctly calls for is that we are called upon to justify the need for such studies usually by explaining how this is going to serve public welfare and public health. To do this, value issues creep back in but are often not directly addressed. I have noticed this in our team's pursuit of research funding, where we have had multiple audiences. Sometimes the NIH, sometimes foundations that have a national and international perspective, sometimes foundations with a local perspective. Each time, we've had to think about who the audience is and what justification they will accept. While we've tried to hold onto our own views of what is important, we have also been very conscious of what others will see as justified.

Another place in my experience where issues of values have come up and had to be clarified has been in dealing with the media. As the publication of the books from the U.S. national survey neared, Ed and I and our co-authors were faced with the realization that this study was going to make a big splash and we were totally unprepared and untrained to deal with that. So with Ford Foundation support, we contracted with public relations experts for some media training. I found this very revealing in terms of defining what our message should be, what we could all agree on. When we (Ed Laumann, John Gagnon, Bob Michael, and I) first got together with Gina Kolata and the media consultants, what struck me was how different we all were, even the four social scientists. We come from very different perspectives. In terms of being all social scientists of the same gender and color, you could say we were a homogeneous group. But ideologically, theoretically, in terms of our training we were actually quite varied. We had lots of unresolved differences, even after the book was written. The thing that amazed me was that immediately when faced with the prospect of facing the public, at the level of abstraction and brevity that we would have to be communicating, there was complete agreement amongst us about the basic scientific issues and especially the importance of the scientific study of sexuality. I don't think any of us had expected this, but that became one of our primary messages. I'm not sure that we always succeeded in getting this message out through the media, but more than specific findings, more than a specific meaning or interpretation, we wanted to convince people of the need for and importance of rigorous research and information about sexuality. Outside this room that isn't a totally uncontroversial message; it involves a lot of political issues. I don't think that we can assume that the public accepts the need, importance, value of the study of sexuality per se. We're still in a period of needing to justify ourselves in terms of some other benefit or policy need, be it AIDS or public health. Hopefully we can, but I'm not sure how we get further than that at the moment.

Leonore Tiefer: The challenge that we're facing is how to acknowledge that we do not engage in value-free research and how we should promote more intentional values for our research. The reality is that respect for our research rests on the misguided assumption that it is value-free, the very narrow-minded views of the media which see science as pure and politics as biased.

Richard Parker: At some level, my thoughts are from a space radically different to this meeting because, to use Rorty's phrase, I am committed to an epistemology of solidarity as opposed to an epistemology of objectivity. Much of the research related to sexuality that I've been involved in really has emerged clearly linked to specific social movements, particularly feminism and the gay and lesbian movements. Most of the work on reproductive health and reproductive rights is linked to feminist organizations internationally. Much of the international work on HIV-AIDS has been linked either to emerging gay communities or to feminism. There are very clear linkages between social movements and research, so what researchers are trying to accomplish with their research is in some ways more straightforward. It seems to me that in the comparable context here in the United States or in Europe, those connections aren't nearly as simple and the fire that one comes under for not being value-free is perhaps more intense. Where I am working, we can be more open about what it is we're doing because it's more obvious and there's no way of concealing it in any case. In the U.S. and in Europe, you come under fire for not being value-free in a variety of powerful ways.

Ed Laumann: I think it would be a big mistake to attempt to devise a more effective science of sexology or human sexuality that is constrained within a frame constructed around the problems of AIDS, STDs, gender politics, and public health. We risk a lot by adopting the perspective of identity politics, which is really what Richard has been describing. While this is probably the nature of the beast, certainly internationally and even for much of the U.S. situation in the current period, there is a wide range of human sexuality issues that have nothing to do with particular sexual orientations or gender politics but everything to do with advancing our fundamental understanding of human sexuality. Let's take, for example, the increasingly controversial issue of male circumcision (see Laumann et al., 1996, in press). We happened to ask a question about male circumcision in our survey (the National Health and Social Life Survey, see Laumann et al., 1994). Over the years, the U.S. has spent many billions of dollars in snipping male foreskins, almost always neonatally. But in reviewing the relevant biomedical literature, we found that much of the biomedical rationale for circumcision is weak and unpersuasive, especially with respect to its empirical grounding in adequate research studies. The dominant praxis of male circumcision in the U.S., where well over 70 percent of native-born adult men are circumcised, is grounded in profoundly social, rather than narrow biomedical, considerations. In fact, we found circumcision is highly patterned according to different social attributes, such as race, ethnicity, and education, and strongly correlated with certain sexual practices, such as oral sex, although it does not appear to confer any protection against STDs per se—the presumptive biomedical rationale for doing it originally. Moreover, it is related to sexual dysfunction (especially among older men), but that may be because men who are circumcised masturbate more than men who are uncircumcised. A range of intriguing issues has been opened up in examining our wide-ranging data base that permits us to see what is related to what among the circumcised and the uncircumcised. The point here is that since sexuality expresses itself in so many, often unanticipated, ways in the human condition, we need to assert that there is a value to systematic inquiry about sexuality that may not be in the service of any particular group's preferences or identity. We will probably gain better access to the media by keeping the mystique of the white coat than by tossing it aside to advance limited political goals whose very grounding and direction may shift from moment to moment in response to changing political circumstances.

John Bancroft: Do you think that there is a middle ground? Kinsey was an example of a person who tried to eliminate all values from his reporting of behavior. Ever since, people have been attributing values to him and there are some horrendous examples. To what extent has that happened with your work? To what extent have people been attributing motives or political agendas to your work which you had tried to put forward in a value-free way?

Ed Laumann: There certainly has been some sense of alienation from what could be termed the more "progressive" or "liberated" elements who didn't like some of our results or our discussion of them, and some acceptance by more tradition-oriented institutions, such as churches of moderate conservative orientation. There clearly is evidence for a restructuring of public opinion and beliefs about typical sexual conduct in the populations at large, with changes in the ways it is being framed, debated, and so on. But in our media planning for the release of the study, we really couldn't scope out the public response because we had no way of anticipating our findings and their remarkable consistency nor how they would play in the public arena.

Anke Ehrhardt: I would disagree with Ed in saying that anything we find out about human sexuality is likely to be used for some agenda. I think the challenge is really how we can apply methodologies which are relatively free of bias. From the beginning we should train young people that there are always policy implications rather than pretend that good science is value-free. The kind of interdisciplinary forum that Ed described is critical. What do we do with young people? We split into different camps. Either it's social constructionism and the body is not relevant or it is biomedical with "stay away from anything which is social." The challenge is to expose young people to interdisciplinary thinking and to good, solid methodology relatively free of bias.

Stuart Michaels: I would like to comment on the issues we often deal with as researchers in getting funding. This is also a very political process. I think we're all reflecting on what we've been through especially in the period of AIDS and how that's influenced the research that we've been able to do. This theme that Diane developed is a major one. Too often this has shaped the research that we've done and made it into a study of problems and risk behavior and narrowed and contorted the notions of sexuality that inform the research. We are all sympathetic to your call for studies on the positive side, but the moment you raise the issue in your fairly political, public report, you're explaining how this is going to serve public welfare and public health; the value issues creep back, but are not directly addressed. I'm only saying this because it's incredibly real. In our pursuit of research funding, we have multiple audiences. Sometimes the NIH, sometimes foundations that have a national and international perspective, sometimes foundations with a local perspective. Each time, you have to think about who the audience is and what justification they will accept.

The issue of values versus value-free is not the total story of what's going on in science; science has other kinds of conflict at a more middle-range level, and of the need for a scientific environment in which we can function effectively. I don't see that we're anywhere close to convincing the public that's a value, that we can just state and expect to be supported. We're always justifying ourselves in terms of some other policy need, be it AIDS or public health in some more abstract way. I'm not sure how one gets further than that.

Anne Johnson: Let me reflect on some of these issues, in relation to the British survey on sexual behavior. There seems to me to be a real problem here because we have to define our research policy, but in doing so, we are products of the policy issues of the time, and these are not likely to be highly innovative. Health issues have driven research for most of the people in this room. The renewed interest in sex research has made quite a few careers and we've all been confined in our research by the agenda of the day, which has been driven by the negative outcomes of sexual behavior. Certainly that's what happened in Britain; if you get policymakers involved, the problems that you address will be in the context of their agenda. In the end, the political controversy was probably a good thing for us. Because our then prime minister, Margaret Thatcher, turned down our study, and we were funded by a nongovernment source, the Wellcome Trust. In some ways, that gave us a much freer hand, both in the way that we developed the study and in the way that we published it, the speed of publication, and its dissemination. What limited the survey content was our own nervousness and personal values about what we could and couldn't ask in this context; and that we could only justify the research on the basis of benefiting public health. Thus it probably partly reflects our own backgrounds. Most of us were in sex research because of HIV and AIDS.

Carol Jenkins: In Papua New Guinea, the purpose of our research has been to look at the risk of AIDS for women. And it was the ICRW, the International Center for Research on Women, that funded that research.

The Papua New Guineanians themselves have pushed the research toward establishing a much more holistic view of their own sexuality because they wanted to know about it. Many of you have talked about the problems of framing research questions because of the influence of the funding agencies. But isn't there a wellspring of curiosity from the public itself that wants to know about its own sexuality, and where does that lead research? I should think that some way of getting that expressed may be of some use. It certainly helped me because I was being pushed by the funding to aim at problems in sexuality. Being a foreign researcher, I wanted the Papua New Guineanians to help me figure out what this was all about. In so doing, they broadened the framework in which we were working so it came to cover sexual life histories and developmental aspects of sex, and a great deal about the social construction of sex that crossed cultures within Papua New Guinea.

Alfred Spira: I just want to give you some information about how things went in France. We've had, I think, a unique situation in this country for three reasons. First, our sexual behavior research has always been completely publicly funded. We didn't receive any money from private foundations. We received all of our money through an AIDS research agency, but we were able to incorporate questions and concepts about human sexuality not directly related to AIDS or to prevention. As money came from the government, we were obliged to report very closely to the government, but at the same time we have been completely free in disseminating the information and the publication of the results. I was surprised when Anne Johnson said that in England they were able to disseminate the results more quickly because their study was privately funded. We didn't experience any limitation of this kind. The only limitation we experienced because of the public origin of funding was to submit our projects to different kinds of ethical committees and national scientific bodies. But this seemed to be completely normal. The second reason is that the research we did in France at the end of the 1980s and beginning of the '90s was not the first national sexual behavior survey. There had been a survey in the early '70s just at the beginning of dissemination of medical contraception, so there was actually a background for quantitative research in sexual behavior. It's interesting to note that nothing happened between 1970 and 1988–89, but there was a background for sexual behavior quantitative research. The last point which is of interest is the relation to policymakers and prevention bodies. It took us a very, very long time to have results of our research incorporated in prevention strategies in the country. It took at least two years of repeated meetings and we asked very, very often to have meetings with policymakers and with persons in charge of prevention strategies. But after two years, finally some results of the research have been incorporated in prevention strategies and they are now being used by policymakers. We were lucky enough to work with rather clever politicians and policymakers who understood that they were facing a problem in which they didn't understand anything. It was related to sexual behavior and to social problems and one of the ways for them to say that they did their job was just to provide funds and to leave researchers to do their job. So, until now, the situation was rather satisfying. Now, of course, the situation is that we want to go further, to move out of AIDS and HIV prevention problems, and it's again very difficult to find money for new research.

Theo Sandfort: On the issue of how research and policy relate to each other, I want to share my experience of working with policymakers on a rather concrete level, people who have to design prevention campaigns or interventions. It's my experience that there are a lot of communication problems between policymakers and researchers. They speak different languages and they have a different understanding of what each party is doing. The prevention workers want data now; they want answers to all their questions; they don't understand the logic of research, all the things you have to take into account; and they want to know many things. What I always try to do is to spend time finding out what they want to know and why they want to know it and what effect the outcome of the study will have on their policymaking. So they should focus their questions in a sense that they should know what to do with the data. They want to know everything and you have to help them focus their questions. When I work with prevention workers, that's what most of my energy goes into, and then at the end of the study we sit together and interpret the findings. We try to arrive at a common understanding of its relevance to what they are going to do. One basic problem with that is that they want data and findings and there is a potential risk that we become some kind of "data farmers," we deliver the data. We need to keep in mind that we have to develop theories because data without theory are worthless and that's a big risk in these situations of collaboration with policymakers.

Diane di Mauro: You raise some very crucial points that we also addressed when planning the brainstorming sessions for the Sexuality Research Assessment Project. It was very important that the participants of these discussion sessions consisted of both researchers and policymakers. What became evident was the tremendous need for these kind of forums or arenas in order to familiarize the participants with the vocabulary, the theoretical constructs and the ideas that both policymakers and researchers make use of. A number of suggestions came out of these sessions on this point, such as having some kind of traveling seminar to engage the policymakers in Washington and in other parts of the country in a discussion of specific themes and issues relevant to both researchers and policymakers. Unfortunately, as of this date, there has not been much interest expressed in providing support for such endeavors, but to be able to move beyond that division of researchers and policymakers would require a discussion of that sort.

Theo Sandfort: From my experience, it is a discussion that has to be organized by a third party; it doesn't happen automatically. And the different parties have different priorities.

Ed Laumann: I would like to underscore that we need to distinguish among different types of public and private policymakers. There's been too much job-shopping where, for example, people at the Centers for Disease Control and Prevention or elsewhere identify some need that they want to address and then ask researchers to make proposals for doing the work. The research community is often left in the situation of deciding that "if we want research funding, we will have to do it on their terms," often with little active participation in formulating the research problem. We need a much better appreciation of the fact that, at least in this country, not all policymakers wear federal government hats. As we speak, a major decentralization of a broad portfolio of responsibilities to the states is going on. Most of us have not even begun to think about how to develop research/advisor relationships at that level. I think this is a terrific opportunity because there are states like California and New York which have policymakers with forward-looking and creative interests in issues with which we are concerned. There are also religious groups and other community-related groups (that most of us don't even think about) who are very interested in these issues and who are often much more willing and able to try new things that a governmental unit simply can't do in a politically uncertain environment. This could provide another basis for trying out new alternatives that can then become pretested models for dissemination at the federal level. In short, I think we should move away from the idea that there are only federal-level policymakers and explore other state-level and private avenues for support of innovative research with policy relevance.

Alfred Spira: In France, we have had experience which is not far from yours. For the past five years, we have had two kinds of problems. The first one is a problem of language; we don't speak the same language which means that we don't think in the same way. You say that you believe the policymakers need the results very quickly; I'm used to saying they needed the results yesterday! Because they have a meeting with a minister or they have to decide very, very important things. So I say to them, if you want to have the results for the next year or the next two years, just let us begin to work together today and it will be okay. So the first problem is a problem of language, and we decided to set up a small group, a commission, which regularly meets twice a year. Sitting in this group, persons from the prevention agencies and the government and researchers and each party presents what has been going on during the last six months. They explain to us their problems, what they are thinking to do and how, and we explain to them what we have been doing since the last meeting, what the new results are, the new projects, and we try to see if these things are fitting well. The second problem is the time problem; the speed of time is not the same for them and for us. So what we decided is to raise a governmental committee which meets once a week to take the decisions concerning public interventions and prevention. There would be one researcher sitting on this committee just to be aware of the problems they were dealing with and to provide information coming from the researchers when it is available. That now is working, I cannot say it's working well, it's working not too badly with some crises from time to time because they make big mistakes. For example, one year ago, they decided to communicate about oral sex and condom use in the general population and they wanted to advertise that nobody should have any form of sex, including oral sex, without a condom and they wanted to advertise this to the general population. We were able to convince them quite quickly that this was going to be a big mistake and finally they stopped the communication on this. But we have found that it's useful to have regular places to speak together, to meet together, and to explain our differences.

Diane di Mauro: Our plan for the Sexuality Fellowship Program at the SSRC is to host a fellows' workshop at the end of each fellowship year that would include a component on how to publicly represent oneself as a sexuality researcher. This component would help those scholars new to this work to become more well-versed and comfortable "wearing the hat" of sexuality researcher and, as well, to become familiar with how to discuss their work with media representatives.

Françoise Dubois-Arber: Coming back to our role in the relationships with policymakers/politicians, being in evaluation, we are totally involved in this type of reflection. Policymakers see us as data providers and less as theory developers (it is not their problem). They also see us as evaluators of what they are doing but, more and more, expect answers from us about what they should do, and about what should be the criteria of judgment about a policy (what is a success, what is a failure) as if we were to assume the role of counselors in policymaking. Even in the university, the pressures towards a more active role in policymaking are great and it's extremely difficult to stay with the same role of "researcher" year after year, not to try to influence the policymakers too much, not make the policy for them. It's tempting sometimes; when you have been accumulating a lot of different data for years in the context of a global evaluation, you begin to have your own overall perspective on the field. I'm not sure that as researchers we are prepared for that and I would advocate that we reflect on how to better manage our roles. Another thing is that policymakers are asking us to take on new roles: for example, they are asking that we do our research, but also that we prepare the results differently for different audiences. We are not prepared for the task of "translating" our research in something accessible to politicians, to policymakers, to professionals, to the general public.

John Bancroft: We have no training for that.

Françoise Dubois-Arber: Absolutely. And we are also very naive about how our data can be misused. That can happen and we have to be prepared for it. Okay, we are researchers, but we are de facto involved in this sort of thing and we should be better prepared to deal with it.

Alfred Spira: One important issue is our role in the evaluation of policies and interventions. In my country at least, policymakers and those who are responsible for interventions in the field have absolutely no idea of what scientific evaluation means. For them, once something is done, once they've spent the money, it's done and they don't ask themselves about efficacy and results. And I think that this discipline, sexology, would be viewed completely differently if we were able to show that it's a scientific discipline which is useful in designing new policies and in spending money in more efficient ways.

Theo Sandfort: Those of us in the field of sexology feel we deserve a better status, but before we can accomplish that, it's important to think about the relationship between sexology and the traditional disciplines. And we will have to reflect much more before we can really understand what the problem is. The traditional disciplines distinguish themselves from each other by saying this is the glass through which we look at certain things, and we as sexologists have a lot of glasses to look at the same thing. So in a way, sexology is a completely different discipline to the traditional disciplines and it's important to reflect on what that means.

John Bancroft: Just let me finish off this session with a comment on something that Anke Ehrhardt said about the importance of being able to demonstrate that we had methodology which wasn't distorted by our own value systems. One of the people who for many years has been particularly and consistently attacking Kinsey and sex education is Judith Reisman. Reisman has done some sex research which provides an example of how research, driven and shaped by a political agenda which you don't happen to agree with, can offend you in terms of its methodology. That is an example of what we all have to be careful about.

Part 2.
Methodology for the Individual

Survey Measurement of Sexual Behavior

Problems and Progress

CHARLES F. TURNER, HEATHER G. MILLER, AND SUSAN M. ROGERS

Overview

In this chapter, we review evidence of the biases that attend common measurements of sexual behavior, as well as new developments that hold promise of reducing these biases. Given the underinvestment in research on sexual behavior during the past four decades, this area today is informed by only a thin substrate of methodological studies. For this reason, much of the evidence we adduce to support inferences about biases in such measurements must be drawn from parallel experience in measuring other sensitive behaviors—for example, drug use. We subsequently describe promising technologies for improving survey measurements of sexual behavior and present data from a pilot study that examined the impact of one approach in reducing bias in such measurements.

Central Role of Surveys

Surveys of the sexual and drug-using behavior of large, representative samples of the U.S. population have long been recognized as a prerequisite for understanding and retarding the spread of the human immunodeficiency virus (HIV). Indeed, at present, all means of controlling the spread of HIV, the most deadly of sexually transmitted pathogens, rely on our ability to influence human behavior. Even if a fully effective vaccine or therapy becomes available, the history of other sexually transmitted diseases, or STDs (Brandt, 1987), suggests that the need for protective behavioral change will persist. So, too, will the need for a reliable technology to monitor the effectiveness of our efforts to encourage such changes in behavior.

Groups that have reflected on the research required to combat the epidemic of acquired immunodeficiency syndrome (AIDS) have echoed those arguments for survey research that investigates sexual and drug-using behavior. Such bodies include numerous committees of the National Academy of Sciences and the Institute of Medicine (IOM, 1986, 1988; Turner, Miller, & Moses, 1989; Miller, Turner, & Moses, 1990; Auerbach, Wypijewska, & Brodie, 1994), Ronald Reagan's Presidential Commission on the

HIV Epidemic (1988), the National Commission on AIDS (1993), and the General Accounting Office (1988). Among the major reasons those groups cite for conducting surveys are the following:

- Understanding the spread of the HIV epidemic (and its *potential* for spread) requires knowing some simple "facts" about sex, such as the size of key population groups, including men who have sex with men and heterosexuals with multiple partners; the rates of new partner acquisition; and so forth. Population-based surveys of sexual behavior can supply estimates of the prevalence and patterns of behavior that affect the velocity and breadth of spread of HIV and other STDs.
- Inducing behavioral change requires an understanding of what motivates and constrains behavior that risks transmission of HIV and how behavioral change can be made more attractive. Surveys can provide information about the factors that shape risk-taking behavior and thus help researchers to develop hypotheses about the sorts of behavioral interventions that may motivate individuals to change that behavior.
- Measuring the effectiveness of prevention efforts requires data collected at one point in time as a baseline and data collected at regular intervals thereafter to assess whether protective change is occurring in the population's patterns of sexual behavior. Continued monitoring of behavior through population surveys allows scientists to gauge the persistence of change and risk-taking as new people enter the at-risk population, as the current at-risk population ages, and as secular events modify people's responses to this epidemic.

The National Institutes of Health (NIH) has responded to the need for such data by funding several major research projects to survey AIDS-related sexual and drug-using behaviors in the U.S. population. Because of the substantial cost of sending field interviewers to tens of thousands of households across the country, the largest surveys of the U.S. adult population have used telephone survey techniques. In the National AIDS Behavioral Survey (NABS) research program (Catania et al., 1992b), telephone interviews were conducted with 10,630 respondents in 1990; currently, telephone interviews are proceeding among a new probability sample of 6,400 U.S. adults. These NIH-funded telephone surveys are substantially larger than the surveys of adults that have collected data on AIDS-related behavior during personal visits.[1] Because of the great efficiency of tele-

---

1. So, for example, Tanfer's (1993) National Survey of Men conducted in-person interviews with 3,321 men, and the University of Chicago team of Laumann and colleagues (1994) interviewed 3,432 adults in the National Health and Social Life Survey. The lone exception to the generalization that in-person surveys of adult sexual behavior have been conducted with much smaller samples than comparable telephone surveys is the British National Survey of Sexual Attitudes and Lifestyles (Johnson et al., 1994), which undertook in-person interviews with 18,876 respondents.

phone survey methods, the NABS research program surveyed samples that were large enough to permit analyses of key subpopulations (for example, people with multiple new sexual partners in the past year); surveys of samples of comparable size would be almost prohibitively expensive to conduct using personal interviews. Telephone surveys have also played a crucial role in shaping our understanding of AIDS-related behavior in other nations (see Table 1).

Because of the importance of telephone surveys in monitoring AIDS risk behaviors, emerging evidence suggesting the possibility of nontrivial reporting biases has caused substantial concern. Interview modes that require respondents to disclose sensitive, stigmatized, or illicit behavior to a human interviewer appear to affect the quality of the data. In particular, requiring respondents to disclose to a human interviewer that they have engaged in such behavior seems to greatly diminish the willingness of respondents to report those activities.

Quality of Survey Data: Issues and Concerns

Concerns persist regarding the quality of survey measurements of sexual behavior. We know that adults typically underreport many sexual activities[2] and that important gender-related differences are present in the error structure of the data. In national probability surveys in the United States and Europe, for example, studies found that men consistently reported more heterosexual partners than did women—an algebraic impossibility.[3] Similarly, among individuals who reported risk factors for HIV and other STDs, men were more likely than women to report using condoms during heterosexual sex (Catania et al., 1992b). In both of these cases, the extent to which the difference in results by gender reflects overreporting by men or underreporting by women is not known.

Although a complex array of factors can distort survey measurements of sexual behavior, there are only a few ways to independently corroborate the accuracy and reproducibility of those measurements. To date, evidence of validity and reliability has been gleaned largely from reports by regular sexual partners, test-retest reliability studies, and independent replication of surveys within the same population.[4] A review by the National Academy of Sciences of studies conducted before 1990 concluded that surveys of sex-

2. For reviews, see Chapter 6 in Miller, Turner, & Moses, 1990; Turner, Danella, & Rogers, 1995; Catania et al., 1990; and Bradburn & Sudman, 1979. See also Johnson et al., 1994; and McQueen et al., 1989.

3. See Smith, 1992; Dolcini et al., 1993; and Morris, 1993. However, for a proposed resolution of the paradox, see Wadsworth et al., 1996.

4. See Clark & Wallin, 1964; Levinger, 1966; Jacobson & Moore, 1981; Blumstein & Schwartz, 1983; Coates et al., 1988; Kahn, Kalsbeek, & Hofferth, 1988; and Seage et al., 1989. For reviews, see Chapters 2 and 6 in Turner, Miller, & Moses, 1989; and Turner, Danella, & Rogers, 1995.

Table 1. *Selected Major Telephone Surveys of AIDS-Related Behaviors*

Survey	N	Population	Reference
1990 National AIDS Behavioral Survey (NABS)	10,630	U.S. adults, ages 18–75	Catania et al., 1992b
Analyse des Comportements Sexuels en France (ACSF)	20,055	French adults, ages 18–69	ACSF Investigators, 1992
New Zealand Partner Relations Survey	2,361	New Zealand adults, ages 18–54	Davis et al., 1993
Los Angeles Men's Survey	1,610	Los Angeles males, age 18 and older	Montgomery, Lewis, and Kirchgraber, 1991
Australian Survey of Sexuality and Menopause	2,001	Australian women, ages 45–55	Dennerstein et al., 1994
California AIDS Survey	2,012	California adults, age 18 and older	Communication Technologies, 1987

ual behavior could certainly enlist the cooperation of research subjects and that resulting data could be consistent across surveys and couples, as well as within subjects interviewed prospectively over time (Miller, Turner, & Moses, 1990, pp. 359–471). Nevertheless, the review also noted that consistency did not guarantee accuracy, that there was ample evidence of error and bias in existing surveys of sexual behavior, and that such evidence should be of concern to investigators.

An interview procedure that requires subjects to report sensitive or illegal behavior to a live interviewer invites concerns about response biases. In general, survey methodologists accept that biases in the reporting of illicit or stigmatized behavior in general population surveys produce a net negative bias in estimates of the prevalence of those behaviors in the population. The negative bias occurs because the number of survey respondents who deny engaging in stigmatized or sensitive behavior that they in fact have engaged in is expected to be larger than the number who falsely report behavior that they have not engaged in (Turner, Lessler, & Gfroerer, 1992; Catania et al., 1990; Miller, Turner, & Moses, 1990; Bradburn & Sudman, 1979). Thus researchers interpret higher rates of reporting of sensitive behaviors under more private survey conditions as reflecting a reduction in the reporting bias and thereby an increase in the accuracy of the measurements. For highly normative behavior, the reverse situation would be expected.

In the past two years, strongly suggestive evidence has become available concerning the magnitude of the biases that can afflict survey measurements of sexual behavior requiring disclosure to a live interviewer. We believe that, for our purposes, this evidence is properly termed "suggestive" rather than "conclusive" because most of it is derived from studies of sensitive behavior other than sexual behavior.

Evidence of Bias in Measurements from Personal Visit Surveys

A number of recent studies have found evidence of self-disclosure bias in interviewer-administered surveys that ask respondents to report on sensitive behavior. These studies also demonstrate that the level of privacy the interviewing mode affords can affect survey measurements dramatically. Results from a large-scale, randomized experiment embedded in the National Household Survey on Drug Abuse (NHSDA) indicate that measurements made with self-administered questionnaires (SAQs) yielded higher estimates of the prevalence of illicit drug use than measurements made with interviewer-administered versions of the same questionnaire (Turner, Lessler, & Devore, 1992). The relative advantage of SAQs in encouraging more complete reporting of drug use appears to be a direct function of the sensitivity of the behavior being reported. Thus the effect of the mode of survey administration was greatest for reports of cocaine use—particularly recent use. SAQs yielded estimates of the prevalence of recent cocaine use that were 2.4 times higher than estimates obtained with interviewer-administered questionnaires (IAQs). The effect was less pronounced for reports of marijuana use, and it was almost nonexistent for reports of alcohol use by adults.[5] Recent analyses of a parallel experiment embedded in the National Longitudinal Survey of Labor Market Experience, Youth Cohort (NLS-Y), also found that SAQs yielded more frequent reports of illicit drug use than did IAQs (Shober et al., 1992).

Dramatic mode effects have also been seen when women are offered an SAQ to report on abortion. Jones and Forrest (1992) have used data from abortion providers to estimate the extent of bias in reports of abortions in three major national survey programs: the National Survey of Family Growth (NSFG), the NLS-Y, and Kantner and Zelnik's national surveys of young women. They found substantial biases in reports of abortion in all of those surveys. Estimates derived from women's self-reports in the 1988 NSFG, for example, included only 37% of the abortions reported annually by abortion providers during the 1984–1987 period. In that same wave of the survey, women were also given an SAQ to offer a second, private opportunity to report past abortions (London & Williams, 1990). Jones and Forrest note that use of SAQs increased reporting of abortions from 39% to 71% of the level reported by abortion providers.

Evidence of Bias in Measurements from Telephone Surveys

Although the need for economy argues for use of telephone survey methodology to collect AIDS behavioral data from the population, such surveys may be vulnerable to serious biases. Two major studies compared estimates of the prevalence of illicit drug use obtained from interviewer-administered telephone surveys with estimates obtained from self-administered questionnaires during in-person surveys. (Table 2 summarizes the relevant results.) Gfroerer and Hughes (1992) compared results from the 1988 National Household Survey on Drug Abuse, a survey conducted in person that uses self-administered questionnaires, with results from a 1988 national telephone survey conducted for the Food and Drug Administration (FDA). The FDA survey used questions modeled on those in the NHSDA, and Gfroerer and Hughes went to considerable lengths to match the composition of the two samples.[6] With fairly large samples (ns = 5,018

---

5. However, even for alcohol use, SAQs appeared to encourage more reports by 12- to 17-year-olds—a group for whom the use of alcohol is illicit. For this group, estimates of the prevalence of recent alcohol use were 1.4 times higher when SAQs were used.

6. For example, households without telephones were excluded from the NHSDA database, and re-editing and poststratification weighting were used to make the data processing and sample composition for the surveys comparable.

Table 2. *Prevalence Estimates for Sensitive Alcohol and Drug Use Behaviors Derived from Telephone Surveys and Relative Increases in Prevalence Observed When Estimates Are Derived from Self-Administered Questionnaires in Personal Visit Surveys*

Measurement	Gfroerer and Hughes (1992) (a)		Aquilino (1994) Total Sample (b)		Aquilino (1994) Black Sample (c)	
	Prevalence Estimate from Telephone Survey (Per 100)	Relative Increase with Self-Administration (d)	Prevalence Estimate from Telephone Survey (Per 100)	Relative Increase with Self-Administration (d)	Prevalence Estimate from Telephone Survey (Per 100)	Relative Increase with Self-Administration (d)
Drunk 1+ times per month in past year	n.a.	n.a.	11	36%	4	275%
Ever used marijuana	25.8	33%	56	4%	46	26%
Used marijuana in past 12 months	5.2	54%	8	63%	5	200%
Ever used cocaine	7.9	43%	19	32%	12	92%
Ever used crack	n.a.	n.a.	2	100%	1	700%
Used cocaine in past 12 months	1.4	121%	3	0%	2	150%

Note. All estimates exclude households that do not have working telephones; n.a. = not available.

(a) Gfroerer and Hughes (1992) compared results for 5,018 respondents age 18 and older (living in households with a telephone) in the National Institute on Drug Abuse's (NIDA's) 1988 National Household Survey on Drug Abuse (NHSDA) with results obtained in a Food and Drug Administration (FDA)-sponsored telephone survey of a national probability sample of 1,965 adults conducted in 1988. The latter survey used NHSDA questions reformatted for computer-assisted telephone interviewing. Reported response rates for the adult sample varied somewhat (71% in the NHSDA versus 66% in the FDA telephone survey). Prevalence estimates were derived after re-editing datasets and re-weighting samples to ensure that they were comparable.

(b) The Aquilino (1994) sample included 2,417 adults ages 18 to 45 drawn as a multistage area probability sample of the 37 largest metropolitan statistical areas in the United States. Sampled respondents were randomly assigned (within sample clusters) to one of three experimental treatments: telephone survey; in-person, interviewer-administered questionnaire survey; or in-person survey with an SAQ. Samples in the two treatment conditions (telephone vs. SAQ) presented in this table represent approximately two thirds of the total n of 2,417.

(c) The survey oversampled African Americans and Hispanics. Aquilino (see his Table 1) indicates that 22% of 2,417 respondents were African American (i.e., n = 532). As with the total sample, the two (randomly assigned) treatment conditions presented in this table would represent roughly two thirds of the total sample of African Americans.

(d) Relative percentage increase in reporting defined as {100 * (SAQ [self-administered questionnaire] Estimate − Telephone Estimate)} divided by Telephone Estimate.

and 1,965), Gfroerer and Hughes found that SAQs yielded significantly and substantially higher estimates of illicit drug use. The relative increase in estimated prevalences ranged from 33% for reporting any lifetime use of marijuana to 121% for reporting use of cocaine in the past 12 months.

Aquilino (1994) has recently reported similar results from an experiment in which respondents were randomly assigned to different modes of survey administration. The experiment was embedded in a probability survey of households in the 37 largest metropolitan areas in the United States. To remove the impact of differences in recruitment by survey mode, the experiment began with an initial in-person household contact to screen and recruit respondents, who were then randomly assigned to a survey mode.[7] Aquilino's results were generally consistent with those of Gfroerer and Hughes, although Aquilino's estimated prevalences of drug use were higher and there was some variation in the observed mode differences. Overall, Aquilino found that self-administered surveys produced higher estimates of prevalence for most measurements of drug use. So, for example, self-administered surveys produced a 63% relative increase in reports of marijuana use in the past 12 months and a 32% relative increase in reports of any lifetime cocaine use. Aquilino also reported similar results for his oversampling of 532 African American respondents. Although the small samples in that subanalysis make the estimates rather unstable, the analyses offer highly suggestive evidence that African American respondents may be more sensitive than the rest of the population to the mode of survey administration and more likely to report drug use in a self-administered survey than in a telephone survey.

Limitations of In-Person Surveys Using SAQs

Given this litany of potential measurement biases, one might wonder whether we should retreat to conducting only in-person surveys that use self-administered questionnaires. For several reasons we should seek alternative solutions. First, using only in-person surveys with SAQs would mean substantially higher costs for those surveys that are now conducted by telephone. Second, although SAQs constitute a reasonable technology for surveying sexual, contraceptive, and other sensitive behavior, they have important drawbacks. Extensive use of contingent questioning—that is, branching or skip patterns—may not be possible in SAQs because some respondents have trouble following the complex instructions necessary to navigate their way through a self-administered form (Lessler & Holt, 1987). This limitation makes it difficult to match the questions that are asked of a respondent with the particular behavior they report—for example, by asking detailed follow-up questions.

7. Households without a telephone were excluded from analyses.

Even more important, according to the National Center for Education Statistics (1993), the reading skills of a sizable segment of the U.S. population are limited. Literacy problems are particularly severe among some of the populations of special interest in studies of sexual behavior, including people whose history of STDs or drug use places them at greater risk of HIV infection. (In studies of intravenous drug users in Baltimore, for instance, AIDS researchers[8] estimated that between 30% and 50% of study participants could not reliably complete a self-administered survey form.) The extent of reading problems in such populations means that a sizable proportion of the respondents in national surveys and other kinds of research must be questioned by an interviewer. This requirement introduces potential bias into the resultant measurements of stigmatized sexual, drug use, and related behavior. Furthermore, the bias that is introduced when an SAQ must be administered by the interviewer will be correlated not only with the respondent's level of literacy but with other important variables associated with literacy, such as education and related socioeconomic and demographic characteristics.

For respondents who are able to complete SAQs, the available evidence suggests that this survey mode invites other data-quality problems. For example:

- Attempts to derive national estimates of the prevalence of male-male sexual contact from the 1970 Kinsey Institute survey required more than a year of statistical effort to impute values for the 20% of cases in which key data elements were missing on the SAQ (Fay, Turner, Klassen, & Gagnon, 1989; Turner, Miller, & Moses, 1989, pp. 122–128).
- Analysis of more recent SAQ data on sexual behavior (Rogers & Turner, 1991) indicated that the nonresponse problem had not improved markedly over the past 20 years. For instance, we found that questions on male-male contact were not answered by 19% of men completing the sexual behavior SAQs used in the 1989 and 1990 General Social Surveys conducted by the National Opinion Research Center. Similarly, Cox and colleagues (1992) found that 14% of the respondents to the 1988 NHSDA did not answer one or more SAQ questions about cocaine use.
- Analyzing the patterns of response in major surveys that use SAQs indicates that substantial proportions of respondents give logically inconsistent answers. Cox and coworkers found, for example, that of 946 respondents who reported cocaine use on one or more questions in the

---

8. David Celentano, School of Public Health, Johns Hopkins University, in discussions with the steering committee for the Multisite Trial of Behavior Interventions to Halt the Spread of HIV, sponsored by the National Institute of Mental Health, February 1991.

1988 NHSDA, more than 14% gave logically inconsistent answers—that is, their responses to one or more questions indicated that they had never used cocaine. Similarly, Smith (1989) reported evidence suggesting that approximately one half of the men who reported male-male contact in the 1988 General Social Survey gave responses to other questions in the face-to-face segment of the survey that raised doubts about the validity of their reports of homosexual contact on the SAQ.

Until recently, these problems were unavoidable. Now, however, advances in survey technology offer hope that they can be overcome in the future. Specifically, audio computer-assisted self-interviewing (audio-CASI) and telephone audio-CASI (T-ACASI) appear to promise a reduction of the measurement biases that have plagued surveys of sensitive behavior in the past.

In-Person Audio-CASI

Over the past five years, researchers at Research Triangle Institute (RTI)[9] have developed the audio-CASI technology to administer complex questionnaires in personal interview surveys (Turner, Lessler, & Gfroerer, 1992; O'Reilly & Turner, 1992; O'Reilly et al., 1994; Cooley et al., 1996). Using portable laptop computers, respondents listen to questions through headphones and enter their answers by pressing labeled keys. The recorded audio component has high-quality sound; it does not rely on synthesized voices and presents no significant delays in playing back the audio-delivered questions.[10] This private interview mode can be used with any respondent who can hear and speak; it does not require literacy in any language.[11]

---

9. A parallel effort was under way at the University of Michigan (Johnston, 1992) during the period. That effort implemented audio-CASI on the Apple Macintosh platform.

10. Although the new technology bears a superficial resemblance to attempts to use Sony Walkmen to read survey questions (Camburn, Cynamon, & Harel, 1991), it is, in fact, fundamentally different. In particular, audio-CASI is computer-controlled and thus capable of executing skip patterns, checking for out-of-range responses and inconsistencies across similar questions, and generating data files.

11. Because of audio-CASI, interviewers who spoke only English were able to interview subjects who spoke only Korean or Spanish (Turner et al., 1996b; Hendershot et al., 1996). English-speaking field interviewers carried cellular telephones when recruiting and interviewing Korean- or Spanish-speaking subjects. If the interviewers encountered problems rostering the household, recruiting subjects, or conducting the interview, they could call the study office, where Korean- and Spanish-speaking interviewers were available for help. The audio-CASI computer was programmed to read questions and answers in both Spanish and Korean. We believe that extensions of this method will provide an efficient, cost-effective way to include linguistic minorities who would otherwise be excluded from national samples.

Our in-person audio-CASI technology is robust, and the average field interviewer can use it in a broad range of environments. The audio software is integrated with a standard software system for computer-assisted interviewing. A number of support capabilities are provided through the personal computer (PC) function keys: the screen display can be blanked out or left on; the audio can be turned on or off; questions can be repeated; and the respondent can back up through the questionnaire or can elect to refuse to answer a particular question. Our early audio-CASI pilot tests indicated the following:

- The technology was stable and could be used without disrupting typical survey and research routines.
- Virtually without exception, respondents had no trouble using the new technology. That was true for both educated people and people with substantial reading problems, for the young and the old, and for English-speaking respondents and respondents who spoke only Spanish or Korean.
- Even literate respondents reported that they preferred the new technology to paper-and-pencil SAQs.
- Although the samples for the pilot test were small, statistically significant increases were found in reports of some sensitive behavior (such as abortion) when audio-CASI was used.

During 1995, RTI's in-person audio-CASI technology was adopted for use in two major national surveys: the National Survey of Family Growth, sponsored by the National Center for Health Statistics of NIH (Cycle V; n = 10,000 females, ages 15 to 44), and the NIH-funded National Survey of Adolescent Males, or NSAM (new cohort; n = 1,741 males, ages 15 to 19). Preliminary data from these surveys indicate that the audio-CASI technology was well accepted by field interviewers and survey respondents in personal visit surveys and that it substantially increased reports of sensitive behavior. In the NSFG, for example, one fifth of women increased the number of abortions or sexual partners they reported during reinterviews that used audio-CASI to administer the survey questions (Kinsey, Thornberry, Carson, & Duffer, 1995). Similarly, preliminary data from a randomized experiment embedded in the NSAM also indicated a substantial increase in the number of adolescent males who reported having male-male sexual contacts (Turner, Ku, Sonenstein, & Pleck, 1996a).

Table 3 presents the results obtained from the first 928 respondents in the 1995 NSAM.[12] The table shows the percentage of respondents who re-

---

12. The two paragraphs that follow, which describe the 1995 NSAM, are excerpted from Turner and colleagues (1996a).

ported engaging in each of six types of male-male sexual contact: masturbating another male, being masturbated by another male, insertive oral sex, receptive oral sex, insertive anal sex, and receptive anal sex. The final line of the table shows the results for a composite measure comparable to that reported for the 1988 NSAM. The measure indicates whether the respondent reported at least one type of male-male contact.

As Table 3 shows, there were substantial and statistically reliable differences between the reports given in the audio-CASI interview and those provided in the paper-and-pencil SAQ. Respondents were more than four times more likely to report some male-male contact in the audio-CASI interview. Although the odds ratios for the individual behaviors varied somewhat (from 2.1 to 5.4) and several were statistically unreliable with our incomplete sample size of 928, it appears that audio-CASI will reduce the underreporting of male-male sex in the 1995 NSAM.

Telephone Audio-CASI Technology

In the winter of 1994–1995, researchers at RTI enhanced their in-person audio-CASI system to allow it to conduct complex call-in or call-out telephone audio-CASI surveys.[13] (In a call-in survey, the respondent initiates the interview by calling a number that is answered by the T-ACASI interviewing system. In a call-out survey, a human telephone interviewer calls the respondent and subsequently transfers the call to the T-ACASI system.)

Our T-ACASI system is an outgrowth—both in motivation and architecture—of the technology RTI developed for in-person audio-CASI surveys of sexual and contraceptive behavior. Those efforts resulted in development of a software platform that fully integrates audio-CASI and

---

13. Early experimentation with T-ACASI began at the Bureau of Labor Statistics (BLS) during the late 1980s under the rubric of touch-tone data entry (TTDE) surveys (Werking, Tupek, & Clayton, 1988; Werking et al., 1988; Clayton & Harrell, 1989; Werking & Clayton, 1990; Clayton, 1991). In the early 1990s, RTI adopted an analogous touch-tone data entry procedure for call-in randomization of subjects for clinical trials. Such early systems are currently being used by the BLS in its monthly collection of data from the vast majority of the 350,000 establishments that respond to the Current Employment Survey. Methodological research indicates that error rates using TTDE technology are low (Phipps & Tupek, 1990) and that TTDE has a considerable advantage over other methods in terms of cost and timeliness of data reporting (Werking & Clayton, 1990). Initial T-ACASI applications were limited to simple data-collection tasks, typically involving only 5 to 10 questions that were asked without skip patterns or other tailoring of the survey instrument (Weeks, 1992). The Current Employment Survey, for example, requires only 1 minute and 45 seconds for the average respondent to complete. In addition, both the subject populations and the subject matter for those early T-ACASI efforts were limited to routine, nonsensitive reporting of commercial or technical data by trained, highly literate respondents.

Table 3. *Estimates of Prevalence of Different Types of Male-Male Sexual Contact in a National Sample of Males Ages 15 to 19, by Mode of Data Collection (Self-administered Questionnaire or Audio-CASI): Preliminary Results from the 1995 National Survey of Adolescent Males*

	Estimated Prevalence (Per 100)					
	Paper SAQ		Audio-CASI			
Measurement	Est.	(N)	Est.	(N)	Odds Ratio	p
Ever masturbated another male	1.1	(176)	2.3	(731)	2.07	0.29
Ever been masturbated by another male	0.6	(176)	3.0	(730)	5.44	0.03
Ever had insertive oral sex with another male (your penis in his mouth)	0.6	(176)	2.5	(730)	4.42	0.07
Ever had receptive oral sex with another male (his penis in your mouth)	0.6	(176)	2.1	(730)	3.67	0.13
Ever had receptive anal sex with another male (his penis in your rectum or butt)	0.0	(176)	1.2	(730)	(b)	0.05
Ever had insertive anal sex with another male (your penis in his rectum or butt)	0.6	(176)	1.6	(729)	2.93	0.23
Any male-male sex (a)	1.1	(176)	4.7	(728)	4.26	0.01

Note. Preliminary data from the first 928 cases of the 1995 National Survey of Adolescent Males. *p*-values are those for likelihood ratio chi-square for fit of independence model to the two-way table of mode by reporting of behavior. SAQ = self-administered questionnaire; CASI = computer-assisted self-interviewing.
(a) This composite measure of any male-male sex is derived from the six individual measurements. Cases with missing data for any of the six behaviors were excluded from the analysis of the composite measure.
(b) An odds ratio cannot be calculated because of the zero denominator.

Source. Turner, C. F., Ku, L., Sonenstein, F. L., & Pleck, J. H. (1996a). Impact of audio-CASI on bias in reporting of male-male sexual contacts: Preliminary results from the 1995 National Survey of Adolescent Males. In R. B. Warnecke (Ed.), *Health survey research methods.* Hyattsville, MD: National Center for Health Statistics.

T-ACASI capabilities and that can be implemented on a wide array of hardware. By merely cloning the relevant software and digitized voice files, the administration of a survey can be painlessly transferred among (1) laptop PCs used in the field, (2) desktop systems used in clinics, and (3) telephone audio-CASI systems used for call-in or call-out surveys.

Pilot Test of T-ACASI

Encouraging preliminary results are available from a pilot study that implemented the questionnaire from the National AIDS Behavioral Survey (Catania et al., 1992b) under T-ACASI.[14] (The NABS survey includes a wide variety of questions on sensitive issues, including heterosexual and same-gender sexual experiences, HIV serostatus, and drug use.) The pilot study used a cross-over experimental design in which a live telephone interviewer first asked each respondent[15] a standard set of introductory questions (section A) to elicit nonsensitive personal characteristics and attitudes. The sensitive questions in the survey were divided into two sections (B and C), and subjects were randomly assigned to one of two experimental conditions: (1) all questions in section B were administered by a human interviewer, and all questions in section C were administered using T-ACASI; or (2) all questions in section B were administered using T-ACASI, and all questions in section C were administered by a human interviewer. At the conclusion of the interview, a human telephone interviewer asked respondents a final series of questions (section D) to evaluate their experience with each mode of interviewing.

In addition to assessing the feasibility of implementing the new technology, the pilot study was intended to test two hypotheses:

H_1 Respondents will feel more comfortable reporting sensitive sexual behavior to a computer in a T-ACASI interview than to a human interviewer in a standard telephone interview.

14. In this section, we draw on material reported in Turner and coworkers (1996c).
15. The sample for this experiment was restricted to people ages 18 to 49. People under the age of 18 were excluded because of the difficulties in obtaining written parental consent in a telephone survey. People over the age of 45 were excluded because they have a low incidence of STDs and of risky sexual practices (Catania et al., 1992b:1103; Laumann et al., 1994:Tables 5.4a and 11.2). The pilot study used a composite sample with two strata. The first and largest stratum (target n = 200) was recruited from a probability sample of households with listed telephones in Cook County, Illinois (which comprises the city of Chicago and surrounding areas). The second stratum (target n = 50) was made up of patients recruited from the Wake County STD Clinic in Raleigh, NC. We included that group in the experiment to gain information on the impact of T-ACASI in a population that has a history of HIV risk behavior. We report here the results of a preliminary analysis of data from the first 142 interviews conducted in the pilot study.

H₂ Respondents will be more likely to report engaging in stigmatized or sensitive behavior (e.g., anal intercourse) and less likely to report engaging in normative behavior (e.g., always using condoms) in the more private T-ACASI interview mode than in a standard telephone interview with a human interviewer.

Results from preliminary analyses of the first 142 interviews in the pilot study encourage us to believe that T-ACASI surveys of sexual behavior are both feasible and likely to improve the quality of the resultant data. First, we found that touch-tone telephones were widely available in the "younger households" in the study—that is, households with an adult aged 18 to 49. Second, we found that the T-ACASI system was stable and that interviewers had relatively little difficulty in using it.[16] Third, our substantive hypotheses were generally confirmed by the study (see Table 4):

- By an odds ratio of 4.5, those who judged one method superior thought T-ACASI protected respondents' privacy more effectively than standard telephone interviewing.
- By an odds ratio of 4.4 among respondents who had an opinion, T-ACASI was considered more likely to elicit honest reporting of sexual and drug use behavior.
- By an odds ratio of 2.9, respondents who preferred one method reported that T-ACASI was better than standard telephone interviewing for collecting information about sensitive behaviors.
- By an odds ratio of 1.8 among respondents who reported a preference, T-ACASI was thought to provide a more comfortable environment for answering sensitive questions.

Given the small number of interviews used for these analyses (the maximum number for each condition was 62 and 80), we initially feared that their statistical power would be inadequate to detect differences across interview modes. On the contrary: our preliminary analyses indicated that there were significant (or bordering on significant) differences in the

---

16. During the study and the poststudy reviews, we discovered, for example, that respondents with two-line phones or call-waiting would occasionally discontinue the interview to take another call. The T-ACASI system initially treated such lengthy "silences" on the line as terminated interviews. We have altered our system so that after waiting several minutes for the respondent to come back on the line, the T-ACASI program will notify the telephone interviewer of the interruption so that the interviewer can recontact the respondent to complete the interview. We also encountered instances of "dropped connections" during the first days of interviewing, but they were not so frequent as to disrupt our operations. To deal with these occasional glitches, our hardware interface has been "trained" to adapt better to the telephone switching system environment in which it is working (that is, the electronic characteristics of telephone lines when they "hang up," generate flash tones, busy signals, and so forth).

Table 4. *Respondent Preferences for T-ACASI Versus a Standard Telephone Interview Using a Human Interviewer*

Dimension	Preference for			Odds Ratio (a)
	T-ACASI	Human	Indifferent	
Best at protecting your privacy	49%	11%	40%	4.53
Best for getting honest answers	73%	17%	10%	4.39
Best for asking about sensitive topics like sexual behavior	66%	23%	11%	2.88
More comfortable giving your answers	44%	24%	31%	1.82
Easier to use	30%	59%	11%	0.51
Most interesting to use	27%	50%	23%	0.54
Easiest to change answer (b)	1%	61%	37%	0.02

(a) Odds ratio for preference of T-ACASI to human interviewer; indifferent responses were excluded.
(b) This question asked respondents to rate which was the "hardest" mode in which to change answers. We report responses for the "easiest" mode to make them consistent with the coding of other dimensions in the table.
Source. Turner, C. F., Miller, H. M., Smith, T. K., Cooley, P. C., & Rogers, S. M. (1996c). Telephone audio computer-assisted self-interviewing (T-ACASI) and survey measurements of sensitive behaviors: Preliminary results. In R. Banks, J. Fairgrieve, L. Gerrard, et al. (Eds.), *Survey and statistical computing*, 1996. Chesham, Bucks, U.K.: Association for Survey Computing.

responses to many of the most sensitive questions in the survey. Anal intercourse among heterosexuals is probably the most sensitive behavior reported by a sizable proportion of the U.S. population[17] and thus the behavior that should be most likely to show the effects, if any, of the increased privacy afforded by T-ACASI. As Table 5 shows, the pilot study found a difference of almost 17 percentage points in the proportion of respondents who reported engaging in anal sex during their lifetime in the interviewer-administered questioning (25.4%) compared with the T-ACASI mode (42.0%).[18] T-ACASI also substantially increased the likelihood that respondents would admit that:

---

17. Laumann and colleagues (1994) note that 25.6% of men and 20.4% of women (ages 18 to 59) report having had anal intercourse.
18. Our ongoing analyses of data for the full experiment suggest that this result is attenuated in the sample from the full study.

- They never used a condom (18.4% for the T-ACASI mode versus 8.1% for the interviewer-administered mode).
- They had infrequent (less than once a month or never) discussions of their sex lives with their most recent partner (64.0% versus 30.7%).
- Their most recent sexual relationship lasted less than 6 months (21.3% versus 5.8%).
- They had very limited sexual experience (that is, no sexual partners in adulthood [7.6% in the T-ACASI mode compared with 1.6% with a human interviewer]; no sexual intercourse in the past 6 months [8.0% versus 1.5%]; or intercourse 10 or fewer times in the past 6 months [41.3% versus 22.7%]).

T-ACASI also appears to lessen the likelihood that respondents will overreport normative behavior. For example, although 14.8% of respondents told a human interviewer that they had "used a condom every time they had sex in the past 6 months," only 6.8% of respondents made that claim when they were interviewed using T-ACASI.

Although the results from this small number of interviews must be viewed cautiously, they appear to support our hypotheses that subjects prefer a T-ACASI interviewing mode when answering sensitive questions and that T-ACASI increases the likelihood that subjects will report sensitive behaviors and decreases overreporting of normative behaviors. Such results indicate the potential value of T-ACASI for improving data quality in telephone surveys of sexual behavior.

Future Research

The studies are part of our current program of research aimed at improving the quality of survey measurements of sexual and other sensitive behavior. Among the activities presently under way are:

- A large-scale national survey of sexual behavior conducted as a randomized field experiment in which one-half of respondents will be interviewed using standard telephone survey procedures and one-half will be interviewed using T-ACASI.
- Experimental comparison of audio-CASI with both interviewer-administered and paper-and-pencil self-administered measurements in a large-scale, in-person survey of sexual behavior.
- An experimental test of the impact of telephone audio-CASI on the reporting of HIV status and of sexual, drug use, and other sensitive behavior, which is being conducted as a methodological add-on to the Urban Men's Health Survey (with J. Catania and colleagues).
- Tests of the impact of audio-CASI on reports of sexual behavior and

Table 5. *Estimates of Prevalence of Sensitive Behaviors Obtained from Telephone Interviews Using Human Interviewers and Telephone Audio-CASI (T-ACASI)*

	Estimated Prevalence (Per 100)						
	Human Interviewer		T-ACASI		Odds Ratio	p	
Measurement	Estimate	(Base N)	Estimate	(Base N)			
Anal Intercourse							
Ever had anal intercourse	25.4	(67)	42.0	(50)	2.13	0.03	(a)
Had anal intercourse in past 6 months	3.0	(67)	12.0	(50)	4.43	0.03	(a)
Oral Sex							
Given oral sex (since age 18)	79.7	(59)	79.5	(73)	0.99	ns	(b)
Received oral sex (since age 18)	89.8	(59)	89.0	(73)	0.92	ns	(c)
Limited Sexual Experience							
Had no sex partners since age 18	1.6	(61)	7.6	(79)	4.93	0.09	(d)
Had no sex in last 5 years	4.8	(62)	11.4	(79)	2.53	0.15	(e)
Did not have sex in past 6 months	1.5	(67)	8.0	(50)	5.74	0.01	(f)
Had sex fewer than 10 times in past 6 months	22.7	(67)	41.3	(50)	2.51	0.01	(f)
Condom Use							
Never used a condom in lifetime	8.1	(62)	18.4	(76)	2.57	0.07	(g)
6 months: Used condom every time had sex	14.8	(54)	6.8	(44)	0.42	0.14	(h)
6 months: Almost every time or every time had sex	27.8	(54)	15.9	(44)	0.49	0.14	(h)
Stability and Quality of Relationships							
Most recent sexual relationship lasted less than 6 months	5.8	(52)	21.3	(61)	4.42	0.01	(i)
Never discussed sex life with most recent partner	1.9	(52)	14.8	(61)	8.83	0.03	(j)

Estimated Prevalence (Per 100)

Measurement	Human Interviewer		T-ACASI		Odds Ratio	p
	Estimate	(Base N)	Estimate	(Base N)		
Discussed sex life less than once a month	28.8	(52)	49.2	(61)	2.39	0.03 (j)
Ever had a one-night stand since age 18	59.0	(61)	64.4	(73)	1.26	ns (k)

Notes. p-values are those for statistical tests of association in 2-way tabulations of Interview Mode by Question Response. In cases in which the response distributions have more than two categories, these p-values do not apply to each individual odds ratio. ns = not significant.
(a) MH = 4.97, d.f. = 1. Mantel-Haenszel test for trend in 2×3 table (Interview Mode by Reporting of Anal Sex). Categories of anal sex were (1) never experienced, (2) experienced but not in past 6 months; and (3) experienced in past 6 months. Note that the anal sex questions were not asked of people who reported no heterosexual sex in the previous 12 months or who reported only female-female sex in the past 5 years.
(b) L^2 = 0.00, d.f. = 1. Likelihood ratio chi-square test of independence model for 2×2 tables (Interview Mode by Given Oral Sex: Yes/No). The question was not asked of people who reported having no sex partners since age 18.
(c) L^2 = 0.02, d.f. = 1. Likelihood ratio chi-square test of independence model for 2×2 tables (Interview Mode by Received Oral Sex: Yes/No). The question was not asked of people who reported having no sex partners since age 18.
(d) L^2 = 2.91, d.f. = 1. Likelihood ratio chi-square test of independence model for 2×2 tables (Interview Mode by Had Any Sex Partners since Age 18: Yes/No).
(e) L^2 = 2.02, d.f. = 1. Likelihood ratio chi-square test of independence model for 2×2 tables (Interview Mode by Had Sex in Past 5 Years: Yes/No).
(f) MH = 7.27, d.f. = 1. Mantel-Haenszel test for trend in 2×3 table (Interview Mode by Frequency of Sex in Past 6 Months). Categories for frequency of sex were 0; 1–10; and 11+ times. Note that this question was not asked of people who reported no heterosexual sex in the previous 12 months.
(g) L^2 = 3.23, d.f. = 1. Likelihood ratio chi-square test of independence model for 2×2 tables (Interview Mode by Ever Used a Condom: Yes/No).
(h) MH = 2.13, d.f. = 1. Mantel-Haenszel test for trend in 2×4 table (Interview Mode by Condom Use in Past 6 Months). Categories for condom use were never; sometimes; almost always; and every time. Note that these questions were asked only if the person reported having one or more sex partners in the past 6 months.
(i) L^2 = 6.03, d.f. = 1. Likelihood ratio chi-square test of independence model for 2×2 table (Interview Mode by Most Recent Relationship Lasted More than 6 Months: Yes/No). The question was not asked of people who reported that they did not have a person that they had had sex with most often in the past year.
(j) L^2 = 9.00, d.f. = 1. Likelihood ratio chi-square test of independence model for 2×4 table (Frequency of Discussion by Interview Mode). Categories for frequency of discussion were never; less than 1 a month; 1–2 times a month; and 1+ times a week. Note that this question was not asked of people who reported that they did not have a person that they had had sex with most often in the past year.
(k) L^2 = 0.41, d.f. = 1. Likelihood ratio chi-square test of independence model for 2×2 table (Interview Mode by Ever Had a One-Night Stand: Yes/No). This question was not asked of people who reported that they had not had sex since age 18.

Source. Turner, C. F. Miller, H. M., Smith, T. K., Cooley, P. C., & Rogers, S. M. (1996c). Telephone audio computer-assisted self-interviewing (T-ACASI) and survey measurements of sensitive behaviors: Preliminary results. In R. Banks, J. Fairgrieve, L. Gerrard, et al. (Eds.), *Survey and statistical computing, 1996.* Chesham, Bucks, U.K.: Association for Survey Computing.

condom use during clinical interviews in STD clinics (with R. Jadack and colleagues).
- Assessment of the impact of audio-CASI on reports of HIV risk behaviors in the HIV Vaccine Preparedness Study (with D. Metzger, B. Koblyn, and coworkers).

Over the next two years, we hope that this research will provide a firmer foundation for drawing inferences about the extent, if any, to which audio-CASI and T-ACASI technology may increase the validity and reliability of survey measurements of sexual, contraceptive, and other related behaviors. We also hope such studies can help to identify the types of measurements and research contexts for which those technologies are best suited and the costs and barriers to their adoption.

Author Note

Research Triangle Institute was established in 1958 by Duke University, North Carolina State University, and the University of North Carolina to foster basic and applied research in science and engineering.

Acknowledgment

Preparation of this chapter was supported by grants to Charles Turner from the National Institutes of Health—specifically, grants RO1-HD/AG31067-01 from the National Institute of Child Health and Human Development and the National Institute on Aging, and RO1-MH56318-01 from the National Institute of Mental Health.

References

ACSF Investigators. (1992). Analysis of sexual behavior in France: A comparison between two modes of investigation—telephone survey and face-to-face survey. *AIDS, 6,* 315–323.

Aquilino, W. (1994). Interview mode effects in surveys of drug and alcohol use: A field experiment. *Public Opinion Quarterly, 58,* 210–240.

Auerbach, J. D., Wypijewska, C., & Brodie, H. K. H. (Eds.). (1994). *AIDS and behavior: An integrated approach.* Washington, DC: National Academy Press.

Blumstein, P. W., & Schwartz, P. (1983). *American couples: Money, work, and sex.* New York: Morrow.

Bradburn, N., & Sudman, S. (1979). *Improving interview methods and questionnaire design.* Washington, DC: Jossey-Bass.

Brandt, A. (1987). *No magic bullet.* New York: Oxford University Press.

Camburn, D., Cynamon, D., & Harel, Y. (1991, May). *The use of audio tapes and written questionnaires to ask sensitive questions during household interviews.* Presentation to the National Field Technologies Conference, San Diego, CA.

Catania, J., Dolcini, M., & Coates, T. (1992). Response to Cohen and Dent: The validity of self-reported condom use. *American Journal of Public Health, 82,* 1564.

*Catania, J., McDermott, L., & Pollack, L. (1986). Questionnaire response bias and face-to-face interview sample bias in sexuality research. *Journal of Sex Research, 22,* 52–72.

Catania, J., Coates, T., Kegeles, S., Thompson-Fullilove, M., Peterson, J., Marin, B., Siegel, D., & Hulley, S. (1992a). Condom use in multi-ethnic neighborhoods of San Francisco: The population-based AMEN (AIDS in Multi-Ethnic Neighborhoods) study. *American Journal of Public Health, 82,* 284–287.

Catania, J. A., Coates, T., Stall, R., Turner, H., Peterson, J., et al. (1992b). Prevalence of AIDS-related risk factors and condom use in the United States. *Science, 258,* 1101–1106.

Catania, J. A., Gibson, D. R., Chitwood, D. D., & Coates, T. J. (1990). Methodological problems in AIDS behavioral research: Influences on measurement error and participation bias in studies of sexual behavior. *Psychological Bulletin, 108,* 339–362.

Clark, A. L., & Wallin, P. (1964). The accuracy of husbands' and wives' reports of the frequency of marital coitus. *Population Studies, 18,* 165–173.

Clayton, R. L. (1991, April). *Developing CASI data collection methods in the Current Employment Statistics Survey.* Paper presented to the CASIC Methodology Panel, U.S. Bureau of the Census, Suitland, MD.

Clayton, R. L., & Harrell, L. (1989). Developing a cost model of alternative data collection methods: Mail, CATI, and TDE. In *Proceedings of the American Statistical Association,* Section on Survey Research Methods.

Coates, R. A., Calzavara, L. M., Soskolne, C. L., Read, S. E., Fanning, M. M., et al. (1988). Validity of sexual histories in a prospective study of male sexual contacts of men with AIDS or an AIDS-related condition. *American Journal of Epidemiology, 128,* 719–728.

Communication Technologies. (1987). *A report on designing an effective AIDS prevention campaign strategy for San Francisco: Results from the fourth probability sample of an urban gay male community.* San Francisco AIDS Foundation, San Francisco.

Cooley, P. C., & Turner, C. F. (1996). Implementing audio-CASI on Windows' platforms. *Technical Papers on Health and Behavior Measurement,* no. 25. Rockville, MD: Research Triangle Institute.

Cooley, P. C., Turner, C. F., O'Reilly, J. M., Allen, D. A., Hamill, D. N., & Paddock, R. E. (1996). Audio-CASI: Hardware and software considerations in adding sound to a computer-assisted interviewing system. *Social Science Computer Review, 14*(2), 197–204.

Cox, B., Witt, M., Traccarella, M., & Perez-Michael, A. (1992). Inconsistent reporting of drug use in the 1988 NHSDA. In C. F. Turner, J. T. Lessler, & J. C. Gfroerer (Eds.), *Survey measurement of drug use: Methodological studies* (DHHS Publication No. ADM 92-1929). Washington, DC: U.S. Government Printing Office.

Davis, P. B., Yee, R. L., Chetwynd, J., & McMillan, N. (1993). The New Zealand partner relations survey: Methodological results of a national telephone survey. *AIDS, 7,* 1509–1516.

Dennerstein, L., Smith, A. M., Morse, C. A., & Burger, H. G. (1994). Sexuality and the menopause. *Journal of Psychosomatic Obstetrics and Gynaecology, 15,* 59–66.

Dolcini, M., Catania, J., Coates, T., Stall, R., Hudes, E., et al. (1993). Demographic characteristics of heterosexuals with multiple partners: The National AIDS Behavioral Surveys (NABS). *Family Planning Perspectives, 25,* 208–214.

Fay, R. E., Turner, C. F., Klassen, A.D., & Gagnon, J. H. (1989). Prevalence and patterns of same-gender sexual contact among men. *Science, 243,* 338–348.

General Accounting Office. (1988). *AIDS forecasting: Undercount of cases and lack of key data weaken existing estimates.* Washington, DC: General Accounting Office.

Gfroerer, J. C., & Hughes, A. L. (1992). Collecting data on illicit drug use by phone. In C. F. Turner, J. T. Lessler, & J. C. Gfroerer (Eds.), *Survey measurement of drug use: Methodological issues* (DHHS Publication No. ADM 92–1929). Washington, DC: U.S. Government Printing Office.

Hendershot, T., Thornberry, J., Miller, H., Rogers, S. M., & Turner, C. F. (1996). Multilingual audio-CASI: Using English-speaking field interviewers to survey non-English-speaking households. In R. B. Warnecke (Ed.), *Health survey research methods: Conference proceedings* (DHHS Publication No. PHS 96–1013). Hyattsville, MD: National Center for Health Statistics.

IOM (Institute of Medicine). (1988). *Confronting AIDS: Update 1988.* Washington, DC: National Academy Press.

IOM (Institute of Medicine). (1986). *Confronting AIDS.* Washington, DC: National Academy Press.

Jacobson, N. S., & Moore, D. (1981). Spouses as observers of the events in their relationship. *Consulting and Clinical Psychology, 49,* 269–277.

Johnson, A., Wadsworth, J., Wellings, K., Field, J., & Bradshaw, S. (1994). *Sexual attitudes and lifestyles.* London: Blackwell.

Johnston, G. (1992, January). *Demonstration of computer-administered audio survey technology.* Seminar presented at the National Center for Health Statistics, Hyattsville, MD.

Jones, E. F., & Forrest, J. D. (1992). Underreporting of abortion in surveys of U.S. women: 1976 to 1988. *Demography, 29,* 113–126.

Kahn, J. R., Kalsbeek, W. D., & Hofferth, S. L. (1988). National estimates of teenage sexual activity: Evaluating the comparability of three national surveys. *Demography, 25,* 189–204.

Kinsey, S. H., Thornberry, J. S., Carson, C. P., & Duffer, A. P. (1995). *Respondent preferences toward audio-CASI and how that affects data quality.* Paper presented at the 50th Conference of the American Association of Public Opinion Research, Fort Lauderdale, FL, and at the International Field Directors and Technologies Conference, Deerfield Beach, FL.

Laumann, E., Gagnon, J., Michael, R., & Michaels, S. (1994). *Social organization of sexuality.* Chicago: University of Chicago Press.

Lessler, J. T., & Holt, M. (1987). Using response protocols to identify problems in the U.S. Census long form. In *Proceedings of the American Statistical Association,* Survey Research Methods Section (pp. 262–266).

Levinger, G. (1966). Systematic distortion in spouses' reports of preferred and actual sexual behavior. *Sociometry, 29,* 291–299.

London, K. A., & Williams, L. B. (1990). *Comparison of abortion underreporting in an in-person interview and a self-administered questionnaire.* Paper presented at the annual meeting of the Population Association of America, Toronto.

McQueen, D., Gorst, T., Nisbet, L., Robertson, B., Smith, R., & Uitenbroek, D. (1989). *A study of lifestyle and health.* Interim report no. 1. Research Unit in Health and Behavioral Change, University of Edinburgh, U.K.

Miller, H. G., Turner, C. F., & Moses, L. E. (Eds.). (1990). *AIDS: The second decade.* Washington, DC: National Academy Press.

Montgomery, K., Lewis, C. E., & Kirchgraber, P. (1991). Telephone screening for risk of HIV infection. *Medical Care, 29,* 399–407.

Morris, M. (1993). Telling tales explains the discrepancy in partner reports. *Nature, 365,* 437–440.

National Center for Education Statistics. (1993). *Adult literacy in America: A first look at the results of the National Adult Literacy Survey.* Washington, DC: U.S. Department of Education.

National Commission on AIDS. (1993). *Behavioral and social sciences and the HIV/AIDS epidemic.* Washington, DC: National Commission on AIDS.

O'Reilly, J., & Turner, C. F. (1992, March). *Survey interviewing using audio-format, computer-assisted technologies.* Presentation to the Washington Statistical Society.

O'Reilly, J., Hubbard, M., Lessler, J., Biemer, P., & Turner, C. F. (1994). Audio computer-assisted self-interviewing: New technology for data collection on sensitive issues and special populations. *Journal of Official Statistics, 10,* 197–214.

Phipps, P. A., & Tupek, A. R. (1990). *Assessing measurement errors in a touch-tone recognition survey.* Paper presented at the Measurement Error Conference, Tucson, AZ.

Presidential Commission on the HIV Epidemic. (1988). *Final report of the Presidential Commission on the HIV epidemic.* Washington, DC: Government Printing Office.

Rogers, S., & Turner, C. F. (1991). Male-male sexual contact in the U.S.A.: Findings from five sample surveys, 1970–1990. *Journal of Sex Research, 28,* 491–519.

Seage, G. R. III, Mayer, K. H., Horsburgh, C. R., Cai, B., & Lamb, G. A. (1989, June). *Validation of sexual histories of homosexual male couples.* Presentation to the Fifth International Conference on AIDS, Montreal.

Shober, S. E., Fe Caces, M., Pergamit, M. R., & Branden, L. (1992). Effect of mode of administration on reporting in the National Longitudinal Survey. In C. F. Turner, J. T. Lessler, & J. C. Gfroerer (Eds.), *Survey measurement of drug use: Methodological studies* (DHHS Publication No. ADM 92-1929). Washington, DC: U.S. Government Printing Office.

Smith, T. W. (1992). A methodological analysis of the sexual behavior questions on the General Social Surveys. *Journal of Official Statistics, 8,* 309–325.

Smith, T. W. (1989). *A methodological review of the sexual behavior questions on the General Social Survey.* Chicago: National Opinion Research Center.

Tanfer, K. (1993). National Survey of Men: Design and execution. *Family Planning Perspectives, 25,* 83–86.

Turner, C. F. (1989). Research on sexual behaviors that transmit HIV: Progress and problems. *AIDS, 3,* S63–S71.

Turner, C. F., & Martin, E. (Eds.). (1985). *Surveying subjective phenomena,* 2 vols. New York: Russell Sage.

Turner, C. F., Danella, R., & Rogers, S. (1995). Sexual behavior in the United States,

1930–1990: Trends and methodological problems. *Sexually Transmitted Diseases, 22*(3), 173–190.

Turner, C. F., Lessler, J. T., & Devore, J. (1992). Effects of mode of administration and wording on reporting of drug use. In C. F. Turner, J. T. Lessler, & J. C. Gfroerer (Eds.), *Survey measurement of drug use: Methodological issues* (DHHS Publication No. ADM 92–1929). Washington, DC: U.S. Government Printing Office.

Turner, C. F., Lessler, J. T., & Gfroerer, J. C. (1992). Future directions for research and practice. In Turner, Lessler, and Gfroerer (Eds.), *Survey measurement of drug use*.

Turner, C. F., Miller, H. G., & Moses, L. E. (Eds.). (1989). *AIDS, sexual behavior, and intravenous drug use*. Washington, DC: National Academy Press.

Turner, C. F., Ku, L., Sonenstein, F. L., & Pleck, J. H. (1996a). Impact of audio-CASI on bias in reporting of male-male sexual contacts: Preliminary results from the 1995 National Survey of Adolescent Males. In R. B. Warnecke (Ed.), *Health survey research methods: Conference proceedings* (DHHS Publication No. PHS 96–1013). Hyattsville, MD: National Center for Health Statistics.

Turner, C. F., Rogers, S. M., Hendershot, T., Thornberry, J., & Miller, H. (1996b). Improving representation of linguistic minorities in health surveys: A preliminary test of multilingual audio-CASI. *Public Health Reports, 111*(3), 276–279.

Turner, C. F., Miller, H. M., Smith, T. K., Cooley, P. C., & Rogers, S. M. (1996c). Telephone audio computer-assisted self-interviewing (T-ACASI) and survey measurements of sensitive behaviors: Preliminary results. In R. Banks, J. Fairgrieve, L. Gerrard, et al. (Eds.), *Survey and statistical computing, 1996: Proceedings of the Second ASC International Conference.* Chesham, Bucks, U.K.: Association for Survey Computing.

Wadsworth, J., Johnson, A. M., Wellings, K., & Field, J. (1996). What's in a mean? An examination of the inconsistency between men and women reporting sexual partnerships. *Journal of the Royal Statistical Society, 159,* 111–123.

Weeks, M. F. (1992). Computer-assisted survey information collection: A review of CASIC methods and their implications for survey operations. *Journal of Official Statistics, 8,* 445–465.

Werking, G. S., & Clayton, R. L. (1990). Enhancing the quality of time-critical estimates through the use of mixed mode CATI/CASI collection. In *Proceedings of Statistics Canada Symposium 90: Measurement and Improvement of Data Quality.*

Werking, G., Tupek, A., & Clayton, R. L. (1988). CATI and touch-tone self-response applications for establishment surveys. *Journal of Official Statistics, 4,* 349–362.

Werking, G. S., Clayton, R. L., Rosen, R., & Winter, D. (1988). Conversion from mail to CATI in the Current Employment Statistics survey. In *Proceedings of the American Statistical Association,* Survey Methods Section (pp. 431–436).

Surveying Sexuality and AIDS

Interviewer Attitudes and Representations

ALAIN GIAMI, WITH HÉLÈNE OLOMUCKI
AND JANINE DE POPLAVSKY

Surveying sexuality is not a simple act. Asking questions about a subject considered to be private can lead to unexpected or irrational reactions from the respondent, public opinion, and politicians. From the beginning, the ACSF[1] team was aware of the difficulties associated with this work and rapidly recognized the necessity of training, supporting, and listening to the problems of interviewers recruited to administer questionnaires used for the ACSF survey. Completing a questionnaire on sexuality is conceived as a particular way of communicating about sexuality, in a particular cultural context. This context is determined by psychosocial processes, which it is necessary to understand, in addition to the collection of data.

This chapter describes and analyzes the work of the interviewers who administered the questionnaires and collected data for the ACSF survey (Spira, Bajos, & the ACSF Group, 1994; Giami, 1996). The survey is presented, as is the context for the questionnaires. We then analyze the psychological processes and particularly the countertransference attitudes (Devereux, 1967) affecting the interviewers during this work. In particular, we address the interviewers' initial motivations and attitudes to the study, the relationship between the interviewer and respondent, and the representations and fantasies of the investigators concerning the theme of the survey: sexuality and AIDS.

State of the Art

Classic methodological work on questionnaire-based surveys often considers the interviewer to be one of the major sources of measurement error and bias during data collection, independent of the subject of the survey (Hyman, 1954; Turner & Martin, 1984).

Surveying Sexuality

In a text of nearly 40 pages, Alfred Kinsey (1948) defined in detail the ideal personality for an interviewer. He emphasized the value of tolerance

---

1. ACSF: Analyse des Comportements Sexuels en France (Analysis of Sexual Behavior in France).

62 | *Researching Sexual Behavior*

and empathy on the one hand and persuasion and seduction on the other. He described the central contradiction between "standardizing the questions and adapting the form of the questions" (Kinsey, 1948). According to Kinsey, the interviewer should be informed of the aim of the question and the field it is to cover, but almost complete freedom should be given in the formulation of the questions while collecting the data.[2] Note that this was possible in this study only because of the very small number of interviewers used to collect data. The 18,000 people investigated for the Kinsey reports were interviewed by only nine investigators, all experienced researchers engaged in the project. Just two researchers, Kinsey and one of his assistants (W. Pomeroy), were responsible for 15,000 of the interviews (85%) (Pomeroy, 1982).

More recently, Johnson and Delamater suggested that the "major problem is the attitude of researchers and interviewers to research into sexuality." As concerns methodology, they state that "concern with the threat of the subject matter is a projection of the interviewer's own discomfort." They conclude by suspecting "ourselves and our interviewers" of having been "insensitive to the important source of sensitivity in research on sexuality" and of having "overestimated the extent to which our respondents are sensitive to these topics and to reporting them" (Johnson & Delamater, 1976, p. 181).[3]

During the ACSF pilot survey, the formulation of the questionnaire was subject to a linguistic analysis and the interaction of the questionnaire was analyzed from recorded interviews. This confirmed that the interviewer necessarily put his or her own accent on what he or she said (Richard-Zappela, 1994) and that the relationship between the interviewer and the respondent developed as a sort of "conversation" between them (Achard, 1994). This analysis of the problem of collecting data clearly evidenced the need to train interviewers prior to the ACSF survey.

On the other hand, some researchers have chosen to ignore this phenomenon. They consequently propose methods to reduce this type of bias. Sundet et al. (1990), for example, opted for an entirely self-administered questionnaire, sent by post to the respondents. This approach simply eliminates interviewers from the data supply step and leaves the respondent alone with the questionnaire.

---

2. There is a distinction of this type in *The Authoritarian Personality* (Adorno et al., 1950), discriminating between underlying questions and explicit questions. Underlying questions are those that the researchers are trying to answer. The term *explicit questions* describes how the questions are put to the subject.

3. In the light of this, the attitude of Wellings' group is open to question when they state, "It is regrettable that questions about masturbation were excluded from the survey because discussions addressing this practice led to disgust and embarrassment among the subjects questioned during the qualitative pre-survey to establish the formulation of the questions" (Wellings et al., 1990, p. 133).

Issues in Interviewer Training

Bradburn and Sudman (1981) suggest that interviewer training should be central to the preparation of a survey. They recommend: "For surveys involving threatening topics, it would be a good idea to obtain a pretraining measure of the interviewers' expectations about difficulties with threatening questions. Then either those interviewers who expect considerable difficulties should not be assigned to that study, or time should be spent in training sessions to change their expectations and teach them how to handle problems if they should arise" (Bradburn & Sudman, 1981, p. 173).

Training for interviewers which includes increasing awareness of the relational and psychological dimensions of collecting data has been adopted by most major modern surveys on sexual behavior (Simon, Gordonneau, Mironer, & Dourlen-Rollier, 1972; Klassen, Williams, & Levitt, 1989; Laumann, Gagnon, Michael, & Michaels, 1994). In 1970, the Kinsey Institute during routine preliminary testing of NORC[4] interviewers identified anxiety, embarrassment, and a degree of rigidity associated with the research theme, which could potentially result in a large bias during data collection. These attitudes led to problems when formulating questions, hasty interpretations, induction of replies, and an absence of neutrality, all of which reduce the quality of the data collected. The training program used in this case included, in addition to the technical training, identification and evaluation of potential psychological difficulties the interviewers may have. The organizers of this survey, therefore, ran "psychological preparation" sessions during which the interviewers could discuss their difficulties (Shipps, 1989).

Simon believed it important to "defuse affective and moral resistance, and misplaced curiosity which could result from the subject of the survey, taboo for everybody, and which could have a negative effect on the information to be collected" (Simon et al., 1972).

During the preparation of the National Health and Social Life Survey, Laumann, Gagnon, and their team obtained financing for a three-day training session in Chicago for the 220 professional interviewers (mostly women) who had volunteered. This research team noted that the expected difficulty of this study was seen as a stimulating challenge by many of the interviewers. Most had volunteered for the survey because it was in the public interest. The training sessions, animated by psychologists specialized in the field of sexuality, allowed the interviewers to explore their own anxieties and reticence. Furthermore, participation in these sessions seems to have communicated strong motivation, which was maintained throughout the field phase. This research team chose women interviewers who were the most competent, without trying to match sex or race with the interviewees (Laumann et al., 1994).

---

4. National Opinion Research Center of the University of Chicago.

Problematics

The use of interviewers is not only a source of bias in the production of data. The establishment of an interviewer-respondent relationship is also one of the main conditions applying to a survey. We have tried to identify the conditions affecting the progress of the survey, particularly the scientific and technical apparatus which was developed and serves as the social and cultural context. We also assessed the psychological processes and especially the countertransference attitudes affecting the interviewers. The significance of these processes was confirmed by the daily monitoring of the interviewers. On one occasion during the administration of a questionnaire, the following question was posed by the interviewer: "Have you yourself ever been subjected to pornographic conversations or telephone calls?" The respondent replied, "No, today is the first time." This shows that meanings can be attributed to the survey and this can help explain the origin of much reticence, both public and private, concerning surveys of sexuality.

We used as a basis the assumption of Devereux that "an interview about sex even in the case of a scientific interview is in itself a kind of sexual interaction, which can be lived out on a symbolic, verbal and emotional level as shown in the analysis of the sexual transference in psycho-analysis" (Devereux, 1967, p. 29). Countertransference can be defined as "all unconscious reactions of the analyst to the person analyzed and particularly transference from the analyst" (Laplanche & Pontalis, 1967). This definition has the merit of emphasizing the importance of fantasies developed during this type of communication.

Completing the questionnaire involves a relationship between two individuals. The situation is, however, asymmetric. For the interviewer, it is a professional activity, whereas it addresses the private life of the respondent. For telephone interviews, the interviewer is in his/her place of work, covered by his/her professional status. The respondents are questioned in their home in a private situation about the most intimate aspects of their life, not only sexuality. The questionnaire itself serves as mediator of the communication. The interview proceeds according to a well-defined scenario based on progression and the alternation of questions considered to be banal and those considered sensitive.

The professional nature of the involvement of the interviewer does not exclude conscious and unconscious manifestations of his/her subjectivity. We believe it necessary to study the interviewers' representations of sexuality and AIDS to identify both the difficulties with which they expect to be confronted and spontaneous interpretation of replies which could affect the quality of the data collected. There is also interference between the interviewer's subjectivity, derived from representations of sexuality and

AIDS, and the professional dimension of the interviewer's activity aiming at isolating them.

Methods

The apparatus established for the training of the interviewers gave us the opportunity to perform a qualitative survey among these interviewers to identify the psychosocial and some of the unconscious dimensions of their involvement in the survey. The analyses presented in this chapter are based on all our formal and informal contacts with the interviewers, researchers, and the heads of polling institutes throughout the ACSF survey.

We asked the interviewers to comment and give their subjective impressions both before and after the survey. This allowed us to investigate the interviewer-respondent interaction from the angle of its interiorization by the interviewers, rather than from its exteriority. Our position is thus consistent with that of M. Godelier, who states: "Social relations are not only between individuals, they are within individuals. . . . Ideology is the inner framework of social relations and this framework is found as much within the individual as in his or her relationships" (Godelier, 1996, p. 28). Our qualitative study of interviewers was conducted through semistructured interviews to evaluate the importance of countertransference attitudes involved in carrying out the survey. About 30 interviewers were interviewed at different moments of the survey.

Context: The Apparatus of the ACSF Survey

In our approach, the apparatus of the survey can be considered to be a *working situation* characterized by a particular *working organization* (Dejours, 1993). This serves as a framework within which the various participants in the survey act. The research apparatus consists of all the relationships between the various people involved in the project (the researchers, polling institutes, interviewers) as well as the external bodies controlling the research. This is the context for the relationship between the interviewer and respondent.

The interviewers are a sort of open window onto the studied population, in this case representative of the French general population. The interviewer-respondent relationship is mediated by technical (the telephone) and scientific supports (the questionnaire). The interviewers are directly supported by the polling institute supervisors and research teams of the ACSF, who contributed to the training, the monitoring, and control of the survey. This monitoring is not limited to verifying the quality of the data collected but allows effective supervision of the interviewers throughout the survey. Thus ACSF researchers are available both at moments of interest and excitement and periods of discouragement. There are also informal contacts between interviewers and, obviously, they had relationships with their personal entourage which included discussions of the survey. The discussions between the interviewers and the researchers gave the researchers a clearer view of the population surveyed.

The researchers, supervisors, and polling institute heads also have programmed meetings. Within the research teams, the coordinators of the ACSF survey hold a particular position with respect to the researchers, the interviewers, and the polling institute heads and the external bodies. The ACSF survey was evaluated by scientists of the ANRS, was assessed by the national AIDS committee as concerns ethics, and was under the administrative control of the CNIL (the national commission for computer technology and civil liberties) to ensure the confidentiality of the data collected.

INSERM occupies a special place in this structure. The unit organizing the survey is part of INSERM, and it is the client of the polling institutes and manages the public fundings allocated to research. The name INSERM is a symbolic guarantee of the scientific quality of the work. The project would not have been possible except at the request and with the authorization of the government (Got, 1989). Thus throughout the survey the interviewers worked in a context particularly loaded with the symbolic dimension of science, the issues concerning the "fight against AIDS," and public involvement.

Training Interviewers

Defining the objectives of the training and establishing training strategies were subjects of extensive discussion among the ACSF staff and managers of the polling institutes. First, it appeared that providing training for the interviewers would mean a change in the usual work practices of these institutes, which are usually responsible for it themselves. In accordance with their organization culture, the project managers and supervisors wanted to be completely involved in the training process and be technically involved in its management. As two institutes had been engaged to carry out the survey, the managers of both were reluctant to share a common training program which might reveal their expertise to the other. The principle of technical training was immediately and unanimously accepted by the ACSF staff, given the complexity of the questionnaire (filters, precise wording of instructions, selection of questions depending on the respondents' characteristics, etc.). The introduction of a psychosocial and interpersonal dimension, on the other hand, was subject to more reservations. The task appeared even more difficult as the team psychologists could not simply define typical ideal conduct and encourage the interviewers to adopt it. Rather, the interviewers had to be helped to become aware of their own emotional investment in the subject of the survey and to try to avoid defensive attitudes when administering the questionnaire.

Training Program

An initial training program was tested and evaluated at the same time as the pilot survey. The final program had the following direct objectives:

1. Acquiring technical competence in the use of the questionnaire: familiarity with the introductory text, the filters, the forms of answers, etc.
2. Acquiring the interpersonal skills for supporting the respondent in an exercise in which interviewers might be emotionally involved. This skill involves the personalization of each interviewer-respondent interaction. The interviewer must find, for each respondent, the right distance between them. Contrary to what might be thought, this is not contradictory with the requirement for standardizing the administration of the questionnaire.
3. Acquiring specific competence: understanding the survey objectives, knowledge of the structure and logic of the questionnaire.

The program also had the following indirect objectives:

1. Clarifying the interviewer's psychological involvement in the research, in particular interviewer resistance and counterattitudes to the subject matter.
2. Motivating the interviewers, giving them a sense of responsibility as they are participating in a large-scale survey.
3. Providing the necessary information about AIDS so as to better understand the questionnaire and answer questions asked by respondents.

Content of the Training

The training included a plenary session introducing the study, its scientific objectives, and its usefulness to society; giving medical and epidemiological information on AIDS and STDs (plenary session); and answering questions. Small-group workshops were held to provide a detailed analysis of both the procedure for selecting the respondent and the questionnaire item by item; an actual run-through of a questionnaire; and an analysis of this experience, involving identification of interpersonal difficulties, role-playing, and simulations and identification of technical and linguistic difficulties. There were also individual interviews with volunteer interviewers.

Interviewer Interviews

The interviews on which this study was based were done primarily at the request of the ACSF psychologists. Interviewers, however, used the interview time to express themselves, reconsider thoughts evoked by the training, clarify their motivations, reply to questions in the questionnaire, converse with a psychologist, and state their opinion of the training. Such interviews were offered to all the interviewers, and a large proportion volunteered, but only around 30 were actually interviewed owing to lack of resources. Although not all the interviewers were interviewed, these interviews were perceived as an integral part of the support and monitoring of the interviewers as a body. They revealed that the interviewers needed to communicate their experience of the survey. As one interviewer stated, "An interview is like an analysis, or a psychotherapy. . . . Well, I feel that it's a great opportunity to discuss all this with a psychologist from the beginning to the end. I really think, and I say this egotistically, only for myself, that is really good. If everyone had been able to do it, it would have been even better."

Interviewer Motivations

Declared Interest

We picked up what might be defined as the interviewers' public and correct discourse associated with the necessity of convincing the research staff and employers of their competence and motivation. We noted here the importance of participating in a large-scale humanitarian and scientific survey which would mean that human lives can be saved and science is advanced, while also informing the population and making it more aware of the problems of AIDS and the prevention of HIV infection. Thus there was substantial support for the objectives presented during the training sessions. This dimension of the motivation seems to reflect the discourse expressed by the staff in the first session of the training program (presentation of the scope of the survey). Some interviewers expressed here common views about the survey and research against AIDS, views that might be considered as correct by the staff. To a lesser degree, some interviewers were skeptical as to the effectiveness of this kind of survey in modifying sexual behavior and contributing to AIDS prevention. According to this opinion, the survey would give a generalized and vague reflection of sexuality in France.

Personal Interest

In this category, motivation refers much more to the personal experience of the interviewers. This section of the analysis identified motivations less consistent with the demands of the research team. A significant number of the interviewers knew one or more HIV-positive individuals or persons with AIDS. Such proximity was a strong motivation; for them, they would be making a personal contribution to the fight against AIDS. Participating in a large-scale survey gave them a certain pride associated with the desire to be up to the task entrusted to them. Being able to get respondents to answer honestly seemed to be a challenge which they wanted to take up. There was also a certain amount of curiosity and desire to learn about the population's sexual practices, with a hope to make commonplace a subject which may be considered as taboo. The link between the survey subject (sexual behavior) and the prevention of AIDS was an element enabling them to sublimate positively their resistance to and guilt at exploring respondents' sexuality. Finally, it is important to note that participating in the survey was a paid job. This was also a personal motivation for the interviewers.

The Interviewer-Respondent Relationship

The "Hook"

The first contact with the respondent is the most important for establishing the survey relationship. One consequence of the decision to use the telephone is to isolate the voice from the global sensorial perception of the outside world. The voice is then the vehicle of the communication between the two people involved. The voice can, according to the moment, be seductive, harmonious, sympathetic, or rejecting. Emotion and affects are also transmitted by the voice.

The voice is initially persuasive to "hook" the other party. Once involved in the survey, the individual becomes the respondent, and the voice of the interviewer is as neutral as possible when asking the questions. The survey relationship is established and the respondent can respond.

The ideal goal is neutrality, and establishing this is facilitated by styles adopted by the interviewer: according to the case, this could be arguments appealing to thought and logic, altruism, or seduction.

Handling Conflict While Maintaining Neutrality

The interviewers in some cases became involved in discussion with people expressing opinions which shocked them. It is interesting that the interviewers expressed ideological values colored by liberalism and tolerance which were consistent with the social values expressed by the ACSF research team. Some interviewers were shocked by the number of respondents who did not believe themselves concerned by the AIDS problem. The necessity of continuing the survey and the assessment of its objectives helped the interviewers to adopt a neutral attitude, overcoming their reactions to the views of the respondents.

A Double-Bind Situation

This mode of communication involving completing a long questionnaire on sexuality cannot be a simple game of question and answer. From the start, the interviewers developed representations of the study in which they attributed to it meanings other than the simple collection of data. The way the interviewer-respondent relationship was handled depended, among other factors, on the ambiguous nature of the instructions given to the interviewers by the research team. These instructions can be seen as a "double bind":[5] the respondents must be made to talk, but also prevented from talking such that they do not digress, and so only produce usable data.

Getting reliable answers depends on the ability of the interviewers to manage a complex relationship loaded with their own motivation, reticence, representations of the survey developed from the first days, and the demands, expectations, and questions of the respondents. During the survey, the interviewers were confronted with various demands from the respondents. As only the answers to the survey questions are considered as data, the interviewers thus had to restrict to a minimum other confidences, digressions, and confessions brought on by the situation, so as not to interfere with the correct completion of the questionnaire. A certain distance was perceived as being necessary for answering intimate questions. Intimacy risked creating a process of self-censorship.

Experiencing the Interview Process

The interviewers were particularly interested in the working conditions, because they had to be available and listen to the respondents. The necessary productivity (linked in one of the two polling institutes to their remuneration) often appeared to be an obstacle to establishing such a relationship. The time constraints were sometimes perceived as possibly damaging to the climate of confidence, which was difficult to establish in some cases. However, it must be borne in mind that the interviewers often felt some apprehension about managing difficult cases and the time limits imposed by the needs of the survey were undoubtedly reassuring.

Concerns and Embarrassment

The enthusiasm and altruism of the interviewers must be balanced against the legitimate concerns expressed before the beginning of the survey. Making contact with respondents brought some of these into clear focus, particularly the possibility of meeting with refusal and the problems

---

5. The idea of double bind was defined by Bateson as "simultaneously giving two contradictory orders: 'Do this, but whatever you do, don't do it' " (Bateson, "Schizophrenia and Society," p. 525, in *Encyclopedia Universalis*, vol. 16, 1985).

associated with asking such intimate questions. Part of this apprehension was projected onto the respondent. We noted the fear of shocking some people or upsetting them and comments on the crude nature of the questionnaire and its length. Some situations related to interviewers' personal experiences provoked strong feelings of embarrassment, particularly questions dealing with death, rape, and, more generally, sexuality. The interviewers were sometimes worried about the risk of drifting toward coarseness or obscenity. All of them were concerned for the absolute respect of respondents' and their own anonymity.

Ambivalence and Dynamics of the Motivation

The interviewers' involvement seemed to us to be a complex mixture of strong social and personal motivations and an expressed ambivalence composed of enthusiasm and concern. These motivations and the underlying energy changed during the survey. Concern decreased significantly as the work progressed and its feasibility was demonstrated daily. We noted the strongest involvement during collective summing-up sessions and personal conversations at midsurvey time. The interviewers then showed themselves to be particularly stimulated by this exchange. On the other hand, at the end of the survey, weariness and fatigue had set in, due to the progressive difficulty of finding people to question and the repetitive nature of the responses.

Throughout the three months the survey took, there were continuing processes of maturation, investment then disinvestment, excitement, and boredom. It may therefore be necessary to take the time taken by a survey into account, and ensure effective and efficient support for the interviewers so as to maintain their motivation and their competence through to the end.

Fantasies

Administering the questionnaire led to a number of fantasies among the interviewers. Some of these fantasies were associated with situations involving communication on sexuality: using the telephone for sexual abuse; religious confessions; obtaining confessions of sexual guilt; or administering psychotherapy. One interviewer stated: "I didn't dare go as far as say confession, but, I won't go as far as saying we'll be like priests, or psychologists."

Moreover, some of the words used by interviewers imply that the interviewer-respondent interaction might have been experienced (on the level of fantasizing) as a sexual interaction incorporating both excitement and embarrassment. The fantasies can be deciphered from the words and metaphors used by the interviewers. Some were in the category of "survey as coitus." During the training sessions, the interviewers expressed a very strong desire at the same time as expressing their fears linked to the high stakes involved. At the beginning of the survey, there was a fair level of excitement represented by very rich cognitive functioning (construction of spontaneous theories about the respondents). Toward the end of the survey, the interviewers spoke of fatigue and boredom with the repetitiveness of responses. Others were in the category of "interview as coitus." Carried on a wave of excitement, interviewers in some cases fantasized administration of the questionnaire as a sexual relationship between the interviewer and respondent. These fantasies were not directly admitted by the interviewers. They used metaphors for the sexual act: "Well, some people were a bit embarrassed, when asked if they thought that the man was frustrated by not having an orgasm, or for the woman not being penetrated. But then, *once entered into*, once started, *once we'd really got into the subject*, it went better, you know. It's true that some were a bit prudish at the beginning, but there were others that *plunged straight into it*, you know. It just happened. . . . Anyway, *it takes two people*, so I don't know why we use more, we emphasized the man more than the woman . . . and because I'm a woman it just happened. It's true that it was easier when they were alone." The interviewers were thus required to act in a contradictory way, but this seemed to work for the survey. The necessary restriction on confidences served as a reassuring censure for the interviewers (involving asking preestablished questions and not drifting into intimate curiosity which could awaken various fantasies).

The survey relationship required that the interviewers use a rational strategy to establish and maintain contact throughout the questionnaire by handling their own motivations, the demands of the respondents, their personal reactions, and constraints imposed by the scientific structure. The issues they faced included their own fantasies brought on by the situation of the survey on sexuality, reinforced by what they were saying and hearing.

Interviewer Representations

During interviews prior to the survey, the interviewers described their fears and expectations of the survey. These expectations are the expression of the interviewers' initial representations. They were linked both to the interviewer's previous professional experience and to their representations of sexuality. Identifying these representations was useful for two reasons. During the survey they helped elucidate difficulties felt by the interviewers (and this was the subject of work involving role playing during the training sessions). They also helped identify representations of sexuality in the general population. Obviously, the interviewers express representations likely to be found among people of their age and social category.

Sexuality and Age

Respondents more than 20 years older than their interviewer (i.e., a one-generation age difference) are considered here to be in an older age group. Individuals in this group were perceived as not being concerned by sexuality. Thus the interviewers felt that discussion of their past sex life risked upsetting these individuals. Older persons were perceived as belonging to a different cultural world in which talking about sexuality to a younger person is taboo.

Difference between Genders and Communication about Sexuality

The gender difference was raised when the interviewer seemed to perceive possible eroticism in the conversation. Male interviewers presumed that women would have more difficulty replying to a man, and the female interviewers believed that men would have problems confiding in them. Both men and particularly women interviewers emphasized the seriousness of the questionnaire and its scientific context. The involvement of eroticism in the situation appeared to the interviewers as a potential source of difficulty.

The Sexuality of the French

Most interviewers had a representation of a "well-behaved and conformist" France: "the French always have the same classical practices"; "they do not have that much intercourse"; "traditional gender roles are still dominant." However, a few atypical cases were reported as shocking by the interviewers: "very large number of sex partners"; "sexual violence and sexual abuse"; "sexually active Catholic priests." Interviewer surprise evidenced the existence of normative representations, which filtered the respondent replies.

Projection of the Difficulties

The perception of difficulties with communication are frequently projected onto the other party rather than leading to recognition of one's own difficulties with this other party. Interviews with a woman interviewer before and after the survey reveal this type of process. Before the survey this woman stated: "Some of the questions, which are crude, like 'do you suck your partner's penis' . . . I couldn't see any other way of saying it . . . 'fellatio' was suggested, but some people won't understand, so we said it more simply, more, well, directly. It's true that I thought we could have found different words. I said to myself that it's crude and a bit vulgar. It's true, 'suck,' well, it's vulgar . . . I think that I blushed there, but, me, I'm sure I would have blushed if I'd been asked that question like that." After the survey she stated: "I had a North African man who spoke fluent French, but I remember that there were the questions about his sexual activities during his life, what was it . . . 'have you licked your partner's sex', he didn't understand 'licked.' I had the impression he didn't understand . . . finally, I was tired, so I said to him 'listen, you lick an ice cream, it's the same only it's your partner's sex,' and he understood. Well, perhaps it was the situation that he didn't understand." These statements reveal that during the first interview she expressed her embarrassment about a question concerning fellatio and during the postsurvey interview she described a difficulty with the same question but attributed the difficulty to the respondent. Thus the interviewer initially could not attribute the problem to anyone else and was forced to recognize it in herself. Subsequently, it is striking that she chose the same item to report one of the difficulties she had during the survey.

Performing the survey allowed the interviewers to express their representations of sexuality, particularly the relationship between age and sexuality, relationships between the sexes, the place of sexuality in the couple, and the opposition between situations considered to be typical and atypical. The production of objective data by the questionnaire allowed them to see the difference between prior representations and the overall impression gained through this experience. The interviewers seemed to conduct, in their own way, personal research based on the confrontation between initial hypotheses and research data.

Conclusion

Our analysis shows that conducting a survey on sexuality, a particular form of communication about sexuality, is far from being a natural act[6] which can be reduced to the simple materialism of the results presented to the scientific community and to society in general through the media.

The interviews collected allowed us to identify representations and fantasies or metaphors used by the interviewers to interpret their experience. We tried to understand how and why the interviewers gave a meaning to their involvement and subjectively implicated themselves in the ACSF. We know of no analysis of the subjective position of interviewers during a quantitative survey by questionnaire that has used this approach (see Catania et al., 1995). Our work is similar to that of Herdt and Stoller (1990) using an ethnographic approach to eroticism.

The training and support from the research team made it easier for the interviewers to handle the interviewer-respondent relationship in the heat of the action, including the difficulties they imagined at the start of the

---

6. An editorial in the journal *Nature* which described the main results of the ACSF survey and the British survey used the term *natural act* to comment on the fact that both surveys were conducted without major problems.

survey and those encountered during the survey. Collecting data as complex as these depends on establishing a scientific, technical, and relational structure developed for the occasion. The structure restrained the subjective reactions (both psychological and ideological, conscious and unconscious) raised by the subject surveyed. It also channeled eroticism involved in all forms of communication about sexuality. The interviewers were thus in a double-bind situation, or subject to ambivalence, which showed itself to facilitate formulation of the questions, while feeling protected by the scientific context.

Using the telephone, thus hearing, seems to have favored expression of the imagination of the interviewers. The technical language of the survey was not sufficient to contain the unconscious representations which should have used different words and metaphorical strategies for expression. A situation determined by focus on the voice and listening was represented using visual terms (implying a voyeurist position) or active terms (implying genital-type fantasies). The evolution of the psychological investment of the interviewers during the study revealed how a degree of eroticism associated with the situation, which could be seen as a risk of divergence, allowed the survey to develop, proceed, and come to a conclusion. Understanding this dimension could allow better management of secondary effects, particularly embarrassment and guilt, which could impair the progress of scientific work—the perfect subliminatory activity.

The main aim in the development of the questionnaire was the collection of coherent, homogeneous, and quantifiable data. This involved minimizing the personal expressions of the interviewers and respondents. A pilot survey was used to compare face-to-face interviewing with telephone interviews (ACSF investigators, 1992). A study of the interviewer effect evidenced the importance of gender on the data collected, but only for some questions on opinion (Firdion & Laurent, in press). The questionnaire and structure used can be considered to have minimized the effects of the interviewers on the production of data. These effects were not, however, eliminated.

It is surprising that despite the psychological factors at work on the interviewers, quantitative analysis of the interviewer effect, particularly that associated with the interviewer's gender, did not evidence any large bias in the replies obtained. It is possible that the production of reliable data from surveys may be possible only with the participation of trained interviewers who understand the difficulties associated with the relationship they establish with the respondent. The data can only be standardized by appropriate use of flexibility and specificity for each interview.

Our work helps illuminate the complexity of communication about sexuality in a professional context. It mobilizes personal and subjective involvement, representations, and fantasies in the professional interviewers. In addition to the information we collected about the act of surveying, our study opens new fields for work on communication about sexuality. We obtained information about taboos and guilt arising from the curiosity involved and about the satisfaction, possibly mixed with embarrassment, associated with the discovery of details of the sexual life of another. We learned how erotic investment and disinvestment processes work in the individuals in this strictly defined context aimed at describing sexual behavior. Desire finds indirect ways of manifesting itself other than the direct and crude expression of sexuality, which can be compared to certain forms of pornography. The notions of confession, confidence, fault, and surprise described by the interviewers show the extent to which communication about sexuality, whether during a survey or within a relationship between partners, is structured by imaginary significations attributed by the individuals. The voyeuristic and sexual metaphors are evidence of the erotic character of the energy necessary for this work.

References

Achard, P. (1994). Sociologie du langage et analyse d'enquêtes. De l'hypothèse de la rationalité des réponses. *Sociétés Contemporaines, 18/19,* 67–100.

ACSF Investigators. (1992). Analysis of sexual behavior in France: A comparison between two modes of investigation, telephone survey and face-to-face survey. *AIDS, 6,* 315–323.

Adorno, T. W., Frenken-Brunswick, E., Levinson, D., Nevitt Sanfort, R. (1950). *The authoritarian personality.* New York: Harper.

Bradburn, N., & Sudman, S. (1974). *Response effects in surveys.* Chicago: Aldine.

Bradburn, N., & Sudman, S. (1981). *Improving interview method and questionnaire design.* San Francisco: Jossey-Bass.

Catania, J. A., Binson, D., van der Straten, A., & Stone, V. (1995). Methodological research on sexual behavior in the AIDS era. *Annual Review of Sex Research, 6,* 77–125.

Dejours, C. (1993). De la psychopathologie à la psychodynamique du travail. *Travail, usure mentale* (pp. 205–253). Paris: Bayard.

Devereux, G. (1967). *From anxiety to method in the behavioral sciences.* The Hague: Mouton.

Firdion, J.-M., & Laurent, R. (1997). Effet du sexe de l'enquêteur: Une enquête sur la sexualité et le sida. In N. Bajos, M. Bozon, A. Ferrand, A. Giami, & A. Spira (Eds.), *La sexualité aux temps du sida.* Paris: P.U.F. (in print).

Giami, A. (1996). The influence of an epidemiological representation of sexuality: The ACSF survey questionnaire. In M. Bozon & H. Leridon (Eds.), *Sexuality and social sciences—An analysis of the French sexual behavior survey* (pp. 57–82). London: Dartmouth.

Godelier, M. (1996). Sexualité et société. In J. Cournut (Ed.), *Psychanalyse et sexualité. Questions aux sciences humaines* (pp. 27–40). Paris: Dunod.

Got, C. (1989). *Rapport sur le sida.* Paris: Flammarion.

Herdt, G., & Stoller, R. (1990). *Intimate communications—Erotics and the study of culture.* New York: Columbia University Press.

Hyman, H. (1954). *Interviewing in social research.* Chicago: University of Chicago Press.

Johnson, W., & Delamater, J. (1976). Response effects in sex surveys. *Public Opinion Quarterly, 40,* 165–181.

Kinsey, A., Pomeroy, W., & Martin, C. (1948). *Sexual behavior in the human male.* Philadelphia: Saunders.

Klassen, A., Williams, C., & Levitt, E. (1989). *Sex and morality in the U.S.: An empirical enquiry under the auspices of the Kinsey Institute.* Middletown, CT: Wesleyan University Press.

Laplanche, J., & Pontalis, J. B. (1967). *Vocabulaire de la psychanalyse.* Paris: P.U.F.

Laumann, E., Gagnon, J., Michael, R., & Michaels, S. (1994). *The social organization of sexuality: Sexual practices in the United States.* Chicago: University of Chicago Press.

Pomeroy, W. (1982). *Dr. Kinsey and the Institute for Sex Research.* New Haven: Yale University Press.

Richard-Zappela, J. (1994). Linguistic analysis of the questionnaire. In A. Spira, N. Bajos, & ACSF Group. *Sexual behaviour and AIDS* (pp. 33–37). Aldershot: Avebury.

Shipps, J. (1989). Training the NORC field supervisors. In A. Klassen, C. Williams, E. Levitt (Eds.), *Sex and morality in the U.S.: An empirical enquiry under the auspices of the Kinsey Institute* (pp. 295–302). Middletown, CT: Wesleyan University Press.

Simon, P., Gordonneau, J., Mironer, L., & Dourlen-Rollier, A. M. (1972). *Rapport sur le comportement sexuel des français.* Paris: Julliard, Charron.

Spira, A., Bajos, N., and the ACSF Group. (1994). *Sexual behaviour and AIDS.* Aldershot: Avebury.

Sundet, J., Magnus, P., Kvalem, I., & Bakketeig, L. (1990). Self-administered anonymous questionnaires in sexual behaviour research: The Norwegian experience. In M. Hubert (Ed.), *Sexual behaviour and risks of HIV infection* (pp. 79–96). Proceedings of an international workshop supported by the European Community. Brussels: Publications des Facultés Universitaires Saint-Louis.

Tielman, R. (1990). Telephone surveys in comparison with other methods in psycho-social AIDS research. In M. Hubert (Ed.), *Sexual behaviour and risks of HIV infection* (pp. 97–103). Proceedings of an international workshop supported by the European Community. Brussels: Publications des Facultés Universitaires Saint-Louis.

Turner, C., & Martin, E. (Eds.). (1984). *Surveying subjective phenomena.* New York: Russell Sage.

Wellings, K., Fields, J., Johnson, A., Wadsworth, J., & Bradshaw, S. (1990). Notes on the design and construction of a national survey of sexual attitudes and lifestyles. In M. Hubert (Ed.), *Sexual behaviour and risk of HIV infection* (pp. 105–133). Proceedings of an international workshop supported by the European Community. Brussels: Publications des Facultés Universitaires Saint-Louis.

Discussion

John Bancroft: Are there any immediate points people want to raise, directly stemming from Charles Turner's paper?

Anke Ehrhardt: Just a question. Obviously we always assume that reporting of stigmatized behavior is the truth. My question is about the validity of such reporting. You have assumed the method is advantageous because it produces higher reporting. But we really don't know. Maybe on the computer, you flip out and report higher frequency of behavior.

Charles Turner: I have two responses. The first is that it isn't the case that the differences are always in the direction of more reporting of stigmatized behavior. It's not clear that it's always in a direction you can predict beforehand. For example, oral sex shows no difference. The second response is that we want to see, in instances in which we have independently collected data on the behaviors of respondents, whether or not we get better correlations between the survey measures and those independent measures. If, for example, you're looking at the reporting of behaviors that put you at risk for an STD in a population with lots of STDs around and you're getting measures of the numbers of partners, the size of the networks, and so forth that correlate better with actual sero-incidence of gonorrhea, then you have some external validation.

Alain Giami: But, given the usual discrepancies between women and men reporting their numbers of partners, do you observe that men start reporting less and the women more partners?

Charles Turner: We don't know. That's what we're hoping.

Colin Williams: Now, when I'm on the phone with this disembodied voice talking to me, do I have to have touch-tone?

Charles Turner: You have to have a phone that's capable of generating tones. And for the population of households containing a person aged 18 to 49, which is actually, for reasons that you all understand, the population we're interested in, 95 percent of that population nationally reports having such a phone. If you're looking at older folks, it's a tougher problem.

Ulrich Clement : Do you have any idea what the psychological basis of this interaction between the respondent and an interviewer is? There is always an interaction between two persons. What do respondents see as different in a questionnaire compared to an audio-CASI? Do you have any concept of what makes this difference?

Charles Turner: We've done a little qualitative research, but at the moment we're looking at something that is admittedly a black box. It's my impression that if somebody calls me up (as a person who is in a long-term relationship and has a couple of kids) and asks how many times I have had sex in the past 30 days, I may feel some pressure to give a number larger than the truth. Similarly, if somebody calls up and asks, "Have you had any sexual partners in the past year?" there may be a psychological or normative pressure to say that you're sexually active. That's our guess as to why the distribution is moving down with T-ACASI surveys. I think some people would find it a bit hard to tell a stranger that they were in a marriage and hadn't had sex in the past month.

Ulrich Clement: But why should they tell this to an audio-CASI?

Anne Johnson: Because the audio-CASI doesn't form an opinion.

Ulrich Clement: But it's a human voice, isn't it?

Charles Turner: Sure, it's human.

Ulrich Clement: Do you think it's the interaction? The fact that in one case there's interaction and in the other there's not?

Charles Turner: I can only speculate, but I think it's the elimination of someone being in a position to judge what's going on. And it's probably a certain degree of confidence that the researchers are doing research that is never going to be associated with the respondent and that nobody, not even the interviewer, will know what the respondent said. If you think about a face-to-face interview, you may promise total confidentiality, but there's still one person who knows about your sex life. In our case, that's usually the middle-aged woman standing at the door saying, "Well, how many times have you had anal sex in the past month?"

Leonore Tiefer: Do they think the machine is a lie detector?

Charles Turner: We don't know; I don't think so, but . . .

Theo Sandfort: I think that personal interviews are much more rewarding than being interviewed by a computer.

Charles Turner: There's a table in the paper that shows that respondents do, in fact, say that. But they also say that they are more comfortable reporting on these issues to the computer than to a human interviewer and that they believe that the computer will get most people to provide more honest reports. In addition, to the extent that you worry about idiosyncrasies of interviewer behavior and what that does to the error structure of the data in the computerized interviews (both the bias and the variance), you get a completely standardized stimulus.

Barbara Marín: Alain, you have focused on the perspective of the interviewer, the ways in which interviewers attach meanings to the task that they're doing. I'm wondering if you have any insights, from the perspective of the respondent, about these meanings? It was very intriguing to hear that someone thought of the interview as a pornographic telephone call, and I'm wondering if you have guesses about how common that might be.

Alain Giami: We consider the interviewer's attitudes and representations while interviewing to be a topic of interest in its own right. From this perspective, interviewers reported that some respondents represented their participation in the survey as a therapy process. This seems to have facilitated the questionnaire interaction in some cases. But it is difficult to assess and, in the case of the French survey, we could not interview respondents after the questionnaire itself due to the constraints of anonymity. We didn't inquire about the opinions or impressions of the respondent, so I cannot say.

John Bancroft: I think the point you made, Alain, about sexual interaction is a very important one, and it is perhaps relevant to the question about the difference between interviewer and computer. I'm not certain about contrasting questionnaire and computer, but as somebody who's been talking to people all through my professional life about their sexuality, you become very conscious of the sexuality of that process and it requires professional skills to contain it and to manage it in order to establish a situation which makes it safe for people to talk. This is a very important part of a clinical interview, and I don't see that that would be fundamentally different in a research-based interview. The sort of research that I have been involved in which uses such interviews has not been large-scale survey but rather looking at change in response to a treatment, so the constraints are very different. In our training of interviewers, we encourage them to establish rapport with the interviewee first to enable them to talk about their sexuality in terms and in words with which they feel comfortable and really establish a comfortable empathic person-to-person relationship before moving in with very precise questions about how many times something is done during what period. If you go straight into such precise questioning, you have a very strange interaction between the interviewer-interviewee. And I'm just wondering whether a computer somehow or other cuts that out and enables the respondent to answer questions without being inhibited or affected by an uncomfortable interaction with the interviewer.

Alain Giami: In a review of the French research on sex and AIDS that we made recently (Bajos, Bozon, & Giami, 1995), we found that in qualitative research conducted with semistructured interviews, there were no questions about sexual practices. Qualitative research does not take into account sexual practices. It seems that sexual practices are principally investigated in questionnaire surveys using closed questions. Second, when we study the history of the surveys, we can observe that the questions are not framed the same way. We do not ask the same questions now that we asked 25 years ago. For example, there are no longer any questions about coital positions. In the era of AIDS, we ask about contacts between organs and body fluid exchange. An explanation of this state of the art can be found in the fact that qualitative research is focused more on attitudes, representations, and relationships than on practices, while quantitative and large-scale surveys are more medically driven and epidemiologically oriented. There is also the assumption that interviewers and researchers are resistant to asking such questions.

Alfred Spira: I would like to stress two points. The first one is that nobody is used to speaking about his or her own sexual life, absolutely nobody. Usually, and this is what we've observed in our survey, the person answering our questions was speaking about their own sexual life for the first time. Before the survey, we did not think we could interview a person for more than one hour. We were very surprised to have two-hour interviews and the person say, "Is it already finished?" So this is very difficult to take into account in designing the interview, but I think it's very important. My second point is that we are working on sexuality as related to disease, not sexuality as a part of life. I was very surprised when I realized that medical doctors, physicians, never, never ask questions about sexual life, and one of the reasons why they don't do this is they don't know how to do this. Those of us who are physicians know that we learn a lot of things in medical schools, but never how to ask questions about sex. Sex didn't exist during my medical school years. And the second reason why physicians don't do this is because of this sexual interaction with the patient, which occurs if we ask questions about sexual life.

Alex Carballo-Diéguez: It has been my experience that when people start giving information, for example, on how many partners they had in the last year or what they did with them, often they are surprised about what they recall, and that seems to lead them to reflect on their behavior. Would you comment more on that issue?

Alain Giami: It's again a question about the respondents, and not about the interviewers. What I can say is that for the young interviewers that we recruited for this survey one of the incentives that they had for being part of this enterprise was that we gave them information about AIDS, about sex, about a lot of things related to the surveys. The assessment they got from this information helped them at the same time to assume the legitimacy of the questions that they would have to ask. For example, we have a question about fist fucking that was asked only of gay men, and most of the interviewers and some of the researchers had never heard of this sexual practice. At the beginning, it was very difficult for people to be able to ask such questions, so they had to understand the rationale for doing so.

John Bancroft: What is "fist fucking" in French? It might sound better.

Alain Giami: There's no French word for it!

Carol Jenkins: I'd like to ask if you had data on the sexual activity levels of your interviewers and if there was any evidence, as some people have told me about work they've done in Thailand, that the more sexually active interviewers elicit a greater number of partners in their interviews. If the interviewer is more sexually active, he or she seems to be able to make people relax, at least that's the hypothesis, so that they elicit more partners.

Alain Giami: No, we don't have data on that topic. Some interviewers reported that their training and the experience of performing the survey during three and a half months changed their attitude towards sexual words. Some of them were concerned about the reactions of their relatives to this. There is something sexual in sexual interviewing and we should not deny it.

Ulrich Clement: I think we are now implicitly discussing the theory of the sexual interview and we are lacking such a theory, basically. We all are doing sexual interviews without a theory of what it is we are doing. You started the idea when you said that a sexual interview is a sexual interaction, but as we said before, Alain, even in a computer-assisted interview there is an interaction component. A computer might be a seducer for some people and there might be a tendency that the computer-assisted interview biases all reporting of sexual interactions because it's seducing or sexualizing to interact with a computer. It would be an interesting question, what type of seduction the sexual interview is. We have emphasized much more the question of underreporting and of inhibited respondents, but we also should consider the other possibility that our respondents could be excited or seduced by this or that assessment.

Leonore Tiefer: If we're developing a theory of the interview and we talk about the sexual aspects of the interview, we must also talk about the educational aspects of the interview, and I think also of the beneficial/therapeutic effects when, in the context of a clinical setting, we take a history from somebody. It's a purely information-gathering segment, and yet we all know that it's a component of the therapeutic interaction that by asking the questions, we are communicating permission-giving by saying the words, without falling apart or laughing. We are communicating a certain way of thinking about sex that I would suggest is a form of education, and it seems to me that we can do this in a more intentional way. To go back to what we were saying at the beginning about policy, the educational component of sex research does not have to be totally incidental. It can be in some way intentional. And this brings us then to the question of whether a machine is likely to incorporate the same potential for education as a human being. So when we think about the multiple roles of the research, I think it's wrong for us to say we're only interested in one role and the rest of them just kind of fall out the way they fall out. I think we have to be more respectful of the multiple realities of the interview and then we can be more intentional about maximizing the social benefits.

Stuart Michaels: I think this is a very interesting discussion and certainly issues that all of us in various ways have confronted in the course of our work. Our experience with the face-to-face survey in the U.S. led us to think of the "professional stranger" as the model for the role of the interviewer. Rather than a friend or even a clinician, we were thinking of the model for the interviewer as a skilled person doing their job, a job that involved neutrality, unflappability, some social distance, and especially someone whom the respondent was unlikely to ever encounter again. I think in response to Ulrich's question, that the theory behind the audio-CASI method is partially explainable as the flip side of rapport. The more you establish a personal rapport, the more you create reasons for a person to want the other to like them and, therefore, pressures to present an image of oneself that will be more pleasing to the other person. I think with the computer that it is that dimension that you're trying to decrease. That is, the attempt is to decrease "social desirability" pressure, the tendency to either under or over report behavior or shape attitudes depending on perceptions of what are general social norms and respectability. As Charles points out, sometimes computer interviewing produces reports of less sexual activity because the demands in the interview situation to present yourself as sexual are somewhat lessened. Another thing that may help promote the acceptability of audio-CASI is a more general transformation of society, substituting machines for people. I am thinking about ATM machines and other kinds of machines. But computers and audio-CASI don't solve all our problems. We are still faced with all the problems of questionnaire construction. All the issues about how you ask questions, what the focus of the research is, how it's framed, in what language the interview is conducted remain. In some ways these problems are worse because of the computer's lack of flexibility. There's no compensation by human beings mediating the respondent's understanding of the questionnaire as written. The computer can't perceive any lack of understanding of the questionnaire by the respondent and therefore once you've written the questionnaire and programmed it into the computer, it's there and every single respondent hears the question that way.

Reference

Bajos, N., Bozon, M., & Giami, A. (Eds.). (1995). *Sexualité et sida—Recherches en sciences sociales*. Paris: ANRS.

Part 3.
Methodology in Specific Contexts

Measuring Sexual Behavior among Teenage Males in the United States

FREYA L. SONENSTEIN, LEIGHTON KU,
AND JOSEPH H. PLECK

This paper summarizes strategies developed to measure sexual and contraceptive behavior, particularly condom use, among young men in the United States. It is based on our experience with the National Survey of Adolescent Males, which was first fielded in 1988. Since that time we have conducted two follow-up surveys with the original cohort of males 15 to 19 years old in 1990–1991 and in 1995. We also conducted a new survey of 15- to 19-year-old males in 1995. Over the course of the survey's existence, substantial efforts have been made to develop sound survey methods and to improve incrementally the validity or reliability of the data.

Background

Serious scientific studies of sexual behavior must contend with a volatile political environment in the United States. For example, government funding for two national surveys of sexual behavior was withdrawn in 1991 (Laumann, Gagnon, Michael, & Michaels, 1994). Nonetheless, many sample surveys of U.S. teenagers conducted since the early 1970s have included measures of sexual behavior. By contrast, there have been very few scientific sample surveys of adults' sexual behavior in the United States. The surveys of teenagers' sexual behavior have included nationally representative samples of teenagers, such as the studies by Sorensen (1973), Zelnik and Kantner (1980), Mosher (1990), Sonenstein, Pleck, and Ku (1989), Furstenberg, Moore, and Peterson (1985), as well as the new Add Health Study, discussed by Richard Udry in this volume (see part 7). Studies of teenagers representing state or community populations have also been conducted, including those by Miller and Simon (1974) in Illinois; Vener and Stewart (1974) in three Michigan communities; Jessor and Jessor (1975) in a Rocky Mountain city; Udry and Billy (1987) in a North Carolina community; and Hingson, Strunin, Berlin, and Heeren in Massachusetts (1990). Many multipurpose surveys of teenagers, such as the National Longitudinal Survey of Youth (Mott, 1983), High School and Beyond (Hanson, Morrison, & Ginsburg, 1989), and the Youth Risk Behavior Survey (CDC, 1995) include at least some questions about sexual behavior.

The major stimulus behind these studies of adolescent sexual behavior is the view that early and unprotected sexual intercourse is a major public health and social welfare problem. Since the mid-1970s, high rates of teenage and out-of-wedlock pregnancies and births have been associated with a number of social problems, including higher welfare costs and poorer child health outcomes (Hayes, 1987; Moore & Burt, 1982; Maynard, 1996). In the 1980s, the HIV epidemic and the high prevalence of STDs among teens further strengthened the rationale for a public health interest in monitoring and understanding the sexual behavior of teenagers.

Because public health concerns have guided most of the data-collection efforts, the kinds of questions that are asked about sexual behavior have been limited. Even studies containing larger batteries of questions about sexual behavior have been primarily driven by public health interest in fertility and STD transmission and not broader issues regarding sexuality. For example, studies typically do not ask teenagers about their sexual feelings or how they are expressed, but focus on sexual and contraceptive behaviors. The National Survey of Adolescent Males (NSAM) falls squarely among the surveys that have been motivated by concern about teenage pregnancy and STD transmission. It is one of the few national surveys of teenagers that focuses primarily on measuring sexual and contraceptive behavior.

Since it is unusual for surveys to study only males, it is useful to explain why NSAM developed in this way. NSAM was begun in the mid-1980s because the national surveys that tracked teenagers' fertility behaviors interviewed only females. The gathering of data about trends in young women's sexual activity, contraceptive use, pregnancies, and births began in the United States with the National Surveys of Young Women in 1971, 1976, and 1979 conducted by Zelnik and Kantner (1980) at Johns Hopkins University. Later the National Survey of Family Growth (NSFG) conducted by the National Center for Health Statistics took over, collecting this information for teenagers, and older women too, in Cycle III in 1982, Cycle IV in 1988, and Cycle V in 1995 (Mosher, 1990; Mosher & Bachrach, 1996). With the exception of a male component that was added to the 1979 survey by Zelnik and Kantner, national data from men about sexual behaviors were not collected until we fielded NSAM in 1988.

NSAM's primary objectives were to obtain information about patterns of sexual activity and condom use among U.S. teenage males 15–19 years old; to assess their knowledge, attitudes, and risk behaviors relative to AIDS; and to conduct analyses which would identify determinants of condom use. These data were intended to complement comparable information from the NSFG that would be available for teenage females ages 15–19 for the same year, 1988. They were also intended to provide trend information for teenage males through comparisons with the results of the earlier survey of males conducted by Zelnik and Kantner in 1979. Since the first NSAM survey was conducted in 1988, the original cohort of teenage males has been reinterviewed in 1990–1991 and in 1995. In addition, a new cohort of 15- to 19-year-old males was interviewed in 1995 to coincide with the fielding of Cycle V of the National Survey of Family Growth, which collects information from female teenagers as well as adults.

In developing the NSAM survey, we had to confront a number of challenges which were posed because the survey respondents were young and male and because the information we were seeking was sensitive. One reason males had not been included in teenage fertility surveys earlier was researchers' beliefs that males, young males in particular, were a difficult survey population. Men were believed to be especially poor respondents in fertility studies because their answers may be less reliable than women's answers (Cherlin, Griffith, & McCarthy, 1983; Lerman, 1993; Mott, 1983; Sweet, 1996). There was concern that adolescent males might exaggerate their reports of sexual activity. In addition, they might have inadequate knowledge of the pregnancies and births to which they had contributed. The relative youth of the NSAM population posed special problems because young men were also believed to be a particularly difficult population to find and to engage in interviews (Micklin, Gardner, & Thomson, 1977). Potentially, a survey of teenage males might have a poor response rate which would threaten the representativeness of the sample.

This paper describes the NSAM experience as we developed a survey that would capture the relatively difficult teenage male population and would obtain truthful reports about their sexual behaviors. We will first discuss the access question—how to obtain interviews with teenagers about their sexual behaviors. Then we will discuss the content question—how to obtain reliable and valid information about sexual behavior from adolescent respondents. Throughout, the primary focus of the discussion will be on male teenagers' heterosexual behavior. NSAM also contains measures of homosexual activity, but another paper in this volume, by Charles Turner and colleagues (see part 2), presents some of these results.

Gaining Access to Teenage Respondents

NSAM was designed as a survey of males ages 15 to 19 living in households in the United States at the dates of original sample selection in 1988 and 1995. In both years, the surveys used stratified, multistage national probability samples that oversampled for black and Hispanic youths. Sample weights were developed to adjust for probability of selection and nonresponse and are poststratified to correspond to census target totals. Interviewers contacted selected housing units, screened for eligible youths, and obtained interviews with them. In 1995, a lead letter introducing the study was sent to each selected housing unit to enhance the receptivity of the person answering the door.

Response Rates

When we began NSAM, the survey lore was replete with stories about how difficult it was to interview teenage males. Our experience is that interviewing teenage males requires patience; a substantial number of broken appointments occur and multiple callbacks are required. However, the standard procedures used by professional survey research firms to obtain high response rates work as well with teenage males as with other populations. The Institute for Survey Research at Temple University, our data collection subcontractor in 1988, obtained interviews with 73.9 percent of the eligible males living in households, and the Research Triangle Institute (RTI), the subcontractor in 1995, obtained a 74.65 percent response rate.[1] These response rates are judged acceptable by most survey experts and are comparable to or better than response rates for most in-person household surveys other than those conducted by the U.S. Census Bureau.

Follow-up rates for the longitudinal component of the NSAM survey have been relatively high. When we returned to reinterview the 1988 respondents 2.5 years later, 89 percent of those originally interviewed who were still living consented to a second interview. Those lost to follow-up tended to be slightly older. Longitudinal weighting has been used to adjust for this problem. More important, there was no attrition bias by race or by behavioral outcomes, such as sexual activity or condom use (Ku & Kershaw, 1991). In 1995, 74.8 percent of the living 1988 respondents were reinterviewed. Analyses of attrition have not yet been completed for the 1995 wave of the original cohort.

The experience of NSAM suggests that earlier concern about the difficulty of getting teenage males to participate in sample surveys was overblown. Most teenage males, when approached as members of randomly selected households, will participate in a survey about sexual and contraceptive behavior. Not only will they talk to interviewers once, but they are willing to participate twice and three times. We think that the high proportion of young men willing to be reinterviewed demonstrates that most found the subject matter to be interesting rather than painfully embarrassing.

Parental Consent

A particular issue for conducting surveys of teenagers is obtaining parental permission. In 1996, the U.S. Congress considered legislation, the Family Privacy Act, to bar any surveys of minor teenagers about sensitive topics unless parental permission is obtained. The surveys that are particu-

---

1. In 1995 we changed our survey contractor to RTI, which had recently developed an audio computer-assisted self-interview (ACASI) technology. See Charles Turner's paper in this volume (part 2).

larly affected by this legislation are those that collect data in schools and rely on classroom administration of paper and pencil instruments. Typically these surveys of students in school use passive parental-consent procedures. Parents are notified that the study will be conducted, but they must contact the school if they do not wish their child to participate in the study. The Youth Risk Behavior surveillance data collected by the Centers for Disease Control (1995) rely on these types of procedures.

NSAM has always used active parental-consent procedures for all teenage respondents under the age of 18. The parents of the teens had to sign an informed consent form before their sons were interviewed. We believed that active consent was necessary and appropriate because the survey questions about sexual behavior were more extensive in 1988 than had ever been used before in a national survey of teenagers. As a household-based survey, NSAM was usually conducted in person in the teenager's home. Thus some parents were readily available to be told about the study and solicited for their permission. Many, however, were not home on the first or even subsequent visits. Thus the commitment to obtaining parental consent for respondents under the age of majority was not without cost; it required a substantial investment of the project's resources.

The procedures developed in 1995 required that a parent or guardian had to sign a consent form before the interviewer talked to the minor adolescent. The parent kept one copy of the form and the original was returned by the interviewer to RTI. Its use ensured that parents were uniformly informed about the purposes and procedures of the NSAM study. The main components of the form were:

- Frankness about the purpose of the study. The parental consent form said that the son had been randomly selected to participate in a survey whose purpose was "to get information about young men's knowledge, attitudes and behaviors that relate to current health issues, such as alcohol and drug use, sexual behavior, sexually transmitted diseases and AIDS." This provides a clear statement that sexual behavior will be a topic in the survey.
- Assurance that permission is required. The parent was told that the son would not be asked to participate if consent was not given.
- Assurance that the child still needed to provide his own consent. If parental permission was given, the teenager could still decide whether or not he wished to participate in the survey. Having started the interview, he could refuse to answer any question.
- Assurances about confidentiality. Answers to the interview would be treated as confidential and would not be associated with the son's name in any reports. Indeed, parents were told that they would not have access to their own children's answers.

92 | *Researching Sexual Behavior*

- Contact names to obtain more information. The parent was given the name and telephone number of the study director at RTI and the Institutional Review Board chairperson at RTI.

Although this form was quite long and covered a number of potentially sticky points, study participation was not hindered for most of the eligible respondents. Initially, we worried that the parents of teenagers, especially 15-year-olds, would be reluctant to provide access to their children. These fears proved to be unfounded. After being provided with a description of the study, most parents agreed to have their sons participate. In 1988, only 6.1% of households with eligible respondents did not participate because a parent withheld consent for his or her minor child; in 1995 this proportion was 5.6%. We believe that these high rates of cooperation are a tribute to the professional skills of the interviewers, who did an excellent job conveying the importance of the study. We also think that the high proportion of parents providing permission demonstrates the level of support that parents of teenagers have for public health efforts to address adolescent sexual health issues.

Incentives

Another issue in obtaining the participation of teenagers in a survey is the use of incentives, such as gifts or cash paid to respondents. Originally, in 1988, we had not planned to offer incentives. However, during the debriefing with interviewers after the pretest, they strongly endorsed offering the teenagers some token in recognition of the time and information that the respondents had provided to the study. Since the budget did not contain a provision for this expenditure, the token necessarily had to be inexpensive. Luckily for us, in 1988 Temple University was in the national collegiate basketball playoffs. We gave each respondent a Temple University basketball shirt, which proved to be a great incentive, according to the field staff. The use of this incentive had the added benefit of providing name recognition when the Temple University interviewers returned 2.5 years later to conduct a second interview. At the second interview, having budgeted a modest amount for incentives, we provided a Temple University athletic bag.

In 1995, we offered cash incentives for interviews, based on RTI's advice that cash was simple to administer and would be popular with respondents. Respondents were first offered $10. If they said they were not interested in participating in the survey for $10, the interviewer was authorized to offer $20. We used a sliding scale like this because it was difficult to select a single payment level as appropriate. Ten dollars may seem like a lot of money to a 15-year-old but not to a 19-year-old. In practice, most of the interviews were conducted with a $10 incentive. When, in 1995, we began collecting urine specimens for STD testing for those 18 years or older, separate incentive payments, set at the level of the interview incentive payment, were provided.

Obtaining Information about Sexual Behavior

Once a teenage male has agreed to be interviewed, challenges remain in terms of keeping him motivated to respond completely and accurately to the questions. Interviewing is a social-interaction process, and sample household surveys rely heavily on the quality and training of the interviewer, who must manage this interaction process so that the research protocol is carried out. Furthermore, the protocol itself must be carefully developed so that it provides the most reliable and accurate measures possible of the behavior being studied.

Interviewer Selection and Training

To enhance the comparability of this experience across respondents, the interviewers who carry out national surveys undergo extensive training in uniform survey research practices as well as in the protocols associated with particular surveys. For the NSAM, interviewers participated in three days of training in 1988 and 1991 and five days of training in 1995. The training was more extensive in 1995 because the protocol had new features such as the use of ACASI (see Turner chapter in part 2) and the collection of urine samples. Part of this training addressed the issue of the sensitive nature of the survey and the importance of not appearing judgmental. Interviewers were allowed to self-select into this survey so that no interviewer was assigned to the project who had reservations about the sexual content of the study. During and after the training session, supervisors further screened out interviewers who had difficulty with the survey content or who had other performance problems.

Questionnaire Mode

At the core of any survey about sexual and contraceptive behavior is a detailed questionnaire, administered by an interviewer (i.e., in person or by telephone) or self-administered by the respondent (e.g., a written or computer-assisted questionnaire). The arguments in favor of interviewer-based questionnaires are that professional interviewers are more capable of handling complex questionnaires and skip logic, and that personal rapport between the interviewer and subject can yield greater commitment to the interview process. Further, the interviewer can provide additional explanation or guidance if the respondent has questions. The main argument in favor of self-administered questionnaires is that they ensure greater privacy for the respondent and reduce the risk that respondents will give only socially desirable responses. This could be particularly important for sensitive subjects, such as sexual behavior or drug use, but might be less important in less sensitive areas such as family background or attitudes.

In planning the 1988 survey, we reviewed the methods used by our predecessors. In 1976, Zelnik and Kantner used interviewer administration for all questions, including those about sexual activity and contraceptives, in their National Survey of Young Women. But when they added a young men's sample in 1979, they adopted a self-administered format. The apparent concern was that using female interviewers to pose these questions to young men would be problematic. Then, as now, the great majority of professional interviewers were females. The researchers experimented with recruiting and training male interviewers to conduct the interviews but abandoned this strategy after poor experiences (Tanfer, 1983). The 1987 Planned Parenthood Poll by Louis Harris and Associates (1987) used female interviewers to obtain these types of information from young men and women. Our conversations with one of the project directors of the poll indicated that there had been no difficulties using female interviewers. Based on this experience, we elected to use the national cadre of professional female interviewers employed by the survey research firm ISR Temple to conduct the interviews with adolescent males in 1988 and 1991. In 1995, RTI had a pool of trained male and female interviewers; therefore the interviews were conducted by both male and female interviewers in the most recent round of the survey.

For the first NSAM survey in 1988, we elected to use both interviews and self-administered questionnaires. Many of the core behaviors, including most heterosexual behaviors and condom use, were asked about in the face-to-face interviews. A paper-and-pencil self-administered questionnaire (SAQ) was used for the most sensitive behaviors, including homosexual behavior, riskier sexual behaviors (e.g., sex with prostitutes or sex while under the influence of alcohol or drugs), and other illicit behavior (e.g., drug use). To cross-check data about sexual activity reported to the interviewer, the SAQ also repeated questions about ever having sexual intercourse and using a condom at last intercourse.

At the end of the oral interview, which usually lasted one hour, interviewers were instructed to explain that there were additional questions that we would like the respondent to answer in private. The respondents were handed the SAQ. The front page of the SAQ included assurances of confidentiality and instructions about how to complete the form. The interviewer reviewed these assurances and instructions with the respondent before leaving the respondent to complete the form in private. To ensure privacy, the interviewers were instructed not to read the questions in the SAQ to the respondents if they had difficulty reading. Instead they were to note when a respondent had reading problems with the SAQ. When the respondent had completed the SAQ, he put it directly into a mailing envelope. The interviewer placed the completed interview schedule and the other study forms into the same envelope. Then the respondent sealed the envelope so that it was ready to be mailed to the survey research firm. In 1988, all but 21 of the 1,880 respondents (99%) completed the SAQ and item nonresponse was never higher than 5%.

For the new cohort of teenage men sampled in 1995, we modified the self-administration methodology. Based on promising initial results, we primarily used RTI's new ACASI technology to ask about the most sensitive subjects. To test the impact of this change, about one fifth of the sample was randomly assigned to use the paper-and-pencil SAQ mode. The paper by Turner in part 2 discusses this methodology in more detail. In 1995, 98% of the respondents completed the self-administered questions, using either ACASI or paper-and-pencil SAQs. Preliminary results indicate that use of ACASI has substantially increased reporting of stigmatized behaviors, such as homosexual intercourse, but made little difference in the reporting of less-stigmatized behaviors, such as heterosexual intercourse and condom use (Turner, Ku, Sonenstein, & Pleck, 1996).

Question Wording

One challenge faced by researchers who attempt to study trends in sexual behavior over time is that terminology and sensitivities can also change. In our study, we wanted to make comparisons to the 1979 baseline information from males collected by Zelnik and Kantner, and we also wanted to use items comparable to those used for teenage females in the National Survey of Family Growth Cycle IV (NSFG), which was also fielded in 1988. The wordings in these two surveys were roughly comparable. In 1979, Zelnik and Kantner used the following question: "Have you ever had sexual intercourse (sometimes this is referred to as 'making love,' 'having sex' or 'going all the way')?" In 1988, the National Survey of Family Growth asked: "At any time in your life, have you ever had sexual intercourse (that is, made love, had sex or gone all the way)?" We considered dropping the old-fashioned term "going all the way," but concluded that although the language was dated, most teenagers understood its meaning. We also thought about using more slang terms and decided not to because there is considerable variation among subgroups in their usage and because participants in focus groups that we ran in 1987 advised us to use formal rather than informal terminology to maintain a neutral, professional tone in the interview.

Another challenge posed by studying adolescents is whether young people, especially those who have not engaged in sexual intercourse, share common definitions of the behaviors under study. This point was driven home by some of the responses that we were given in the qualitative interviews with 15–19-year-olds that we conducted prior to the 1995 fieldwork. Some respondents appeared to have different interpretations of what "having sex" meant. For example, one teen thought that touching a female's breast counted. Others in the preliminary pilot test of the interview were unsure whether certain behaviors such as receiving masturbation or oral sex should be included as "sexual intercourse." We received similar feedback from focus groups we ran in 1987. Similar problems were encountered in the respondents' definitions of sexual partners. One respondent in 1994 thought that a sexual partner was anyone that he "went on a date with, kissed or had sexual intercourse with." Still another said that a "partner" implies that there is an investment of meaning in the relationship; a meaningless sexual experience in which there are no feelings involved might be excluded from the partner designation.

These examples demonstrate the potential misunderstandings that occur because of differing interpretations of questions. Several approaches were used to mitigate these problems:

- Important components of questionnaire development before fielding the 1988 and 1995 surveys were qualitative assessments, such as focus groups, and pretests of small samples of young men to identify concepts, questions, or other procedural aspects that might cause problems.
- After we encountered the problems that some teenagers were having defining sexual intercourse in 1988, we opted for a simple definition using vaginal intercourse as the criterion. We added instructions in the interviewers' manual: If the respondent asks, the interviewer is instructed to say that "sexual intercourse includes vaginal intercourse only. It does not include anal intercourse, heavy petting, or oral sex." To maintain comparability over time, we repeated these interviewer instructions in 1995.
- To obtain other measures of sexual behavior, we added questions to the SAQ that asked the respondent whether he had ever engaged in specific sexual acts: Kissed a female on the mouth? Touched a female's breast? A female touched your penis until you ejaculated or came? Put your penis in a female's vagina (vaginal intercourse)? A female put her mouth on your penis? Put your mouth on a female's vagina (oral intercourse)? Put your penis in a female's rectum or butt (anal intercourse)?[2]

Finally, it is useful to illustrate potential pitfalls by describing question wording that was not successful. Because a number of respondents in the pilot work we conducted in 1995 appeared to be confused about whether other forms of sexual expression beyond vaginal intercourse counted as "sexual intercourse," we added this question to the SAQ: "Have you ever

2. These items were adapted from an instrument used by Udry and Billy (1987).

had sexual intercourse, including vaginal, oral and anal intercourse, with a female?" Fifteen percent of the respondents provided answers to this question that were inconsistent with their other answers. Ten percent, for example, answered no to this question, although they had said that they had put their penis in a female's vagina. We think that these respondents were confused and thought that we were asking whether they had experienced all three types of intercourse. In this case, the rewording of a question to address issues raised by a few respondents in the focused preliminary interviews resulted in confusion for other respondents. The most important lesson to be learned from this failure is the value of adhering to the principal of keeping the questions simple.

Measuring Levels of Sexual Experience

The NSAM survey attempted to do more than just measure how many teenage males had experienced sexual intercourse, the standard measure used in many surveys. Our challenge was to construct a 60–75-minute instrument which replicated the standard items that had been used in surveys of female fertility behavior as well as expanding available information to include measures of (1) patterns of sexual activity across time and across partners, (2) consistency of contraceptive use across time and across sexual partners, and (3) experience with condoms.

We struggled to develop items measuring patterns of sexual activity and contraceptive use across time and across partners within the time constraints of the interview and what we believe to be genuine recall constraints. The approach we finally selected was to focus sequentially on the respondent's experiences with his most recent sexual partners starting with the last sexual partner—the one with whom he most recently had sex. The most detailed information was collected for the two most recent relationships and more limited information was collected for up to four more partner relationships if they occurred in the last 12 months. Limited information was also collected about the respondent's first experience with sexual intercourse if it had not occurred with a partner that he had in the last 12 months. This approach balances the need for complete information about partners with a recognition that recall about more recent partners is going to be better.

We felt that a partner-by-partner recall method was more consistent with respondent's cognitive processes: that they tended to recall experiences by relationships rather than summatively. For example, more accurate information might be obtained by asking how often a person used a condom with each partner rather than asking how often a condom was used overall. In addition, the partner-by-partner data provide richer information to examine changes in behaviors during or between relationships. The partner-by-partner accounts of sexual behavior can be used to construct measures of the patterns of sexual activity and contraceptive use within and across partners in the last 12 months. For example, we have done analyses of the consistency of condom use with all partners over the last 12 months (Ku, Sonenstein, & Pleck, 1992), the consistency of condom use over the last partner relationship (Pleck, Sonenstein, & Ku, 1991), and the decay of condom use as relationships last longer (Ku, Sonenstein, & Pleck, 1995).

Constructing measures of behavior across partners for the last year is difficult in NSAM when a respondent has had more than 6 partners in the last year. Fortunately, very few of the 15–19-year-olds had more than 6 partners in the last 12 months. Only 8 percent of the 15–19-year-old respondents in 1988 reported more than 6 partners. The majority (72 percent) of those who were sexually experienced reported one or two partners in the last year. Thus we were able to collect information about all partners in the last 12 months for the great majority of the study participants. For respondents with more than 6 partners in the last 12 months, we have imputed measures of their sexual activity with the additional partners based on their behaviors with partners that they do report.

The problem of missing information about additional partners for respondents with many partners cannot be solved by simply asking about the other partners. The more partners a respondent has, the harder it is for him to remember details about each relationship. The partner-by-partner questions are also very repetitive if the respondent has had a lot of partners. Thus he may get tired or bored with the question series, and the quality of the information he provides will decay. One solution is to shorten the recall period so that behavior with fewer partners will be fully captured, but this approach is not well suited to teenagers who have sex infrequently and episodically. The challenge is to develop measures for teenagers and young adults that can capture information across time for respondents who may have quite varied levels of sexual activity. For the young teenage male who may have sex very episodically, a 12-month time window will provide a better picture of his behavior and will not tax his memory. The 12-month time frame works less well for the highly sexually active youth and for a person in a long-term relationship. For the latter cases, a description of the most recent 1–3 months might provide a more accurate measure of behavior. The difficulty is that the population of teenagers includes all types of respondents, and a survey instrument needs to accommodate all so that uniform measures of sexual behavior can be constructed.

Reliability of Male Reports about Sexual Experience

Because we embedded alternative measures of sexual experience in the NSAM interview and SAQ protocols, we are able to compare a respondent's report about his sexual experience provided under different conditions. There has been considerable speculation that teenage males in the United States exaggerate their levels of sexual experience (Newcomer & Udry, 1988). We can compare a respondent's report to an interviewer with his answers on the SAQ, where presumably he is not as motivated to provide socially acceptable answers because of the privacy of the reporting situation.

Our analyses indicate very high consistency between the respondents' reports to the interviewer of having engaged in sexual intercourse with a female and their SAQ reports of having put their penis in a female's vagina. In 1988, there was 96% consistency and in 1995 there was 95% consistency.

Furthermore, in 1995 we examined the 76 inconsistently reporting respondents in more detail to see if the bias was toward under- or overreporting of sexual experience. Just over half of the respondents (n=43) who told the interviewer that they had not had sexual intercourse said on the SAQ that they had had vaginal intercourse. These respondents appear reluctant to talk about sex to an interviewer; they are underreporting their sexual experience. The remaining 33 respondents told the interviewer that they had experienced sexual intercourse with a female but recorded no vaginal intercourse on the SAQ. Almost half of this group, 15 respondents, indicated on the SAQ that they had experienced mutual masturbation or oral or anal sex with a female. These males appear to be sexually experienced but are using a definition of sexual intercourse more broadly defined than vaginal intercourse to place themselves in this category. An additional 11 members of this inconsistent group reported having either kissed a female or touched a female's breast. This group may genuinely misunderstand commonly held definitions of sexual intercourse or they may have exaggerated their reports of experience to the interviewer. The remaining seven inconsistent respondents told the interviewer they were sexually experienced but reported no sexual behaviors at all on the SAQ. These respondents appear to be exaggerating their level of sexual experience in the interview situation.

Overall, there is strong consistency between the respondents' reports to interviewers and on the SAQ about whether they have experienced sexual intercourse with a female. When inconsistencies exist, the bias does not appear to work in a single direction. More than half the respondents appeared reluctant to tell an interviewer that they had sexual intercourse. Of the remaining respondents, more than half had some sexual experience with a female but no vaginal intercourse. Only a few respondents were clearly overreporting their experience to the interviewer. It is important to note, however, that consistency of reporting across the same interview is not necessarily a measure of whether the respondent is telling the truth. It is simply a measure of the reliability of his reports—that he will give the same answer on multiple occasions.

Validation and Alternative Measures of Sexual or Contraceptive Behaviors

A common criticism of interview or questionnaire-based survey data is "How can you believe what they are saying?" Sexual behavior is one of the most private areas of human experience, and many persons are particularly skeptical of teenage males' responses. Researchers must be both rigorous and creative in considering ways to assess the validity of self-reported behaviors. Our earlier discussion showing the consistency of measures between the interviews and the SAQs demonstrates good reliability of results but does not indicate validity by any external standards. For example, a young man might say both in the interview and the SAQ that he always uses condoms but still be dishonest on both occasions.

Validation might be based on measures within the sample or inferred through comparisons with other population measures. For example, when we initially reported that condom use by adolescent males more than doubled between 1979 and 1988, it was useful to be able to cite reports that condom sales nationwide grew substantially over that period in a consistent fashion (Sonenstein, Pleck, & Ku, 1989). This greatly improved face validity for the survey results.

In more recent analyses, we have found that levels of self-reported unprotected sex among our respondents in 1988 are strongly correlated with reports of pregnancies and births that occurred between 1988 and 1991. Other analyses comparing births reported by males in our survey are consistent with levels of births (fathered by men of ages similar to our sample) reported by women in the 1988 National and Maternal Infant Health Survey (Lindberg et al., in preparation). That is, we can demonstrate not only that males' reports of births are broadly consistent with females' but also that the males' fertility experiences can be predicted based on their earlier self-reported sexual and contraceptive behaviors.

On the other hand, it is troubling that data from our survey and others such as the National Survey of Family Growth tend to indicate that although contraceptive use, including condoms, rose substantially among teenagers in the late 1980s and early 1990s, teenage birth and pregnancy rates nonetheless also rose (Alan Guttmacher Institute, 1994). Part of this rise might be due to modest increases in the proportion of sexually active adolescents, substantial decreases in the abortion rate, and increased reliance on condoms, which have higher failure rates than other methods of contraception. It is nonetheless difficult to understand how pregnancy rates could rise at the same time that use of contraceptives rose. We continue to worry that teenagers may be overreporting condom use because it has become a socially approved behavior.[3] However, further analyses conducted with NSAM indicate that respondents scoring higher on a measure of the tendency to give socially desirable answers do not show differences from other young men in their reports of condom use (Pleck, Sonenstein, & Ku, 1993).

For the 1995 surveys, we added yet another method of validation: we collected urine specimens from respondents over the age of 18 in order to conduct tests of infection by two common STD agents: *Chlamydia trachomatis* and *Neiserria gonorrhoeae*. New DNA-based technologies, Polymerase Chain Reaction and Ligase Chain Reaction tests, have been developed that can use simple urine specimens and are highly sensitive and specific. Both types of tests first replicate DNA strands manifold, then measure the presence of highly specific DNA sequences that indicate presence of the STDs (Bauwens et al., 1993; Chernesky et al., 1994). If the diagnostic tests identify people who are infected but who claim they are not sexually active or have used condoms 100% of the time, then their responses need to be viewed as suspect. For example, a recent study of clinic patients found that many of those who became infected with an STD reported 100% condom use and found that there was essentially no correlation of self-reported condom use and STD acquisition (Zenilman et al., 1995). In other areas of research, use of biomarkers to validate self-reported behaviors has been common for a long time. For example, smoking researchers routinely collect saliva or other biological specimens to measure tobacco metabolites to verify smoking status.

Conclusions

Survey research about the sexual behavior of adolescents in the United States has been accumulating over the last twenty-five years. A number of studies have demonstrated these points:

- Representative samples of teenage females and males can be recruited to participate in studies of sexual behavior.
- Obtaining parental consent is not a major obstacle for conducting studies with children under the age of 18 years.
- Asking teenagers questions about sexual behavior and contraceptive use does not have a major impact on further participation in longitudinal surveys.
- The majority of teenagers share a common understanding about what sexual intercourse is, even if they have not yet engaged in it.
- Self-reports of sexual activity and contraceptive use to interviewers and in self-administered surveys tend to be internally consistent.

3. Increased social approval of condoms could also be viewed as a desirable trend.

- Teenage males' reports of paternity experiences are consistent with those of teenage females.

While there is some evidence of the broad validity of adolescents' self-reports of sexual and contraceptive behaviors, the evidence must still be considered mixed. In particular, it is not clear how much measurement error is implicit for respondents in general and how much might be specifically occurring among adolescents or males. Methodological work is needed in this area.

As noted at the beginning of this paper, the recent resurgence of interest in surveys of sexual behavior has been generated by public health concerns such as HIV infection, STDs, and teenage pregnancy. The research, led by behavioral scientists, has mostly focused on individuals' self-reports of sexual behaviors, complemented with other demographic, attitudinal, and behavioral data. While this was a relative black box as recently as the late 1980s, there has been a virtual explosion of survey research since then.

What will the next generation of survey research look like? One reasonable speculation is that more studies will use new interview technologies, such as ACASI or telephone analogues of this method, because of the relative ease of administration and the apparent improvement in reporting of the most sensitive behaviors. Thus technological advances may improve our ability to obtain valid descriptions of teenagers' sexual behavior.

Progress must also be made in the development of explanations of sexual behavior. The development of conceptual models of the important determinants of sexual behavior might motivate changes in types of data being collected. Here multiple frameworks are possible. Some behavioral researchers, such as psychologists, may want to increase the emphasis on measuring feelings about sexuality and sexual identity as opposed to behaviors alone to help understand how sexual behavior and sexuality relate to personality and other psychological domains. Others, such as sociologists, may want to gather more data about respondents' social environment, including home and school environment, or to look at social aspects of sexual relationships, such as power. This might require collecting data from or about parties other than the respondent—e.g., his family, teachers, or sexual partners. Biomedical researchers, such as clinical researchers or epidemiologists, may be interested in obtaining clinical data, such as STD and HIV tests, or other biological markers, such as hormone levels. The recent development of simple urine-based STD and HIV tests makes this much more feasible. In order to develop a full understanding of sexual behavior, multiple conceptual approaches are worthy of further development and testing.

A more vexing problem, which might ultimately be beyond the capability of most nationally representative or other sample-based surveys, is the problem of getting information about sexual partners. From a social perspective, the partner and relationships with the partner have a strong and direct impact on sexual practices. From a health perspective, the infectivity or fecundity of the partner is an important determinant of the eventual outcome of infection or pregnancy. The problem is that it is difficult to identify simple and effective means of surveying respondents *and* their partners that do not seem to violate basic rules of confidentiality and protection of privacy. Contacting both partners is more feasible among established dyads, such as married couples, but becomes more difficult for transitory relationships, which are more common among adolescents.

The scientific study of the sexual behavior of U.S. adolescents has progressed over the last 25 years, with improvements registered in the collection of trend data and in measurement technology. Much more work is needed to broaden the conceptual models used to test explanations of this behavior. The HIV epidemic has required researchers from many disciplines, including psychologists, sociologists, public health workers, and survey researchers, to collaborate to understand the dimensions of sexual and contraceptive behaviors. Further progress in the field will necessitate and even heighten the need for multidisciplinary approaches to research.

Author Note

The opinions expressed in this paper are solely those of the author and do not represent the views of the Urban Institute, University of Illinois, or their funders. We would also like to acknowledge the intellectual contributions of Koray Tanfer (now at the Battelle Memorial Institute) and Charles Turner (of Research Triangle Institute) in methodology development. Survey development and data collection have been supported by grants from the National Institute of Health and Human Development.

References

Alan Guttmacher Institute. (1994). *Sex and America's teenagers*. New York: Alan Guttmacher Institute.

Bauwens, J., Clark, A., Loeffelholz, M., et al. (1993). Diagnosis of Chlamydia trachomatis urethritis in men by Polymerase Chain Assay of first-void urine. *Journal of Clinical Microbiology, 31,* 3013–3016.

Centers for Disease Control. (1995). Youth risk behavior surveillance—United States 1993. *Morbidity and Mortality Weekly Report, 44,* SS-1, March 24.

Cherlin, A., Griffith, J., & McCarthy, J. (1983). A note on maritally disrupted men's reports of child support in the June 1980 Current Population Survey. *Demography, 20,* 3.

Chernesky, M., Jang, D., Lee, H., et al. (1994). Diagnosis of Chlamydia trachomatis infections in men and women by testing first-void urine by Ligase Chain Reaction. *Journal of Clinical Microbiology, 32,* 2682–2685.

Furstenburg, F., Moore, K., & Peterson, J. (1985). Sex education and sexual experience among adolescents. *American Journal of Public Health, 75*(11), 1331–1332.

Hanson, S., Morrison, D., & Ginsburg, A. (1989). The antecedents of teenage fatherhood. *Demography, 26*(4), 579–596.

Hayes, C. D. (Ed). (1987). *Risking the future: Adolescent sexuality, pregnancy and childbearing.* Washington, DC: National Academy Press.

Hingson, R., Strunin, L., Berlin, B., & Heeren, T. (1990). Beliefs about AIDS, use of alcohol and drugs and unprotected sex among Massachusetts adolescents. *American Journal of Public Health, 80,* 295–299.

Jessor, S. L., & Jessor, R. (1975). Transition from virginity to nonvirginity among youth: A social-psychological study over time. *Developmental Psychology, 11,* 473–484.

Ku, L., & Kershaw, J. (1991, November). *Notes on attrition bias and weighting in Wave 2 of the National Survey of Adolescent Males.* Paper written for the Urban Institute.

Ku, L., Sonenstein, F. L., & Pleck, J. H. (1992). The association of AIDS education and sex education with sexual behavior and condom use among teenage men. *Family Planning Perspectives, 24*(3), 100–106.

Ku, L., Sonenstein, F. L., & Pleck, J. H. (1994). The dynamics of condom use among young men during and between relationships. *Family Planning Perspectives, 26*(6), 246–251.

Laumann, E. O., Gagnon, J. H., Michael, R. T., & Michaels, S. (1994). *The social organization of sexuality: Sexual practices in the United States* (pp. 40–41). Chicago: University of Chicago Press.

Lerman, R. I. (1993). A national profile of young unwed fathers. In R. I. Lerman & T. J. Ooms (Eds.), *Young unwed fathers: Changing roles and emerging policies* (pp. 27–51). Philadelphia: Temple University Press.

Lindberg, L. D., Sonenstein, F. L., Martinez, G., & Marcotte, J. (1996). Accuracy of fathers' reports of fertility. Washington, DC: Urban Institute.

Louis Harris and Associates. (1987). *American teens speak: Sex, myths, TV and birth control: The Planned Parenthood Poll.* New York: Planned Parenthood Federation of America.

Maynard, R. (1996). *Kids having kids.* New York: Robin Hood Foundation.

Micklin, M., Gardner, J. S., & Thomson, E. (1977). Problems in surveying adolescent sexual behavior: A case study. Seattle: Battelle Human Affairs Center.

Miller, P. Y., & Simon, W. (1974). Adolescent sexual behavior: Context and change. *Social Problems, 22*(1), 58–75.

Moore, K. A., & Burt, M. R. (1982). *Private crisis, public cost: Policy perspectives on teenage childbearing.* Washington, DC: Urban Institute Press.

Mosher, W. D. (1990). Contraceptive practice in the United States, 1982–1988. *Family Planning Perspectives, 22,* 198.

Mosher, W. D., & Bachrach, C. A. (1996). Understanding U.S. fertility: Continuity and change in the National Survey of Family Growth. *Family Planning Perspectives, 28*(1) 4–12.

Mott, F. L. (1983). *Fertility related data in the 1982 National Longitudinal Survey of*

Work Experience of Youth: An evaluation of data quality and some preliminary analyses. Paper prepared at Ohio State University.

Newcomer, S., & Udry, R. (1988). Adolescent honesty in surveys of sexual behaviors. *Journal of Adolescent Research, 3,* 4.

Pleck, J. H., Sonenstein, F. L., & Ku, L. (1991). Adolescent males' condom use: Relationship between perceived cost-benefits and consistency. *Journal of Marriage and the Family, 53*(4), 733–746.

Pleck, J. H., Sonenstein, F. L., & Ku, L. (1993). Changes in adolescent males' use of and attitudes toward condoms, 1988–1991. *Family Planning Perspectives, 25*(3), 106–110,117.

Sonenstein, F. L., Pleck, J. H., & Ku, L. C. (1989). Sexual activity, condom use, and AIDS awareness among adolescent males. *Family Planning Perspectives, 21,* 152.

Sorensen, R. (1973). *Adolescent sexuality in contemporary America.* New York: World.

Sweet, J. (1996). Testimony at the Town Meeting on fathering and male fertility sponsored by the Interagency Forum on Child and Family Statistics, March 27. Washington, DC.

Tanfer, K. (1983). Presentation on using male interviewers in the 1989 National Survey of Young Men. Washington, DC: National Institute on Child Health and Human Development.

Turner, C. F., Ku, L., Sonenstein, F. L., & Pleck, J. H. (1995). Impact of audio-CASI on reporting of male-male sexual contacts: Preliminary findings from the National Survey of Adolescent Males. In R. B. Warnecke (Ed.), *Health survey research methods: Conference proceedings* (pp. 171–76). Hyattsville, MD: National Center for Health Statistics.

Udry, J. R., & Billy, J. (1987). Initiation of coitus in early adolescence. *American Sociological Review, 52,* 841–855.

Vener, A. M., & Stewart, C. S. (1974). Adolescent sexual behavior in middle America revisited: 1973. *Journal of Marriage and the Family, 36,* 728–735.

Zelnik, M., & Kantner, J. F. (1980). Sexual activity, contraceptive use, and pregnancy among metropolitan area teenagers: 1971–1979. *Family Planning Perspectives, 12,* 230–237.

Zenilman, J., Weisman, C., Rompalo, A., et al. (1995). Condom use to prevent incident STDs: The validity of self-reported condom use. *Sexually Transmitted Diseases, 22*(1), 15–21.

Item Nonresponse in the National AIDS Behavioral Surveys among African American and White Respondents

JOHN PETERSON AND JOSEPH A. CATANIA

In assessments of human sexual behavior, two types of purposeful response biases may occur.[1] One type is a direct nonresponse, either refusing to answer a question or answering "don't know." The second is to confabulate answers that may conform to normative expectations about what is desirable behavior or belief. In this paper we explore the former type of response bias, focusing on "decline to answer" and "don't know" responses to various sexual questions and contrasting social demographic items. In particular, we examined African American respondents 18–75 years of age in a phone interview and report on the patterns of response bias that occur in that portion of the U.S. population. In addition, we have comparative data from white adults. We're interested in how ethnic or racial patterns of response bias vary by gender and age. Evidence indicates that males and females differ in their willingness to disclose sensitive information. In general, women tend to be more willing to disclose such information than males. There is also evidence for differences in self-disclosure of sensitive topics with age, perhaps reflecting differences in historical experiences. Older age cohorts grew up in times when discussion and disclosure of sexual information was considered to be more taboo than it is today among younger age cohorts.

The data we are commenting on come from the National AIDS Behavioral Survey baseline study, a Random Digit Dial telephone survey conducted in the United States in 1990–1991. Our sample involves large oversampling of African Americans and older Americans.

To provide an anchor for nonresponse bias in this sample of African Americans and whites, we considered nonresponse for the question "How old are you?"—a fairly innocuous question for both African Americans and whites. The decline-to-answer response is given by a very small number of respondents, fewer than 1%—approximately 0.1% to 0.2% for males and slightly higher for females, around 0.8%. This is what one might expect in terms of gender bias and reporting one's age. In contrast, ques-

---

1. John Peterson was unable to present this paper because of health problems. It was presented at the meeting by Joseph Catania.

tions about income exhibit much higher levels of "don't know" and "decline to answer" responses. In general, the total amount of nonresponse is fairly equivalent for African American males and females and for white males. However, it nearly doubles for white females, approaching 6.4%.

In contrast to nonresponse patterns for demographic variables, we found very little nonresponse for the fundamental sexual question asked of all respondents: "Have you had sex of any kind in the past 5 years [for those under 50 years] or the past 15 years [for those over 50 years of age]?" This nonresponse pattern was similar for males and females and for whites and African Americans.

We also found very low levels of nonresponse across ethnic and gender groups for the question concerning sexual orientation defined behaviorally in terms of the gender of one's sexual partners. Fewer than 1% of African Americans and fewer than 1% of whites, either male or female, declined to answer this question. It is important to keep in mind that for questions about behavior, people could make up answers instead of giving a "decline to answer" response.

We also asked a large segment of respondents about how many sexual partners they had had in the last 12 months. Nonresponse was highest for African American males; approximately 0.9% declined to answer or said they didn't know how many partners they had had in the past 12 months. Overall, however, there was very little nonresponse to this question.

We would have liked to gather data on other types of sexual behavior questions, such as condom use and anal intercourse. However, this study, which focused on AIDS, screened respondents on risk factors for HIV or other STDs. Only those who had such a risk factor were administered a more intensive battery of sexual questions. As one might expect, this more selected population had very low levels of nonresponse to even the most sensitive items. Our inclination is to believe that respondents who report none of the standard HIV/STD risk factors would be the ones most likely to have difficulties with more sensitive questions.

Sexual behaviors aside, another area of sexual inquiry stood out as an exception to the low levels of nonresponse obtained on the behavior questions. On some of the condom attitude items, we found relatively high levels of nonresponse. This was not a consistent finding across all attitudinal questions. In general, questions which ask for intimate details about the person's sexual life seem to elicit higher levels of nonresponse. To provide an anchor, consider the item "using condoms is immoral." Although the absolute levels of nonresponse may be a bit higher for some of the demographic variables, with a high of 2.3% for African American males and 1% or less for all others, these are not nonresponse levels that raise eyebrows.

For a more intimate attitudinal item, such as whether one believes that condoms take all the fun out of sex, nonresponse increases substantially.

Here we see both gender and ethnic differences. For instance, among African Americans, females are more likely than males to decline to answer this question. This is also true among whites. White females are the most likely, with almost 8% declining to answer such a question.

A similar pattern emerges for an item on whether the person says he or she believes that condoms are very likely to slip off during sex. Like the question about fun, it implies experience with condoms and is asking about more intimate details. Again, female nonresponse is higher than male nonresponse: almost 8% of African American females and white females declined to answer that question compared with 5% to 6% for males. And again, whites are slightly higher than African Americans. This slightly higher tendency toward nonresponse for whites might be expected. Attitudinal research has suggested that African Americans are more sex-positive than whites, responding a bit more like people from Scandinavian countries than like whites from the United States.

Age also produces interesting patterns. To provide an anchor, consider the education variables. Although the overall level of nonresponse is relatively low, 1% or less, there is a slight increase in the amount of nonresponse that occurs as we move across age cohorts. This pattern is accentuated with more sensitive items. The income question, for instance, has substantially more nonresponse with increasing age. This increase is greater for whites than African Americans. For instance, for respondents aged 60 and above, approximately 9% of whites compared with 5% of African Americans refused to answer.

On the other hand, for the item on whether the respondent had sex in the past 5 years (or, in the case of people over the age of 50, in the past 15 years), we see extremely low levels of nonresponse and very little shift in willingness to answer that question across age groups. The sexual orientation question also was associated with relatively low levels of nonresponse across age groups for both African Americans and whites. Although there is a slight tendency for whites to be less likely to answer this question, approximately 0.9% declined to answer versus 0.3% for African Americans. Overall these percentages are so low that they are of little concern.

For the item on number of partners people had sex with in the past 12 months, we see that African Americans are slightly more likely to refuse to answer this question than whites. However, this occurs only at the extreme age group, where 2.6% of African Americans over the age of 60 refused to answer this question as compared with 0.3% of whites.

For the condom attitude items, we see a clear pattern with age. For the item on whether using condoms is immoral, significantly more older individuals declined to answer this question than younger individuals. Approximately 4.6% of African Americans and 3.4% of whites over the age of 60 refused to answer this question, compared with fewer than 1% of people 18–29 years of age. For the item on whether condoms take all the fun out of sex, we also see an increase in nonresponse with age, reaching a maximum among whites of 11.8% versus 9.9% for African Americans. For the item on whether condoms slip off during sex, we see substantial increases in nonresponse with age. Unfortunately this item was asked only of younger adults. (There was a split battery, and younger adults got some items that older adults didn't.) But the age pattern emerged with some modification by ethnicity, with older whites evidencing more nonresponse than older African Americans. For instance, for white individuals 40–49 years old we found 12% declined to answer versus 9% for African Americans. This compares to values respectively of 4.5% and 2.7% for individuals 18–29 years of age.

Although we see ethnic differences in nonresponse, these are evident only on the more sensitive questions. Particular types of attitudinal context appear to be slightly more sensitive to ethnic differences. However, these are all modifiable by gender and age of the respondent, with older respondents being generally less likely to answer the most sensitive questions and males less likely to answer some types of questions. There are exceptions to these rules. With some of the condom attitudinal questions, we find that females are less likely to answer the questions than are males.

Our continuing work in this area will examine the joint effects of age and gender. We suspect that prohibitions on discussing sex may be greater for older women than for older men. We also are considering looking into the issue of social class, particularly the effects of education on nonresponse. It may be that some of the nonresponse simply reflects comprehension problems, although a fair amount of work was done on looking at comprehension issues in the pilot research for this study.

Our general conclusion is that differences between ethnic groups are most evident in older age cohorts. Historical changes may have had a leveling effect to some extent such that younger people are becoming more sex-positive in the United States. Gender differences are clear across both ethnic groups, and such differences may transcend ethnic influences.

The Effects of Question Wording, Interviewer Gender, and Control on Item Response by African American Respondents

JOSEPH A. CATANIA, DIANE BINSON, JOHN PETERSON, AND JESSE CANCHOLA

The National AIDS Behavioral Methodology Surveys consist of two distinct Random Digit Dial (RDD) telephone surveys conducted at a national level, first of the general population and then of African Americans. Both surveys represent large-scale field experiments that looked at the following questions:

1. How does gender of the interviewer affect respondents' answers to questions on various topics of sexuality?
2. Are there ways to ask sexual questions in a manner that is more emotionally supportive to respondents?
3. If we give respondents more control over the research situation, will they feel more comfortable and therefore provide more honest self-disclosures?

This work is based on the notion that if you give people some control in situations where they might be anxious they will feel less anxious. In this instance, we gave respondents control by giving them the option to choose the gender of their interviewer. Respondents were randomized to all conditions, and all conditions are crossed. We also examined gender interactions, and all analyses control for time of interview and interviewer cluster effects. Three examples that are illustrative will be discussed.

Self-disclosure theory suggests that the more trusting and comfortable persons feel with someone, the more likely they are to be honest in their self-disclosures. Psychological control theory also contends that in ambiguous or potentially stressful situations, the more control given to persons over some aspect of the situation, the more comfortable they're going to feel. Consequently the more comfortable they feel, the more likely they will be able to make honest disclosures in that particular situation.

Both surveys were RDD surveys that produce probability samples. The first study, the general population survey, interviewed 2,000+ respondents aged 18–49 years. The African American survey, also conducted at the national level, interviewed approximately 1,300 African Americans 18–49 years of age.

We will first give evidence and examples of the item context manipulations which were designed to give respondents more emotional support. An example of a standard context in asking about condom use is the following item: "Thinking about all of the times you've had vaginal intercourse during the last 6 months, how often would you say you used a condom?" The respondents would then indicate what percent or how frequently they used condoms. The supportive, or what we refer to as the enhanced, item goes like this: "Many people these days have thought about the need to use condoms. Some people have decided to use condoms, some are undecided about the need to use them, and others feel they have no real need to use condoms." This type of supportive item tries to give people a sense that there are multiple possible answers to these questions and no single right answer.

This context manipulation had a significant effect on respondents' answers to questions on condom use. For men in the general population, 66% reported no condom use with the enhanced item, 60% with the standard. For African American men, this percentage was 40 versus 28. So the effect appears to be larger among African Americans than among the general population. There was very little effect for women, though in the general population survey we did find an effect for women who had some type of risk factor for HIV.

There was also a significant effect for gender of interviewer on people's tendency to report nonuse of condoms. Again, this effect was observed primarily for men. In the general population, a same-gender interviewer elicited significantly more responses of nonuse of condoms than an opposite-gender interviewer, 63% versus 57%. Among African Americans we obtained the opposite effect: African American men were significantly more likely to report condom nonuse to an opposite-gender interviewer than to a same-gender interviewer. There was no effect for giving respondents the option of selecting the gender of their interviewer on condom use responses.

Another item we looked at was the question on age at starting coital activity. In a sense, this can be used to index whether a person was a virgin during adolescence. We looked at the specific issue of whether people were virgins before age 18. The standard way interviewers have asked this question in the past is along the lines of "How old were you when you first had sex with another person?" The enhanced version asks, "People start having sexual intercourse at different ages, for instance, some people start having sexual intercourse when they are very young, others during their teen years, some not until they're adults, and others decide not to have sexual intercourse at all. How old were you when you had sexual intercourse with another person?"

What we found in both the general population and the African American population is that the enhanced item had opposite effects for men and women. Men were significantly more likely to report being virgins during adolescence in the enhanced condition than in the standard condition. The opposite was true for women: significantly more women reported being sexually active during adolescence in the enhanced condition than in the standard condition. For African American males, 33% reported sexual inactivity during adolescence in the enhanced version versus 17% in the standard condition. In the general population, these numbers were 46% versus 37%. For African American women, 42% said they were sexually inactive during adolescence in the enhanced condition versus 50% in the standard condition. In the general population, these numbers were 55% versus 60%.

These findings are interesting on at least two accounts. First, they illustrate that a simple manipulation, such as giving people a little more supportive type of question context, can reduce the gender differences in reporting sexual activity. Second, it is also interesting that these effects on people's reporting of adolescent sexual behavior do not extend to reports of their adult sexual behavior. These manipulations had no effects on reports of numbers of partners in adulthood. It appears that the fictions or the myths that people develop during adolescence are carried forward by them in time.

Another topic area of substantial interest in the field of human sexuality and AIDS research is assessment of sexual orientation. One way of assessing this is to ask people the basic question about the gender of their sexual partners. The standard way this has been asked in numerous surveys is with the question: "Have you ever had sex of any kind with another male?" The enhanced way of assessing these lifetime reports is to ask people in surveys: "In past surveys, many men have reported that in some point in their life they have had some type of sexual experience with another male. This could have happened before adolescence, during adolescence, or as an adult." This kind of item, following as it does the suggestions made by Bradburn and Sudman (1979), may be less threatening to some respondents, since the interviewer sets norms for the sensitive item by letting the respondent know that a fair number of other respondents have reported this behavior in the past.

We have observed significant effects for men in a variety of combinations of manipulations on this item. But there were no significant effects for women with any of the manipulations. For men we found that an opposite-gender interviewer and a standard survey item get identical values in the general population and among African Americans (3.2%). We found a nearly threefold increase in both the general population and in African Americans when we moved to an enhanced interview with a same-gender interviewer (8% for general population and 9% in the African American population).

In general, the patterns that we have observed in the general population are very similar to what we are seeing among African Americans, right down to the gender effects. One problem, however, is that we do not have as large a sample of African Americans as we would like to have. If we had another couple of hundred respondents, particularly men, we would be detecting substantially more significant effects. So far, there has been only one case where the effects found in African Americans are opposite to those found in the general population, and that is with the reports of nonuse of condoms and the effects of gender of interviewer.

Overall, the largest number of significant effects that we have observed are due to either the enhanced item or the gender of interviewer. The experiment with choosing the gender of the interviewer showed little. However, control issues were important in at least three topics that might be construed as being highly sensitive: rape, sexual dysfunction, and extramarital sex. For these areas, giving people a little more control appears to have a significant effect. In general, it appears that being interviewed by people of the same gender makes respondents feel a bit more comfortable and more willing to disclose information in directions that we presume to be more honest. The consistency of the findings lends support to the validity of our assertion that the differences in the answers we're observing are in the direction of more honest self-disclosure. Generalization of these findings to other data-collection modes would be an important next step, as well as examination of these types of manipulations in other populations, such as Hispanic and Asian Americans.

Reference

Bradburn, N., & Sudman, S. (1979). *Improving interview methods and questionnaire design.* Washington, D.C.: Jossey-Bass.

Researching Sexual Behavior
Methodological Issues for Hispanics

FABIO SABOGAL, DIANE BINSON, AND
JOSEPH A. CATANIA

The Hispanic Population

The terms *Hispanic* and *Latino* denote current residents of the United States who trace their background to a Latin American country or to the Iberian peninsula of Europe (Spain and Portugal). The Hispanic/Latino population grew more than seven times faster than the rest of the population during the last two decades, with 22.6 million enumerated in the 1990 census (Bureau of the Census, 1993a, 1993b). Demographic projections estimate that Hispanics may be the largest minority population in the United States by the year 2010 (Day, 1993; Campbell, 1994). Hispanics belong to all races—white, black, Asian, and Native American. The Hispanic/Latino population in the United States consists of the following groups: Mexican (61.2%), Puerto Rican (12.1%), Central American (6.0%), Cuban (4.8%), South American (4.7%), Spanish (4.4%), other Hispanic (3.9%), and Dominican (2.4%) (Bureau of the Census, 1993b).

The majority of Hispanics share a common cultural heritage, the Spanish language and the Catholic religion, and have core cultural values, such as unity, reliance, and the central role of the family (*familismo*) (Sabogal, Marín, Otero-Sabogal, Marín, & Pérez-Stable, 1987). In spite of Hispanic homogeneity, there is also great diversity among and within the various Hispanic subgroups. For example, a large proportion of Mexican Americans have lived in the Southwest since the nineteenth century or earlier, have the youngest populations of all Hispanic subgroups (median age, 23.5), have very high birthrates, have the lowest birth weight incidence among Hispanic subgroups, have larger families, and rely on an extended family structure that includes godparents (Bureau of the Census, 1993b; Molina & Aguirre-Molina, 1994). Puerto Ricans are more concentrated in major northeastern urban areas and Puerto Rico, are U.S. citizens, have the highest rate of female family headship, and are the most disadvantaged Hispanic subgroup in terms of socioeconomic status (Comas-Díaz, 1988; Chapa & Valencia, 1993). Cuban Americans are concentrated in Florida (43% of Hispanics in Florida are Cuban), tend to be older (median age, 35.8 years), have a high rate of labor force participation, are more likely to live in extended families, have higher educational levels, and are less likely to be living below the poverty level than other Hispanic subgroups (Bureau of the Census, 1993b). Central Americans, especially from Salvador, Guatemala, and Nicaragua, are the newest Hispanic arrivals. South Americans have the highest education among Hispanics.

Sexual Attitudes and Behaviors

Hispanics are less knowledgeable about sex, have less exposure to sexual education, exhibit stronger traditional family attitudes, and have more conservative attitudes toward sexuality than non-Hispanic whites (Amaro, 1988; COSSMHO, 1991; Sabogal & Otero-Sabogal, 1989). Although gender differences in sexual behavior and sex role attitudes among Hispanics have been reported (Pavich, 1986), other studies have challenged the rigid gender roles attributed to Hispanics (Cromwell & Ruíz, 1979; COSSMHO, 1991). Acculturation and socioeconomic factors play a key role in explaining traditional gender roles (Vásquez-Nuttall, Romero-García, & De León, 1987). Egalitarian sex roles increase with education (Rogler & Cooney, 1984). Sex role differences are more accentuated among less acculturated Hispanics who are more likely to adhere to traditional gender roles (Pavich, 1986; Sabogal & Otero-Sabogal, 1989). Adherence to traditional sex roles among Hispanic women decreases as immigrants are acculturated to a culture with less rigid sex roles and more permissive sexual attitudes (Sabogal, Pérez-Stable, Otero-Sabogal, & Hiatt, 1995). Among Hispanic women, having more sexual partners is associated with increased acculturation (Sabogal, Faigeles, & Catania, 1993; Van Oss-Marín, Tschann, Gómez, & Kegeles, 1993; Ford & Norris, 1993).

Hispanics have a relatively high rate of sexually transmitted diseases (STDs). The incidence of AIDS in the United States is three times higher for Hispanics (Díaz, Buehler, Castro, & Ward, 1993; Gayle, Selik, & Chu, 1990) and the number of heterosexually acquired HIV infections reported in Hispanics is 10 times the rate for non-Hispanic whites (CDC, 1989). The incidence of syphilis and gonorrhea is greater among Hispanics than among non-Hispanics (Moran, Aral, Jenkins, Peterman, & Alexander, 1989; Rolfs & Nakashima, 1989). Hispanic women have one of the highest rates of cervical cancer in the world (Zunzunegui, King, Coria, & Charlet, 1986).

Lack of Methodological Studies

Over the last decade, there has been an increased interest in collecting information about Hispanic health, including sexual behavior, AIDS, and reproductive health behaviors. For example, telephone surveys have been used successfully in Hispanic populations (Catania et al., 1992a; Marín, Turner, & Moses, 1990; Sabogal et al., 1995), and a number of telephone surveys of AIDS-relevant sexual behavior that include Hispanic populations have been completed: the National AIDS Behavioral Surveys (NABS) and the Family of AIDS Behavioral Surveys (FABS) (Catania et al., 1992b; Catania et al., 1995), and general populations surveys in Massachusetts (Hingson et al., 1989), Los Angeles (Kanouse et al., 1991), and Chicago (Ostrow, 1989).

The increased use of telephone interviews to assess sensitive topics has not been accompanied by related methodological work. Methodological issues pertinent to asking sensitive and threatening questions have been set aside in the rush to collect data. For example, studies of participation bias and measurement error in telephone surveys that ask sensitive AIDS and sex information questions among Hispanic populations are rare, despite the need to collect accurate information on a population that has a high prevalence of STDs. Similarly, in studies of sexual abuse and harassment, respondents are self-selected and therefore not representative of the general or minority populations (Russell, 1984) or, as in a recent national sexual behavior survey (Laumann, Gagnon, Michael, & Michaels, 1994), respondents were interviewed in English only.

This paper describes the challenges, problems, and methodological issues in researching Hispanic sexual behavior, including (a) definition of the Hispanic population, (b) great diversity among Hispanic subgroups, gender, and acculturation levels, (c) Hispanic cultural values and beliefs, (d) translation procedures and language, (e) literacy and educational achievement, (f) nonresponse bias, and (g) additional methodological issues.

Identifying Ethnicity

There is a lack of scientific consensus on the measurement of race and Hispanic ethnicity (Hahn & Stroup, 1994). Methods that have been used to identify Latino ethnicity include birthplace, family origin of parents and grandparents, generation, language use, Hispanic surname, self-identity, perceived ethnicity by staff, skin color, cultural values, and physical characteristics. Overall, a combination of multiple indicators is preferred. Self-declared ethnic identity is one of the best methods and has been used as a gold standard for validity studies (Pérez-Stable, Hiatt, Sabogal, & Otero-Sabogal, 1995).

Many Hispanics/Latinos do not distinguish between the current race and ethnic categories used by the Office of Management and Budget (OMB) (Harris et al., 1993; Rodriguez & Cordero-Guzman, 1992). The U.S. census asks respondents to self-categorize their race (white, black, Asian, or Native American) and then determine Hispanic ethnicity (e.g., "Is this person Spanish/Hispanic/Latino?"). When Hispanics are asked whether they are black, white, Asian, or Pacific Islander, a high percentage check "other."

Hispanics write their nationality—Mexican, Salvadoran—and when asked the Hispanic origin question, approximately 10 million Hispanics skip the question. Research shows that Hispanics think they have already answered it. Eliminating the separate Hispanic question reduces the number of Hispanics because, in general, Cuban Americans and people who trace their ancestry to Spain tend to pick "white" over "Hispanic" when forced to choose.

The distribution of self-identified Hispanics varies depending on the way researchers ask the question. The distribution could be affected by the presence or absence of a Hispanic category, a multiethnic category, the order of the ethnic and racial questions, and the Hispanic group. For example, a greater percentage of respondents consider themselves Hispanics when asked a separated question (e.g., "Are you Hispanic, Latino, or of Hispanic origin?") than when "Hispanic" is included as a racial category in a single question combining race and ethnicity (e.g., white, black, Hispanic, American Indian, Asian). A combined race and ethnicity question may reduce the count of Hispanics by approximately 14%. A recent federal survey of nearly 60,000 households found that making Hispanic origin a category listed alongside white and black reduced the estimation of Hispanics from 11% to 7.5%.

Multiracial or biracial categories are absent in the current racial/ethnic categories used by OMB. Some critics consider that actual categories do not reflect the increasing racial and ethnic diversity of the United States (U.S. Department of Labor, 1995). People with a mixed ethnic or racial background may be misclassified. For example, a black Hispanic may be classified as black in one study but as Hispanic in another. There is a lack of information regarding attitudes and behaviors among multiracial Hispanics.

Ethnic self-identification also varies by level of acculturation. Many recent immigrants are not familiar with the established ethnic categories. The concept of ethnicity is uncommon in Latin America. For some immigrants, ethnicity is a concept that is learned in the United States when individuals enter a host culture that is sensitive to ethnic and racial categories. Abstract concepts such as "national ancestry, race, Spanish origin, ethnic group, ethnicity, multiethnic, Hispanic origin, and other Hispanics" are unfamiliar and produce confusion for many Hispanics.

There is a lack of consistency among the terms used to identify Hispanic/Latino populations. The confusion in terminology (e.g., Chicano, Raza, Hispanic surnames, Spanish American, Latino, U.S.-born Hispanics, white person of Hispanic origin, Boricua, Mexican American, Spanish-speaking) produces noncomparable samples among researchers (Hayes-Bautista, 1980). A recent study suggested that Hispanic (58%) was preferred over Latino (12%) or Spanish origin (12%).

There is also a lack of consistency in the way Hispanics have been identified in sex research surveys. For example, the NABS used only a race question (Sabogal et al., 1993; Sabogal & Catania, 1996). The NABS II included a race, a race and ethnicity, and a race and ethnicity of the partner question. The National AIDS Methodological Survey included a race and a Hispanic group question. The National Health and Social Life Survey included race, ethnicity, and race and ethnicity of the partner questions (Laumann et al., 1994).

Diversity

The Hispanic population is a heterogeneous, multiethnic, and multicultural population from many national communities, reflecting diversity in race, nationality, ethnicity, culture, religion, geography, socioeconomic status, and social class. Hispanics belong to any racial group. There are Hispanics who are of Asian, American Indian, African, or European background. Many Hispanics have a mixed ethnic or racial background. There is no one Hispanic population, but several Hispanic subgroups.

One of the implications of the great diversity among Hispanic subgroups is that sex researchers need a large sample and enough financial resources to study a particular sex outcome across social strata, including the major U.S. Hispanic subgroups, acculturation levels, and gender. For example, a power calculation for the FABS for the outcome of number of people who had vaginal or anal intercourse in the previous 12 months showed that the required number of subjects was 1,664 to study a 2×2 gender by language interaction. Larger samples were also needed to study the main effects of church attendance ($n = 2,122$) or sexual problems ($n = 2,431$). Large sample sizes, both in English and Spanish, have been used successfully with Hispanics at a national (NABS: $n = 4,658$; 2,645 Spanish-speaking and 2,013 English-speaking Hispanics), nine-state ($n = 1,592$; Van Oss-Marín et al., 1993), and regional ($n = 1,646$; Sabogal et al., 1995) level. Although nearly 90% of Hispanics are concentrated in 10 states, to oversample the major Hispanic subgroups across geographical areas, a large amount of resources is generally needed.

Hispanic subgroup, acculturation/language of interview (e.g., Spanish—low acculturation vs. English—high acculturation), and gender are three important dimensions that need to be included when researching Hispanics. Researchers may bias a study by taking only English-speaking Hispanics. We found in the NABS, for example, that age of sexual initiation varies by language preference and level of acculturation (Sabogal et al., 1995). We also found that 60% of Hispanic respondents preferred to answer the NABS questions in Spanish (Sabogal et al., 1993). It is estimated that 63% of Hispanics speak Spanish at home and 25% speak little or no English. It is essential to include Spanish-speaking Hispanics, as their attitudes and behaviors differ from those of English-speaking Hispanics.

Cultural Values

The core cultural scripts of *simpatía* and *respeto*, a pattern of social interaction that promotes smooth, pleasant, and respectful social relationships emphasizing positive behaviors in agreeable situations and avoiding confrontation, may affect the validity of responses to sensitive questions (Triandis, Marín, & Betancourt, 1984; Paz, 1993). *Simpatía* and *respeto* are types of image management characterized by conformity and the presentation of an amiable attitude in social interactions with outsiders to create a favorable impression. Hispanics stress the importance of a proper image and tend to report socially desirable and acquiescent responses (Ross & Mirowsky, 1984). In survey research on threatening behavior, Hispanic respondents may, for example, underreport by denying that they have engaged in a socially undesirable behavior (e.g., extramarital sex) because it is contranormative to disclose this private information to a stranger (Bradburn, Sudman, Blair, & Stocking, 1978). For example, low-acculturated Hispanic women reported almost zero percent of multiple sex partners in the prior twelve months in the NABS (Sabogal et al., 1993). *Simpatía* may explain anecdotal reports that Hispanics tried to please the interviewer, giving them socially desirable answers, saying "yes" when they mean "maybe or maybe no," using a more indirect and polite language, and making several "excuses" (e.g., "Please call me next week," "she is on vacation in Mexico") instead of refusing the interview directly.

Cultural values such as *simpatía* and *respeto* may also explain high levels of "yea-saying" found in Hispanics, who tend to agree with statements regardless of their content *("Como usted diga, si usted lo dice es verdad,"* "If you have said it, then it must be true. It is true if you say so") (Marín & Marín, 1991). Hispanic populations may often produce socially desirable responses (Ross & Mirowsky, 1984), may show low self-disclosure to a stranger (Franco, Malloy, & Gonzalez, 1984), and may produce extreme responses (Yang & Bond, 1980; Marín, Triandis, Betancourt, & Kashima, 1983). Research shows that Hispanics are more likely than non-Hispanic whites to use extreme response categories, particularly the positive end of agree-disagree scales (Bachman & O'Malley, 1984), and to agree with a given item to a greater extent than non-Hispanic whites (Marín, Gamba, & Marín, 1992). The tendency to give socially desirable responses among Hispanics coincides with meta-analysis procedures that show that in 81% of the studies, Hispanics scored significantly higher on a lie scale than non-Hispanic whites (Campos, 1989). Respondents who are older, Mexican, Puerto Rican, or of lower socioeconomic status are more likely to acquiesce and give socially desirable responses (Ross & Mirowsky, 1984; Carr & Krause, 1978).

Traditional Hispanic culture is also characterized by a male-centered view in which men tend to prove their virility by having multiple sex partners (Carrier & Magaña, 1991; Sabogal & Otero-Sabogal, 1989). It is possible that societal machismo norms may reflect reporting biases in which Hispanic women underreport while Hispanic men overreport. For example, only 1% of Cuban women reported multiple sex partners in the past year compared with 28% of Cuban men (Sabogal et al., 1993). One possible explanation for this large discrepancy is that Hispanic women with low acculturation are less likely to admit having multiple sexual partners than those with high acculturation.

Hispanic culture has a flexible attitude toward time. Hispanics may overestimate time to complete a task, while non-Hispanics may underestimate. Differential temporal orientation may be related to differences in time estimation, punctuality, planning, length of time spent at a task, and estimation of behavioral frequencies among ethnic groups. For example, compared with whites, Hispanics were more likely to decline to answer when asked in the NABS to estimate the number of times they had vaginal intercourse in the previous six months.

Hispanic cultural characteristics such as *simpatía, respeto,* machismo, and time flexibility may increase self-disclosure bias, producing normative answers to sensitive or stigmatized questions (e.g., extramarital sex, abortion).

New technologies in questionnaire administration and research on item context offer possibilities in reducing measurement bias. Audio computer-assisted self interview (audio-CASI), in which respondents listen to questions through headphones and respond on portable laptop computers, and telephone-audio (T-ACASI) technology, in which respondents listen to computer-controlled questions and respond by pressing keys on a touchtone telephone, have produced more accurate self-reported estimates of male-male contact than paper-and-pencil measures (Turner, Ku, Sonenstein, & Pleck, 1995). Audio-CASI and T-ACASI have been shown to substantially increase the likelihood that respondents report engaging in sensitive, infrequent, stigmatized, or illicit behaviors, decreasing socially desirable or normative behaviors (Turner, Miller, Smith, Cooley, & Rogers, 1996). Preliminary evaluation of multilingual audio-CASI procedures with a limited sample of Spanish-speaking Hispanics suggests that this new technology can be used successfully with monolingual Hispanics, who indicated adequate comprehension of the questions asked in the audio-CASI interview and comfort using the equipment (Hendershot, Thornberry, Rogers, Miller, & Turner, 1995; Turner, Rogers, Hendershot, Miller, & Thornberry, 1995). More research is needed to adequately test this new technology in low-literacy, multiethnic communities.

Survey instruments that use "enhanced" questions that are "supportive" of what may be perceived as nonnormative or stigmatized behavior have increased data quality compared to standard worded items (Catania et al., in press). One hypothesis is that permission-giving questions allow respondents to feel more comfortable disclosing personal information. Methodological studies that test different conditions (e.g., survey mode, item context, interviewer ethnicity) to reduce measurement bias among Hispanics are urgently needed.

Translation Procedures

Research instruments that are developed only in English have the disadvantage of not reaching recent immigrants with limited English who are less acculturated to U.S. mainstream culture. Nationally, about 78% of Hispanics speak a language other than English at home (U.S. Department of Commerce, 1993), about 65% prefer to use Spanish in daily social interactions (Marín & Marín, 1991), and approximately 60% in the NABS answered the questionnaire in Spanish (Sabogal et al., 1993; Sabogal & Catania, 1996).

Research instruments should be developed in the first language of the target audience, as the native language reflects values and beliefs intrinsic to that group. However, when translations are required, there are four tools that researchers should use to produce equivalent bilingual instruments: revision by an internal and external panel of experts, back-translation, decentering, and extensive pretesting.

It is essential that instruments be reviewed by a diverse team of native bilingual and bicultural people who are representative of the different ethnic groups or dialects of the target population. Even among native speakers, people from different educational backgrounds or regions of a country will disagree about how something should be said. The dialogue that ensues during resolution of these differences results in an improved translation that can be easily understood by a wide variety of people. Consensus should be reached among translators on the best way to communicate the meaning of the original English-language instrument (Pasick, Sabogal, et al., 1996).

Back-translation is the process by which original instruments are translated into another language, then translated back into the first language. Back-translations are very useful in identifying discrepancies in meaning and equivalence among languages.

Decentering is a process of simultaneous translation of instruments into both languages, adjusting both until they have equivalent meanings and are appropriate for their respective cultures (Ferketich, Phillips, & Verran, 1993). Decentering requires flexibility, as researchers may change both versions at the same time without knowing how the final questionnaire will look. The decentering process, in which successive iterations of translations are performed, improves the final product because instruments must undergo a quality-control process at least twice (Pasick, Sabogal, et al., 1996).

Extensive pretesting elicits feedback from members of the target group. Pretesting during all phases of survey development is one of the most critical aspects of producing valid bilingual instruments. For example, when pretesting the FABS we found that "to have an orgasm (cum)" was better translated as *"tener un orgasmo, derramarse, venirse"* than as *"correrse, eyacular, tener un espasmo."* Also, "dildo" was better translated as *"pene artificial o dildo"* than as *"pene postizo."* New strategies for pretesting survey questions, such as cognitive research (Lessler, Tourangeau, & Salter, 1989), "think-aloud" techniques, coding respondent behaviors (e.g., adequate answer, interrupts, requests clarification, qualified answer, inadequate answer, distressed, angry, defensive, fatigued, redundant questions), coding interviewer question-reading behaviors (no change, slight change, and major change), and special probe questions to explore respondents' understandings of questions, need to be explored when designing culturally equivalent instruments (Oksenberg, Cannell, & Kalton, 1991; Fowler, 1989).

The translation process used for the FABS serves as a good example. The FABS Spanish translation used a universal, broadcast-Spanish language, avoiding colloquial words and regionalisms (Sabogal, Otero-Sabogal, Jenkins, & Pérez-Stable, 1996) and is directed toward all Hispanic groups regardless of region of origin or nationality. Rather than a literal, word-for-word translation, which can be culturally offensive, incomprehensible, or culturally irrelevant, we followed a more conceptual translation process (Hendricson et al., 1989). Two groups of expert panels, a local internal and a national external, were consulted to review the initial Spanish draft. We worked with a diverse team of native bilingual individuals who were representative of the different ethnic groups or dialects of Hispanics. The team was instructed to identify colloquial words, regionalisms, and culturally offensive terms. The team originally identified a list of words that were difficult to translate into Spanish because: (a) there was not an equivalent Spanish word (e.g., dildo), (b) they were very clinical or technical words (e.g., dental dam, mutual masturbation, anus or rectum), or (c) there were several possibilities in the translation (e.g., condom: *condón, preservativo, profiláctico, hule, o caucho*). Extensive field pretesting with Hispanics from all subgroups ensured a universal, broadcast-Spanish language in the FABS translation.

Bilingual Hispanics provided different responses depending on the language of interview. Some studies with Hispanics have suggested that responding to a survey in a secondary language elicits the respondent's awareness of his/her ethnicity and produces more extreme and ethnic responses than when answering the same instrument in the respondent's primary language (Yang & Bond, 1980; Marín et al., 1983; Marín & Marín, 1991). Thus the fact that bilinguals provide different responses when answering in each of their languages is an additional concern when doing research with Hispanic populations.

Low Literacy

Although low levels of literacy are found across ethnic levels, poorly educated individuals experience major difficulties with research instruments that require high-level reading, writing, computational, and information-processing skills. A great proportion of Hispanics are not literate in Spanish or English. Statistics on literacy and school achievement indicate that only 9.2% of Hispanic adults have attained a bachelor's degree or higher (compared with 22% of non-Hispanics), and about 50% of Hispanics have received a high school diploma (compared with 80% of non-Hispanics). Educational problems are most acute among Mexican-origin individuals, reflected in a 6% university graduation rate and 44% high school graduation rate (U.S. Department of Commerce, 1993).

Methodological problems associated with low literacy and poor school achievement among Hispanics include lack of familiarity with questionnaires, tendency to think in concrete and immediate terms, difficulty with complex response scales, problems with comprehension of tasks to be completed, insufficient language fluency, difficulty recalling time periods and events, longer periods of time to complete a task, difficulty with abstract hypothetical scenarios and multiple choice questions, and great effort with comprehension of tables, probabilities, labels, menus, instructions, and graphics (Marín & Marín, 1991; Canales, Ganz, & Coscarelli, 1995). For example, Hispanics reported difficulty with Spanish instructions provided with condoms that required a high-school-level reading ability to comprehend them fully (Richwald, Schneider-Muñoz, & Valdez, 1989). Difficulty understanding clinical or technical words (e.g., mutual masturbation, bisexual, dental dam, vaginal intercourse, oral sex, pelvic exam, anus, and rectum) and unfamiliar "legal" research consent forms are very often reported by low literacy individuals. A recent study found that Hispanics, especially those with fewer than 12 years of education, reported comprehension difficulty with technical terms such as "vaginal intercourse" and "anal intercourse" (Binson & Catania, under review).

Research instruments must be designed to match the literacy, cultural, and language needs of the target population. Innovative methods, such as Fotoplatica for Hispanic families with low literacy (Harlander & Ruccione, 1993) and Talking Posters, a Freirean approach using printed media as triggers to start a dialogical process (Bialik-Gilad, Magaña, & Batista-Pinto, 1990), need to be explored in sex research with low-literacy individuals.

Response Bias

An additional concern when conducting research with Hispanic populations is the method for selecting potential eligible Hispanics to participate in survey research, for the method may introduce measurement error and participation bias. Respondent selection is of critical concern to AIDS and sex research. Survey interviewers from the Sex and AIDS Methodology Survey reported that in Hispanic households, respondents who answered the phone were more likely to say that they were the eligible subject with the "last birthday" or the "next birthday" regardless of their actual birthday. Thus it is probable that some Hispanic respondents (e.g., housekeepers) who answer the phone simply gave the interviewer false information (e.g., "I'm the one with the most recent birthday") because they wanted to be interviewed, wanted to receive more information about the study, or had nothing else to do. Anecdotal reports suggest that the "last birthday" or the "next birthday" method identified different eligible respondents than the standard Kish method (i.e., complete enumeration). If, for example, large percentages of housekeepers are more likely to say that they "have the last birthday," then predictions of risk factors in the Hispanic population will be underestimates. Volunteer and response bias (systematic error) in Hispanic populations may distort estimates of high-risk sexual practices, and that may have serious consequences for policy and planning (Catania, Gibson, Chitwood, & Coates, 1990; Catania, Gibson, Marín, Coates, & Greenblatt, 1990).

Nonresponse Bias

Nonresponse bias may compromise estimates from sex and seroprevalence surveys. Nonresponse bias occurs when the distribution of responses obtained from respondents who complete the survey is different from what would have been obtained if all respondents had participated. Nonresponse also occurs when there is selective participation with respect to attributes (e.g., ethnicity, acculturation, gender) that are directly related to sexual behaviors or HIV infection (Miller, Turner, & Moses, 1990). We describe nonresponse bias in the NABS by ethnicity, gender, and acculturation levels among Hispanics. We hypothesized that Hispanics would be more likely to decline to answer sensitive demographic and sex questions than whites or African Americans and that gender and acculturation levels among Hispanics are important variables that correlate with selective participation in sex surveys.

The NABS is one of the largest general-population surveys of HIV-relevant sexual behavior in the United States. The objective of the NABS was to examine correlates of HIV-relevant risk factors for the nation and for selected "high-risk" cities. The survey sample was constructed by oversampling Hispanics and African Americans to estimate the prevalence within the general heterosexual population (Catania et al., 1992b).

Analysis of the NABS (n = 10,418) comparing nonresponse rates (e.g., missing values and "don't know" answers) showed nonresponse bias among Hispanics when compared with whites and African Americans for sensitive demographic and sex questions. Hispanics were more likely than whites or African Americans to decline to answer when asked at the end of the survey how difficult or easy it was to talk about sex. In comparison, there were no significant differences between whites and African Americans in missing data for that variable. Compared with whites, Hispanics were also more likely to decline to answer when asked to estimate the number of times they had vaginal intercourse in the previous six months. However, Hispanics were more likely than whites to answer when asked the number of different people they had vaginal or anal intercourse with in the previous year or in the previous five years, or if they had ever received the HIV antibody test.

Hispanic women were more likely to decline to answer when asked if they thought their answers to the AIDS survey were kept confidential than were white and African American women. There were no significant differences in missing values between whites and African Americans. Compared with whites and African Americans, Hispanics declined to answer sensitive demographic questions more often. For example, Hispanic males were more likely than white and African American males to decline to answer the household income question. In comparison, there were no differences between white and African American males. This pattern was more accentuated among women, especially among Hispanic women, who were more likely to decline to answer the income question than white and African American women. In the same way, Hispanics were more likely than whites and African Americans to decline to answer when asked their zip code. There were no significant differences in missing values between whites and African Americans for the zip code question.

Differential responses among Hispanics were observed when analyzing nonzero responses compared with zero responses. For example, compared with whites, Hispanics were more likely to give a zero response when asked the number of sexual partners they had in the last five years, if they had used alcohol or drugs before sexual intercourse, if they believed the AIDS survey was confidential, if they identified as gay, lesbian, or bisexual, and whether condoms were used during vaginal intercourse. Hispanic men were more likely than white and African American men to give a zero answer when asked how often they used condoms during vaginal intercourse. Hispanic women were more likely to give a zero response when asked how many times they had sexual intercourse in the last 5 years or how many times they had anal intercourse than were white or African American women. Hispanic women were far more likely to report a zero response when asked if condoms were used during vaginal intercourse compared with white and African-American women. In brief, a higher proportion of nonresponse rates and zero responses was found among Hispanics for some of the demographic and sex questions from the NABS and in several other studies (Aday, Chiu, & Anderson, 1980; Marín & Marín, 1991).

Nonresponse Bias by Acculturation and Gender

Analysis of the Hispanic NABS data (n = 4,655) showed differential nonresponse rates and nonzero responses by acculturation and gender among Hispanics. Overall, women and low-acculturated individuals were more likely to give nonresponses and zero answers to sensitive questions. For example, low-acculturated Hispanics were more likely to decline to answer to the number of times they had sexual intercourse in the previous six months and if they thought their answers to the AIDS survey were kept confidential than high-acculturated Hispanics. Low-acculturated respondents were considerably more likely to decline to answer when asked the degree of difficulty when talking about sex in AIDS surveys than high-acculturated Hispanics. However, low-acculturated Hispanics were more likely to answer when asked to estimate the number of intercourse partners in the last 5 years than high-acculturated Hispanics. Low-acculturated Hispanic women were more likely to decline to answer the household income question than high-acculturated Hispanic women. Hispanic women were more likely to decline to answer when asked if they had ever received the HIV antibody test than Hispanic men.

There was a higher proportion of "zero answers" among Hispanic women and low-acculturated Hispanics. For example, Hispanic women were more likely than Hispanic men to give a zero response when asked if they had sex in the last 5 years, if they had sex in the last year, if they used condoms during vaginal intercourse, when estimating the number of partners they used condoms with during vaginal intercourse, and when answering how difficult it was to talk about sex in AIDS surveys. Hispanic men and highly acculturated Hispanics were more likely to identify themselves as gay, lesbian, or bisexual than women and low-acculturated Hispanics. High-acculturated Hispanics were also more likely to report not being tested for HIV than low-acculturated Hispanics. The difference was greater among women than among men. High-acculturated Hispanics were more likely to disagree when asked if they thought their answers to the AIDS survey were kept confidential than low-acculturated Hispanics.

Low-acculturated Hispanics were more likely to give a zero response (e.g., "no") when asked if they used condoms during vaginal intercourse, if they used condoms during anal intercourse, and how difficult it was to talk about sex in AIDS surveys than high-acculturated Hispanics. Low-acculturated Hispanics were more likely to give a zero response when asked if they used alcohol or drugs before sexual intercourse. This difference was greater among Hispanic women than among Hispanic men. Low-acculturated Hispanic women were more likely to give a zero response when asked if they have ever had anal intercourse than high-acculturated Hispanic women.

In summary, we found that nonresponse to sensitive demographic and sex questions was more likely among Hispanics, especially among women and low-acculturated, Spanish-speaking Hispanics. Nonresponse among this group may be related to maintaining traditional gender roles and conservative attitudes toward sexuality, being less knowledgeable about sexuality, and having greater difficulty disclosing personal information. Nonresponse to sex and sensitive demographic questions such as income, especially among low-acculturated women, may be related to traditional cultural characteristics such as machismo and *marianismo* in which "good" women are not supposed to be interested in sex or personal finances. There is a lack of methodological studies that test different experimental conditions in which Hispanics may be more likely to reduce their nonresponse bias. Carefully designed experiments that test methods of asking questions, respondent selection, respondent control of interviewer selection, cultural characteristics, and question context (e.g., permission giving) are needed.

Additional Methodological Issues

Some further important issues need to be addressed when studying Hispanics:

1. Ethnographic approaches and extensive pretesting using cognitive research, special probe questions to test for comprehension, and interview behavior coding, have been successful methods to improve the design of large-scale surveys and develop culturally equivalent instruments (Sabogal & Otero-Sabogal, 1989; O'Donnell, Sandoval, Vornfett & DeJong, 1994; Flaskerud & Calvillo, 1991; Van Oss-Marín et al., 1993).

2. Sex and AIDS-related telephone surveys have been used successfully in Hispanic populations (Catania et al., 1992a; Marín et al., 1990; Sabogal et al., 1995). Compared with face-to-face interviews, telephone surveys among Hispanics may provide more accurate results (Marín & Marín, 1989) but higher refusal rates, especially among Hispanic women. Response rates in national telephone surveys of sexual behavior among Hispanics have not been reported in the sex-research literature questioning the validity of survey measurements of AIDS-related and other sensitive behaviors among Hispanics (Catania et al., 1992b; Laumann et al., 1994; Billy, Tanfer, Grady, and Klepinger, 1993).

3. Sex studies with few Hispanic respondents, with specific Hispanic subgroups, or with only English-speaking Hispanics have limited external validity. When possible, both Spanish- and English-speaking Hispanics should be included in sex studies.

4. There are few standardized sexual-behavior scales for Hispanics that

have undergone a complete psychometric and cultural analysis. Cultural equivalency of instruments is a prerequisite to obtain valid responses across ethnic and racial groups.

5. Hispanics often agree to participate in survey research (Aday et al., 1980; Marín, Pérez-Stable, & Marín, 1989). Once Hispanics are contacted, refusal rates are generally low. Hispanics are very open to talk about sex individually or in groups under conditions of credibility, respectability and confidentiality.

6. Cohort recruitment and maintenance in longitudinal studies is a major problem for Hispanics. Future studies should explore effective tracking strategies among Hispanics.

7. Studies of Hispanic populations regarding sexual behavior must include Hispanic researchers, interviewers, and community support to enhance the quality of the research.

8. Cultural competence of researchers regarding the Hispanic culture is imperative to develop appropriate research instruments that reflect the linguistic, cultural, and literacy needs of the target population (Rogler, 1989; U.S. Department of Health and Human Services, 1992).

Acknowledgments

This study was funded by NIMH grant MH43892 and NIMH/NIA grant MH46240. We thank Lance M. Pollack, Ph.D. for his work analyzing the NABS data.

References

Aday, L. A., Ciu, G. Y., & Andersen, R. (1980). Methodological issues in health care surveys of the Spanish heritage population. *American Journal of Public Health, 70,* 357–364.

Amaro, H. (1988). Women in the Mexican-American community: religion, culture, and reproductive attitudes and experiences. *Journal of Community Psychology, 16,* 6–20.

Bachman, J. G., & O'Malley, P. M. (1984). Yes-saying, nay-saying, and going to extremes: Black-White differences in response styles. *Public Opinion Quarterly, 48,* 491–509.

Bialik-Gilad, R., Magaña, R., & Batista-Pinto, J. (1990). Talking posters: A Freirean approach. *Border Health Special* (pp. 14–18).

Billy, J. O. G., Tanfer, K., Grady, W. R., & Klepinger, D. H. (1993). The sexual behavior of men in the United States. *Family Planning Perspectives, 25,* 52–60.

Binson, D., & Catania, J. A. (Under review). Respondents' understanding of the words used in sexual behavior questions. *Public Opinion Quarterly.*

Bradburn, N. M., Sudman, S., Blair, E., & Stocking, C. (1978). Question threat and response bias. *Public Opinion Quarterly, 42,* 221–234.
Bureau of the Census. (1993a). The Hispanics population in the United States: March 1992. *Current Population Reports* (pp. 20–465RV). Washington, DC: U.S. Bureau of the Census, U.S. Government Printing Office.
Bureau of the Census. (1993b). Hispanic Americans today. *Current Population Reports* (pp. 23–183). Washington, DC: U.S. Bureau of the Census, U.S. Government Printing Office.
Campbell, P. A. (1994). Population projections for states, by age, race, and sex: 1993 to 2020. *Current Population Reports* (pp. 25–111). Washington, DC: U.S. Bureau of the Census, U.S. Government Printing Office.
Campos, L. P. (1989). Adverse impact, unfairness, and bias in the psychological screening of Hispanic peace officers. *Hispanic Journal of Behavioral Sciences, 11,* 122–135.
Canales, S., Ganz, P. A., & Coscarelli, C. A. (1995). Translation and validation of a quality of life instrument for Hispanic American cancer patients: Methodological considerations. *Quality of Life Research, 4,* 3–11.
Carr, L., & Krause, N. (1978). Social status, psychiatric symptomatology, and response bias. *Journal of Health and Social Behavior, 19,* 86–91.
Carrier, J. M., & Magaña, J. R. (1991). Use of ethnosexual data on men of Mexican origin for HIV/AIDS prevention programs. *Journal of Sex Research, 28,* 189–202.
Catania, J. A., Coates, T. J., Kegeles, S., Fullilove, M. T., Peterson, J., Marín, B., Siegel, D., & Hulley, S. (1992a). Condom use in multi-ethnic neighborhoods of San Francisco: The population-based AMEN (AIDS in Multi-Ethnic Neighborhoods) study. *American Journal of Public Health, 82,* 284.
Catania, J., Coates, T., Stall, R, Turner, H., Peterson, J., Hearst, N., Dolcini, M., Hudes, E., Gagnon, J., Wiley, J., & Groves, R. (1992b). The prevalence of AIDS-related risk factors and condom use in the United States. *Science, 258,* 1101.
Catania, J., Gibson, D. R., Marín, B., Coates, T., & Greenblatt, R. (1990). Response bias in assessing sexual behaviors relevant to HIV transmission. *Evaluation and Program Planning, 13,* 19–29.
Catania, J. A., Binson, D., Dolcini, M. M., Stall, R., Choi, K-H., Pollack, L. M., Hudes, E. S., Canchola, J., Phillips, K., Tedlie Moskowitz, J., & Coates, T. J. (1995). Risk factors for HIV and other sexually transmitted diseases and prevention practices among US heterosexual adults: Changes from 1990 to 1992. *American Journal of Public Health, 85,* 1492–1499.
Catania, J. A., Gibson, D. R., Chitwood, D. D., & Coates, T. (1990). Methodological problems in AIDS behavioral research: Influences on measurement error and participation bias in studies of sexual behavior. *Psychological Bulletin, 108*(3), 339–362.
Catania, J. A., Binson, D., Canchola, J., Pollack, L. M., Hauck, W., & Coates, T. (in press). Effects of interviewer gender, interviewer choice, and item context on responses to questions concerning sexual behavior. *Public Opinion Quarterly.*
CDC (Centers for Disease Control). (1989). Update, heterosexual transmission of AIDS and HIV infection. *U.S. Morbidity and Mortality Weekly Report, 38,* 423–434.

Chapa, J., & Valencia, R. R. (1993). Latino population growth, demographic characteristics, and educational stagnation: An examination of recent trends. *Hispanic Journal of Behavioral Sciences, 15,* 165–187.

Comas-Díaz, L. (1988). Mainland Puerto Rican women: A sociocultural approach. *Journal of Community Psychology, 16,* 21–31.

COSSMHO. (1991). Hispanic sexual behavior. *Implications for Research and HIV Prevention.* Washington, DC: National Coalition of Hispanic Health and Human Services Organizations.

Cromwell, R. E., & Ruíz, R. A. (1979). The myth of macho dominance in decision making within Mexican and Chicano families. *Hispanic Journal of Behavioral Sciences, 1,* 355–373.

Day, J. C. (1993). Population projections for states, by age, race, and sex: 1993 to 2050. *Current Population Reports* (pp. 25–104). Washington, DC: U.S. Bureau of the Census, U.S. Government Printing Office.

Diaz, T., Buehler, J., Castro, K., & Ward, J. W. (1993). AIDS trends among Hispanics in the United States. *American Journal of Public Health, 83,* 504–509.

Ferketich, S., Phillips, L., & Verran, J. (1993). Development and administration of a survey instrument for cross-cultural research. *Research in Nursing and Health, 16,* 227–230.

Flaskerud, J. H., & Calvillo, E. R. (1991). Beliefs about AIDS, health, and illness among low-income Latina women. *Research in Nursing and Health, 14,* 431–438.

Ford, K., & Norris, A. (1993). Urban Hispanic adolescents and young adults: Relationship of acculturation to sexual behavior. *Journal of Sex Research, 30,* 316–323.

Fowler, F. J. (1989). Coding behavior in pretests to identify unclear questions. In F. J. Fowler (Ed.), *Health survey research methods.* National Center for Health Services Research and National Health Care Technology Assessment. U.S. Department of Health and Human Services. DHHS Publication N. (PHS) 89–3447.

Franco, J. N., Malloy, T., & González, R. (1984). Ethnic and acculturation differences in self-disclosure. *Journal of Social Psychology, 122,* 21–32.

Gayle, J., Selik, R., & Chu, S. (1990). Surveillance for AIDS and HIV infection among Black and Hispanic children and women of childbearing age, 1981–1989. *Morbidity and Mortality Weekly Report, 39,* 23–30.

Hahn, R. A., & Stroup, D. F. (1994). Race and ethnicity in public health surveillance: Criteria for the scientific use of social categories. *Public Health Reports, 109,* 7–15.

Harlander, C., & Ruccione, K. (1993). Fotoplatica: An innovative teaching method for families with low literacy and high stress. *Journal of Pediatric Oncology Nursing, 10,* 112–114.

Harris, M., Consorte, J. G., Lang, J., & Byrne, B. (1993). Who are the Whites? Imposed census categories and the racial demography of Brazil. *Social Forces, 72,* 451–462.

Hayes-Bautista, D. E. (1980). Identifying Hispanic populations: The influence of research methodology upon public policy. *American Journal of Public Health, 70,* 353–356.

Hendershot, T. P., Thornberry, J. P., Rogers, S. M., Miller, H. G., & Turner, C. F. (1995). Multilingual Audio-CASI: Using English-speaking field interviewers to survey elderly Korean households. *Technical Papers on Health and Behavior Measurement.* (Technical Paper No. 18.) Rockville, MD: Research Triangle Institute.

Hendricson, W. D., Russell, I. J., Prihoda, T. J., Jacobson, J. M., Rogan, A., & Bishop, G. D. (1989). An approach to developing a valid Spanish language translation of a health-status questionnaire. *Medical Care, 27,* 959–966.

Hingson, R., Strunin, L., Craven, D., Mofenson, L., Mangione, T., Berlin, B., Amaro, H., & Lamb, G. (1989). Survey of AIDS knowledge and behavior changes among Massachusetts adults. *Preventive Medicine, 18,* 806.

Kanouse, D., Berry, S., Gorman, E., Yano, E., Carson, S., & Abrahamse, A. (1991). *AIDS related knowledge, attitudes, beliefs, and behaviors in Los Angeles County.* Santa Monica, CA: Rand Corporation.

Laumann, E. O., Gagnon, J. H., Michael, R. T., & Michaels, S. (1994). *The social organization of sexuality.* Chicago: University of Chicago Press.

Lessler, J., Tourangeau, R., & Salter, W. (1989). Questionnaire design in the cognitive research laboratory. *Vital and Health Statistics,* (Series 6, N. 1). Washington, DC: National Center for Health Statistics.

Marín, G., & Marín, B. V. (1989). Comparison of three interviewing approaches for studying sensitive topics with Hispanics: Refusal rates, interviewee discomfort, and perceived accuracy. *Hispanic Journal of Behavioral Sciences, 11,* 330–340.

Marín, G., & Marín, B. V. (1991). *Research with Hispanic populations.* Newbury Park: Sage.

Marín, G., Gamba, R. J., & Marín, B. V. (1992). Acquiescence and extreme response sets among Hispanics: The role of acculturation and education. *Journal of Cross-Cultural Psychology, 23,* 498–509.

Marín, G., Marín, B. V., & Pérez-Stable, E. J. (1990). Feasibility of a telephone survey to study a minority community: Hispanics in San Francisco. *American Journal of Public Health, 80,* 323–326.

Marín, G., Pérez-Stable, E. J., & Marín, B. V. (1989). Cigarette smoking among San Francisco Hispanics: The role of acculturation and gender. *American Journal of Public Health, 79,* 196–198.

Marín, G., Triandis, H. C., Betancourt, H., & Kashima, Y. (1983). Ethnic affirmation versus social desirability: Explaining discrepancies in bilinguals' responses to a questionnaire. *Journal of Cross-Cultural Psychology, 14,* 173–186.

Miller, H. G., Turner, C. F., & Moses, L. E. (Eds.). (1990). *AIDS: The second decade.* Washington, DC: National Academy Press.

Molina, C. W., & Aguirre-Molina, M. (1994). Latino populations: Who are they? In C. W. Molina & M. Aguirre-Molina (Eds.), *Latino health in the U.S.: A growing challenge.* Washington, DC: American Public Health Association.

Moran, J., Aral., S., Jenkins, W. C., Peterman, T. A., & Alexander, E. R. (1989). The impact of sexually transmitted diseases on minority populations. *Public Health Reports, 104,* 560–565.

O'Donnell, L., Sandoval, A., Vornfett, R., & O'Donnell, C. R. (1994). STD prevention and the challenge of gender and cultural diversity: Knowledge, attitudes, and risk behaviors among black and Hispanic inner-city STD clinic patients. *Sexually Transmitted Diseases, 21,* 137–148.

Oksenberg, L., Cannell, C., & Kalton, G. (1991). New strategies for pretesting survey questions. *Journal of Official Statistics, 7,* 349–365.

Ostrow, D. (1989). Personal communication.

Pasick, K. J., Sabogal, F., et al. (1996). Problems and progress in translation of health survey questions: The Pathways experience. *Health Education Quarterly, 23* (supplement), S5.

Pavich, E. G. (1986). A Chicana perspective on Mexican culture and sexuality. *Journal of Social Work and Human Sexuality, 4,* 47–65.

Paz, J. (1993). Support of Hispanic elderly. In H. P. McAdobo (Ed.), *Family ethnicity* (pp. 177–183). Newbury Park: Sage.

Pérez-Stable, E. J., Hiatt, R. A., Sabogal, F., & Otero-Sabogal, R. (1995). Use of Spanish surnames to identify Latinos: Comparison to self-identification. *Monographs: Journal of the National Cancer Institute, 18,* 11–16.

Richwald, G. A., Schneider-Muñoz, M., & Valdez, R. B. (1989). Are condom instructions in Spanish readable? Implications for AIDS prevention activities for Hispanics. *Hispanic Journal of Behavioral Sciences, 11,* 70–82.

Rodriguez, C. E., & Cordero-Guzman, H. (1992). Placing race in context. *Ethnic and Racial Studies, 15,* 523–542.

Rogler, L. H. (1989). The meaning of culturally sensitive research in mental health. *American Journal of Psychiatry, 146,* 296–303.

Rogler, L. H., & Cooney, R. (1984). Spouse relationships. In L. H. Rogler & R. Cooney (Eds.), *Puerto Rican families in New York City: Intergenerational processes* (pp. 99–123). New York: Hispanic Research Center.

Rolfs, R. T., & Nakashima, A. K. (1989). Epidemiology of primary and secondary syphilis in the United States, 1981 through 1989. *Journal of the American Medical Association. 264,* 1432–1437.

Ross, C. E., & Mirowsky, J. (1984). Socially-desirable response and acquiescence in a cross-cultural survey of mental health. *Journal of Health and Social Behavior, 25,* 189–197.

Russell, D. (1984). *Sexual exploitation.* Newbury Park: Sage.

Sabogal, F., & Catania, J. (1996). HIV risk factors, condom use, and HIV antibody testing among heterosexual Hispanics: The National AIDS Behavioral Surveys (NABS). *Hispanic Journal of Behavioral Sciences, 18*(3), 367–391.

Sabogal, F., & Otero-Sabogal, R. (1989). *Latin sexuality, AIDS and drug use in gay males, IV drug users and heterosexual males: A focus group approach.* University of California, San Francisco, Center for AIDS Prevention Studies.

Sabogal, F., Faigeles, B., & Catania, J. A. (1993). Multiple sex partners among Hispanics in the United States, The National AIDS Behavioral Surveys. *Family Planning Perspectives, 25,* 257–262.

Sabogal, F., Marín, G., Otero-Sabogal, R., Marín, B., & Pérez-Stable, E. J. (1987). Hispanic familism and acculturation: What changes and what doesn't? *Hispanic Journal of Behavioral Sciences, 9,* 397–412.

Sabogal, F., Otero-Sabogal, R., Jenkins, C. N. H., & Pérez-Stable, E. J. (1996). Printed health educational materials for diverse populations: Suggestions from the field. *Health Education Quarterly,* S123–S141.

Sabogal, F., Pérez-Stable, E. J., Otero-Sabogal, R., & Hiatt, R. (1995). Gender, ethnic, and acculturation differences in sexual behaviors: Hispanic and non-Hispanic White adults. *Hispanic Journal of Behavioral Sciences, 17*(2), 139–159.

Triandis, H. C., Marín, G., & Betancourt, H. (1984). Simpatía as a cultural script of Hispanics. *Journal of Personality and Social Psychology, 47,* 1363–1375.

Turner, C. F., Rogers, S. M., Hendershot, T. P., Miller, H. G., & Thornberry, J. P.

(1995). Improving representation of linguistic minorities in health survey: A preliminary test of multilingual Audio-CASI. *Technical Papers on Health and Behavior Measurement* (Technical Paper No. 19). Rockville, MD: Research Triangle Institute.

Turner, C. F., Ku, L., Sonenstein, F. L., & Pleck, J. H. (1995). Impact of Audio-CASI on bias in reporting of male-male sexual contacts. *Technical Papers on Health and Behavior Measurement* (Technical Paper No. 17). Rockville, MD: Research Triangle Institute.

Turner, C. F., Miller, H. G., Smith, T. K., Cooley, P. C., & Rogers, S. M. (1996). Preliminary evaluation of a new technology for surveys of sexual and other sensitive behaviors. *Technical Papers on Health and Behavior Measurement* (Technical Paper No. 21). Rockville, MD: Research Triangle Institute.

U.S. Department of Commerce. (1993). *We the American . . . Hispanics* (pp. 300–641). Washington, DC: U.S. Bureau of the Census, Ethnic and Hispanic Statistics Branch, Population Division. U.S. Government Printing Office.

U.S. Department of Health and Human Services. (1992). *Cultural competence for evaluators: A guide to alcohol and other drug abuse prevention practitioners working with ethnic/racial communities.* M. A. Orlandi (Ed.), (DHHS Publication No. ADM 92–1884). Rockville, MD: Office of Substance Abuse Prevention.

U.S. Department of Labor. (1995). *A CPS supplement for testing methods of collecting racial and ethnic information: May 1995.* (USDL Publication No. 95–428). Washington, DC: Bureau of Labor Statistics.

Van Oss-Marín, B., Tschann, J. M., Gómez, C., & Kegeles, S. (1993). Acculturation and gender differences in sexual attitudes and behaviors: Hispanics vs. non-Hispanic White unmarried adults. *American Journal of Public Health, 83*(12), 1759–1761.

Vásquez-Nuttall, E., Romero-García, I., & De León, B. (1987). Sex roles and perceptions of femininity and masculinity of Hispanic women. *Psychology of Women Quarterly, 11,* 409–425.

Yang, K., & Bond, M. H. (1980). Ethnic affirmation by Chinese bilinguals. *Journal of Cross-Cultural Psychology, 11,* 411–425.

Zunzunegui, M., King, M. C., Coria, C. F., & Charlet, J. (1986). Male influences on cervical cancer risk. *American Journal of Epidemiology, 123,* 302–307.

Sexual Research with Latino Men Who Have Sex with Men

Methodological Issues

ALEX CARBALLO-DIÉGUEZ

A decade ago, whenever I expressed interest in the study of Latino gay men, people smiled at me and replied: "There aren't any." This frequent reaction was based both on the invisibility of Latino gay men in the United States and on the assumption that if there were any, they were closeted, married, and impossible to reach.

As we approach the end of the century, the cultural landscape has changed. Due mainly to the high incidence of AIDS among Latino men who have sex with men (MSM), but also to increased social and political maturity, this population now has a clear presence. There are numerous Latino gay organizations, some of them with national reach. Latino gay entertainment places abound on both coasts. Latino contingents customarily participate in annual gay parades and even hold parades of their own. Spanish TV talk shows frequently feature Latino drag queens, Latino leather queens, and plain everyday Latino gays. And revisionism is rescuing documentation on the presence of Latinos from the very beginning of the gay liberation movement. I found a great anecdote in Dick Leitsch's report of the Stonewall riots published in *The Advocate* in 1969:

> At one point, a cop grabbed a wild Puerto Rican queen and lifted his arm to bring a club down on "her." In his best Maria Montez voice the queen challenged, "How'd you like a big Spanish dick up your little Irish ass?" The cop was so shocked he hesitated in his swing, and the queen escaped.

Although the higher visibility of Latino MSM has facilitated their study, a number of methodological issues still remain, some common to all cross-cultural or gay men's studies, others specific to Latino MSM. To facilitate the exposition, I will discuss these issues separately, although there is considerable overlap between them. They are:

1. Sexual self-identity of target population
2. National ancestry
3. Language
4. Recruitment strategies
5. Interviewer issues

Sexual Self-Identity

Who are we trying to study? Latino gay men? Latino homosexuals? Latino "straight" men who have sex with men? Latino drag queens? Or Latino bisexuals? It is important to define clearly our target population because recruitment strategies, assessment characteristics, payment, interpretation of results, etc., will be contingent on the target population.

For most Latinos, *gay* and *homosexual* are synonyms that refer to men who feel sexually and emotionally attracted to other men. Only a few of the participants in a study of Puerto Rican MSM I conducted in the early 1990s (n = 182) made a distinction between the two terms, stating that a gay man is a homosexual with political and community involvement. Inherent in the idea of a homosexual Latino man is that he shows some degree of effeminacy.

If, by contrast, a Latino MSM has a masculine demeanor, always takes the insertor role in oral or anal sex, does not kiss his male partners, and has no tender feelings toward them, he may comfortably call himself *hombre normal* (there is no equivalent to *straight* in Spanish). Most Latin American cultures are quite tolerant of men's sexual exploits; and, provided that the restrictions are maintained, the more experience the man has the more macho he is reputed to be, even if some of this experience is with other men. Straight MSM have a strong emotional investment in distinguishing themselves from gays and are unlikely to respond to recruitment material addressed to gays.

Latinos who customarily dress in female clothes resent being called men. Frequently they do not see themselves as gay, either, but as women, female impersonators, drag queens, transgenders, and occasionally transsexuals. Given that they generally resort to commercial sex to support themselves, they have a different lifestyle from most gay Latinos. They feel discriminated against by Latino gay men who reject their "obviousness," and they are also unlikely to respond to a recruitment targeted at gays.

Finally, the concept of bisexuality as a distinct type of sexual orientation is often absent in Latin American cultures. Individuals who have been exposed to academic writings or who are U.S.-acculturated seem to use this term. Occasionally, some individuals who see themselves in transition from *normales* to gay may call themselves bisexuals, as well as MSM with strong internalized homophobia who feel that being bisexual is not as "bad" as being a "complete" homosexual.

If we ask Latino MSM, "Are you straight, gay, or bisexual?" we present to them a categorization to which they may respond but one that is most likely alien to their culture. A categorization based on gender roles, particularly degree of effeminacy and penetrative versus receptive sexual role, may be more culturally consistent. This was pointed out by Parker in his studies in Brazil, by Lancaster in Nicaragua, and by Carrier in Mexico. In my current work, I recruit study candidates who acknowledge having sex with men or with men and women. Then, in the course of the interview, I present to each participant a list of grouped self-identity labels (discussed later in the section on Language) according to his nationality, ask him whether he agrees with the classification, then ask him what word he would use to call himself. It is not a simple method, but I believe it is closer to the Latin American semantic structure of sexual orientation than the choices used in the United States.

National Ancestry

Some people prefer *Latino* to *Hispanic* or vice versa. Others like neither term. *Hispanic* is a term favored by government agencies, mainly the Census Bureau, to label people bearing Spanish surnames or those whose ancestry can be traced to Mexico, Puerto Rico, or Cuba. Critics claim that this label mixes Europeans born in Spain and people from Latin America, an important distinction, for example, when it comes to programs targeted to Hispanic minorities but not to Europeans. The term *Latino* was proposed as an alternative, with its use restricted to people born in the Americas or their descendants. However, it includes Brazilians, who consider themselves Lucios rather than Latinos, and bears the masculine *o* ending, which can be understood as being sexist. Those who dislike both *Hispanic* and *Latino* state that they obscure important ethnic differences which are preserved by using descriptors of national origin (Puerto Rican, Cuban, Mexican, etc.). Furthermore, these labels confound race and ethnicity, especially when used as an alternative to *white* or *black*. However, those who see power in numbers still prefer pan-ethnic labels.

When the Latino National Political Survey (González, 1992) posed the question to people in the survey, the majority chose to identify themselves by their place of origin (as Puerto Rican, Mexican, Cuban, etc.) regardless of whether they had been born in the United States or in Latin America. It should also be noted that outside the United States the expression *Latin American* (*latinoamericano* or its feminine declension, *latinoamericana*) creates no controversy and is widely accepted as a group label for most nations with Latin roots, whether they speak Spanish, Portuguese, or French (French Canadians would probably take exception to this label).

Beyond the controversy concerning umbrella labels, consensus exists that there are significant differences among the various national groups. Besides language use, other important differences are the country of origin's historical and political past, the kind of racial and ethnic mixing of the population, the immigration barriers set up by the United States, the food preferences, and the types of music and dance favored by each group.

Some of these differences are quite obvious to the people in the various national groups and constitute a source of curiosity, amusement, jokes, and criticisms. Other possible differences—for example, in terms of behaviors that expose people to HIV—are less well known.

Sumaya and Porto (1989) and Díaz et al. (1993) note that people of different Latin American backgrounds appear to have contracted HIV by behavioral routes that vary widely according to national origin. For example, the largest percentage of Puerto Rican men diagnosed with AIDS seem to have been infected through needle sharing, while the largest percentage of Mexican men with AIDS report same-sex behavior as the main route of HIV transmission. The available statistics concerning people of Latin American ancestry born in the United States are not, however, broken down by ethnic heritage, and therefore a comparative analysis of risk behavior is not possible (Sumaya & Porto, 1989). The data nevertheless point out that interethnic differences most likely exist. These differences should be taken into account in doing research with Latinos.

In New York City, Puerto Ricans and Dominicans constitute the two largest groups of Latin American descent. They share many characteristics, such as being nationals from Caribbean countries with similarities in music and food. However, while Puerto Ricans are U.S. citizens who can commute between the island and the mainland at will, Dominicans require visas, which are frequently denied. Dominicans who manage to enter the United States with the purpose of staying as residents are often unable to return to their country for many years until an amnesty or other circumstance allows them to legalize their immigration situation. One third of the Dominicans who live in New York City reside in the Washington Heights area of Manhattan (New York City Department of City Planning, 1992). Only anecdotal information is available concerning the behavior of Dominican MSM; they are reported to be more secretive than Puerto Ricans or Colombians and to wish to "pass for straights." They are less likely to socialize in gay bars.

Colombians and Mexicans constitute two other important groups in New York. Colombia's history is intertwined with that of other mainland South American countries much more than with Caribbean nations. Colombians living in New York appear to be somewhat more affluent than Dominicans. Half of them live in Jackson Heights and nearby areas of the Queens borough, where there are a number of Latino gay entertainment places. Some of these bars are more formal than Latin bars in Manhattan: men dress up when they go to them and behave in a conservative manner. Yet the presence of X-rated movie houses and street cruising tell about other aspects of homosexual interaction in the area.

Mexicans constitute an increasingly visible community in New York. Many Mexican men are recent immigrants who live in crowded hotels in various parts of the city, saving as much money as possible to send to their wives and children back home. They can be seen late at night socializing on street corners or in public plazas, drinking beer and conversing among themselves. People in the gay community report that many of these men, who do not self-identify as gay, will, after enough drinking, end up engaging in sex with other men.

In sum, national ancestry may contribute to explain cultural, behavioral, and sociodemographic differences found in the study of Latino MSM. Interethnic variations, however, are not sufficiently known.

Language

The obvious initial step to effective assessment of a population is to do it in a language understandable to the respondent. This task is far from being as simple as it sounds. Some Latinos are new immigrants who hardly manage a few words in English. Others are second- or third-generation Latinos born in the United States who are unable to speak Spanish but who nevertheless identify with Latino cultural values. Between these two extremes there are different levels of bilingualism. Some Latinos master both English and Spanish artfully. Others speak Spanglish, a mixture of the two languages used by people who borrow words from one or the other language and are often unable to speak either one correctly. Spanglish has produced frequently heard hybrid constructions such as *rufo* (English word *roof* plus the last vowel of *techo*, Spanish for roof) and *liquea* (English *leak* with the Spanish conjugation of *gotear*, "to leak"). A careful analysis of the language dominance of the respondent is necessary before choosing the language vehicle for a survey, but even then it may be problematic. A participant may initially appear quite comfortable in both languages, but when it comes to specific questions on sexual practices and safer sex he may know the vocabulary in only one language and the questionnaire may need to be continued in that language.

Another level of difficulty stems from national variations in the use of Spanish. For example, *no te apures* means "don't hurry" in Argentina but "don't get annoyed" in Puerto Rico. *Me dá coraje* means "it makes me angry" in Puerto Rico, whereas it translates as "it gives me courage" when used by an Argentine. Because these are accepted meanings for the same words, we need to understand the regional uses to make sense of questions and answers.

When we consider slang, we add a further twist to the matter. Slang is formed by using words and neologisms idiosyncratically. For example, *coger* means "to take, to grab" in its literal sense, but it means "to fuck" in Mexico and Argentina. Being Argentine, I was amused the first time I went to Puerto Rico and read a sign in a public square: *"No coger las palomas"* ("Don't fuck the pigeons," in my slang).

I know of only two nonderogatory Spanish expressions to refer to homosexuals: *entendido* (the one who "understands," presumably the same sex interest of another man) and *de ambiente* (literally belonging to the ambient, the surrounding; one who is "in" what is happening). Both these locutions are used almost exclusively among homosexuals to indicate to one another that someone shares their sexual orientation. Lately these expressions have been replaced by the simpler English term *gay* (sometimes spelled *gai*), which is widely used. Most of the remaining words, which vary widely in different countries, have pejorative meanings. For illustration purposes, Table 1 presents the words most commonly used in four Latino ethnic groups. This vocabulary was elicited during focus groups. The same word may apply to different types of men in different countries, as is the case with *loca* and *bisexual*.

Many fully bilingual Latinos use English as the main vehicle to express their thoughts but switch to Spanish for all the emotionally charged expressions. For example, "And I told him, *Dias mío!* you got to see a doctor, *chico*, you need help." Rogler, Malgady, and Rodriguez (1989) reported that bilinguals frequently experience a loss in second-language fluency under stressful conditions, such as in a psychiatric interview. This observation coincides with research findings that support the notion that early traumatic events are recorded in one's memory in the mother tongue. A group of fully bilingual Latinos was asked to respond to a word-association task both in English and Spanish. Some of the words were apparently innocuous, whereas others were likely to elicit emotional responses *(breast, cut dodo)*. The reaction time for the latter was significantly longer in Spanish than in English, whereas there was no difference for the former. These results seem to support the hypothesis that traumatic and emotionally charged concepts are encoded in the mother tongue (A. Brok, personal communication, 1985).

In the course of psychotherapeutic treatment, gay Latinos have expressed more distress at being called *maricón* than *faggot*, the equivalent English term. An AIDS researcher confided to me that he had more difficulties asserting himself as a gay man in Spanish than in English.

Spanish has two forms for "you": *tú* and *usted*. A few countries use *vos* instead of *tú*. *Tú* is used when there is a familiar relationship between people, whereas *usted* is used mainly in formal circumstances. This usage varies in different nations. Puerto Ricans tend to use the familiar form *tú* regardless of whom they are addressing. Colombians use the formal *usted* even among family members. The choice of *tú* or *usted*, when not determined by usage in the country of origin, is a way of showing the psychological distance between the persons engaged in the conversation. In the course of data collection, the dynamics between interviewer and interviewee or the group characteristics (e.g., in the case of written questionnaires) may determine whether colloquial or formal usage is more appro-

Table 1 *Words Frequently Used by Four Latino Ethnic Groups to Refer to Men Who Have Sex with Men (MSM)*

	Colombians	Dominicans	Mexicans	Puerto Ricans

Generic words	**de ambiente**[a]
	gay
	homosexual
	flojo de la cola
	medio raro
	volteado
	delicado
	dañado
		gay
		homosexual
			gay
			homosexual
			se le hace
			  agua la canoa
			le gusta el
			  arroz con
			  popote
				gay
				homosexual

Masculine men	**cucarrón** cacorro	**bugarrón** bisexual	**mayate** puñal machines ponedores chacales chichifo	**bugarrón** normal macho varón chillo hombre
Effeminate men	**fifi** mariposo brinca loca maricón	**pájaro** maricón	**joto** maricón lilo manfloro mayuyo tortillero puto sidral	**loca** pato maricón entendido
Men who wear women's clothes	**vestida** perversa de la movida	**loca** mujercita afeminado travesti se disfraza	**vestida** torcida transvesti jota	**draga** mujer transexual drag queen
Men who have sex with men and women				**bisexual** lo mismo raspa que pinta

(a) Bold type indicates the most popular word in each category.

priate. A young Latino gay man may feel uncomfortable disclosing sexual intimacies to an older Latino interviewer who uses formal language reminiscent of teacher-student or angry-parent-punished-child relationships. Conversely, the use of familiar language may impress some interviewees as a lack of respect for a stranger.

Finally, the educational level of the respondent has a strong influence in the characteristics of the language to be used for data collection. In my current study, paper-and-pencil self-assessment needed to be read to respondents whose reading skills were poor. Less-educated participants may understand only vernacular language for sexual matters and may feel intimidated by formal language. Conversely, vernacular language may seem offensive to more educated respondents.

I generally start my first contact with study participants by asking them which language they prefer to use. I pose the question both in English and in Spanish to avoid biasing their choice and to show that I feel at ease in both languages, since participants have reported how uncomfortable it is for them to be interviewed by someone with poor command of Spanish who nevertheless insists on using it. If Spanish is chosen, my second question is "*¿Nos trataremos de tú o de usted?*" to establish whether the respondent prefers familiar or formal language. The choice of vernacular versus formal language can be determined during the vocabulary elicitation section of the sexual interview with questions such as "When a man puts his penis in someone's mouth, how do you call it? (oral sex/blow job)".

Recruitment

Most studies of Latino MSM rely on convenience samples. That imposes serious limitations on the generalization of results. Some attempts are under way to obtain random samples of Latino gay men. One creative approach being used by West Coast researchers (R. Díaz, personal communication) consists in targeting recruitment areas where Latino gay men are likely to live. These areas are cross-identified, taking into account those neighborhoods that the national census detected as having high concentrations of Latinos, the places of residence of Latinos reported with AIDS, and the areas where entertainment places catering to gay Latinos exist. Once the areas are identified, random telephone calls are made to their households inquiring about the presence of unmarried males. These men are then asked to respond to a phone survey that includes, among others, some questions on same-sex sexual behavior.

The method is appealing, and it will be interesting to analyze, after its implementation, how successful it is. However, besides its cost, several problems can be anticipated. It is known that the last census seriously undercounted minority sectors of the population, particularly in urban areas. Additionally, fear of deportation may have led undocumented Latinos not to answer questionnaires, to answer partially, or to give false information during the census. Most Latinos of limited financial resources get medical attention through public hospitals rather than private physicians. These hospitals often have "catchment areas": only those individuals living within a certain radius of the hospital are admitted for treatment. Latinos who may have heard that one hospital is better than another (because of technical skills of the personnel or because it is a richer hospital that gives more *ayuda* [help]) may without much effort find a relative living in the hospital vicinity who may "lend" his or her address. Also, Latinos who have fallen ill and originally lived on their own may have moved to relatives' residences. Therefore the residence of a person diagnosed with AIDS may not be the one that appears in medical records. Economic advantages and social tolerance may be some of the reasons determining the location of gay entertainment establishments. For example, Jackson Heights, Queens, has more Latino gay establishments than any other area in the city, and an annual local gay parade is held there. Yet Latino MSM who patronize these gay establishments travel from distant places, sometimes staying overnight or weekends at friends' homes.

Another inconvenience consists in being interviewed over the phone by a stranger. Marín and Marín (1992) from UCLA obtained good response rates to phone interviews of Latinos; yet they were unable to determine what proportion of gay Latinos would disclose their sexual behavior over the phone. Given the high levels of homophobia present in Latin American environments, reluctance to disclose can be anticipated. This homophobia is portrayed in many popular expressions.

An important issue to analyze in data collected through phone surveys is the degree of acculturation of the MSM who acknowledge their behavior; most likely they will be highly acculturated to the United States. MSM from Latin America tend to distrust the system, to give evasive responses, and to try to guess what the interviewer expects them to say. Once I asked a Dominican gay man why it was so difficult to recruit other men like him. He replied: "If you approach me in the street, I will deny I am gay; and if you approach me in a gay bar, I will deny I am Dominican." Latino MSM who perceive the police as death squads and U.S. citizens as CIA agents will be unlikely to openly report same-sex behavior.

Acculturation to gay culture is also important. Some participants in our study who were asked about fist fucking inquired with disbelief, "Do people really do that?"

Short of geographical randomization, another strategy could be to randomly select Latino gay men from mailing lists of Latino gay organizations. However, many of these lists are confidential, and Latino gay organizations are quite young and have a limited number of affiliates. If one is interested in recruiting a specific national group, the problems multiply.

Different recruitment strategies are needed for people with different self-identities. Although Latino gays may be recruited with fliers distributed in gay bars, drag queens do not respond to such an approach and often need to be reached by word-of-mouth by other drag queens who participated in the study and who say "it's OK." Both drag queens and straight MSM may see little incentive in the customary $10-per-hour participant fee and may require more money.

Despite the problems endemic to convenience samples and snowball techniques, at present they may be the few recruitment strategies likely to generate sufficient numbers of Latino gay men to undertake a study. To recruit Dominican MSM, we helped one of them organize a party with typical food at his home in East Harlem to which he invited a number of friends. After socializing with my research team and myself for several hours and asking questions about our work, they volunteered to introduce us to their acquaintances and even to integrate a committee of community advisors for our project. The method of gaining the trust of a gatekeeper, frequently used in anthropological studies, was very effective in this case.

Interviewers

Obviously, the interviewers need to be fully bilingual, hopefully bicultural, and gay-sensitive. It is not always easy to find such interviewers. Many of the issues discussed above concerning language dominance and lack of knowledge of sexual terms in the secondary language apply to interviewers as well. Often, after an English-dominant interviewer has conducted the first dozen interviews, we observe, without surprise, that most of his respondents "happened" to choose English. The same happens with Spanish-dominant interviewers.

Matching interviewer and interviewee by ethnicity can be a tricky business. There are advantages in matching in terms of knowledge of similar slang and cultural references. Furthermore, a Puerto Rican interviewer, for example, may quickly recognize a non–Puerto Rican trying to pass for one in order to cash the money incentive for the study. However, ethnic match may also bring problems; I interviewed a Dominican gay man who told me that had I been Dominican he would have been reluctant to disclose information because I might have known someone who might tell someone else who might inform his grandmother in the island that he was gay. Computer-assisted methods with audio capabilities may be a solution to these interviewer-related problems.

Although many of the issues I have discussed are pertinent to other ethnic groups as well and not exclusively to MSM, they should not be overlooked in studies of Latino MSM.

Author Note

Some parts of this paper have been published in Carballo-Diéguez, A. (1989), Hispanic culture, gay male culture, and AIDS, *Journal of Counseling and Development, 68,* 26–30, and Carballo-Diéguez, A., & Dolezal, C. (1994), Contrasting types of Puerto Rican men who have sex with men (MSM), *Journal of Psychology and Human Sexuality, 6*(4), 41–67.

References

Díaz, T., Buehler, J., Castro, K., & Ward, J. (1993). AIDS trends among Hispanics in the United States. *American Journal of Public Health, 93*(4), 504–509.

González, D. (1992, November 15). What's the problem with Hispanic? Just a Latino. *New York Times.*

Marín, B. V., & Marín, G. (1992). Predictors of condom accessibility among Hispanics in San Francisco. *American Journal of Public Health, 82*(4), 592–595.

New York City Department of City Planning. (1992, June). *The newest New Yorkers: An analysis of immigration into New York City during the 1980s.* New York: Department of Planning, Publication DCP92–16.

Rogler, L. H., Malgady, R. G., & Rodriguez, O. (1989). *Hispanics and mental health: A framework for research.* Malabar, FL: Robert E. Krieger.

Sumaya, C. V., & Porto, M. D. (1989). AIDS in Hispanics. *Southern Medical Journal, 82*(8), 943–945.

Sexual Behavior Research

Studying Bisexual Men and Women and Lesbians

LYNDA S. DOLL

Research on the sexual behavior of bisexual men and women and lesbians has lagged behind research on other populations. Issues important to our understanding of human sexuality—the frequency, development, contexts, and cultural meanings of sexual behaviors—have been examined among male and female heterosexuals and homosexual men. In this chapter, we review trends in recent sexuality research related to bisexual men and women and lesbians and assess the extent to which important research questions have been studied in these populations. Our goal is not to examine the research findings themselves but rather to qualitatively assess the topics under study during the last 10 years in the United States and the methodological approaches used to study them.

Two procedures were implemented to assess recent trends in sexual behavior research conducted in the United States for these populations. First, reports were collected from national probability surveys of the general population published in books and peer-reviewed journals. These reports permit an assessment of data on the frequency and demographic distribution of male and female bisexual behavior as well as exclusively homosexual behavior among women. Second, computer searches of peer-reviewed journals were conducted using the PSYCHLIT and MEDLINE databases for the last 10 years (1986 through July 1996). Broad searches of these databases were conducted utilizing the search terms "bisexual men," "bisexual women," and "lesbian or homosexual women." After the exclusion of citations related to specific medical conditions (e.g., HIV disease progression and opportunistic infections), employment and career choices, civil rights and legal issues, and interpretations of sexuality themes in literature, 166 citations were identified that mentioned bisexual men, 61 that mentioned bisexual women, and 396 that mentioned lesbians. These citations covered a range of behavioral and social issues related to these populations, including sexual behavior. This snapshot of recent research gives us a broad picture of what has and has not been studied related to these populations, as well as the variety of methods utilized. This larger body of behavioral or social science literature is often critical to the interpretation of data on sexuality. The snapshot also gives us a perspective on the support and interest in conducting sexuality research relative to research on other topics.

General Population Surveys

Political concerns have slowed or halted many attempts to conduct general population sexuality surveys (Laumann, Gagnon, & Michael, 1994). Despite these constraints, sexual behavior data have now been reported from several surveys in the United States (e.g., General Social Surveys [Smith, 1991; Turner, Danella, & Rogers, 1995], National Health and Social Life Survey [Laumann, Gagnon, Michael, & Michaels, 1994], National AIDS Behavioral Survey [Catania et al., 1992; Dolcini et al., 1993], National Survey of Adolescent Males [Sonenstein, Pleck, & Ku, 1989], National Survey of Men [Billy, Tanfer, Grady, & Klepinger, 1993], the National Surveys of Family Growth [Campbell & Baldwin, 1991; Seidman & Rieder, 1994; Turner, Danella, & Rogers, 1995], and the Project HOPE Survey of AIDS-Risk Behaviors [Sell, Wells, & Wypij, 1995]). Although the preponderance of published reports focus on heterosexual men and women, since 1990 a growing number of relatively in-depth summaries of male homosexual behavior have emerged from these surveys. Data have also been reported on bisexual behavior and female homosexuality within several reports; however, these findings tend to be limited to a single prevalence rate at one point in time. Prevalence figures for bisexual behavior among men are available through the National Health and Social Life Survey (Laumann et al., 1994), the General Social Surveys (Rogers & Turner, 1991), the National AIDS Behavioral Survey (Binson, Michaels, Stall, Coates, Gagnon, & Catania, 1995), Kinsey Institute Surveys (Fay, Turner, Klassen, & Gagnon, 1989; Turner et al., 1995), the 1989 National Household Seroprevalence Survey Pretest (Turner et al., 1995), and the Project HOPE Survey of AIDS-Risk Behaviors (Sell et al., 1995). Data on the prevalence of homosexual behaviors among women are available in fewer reports, including the National Health and Social Life Survey (Laumann et al., 1994), the General Social Surveys (Smith, 1991; Turner et al., 1995), the 1970 Kinsey Institute Survey (Turner et al., 1995), the 1989 National Household Seroprevalence Survey Pretest (Turner et al., 1995), and the Project HOPE Survey of AIDS-Risk Behaviors (Sell et al., 1995). Two recent reports on women, entitled "The Response of American Women to the Threat of AIDS and Other Sexually Transmitted Diseases" (Campbell & Baldwin, 1991) and "American Women's Sexual Behavior and Exposure to Risk of Sexually Transmitted Diseases" (Kost & Forrest, 1992), failed to mention women with same-sex contact. Given the sensitivity to adolescent sexuality, it is not surprising that national data on adolescent bisexuality and female homosexuality are primarily available through retrospective reports such as those mentioned above. Only one state-based report was identified reporting male and female bisexuality and female homosexuality among in-school adolescents (Remafedi, Resnick, Blum, & Harris, 1992).

In addition to data on overall prevalence rates, these national surveys have provided information on the frequency of sexual behaviors among regional and racial/ethnic subgroups (e.g., number and characteristics of partners, type and frequency of penetrative and nonpenetrative sexual contact, AIDS risk behaviors, sexual fantasies and attractions). Perhaps because of sample size constraints, almost no such data have been reported for subpopulations of the three populations covered in this chapter.

Our understanding of sexual behaviors among bisexual men and women and lesbians is clearly hampered by the limited amount of data available. However, methodological limitations in existing surveys also make interpretation of data difficult. The lack of a generally agreed-upon definition of bisexuality hampers comparisons across surveys. While most surveys use a behavioral definition, namely, gender of partners, to define bisexual contact, others use sexual-identity categories (Billy et al., 1993). Some surveys define sexual contact as intercourse to the point of orgasm; others do not require orgasm. Still others fail to clarify how they define sexual contact. Reporting periods also differ considerably across studies, including the last year, five years, ten years, since 18, and during adulthood, and few investigators report prevalence rates for more than one time period. This lack of standardization means that, at best, only gross comparisons of rates of sexual behaviors can be made across studies.

In sum, there are growing numbers of studies reporting national survey data on bisexual behavior among men. Lack of theory development has resulted, however, in ambiguity about what constitutes bisexuality and how to measure it. Questions currently used on surveys often do not provide meaningful or extensive information on these behaviors. Moreover, national surveys have been limited in their ability to assess bisexual behavior among adolescents and racial/ethnic subgroups—two groups of particular interest in the study of male bisexuality (Doll & Beeker, 1996). Homosexual behavior among women remains particularly understudied in national surveys relative to such behavior in men.

Peer-Reviewed Literature, 1986–1996

In addition to these national surveys, there is a large body of behavioral and social science literature in which bisexual men and women and lesbians are mentioned. This literature includes descriptions of quantitative and qualitative studies, literature reviews, and theoretical and other discussion papers. With regard to the study of human sexuality, this literature provides critical information for understanding the development, contexts, and cultural meanings of sexual behaviors.

Single versus Multiple Populations

Historically, data on bisexual men and women have been aggregated with that of exclusively homosexual persons, with few, if any, comparisons made across behavioral groups. Thus the first question assessed in this second body of literature was the extent to which the three populations of interest in this chapter were included as a major focus of study in published articles. We examined the percentage of articles that focused exclusively on one of the three populations (i.e., bisexual men, bisexual women, or lesbians) or described multiple populations (i.e., bisexual *and* gay men or bisexual women *and* lesbians). Additionally, in articles reporting on two populations we examined the percentage of articles that aggregated populations with no assessment of differences versus the percentage that drew comparisons between groups. Separate analyses as well as group comparisons are critical not only to better understand each group but also to understand the extent of overlap across time between populations. To test hypotheses about the stability of bisexual behavior it is important to understand patterns of bisexual versus exclusively homosexual contact over time.

Of the 166 articles mentioning bisexual men, 8 (5%) included information only on bisexual men and 158 (95%) examined both gay and bisexual men. Among the latter articles, 137 (87%) aggregated information on homosexual and bisexual men without separate analyses or conclusions specific to bisexual men, and 21 (13%) specifically discussed population differences. Thus 29 articles, only 18% of articles mentioning bisexual men in the last ten years in these two databases, actually discussed information specific to that population.

Among the 61 articles mentioning bisexual women, 3 (5%) reported exclusively on bisexual women, with 58 (95%) including information on both bisexuals and lesbians. Among the latter group, 36 (62%) aggregated information on lesbian and bisexual women, while 22 (38%) compared differences. Thus compared to the literature on bisexual men, over twice as many articles (41%) purportedly reporting on bisexual women actually contained information specific to these women. The data on lesbians provide an interesting comparison. Among the 396 published articles, 337 (85%) featured lesbians exclusively, with only 59 (15%) aggregating populations. Among these 59 articles, 23 (39%) specifically drew comparisons between lesbians and bisexual women. Thus 91% of the literature purportedly reporting on lesbians provided population-specific information.

In sum, in the published literature covering the last ten years, few articles were found that mentioned bisexual men or women. Of these, even fewer actually provided population-specific information. Reasons for this apparent lack of interest are unclear. The ambiguity over what constitutes bisexuality may hinder active research on these populations. More pragmatically, the applied focus of recent funding for sexuality research may have discouraged basic research and theory building. In contrast, however, despite these funding constraints, nearly 400 articles have been published during this same period that mentioned lesbians, the majority of which provide population-specific information.

In the remainder of this chapter the range of topics and the study methods reported in the articles containing population-specific information (bisexual men: 29 articles; bisexual women: 25 articles; lesbians: 359 articles) will be examined. Of particular interest are the following questions: What percentage of articles published since 1986 focused on topics under the broad category of human sexuality? What percentage of articles were HIV-related? What methodological approaches have been used in this body of literature?

Topics Covered

Table 1 describes the broad topic categories discussed in articles during the 10-year period. For bisexual men, 48% of the 29 articles concentrated on sexuality topics, including articles on HIV risk behaviors (10 articles), sexual identity development and coming out (2 articles), and the origins of sexual orientation (2 articles). The only other topic covered with any frequency was relationship issues (17%). The literature that has emerged on bisexual women has also focused primarily on sexuality topics (48% of 25 articles), but with less emphasis on HIV. Sexuality topics covered included origins of sexual orientation (4 articles), sexual identity development (3 articles), HIV risk behaviors (3 articles), and non-HIV-related sexual practices (2 articles). The only other category to emerge with any frequency in the literature on bisexual women was that of relationship issues, accounting for 4 articles.

The literature on lesbians presents a somewhat different picture, with sexuality-related topics representing only 17% of articles. Among the topics covered in the sexuality category were sexual-identity development (30 articles), origins of sexual orientation (16 articles), non-HIV-related sexual practices (5 articles), and HIV risk behaviors (3 articles). The most frequently covered category overall was relationship issues, representing 24% of all articles. Specific topics under this category included parenting (32 articles), couples' issues (31 articles), partner abuse (11 articles), and friendships (7 articles). Less frequently covered topics included interventions: psychotherapy (12%), mental health/coping (11%), health care (8%), and substance abuse (7%).

HIV-Focused Articles

In recent years, sexuality research has in some respects been in a boom period in the United States, with numerous studies examining HIV risk behaviors. Clearly the field of sexuality research has benefited enormously from this infusion of resources. Among the 29 articles on bisexual men, fully 48% (14 articles) were focused on HIV; 71% of these assessed the prevalence of risk behaviors or their determinants. In striking contrast is the literature on women; only 12% (3 articles) on bisexual women and 2% (8 articles) on lesbians, respectively, were HIV-focused. The majority of

Table 1 *Research Topic by Population Type, Published Literature, 1986–1996*

Topic	Bisexual Men N = 29 Articles	Bisexual Women N = 25 Articles	Lesbians N = 359 Articles
Aging	—	—	4%
Body imagery	3%	—	2%
Cognitive/motor/ spatial functioning	—	4%	<1%
Culture/community	—	—	3%
Health behaviors/care	3%	8%	8%
Interventions	7%	12%	12%
Knowledge/attitudes	—	—	1%
Mental health/coping	7%	—	11%
Relationship issues	17%	16%	24%
Sexuality-related	48%	48%	17%
Specific populations	3%	8%	5%
Stigma/homophobia	3%	—	3%
Substance use	—	—	7%
Theory/methods	7%	4%	3%

articles on all three populations are epidemiologic descriptions of risk behaviors.

Methodological Approaches

In Table 2, categories of methodological approaches or formats are reported for the entire 10-year period and for two shorter periods, 1986 to 1990 and 1991 to 1996. Changes were examined over the two periods to assess the emergence of new research methods. For purposes of this chapter, articles were categorized into one of four broad categories: (1) quantitative methods (surveys, biological testing, chart reviews, experiments); (2) systematically conducted qualitative methods (in-depth interviews, focus groups, case studies); (3) literature reviews; and (4) discussion formats, including theoretical papers. Questions of particular interest related to methods are these: What are the relative percentages of the four methods or formats in these reports? What changes have occurred in methodological approaches over the 10-year period? What approaches were used in the sexuality-related literature specifically?

Looking first at the entire period, the methodological approaches used

Table 2 *Methodological Approaches in Published Literature, 1986–1996*

Method	Total	1986–1990	1991–1996
	Bisexual Men		
	N = 29	N = 11	N = 18
Quantitative reports	72%	63%	78%
Qualitative reports	10%	27%	0%
Literature reviews	3%	0%	6%
Discussion papers	14%	9%	17%
	Bisexual Women		
	N = 25	N = 11	N = 14
Quantitative reports	60%	64%	57%
Qualitative reports	20%	27%	14%
Literature reviews	0%	0%	0%
Discussion papers	20%	9%	29%
	Lesbian Women		
	N = 359	N = 178	N = 181
Quantitative reports	32%	37%	27%
Qualitative reports	18%	14%	22%
Literature reviews	11%	7%	14%
Discussion papers	39%	42%	36%

in reports on bisexual men and women were more similar to each other than those used in papers on lesbians. For example, 72% and 60% of reports on bisexual men and women, respectively, used quantitative methods (e.g., surveys: men, 66%; women, 52%; biological testing: men, 6%; women, 4%). In comparison, only 32% of reports on lesbians used quantitative methods (e.g., surveys: 30%; biological testing: 1%; chart reviews/experiments: 1%). Qualitative methods ranged from 10% to 20% in reports on bisexual men and women, respectively, but the relative percentages of review and discussion papers were somewhat lower. Among bisexual men, 3% of papers were reviews and 14% were discussion papers. Among bisexual women, 20% were discussion papers. Approximately 18% of reports on lesbians used qualitative methods and another 50% were either review (11%) or discussion papers (39%).

Trends in methodological approaches are difficult to establish with the small number of articles found on bisexual men and women. For bisexual men, the number of reports using quantitative approaches increased and, for both groups, the number of discussion papers doubled between the two periods. The number of qualitative reports decreased for both. In contrast, the number of quantitative reports and discussion papers on lesbian women decreased between the two periods and the number of qualitative reports and reviews increased.

Looking specifically at the sexuality-related literature (Table 3), the bulk of the published articles on bisexual men and women reported quantitative methods, with very few discussion papers (men: 86%; women: 75%). Sexuality-related articles on lesbians were more equally split between quantitative (40%), qualitative (20%), and discussion papers (33%).

In sum, quantitative research on sexuality themes dominated the small body of literature on bisexual men and women; however, most of the articles were HIV-focused. Our knowledge has advanced through this HIV-related research, but very little has been published about sexual behaviors (or, indeed, much of anything else about bisexual men or women) outside of these more problem-focused areas. It is hoped that the excellent applied research that has emerged in the last few years on these two populations will stimulate more basic research as well.

In an article published in 1988, Risman and Schwartz noted the paucity of research on homosexual women. Nonetheless, in this review we identified nearly 400 articles mentioning lesbian or bisexual women. Themes identified in this body of literature seem to represent a continuation of earlier research. In 1988, Risman and Schwartz noted four themes that dominated sociological research on homosexual men and women in the decade prior to the publication of their article: (1) the essentialist/constructionist debate on the origins of homosexuality, (2) gender role nonconformity, (3) studies of intimate relationships, and (4) AIDS. There is clearly a similarity between these themes identified eight years ago and the themes identified in this more recent search of the literature on lesbians. From 1986 through 1996, articles on intimate relationships, in particular those focusing on couple and parenting themes, dominated the literature on lesbians and were frequent themes in articles on bisexual women. Sexuality themes became more salient in recent years, but the majority of articles focused on sexual-identity development and coming out, not on the origins of homosexuality and gender roles.

Risman and Schwartz (1988) also note the paucity of articles on gay and lesbian organizational issues. No articles on bisexual men or women and only 3% of articles on lesbian women covered community or cultural issues. Indeed, the existing literature on all populations focused on individual or interpersonal issues. Social or structural issues were simply not salient. Research on organizational roles and structures, institutional affiliations, and social and sexual networks would provide much needed information on all three populations.

Table 3 *Methodological Approaches by Sexuality Topic, Published Literature, 1986–1996*

Topic	Quantitative	Qualitative	Review	Discussion
Bisexual Men (N = 14 Articles)				
Origins of sexual orientation	14%	—	—	—
Sexual practices	—	—	—	—
Sexual abuse	—	—	—	—
HIV risk behaviors	64%	—	7%	—
Sexual language	—	—	—	—
Gender roles	—	—	—	—
Identity development/ coming out	7%	7%	—	—
Total	86%	7%	7%	—
Bisexual Women (N = 12 Articles)				
Origins of sexual orientation	25%	—	—	8%
Sexual practices	17%	—	—	—
Sexual abuse	—	—	—	—
HIV risk behaviors	25%	—	—	—
Sexual language	—	—	—	—
Gender roles	—	—	—	—
Identity development/ coming out	8%	17%	—	—
Total	75%	17%	—	8%
Lesbian Women (N = 60 Articles)				
Origins of sexual orientation	13%	3%	2%	8%
Sexual practices	7%	—	—	2%
Sexual abuse	3%	—	—	—
HIV risk behaviors	3%	—	—	2%
Sexual language	2%	—	—	—
Gender roles	2%	—	—	3%
Identity development/ coming out	10%	17%	3%	20%
Total	40%	20%	5%	33%

Implications

In this chapter, the peer-reviewed literature from two databases was examined to assess broad trends in topics and methods. Given the number of articles identified, particularly on lesbians, it was not possible to examine book chapters as well as other reports that might not have entered the two databases. These databases may have excluded articles that described one of the populations behaviorally but did not mention the population by name. Furthermore, data published in the popular press were excluded (Lever, 1995a; 1995b). However, even with these caveats about the incompleteness of the database, several implications can be suggested.

Need for More Complex Research on Bisexuality

In the first sections of this chapter, it was noted that ambiguity over what constitutes bisexuality and theory development related to this phenomenon have hampered the collection of detailed empirical data on bisexual behavior. That in turn has hampered further theory development. In the next sections, an additional theme arose. Most recent literature on bisexual men and women has been dominated by epidemiologic research on HIV-related topics. These concerns—lack of empirical data and the emphasis on epidemiologic approaches—argue both for more research and for taking a more complex approach to conceptualizing and conducting research on bisexual behavior. That is, in order to advance our knowledge, it is critical that we expand beyond the strictly quantitative approaches of epidemiology and demography that characterize much of the recent research on these populations. Very frequently, researchers (particularly in the "HIV world") state that they are "describing a population" (e.g., bisexual men, lesbians). This usually means describing rates of sexual behavior and very little else. Using complementary qualitative and quantitative methods is critical, as is the use of theory in posing research questions.

In earlier sections, the tendency to aggregate information on bisexual men and women with exclusively homosexual persons was discussed. Another concern that is related to the need for more complex approaches to research is the aggregation of diverse groups of individuals who are behaviorally similar (e.g., they engage in sex with men and women) into a single group of individuals, labeled bisexuals. That is, the construct of bisexuality is frequently defined by this very narrow behavioral feature without understanding the psychological and social contexts of the lives of these men and women. This tendency may in part result from the heavy emphasis on HIV-focused, epidemiologic research with these populations. Heckman et al. (1995) compared rates of HIV risk behaviors between exclusively homosexual and behaviorally bisexual men. As noted earlier, disaggregating data on homosexual and bisexual men is a step forward; however, the authors then aggregated all bisexual men together. Can we assume that a man with a steady female partner who occasionally hustles male partners for money or drugs is more similar to a gay-identified man who had sexual contact with both men and women during his early 20s than to an exclusively heterosexual man? These questions about overlapping populations and contexts of sexual and social contacts have not been systematically addressed in the research conducted in the United States to date.

In 1988, Risman and Schwartz criticized the tendency to use the term *homosexual* as a noun rather than an adjective. They suggested that in using the term as a noun, homosexual desire is reified into a type of human being. The current tendency to aggregate bisexuals into a single category reinforces this same tendency and does little to advance our theoretical understanding of this phenomenon. A recent book edited by Peter Aggleton (1996) entitled *Bisexualities and AIDS* is perhaps a good role model for the type of approach that is needed in research on bisexuality. In this book, not one but numerous patterns of male bisexual behavior are described from locations throughout the world. Such wide diversity may not be found in the United States, but the number of different patterns of male and female bisexuality is probably far more extensive than has been documented through epidemiologic research to date.

Bias of HIV-Focused Research

It is critical to assess how much bias the HIV focus in research, particularly on bisexual men, has produced. In HIV-focused studies, research questions are developed with the goal of understanding HIV transmission dynamics, not sexual behavior. Furthermore, samples are recruited to maximize knowledge about at-risk populations, not to gain an understanding of sexual expression. The consequences of these and other biases have rarely been discussed, but they are important because they skew what we understand about populations. This is particularly true for populations that have received new attention during the HIV epidemic. Research on bisexual men is an excellent example. In a recent review of the relationship between male bisexual behavior and HIV risk, four contexts were identified in which rates of both bisexual behavior and HIV risk may be elevated: in sex trading, drug use, sexual-identity exploration, and communities of color (Doll & Beeker, 1996). At a recent meeting, a colleague pointed out to the first author that emphasizing the first two contexts (sex trading and drug use) may be perceived as "criminalizing" bisexuality—a very thoughtful comment on the implications of HIV-focused studies for the broader field of sexuality research. Certainly HIV researchers must take care in generalizing results from biased samples to entire populations. Furthermore, it is important to emphasize repeatedly that much of HIV research does not explore the full range of contexts and types of sexual expression engaged in by bisexuals and lesbians. Indeed, what is published is, by definition, problem-focused.

Research on bisexual women and lesbians in the context of HIV is even fundamentally more troublesome—that is, it hasn't been conducted for a variety of reasons, including assumptions about the prevalence of homosexual behavior as well as HIV risk levels among women. More recently, research has begun to focus on lesbians, perhaps because of the advocacy of community groups. But the emphasis continues to be on problem-focused behaviors, such as drug use. The critical issue here is that depending upon HIV funds for support of sex research, while necessary, may not always advance our understanding of human sexuality as we would like.

Methodological Balance

Finally, in this chapter only very broad categories of methodological approaches could be examined. Specific details related to sampling, research design, and statistical approaches would need to be scrutinized to comment on the quality of the work published. However, if one assumes that a combination of qualitative and quantitative approaches are necessary to adequately describe a given population, then some tentative suggestions can be made. To date, the limited data on bisexual men and women is overwhelmingly quantitative. Further qualitative research is needed to better clarify the contexts and meanings of these behaviors. Work by Blumstein and Schwartz (1977) and Weinberg, Williams, and Pryor (1994) are excellent examples of research that needs to be expanded with these populations. Overall, the literature on lesbians during this 10-year period suggests some imbalance toward discussion formats, though the sexuality-specific work has a higher percentage of both quantitative and qualitative work. The emergence of qualitative research with this population as well as the growing number of reviews may suggest a maturing of the field of research on lesbians with more emphasis on synthesizing research findings and clarifying cultural and other meaning of behaviors. However, overall, additional quantitative research with nonclinic-based samples would advance our understanding of women with same-gender contact.

References

Aggleton, P. (1996). *Bisexualities and AIDS: International perspectives.* London: Taylor & Francis.
Billy, J. O. G., Tanfer, K., Grady, W. R., & Klepinger, D. H. (1993). The sexual behavior of men in the United States. *Family Planning Perspectives, 25,* 52–60.
Binson, D., Michaels, S., Stall, R., Coates, T. J., Gagnon, J. H., & Catania, J. A.

(1995). Prevalence and social distribution of men who have sex with men: United States and its urban centers. *Journal of Sex Research, 32,* 245–254.

Blumstein, P. W., & Schwartz, P. (1977). Bisexuality: Some social psychological issues. *Journal of Social Issues, 33,* 30–45.

Campbell, A. A., & Baldwin, W. (1991). The response of American women to the threat of AIDS and other sexually transmitted diseases. *Journal of Acquired Immune Deficiency Syndromes, 4,* 1133–1140.

Catania, J. A., Coates, T. J., Stall, R., Turner, H., Peterson, J., & Hearst, M. (1992). Prevalence of AIDS-related risk factors and condom use in the United States. *Science, 258,* 1101–1106.

Dolcini, M. M., Catania, J. A., Coates, R. S., Hudes, E. S., Gagnon, J. H., & Pollack, L. M. (1993). Demographic characteristics of heterosexuals with multiple partners: The National AIDS Behavioral Surveys. *Family Planning Perspectives, 25,* 208–214.

Doll, L. S., & Beeker, C. (1996). Male bisexual behavior and HIV risk in the United States: Synthesis of research with implications for behavioral interventions. *Aids Education and Prevention, 8,* 205–225.

Fay, R. E., Turner, C. F., Klassen, A.D., & Gagnon, J. H. (1989). Prevalence and patterns of same-gender sexual contact among men. *Science, 243,* 338–348.

Heckman, T. G., Kelly, J. A., Sikkema, K. J., Roffman, R. R., Solomon, L. J., & Winett, R. A. (1995). Differences in HIV risk characteristics between bisexual and exclusively gay men. *AIDS Education and Prevention, 7,* 504–512.

Kost, K., & Forrest, J. (1992). American women's sexual behavior and exposure to risk of sexually transmitted diseases. *Family Planning Perspectives, 24,* 244–254.

Laumann, E. O., Gagnon, J. H., Michael, R. T., & Michaels, S. (1994). *The social organization of sexuality: Sexual practices in the United States.* Chicago: University of Chicago Press.

Laumann, E. O., Gagnon, J. H., & Michael, R. T. (1994). A political history of the National Sex Survey of Adults. *Family Planning Perspectives 26,* 34–38.

Lever, J. (1995a, March 21). The 1995 Advocate survey of sexuality and relationships: The women. *Advocate* (pp. 37–40, 45–50).

Lever, J. (1995b, August 22). Lesbian sex survey. *Advocate* (pp. 22–30).

Remafedi, G., Resnick, M., Blum, R., & Harris, L. (1992). Demography of sexual orientation in adolescents. *Pediatrics, 89,* 714–721.

Risman, B., & Schwartz, P. (1988). Sociological research on male and female homosexuality. *Annual Review of Sociology, 14,* 125–147.

Rogers, S. M., & Turner, C. F. (1991). Male-male sexual contact in the U.S.A.: Findings from five sample surveys, 1970–1990. *Journal of Sex Research, 4,* 491–519.

Seidman, S. N., & Rieder, R. O. (1994). A review of sexual behavior in the United States. *American Journal of Psychiatry, 151,* 330–341.

Sell, R. L., Wells, J. A., & Wypij, D. (1995). The prevalence of homosexual behavior and attraction in the United States, the United Kingdom and France: Results of national population-based samples. *Archives of Sexual Behavior, 24,* 235–248.

Smith, T. W. (1991). Adult sexual behavior in 1989: Number of partners, frequency of intercourse in risk of AIDS. *Family Planning Perspectives, 23,* 102–107.

Sonenstein, F. L., Pleck, J. H., & Ku, L. C. (1989). Sexual activity, condom use and AIDS awareness among adolescent males. *Family Planning Perspectives, 21,* 152–158.

Turner, C. F., Danella, R. D., & Rogers, S. M. (1995). Sexual behavior in the United States, 1930–1990: Trends and methodological problems. *Sexually Transmitted Diseases, 22,* 173–190.

Weinberg, M. S., Williams, C. J., & Pryor, D. W. (1994). *Dual attraction: Understanding bisexuality.* New York: Oxford University Press.

Discussion

Barbara Marín: Have you looked at whether the people who are nonresponders were more likely to be those who had never in their life used a condom? Both the age data and the gender data would suggest that nonresponders often might be never users. It makes sense that people who had never used condoms might simply say, "I don't know" or "I can't answer."

Joe Catania: That's a good question. We've got the data to look at that, but haven't yet done so.

Alex Carballo-Diéguez: I was wondering if your attitude questions were at the end of the interview and people who are older got tired and stopped answering.

Joe Catania: It's possible. However, it's a relatively short interview. We were concerned about respondent fatigue, so the interview could be done in 10–15 minutes. For older respondents, because they didn't have risk factors for HIV, they did not get the more extensive battery of sexual behavior questions which raises another possibility. These additional items on sexuality may have desensitized respondents who received them, with the consequence that the condom items did not have as much of an impact on these individuals as on those who did not receive the additional sexual behavior items. The elderly would have been disproportionately represented among the latter.

Colin Williams: I'm worried about two things. First, are you going to control for class?—because we know that race and social class are highly correlated. Second, I want to know who these people are who are called "whites," or even "African Americans." These seem to be such large categories within which there are a lot of differences which might be relevant to the interpretation of your data.

Joe Catania: Yes, we will be controlling for social class. On the other issue, we didn't collect detailed data on subethnic groups. That would be fascinating data to have. It's also fascinatingly difficult to collect.

Ulrich Clement: Do you have any ideas or empirical indicators of whether the nonresponse is more likely to be an implicit "no" or an implicit "yes" or is it probably uncorrelated to either?

Joe Catania: The respondent has to verbalize, "I don't want to answer that question."

Ulrich Clement: So what's your idea about what it means? What's behind the nonresponse? Might a nonresponse mean yes, I have something to hide and I don't want to tell you? Or is it I don't have anything to say, so this is why I say just no.

Joe Catania: That's a multivariate question. Take, for example, older respondents. If you believe that there are historical differences in how people were reared and the experiences they might have had in talking about sex while growing up, and if you believe that older folks generally grew up in a more sex-negative culture than younger respondents in our sample, then you arrive at a set of explanations that might focus on historical differences in rearing practices around sexuality and the effects these practices have on comfort with sexual topics. People might be willing to disclose on some sexual topics they hear a lot about in the media, because media exposure may create a positive norm about disclosing some sexual information. But when you get into the more intimate kinds of questions like "do condoms slip off," "are condoms fun," those aren't the kinds of questions that people typically hear being bantered around on television or radio, or in the newspaper. There would be reason to believe that older folks might find it easy to answer some types of sex questions and not others.

Theo Sandfort: I think what you're doing is very important, but I think that the importance would increase if your analyses were theory driven rather than fact-finding, and I think it's very important that this methodological research be developed from a theoretical perspective.

Joe Catania: There is a theoretical framework, but it is thin with regard to ethnic differences. There is a body of evidence (in the U.S.) on sexual attitudes among different ethnic groups; attitudes of African American males appear to be much more sex-positive than African American females, white males, and white females; they look more like Scandinavians than U.S. Caucasians. That's not exactly a theory. Theories are needed to address the possible cultural experiences that might make African American males feel better about their sexuality and more comfortable talking about sex.

John Bancroft: That's going to be more easily answered by the people who expressed those attitudes in the first place, isn't it, rather than by considering those who don't respond?

Joe Catania: Well, if they're good observers of their own behavior.

Ann Stueve: I found your paper fascinating because I'm doing very similar analyses looking at pencil/paper questionnaires of seventh- and eighth-grade inner city kids. Three of our preliminary findings I thought might be of interest. First, we get much more missing data on questions about sex with seventh and eighth graders than we do on substance use or violence. Whereas we have missing data in the range of 1% to 3% on cigarettes, alcohol, marijuana, cocaine, it's upwards of 6%–10% when we move into the domain of sexual behaviors, suggesting for this age group that it's a sensitive issue [see Stueve's paper in this volume]. However, given the later placement of these questions in the survey, this may be a fatigue effect. Like some of your data, we too find girls to be more compliant; they're less likely to have missing data. One of the really interesting things we started to find is that children who do not answer a question at baseline are more likely to endorse the risk behavior six months later, so that missing data is a fairly consistent predictor of initiation of the behavior or, if not, at least the willingness to report the behavior. It looks like this works across substance-use items as well as the sex items we have in the survey, which has made us much more interested in looking at them.

Richard Parker: I don't want to discuss these issues in terms of blacks or whites. What I'm interested in are the methodological issues in terms of cross-cultural or cultural differences. One of the conclusions that has been reached looking cross-culturally is that the same instruments don't necessarily work in different cultural contexts. What I'm curious about in this kind of comparative work is if indeed you've made an effort to look at the ways in which cultural differences between the black community and white Americans may relate to their different responses.

Joe Catania: Prior to fielding the NABS, Stuart Michaels and Ed Laumann at NORC very kindly shared some data with us. There were a large number of qualitative studies that had been done with African American men and women, Hispanic men and women, Spanish speakers, English speakers, white males and females, and in different parts of the country looking at comprehension issues (e.g., what do these questions/words mean to you?). Our survey was a distillate of that process. In general, the conclusion that the NORC group and ours reached was that there is a commonly understood language; i.e., although people use lots of other words to describe sexual behaviors, there's still a common language, almost like a trade language, that works for the interview. However, that's not universally true. Diane Binson is looking at issues around people's comprehension of the term *anal intercourse,* and does find comprehension problems with people of low SES. Approximately 25% of low SES respondents really don't understand the term.

Cynthia Graham: I am very interested in your results obtained from varying the item wording and wondered if there had been any other studies that have looked at such enhanced conditions of questionnaires, because it seems such a simple manipulation, one that you would normally do in a clinical interview. It's had such an impact on your results.

Joe Catania: There is a predecessor; Bradburn and Sudman (1979) did a nice study. They expressed their work in terms of length of item wording, but they were looking specifically at one item on sexual intercourse. They didn't look across a wider range of reported activities.

Cynthia Graham: What about the surveys of sexual behavior, then? Have they used this type of enhanced question?

Joe Catania: Not that I'm aware of. By and large, surveys use an economy of words because of costs. Indeed, there are costs to having too many of these enhanced, long items. If you have too many of them, people start getting frustrated with the interview and begin dropping out.

Ulrich Clement: I would like to know about the concept behind this enhanced question. You presented this table on percentage who were virgins at 18, but under the enhanced condition that men reported a higher percentage at 18 than the women.

Joe Catania: Correct, you get a gender interaction.

Ulrich Clement: The enhanced condition does not necessarily lead to more reporting, but is there something else that is happening? What does it enhance? Do you invite people to report on more sexual behavior or do you enhance a tendency to report more gender-stereotyped answers?

Joe Catania: The enhanced condition actually produces less gender-stereotyped answers. There was an increase in male reports of virginity during adolescence but a decrease in reports by female respondents.

Anne Johnson: One interpretation might be that it gives people time to think, particularly if you're asking a question that asks them something about their adolescence which happened many years earlier. Because the enhanced condition in a sense clues people in to what that question is going to be, you should be able to tease out whether it's norm setting or thinking time which is relevant. If it's norm setting, then it should work better for the more stigmatized behaviors than for less stigmatized behaviors. If it's time to think, it should be more apparent for those questions that have more difficult recall demands.

Joe Catania: It does work better for more stigmatized behaviors. That's true. There's a third view, which is that these particular items may not necessarily be norm setting but permission giving. They're telling people that there's a wide range of experiences, and that their experience isn't alien.

Alex Carballo-Diéguez: We had a similar experience in a study of Puerto Rican men who have sex with men. We asked first in structured fashion, "How often do you use condoms for anal sex?" and many of the interviewees said always. At a later point we said, "Most men don't use condoms 100% of the time they have anal sex. Now, tell me about the occasions when you didn't use them and why was that the case?" and then many people who had said "I always use condoms" would say, "Well, you know, I was drunk." When we normalized the situation, it was okay to acknowledge risky behavior.

Richard Udry: There are limits to how far you want to play this game. For example, you might say, "Many people find it sexually exciting to hit their sex partners while they have sex with them. How often have you done this?" It might not change your answers, but do you not have some kind of responsibility for the kind of information you're spreading in the population in this fashion?

Joe Catania: We didn't use that approach when we asked about sexual violence. We tried to be a bit more empathic about how difficult this question might be for some folks. That is, we acknowledged that this is an uncomfortable topic. That had no effect for females, but there was an effect for males: an increased percentage of males reported a history of sexual violence.

Theo Sandfort: I'm not sure whether you looked at it, but I can imagine that having enhanced questions has a generalizing effect on the whole questionnaire. Did you check that? Can you check it?

Joe Catania: Well, there was a whole range of items in which there were no differences between conditions, so if it was having a general effect, we didn't see it across this range of items. There may be effects on things that are a bit more sensitive. In our study with African Americans, we have additional data on people's perceptions of the sensitivity of sexual questions, using a couple of different techniques for assessing them. We haven't analyzed those data yet, but what we want to be able to do is see if in fact our assumption is correct, that if you simply array the items along a sensitivity dimension the effects that you see are with the questions and in the upper range.

Theo Sandfort: My idea is that you express an attitude in response to one of these questions which generalizes to other items as well, because not all items have been enhanced in the same way.

Joe Catania: It may be. What I'm saying is that there's no evidence to indicate that it's true. And I think if it was true you would expect a particular pattern that we don't see.

Anne Johnson: I was quite surprised that you had a 9% nonresponse to the item on income and a 0.9% item nonresponse to numbers of partners.

Joe Catania: You're surprised in what way, good or bad?

Anne Johnson: The high item nonresponse to income sounds more like the British when they talked about how much they earned. But the partners item's nonresponse seems low.

Joe Catania: It's 9% amongst the older folks.

Anne Johnson: But what I really want to know is were the questions always asked in the same way? One of them in the self-completion part and another face-to-face?

Joe Catania: They're all asked the same way. We actually found lower nonresponse than people typically find in these surveys, and part of it's because we embedded the question in a health context. We gave people more of a rationalization for why we were asking about their income as opposed to just diving right into it. It's the same thing with sex questions; people like to have some general rationale for why you're asking them these questions.

Anne Johnson: So how do you explain such a big difference in item nonresponse? I mean to income versus number of partners.

Joe Catania: You see the big increase in nonresponse in the income item, typically among older respondents. And you see a difference between white females and white males. It looked like females are the highest; it was around 6% for white females. It's with the older folks that you see the most nonresponse. They're the most conservative about that particular type of question.

John Bancroft: The general picture that seems to be emerging from these studies is that there are relatively small differences between whites and African Americans but substantial differences between both those groups and Hispanic Americans. Would that be a fair comment?

Fabio Sabogal: Yes, I think it is true, especially among the low-acculturated Hispanics and among Hispanic women. Analyzing the National AIDS Behavioral Surveys (NABS), we found that women and low-acculturated individuals were more likely to give nonresponses and zero answers to sensitive questions [see chapter by Sabogal, Binson, & Catania in this volume]. In other studies (Sabogal, Perez-Stable, Otero-Sabogal, & Hiatt, 1995), we found, for example, that although gender differences in sexual behavior were present among non-Hispanic whites and Hispanics, these differences were greater among Hispanics. Hispanic men, especially unmarried and acculturated, reported a considerably higher number of sexual partners when compared with Hispanic women than did non-Hispanic white men when compared with non-Hispanic white women. Women's sexual behavior differed by ethnic group much more than men's. Non-Hispanic women have more liberal attitudes toward sexuality and more information about sex than do Hispanic women. Traditional machismo attitudes and less-flexible gender roles are also more prevalent among Hispanics, especially the low-acculturated and less-educated (Sabogal et al., 1995).

John Bancroft: Could I ask Richard if that would extend to Latin America?

Richard Parker: It's tricky, actually. I'm going to turn your question back into a question for Fabio. I was interested in your early comment about the differences between Mexicans and other Latino groups, including South Americans, in terms of greater conservatism. To what kinds of factors are you folks attributing that type of difference within the broader category of Hispanic or Latino—to differences in national cultural traditions, to differences in terms of the influence of different types of Catholicism, how are you trying to read those differences?

Fabio Sabogal: I think there are major geographical, cultural, economic, and educational differences among Hispanics. Hispanics belong to many racial groups. There is no one Hispanic culture but several cultures. The Hispanic population is a heterogeneous, multiethnic, and multicultural population, comprising many national communities and reflecting diversity of race, nationality, ethnicity, culture, religion, geography, socioeconomic status, and social class. For example, a large proportion of Mexican Americans, who make up 62% of the Hispanic population in the United States, live in the Southwest. They have the youngest median age (24 years) among Hispanic subgroups, a very high birthrate, and large extended families that include godparents. Puerto Ricans, who represent 13% of U.S. Hispanics, live in major northeastern urban areas and in Puerto Rico, are U.S. citizens, have the highest rate of female-headed families, and are the most economically disadvantaged Hispanic subgroup. Cuban Americans (5% of U.S. Hispanics) live primarily in Florida, have higher educational levels, and are less likely than other Hispanic subgroups to live below the poverty level. Central and South Americans represent 10.7% of the Hispanics. Central Americans, especially from Salvador, Guatemala, and Nicaragua, are the newest Hispanic arrivals (Sabogal, Faigeles, & Catania, 1993). People from South America have the highest level of education among Hispanics. They are more distanced geographically from their original family and are more likely to move by themselves. In another study (Sabogal & Catania, 1996), we found that Hispanics classified as "Other Hispanics" (e.g., South American, Caribbean, and European Hispanics) reported the highest prevalence of HIV risk factors, followed by Cuban and Puerto Rican Hispanics. The lowest prevalence of HIV risk factors was reported by Mexican and Central American respondents, corroborating previous studies in which Mexican-born Hispanics residing in the South and West of the U.S. reported the lowest rates for AIDS among Hispanics. Acculturation to the U.S. mainstream, the process of cultural exchange by which immigrants modify their attitudes, cultural norms, and behaviors as a result of the interaction with a different culture, may be an important factor that correlates with changes in sexual attitudes and behaviors (Sabogal et al., 1995). Acculturation may be viewed as a vulnerable period of stressful transitions and readaptations to unfamiliar and changing environments during which immigrants are in new situations where they try to experiment with different behaviors. For example, the number of sexual partners, smoking, and alcohol and drug consumption increase with acculturation. Other key variables are the motivation to immigrate, age, and if you immigrate by yourself or with your family. Religiousness continues to be a central factor for Hispanics that influences their mental, spiritual, and physical health. For example, the Catholic Church has a strong authority on behavioral standards for Hispanics prescribing sexual attitudinal and behavioral norms.

Colin Williams: Do you have any measure of acculturation other than length of time in the country? I recall a study of Mexican gays who were in the L.A. area. There was a marked difference in the kinds of sexual practices that they would do which depended on how long they had been in the country. Do you take this aspect of acculturation into account?

Fabio Sabogal: In general, in the area of acculturation there have been a lot of studies (e.g., Marín, Sabogal, Marín, Otero-Sabogal, & Pérez-Stable, 1987) developing an acculturation scale for Hispanics. We found that acculturation is strongly related to language. For example, a factor analysis revealed three major factors: language use, media, and ethnic social relations. Our scale correlated highly with respondents' generation, length of residence in the U.S., age of arrival, ethnic self-identification, and an acculturation index. A lot of these acculturation scales are related to language, maybe because language is one of the most sensitive factors that change with acculturation. Also, we are finding that the preference for answering the National AIDS Behavioral Survey in Spanish or English is important. For example, there is a high correlation (e.g., around .82) between language preference in the questionnaire and the acculturation score. Language preference is a proxy for acculturation. Age of arrival in this country (e.g., the younger you are, the more acculturated), number of years in the U.S., generation, language, and acculturation are highly correlated. Besides language, other factors such as beliefs, values, and attitudes (e.g., family attitudes, ethnic self-identity) should be incorporated in the development of future acculturation scales. In general, the literature shows that acculturation is related to changing traditional sexual attitudes and beliefs and an increasing number of STD risk factors in studies with heterosexual, adolescents, and gay Hispanics. Acculturation is a key variable and should be included in studies of sexual behavior among Hispanics and other immigrant groups.

Leighton Ku: I'm curious about other risk behaviors. Things like drug use, alcohol, cigarettes, which are not so socially tainted as sex, or are in different ways. I'm wondering whether there are similar patterns of nonresponse or whether there are gender-oriented patterns?

Fabio Sabogal: We haven't done nonresponse analysis of all the risk behaviors. In general, survey questions related to highly sensitive and stigmatized behaviors such as drug and alcohol use and sexual behavior are more likely to produce socially desirable responses. There are studies that point out that Hispanics also underreport cigarette smoking. It does depend on the way that you ask the question. For example, focus groups with credible Hispanic moderators are really popular now in the Hispanic community, and people start talking about sexual behavior, drug use, and alcohol use in such groups. So it all depends on the method that you are using. Also the words and tone that the researcher uses in the questions are very important.

Barbara Marín: I find the issue of language and meaning really interesting. I don't know that we really pay enough attention to the kinds of answers we might get when we word our questions. This becomes something of paramount importance when translating a questionnaire into another language. It really concerns me that there's so much of the culture embedded in the words that are used. Think about certain anal-oral practices, for example, and about the kinds of words that would be acceptable to or understood by a less-acculturated Latino woman versus a gay man in the Castro District of San Francisco. Research becomes complicated because language is where the meaning and culture are expressed.

Fabio Sabogal: Extensive pretesting is the key to solving problems associated with language and meaning. In our research, we use pretesting to elicit feedback from members of the target groups during all phases of research development. We use subjective culture methodology to study beliefs, perceptions, attitudes, roles, social norms, expectancies, stereotypes, cognitive associations, and values shared by a segment of the population. Especially at the beginning of the research, we use these qualitative methods to do ethnographic, open-ended, in-depth individual interviews, focus groups, and extensive pretesting. Then we use more quantitative approaches such as survey research methodology.

Barbara Marín: By the way, in one of our focus groups of Latinos, one man thought "oral sex" meant "sex by the hour."

John Bancroft: Not sex by the ear?

Stuart Michaels: I wonder if we can't learn something from possibly similar processes in other domains. I understand there is a standardized form of Spanish that's used on international television broadcasts. This strikes me as interesting because this is an example of an external social process that is generating or trying to find a common language across different national dialects and cultures. My guess is that this hasn't had much impact specifically on sexual language, but I'm not sure and it still seems worth investigating. Some of the things we're doing when we construct sexual behavior questionnaires are a kind of cross-cultural communication for specific purposes. Is it possible to study other such processes or to look at what happens when you try to create this kind of language that's going out to many culturally different national groups and communities?

Fabio Sabogal: I think that that's very important. For example, in the development of educational materials, we don't create a specific booklet just for Mexican Americans that are in San Francisco, but we try to develop more general, cost-effective booklets or questionnaires. When we developed *HIV Prevention for the Family* with the American Red Cross (see Sabogal & Otero-Sabogal, 1990), there were 120 different places where we sent the 32-page booklet. You don't consider the amount of different ways that people think and analyze the language, and we just tried to get the general meaning from all these groups, the common denominator. It is very important to work with people from all over the country and from all these groups—Mexican Americans, Puerto Ricans, South Americans. This takes a lot of time and money and resources, and sometimes we are working with the Spanish translation and the English translation of the questionnaire needs to be ready tomorrow. It's time consuming, but we need to find a common language if you want to do cross-cultural research. A good review of the process of developing culturally appropriate educational materials for a multicultural population, which includes pretesting and cross-cultural research, will be printed in this year's *Health Education Quarterly*.

Leonore Tiefer: Barbara's question about language made me think of the larger question. It's obvious when we have different languages, Spanish, English, French, German, that we may not be using the same words, but the subtle question is within the language—do the words mean the same thing, and this is always the problem. It's obvious to us in a clinical setting when we may use several different euphemisms or synonyms before we finally seem to communicate. But in the questionnaire it is not so obvious. It has been my experience that the word *masturbation* means such different things to different people and I think that we tend to assume that monolingual problems are less difficult than multilingual problems. It's not necessarily the case.

Fabio Sabogal: The problem is even worse when you have bilingual Hispanics answering in Spanish and in English. There are differences in the way that people answer. If bilingual Hispanics answer in Spanish, they tend to be more like Latin, in general.

John Bancroft: You mean you get a different response depending on the language they use.

Fabio Sabogal: Yes. Bilingual Hispanics provided different responses depending on the language of interview. Some studies with Hispanics have suggested that responding to a survey in a secondary language elicits the respondent's awareness of his/her ethnicity and produces more extreme responses and ethnic responses than when answering the same instrument in the respondent's primary language.

Ted Myers: From my experience working with different cultural groups, meaning is very important. In this discussion, the meaning of various words has received a lot of attention. But there are other issues that we also have to deal with and I don't know in what order of importance we should put them. The language for a bilingual person, for example; if you were to ask a question in English or say in an Asian language, you may get a different response. This may not have to do so much with meaning as with disclosure or fear of disclosure to someone of their own (or opposite) type. We may get some clues about how individuals may respond by looking at their group behavior. There are differences in patterns of socializing between sociocultural groups related to their sexuality. For example, amongst the gay Latino-Hispanic community in Toronto, there have recently been a number of gay bars established where members of the community may group together. The gay Asian community for some time has resisted the formation of such a strong gay-community identity and may be seen to be slowly integrating into the mainstream gay bars. Is this perhaps because they don't want to disclose to others from their cultural community? From my research experience with aboriginal populations, I would say that there is resistance to speaking to outsiders who are not aboriginal and trusted. This presents a different challenge for research. These reserve communities were very isolated. There may be a limited number of people in these communities who speak the aboriginal language and many who may be related (aunts, uncles, nephews, etc.). For sex research, this may present tremendous problems, as disclosure to such a person, who may speak the language or who would normally be trusted or respected, may raise a personal issue. We had to develop special nonverbal techniques that permitted the self-report for those with limited literacy or for those who spoke a native language.

Fabio Sabogal: I think all the aspects that you mention are important, but especially the interviewer-interviewee ethnic and cultural concordance. In general, people feel more comfortable and able to disclose sensitive information if they share a common language and have similar cultural experiences.

Richard Parker: In work in Latin America, as in Britain, social class is extremely important in terms of stratifying a sample; you get very different kinds of responses in different classes. When we come to the United States, often class seems to disappear and ethnicity becomes the center of attention. So I'm curious to what extent you find in the work that you've been doing that the kinds of class differences that are so prevalent in Latin American societies are reproduced in the U.S. and to what extent the acculturation process changes that or has an influence on that.

Fabio Sabogal: Although acculturation may play a strong role to diminish class differences, class differences are also reproduced in the U.S. Among Hispanics, there is a high correlation between social class and acculturation. Education is a major component in this association. High education is associated with higher acculturation levels and social class. Besides acculturation and social class, ethnicity is an important variable in the U.S., but not so in Latin America. Social class, more than ethnicity, seems to be more salient in Latin America. To understand the interactions among these variables in sex research, our data need to be broken down by social class, ethnicity, education, and acculturation. We need to distinguish and control for these complex effects.

Richard Parker: Both Fabio and Alex commented on acculturation and length of time since immigrants arrived, which led me to think about the process of historical change in sexualities taking place in the Latin American countries of origin as well. Certainly in some of the larger countries, like Brazil, probably Mexico, there are emerging gay and lesbian communities which are changing the ways in which people classify and categorize themselves at home and it would be important also to try and think about what they bring with them as being something that changes over time. And then a question to Alex Carballo-Diéguez about the matching of interviewer and interviewee. I think this is interesting, but I wonder if it doesn't cut in a number of different ways. It gets back to the earlier discussion about the sexuality of the interview. At least in our experience in Brazil working with men who have sex with men, we've talked a lot with our research team and interviewers about the extent that the whole process, from recruitment through interview, is a highly sexualized and, in fact, eroticized kind of process. Within this sexual landscape, we did some analysis of the effectiveness of different modalities of "more masculine," "more feminine," the different characters in that particular sexual drama that you described well in your talk. We found, for example, that with the more effeminate informants, transvestite or not, but effeminate, sometimes very masculine interviewers were able to work much more effectively with those more effeminate informants. It would be interesting to look at how that may vary.

Alex Carballo-Diéguez: I agree with that, Richard, because I think that many times the pairings that you see are between a masculine-acting guy and a transvestite, and he's the pimp and she's the sex worker. The drag queens say often that they feel discriminated by gays who look at them as if to say, "You're too much; we cannot tolerate you." As far as the issue of matching is concerned, it's very difficult sometimes. For example, for my current project, which is a comparison between Dominicans, Colombians, Puerto Ricans, and Mexicans, I have hired interviewers of each one of these national groups because they are able to understand regional language variations, and I assumed the respondents would feel more comfortable. Yet I interviewed someone who is Dominican and he said, "I'm so glad that you're not Dominican, because if you were, I would be afraid that you might know someone who knows someone, who knows my grandmother in the island." So you can never win. The other issue that you mentioned, the changes in Latin America, are very important, particularly the political changes. Many people came here, including myself, during a time in which Latin America was a dictatorship throughout. The experiences that we had under dictatorships were quite different from those of younger people who have grown up during a time of relative democracy. And I'm sure that has a strong impact on how they see themselves.

Richard Parker: That and also HIV, because one of the things that AIDS has done is to make the discussion of homosexuality in Latin America much more common and open.

Alain Giami: A question for both of the Hispanic researchers. You said that it was necessary to train Hispanic interviewers to get better information about the behavior of Hispanic subjects, and you also said that sometimes it might be difficult for a Dominican to be interviewed by a Dominican about gay sexual behavior. My question is whether the interviewer and interviewee belonging to the same community would raise more difficulties in obtaining information about a stigmatized behavior. A Hispanic man might feel more ashamed to speak about his homosexuality to another Hispanic man because he would know the values attached to homosexuality in the Hispanic culture. I make the assumption that reporting homosexual behavior might be easier with a person from another community.

Alex Carballo-Diéguez: I think that depends on how they perceive you. If they perceive me as being gay, then probably there is a sense of camaraderie, and we can talk about these issues. We were doing a study with couples. We had an interviewer who was straight but very gay-sensitive. At the interview, in the debriefing, he would ask people how they felt during the interview. People answered, "Oh, great!" In that case, the fact that he wasn't gay didn't seem to bring any problems. If the interviewer is adequately trained, I don't think that there will be much difficulty in disclosing same-sex behavior to another Latin American man.

Alain Giami: Yes, but what if a gay-looking Latino interviews a non-gay Latino man?

Alex Carballo-Diéguez: That depends on how much it shows, I guess.

Richard Parker: We have a Brazilian example of that in the general population survey we did in Rio a few years ago. We got more men in the general population to report same-sex interactions to our gay, more or less obvious gay, interviewers than we did with interviewers who weren't perceived to be gay.

Anke Ehrhardt: On the issue of matching interviewer and interviewees, we don't really have solid data. We have a lot of intuitions. We are now beginning some careful studies such as Joe Catania's, and we may see that some of these variations are not as simple as matching by gender or culture. I'm reminded of another time when everybody thought sex therapists should do sex therapy in a certain way. Masters and Johnson had come out saying you had to have a woman and a man as a therapy team to treat the male-female couple with sexual dysfunction. And that went on for years; that was the bible. Then people did other things because it was so expensive, until the Institute of Sex Research in Hamburg, spearheaded by Gunter Schmidt, did a very careful study comparing gender of therapist, one or two, and experience of therapist. As you might guess, training and experience knocked out all the other variables. So, clearly in terms of interviewing, we need to get beyond the idea that somehow it needs to be a perfect match, gender match, etc. We need to look at what is important. I think training and experience and comfort for the interviewee are very important. And we need to test such ideas.

John Bancroft: Presumably, some of the training should be dealing with gender and ethnic differences.

Anke Ehrhardt: Of course, and language and all of those kinds of issues. But the things which we hear which are important for the interviewee don't necessarily need to be captured by this kind of perfect match.

Stuart Michaels: In trying to think about the case of the American gay man (as opposed to some of the Latin American variants both within and outside the United States being discussed before), I would say the folk theory of homosexuality in the United States among gay men is essentialist. That is, homosexuality is some independent presocial underlying categorical trait defined not in terms of gender role, femininity versus masculinity, but rather simply on the basis of the presence or absence of sexual desire for another man. In the Chicago study, we have had the experience when we speak to respondents or informants from other groups or cultures where it appears as if they understand us to be asking questions about this specific meaning of homosexuality. We've had the experience of asking "Are there any homosexuals in your community?" And we get the answer "no." Yet the person we are talking to clearly understands that there are men who have sex with men in this community, but what they seem to be saying is that there are no gay men of a particular type that they think we are really interested in. I think a lot of this type of confusion crops up in the AIDS intervention and education area, where you have competing paradigms of sexuality. For example, there's a conflict between the organized "gay community" that's currently predominantly white and often perceived as white versus "men who have sex with men" linked to various ethnic or racial groups in this country. There's a lot of conflict between those communities. Sometimes they overlap, sometimes they are quite distinct and in conflict; some people move from one to the other and this seems to me to be in process of relatively rapid change. And I think AIDS is having a major impact. But some of the issues raised by AIDS are very difficult to clearly distinguish because of the different ways we use language. While we may try to maintain an open-mindedness and cultural sensitivity to what the various possibilities of sexual organization and categories are, often in the rush to stop AIDS, one finds what I see happening in Chicago sometimes: gay male organizations begun within the predominantly white organized gay community setting up interventions in African American and Hispanic neighborhoods and bringing along their model of what gay sexuality is. I don't know where that story ends. I don't know if the people in the Hispanic and black communities in Chicago end up conforming or whether they're resisting or maybe creating a hybrid.

Alex Carballo-Diéguez: Sometimes you learn the language of the oppressor. When I first came to this country I had to report whether I was white, black, or Hispanic. I thought that the list included apples, oranges, and potatoes, which are not in the same category. But I understood what they were asking. If I give interviewees the choices straight, gay, or bisexual, they may be able to fit themselves in as one of these. But if I ask a drag queen "Are you gay?" she may say, as some have said, "I'm a heterosexual drag queen." Or a straight-identified man will say, "I'm neither of those; I'm normal, I'm a man, what are you asking me?" Also there is no translation for the word *straight* in Spanish.

Anne Johnson: I think it's of interest to ask whether we can in fact construct the same sort of scheme for lesbians that has been used for gay men. I don't think it's the same because lesbian women don't congregate in the same way, and probably a smaller proportion are gay-identified in the way that gay men are. There are some very interesting issues about the different behavior patterns that emerge from large representative population samples and from convenience samples. But there are in the European literature, which you didn't cover, some very large population samples which do give you the kind of sample sizes based on general population surveys which enable you to draw conclusions about patterns of lesbian relationships. I don't think we have fully exploited our data from the British Survey in this respect and I would absolutely agree with you about the HIV focus in much of this data. But we did write one of the chapters in our book (Johnson et al., 1994) on that subject. It shows some glimpses of fascinating differences between same-sex behavior amongst women and men. For example, initiation into same-sex behavior continues throughout the life course for women, with some women first becoming homosexually active in their late 20s, 30s and 40s. The shape of the curve is very different from male homosexual behavior with most initiation occurring in the teen years, and the whole pattern of subsequent partnerships is different. It would be good to see you draw on the European literature in this context. In addition, the various surveys represented here and done in the U.S. could be combined so that the small samples that each can contribute would in combination allow you to answer some of the questions you raise on a population basis even though the surveys may not have asked quite the same questions.

Lynda Doll: I very much agree with what you're saying, and I appreciate you saying that. I would like to see what could be accomplished if we could gather together data, just taking lesbian women as an example. I don't think that we really have a good overall picture. We have snapshots—we've got this convenience sample and that convenience sample, and no one at this point that I'm aware of has really done a very good job, and this is certainly true of bisexual men as well as lesbian or bisexual women. I'm really reporting from here in the States, but I don't think we've done a very good job of synthesizing the data to give a sense of the overall picture. And maybe we can do that.

Anne Johnson: Charles Turner wrote a fascinating paper (Fay, Turner, Klassen, & Gagnon, 1989) where he put together all the U.S. data from a lot of bad (meaning methodologically weak) studies. Another good example is the U.S./U.K. paper we're working on with the Laumann/Michaels group here. What is extraordinary is that the similarities between these data sets are much greater than the differences. So there's an opportunity to put together some of these data sets from different population samples between us in this room. Together we must have quite a large population-based sample of lesbian women. It would be interesting.

Alex Carballo-Diéguez: Venue sampling is contingent on the number of people that you have in the venue. For example, if I am trying to sample Dominican men who have sex with men, it would be lovely if I could go to a bar or street corner or neighborhood where there are many and then choose one in every four. But the reality is that it's difficult to find them. Not because they don't exist; on one occasion I said to one of them, "Why is it so difficult to identify Dominican gay men?" He said, "Because if you approach me in the street I will say that I'm straight and if you approach me in a gay bar I will say I'm not Dominican, I will say I'm Puerto Rican." So the only way that we've been able to get this sample is through someone who knows someone else who has a party in his home, and then we go and we explain the study and then we get them to come. Otherwise, even going to many different venues it's very difficult to find them. And Dominicans are the second-largest Latino population in New York City, so it's not that there are not enough. There is something about the culture that makes them very closeted, and it's very difficult to reach them. So although I think that the idea of venue sampling is very interesting, I do not know how to deal with this problem.

Colin Williams: One of the things that bothers me about what you've been saying is that you want a representative sample of bisexuals. What is that? And what would it mean? And you say that we have all these other studies that we should put together. Exactly, we should, but you seem to imply that they're bad studies because they don't involve some kind of representative sampling. So the larger picture is no more than a piece. What do you call the larger picture? A representative sample?

Lynda Doll: In the best of all possible worlds, I would want to have a representative sample. I'm very much aware that that is an ideal.

Colin Williams: What's the interest? What would it mean? You have all these people who were atomized, isolated, behaving in a bisexual way, but that rips the meaning of bisexuality from its context, I think. Your point about the community; I think this is where you understand what bisexuality is all about, but it's located within a particular meaningful community. To say "Well, I need a representative sample" I think belies the thing that you say about AIDS. What would you do with it? Isn't this the way an AIDS researcher thinks, that I want quantity, frequency, kind of thing? What questions would you ask of this wonderful representative sample that would give more of an idea of bisexuality than you would get struggling to look at your community and other communities and conclude: "look at the tremendous variety of bisexuality." There is no such thing as a representative bisexuality, I think, is the answer. Now we're trying to push it into a mold which doesn't exist and we're constructing something that we're going to take as knowledge, which is going to be simply the results of our own methodological assumptions and I think we should be aware of that.

John Bancroft: Let's try to get you clear on this, Colin, because this is obviously an intense and important issue. You would agree that with the venue sampling of gay men in particular the attention has tended to focus on subsets of gay men and that there are large parts of the gay population in rural areas and suburban areas that are getting missed. If you went to look at them, their sexuality or their bisexuality would be different anyway because of their different setting and context.

Colin Williams: I think the problem is that we add apples and oranges, but the meaning of bisexuality in a rural area is probably a lot different from the meaning of bisexuality in a city or whatever. Let's put all this stuff together, add it together, and perhaps somehow we get a picture. But I'm not sure that you can get a picture unless you ignore the social reality that surrounds the behaviors that you're studying.

Stuart Michaels: Not surprisingly, I will try to defend surveys. I'm very sympathetic to one point that you're making, if I understand it correctly. There is a tendency in surveys to decontextualize. But I think we should recognize that there are certain advantages that surveys have, and I think they are important to recognize as well. These relate to sampling and the fact that probability sampling can produce representative samples of all groups in the population that the sample is drawn from at the same time. There are many other problems that sampling does not solve for you. You still need theory to tell you what are the important questions to ask and variables to measure. It does not automatically solve the problems we were discussing about how to ask questions and elicit unbiased responses. But ideally it does allow one to have a sample that has persons defined by any criteria in the same proportion as they appear in the population. It also means that relationships between variables that are discovered are not likely to be a function of the particular characteristics of the group one happened to select. One problem and limitation does have to do with sample size. In the U.S. study we were not able to collect a sufficiently large sample to address many of the basic sexual behavior and AIDS-related questions we wanted to because of the government refusing to fund the study and having to scale it down to the size the private funding could afford. In the United States, we sat down and we figured out what we would need as a reasonable sample size to address some of the basic questions about certain sexual practices. We came to the exact same conclusion as the British and the French, because sample size is independent of the size of the population you're sampling; it has to do with the statistical power that you achieve from the sample you get. We all came up with 20,000 as the basic sample size needed. Now this would not solve all the problems. However, it would allow one to address some of the issues about homosexual and bisexual behavior being raised here. We could define certain objective criteria like behavior. We could also then measure a number of other factors—urban/rural, gender, race, ethnicity, age, etc. We could then look at whether or not people who have sex with both men and women in certain conditions think about themselves or define themselves in different ways. Do they then engage in different sexual practices, in different amounts, in different types of relationships, etc.? I don't see that you could ever ask these questions when you only go to organized preexisting groups. The understanding of what differences we might be looking for do come out of research that is more qualitative and ethnographic and done in specific contexts or sites. But if we want to know about relative prevalence and the relationship between behaviors, attitudes, and social networks, we need some method of studying unbiased, representative samples.

Lynda Doll: Understand that I am not in any sense saying that there should not be qualitative research. It is absolutely critical that we have both.

Colin Williams: I'm not defending qualitative research against quantitative; I just want to know what it means, that's all. If I'm understanding Stuart correctly, are you saying that these smaller things will only become understandable if we could put them in the context of a larger whole?

Stuart Michaels: I thought that part of the issue here was the mixture of apples and oranges. And so, if you want to ask questions about whether there are these kinds of differences, then you have to provide the opportunity to find these people. I think that John's example was an appropriate one. If you want to compare the homosexually active men who do not show up in gay venues with the homosexually active men who do, then you need a system that allows both of them to come in independent of that factor and then to compare those groups. And that's one of the things that a probability sample drawn from a population independent of sexual behavior allows one to do, assuming it is large enough.

Richard Parker: It seems to me that this is an area where more than most we start talking about what we need to do before we think very carefully about what we want to know and why we want to know it. If what we want is a study that's going to help us design more effective HIV-prevention interventions, it may not be terribly important what the frequency is. It may be more important to have an understanding of the dynamics of desire and the meanings associated with sexual relations with both genders. There may be other kinds of things that we want to ask. It's an area which I think is especially difficult because so much falls through the cracks of the present way in which research has been implemented. Look at the classic example of female bisexuality. The HIV/AIDS agenda has been developed around HIV transmission and assumed that female-female transmission doesn't happen and so it's not important there. The reproductive health agenda has been organized around reproduction and assumed that female-female sexuality isn't important there. So it's the sort of thing that falls through the cracks. Then we find we've got this huge area that's unknown, this black hole that we now want to do something about. We start running very quickly to try and do it, but we have to ask ourselves exactly what it is we want to know and why, for what purposes.

Lynda Doll: To follow through on that example, one of the things that the very few studies we have on bisexual women in the United States seem to suggest is that bisexual women are more likely to use drugs, and yet I have no context in which to understand that. I don't know whether to believe it. I have a sample of 25 over here and maybe a sample of 40 over there. Do I truly believe that bisexual women are more likely to use drugs? We've got to have a combination of the quantitative and qualitative, but I completely agree with you, Richard, we've got to start asking what we need this information for. If you think back to the beginning of the HIV epidemic, and I was at CDC in the middle of that, we had very few data at that time to enable us to estimate how many men had anal sex and so on and so forth. If we'd had surveys addressing such issues as well as qualitative research, how different would our response have been to the HIV epidemic?

Anke Ehrhardt: It's not that nothing is known. Schwartz and Blumstein carried out a large bisexual survey 15 or so years ago. But suddenly there is this specific perspective. There was a whole literature before HIV which has been ignored. There is a lot in the European literature. I agree with Colin on this: what is the question that we want to answer? If we want to understand the phenomenon, then there are quite a few sources on which we can draw.

John Bancroft: Confronting the question of high-risk sexual behavior and, in particular, why some people continue to expose themselves to risk even when they're aware of the risk is fundamental to the problem of changing behavior. When I took this question and looked at the large surveys, and I've looked at the University of Chicago survey and I've looked at the French survey and to a limited extent the British, in attempting to answer that fundamental question I found relevant information of a very limited kind. One was left with very simple questions like numbers of partners and whether you use condoms. Maybe the fundamental questions had not been on the agenda when these surveys were designed. Echoing Richard's comment, was there enough setting out of the fundamental questions and how they should be addressed before you launched into those huge and extremely expensive surveys? This sounds provocative. Actually, I found more indication of that basic process in the French survey than I've seen in the English language ones.

Colin Williams: What I'd like to see is the Kinsey Institute researching theoretical issues relevant to sexual behavior dealing with the questions that we should be asking before we decide what methods are going to be used. We seem to have methods now. We have this wonderful toy, we have this, that, and the other; let's go out and use them. But we don't necessarily think, "Well, what are the questions going to be then?"

Anne Johnson: I feel I precipitated some of this, though I didn't mean to, when I talked about the Turner paper, calling some of the pre-AIDS work "bad surveys." What I meant was surveys that weren't set up for the question that Charles was trying to answer. I should have said nonideal rather than bad surveys. One of the things that occurred to me as we sat here talking about lesbian women, and something that interests me in our data, is what the differences between expressed female homosexuality and expressed male homosexuality tell us about the difference between female sexuality and male sexuality. It's very interesting that we've heard a lot of discussion about homosexual versus heterosexuality. We've heard a lot about ethnic differences, but we haven't had a discussion about the fundamental issue of differences in how men and women feel sexuality should be expressed. This issue is essential to all the work on how women report differently from men and what the different gender biases are.

Lynda Doll: It's not just HIV surveys that are problem-driven. There's a great tradition and the surveys of sexual behavior have almost always been problem-driven—the problem of teen pregnancy, the problem of this or that or the other thing. So it's following in a fine tradition. It's not looking, as Ed Laumann described it, at the human condition and sexual behavior as an integral part of it, or the organizing factors around which it exists.

Richard Udry: The question of sampling continues to come up in our discussions in whatever group we're talking about. I think we've sometimes got the idea that this problem of sampling is somehow unique to sexual behavior and I don't know where that idea came from in the first place. The strategy of sampling has always been to decide what it was you wanted to survey and then to organize a way to get a sample of people who had that characteristic. Many of the problems that we have in studying sexual behavior and imagining how we could do that with a representative sample can be dissolved fairly easily if one accepts that one is trying to identify a group within a population so that one can then study it. For example, we all talk about the huge surveys that are being done for various purposes. The huge surveys can identify special populations of fairly large numbers. If you have a sample of let's say 20,000, you can identify, by asking one or two questions, a small group in that population, maybe 1% of that population which has the characteristic that you want. So you use your big survey as a sampling frame. You can use that big survey as a sampling frame for smaller studies which take the group that you want that has the characteristic and some other representative sample that doesn't have that characteristic or has some third characteristic and you can do a study of them. You can either do it in the same survey by pop-out sections that nobody else gets or you can go back and get them for another survey and you can get a representative sample of whatever you want. In a sample of 20,000, if there's a characteristic present in 1% or 2% of the population, you can find it. This is a technique that works. It can give you a representative sample of women who have sex with women. You can ask two or more questions on a general survey and identify them. It would be the same if you were trying to get a population of kids who play baseball. I don't see anything peculiar about sexual behavior that puts it in a category that you can't solve.

John Bancroft: If you're going to identify a group on the basis of a few questions and then study them, it becomes a confidentiality issue. The University of Chicago survey and the French survey basically eliminated any chance to contact people after the survey was done. Is that right?

Richard Udry: That may well have been, but that is an unnecessary condition.

Anne Johnson: In the British survey, it was possible to go back to people, and the vast majority of respondents expressed willingness to be contacted again.

Alain Giami: It seems that we have reached a new consensus in this group. We assume that we have done enough AIDS-oriented research. But we must bear in mind that most of the revival of sex research and particularly large-scale surveys could not have been done if there had not been the AIDS crisis. Being one of those who are more interested in sexuality research than AIDS research, I think we should try to establish what we have learned and what we have not learned about sexual behavior from this AIDS-oriented research. It is time to start secondary analyses to establish what we have learned about sex from the AIDS research. Sex research has always or most of the time been problem-oriented, but what would be non-problem-oriented sex research? Can we say the Kinsey surveys were non-problem-oriented?

John Bancroft: Yes, they were non-problem-oriented, and there is serious trouble because of that.

Alain Giami: We should define what we mean by problem-oriented.

John Bancroft: Kinsey didn't go out to establish anything to do with problems; he went out to find out what people did. I think it's fair to say that.

Leonore Tiefer: I think he went out to find what people did because he thought that there was a problem.

John Bancroft: Well, the main problem as far as he was concerned was that we didn't know what people did!

Leonore Tiefer: That's a problem of knowledge: we don't know what people do, and therefore we want to find out what people do. There is no research that doesn't have some problem.

Alfred Spira: I want to stress the point raised by Richard Udry. The reason why we arrived at our sample size of 20,000 is that we wanted to have enough subjects in our survey to be able to compare small groups. The smallest groups we thought we could compare would be groups for which the prevalence in our sample would be around 1% in each gender and in each sex. From that point we arrived at 20,000. What we can do with this survey is not only to describe the population to know what people do, but also to try to understand the determinants of their behaviors. And I do not mean why do men have sex with men, or why do women have sex with women, but why do some persons protect themselves and others not? This is the reason why we arrived at these sample sizes of 20,000.

Richard Udry: Absolutely, I agree. It's nonsense to say that you can't go back to them. It's just not true. There are lots of surveys that contain questions on sexual behavior, and you go back to the individuals who answered them. I've got back to one group of adolescents, I went back to them every week for two years, and the sample I'm working on now, I am going back to them for the third time, and there are 20,000 of them. So to say you can't do it is just not true, and your IRBs will approve it. You just have to set up the conditions under which it's possible.

John Bancroft: I wasn't suggesting you couldn't do it, I was saying that in many respects people feel that they should take steps which would make it difficult to do or impossible.

Richard Udry: I understand that.

Alain Giami: From the very beginning, the system we developed meant that we were able to gather data anonymously. We had intended to destroy the telephone number after the last question of the questionnaire. By so doing, we would be able to recontact respondents if the phone call was accidentally disconnected or the respondent wished to continue the interview at a later date. Ultimately, so that there could be total anonymity, the telephone numbers were destroyed after the first question. As a result, people could not be recontacted if the call was accidentally disconnected. An interrupted interview could only be continued if the respondent called a hotline number arranged for this purpose and stated the registration number which the interviewer had previously assigned. Although monitoring the work of researchers is desirable, given the social stakes and the difficulty of this type of survey, such strictness does pose problems. The entire basis for the regulations in force was the protection of the individual. This is incompatible with the collecting of information which is available to any public body not bound to secrecy and which may therefore be detrimental to the professional, civil or personal lives of citizens. The law did not allow for public health concerns, nor research in the collective interest, where data are never treated individually and cannot be matched up with the individuals. This significant flaw requires researchers to conform to laws written in such a way that individual interests may conflict with collective interests.

John Bancroft: I'd like to hear Alfred Spira and Anne Johnson comment on what seems to me to be very interesting differences between the

English and French surveys which go back to the issues we were talking about this morning, the impact of the interview. If I understand correctly, in the French survey you used a brief screening interview on the telephone for your 20,000, which established by asking basically highly sensitive questions whether they came into a high-risk group and then you went into a more detailed interview with that high-risk group. Whereas, unless I'm mistaken, Anne, you interviewed everybody and you kept your highly sensitive questions to the end in a self-addressed questionnaire. That seems to be a very fundamental difference between those two surveys.

Anne Johnson: Yes, we did interview everyone in detail in the British surveys. With respect to prevalence of risk behaviors, we found very similar results between French and British surveys (Bajos et al., 1995).

Alfred Spira: Our thinking was that in the general population, maybe 75% of a population is not at risk. We were doing a survey for the AIDS national agency, so we thought that we should have complete information about all at-risk persons plus a subsample of what we called the controls, not-at-risk persons. So, we used a filter after 10–12 minutes asking very sensitive questions, but we didn't record the answers; we just said to the persons, "Have you ever made this and this and this in your life, I do not want to know exactly what you did." But if the answer to one of these questions was yes, the person was directed to a long questionnaire. Otherwise he or she was directed to the short questionnaire, apart from a subsample of controls who were directed to the long questionnaire.

Anne Johnson: That method still depends a lot on somebody who has a high-risk behavior being picked up at that point. The method which seemed to have worked very well still depends on somebody making the decision to answer yes at that point. If you want to pick up the drug users, it's one chance and one chance only for them to understand that question.

Alfred Spira: Yes, but they did not know what was going to happen to them.

References

Bajos, N., Wadsworth, J., Ducot, B., John, A. M., le Pont, F., Wellings, K., Spin, A., Field, J., & the ACSF Group. (1995). Sexual behaviour and HIV epidemiology: Comparative analysis in France and Britain. *AIDS, 9,* 734–743.

Bradburn, N., & Sudman, S. (1979). *Improving interview method and questionnaire design, 42,* 221–234. Washington, DC: Jossey Bass.

Fay, R. E., Turner, C. F., Klassen, A.D., & Gagnon, J. H. (1989). Prevalence and patterns of same-gender contact among men. *Science, 243,* 338–348.

Johnson, A. M., Wadsworth, J., Wellings, K., & Field, J. (1994). *Sexual attitudes and lifestyles.* Oxford: Blackwell Scientific Press.

Sabogal, F., & Catania, J. A. (1996). HIV risk factors, condom use, and HIV antibody testing among heterosexual Hispanics: The National AIDS Behavioral Surveys (NABS). *Hispanic Journal of Behavioral Sciences, 18*(3), 367–391, August.

Sabogal, F., Faigeles, B., & Catania, J. A. (1993). Multiple sexual partners among Hispanics in high-risk cities. Data from the National AIDS Behavioral Surveys. *Family Planning Perspectives, 25*(6), 257–262, November.

Sabogal, F., & Otero-Sabogal, R. (1990). *HIV prevention for the family.* Washington, DC: American Red Cross.

Sabogal, F., Otero-Sabogal, R., Pasick, R., Jenkins, C. N. H., & Perez-Stable, E. (in press). Printed health education material for diverse communities: Suggestions learned from the field. *Health Education Quarterly.*

Sabogal, F., Perez-Stable, E. J., Otero-Sabogal, R., & Hiatt, R. (1995). Gender, ethnic, and acculturation differences in sexual behaviors: Hispanics and non-Hispanic White adults. *Hispanic Journal of Behavioral Sciences, 17*(2), 139–159.

Part 4.

Change in Behavior over Time

Pooling Information from Repeated Population Surveys

Its Use in the Evaluation of the Efficacy of AIDS Prevention Campaigns

ALFRED SPIRA

The study of the efficacy of prevention campaigns, especially those concerning AIDS, can be undertaken in three directions: epidemiological, sociological, economic.

From an epidemiological point of view, efficacy is usually measured through the evolution of the incidence of the disease for which a prevention program is undertaken. When working on sexual behaviors in relation to sexually transmitted diseases (STDs) and AIDS, two main problems arise.

First, sexuality is not a disease. However, it can lead to the occurrence of unexpected events, such as an unwanted pregnancy or, more seldom, an STD, among which AIDS is the more life-threatening. The potential efficacy of AIDS prevention campaigns aimed at modifying sexual behavior can hence be evaluated either through the evolution of AIDS incidence or through the evolution of at-risk behaviors, as measured on target populations (this, of course, implies a strong relationship between sexual behavior and AIDS, which is usually accepted). The direct measure of AIDS incidence (and that of the other STDs as well) is usually impossible in the general population, since it would require repeated and systematic HIV blood testing, which is possible only on volunteers, who represent a highly selected subsample of the general population. It can be performed only on selected cohorts of individuals who are informed of such a survey and agree to be followed up. The measure of at-risk behaviors can only rely on repeated sexual-behavior surveys on subgroups of the population, including the same subjects or different samples of the same population. The repetition of such surveys induces specific problems, which will be examined in this chapter.

Second, the measure of efficacy of any intervention poses the problem of the causal relationship between an action, here a prevention campaign, and an observed modification (concerning either a disease incidence or a behavioral modification). The only design which allows for a causal relationship to be suspected to be at play is that of the randomized comparative study. Otherwise, confounding factors may be suspected to be involved in the observed relationships. Nevertheless, such a randomized design may not be feasible, either for ethical or for practical reasons. In such a case, a so-called process analysis is generally undertaken in order to try to relate the observed modifications to their putative origin and to understand the modifications which have occurred.

These two kinds of problems will be studied in this chapter and further illustrated by examples from the literature.

Repetition of Surveys

At least four problems can be induced by the repetition of sexual behavior surveys on the same subgroups of the population.

1. It is acknowledged that the introduction of any measurement device modifies the environment of the milieu in which it is introduced. This general principle, first developed in the physical sciences, also applies to the medical and sociological sciences. Thus one can expect that once a sexual questionnaire has been administered to an individual, his/her sexual behavior will subsequently be modified. Moreover, one can suspect that the use of this questionnaire may have some influence on sexual networks and on the verbal exchanges about sexuality in these networks, since the subjects may speak about it and comment on it among themselves.

2. The repetition of the same questionnaire over time implies that the individuals responding to this questionnaire will be more and more aware of its objectives and content, even of the wording of the questions. Thus it can be feared that the answers will be modified by this increasing acquaintance with the questionnaire. Even if the same questionnaire is used only two times, the responses gathered on the second instance can be influenced by the fact that the questionnaire has already been used for the same purpose on the same individual. However, if such a process occurs in a comparative randomized design, it can be postulated that this "order effect" of the questionnaire could be the same in the two groups which are to be compared.

3. It has been demonstrated on many occasions and in different instances, including sexual behavior surveys (ACSF, 1992), that a "social acceptability" effect can modify the answers of respondents. This effect is the result of a complex interaction between the interviewers and the interviewees. It is to be feared that such an effect can be increased by the repetition of the same kind of inquiry on the same subjects. If the subjects agree several times to participate in the survey, they will be more and more prone to adopt the objectives of the survey and thus to modify their answers in the expected direction. This kind of bias will be enhanced in comparative surveys, especially if there is an intervention group which receives something and a control group which is not submitted to any specific intervention. In this case, the "acceptability effect" may be more important

in the intervention group than in the control group, leading to an interaction confusing the analysis.

4. Repeated sexual behavior questionnaires will be used at time intervals long enough to allow the behavior under study to have evolved. Usually this time lag is not shorter than 6 months, more often it is as long as 18 months to 2 years. During this time, everything will have been modified. First, of course, the age of the subjects and their situation in their sociobiographies. But also the society itself and the perception of AIDS in this society will have been modified. This makes the comparison of repeated sexual behavior questionnaires a very difficult enterprise to undertake. However, in comparative randomized surveys, it can be postulated that these changes related to time occur at the same speed in both groups. This seems to be a quite reasonable assumption, at least in a first instance.

Random Allocation of Subjects

A random allocation of subjects to an intervention group or to a control group will be undertaken each time that a causal relationship between the intervention and the measured outcome is to be demonstrated. However, this design, though it seems to be appropriate from a theoretical point of view, raises some important problems which are going to seriously limit its use.

1. A randomized design can be ethically undertaken only if there is, a priori, a complete ignorance of any potential superiority of one "treatment" over the other. In all other circumstances, such a design could be ethically addressed. This point seems to be of paramount importance in the field of prevention of STDs and AIDS, since prevention strategies are going to be tested only if there is sufficient evidence to suggest their potential efficacy. Nobody is going to try to promote any prevention strategy if there is not sufficient evidence in its favor or if one can suspect that it will bear more drawbacks than benefits. However, two considerations are going to modify this judgment. First, even if a prevention strategy is well justified from a theoretical point of view, its practical use may reveal completely unexpected effects, which is a strong argument in favor of the scientific evaluation of all the new strategies to be used. Second, if a prevention strategy is to be generalized without a previous evaluation undertaken with the stronger requirements, there is a risk of promoting ineffective (or even counterproductive) strategies, at an individual and collective cost.

2. Randomization postulates the comparison of at least two groups of individuals. The randomization process can involve the subjects themselves or the groups to which they belong. In the first instance, this is a classical randomization as in medical controlled trials; in the second instance, a randomization by groups or by communities is undertaken (*American Journal of Epidemiology*, 1995). Whatever the method used, prevention strategies

usually rely on communication and information. This is completely different from the administration of a medicine and bears a risk of "contamination" from one group to the other. If the information concerning the intervention designed for the individuals of one group is disseminated among some or all individuals of the other group, this will result in a bias, the effect of which will be to lower the actual difference between the groups. The minimization of this bias requires work with individuals or groups of individuals which are well separated from one another, in order to minimize the occasions for communication between them. This implies that the randomized comparison of very large segments of a given population will be almost impossible. Moreover, if prevention strategies are going to involve a whole country, their randomized evaluation will be an impossible task.

3. The proposed behavior modification intervention strategies are generally expected to induce very small actual changes in the target population. A direct consequence of this situation is that a large number of statistical units will be required to be able to demonstrate a statistical difference between the compared groups. This would be easily undertaken if the individuals were going to be the statistical units. But since the prevention strategies are generally publicized through communication tools, such as advertisements in journals, TV programs, and posters, the randomization process will concern communities more often than individuals. In such designs, the statistical unit is the community and not the individual, thus drastically reducing the number of statistical units involved in the study and the power of the comparison undertaken.

4. Even if an intervention is very limited and well defined, it is usually impossible to isolate an intervention aimed at modifying behaviors from its social and psychological environment. Thus the analysis will need to try to measure the effect of the intervention per se, while the effect of the other modifications will tend to confuse if not to interact with these evolutions. Hence even if the design is of the randomized kind, the analysis will have to take into account all the inter-current evolutions, just as if it was a non-experimental design.

Practical Use of Surveys

Nevertheless, the evaluation of AIDS-prevention strategies must be undertaken. We will consider some examples of already published studies using repetition or pooling of information gathered in different sexual behavior surveys.

1. In the field of HIV/AIDS prevention, only a few "experimental" studies, including an intervention group and a control group, with a randomized allocation of the subjects have been published to date.

The first one concerns the prevention of mother-to-child HIV transmission by the administration of AZT during pregnancy, delivery, and the first hours of life (Connor, Sperling, Gelber, et al., 1994). The second one is the study in Tanzania of the efficacy of STD diagnosis and treatment in the prevention of sexually transmitted HIV infection (Grosskurth, Mosha, Todd, et al., 1996). The first of these studies does not include any relevant information on sexual behavior, which is not of interest in the survey. In the latter, one person out of eight in the cohort has been interviewed by means of a detailed sexual questionnaire, which has been repeated along time during follow-up. After two years, the incidence of HIV seroconversions was 1.2% in the intervention group and 1.9% in the control group ($p<0.05$). Nevertheless, the results did not show any significant difference between these two groups concerning the incidence of other STDs nor any modification of sexual behavior (Table 1). At baseline, the reported numbers of lifetime sex partners and of sex partners during the past year were similar in the intervention and comparison groups in both sexes. At follow-up, reported partners during the past year showed no change from baseline and there was still no material difference between the intervention and comparison groups. Data were also collected at follow-up on reported "casual" partners during the past two years, defined as all sex partners other than those described as "regular" or living with the respondent. Similar results were again obtained in the intervention and comparison groups.

At baseline, only 2% of men reported sexual contact with bar girls or prostitutes during the past year, and this question was not repeated at follow-up. Information was collected at follow-up on condom use during the follow-up period. Condom use with sex partners other than their spouses was reported by only 2.4% of men (intervention 1.6%, comparison 3.0%) and 2.3% of women (intervention 2.7%, comparison 1.8%). Few individuals reported regular condom use.

This example seems to be the first of the use of repeated sexual behavior surveys specifically designed to help in the evaluation of prevention of STDs and HIV infection. The conclusion of the authors of this survey is that in the absence of sexual behavior change, the most plausible explanation for their results is that the STD treatment program reduced HIV incidence by shortening the average duration of STDs, thus effectively reducing the probability of HIV transmission.

2. However, the design of randomized comparative trials seems unrealistic, if not unfeasible, when considering the potential effects of national prevention campaigns and their relation with modifications of attitudes and behaviors toward HIV/AIDS prevention, since only quasi-experimental designs can be envisaged in such situations. At the level of a whole country, the only way to try to address this concern is the regular repetition, along time, of cross-sectional studies undertaken on samples selected according to the same protocol, using the same sampling frame and the same questionnaire. Even though this design involves important limitations, as al-

Table 1 *Numbers of Sexual Partners Reported in Intervention and Comparison Communities at Baseline and Follow-up, Tanzania*

	Men		Women	
	Intervention	Comparison	Intervention	Comparison
Baseline				
N	237	281	298	301
Lifetime partners (%)				
0	1	3	3	4
1	7	5	28	26
2–4	18	22	47	53
5–19	44	44	19	16
20 +	31	26	3	1
Partners past year (%)				
0	7	10	9	10
1	44	36	78	83
2	22	25	9	6
3–4	18	22	3	1
5 +	10	8	1	0
Follow-up				
N	216	268	248	255
Partners past year				
0	5	4	10	10
1	42	46	81	75
2	27	26	7	12
3–4	18	19	2	2
5 +	8	6	0	0
Casual partners past 2 years				
0	62	55	89	87
1	14	17	6	7
2	10	11	3	3
3 +	14	17	2	3

Source. Grooskurth, H., Mosha, F., Todd, J., et al. (1995). Impact of improved treatment of sexually transmitted diseases on HIV infection in rural Tanzania: Randomised controlled trial. *Lancet, 346,* 530–536.

ready discussed, such an approach was developed in France. In this country, in 1987, a first KABP survey was undertaken on a randomized sample of the general population in the Paris area. This was repeated in 1990 on a national sample of 1,000 individuals aged 18 and over. In 1992, a national telephone sexual behavior survey was undertaken on a very large sample of 20,055 persons aged 18–69. An extra sample of 1,927 persons was interviewed specifically on their knowledge, attitudes, and beliefs toward HIV/AIDS (KABP WHO framework). Such a survey has been repeated in 1994 on a national sample of 1,501 persons.

The analysis of the two last surveys (1992 and 1994) shows interesting results. First, important progress has been accomplished in the evolution of at-risk behaviors. The social representation of the male condom has evolved positively from 1992 to 1994. The proportion of respondents who indicate no more than one reservation about condom use (such as "it is complicated to use" or "it is a limitation to sexual pleasure") has increased from 31.5% to 40.6%. This increase is more important among those persons who declare to have actually used condoms during the preceding year and among those who had used it previously. The repetition of the survey underlines the increase in condom use in the previous year (from 21.9% to 26.8%), mainly among young persons aged under 30 (from 30.1% to 47.6% among women and 48.8% to 63.1% among men), the unmarried (43.8% to 61.4% for women and 60.6% to 81.6% for the men) and those who have had more than one sexual partner during the preceding year (from 58.3% to 75.6%). This increase is in agreement with the change in use of condoms during first sexual intercourse. In 1994, 40.5% of men and 41.3% of women under 30 years of age reported the use of a condom during their first sexual intercourse as compared with as few as 3.2% and 5.9% respectively among the older persons interviewed. The multifactorial analysis undertaken on these data suggests the possible influence of prevention campaigns on these evolutions, even if such changes could have occurred in the absence of any specific prevention campaign (Table 3). Apart from the use of condoms during first sexual intercourse and the number of sexual partners, which is the stronger determinant for condom use, the concern engendered by HIV/AIDS campaigns and the fear of AIDS for oneself are of statistical importance. However, the main limitation of this observation is that it will remain impossible to know if the reported interest in AIDS-prevention campaigns influenced condom use or if the reverse happened.

This survey also underlines the important variability in the strategies adopted by individuals confronted by the development of the AIDS epidemic. Of special importance is the decrease, from 1992 to 1994, of sexual multipartnership (from 20.7% to 15.9% among men and from 9.1% to 6.3% among women). This decrease appears to be of particular importance among middle-class and upper-class men (from 18.9% to 9.9%).

Table 2 *KABP and PR Surveys in France*

	KAPB	PR
1987	Paris	
1990	National	
	N = 1,000	
1992	National	National
	N = 1,927	N = 20,055
1994	National	National
	N = 1,501	N = 1,501

One possible explanation for this phenomenon could be that some men who live in stable couples but have opportunities for sexual encounters have, as a consequence of the AIDS epidemic, reduced their number of extramarital sexual relations.

During the same time, the impact of prevention campaigns seems to have dramatically increased. The proportion of those who declared not feeling themselves concerned by these campaigns fell from 42.5% in 1992 to 25.2% in 1994. On the other hand, there is an increase in those who think that everybody can be HIV infected, including themselves (from 80.2% in 1992 to 86.2% in 1994), or those who think that they actually could be infected (from 24.3% to 42.5%). These results must be compared with the actual epidemiological situation of the persons in the survey: only 8.2% of the studied persons in 1994 are potentially at risk of being infected, as a result of different situations which have occurred since 1980; i.e., men having had sex with men (3.4%), with a drug addict (3.4%), with a person originating from a high prevalence country such as Subsaharan Africa or the Caribbean (4.5%), or men who are intravenous drug users (0.3%). If one adds heterosexual multipartnership to these situations, the total (and actually overestimated) percentage of potentially at-risk persons amounts to 16.1% of the total population.

The discrepancy between self-at-risk perceptions by the individuals and their actual situations results in an increased demand from the general population for social control of HIV dissemination. This becomes particularly evident when considering the population attitudes toward compulsory HIV blood testing, illustrated in Table 4.

So there seems to exist, at the same time in the same population, a double dynamic: an increased concern of the individuals for their own risks

Table 3 *Determinants of Condom Use (1 year), Heterosexual Active Population, France, 1994*

Independent Variables	Men OR*	Women OR
Age < 30 years	1.30	1.44(a)
Number of sex partners >1 (1 year)	2.55(b)	2.79(c)
Feel personally concerned by AIDS campaigns	2.18(b)	1.58
Fear of AIDS for oneself	1.26(a)	1.25(a)
Used condom at first sexual intercourse	2.24(c)	1.04

(a) $p < 0.05$. (b) $p < 0.01$. (c) $p < 0.001$.

*Odds Ratio (OR) of having been a condom user during the past year for those having the specified characteristic (less than 30 years of age, more than one sexual partner, ...), as compared to the others, using a conditional logistic model.

and a general concern about those in the population who are supposed to be the vehicles of infection.

The limitations of this approach are self-evident. The observational nature of the survey designs precludes any causal conclusion. Along the years, everything has been modified, including the epidemiology of the disease itself, the social environment and maybe the sexual behavior. Moreover, an important "social-acceptability" effect could be present in these surveys, and this effect could have increased along time.

3. It is also possible to draw valuable information from the repetition of similar surveys in different settings or countries. Such an exceptional opportunity was provided by the completion of two comparable surveys in France and in Britain, almost the same year (May 1990 to December 1991 in Britain, September 1991 to February 1992 in France), according to comparable protocols (Bajos, Wadsworth, Ducot, et al., 1995).

The basic observation is that the cumulative AIDS incidence is 3.3 times higher in France than it is in Britain. The surveys in the two countries used similar sampling frames and questionnaires, the main difference being that the French interviews took place on the phone, whereas the British survey used face-to-face interviews.

The results can be summarized as follows. Very similar results were found for the prevalence of homosexual partnerships (4.1% in France and 3.9% in Britain respectively), the only major difference being the percentage of individuals reporting more than five partners in a lifetime: 37% of French men compared with 22% in Britain. However, French men who had a homosexual partner in the last year were more likely to have used a

Table 4 *Opinions Concerning HIV Blood Testing, France, 1992–1994*

Should Be Mandatory for These Groups	1992 (%)	1994 (%)	Difference (%)
Prostitutes	94	92	—
Intravenous drug users	91	92	—
Pregnant women	89	93	+4.1
Couples before marriage	80	84	+4.4
Prisoners	76	83	+6.2
Hospitalized persons	75	78	—
Physicians	73	85	+8.8
Foreigners	67	68	—
Soldiers	74	74	—
All population	56	56	—

condom at least once in that time than British men (68.1% versus 58.3%). Anal intercourse and sex with prostitutes were more frequent among heterosexual French people than British people. Condom use among heterosexuals was more systematic in Britain than in France.

So only small differences were found between the two countries, although the prevalence of risk indicators was higher in France. These differences, combined with an early development of prevention policies in Britain together with the timing of virus introduction, may contribute to differences between the epidemics in the two countries.

This example is not, strictly speaking, a repetition of the same survey. However, a rather close collaboration took place between the two research groups while designing the national surveys. It is interesting to note the discrepancy between the large difference between the two countries concerning the epidemiological data, especially the cumulative incidence rates, and the small differences demonstrated by the comparison of the two sexual behavior surveys.

4. In the United States, Catania et al. (in press) were able to perform the National AIDS Behavioral Surveys (NABS) the first time in June 1990–February 1991 and the second time in January to August 1992 on the same individuals and using the same interviewing procedure. They had a total sample of 4,548 subjects, who were interviewed twice. They noted a little reduction in the overall prevalence of various HIV/STDs sexual risk factors in the National or High Risk Cities cohorts over time. However, despite this apparent picture of stability, a small core of respondents main-

tained an at-risk status over approximately one year, and those reducing risk (39% of multiple partners for instance) were essentially replaced by "new" at-risk individuals. There was little change in HIV test seeking or consistent condom use with primary sexual partners. Although the majority of at-risk respondents use condoms sporadically or not at all (65%), the researchers did find a significant increase in condom use among those reporting multiple sexual partners in both waves, particularly among black heterosexuals. Data from other surveys and on condom sales nationally lend support to these findings. However, considering the difficulties of these kinds of studies, which have already been stressed, the reliability of these findings needs to be confirmed by other sources, including a regular monitoring of how the general U.S. population is responding to HIV and other STD prevention.

Conclusion

The evaluation of the efficacy of AIDS-prevention campaigns is indeed a very difficult task to perform. A brief overview of the available designs and of their drawbacks clearly indicates that more theoretical research is badly needed in this field. However, with considerable caution, the pooling of information coming from repeated population surveys can be one tool of this evaluation process. Its conclusions must be analyzed taking into account all the modifications which occurred, both in the epidemiological and sociologic context, and the analysis should consider not only the consequences but also the process of change.

References

ACSF. (1992). A comparison between two modes of investigation: Telephone survey and face-to-face survey. *AIDS, 6,* 315–323.
American Journal of Epidemiology. (1995). *142,* 567–599.
Bajos, N., Wadsworth, J., Ducot, B., et al. (1995). Sexual behaviour and HIV epidemiology: Comparative analysis in France and Britain. *AIDS, 9,* 735–743.
Catania, J. A., Binson, D., Dolcini, M. M., et al. (1995). Changes in HIV/STD risk factors and prevention practices among heterosexual adults in the United States. *American Journal of Public Health, 85,* 1492–1499.
Connor, E. W., Sperling, R. S., Gelber, R., et al. (1994). Reduction of maternal-infant transmission of human immunodeficiency virus type 1 with zidovudine treatment. *New England Journal of Medicine, 331,* 1173–1180.
Grosskurth, H., Mosha, F., Todd, J., et al. (1996). Impact of improved treatment of sexually transmitted diseases on HIV infection in rural Tanzania: Randomised controlled trial. *Lancet, 346,* 530–536.
Moatti, J. P., Grémy, I., Obadia, Y., et al. (1995). Sida: Dernière enquête nationale. *Recherche, 282,* 30–35.

Methodological Problems in Trend Analysis of Sexual Behavior

FRANÇOISE DUBOIS-ARBER, B. SPENCER, AND A. JEANNIN

The AIDS epidemic has triggered renewed interest in the study of sexual behavior, stimulating a need to describe and understand human sexual conduct. Several approaches have been used:

- Ethnographic or psychological studies oriented toward an in-depth understanding of the contemporary meaning of sexuality (Henriksson, 1995; Parker, 1994; Peto et al., 1992; Prieur, 1990; Standing, 1992). Generally, these apply to a specific moment in time.
- National population surveys on sexual behavior, using a more sociological approach and attempting to describe the structure and organization of human sexuality at a defined point in time (Hubert & Marquet, 1993; Laumann et al., 1994; Spira et al., 1994; Wellings et al., 1994). They are generally conceived as cross-sectional, mainly for cost reasons, although repetition is sometimes contemplated.
- National population behavioral surveys (KABP-type) with a more epidemiological approach and public health purpose, mainly restricted to AIDS-related aspects of sexual behavior and often aimed at the early evaluation of prevention measures (Agence Nationale de Recherche sur le SIDA, 1992; Bochow et al., 1994; Bundeszentrale für Gesundheitliche Aufklärung, 1993; Caraël et al., 1995; Catania et al., 1992; De Vroome et al., 1990; Dubois-Arber et al., 1996; Herlitz, 1993; Leigh et al., 1993; McQueen & Uitenbroek, 1992; Robertson, 1995). These have to be repeated regularly in order to conduct trend analysis. Such studies are sometimes criticized for having an overrestrictive and oversimplified view of sexuality. Nonetheless, the issues raised are similar to those addressed in other approaches to sexuality. Such research is complementary to the wider approaches and is of considerable value, providing sufficient thought is given to the quality and interpretation of the data.

Methodological reflection in AIDS behavioral research has been centered mainly on problems related to cross-sectional surveys (ACSF Investigators, 1992; Catania et al., 1990). The purpose of this paper is to present and discuss problems related to trend analysis of sexual behavior, using illustrations from data collected over eight years in repeated surveys conducted to evaluate the Swiss AIDS prevention program (Dubois-Arber et al., 1997).

A baseline telephone KABP-type survey of the general population, aged between 17 and 30 years and living in Switzerland, was first carried out in January 1987, prior to the launch of the first national AIDS campaign. From October 1987 to October 1992, the same survey was repeated, first annually, then biennially (a total of eight consecutive surveys). In 1987 and 1988, the samples included 1,200 persons from the two main linguistic areas (German and French) of Switzerland. The size of the sample has since doubled, with the inclusion in 1989 of the 31–45-year-olds and the further inclusion in 1991 of the Italian-speaking area of the country. The total sample is now 2,800. The sampling technique, the method of data collection (telephone interview conducted by the same agency each year), and the core questionnaire used (wording and sequence of the questions) have remained constant.

Indicators of Sexual Behavior

Public health relevance and evaluation needs were the main requirements for the inclusion of items in the questionnaire. We selected indicators of sexual activity, of potential exposure to risk of HIV transmission, and of condom use in these situations. Low threshold indicators of potential exposure to risk were chosen in order to include all people who, at least once during the survey periods, were in the situation of having to think about AIDS prevention and to take action accordingly (Table 1).

The choice of indicators, in common with most surveys conducted early in the epidemic, was based on models of behavior centered on the individual. This approach has its limitations, since it does not adequately take into account either the environmental context (cultural, social) or the interactional nature of the sexual relationship (structure of the dyad, where sexual interaction takes place, communication, etc.; see Ahlemeyer, 1995; Bajos et al., 1997; Laumann & Gagnon, 1995; Lear, 1995; Peto et al., 1992). It is, however, relatively cheap and simple to implement and relies on well-established statistical knowledge.

The indicators adopted had to be both valid and reliable. Validity was desired both from an epidemiological point of view and in terms of meaning. In other words, indicators should focus on behavior having a clear relationship with the risk of HIV infection. The meaning of questions used as indicators should be unambiguous and the same for all respondents. The questions should also relate to the objectives fixed in prevention programs. In the case of Switzerland, this is condom use: since 1987 the message has been to use condoms in all situations except in the case of a monogamous relationship between two HIV-negative partners who have been tested an appropriate period of time after the start of the relationship. HIV testing

Table 1 *Main Indicators of Sexual Behavior in Swiss Survey*

1. **Sexual activity**
   Lifetime number of partners
   Frequency of sexual intercourse over last seven days

2. **Exposure to potential risk of HIV transmission**
   Number of casual partners in last six months
   Change of or new regular partner in current year (study conducted in October)
   Contact with prostitutes in the last six months (men only)
   Lifetime homosexual contacts (men only)

3. **Protection**
   Condom use with casual partners in the last six months
   Condom use with new steady partner in current year
   Condom use during last intercourse

4. **Possible undesired side-effects of condom promotion**
   Earlier sexual debut: proportion of persons sexually active at age 17

has not been explicitly advocated; neither has a reduction in the number of partners nor a delay in the sexual debut of young people.

The validity of indicators used was checked through interviews designed to ascertain the perceived meaning of terms used in the survey questionnaire. This qualitative study, conducted in 1992, was conducted among the younger part of the survey population (17–22 years; see Jeannin et al., 1994a). For example, the terms *steady* and *casual partners* were found to be generally understood as primary and secondary partners, thus corresponding to what they were intended to measure. On the other hand, the term *to sleep with* (in French, *coucher avec*) had a different meaning for men and women: men were more likely than women to include nonpenetrative sex in the definition.

The reliability of indicators was checked in 1992 using a test-retest procedure, interviews being repeated after six to eight weeks with a subsample of the population. Reliability was good at the individual level. A certain level of change must be expected with individuals, so identical results should not be expected on retest: for example, in the lapse of time between tests, relationships may start or finish. At the population level, the level used to monitor trends, reliability proved to be excellent (Dubois-Arber et al., 1995).

Several cross-checks (comparison with other studies performed at the same time, using the same indicators but other methods of data collection) also allowed assessment of the validity and reliability of the method used. For example, in 1992, using a cluster sample of schools and a self-administered questionnaire, a health survey of Swiss adolescents found similar proportions of behaviors with potential exposure to HIV infection and almost identical levels of protection (Narring et al., 1994).

Bias was also assessed on precise questions. For example, systematic gender differences in number of partners as well as in condom use were found in our surveys, as in many other studies already cited, and the explanations generally suggested (Wellings et al., 1994, pp. 101–102), such as sampling bias, reporting bias, and age differential in couples, may also apply in this case. However, although men reported significantly more condom use than women at last intercourse, no significant difference in rate of condom use during last intercourse was observed in the subsample of men and women living in a stable and faithful relationship and reporting condom use as a means of contraception—a situation where one would expect to find the same proportion for men and women if gender-related reporting bias is not present (Dubois-Arber et al., 1996).

Social desirability—i.e., the propensity to give "expected" answers in a context of intense social pressure toward condom use, for example—was not initially assessed, since it was thought that although it could affect the point values (overestimation of the proportion of condom users, for example) it would not affect the trend. We shall return to this problem.

Trend Analysis

Problems Related to Validity

Significant levels of behavioral change have been obtained in terms of condom use in Switzerland between 1987 and 1994 (Figure 1), but no major changes have occurred regarding sexual activity per se (i.e., number of casual partners and frequency of sexual intercourse). The same may be said regarding the prevalence of behavior with a potential risk of HIV transmission, that is, those situations requiring use of condoms (Table 2; Dubois-Arber et al., 1997).

The first question in terms of validity concerns the observed changes or the observed absence of changes: is the observed trend real? In the case of condom use, a simple triangulation with another source of data, i.e., condom sales, can help to answer the question: condom sales did increase in Switzerland during the period (from 7.6 million items in 1986 to 16 million in 1994). However, such triangulation is not always possible, and more subtle issues must then be addressed.

IS THE INDICATOR STILL MEASURING THE SAME PHENOMENON?

First, questions repeated each year are intended to be constant indicators, but does a question worded in the same way each year retain the same

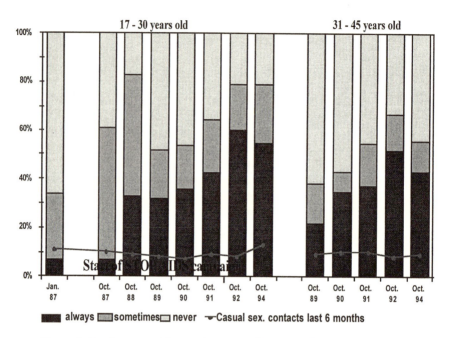

Figure 1. Condom use with casual partners (last 6 months), 1987–1994.

meaning? If the question is held constant but the social context changes, might the indicator still be considered stable? For example, does the term *sexual relationship* or *partner* have the same meaning throughout the years and throughout the population? We have seen that there was a gender difference among young people regarding the meaning of *sleeping with someone*, but this difference may change. We have not yet repeated the complementary qualitative study which would enable us to explore that. Were we to do so, after what interval of time would it be necessary to repeat it? What is meant by *partner* may also be subject to change: what is a steady/primary partner, what are casual partners? For example, are prostitutes included/not included in the same way across time when counting the number of casual partners?

The style, both vocabulary and grammar, used in the wording of the question may influence the speed at which the item will age and lose relevance (this might be called item obsolescence). One may suppose that "colloquial wording" will age faster than "classical wording." This poses the problem of a trade-off between the use of colloquial wording and the use of more academic wording. The former increases current understanding at the expense of future relevance; the latter increases life expectancy of items at the expense of present relevance.

More generally, the concept of *sexual behavior* or *sexuality* may hold different meanings across time and societies (Gagnon, 1995; see also the

Table 2 Indicators of Potential Exposure to Risk of HIV Infection, General Population, 17-30-Year-Olds, Switzerland, 1987-1994 (%)

Category 17-30	January 87 N=1182	October 87 N=1211	October 88 N=1213	October 89 N=1231	October 90 N=1227	October 91 N=1426	October 92 N=1427	October 94 N=1378	P-Value[e]
New steady partner[a]									
17-30			20 ± 2	15 ± 2	17 ± 2	14 ± 2	15 ± 2	14 ± 2	.000
One or more casual partners[b]									
17-30	18 ± 2	14 ± 2	15 ± 2	15 ± 2	12 ± 2	15 ± 2	14 ± 2	13 ± 2	.003
Contact with prostitutes[b,d]									
17-30	2 ± 1	1 ± .6	1 ± .6	2 ± 1	2 ± 1	3 ± 1	2 ± 1	2 ± 1	.160
Homosexual contacts[c,d]									
17-30	3 ± 1	3 ± 1	2 ± 1	4 ± 1	6 ± 1	5 ± 2	4 ± 1	3 ± 1	.245

(a) During the year   (b) During the previous 6 months   (c) During their lifetime
(d) Men only   (e) χ^2 for trend

chapters by Sabogal et al. and Carballo-Diéguez in this book), as well as between researchers (Giami, 1991) in different periods: the Kinsey studies in the United States after World War II, the study of Simon in France at the beginning of the 1970s, and the recent studies in the U.K. and France are at least partly time-dependent in their use of concepts. These differences clearly appear when comparing these studies made at different periods (they were performed at intervals of around two decades) in different places. Just as responses are subject to the impact of changing social desirability, so too is the formulation of questions and response items (Spira, Bajos, & the ACSF Group, 1994, p. 48). The influence of prevailing social mores is apparent in the questionnaires of previous generations. It has been noted how in 1970 the choice of suggested responses concerning the respondents' feelings toward their first sexual intercourse before marriage is formulated in terms of regret. In the same way, future observers may be able to identify some of our questions as reflecting the norms of our time, to which we are currently blind. They may, for example, wonder what led their colleagues in France investigating place of last sexual intercourse in 1991 to attribute one of a limited number of response items to the category "in an elevator"!

The necessity to take into account more subtle shifts in meaning may be obscured in the case of cross-sectional surveys which are repeated more frequently, with the same methodology and within a shorter total time frame.

Second, are most of the changes in the social context surrounding sexuality captured across time when using very broad indicators of individual sexual behavior, such as those chosen? This question arises particularly when looking at trends in indicators of behavior which exhibited little change during the period of observation, i.e., those chosen to measure sexual activity and potential exposure to risk (number and nature of partners over defined period of time, frequency of intercourse). What does this stability mean in terms of population? What may it hide? Qualitative research conducted in different countries has shown how the diverse understanding of sexuality across different individuals and social strata, coupled with the importance of AIDS over the last 10 years, is shaping the way sexuality is thought and experienced (Ford, 1994; Peto, 1992; Pollack, 1988). These alleged changes are said to take place in the interaction (real or perceived) between sexual partners: fear, suspicion, confidence, caution, negotiation, tacit or explicit agreement, etc. Are these characteristics of the interactions really more frequent or just more often cited because of AIDS (reporting bias)? On the other hand, if these changes in the quality of interaction have indeed occurred (e.g., an increase in fear, a decrease in confidence) we would be unable to demonstrate this, since most of these in-depth qualitative studies have not been repeated and give at best a retrospective/reconstructed view of change.

Other studies have also shown how the social discourse regarding sexuality (in the media, in schools, etc.; Savier, Brun, Dezalay, & Loignon, 1992) has recently undergone modification under the pressure of the AIDS epidemic (Kirp & Bayer, 1992). To illustrate, one qualitative study in Switzerland, which was able to be repeated (Weber-Jobé, 1988, 1994), used reports from school sex educators on children's and pre-adolescents' questions on sexuality and AIDS. It was possible to identify interesting qualitative changes in ways of speaking about sexuality. For example, in the later study it was noted that pre-adolescents tended to ask direct questions about sexual practices (e.g., anal and oral sex) or sexual orientation and more precise questions about the limits of safer sex, which was not the case in the earlier study. The AIDS problem legitimated the raising of specific themes, such as homosexuality. These changes may also deeply affect the way sexuality is experienced, but they are not reflected in our indicators.

Third, have changes in the social context surrounding sexuality had a quantitative influence on sexual activity, which we then fail to capture or to interpret correctly by keeping the same set of indicators? Let's take two examples.

1. Faithfulness and reflection before engaging in a new sexual relationship have been largely discussed and/or advocated since the advent of AIDS, but the indicators existing in the repeated studies in Switzerland focus on lifetime number of partners and occurrence of new stable partners. Duration of partnerships or duration of periods without any partner—not included in our set of indicators—may be more accurate indicators of changes resulting from this type of influence.

2. HIV testing has not been specifically promoted as an element of prevention management in Switzerland. Nevertheless, Switzerland has become one of the countries with the highest proportion of tested people, either through voluntary testing or blood donation: 47% of people 17–45 years (Jeannin, Dubois-Arber, & Paccaud, 1994). HIV testing may be increasingly included in individual AIDS risk management, especially at the beginning of new sexual partnerships, in a sequence "condom use during several months—test—give up condom use." This may influence the trend in condom use, particularly the trend of the indicator "condom use during last intercourse" and raises the question of the interpretation of a possible observed decrease of use in this situation.

New indicators capturing these "new" social practices may be needed in the core questionnaire to increase the accuracy of the interpretation of trends in sexual behavior.

Fourth, does social desirability have its own trend? Social desirability is usually measured in individuals in cross-sectional studies in order to evaluate its influence on reported data (Bradburn, 1983). The propensity to give expected (socially desirable) answers is not only individually but also socially shaped and may evolve. In an environment in which in-

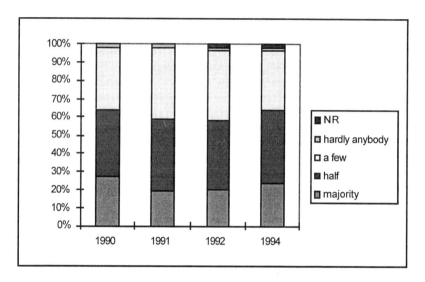

Figure 2. Changes in answer to a question about social desirability of condom use: "In your opinion, how many people in Switzerland use condoms when they have casual sex?" (Switzerland, 17–45 years, 1990–1994).

creased place is given to condom promotion, increased social desirability of condom use is likely. Increased reporting of use, owing to increased social desirability, may precede, replace, or inflate reported actual use. The relationship between reported use and actual use may not be constant. A question attempting to measure this possible evolution of social desirability, by asking what people think about the behavior of the population regarding condom use, was introduced in the survey in 1990 (Figure 2). No significant change was observed between 1990 and 1994. However, condom use also remained stable during this period. The important change had occurred earlier (Figure 1) and was not captured by this late introduction of the question to measure the social desirability of condom use.

Fifth, does the social acceptability of certain types of sexual behavior have its own trend (leading to declaration bias and/or differentials in nonresponse rate)? The AIDS epidemic has increased the visibility of themes such as homosexuality, prostitution, and drug use and partly increased their social acceptability. This may have an influence on trends by changing the nonresponse rate to certain questions (acceptability of the question itself) and/or by modifying the proportion between the yes and the no (acceptability of the disclosure of the "real answer").

In our repeated surveys, there is evidence of changes in the rate of nonresponse for several questions. The rate of nonresponse to the question about lifetime occurrence of homosexual contact among men aged 17–30 years decreased from 15.4 in 1987 to 0.4 in 1994. This was replaced to a very small extent by an increase in the rate of positive response (3.2% in

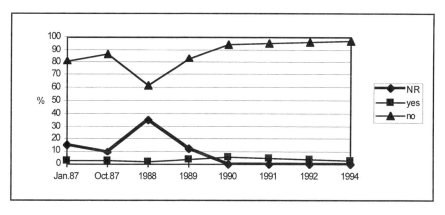

Figure 3. Frequency of nonresponse (NR) and of positive and negative responses regarding lifetime occurrence of homosexual contacts, men 17–30 years, 1987–1994.

1987, 2.8% in 1994; min. 2.1 in 1988 max. 5.6 in 1990; Figure 3) and to a larger extent by an increase in negative response. The same level of change in the rate of nonresponse is seen for the question about male lifetime contact with prostitutes. In this case, however, the increase in positive response seems more clearly related to the decrease in nonresponse (Figure 4). This illustrates how the nonresponse population may either contain a large proportion of those having the marginal behavior or may simply be a reflection of the results of the population as a whole.

Problems Related to Reliability

There is no clear definition of what could be the transposition of the concept of reliability of a single measure to a series of measures. However, we shall retain the term *reliability* to describe phenomena in trend analysis which are similar in nature to those encountered in single measures. Here we are mainly confronted with two types of problem.

(APPARENTLY) "TECHNICAL" PROBLEMS DEALING MAINLY WITH SAMPLE SIZE (PROBLEMS OF STATISTICAL POWER)

Is the trend, or more frequently the absence of trend, real? The relatively modest size of the samples in our repeated surveys allows us to detect changes that are of considerable size, occur over a short period of time, are constant in direction, and affect the whole population. The detection of changes occurring in subsamples of the population may be important in terms of understanding the dynamics of change (for example, changes in behavior among young people which occur earlier than for other generations). However, some changes may be impossible to detect or may remain "unconfirmed" for a long time—see, for example, the change in the number of partners for young people illustrated in Table 3.

No differences in the direction of trends were observed in our surveys

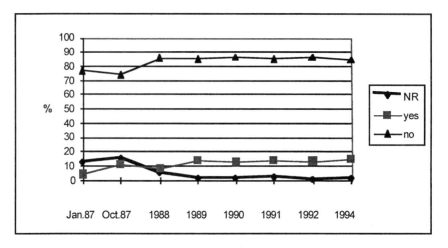

Figure 4. Frequency of nonresponse (NR) and of positive and negative responses regarding lifetime contact with prostitutes, men 17–30 years, 1987–1994.

as regards age, gender, level of education, or linguistic region. However, secondary trends occurring in opposite directions in different subpopulations may be confused with stability at the aggregate level and have to be systematically checked for. These problems point to decisions to be made either at the beginning of a series of surveys or after several years.

Regarding what we actually want to detect, we need to know at the beginning what makes sense (which change, during which period of time, and at what level) and what is the purpose of the study. This is particularly important if we are in an evaluation situation. For example, in Switzerland we have data on age at first intercourse only since 1990 and we lack data on total number of sexual partners over the recent past because, as stated previously, these issues (detection of earlier first intercourse as a secondary effect of wider sex education and condom promotion, detection of decrease in the actual number of sexual partners) did not directly relate to the prevention messages used in campaigns and were not perceived as serious potential problems to be dealt with at the beginning of the implementation of the AIDS prevention strategy. There are limits on the size of the questionnaire, and we had to make choices. These matters only became of interest afterward. It is difficult to predict which type of data will be called for in the future. Very often decisions have to be made rapidly, and intensive validation and pretesting are not possible. We also need information regarding the cost-benefit relationship of increasing samples, or of oversampling certain parts of the population.

After several years, decisions must be made regarding the cost-benefit relationship of changing something in the methodology of the survey, es-

Table 3 Lifetime Number of Partners, 17–20 Years Old, Switzerland, 1987–1994 (%)

N partner	January 1987	October 1987	October 1988	October 1989	October 1990	October 1991	October 1992	October 1994
	N = 344	N = 353	N = 353	N = 428	N = 422	N = 484	N = 492	N = 328
0 part	34 ± 5	32 ± 5	32 ± 5	32 ± 4	32 ± 4	30 ± 4	35 ± 4	34 ± 5
1 part	20 ± 4	22 ± 4	23 ± 4	30 ± 4	26 ± 4	25 ± 4	24 ± 4	27 ± 5
2 part	10 ± 3	11 ± 3	13 ± 3	10 ± 3	10 ± 3	14 ± 3	11 ± 3	14 ± 4
3+ part	33 ± 5	26 ± 5	31 ± 5	26 ± 4	25 ± 4	27 ± 4	29 ± 4	25 ± 5
Nonresponse	3	9	1	2	7	4	1	0

χ^2 for trend: p = .009

pecially concerning the addition, modification, or removal of questions (see the chapter by Catania et al. in this book concerning the effect of changes in the wording of a question to enhance "honest" answers), but also concerning the mode of administration of the questionnaire (see the chapter by Turner et al. in this book concerning the effect of the introduction of new survey methodologies such as audio-CASI on answers to potentially embarrassing questions, such as the practice of anal intercourse).

RELIABILITY OF THE TREND FROM A HISTORICAL POINT OF VIEW
(SHORT-TERM TREND INCLUDED IN A LONG-TERM TREND)

Is an observed trend or absence of trend correctly interpreted? Failure to view an observed trend within a sufficiently long time perspective may lead to errors of interpretation. For example, a trend is observed toward a decrease in the frequency of a phenomenon (see Figure 5). However, study of the progress of the phenomenon over a longer time period may reveal that in the years prior to the set of observations there had been a much more marked secular trend in the decrease of the phenomenon. It then becomes apparent that there has in fact been a slowing down in the decrease of this slope during the period at question. This is a classic example in public health, when observed reduction in the incidence of or the mortality due to a disease is attributed to a given intervention, although this reduction may have begun prior to the intervention and not been influenced by the intervention. A classic example is the case of the temporal relationship between the decrease in mortality due to whooping cough and the introduction of vaccination as observed by McKeown (1974, p. 97); most of the decrease occurred before the intervention (as in the curve *e* of Figure 5).

An example of this "contextualization" of a short-term trend can be drawn from our repeated surveys. A trend was observed between 1987 and 1994 (Figure 6) towards a decrease of the proportion of young people sexually active at age 17. A secondary analysis of studies conducted between 1971 and 1993 on the sexual behavior of Swiss adolescents (Koffi-Blanchard, Dubois-Arber, Michaud, Narring, & Paccaud, 1994) showed that this decrease had to be interpreted in the context of a long-term trend toward an increase in the proportion of adolescents sexually active at 17 years (also observed in the United States by the Centers for Disease Control and Prevention, 1991). This long-term trend had indeed already been reversed by the end of the 1980s when the AIDS prevention campaigns (and the surveys) began (as in the curve *d* of Figure 5). This situation will, of course, need to be reviewed in the coming years, but these findings made it clear that widespread sex education and condom promotion did not increase the level of sexual activity in adolescents, as had been suggested by certain groups.

Unfortunately, data that allow us to interpret a short-term trend in a

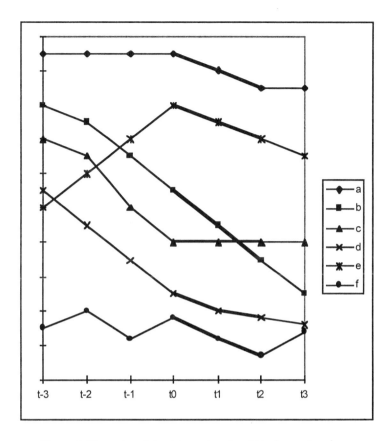

Figure 5. Examples of short-term trends within longer trends.

broader temporal context are frequently not available or are simply not sought out, depending on the interests at stake.

The study of trends in sexual behavior, despite or because of its many uncertainties, poses deep-rooted methodological challenges. It is also essential for the purposes of policy evaluation. It would seem that the instruments at our disposal are not always sufficiently refined to detect subtle changes which may have implications for prevention policy. Whereas adjustments may be made on technical issues, it is not clear how one might adjust indicators to take account of changes in meaning occurring over time. Certain limitations may be overcome by using additional complementary approaches (qualitative, for example) that should also be conceived in terms of trends, i.e., that have to be repeated at appropriate intervals of time. In our eyes, trend studies should be continued, even using a limited

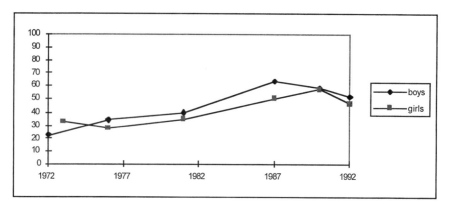

Figure 6. Proportion of 17-year-olds who are sexually active, Switzerland 1972–1992, selected studies.

set of indicators, provided that continuous reflection is conducted about the choice, validity and reliability of these indicators over time.

References

ACSF Investigators. (1992). Analysis of sexual behaviour in France (ACSF): A comparison between two modes of investigation: Telephone survey and face-to-face survey. *AIDS, 6,* 315–323.

Agence Nationale de Recherche sur le SIDA. (1992). *Evaluer la prévention du SIDA en France: Un inventaire des donnés disponibles.* Paris: Agence Nationale de Recherche sur le SIDA, Agence Française de Lutte Contre le SIDA.

Ahlemeyer, H. W. (1995). Heterosexual behaviour and AIDS prevention: The impact of communication. In D. Friedrich & W. Heckmann (Eds.), *AIDS in Europe: The behavioural aspects, Vol. 4.* Berlin: Sigma.

Bajos, N., Ducot, B., Spencer, B., Spira, A., & ACSF Group. (1997). Sexual risk taking, socio-sexual biographies, and sexual interaction: Elements of the French national survey on sexual behaviour. *Social Science and Medicine, 44,* 25–40.

Bochow, M., Chiarotti, F., Davies, P., Dubois-Arber, F., Dürr, W., Fouchard, J., et al. (1994). Sexual behaviour of gay and bisexual men in eight European countries. *AIDS Care, 6,* 533–549.

Bradburn, N. (1983). Response effects. In P. H. Rossi, J. D. Wright, & A. B. Anderson (Eds.), *Handbook of survey research.* New York: Academic Press.

Bundeszentrale für Gesundheitliche Aufklärung. (1993). *AIDS im öffentlichen Bewusstsein der Bundesrepublik.* Köln: BGA.

Caraël, M., Cleland, J., Deheneffe, J. C., Ferry, B., & Ingham, R. (1995). Sexual behaviour in developing countries: Implications for HIV control. *AIDS, 9,* 1171–1175.

Catania, J. A., Gibson, D. R., Chitwood, D. D., & Coates, T. J. (1990). Methodological problems in AIDS behavioral research: Influences on measurement error and participation bias in studies in sexual behavior. *Psychological Bulletin, 108,* 339–362.

Catania, J. A., Coates, T. J., Stall, R., Turner, H., Peterson, J., Hearst, N., et al. (1992). Prevalence of AIDS-related risk factors and condom use in the United States. *Science, 258,* 1101–1106.

Centers for Disease Control and Prevention. (1991). Premarital sexual experience among adolescent women, United States, 1970–1988. *Morbidity and Mortality Weekly Reports, 39,* 929–932.

De Vroome, E. M. M., Paalman, M. E. M., & Sandfort, T. G. M. (1990). AIDS in the Netherlands: The effects of several years of campaigning. *International Journal of STD & AIDS, 1,* 268–275.

Dubois-Arber, F., Jeannin, A., & Konings, E. (1995). Evaluation of the Swiss AIDS prevention strategy: Establishing a system of indicators allowing the monitoring of activities and the assessment of results. In D. Friedrich & W. Heckmann (Eds.), *AIDS in Europe: The behavioural aspects, Vol. 4.* Berlin: Sigma.

Dubois-Arber, F., Jeannin, A., Meystre-Agustoni, G., Moreau-Gruet, F., Haour-Knipe, M., Spencer, B., & Paccaud, F. (1996). *Evaluation of the AIDS prevention strategy in Switzerland: Fifth assessment report 1993–1995.* Lausanne, Switzerland: Institut Universitaire de Médecine Sociale et Préventive (Cah Rech Doc IUMSP, no. 120b).

Dubois-Arber, F., Jeannin, A., Konings, E., & Paccaud, F. (1997). Increased condom use without other major changes in sexual behavior among the general population in Switzerland. *American Journal of Public Health, 87*(4), 558–566.

Ford, N.J., & Kittisuksathit, S. (1994). Destinations unknown: The gender construction and changing nature of the sexual expressions of Thai youth. *AIDS Care, 5,* 517–531.

Gagnon, J. H., & Parker, R. G. (1995). Conceiving sexuality. In R. G. Parker & J. H. Gagnon (Eds.), *Conceiving sexuality: Approaches to sex research in a postmodern world.* New York: Routledge.

Giami, A. (1991). De Kinsey au Sida: L'évolution de la construction du comportement sexuel dans les enquêtes quantitatives. *Sciences Sociales et Santé, 4,* 23–55.

Henriksson, B. (1995). Risk factor love: The symbolic meaning of sexuality and HIV prevention. In D. Friedrich & W. Heckmann (Eds.), *AIDS in Europe: The behavioural aspects, Vol. 2,* pp. 115–131. Berlin: Sigma.

Herlitz, C. (1993). Sexual behaviour in the general population of Sweden. *Social Science and Medicine, 36,* 1535–1540.

Hubert, M., & Marquet, J. (1993). *Comportements sexuels et réactions au risque du SIDA en Belgique: Rapport.* Brussels: Commission des Communautés Européennes (DG-V).

Jeannin, A., Dubois-Arber, F., Konings, E., & Hausser, D. (1994a). *Estimation of the impact of inaccuracy in reporting the number of sexual partners and condom use.* Paper presented at the European Conference on Methods and Results of Psychosocial AIDS-Research: AIDS in Europe—The Behavioural Aspect, Berlin.

Jeannin, A., Dubois-Arber, F., & Paccaud, F. (1994b). HIV testing in Switzerland. *AIDS, 8,* 1599–1603.

Kirp, D. L., & Bayer, R. (1992). *AIDS in the industrialized democracies: Passions, politics and policies.* New Brunswick, NJ: Rutgers University Press.

Koffi-Blanchard, M. C., Dubois-Arber, F., Michaud, P. A., Narring, F., & Paccaud, F. (1994). Hat sich der Beginn der Sexualität bei Jugendlichen in der Zeit von Aids verändert? *Schweizerische Medizinische Wochenschrift, 24,* 1047–1055.

Laumann, E. O., Gagnon, J. H., Michael, R. T., & Michaels, S. (1994). *The social organization of sexuality: Sexual practices in the United States.* Chicago: University of Chicago Press.

Laumann, E. O., & Gagnon, J. H. (1995). A sociological perspective on sexual action. In R. G. Parker & J. H. Gagnon (Eds.), *Conceiving sexuality: Approaches to sex research in a postmodern world.* New York: Routledge.

Lear, D. (1995). Sexual communication in the age of AIDS: The construction of risk and trust among young adults. *Social Science and Medicine, 9,* 1311–1323.

Leigh, B.C., Temple, M. T., & Trocki, K. F. (1993). The sexual behavior of US adults: Results from a national survey. *American Journal of Public Health, 83,* 1400–1408.

McKeown, T. (1974). *An introduction to social medicine,* 2nd edition. London: Blackwell Scientific Publications.

McQueen, D., & Uitenbroek, D. (1992). Condom use and concern about AIDS. *Health Education Research,* 7(1), 47–53.

Narring, F., Tschumper, A., Michaud, P. A., Vanetta, F., Meyer, R., Wydler, H., et al. (1994). *La santé des adolescents en Suisse: Rapport d'une enquête nationale sur la santé et les styles de vie des 15–20 ans.* Lausanne, Switzerland: Institut Universitaire de Médecine Sociale et Préventive (Cah Rech Doc IUMSP, no. 113a).

Parker, R. G. (1994). Sexual culture, HIV transmission and AIDS prevention. *AIDS, 8* (Suppl. 1), 309–314.

Peto, D., Rémy, J., Van Campenhoudt, L., & Hubert, M. (1992). *SIDA, l'amour face à la peur. Modes d'adaptation au risque du sida dans les relations hétérosexuelles.* Paris: l'Harmattan.

Pollack, M. (1988). *Les homosexuels et le sida. Sociologie d'une épidémie.* Paris: Métailié.

Prieur, A. (1990). Norwegian gay men: Reasons for continued practice of unsafe sex. *AIDS Education and Prevention, 2,* 109–115.

Robertson, B. J. (1995). Sexual behaviour and risk of exposure to HIV among 18–25-year-olds in Scotland: Assessing change 1988–1993. *AIDS, 9,* 285–292.

Savier, D., Brun, D., Dezalay, L., & Loignon, H. (1992). De l'influence des mentalités sur l'éducation sexuelle au Planning familial de Grenoble. In A. Ruffiot (Ed.), *L'éducation sexuelle au temps du sida.* Toulouse, France: Editions Privat.

Spira, A., Bajos, N., & the ACSF Group. (1994). *Sexual behaviour and AIDS.* Aldershot, England: Avebury.

Standing, H. (1992). AIDS: Conceptual and methodological issues in researching sexual behaviour in Subsaharian Africa. *Social Science and Medicine, 5,* 475–483.

Weber-Jobé, M., de Vargas, D., & Lehmann, P. (1988). *Image des préservatifs.* Lausanne, Switzerland: Institut Universitaire de Médecine Sociale et Préventive (Cah Rech Doc IUMSP, no.39.20).

Weber-Jobé, M., & Piot-Delbos, I. (1994). *Enfance et adolescence face au sida.* Lausanne, Switzerland: Institut Universitaire de Médecine Sociale et Préventive (Cah Rech Doc IUMSP, no.82.10).

Wellings, K., Field, J., Johnson, A. M., & Wadsworth, J. (1994). *Sexual behaviour in Britain.* London: Penguin Books.

Discussion

Barbara Marín: I have a fairly fundamental concern about measurement. If you use the same question over time, there is the potential for that question's meaning to change over time. The same thing can happen if you're using a question in English and a question in Spanish and it turns out that the Spanish version doesn't mean quite the same thing as the English version. You think you're using the same stimulus, but, in fact, you're not. And so if you get differences in the answers, you don't really know if it's because something has changed over time or is different between English- and Spanish-speakers or because the stimulus changed. Do we have any way of resolving that issue?

Françoise Dubois-Arber: There are two points in your comment: one is the difference in stimulus, i.e., in meaning for people between two cultures, and the other is the difference in stimulus/meaning over time within a culture. We can try to resolve both issues by doing relatively frequent qualitative studies in each culture to be sure that we know exactly what is changing (meaning or behavior or both) and then try to make corrections in our interpretation of the trends. You cannot make quantitative corrections of your trends, but at least you can understand what is happening.

Alfred Spira: I think you are completely right. My feeling is that we have to separate these kinds of questions. If you are asking questions about attitudes or beliefs, this is completely right. If you ask questions about using condoms during the last intercourse, I'm not sure that the meaning can really change from one time to the other.

Françoise Dubois-Arber: Yes, I think that it can change. For example, the reporting by women may become more acceptable over the course of time. But, more generally, we should distinguish the meaning of the question for people (that may not change too much in your example) and the meaning of the act itself, the intercourse. For example, the "burden" of the AIDS problem may have been increasingly included into how the act of intercourse is experienced just as the "burden" of the fear of undesired pregnancy may have been progressively excluded from it after the introduction of the pill. This is not captured in our quantitative studies.

Alex Carballo-Diéguez: I think that even with respect to a question as precise as "Are you using condoms?" we may learn more as time goes

213

by. For example, some men say, "Yes, I use condoms, but at the beginning I penetrate without the condom and I put the condom on before ejaculation." So we may ask the question at a time when we have incomplete knowledge and we think that the question covers everything and then we realize that it doesn't.

Charles Turner: I agree with the spirit of the comment, but if you just consider the wording of the question, you may have the word *condom* and typically use a couple of other alternatives, slang terms, to help people along. Those slang terms may change. For example, if you're working with adolescents and you don't use the term that the kids are using at that time, you may get a decline because some of them may not catch what you're saying. So it's those sorts of changes in the meaning that could have an effect.

John Bancroft: Your response, Françoise, was to say that there had been changes in women in preparedness to say that they had used condoms. That is a change in social acceptability rather than in the meaning of the question, presumably. Whereas Alfred was talking about the meaning of the question changing.

Leonore Tiefer: Do you, the woman, put the condom on the man or do they use the condom in the presence of each other? Conceivably, that type of meaning of the question could change over time were it to become more acceptable or widespread that the woman puts the condom on the man.

John Bancroft: The meaning of the term *use* could change.

Anne Johnson: A more general point about measuring change over time. There's quite a lot of pressure now in Britain to do repeat measures of sexual behavior. If we did so, I feel strongly that we should have another round of methodological work. Measures of socially sensitive behaviors can be quite markedly altered by the method you use, as Charles Turner showed yesterday. But if we change and hopefully improve the methodology, it will be more difficult to compare over time and this is potentially a major problem. Or should you force yourself into the position of doing the same survey again, knowing its weaknesses? Comparisons may be straightforward for time trends, but the overall result inaccurate.

Carol Jenkins: There is an interesting, concrete example of the kind of change in repeated surveys that may not be anticipated, although you're picking up change. The Johns Hopkins group have been doing some remarkable work with the Thai army. They've been looking at each cohort of new recruits and they've certainly seen an increase in condom use and then they tried to validate it with actual condom counting in the brothels, asking individuals, "What brothel did you go to?" "What lady?" "What room?" It was peculiar because they were getting more condoms than men reported using. When they went back to some qualitative in-depth interviewing, the reason was that the men were doubling the condoms and that was not anticipated. When you say, "Did you use a condom the last time you went to a brothel?" "Yes, I used five," did not come out.

Charles Turner: In response to Anne's point, if you're thinking about changing methods, clearly there's always a place for careful, qualitative research at a minimum, in preparing for the research endeavor. Ann, your group was interesting in that you actually managed to publish your qualitative research well before the study was done. I found that enormously helpful for some of the work that we were doing at the National Academy of Sciences. But in terms of thinking about either changing or evolving your methods, clearly what you want to do is to treat every data-gathering activity as a methodological enterprise and build experiments into the main study that will give you the answers you need so you can recalibrate the time series. If you switch your mode of administration or your question, you want to take a portion of the sample and do it the "old" way, so that when you're done, you can say, "This is what the old way showed, and this is what the new way showed." That method can give you some idea of what the time series would look like if you had a constant method. In fact, that is what Freya Sonenstein, Leighton Ku, and we did in the adolescent male study. It's not an innovation. There are a lot of people who worry about time series who have been advocating it for a long time. It is a way to be scientific when trying to make your measures better as well as trying to keep your time series intact.

Alain Giami: We assume that some aspects of sexual behavior can change very quickly from one year to the next. If we turn back to history, especially the French historical school, the work of Jean-Louis Flandrin (1981) in particular, ideas and some behaviors change very slowly. Norbert Elias also gave evidence that it took centuries for some slight changes in what he calls the "process of civilization." If we make the comparison over the last 20 years between the two French surveys, the Simon survey (Simon, Gondonneau, Mironer, & Dourlen-Rollier, 1972) and the ACSF, we can also observe very little change. The main change during the last 20 years was an increase in the number of lifetime partners for women, which increased from 1.8 to 3.2. It stabilized for men, so during the last years there was very little change for them. We try to measure change occurring every two years. We observe an increase in the use of condoms. To what extent can we expect to observe change and is it superficial change or is it some deeper change in the way sexuality is experienced? It seems also that most of these questionnaires are constructed based on the assumption that change occurs. When we ask people, "How many partners have you had during your lifetime, in the last five years and during the last year and during the last month," we make an assumption that change is likely to occur. Change is legitimated. Since the emergence of the AIDS crisis, we have not yet analyzed this process. In the 1970s there was the interaction between militant feminists, gynecologists, and the pharmaceutical companies over the question of chemical contraception. At that time, change was constructed as "sexual liberation." Now we are concerned with protecting life. Or protecting what? What is the relevance of "sexual liberation" today? We were speaking yesterday about value-free research. To what extent are we value free?

Françoise Dubois-Arber: I think it's very difficult to predict what will change over time and the speed of such change. It's especially important when you begin with an idea of doing studies of trends over time. As you say, we are confronted with the fact that a few specific things change, such as condom use and perhaps the number of partners. But I'm more and more convinced that what is really changing are these things about meaning and context, things which are extremely difficult to capture. For example, now we see that we have reached a plateau in the frequency of condom use. We may interpret this as a plateau in AIDS risk reduction. But we also know that young people manage risk in very individual ways, with a tendency to abandon using condoms with established partners. Do they do that "correctly," relying on the result of a test performed by both members of the couple, or "incorrectly," relying only on confidence? In the first case, the couple is no longer a condom user but is still maintaining a risk-reduction strategy; in the second, the couple is no longer a condom user but is now exposed to a risk. We didn't ask a question about that at the beginning of our series of surveys, so we can't interpret the plateau adequately in terms of risk reduction. Now we are thinking about introducing new questions in order to capture these things.

Ted Myers: Any difference found may appear to be much greater than it is. Where we see an increase in risk behavior in certain age groups within either a cohort or repeated cross-sectional study, I'm wondering whether we have adequately assessed the effect of dropout (e.g., HIV-positive individuals because of death) or the group effect. If we repeat a study every five years, then we must consider an "age-generational" effect, as we may be dealing with a different generation or group. We do not have good methodology for analyzing trends in repeated cross-sectional studies.

Alfred Spira: I just want to stress again that we're faced with a real and difficult problem, but we should consider the solutions to this problem found by other disciplines. We know that we cannot measure the exact reality. I took this question about condom use during the last act of sexual intercourse as an example. We will never know exactly what happened during all the occasions of intercourse from beginning to end, but we can use what we call, in epidemiology, proxies. Proxies are variables which we think are highly correlated to what happened. When you work on cardiovascular disease and you measure cholesterol over time, we know that the age of the subjects is increasing over time; they are getting older. There are correlates that we can take into account. But I think it's better to try to measure simple things, even if the meaning is not completely clear, than to measure nothing. And my second comment is, of course when I refer to *condom* in our questionnaires we don't only use that word, we say also *präservativ, capote, condom,* or whatever. The interviewers are trained to use different words, and we don't stick to a single, scientific word which has no meaning for the subjects.

Ann Stueve: We're following three cohorts of youngsters at six-month intervals, and one of the things that is reassuring to us is that when we ask youngsters "Have you ever had sexual intercourse, or used cigarettes, or alcohol or a variety of other risk behaviors?" that we're getting fairly consistent answers from one cohort to the next and from one time frame to the next—spring to fall or fall to spring; that's reassuring. But what we're also seeing, and I know others have seen it in their work as well, is that kids change their stories dramatically from one time frame to another, so that the proportion of kids who at baseline say "Yes, I've had sexual intercourse" [but] who subsequently say "No, I've never done it" is equaling our incidence rates. This is happening for a variety of risk behaviors across a variety of domains, and that's a little unnerving when you see youngsters changing their stories to that extent. There's been a lot of work on what we now call "retraction" in the substance-use field that deals with older adolescents and young adults, and we're seeing the very same pattern. So if we look at the aggregate numbers, things are reassuring, but when we start seeing what children, youngsters, are saying to us and how their stories change, it's a little more unnerving, and it doesn't seem to be simply the phenomenon of changed understanding of what sexual intercourse is because we see the same phenomenon happening with "Have you ever smoked a cigarette?" and seventh- and eighth-graders know what cigarettes are. So it's not just an education issue.

Leighton Ku: Because of the things we've been talking about, and certainly whenever there's an intervention campaign, we hope to change people's ideas and the social acceptability of the practices that we're trying to measure. It seems to me, inevitably, we're confounded when we look at repeated surveys. We can't tell what was actual change versus what was changed because of social desirability. An important way of looking at this, which I haven't seen done enough, is trying to link the behavioral measure to external data, such as condom sales, fertility measures, and STD rates. I know in our work, one of the things that's most persuaded me that our measures of the increase in condom use were reasonable was that condom sales went up when the survey data implied they went up and stayed flat when we said they were supposed to stay flat. On the other hand, the disturbing part was that in addition to showing increased overall contraception use by teenagers, teen pregnancy rates went up, too. So there's something not quite lining up there.

John Bancroft: I would like to ask Ulrich Clement to comment. There have been repeated studies of sexual behavior done before HIV and AIDS, and one of the most striking examples of sequential studies was from Germany. I'm not sure how involved you were, Ulrich, but Gunter Schmidt, certainly, looked at teenagers and students and showed changes. In retrospect, looking back on that, do you think there's anything about those series of studies which needs reinterpretation or were those changes real ones?

Ulrich Clement: There may be different aspects. One aspect that came to my mind when we discussed it was the meaning of *premarital*. In the first study that Gunter Schmidt did with Giese in 1966, the incidence of premarital coitus was a very important question. When I did another survey 15 years later, in 1981, we certainly could not ask the question about premarital coitus because the meaning of *premarital* had simply faded. I mean, historically faded, and it would have been a ridiculous question at that time. There is another aspect in the German language: the term *condom* was introduced with the AIDS crisis. Previously, the term *condom* was unusual in German; we used the term *Präservativ* or *Pariser*. Maybe the meaning has changed and *condom* is in a way associated with AIDS, whereas *Präservativ* was more associated with contraception. Even when you aim at the same thing, the association in the respondent's mind would be different because *condom* is associated with STD prevention whereas *Präservativ* is associated with contraception.

Anke Ehrhardt: I want to come back to what is change. If we look at number of partners, maybe there's very little change, but enormous things have changed over the last 40 years—in terms of gender relations, in terms of with whom people have sex. Gunter Schmidt's study in Germany was most enlightening about teenagers and their first sexual intercourse. Young men are now much more concerned to have sexual intercourse within a romantic context. Much of the real change may be in such aspects of social context rather than in measures of sexual practices and number of partners. There is a whole array of things which can change in a culture which we should keep in mind so that we don't underestimate change.

Alain Giami: To continue with the metaphysics of change, we also have the assumption that every segment of the general population must change equally. As an example, in the French KAPB survey, which was addressed at the general population, we had a measure of the change in condom use. We don't know what proportion of members of the risk groups increased condom use. I'm thinking, for example, of homosexual men, IV drug users, or people coming from African and Caribbean countries who aren't easily identified in those surveys and who are most at risk concerning HIV infection, in France. So I am suggesting that this kind of research is more what Lazarsfeld would have called "administrative research" and is performed to evaluate the politics of the prevention. What are we measuring as change? Are we measuring the effects of the politics or the behavior change that is induced by this politics ? You can also ask,

"Is behavior change needed for everybody?" Some people don't need to change because they are not concerned with HIV risk.

Anne Johnson: This is a question to Alfred on the ethics of randomized controlled trials and prevention. Randomized controlled trials (RCTs) should be used when there's uncertainty about the effects of an intervention, and I think we are very uncertain about the effectiveness of AIDS prevention. A great deal of money is spent in these areas. Good examples would be HIV counseling and sex education in schools. A lot of people say that to do randomized controls in these areas is unethical, but I do not understand why. There is an important opportunity cost in investing in ineffective interventions. I know that some RCTs of behavioral interventions are being done in the United States and we are doing such studies in sex education and intervention among gay men now in England. I would be interested to hear your comments.

Alfred Spira: I've been thinking a lot about this. One of the difficulties is that we cannot randomize an intervention against a placebo. There is no placebo for intervention. But, of course, I think that we can randomize between two interventions—one a real intervention, the other with a small modification of the former. For example, the way you speak with the children or you teach the children. You can speak to them directly or you can use videotapes.

Anne Johnson: We can do RCTs in places where there's very little sex education. What comes to mind are the countries with major HIV epidemics, and for them this really should be a very important agenda. The problem we have in Britain is contamination, i.e., both intervention and control groups are likely to receive education from many sources. All the kids know a lot about HIV, but they know less about the point in their menstrual cycle when they can get pregnant, for example. So they're all really worried about getting HIV, but they're not so worried about getting pregnant or acquiring other STDs. But in many parts of the world there really is an enormous problem amongst adolescents and a very real risk of acquiring HIV, and there is probably not anything like the level of education in the general population seen in the U.S. and Europe. So where I would accept Alfred's comments for the U.S. and much of Europe, in many parts of Africa and Southeast Asia there probably is an opportunity for randomized control trials in education.

Anke Ehrhardt: I think you are always in an enormous dilemma when you have a major social problem, when you want to find out "Does this work?" But I agree with Alfred that you can no longer do nothing as a control condition.

Anne Johnson: We assume that these things do good. I think we have to present the possibility that some of these interventions do harm and there is evidence that some interventions at best do nothing and may do harm. So there is enough uncertainty. If you have limited resources, you have an enormous responsibility to put in the most cost-effective intervention. For example, spending large amounts of money on individualized counseling based on a Western model in an African context could turn out to be inappropriate, and if this were a drug treatment, it might be argued that this was an irresponsible use of resources. The money could have been better spent. So I don't really go along with the unethical argument. I think it's unethical to spend money ineffectively when resources are inevitably scarce.

Anke Ehrhardt: I suppose it varies from case to case. When you have an epidemic like this one, it is very, very difficult. In part, what we need are sound rules for when to stop. For example, when doing a randomized trial, we need an ethics committee or a board which monitors the results and on the basis of established rules tells you when you can stop. With O76, for example, once a decrease of pregnancy transmission by 50% has already been established, it is very hard to go on with the control group.

Charles Turner: I want to echo what Anne was saying. Ethical and social dilemmas are created when you have a massive problem and you think you have some good ideas about where to begin, but you're not sure. There's a need to try and put things out there, but at the same time there's a need to try and do that in a way that's sufficiently constructive. What you need to learn is what works better and what works worse so that you don't end up squandering millions of dollars on mailing a brochure to every household or those other wonderful "interventions" we Americans spend money on like our "Just Say No" campaigns. There are often situations in which you're introducing a program and if you have limited resources to begin with, you don't begin by going nationwide. If you're going to do a staged implementation, you can stage it in a randomized way, which in a way is ethically fairer, so that the geographic locations that get it can be contrasted with those that don't and you can assess the program's impact.

Carol Jenkins: I just wanted to comment on the developing country issue that you brought up. I certainly have found myself in that dilemma, being asked by the EEU to look at peer-education programs for youth, HIV prevention in the Pacific, that were introduced without much thought and without any background from those particular islands. Then they want pre- and posttest evaluations of impact. I clearly saw that was a terrible waste, millions and millions of bucks, and wanted, as we developed our prevention programs for Papua New Guinea, to be able to do something better. So we sat down and attempted to think about controls and randomization. It wouldn't necessarily be too random, but at least we could have a control group and be able to test what we were doing on a small level in one town first. But it became very clear as I was developing these proposals for the program that the ethical board of the country would not accept "empty controls," and this is a nation with zero sex education. So we have to do a small sex education program in one and a more complicated attempt at behavior change in another, but we certainly couldn't get away with nothing.

John Bancroft: While recently looking at the literature on randomization of methods of intervention, I was struck by a profound naiveté in the way huge amounts of money have been spent on doing randomized control trials. A naiveté which I think stems from a lack of recognition of the difference between, on the one hand, comparing treatments for specific illnesses and, on the other hand, providing information or training to try and change a very complex set of behaviors which are influenced by a huge range of factors in an individual's environment. In other words, the sources of variance in the behavior that you're interested in are huge and the contribution that your particular intervention makes is small compared with all these other sources of variance. That, therefore, raises the question of the comparability of your groups. And given the type of information we are considering and the way that it interacts with social processes, it comes back to the point that Alfred was making. Very often you can't randomize individuals because you can't isolate individuals from their peers. So you have to randomize groups, and then it gets very difficult to have any idea whether you can adequately balance your groups for the prognostic factors that are going to influence the likelihood of intervention effects. Unless you can do that, you spend a lot of money doing a randomized control trial which produces inconclusive results.

Barbara Marín: To explain differences between treatment and control groups in randomized trials, we need well-constructed theories of behavior change that allow us to measure the variables that we hypothesize are actually creating the differences, the particular elements in the intervention that are having an impact on people's behavior. My review of the literature of HIV prevention interventions with ethnic minorities (Marín, 1995) suggests that it's rare for researchers to specify a theory of behavior change and actually assess whether their moderating variables change in those people whose behavior changes. If I don't change the things that my theory predicts should change, it doesn't really matter whether behavior changed or not because I may not have had anything to do with it. We need to be incorporating those intermediary elements in our theories and in our instruments if we're going to really understand what's going on.

Ed Laumann: I would underscore the thrust of John Bancroft's remarks. But what I worry about, to return to the discussion about behavior change and the ways we're thinking about changes in sexual behavior, is that we often use one-item measures, which are known to have only modest test/retest reliability and validity, to measure critical variables in our theories. For example, when we look at our data, we find that, across the board, i.e., across the whole age range, roughly 30% of people reported using a condom or other contraceptive during their first act of intercourse.

And, of course, 70% did not. A common interpretation of this majority practice is that the first time for sexual intercourse is likely to be regarded as a romantic, "unexpected" interlude. One simply isn't expected to bring along a contraceptive in anticipation of an event that is supposed to be spontaneous and unplanned. The notion that one can ask a single question to capture this very complex, highly contextualized event strikes me as a highly implausible proposition. This is going to inevitably result in our looking like we can't predict anything very accurately because there are so many things that affect the likelihood of a particular behavioral outcome. I would also urge that we need to do much better theorizing about how behavior changes. And we should be using multiple indicators to access complex situations rather than relying on single-shot measures. The notion that behavioral intervention is analogous to the act of taking a drug, which typically has clear and perceptible effects, has become a kind of prototype model for intervention in ongoing social interaction. To believe this is adequate for social-behavior research is a recipe for disastrous misunderstandings of the underlying phenomena.

Ted Myers: When talking about the need for a theory to guide our research, I think we should look at theories that attempt to integrate a number of disciplines. I believe sex research projects will become increasingly interdisciplinary or multidisciplinary. There are both scientific and economic rationales for this. With regard to the scientific, we know there are many dimensions to the subject—a single focus is unlikely to yield a full understanding. With regard to the economic, because of today's funding environment we are forced to construct and to develop our research in a multidisciplinary way—to become cost effective.

John Bancroft: We've had a number of comments about the need for theory, and it isn't always clear to me just what people are talking about. One of the things that struck me about the field over a long time is the relative lack of an integrated theory underlying sex. The theories we do have are very incomplete, dealing with relatively small parts of the picture. So, Ted, what you are asking for is fairly substantial, but maybe it is something that is lacking and we should be moving towards.

Theo Sandfort: We don't just need to have more facts; we need to understand. And I think there's a big difference between knowing things and understanding things, and I think we are here to help politicians to understand things. We do have the data.

John Bancroft: The point that's being made, if I understand it correctly, is when we think about a theoretical model, we should have an objective which the theoretical model is designed to serve. And there could be many different objectives.

Carol Jenkins: I would totally agree. I'm the only sex researcher in a nation of four million people. I've done national surveys, and I must deal with policymakers all the time. There's no backing out, and there's no saying I'm too academic to be able to answer your questions. They want answers because they want action. A theoretical model can help the educational process between myself and the communities I'm involved with. I think this is a very important process that sexologists are going to have to move on, particularly since the emergence of HIV has brought sexually transmitted diseases to a large consciousness which will become part of a general health and society consciousness, an issue just like diet and cardiovascular disease.

John Bancroft: Just take the rather crucial question of why people continue to behave sexually in a high-risk fashion when they are aware of the risks that they're taking. To address that, you need a theoretical model, but the theoretical model needs to be organized by that question. Anke was talking about the attempts at theory behind the behavioral-change interventions. But those theories have, I think I'm right in saying, largely neglected to look at issues specific to sexuality. But in order to get that sort of theory, I would agree with Ted, we do need to be interdisciplinary; we need to take a number of types of mediating mechanism into account in such a way that it proves useful in generating the testable questions for our research which are ultimately going to help. I think this is a very important task, and I find myself increasingly drawn into this process of working towards a theoretical model or models which will serve the field. Perhaps we're all getting pulled in that direction at the present time, and that's an interesting phase for the field because that hasn't been there before.

Leonore Tiefer: I think there's a pendulum feeling always in sexology—the longer you live, the more swings you ride—and it's my sense that we're interested now in theory because we've just been through this phase of intensive data collection without theory, driven by AIDS. A lot of epidemiologists came into the field whose sole purpose was to document empirically a phenomenon because of its public importance. The phenomenon happened to be about sex and here's all this data. But there wasn't a great need to integrate data into theory before, because we didn't have the data. Now we're overwhelmed with numbers and so the pendulum's swung.

References

Flandrin, J. L. (1981). *Le sexe et l'occident: Évolution des attitudes et des comportements.* Paris: Seuil.
Marín, B. V. (1995). *Analysis of AIDS prevention among African Americans and Latinos in the United States.* Report prepared for the Office of Technology Assessment (OTD), U.S. Congress, Washington, D.C.
Simon, P., Gondonneau, J., Mironer, L., & Dourlen-Rollier, A.-M. (1972). *Rapport sur le comportement sexuel des français.* Paris: Julliard, Charron.

Part 5.
Retrospective versus Daily Assessment

A Comparison of Retrospective Interview Assessment versus Daily Ratings of Sexual Interest and Activity in Women

CYNTHIA A. GRAHAM AND JOHN BANCROFT

Most of the recent AIDS-related research into sexual behavior has involved retrospective, or "recall," methods of data collection. Few of these studies have addressed the reliability or validity of such retrospective assessments, although issues such as underreporting and interviewer effects are acknowledged (Berk, Abramson, & Okami, 1995; Catania, Gibson, Chitwood, & Coates, 1990). The daily diary has been suggested as a more accurate method of assessing frequency of sexual behaviors (e.g., Coxon, 1988); but this is a demanding method requiring high and continuing levels of compliance from subjects, and to date their use in AIDS behavioral studies has been limited. Comparison of retrospective assessments with daily recording of behavior over the same time period does provide one method of assessing the validity of the retrospective method. Most of the studies which have compared daily monitoring with interview or questionnaire methods have used a different time period for the two assessments (McLaws, Oldenburg, & Ross, 1990). Others have used the mean frequency of sexual behavior across a group rather than individual level analyses to compare methods (Hornsby & Wilcox, 1989). Both of these methodologies limit any conclusions regarding recall bias or validity of self-reports. Reading (1983) compared daily ratings of sexual behavior with interview estimates covering the same time period but relied on correlations to compare the two methods, which is an inappropriate method to judge agreement between ratings (Altman, 1991). In this paper we present comparisons of retrospective ratings and daily reports over a one-month period for frequency of sexual intercourse and also for a more subjective variable, frequency of sexual thoughts, used as a measure of sexual interest. The data are taken from the "pretreatment" baseline month in a WHO-funded study evaluating the effects of steroidal contraceptives on the well-being and sexuality of women in two centers: Edinburgh, Scotland, and Manila, Philippines (Graham, Ramos, Bancroft, Maglaya, & Farley, 1995). Thus there is the added interest of the comparison of such assessments in two contrasting cultural settings.

Methods

Subjects

The study recruited women who had been sterilized or whose partners had been vasectomized. These women also were prepared to volunteer to take an oral contraceptive or a placebo pill for four months in a double-blind study. In Manila, recruitment took place at hospital post-sterilization clinics and community-based health centers. In Edinburgh, women were first contacted at the time of their sterilization or via their partners attending vasectomy clinics.

Seventy-five women were recruited in each center (i.e., 150 women in total). All of the women were in an active sexual relationship and in good physical health, and none was using any hormonal or psychotropic medications. Subject characteristics for the two centers are presented in Table 1.

Measures

The data reported in this paper are from the one-month baseline period. The measures described below, as well as a number of other questionnaires and self-ratings, were used throughout the four-month treatment period, but that data will not be reported here.

DAILY DIARY

Frequency of sexual intercourse: Women recorded the occurrence of sexual intercourse with their partners on a daily basis for one month.

Sexual interest: The instructions were as follows: "Apart from the times that your partner first approached you wanting to make love, how often have you found yourself *thinking* about sex with *interest* or *desire*?" Ratings were from 0 (not at all) to 5 (frequently) for each day.

Interviewer Ratings of Sexual Functioning (IRSF)

At the end of the month a semistructured interview, developed in Edinburgh (Bancroft, Tyrer, & Warner, 1982; Tyrer et al., 1983) and modified and checked for interrater reliability for this study, was administered. This type of semistructured interview involves a standard opening question for each item, followed by further probe questions as necessary to allow the interviewer to make the rating. Ratings for frequency of sexual intercourse were made on a 1–7 scale and for sexual interest on a 1–6 scale (see below). Training for the interviewers from both centers was carried out in Edinburgh with further pilot testing in Manila before starting the study.

The interview ratings indicate approximate frequencies. In order to allow comparison with daily ratings, the full range of frequencies have to be

Table 1 *Subject Characteristics*

	Manila (N=75)	Edinburgh (N=75)
Mean age (years)	32.2 (4.2)	32.4 (3.7)
Mean number of children	4.1 (1.2)	2.2 (0.98)
Education (years)	8.4 (2.7)	12.2 (2.0)
Length of current relationship (years)	13.3 (4.8)	10.8 (4.3)
Time since sterilization/vasectomy (years)	5.9 (4.4)	1.0 (2.1)
Employment (%)		
Full-time	24.0	28.0
Part-time	16.0	46.7
None	60.0	25.3
Occupation (employed %)		
Professional	—	1.8
Intermediate	13.3	21.4
Skilled/nonmanual	3.3	26.8
Skilled manual	16.8	12.5
Partly skilled/manual	13.3	28.6
Unskilled/manual	53.3	8.9
Previous oral contraceptive use (%)	33.0	98.7

covered. The equivalent frequencies per month from the daily ratings are therefore given in brackets.

Frequency of Sexual Intercourse: (only 1 occasion per day is counted)
1. None during the month (0)
2. About once a month (1)
3. 2 to 3 times a month (2–3)
4. Once a week (4–5)
5. 2–3 times a week (6–12)
6. 4–6 times a week (13–24)
7. Once a day or more frequently (25+)

For sexual interest, any day on which the rating for sexual interest was 1 or more was counted.

Frequency of Sexual Interest
1. None during the month (0 days)
2. About once a month (1 day)
3. Less than once a week, more than once a month (2–3 days)
4. At least once a week (4–7 days)

230 | *Researching Sexual Behavior*

   5. Several times a week (8–24 days)
   6. At least once a day (25+ days)

Method of Comparing Diary and Interview Data

The frequencies obtained from the daily diaries for a 28-day period were categorized according to the ranges given above and compared with the equivalent interview ratings. The agreement between the diary and interview categories was assessed by means of weighted kappas (Cohen, 1968). These have a maximum of 1.00 when agreement is perfect and a value of zero when agreement is no better than expected by chance; negative values indicate worse than chance agreement. As there were significant center differences for most of the sexuality variables, data from the Edinburgh and Manila samples were analyzed separately.

Results

Frequency of Sexual Intercourse

Tables 2 and 3 show the monthly frequency of sexual intercourse as assessed by the daily diary and the interview. The weighted kappas obtained for Manila and Edinburgh were .71 and .67, respectively; these can be interpreted as indicating "good" agreement (Altman, 1991).

Frequency of Sexual Interest

Tables 4 and 5 contain the number of days (out of a possible 28) on which sexual interest was rated as 1 or more on the daily diary compared with the retrospective interview ratings of frequency. The weighted kappas were .03 for Manila, suggesting agreement between diary and interview no better than chance, and .32 for Edinburgh, indicating only a "fair" degree of concordance. In both Manila and Edinburgh it is apparent that women were most likely to *underreport* the frequency of sexual thoughts on the interview, in comparison with the prospective diary data. The lower kappa value for the Manila women reflects the fact that the discrepancy between the two methods was often by two or three categories. In contrast, for the Edinburgh sample discrepancies were most likely to be by only one category.

The low agreement between diary and interview for sexual interest may in part have been due to our method of counting days of sexual interest; those days rated only 1 or 2 may be less well remembered than those rated 3 or more. To explore this possibility we reanalyzed the data, only counting days on which sexual interest was rated 3 or more on the daily diary. This yielded weighted kappas which were slightly lower (.02 for Manila, and .28 for Edinburgh) than the original kappas; the reason for this was that there were now many more cases where the interview ratings

Table 2 A Comparison of Interview and Diary Methods of Assessing Monthly Frequency of Sexual Intercourse, Manila Sample (N = 75)[a]

Interview	Diary						
	None	Once a month	2–3 times a month	4–5 times a month	6–12 times a month	13–24 times a month	25+ times a month
None							
About once a month	1						
2–3 times a month							
Once a week			2	8	2		
2–3 times a week				2	46	6	
4–6 times a week						7	1
Once a day							

(a) Weighted kappa = .71

Table 3 A Comparison of Interview and Diary Methods of Assessing Monthly Frequency of Sexual Intercourse, Edinburgh Sample ($N = 68$)[a,b]

	Diary						
Interview	None	Once a month	2–3 times a month	4–5 times a month	6–12 times a month	13–24 times a month	25+ times a month
None	1						
About once a month		1					
2–3 times a month		2	3	2	1		
Once a week			3	7	8		
2–3 times a week				3	28	3	
4–6 times a week						6	
Once a day							

(a) Weighted kappa = .67
(b) Seven subjects were excluded because they had more than four days of missing diaries.

Table 4 A Comparison of Interview and Diary Methods of Assessing Monthly Frequency of Sexual Interest, Manila Sample (N = 75)[a]

	Diary					
Interview	None	Once a month	2–3 times a month	4–7 times a month	8–24 times a month	25+ times a month
None	1	1	2	6	15	2
About once a month	2	1		1	10	1
Less than once a week, more than once a month				5	8	1
At least once a week	1			1	6	
Several times a week				3	7	1
At least once a day						

(a) Weighted kappa = .03

Table 5 A Comparison of Interview and Diary Methods of Assessing Monthly Frequency of Sexual Interest, Edinburgh Sample (N = 66)[a,b]

Interview	Diary					
	None	Once a month	2–3 times a month	4–7 times a month	8–24 times a month	25+ times a month
None	2					
About once a month		1	1	1		
Less than once a week, more than once a month				1	2	
					4	
At least once a week				2	17	
Several times a week				1	24	1
At least once a day					3	6

(a) Weighted kappa = .32
(b) Nine subjects were excluded because they had more than four days of missing diary data.

were higher than the diary frequencies (i.e., overreporting); in other words, some women were recalling days on which they had rated sexual interest as only 1 or 2.

Discussion

This study evaluated retrospective assessment by comparing it with daily ratings for the same time period. In such circumstances, the daily ratings are likely to enhance the accuracy of the retrospective assessment. Retrospective reports elicited under different conditions, i.e., when subjects are not concurrently keeping daily records, may be less accurate (e.g., McLaws et al. [1990], who compared a retrospective questionnaire with a diary where the data collected by each covered two different months; this type of design assumes that sexual behavior is relatively stable from one month to the next).

With this qualification, the findings indicate fairly good agreement between diary and interview methods of assessing frequency of sexual intercourse in both centers. A previous study in men, which compared daily diary and monthly retrospective interviews for the same time period, also reported good correspondence between the two methods for coital frequency (Reading, 1983).

For sexual interest, the agreement between the diary and the interview was considerably less in both centers. The discrepancy was particularly striking for the Manila sample, which showed a consistent and marked underreporting of sexual interest on the interview compared with the daily diary. With the exception of sexual intercourse, the Manila women also reported lower ratings on most of the other sexuality variables assessed at the interview (which are not reported here), such as frequency of orgasm, arousal, initiation, enjoyment, and closeness to partner, compared with the Edinburgh sample, suggesting generally less satisfactory sexual relationships. In those circumstances, the reporting of sexual interest at interview may have been more difficult for the Manila women. These findings emphasize the importance of establishing that any method of assessing the quality of sexual life, such as the frequency of sexual interest, is appropriate for a particular cultural setting.

Acknowledgments

This research was funded by the Special Program of Research, Development and Research Training in Human Reproduction, World Health Organization, and carried out in collaboration with Rebecca Ramos, Cesar Maglaya, Primitiva Labudahon, and Rosa Mallari in Manila. We would also like to acknowledge the contribution of Thomas Albright, who developed a statistical program to compute the weighted kappas.

References

Altman, D. G. (1991). *Practical statistics for medical research.* London: Chapman & Hall.

Bancroft, J., Tyrer, G., & Warner, P. (1982). The assessment of sexual problems in women. *British Journal of Sexual Medicine, 9,* 30–37.

Berk, R., Abramson, P. R., & Okami, P. (1995). Sexual activities as told in surveys. In P. R. Abramson & S. D. Pinkerton (Eds.), *Sexual nature, sexual culture* (pp. 371–386). Chicago: University of Chicago Press.

Catania, J. A., Gibson, D. R., Chitwood, D. D., & Coates, T. J. (1990). Methodological problems in AIDS behavioral research: Influences on measurement error and participation bias in studies of sexual behavior. *Psychological Bulletin, 108,* 339–362.

Cohen, J. (1968). Weighted kappa: Nominal scale agreement with provision for scaled disagreement or partial credit. *Psychological Bulletin, 70,* 213–220.

Coxon, T. (1988). "Something sensational" . . . The sexual diary as a tool for mapping detailed sexual behaviour. *Sociological Review, 36,* 353–367.

Graham, C. A., Ramos, R., Bancroft, J., Maglaya, C., & Farley, T. M. M. (1995). The effects of steroidal contraceptives on the well-being and sexuality of women. *Contraception, 52,* 363–369.

Hornsby, P., & Wilcox, A. J. (1989). Validity of questionnaire information on frequency of coitus. *American Journal of Epidemiology, 130,* 94–99.

McLaws, M.-L., Oldenburg, B., & Ross, M. W. (1990). Sexual behaviour in AIDS-related research: Reliability and validity of recall and diary measures. *Journal of Sex Research, 27,* 265–281.

Reading, A. E. (1983). A comparison of the accuracy and reactivity of methods of monitoring male sexual behavior. *Journal of Behavioral Assessment, 5,* 11–23.

Tyrer, G., Steel, J. M., Ewing, D. J., Bancroft, J., Warner, P., & Clarke, B. F. (1983). Sexual responsiveness in diabetic women. *Diabetologia, 24,* 166–171.

Concordance between Self-Report Questionnaires and Coital Diaries for Sexual Behaviors of Adolescent Women with Sexually Transmitted Infections

J. DENNIS FORTENBERRY, HEATHER CECIL, GREGORY D. ZIMET, AND DONALD P. ORR

Introduction

Measurement of sexual behavior is the central methodological challenge of research related to the behavioral epidemiology of sexually transmitted infections (STIs) among adolescents. Production of accurate responses to research inquiries about behavior is a challenging task for subjects, and procurement of valid and reliable data is a daunting responsibility of researchers.

Several aspects of sexual behavior are key factors associated with risk of sexually transmitted infections. Coitus, number of sex partners, substance use in association with sex, and condom use are all identified as risk factors for one or more STI (Aral & Holmes, 1990; Cates, 1990). Frequency of occurrence of these behaviors usually is of greatest interest. Typically, frequency is assessed by asking subjects to report the total number of events in a given time interval. Alternatively, subjects may be asked to provide behavioral frequency as a rate (e.g., intercourse frequency per week).

Relatively little is known about the accuracy of such frequency reports of sexual behavior. Studies from related fields of drug and alcohol use suggest that subjects use a variety of cognitive strategies to produce estimates of behavioral frequency; association, listing, counting, time-based retrieval, and various computational strategies are a few examples (Forsyth, Lessler, & Hubbard, 1992). Intraindividual aspects of the research, such as personal salience, the complexity of patterns of behavior, and emotional responses to sexual behavior questions, may also influence reports of sexual activity (Catania et al., 1990).

Coital diaries represent an alternative measurement technique that allows behaviors to be recorded by the subject within a few hours of occurrence. Temporal proximity of the diary record to the behavioral event may reduce some measurement error associated with recall of behavior over longer periods. Some investigators therefore assume that diaries provide a more accurate representation of actual behavior (Berk, Abramson, &

Okami, 1995; McLaws et al., 1990). Diaries may provide an additional advantage over questionnaires, in that conditional sexual behaviors (such as condom use or change of sex partner) may be linked to individual coital events. Event-specific behavioral detail that is missed by the aggregate assessment provided by typical questionnaire items may thus be captured by diaries.

Coital diaries have their own set of limitations. The requirement of regular diary entry produces a substantial burden for respondents. Failure to record each event obviously represents a threat to the reliability of data. Unless diaries are collected daily (usually an impractical burden for researchers and subjects), additional bias occurs if subjects "fill in" omitted entries at some later date. Confidentiality of diary material is also problematic, especially if stigmatized behaviors are recorded. Since sexual intercourse is generally proscribed for adolescents (whose parents may be unaware of their adolescents' sexual activity or participation in a research study), this issue is especially relevant to the study of adolescents' sexual behavior.

The perspective taken in this paper is that no single approach to measurement is adequate for the array of behavioral issues relevant to sexually transmitted infections among adolescents (Turner, Miller, & Moses, 1989). A more comprehensive research strategy requires complementary measurement approaches. The purpose of this paper is to assess concordance of coital diaries and a self-administered questionnaire for four key risk behaviors for sexually transmitted infections: frequency of intercourse, number of sex partners, frequency of use of alcohol or drugs prior to coitus, and frequency of condom use. Aggregated across events, diaries should provide information comparable to that obtained from retrospective reports obtained by a self-administered questionnaire. Because no gold standard exists for measurement of sexual behavior, the relevant issue becomes one of convergent validity of the diary and questionnaire approaches to measurement. Assessment of concordance enhances confidence in estimates derived from any given method and improves confidence in unique data provided by a given method.

Methods

Data reported here are derived from a longitudinal study of sexually transmitted disease prevention among adolescent women. Subjects were 16 to 19 years of age and were attending one of five clinics in the Indianapolis metropolitan area. Most participants were infected by one or more sexually transmitted organisms at the time of enrollment, although a few were uninfected sexual contacts of infected male partners.

Behavioral data (for the previous three-month interval) were obtained by self-administered questionnaire at enrollment and at three-month follow-up after enrollment. Coital diaries distributed at the enrollment visit were collected at the three-month follow-up visit. Thus items inquiring about sexual behaviors during the previous three months (obtained at the follow-up visit) should correspond to those recorded in diaries during the same interval.

Measures

Research assistants instructed subjects to record each coital event in the appropriate day's square on pocket-sized calendars. Sex partner's initials, alcohol or drug use in association with sex, and condom use were also recorded. In order to maintain confidentiality, subjects were instructed to record the sex partner's initials on the calendar, circle the initials if a condom was used, and make a check mark if alcohol or drugs were used before intercourse. Separate entries were requested for each coital event, even when multiple events occurred on the same day. When diaries were collected at the three-month follow-up visit, research assistants verified the entries with subjects. All subjects entering the larger study were asked to complete diaries; however, most did not return diaries at the follow-up visits.[1]

The total number of intercourse events is the sum of all recorded events for the three-month period. The number of sex partners was computed by assuming that each set of partner initials represented one partner.[2] Substance-associated intercourse was the sum of all events where alcohol or drug use was recorded. Condom use was computed as the proportion of all events where a condom was used.

Questionnaire items addressed number of coital events ("In the past three months, how many times did you have sex?"), number of partners ("How many sex partners have you had in the last three months?"), number of substance-associated coital events ("In the past three months, how many times did you use alcohol or drugs before you had sex?"), and condom use for vaginal intercourse in the previous three months (five categories from "never" to "all of the time"). For all items except condom use,

---

1. Additional follow-up visits occurred at 9, 15, and 21 months after enrollment. Eighty-two subjects completed diaries for at least one follow-up period, but only 48 were obtained for the initial three-month interval. No differences in baseline characteristics were found between 48 subjects who completed diaries during the first three-month interval and the 554 subjects enrolled in the larger study who did not keep diaries. Although they may differ in characteristics that we did not assess, diary completers appear to be representative of the adolescent women participating in the larger study.

2. A potential source of error is our inability to distinguish partners with the same initials; likewise, partners identified by more than one set of initials cannot be distinguished.

subjects were asked to write the number of events in a blank on the questionnaire and were instructed to insert "0" if the behavior in question did not occur during the specified interval.

Concordance was assessed in several ways. First, the direct relationship between two measures was assessed. For number of coital events (which is continuously distributed over a large range), bivariate regression was used. For number of partners, substance-associated coitus, and condom use, cross-tabulation allows assessment of diagonal (exact agreement) and off-diagonal cell counts. Inspection of off-diagonal cells provides an impression of the magnitude of discrepancy between the two measures. The weighted kappa statistic (which is appropriate for categorical data) was used to express agreement between diary and questionnaire reports of condom use (correcting for chance agreement). Fair to good agreement is inferred for weighted kappa values greater than 0.40 (Fleiss, 1981).

Second, relative concordance between diary and questionnaire was expressed as the arithmetical difference between the aggregated diary records and the questionnaire frequency reports. Because exact agreement may be an unnecessarily restrictive requirement for some research applications, the relative differences were recoded to represent close agreement—defined as a relative difference that is not zero but is likely to represent adequate accuracy. Cut-offs to define close agreement were arbitrary and varied with the behavior in question: agreement within five events for coital frequency, within one for number of partners, within two events for substance-associated coitus, and within one category for condom use. A "reasonable" level of concordance is reported as the number of subjects with exact or close agreement between diary and questionnaire for the sexual behavior in question. This approach is similar to that used in other investigations of convergent validity of reports of sexual behavior (Upchurch et al., 1991).

Results

Sociodemographic characteristics of the 48 subjects are shown in Table 1. Seventy-four percent reported African-American racial identity. The average age (at baseline) was 17 years, with an average age at first intercourse of 14 years. At enrollment, the median number of sex partners in the previous three months was one. Almost all subjects reported condom use at least "some of the time."

Comparison of Diary and Questionnaire

NUMBER OF COITAL EVENTS

The number of coital events, range, and average number of coital events (during a three-month interval) for diary and questionnaire are

Table 1 *Selected Sociodemographic and Sexual Behaviors of Diary Completers, at Enrollment*[a]

Age, years (SD)	17.5 (1.1)
Race	
African-American, n (%)	39 (74)
Maternal education	
≥12 years, n (%)	33 (69)
First intercourse, years (SD)	14.6 (1.8)
Coital events,	
Previous 3 months, median (range)	7.0 (0–90)
Number of sex partners	
Previous 3 months, median (range)	1.0 (0–10)
Alcohol/drugs before sex	
Previous 3 months, n (%)	
Never	32 (62)
Once	8 (15)
2 times or more	12 (23)
Regularity of condom use	
Previous 3 months, n (%)	
Never/rarely	18 (34)
Sometimes	12 (23)
Mostly/always	23 (43)

(a) Derived from baseline questionnaire.

shown in Table 2. A substantially greater number of coital events were identified by diaries than by questionnaire. Other analyses (not shown) conducted by withholding data from one subject with a very large number of diary-recorded coital events (n=135, with 18 coital events reported by questionnaire) reduced but did not eliminate the discrepancy between diary and questionnaire reports of coital frequency.

A scattergram (with imposed linear regression line) of the relationship between diary and questionnaire reports of coital frequency is shown in Figure 1. Correlation of the two measures was 0.43.

Because some investigators suggest that the accuracy of questionnaire reports is reduced for higher frequency events (Berk, Abramson, & Okami, 1995), evidence for a nonlinear relationship between questionnaire reports and diary records was assessed. This analysis suggests that concordance between diary and questionnaire counts of coital events decreases at higher levels of sexual activity (see Figure 1). A quadratic polynomial regression

Table 2 *Concordance between Diary and Questionnaire for Number of Coital Events, Number of Sex Partners, and Number of Substance-Associated Coital Events*

	Diary	Self-Administered Questionnaire	Difference[c]
Coital events[a]	1080	665	463
Range	1 to 135	1 to 60	−19 to 117
Mean (SD)	23.5 (25.5)	14.5 (13.0)	9.0 (23.1)
Number of partners[b]	79	77	2
Range	1 to 5	1 to 4	−2 to 3
Mean (SD)	1.7 (0.9)	1.6 (0.7)	0.1 (0.7)
Substance-associated events[a]	46	73	−27
Range	0 to 15	0 to 15	−13 to 4
Mean (SD)	1.0 (2.5)	1.6 (3.8)	−0.6 (3.0)

(a) n = 46 subjects
(b) n = 48 subjects
(c) Diary events minus questionnaire events; negative numbers indicate greater number of questionnaire events than recorded by diary and positive numbers indicate greater number of diary events than reported by questionnaire

showed a total R^2 of 0.33, compared to 0.18 for the linear relationship between the two measures.[3] This significant curvilinear effect remained when the subject with 135 diary-reported events was excluded from the analysis.

For analysis of relative concordance between diary and questionnaire, close agreement was defined as agreement within five events. Exact agreement was found for 22% (10/48) subjects, with close agreement for 27% (13/48). If agreement within five events is defined as a reasonable standard for concordance over a three-month interval, diaries and questionnaires were concordant for number of coital events for 49% of the adolescent subjects.

NUMBER OF PARTNERS

Relatively little difference was noted between diary and questionnaire reports for number of sexual partners (Table 2). The median number of partners (for a three-month interval) reported by each method was one (data not shown).

3. Linear regression parameters were Questionnaire Coital Events = 9.35 + .22 (Diary Coital Events); quadratic polynomial regression parameters were Questionnaire Coital Events = 4.65 + .62 (Diary Coital Events) − 0.004 (Diary Coital Events)^2. Each parameter differs from zero (p<0.05) by t-test.

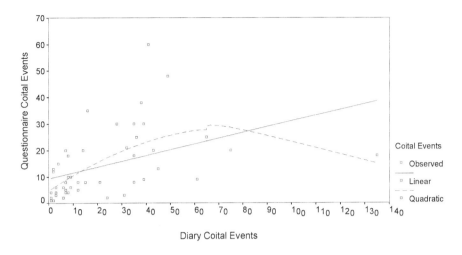

Figure 1. Concordance of Diary and Questionnaire—Number of Coital Events

Agreement between aggregated diary records and questionnaire for number of sexual partners is shown in Table 3. Close agreement was defined as agreement within one partner. There was exact agreement about number of partners for 69% (33/48), with close agreement for 25% (12/48). Thus reasonable concordance between diary and questionnaire was identified for 94% of the subjects.

SUBSTANCE-ASSOCIATED COITUS

Substantially fewer substance-associated coital events were recorded in diaries than were reported by questionnaire (Table 1). However, the majority of subjects (67% and 74% for diary record and questionnaire report, respectively) had *no* substance-related coital events. Two subjects recorded no substance-related coital events who subsequently reported substance-associated coitus by questionnaire, and five subjects recorded substance-associated coitus that was not reported on their subsequent questionnaires (see Table 4).

Diary records and questionnaire reports for number of substance-associated coital events were in exact agreement for 70% of subjects. This was largely due to the high level of agreement (between diary and questionnaire) that no substance-associated coital events occurred.[4] Close agreement (within two events) was found for 20% (9/46).

---

4. Among the 17 subjects with at least one substance-associated coital event (by either method), only three (18%) produced diaries and questionnaires that were in exact agreement.

Table 3 *Concordance between Diary and Questionnaire for Number of Sex Partners in Previous Three Months*

Diary Number of Partners	Questionnaire Number of Partners				
	1	2	3	4	5
1	20	5	1	–	
2	5	10	–	–	
3	–	2	3	1	
4	–	–	–	–	
5	–	1	–	–	–

CONDOM USE

The overall number of condom-protected coital events recorded in diaries was 712/1128 (63%). The proportion of condom-protected events ranged from 0 to 1.00. Regularity of condom use as reported by questionnaire ranged from 1 ("never") to 5 ("all of the time") (median = 4).

The average proportion of diary-recorded condom use for each level of questionnaire-reported regularity of condom use is shown in Table 5. Estimates of the proportion of condom-protected events associated with "never" or "rare" condom use are likely to be unstable because of the small number of subjects. Table 5 demonstrates a general linear relationship between a commonly used ordinal scale for condom use and the proportion of coital events that are condom protected. However, these data suggest that ordinal scale descriptors such as "never" or "all of the time" may not have the substantive meaning for actual behavior that is often inferred by investigators.

In order to assess concordance in condom use between diary and questionnaire, the proportion of condom-protected events obtained from the diaries was recoded to five equal categories: zero to 20%, 21%–40%, 41%–60%, 61%–80%, and 81%–100%. These five ordered categories correspond to the five-point ordinal scale for condom use used in the questionnaire.

Agreement between diary and questionnaire reports of condom use is shown in Table 6. The weighted kappa for these two measures was 0.45. Forty-four percent (20/48) of the subjects had exact agreement between diary and questionnaire, with close agreement (defined as agreement within one category) found for 37% (17/46). Thus 80% of subjects had reasonable concordance between diary records and questionnaire reports.

Table 4 *Concordance between Diary and Questionnaire for Number of Substance-Associated Coital Events in Past Three Months*

Diary Number of Substance-Associated Events	Questionnaire Number of Substance-Associated Events							
	0	1	2	3	4	11	12	15
0	29	–	2	–				
1	4	1	1	–			1	
2	–	–	1	–				1
3	1	–	–	1	1			
4					–			
5					1			
6								1
15						1		–

Discussion

Frequency measures of the same behavior (for the same time interval) should show strong linear relationship for the entire range of behavioral occurrences. Concordance between measures of four sexual behaviors obtained by two methods was demonstrated, although the relationships were not completely straightforward and several nuances were observed that deserve comment.

The observation that diary records identify a substantially greater number of coital events than questionnaire reports suggests adolescents are capable of fulfilling the demands of diary keeping, even when asked to maintain records over a span of several weeks. Although our subjects could have falsified some or all of their diary entries, visual inspection of the diaries showed clear evidence of use over time (such as use of different writing instruments, smudges, and signs of wear). None of the subjects with whom debriefing interviews were conducted admitted to making false diary entries. Empirically, we found evidence that coital events and substance-associated coital events were more common on Fridays and Saturdays, although condom use was evenly distributed through the week. Likewise, a greater proportion of coital events was recorded during spring and summer months, consistent with data from other studies of seasonality of adolescent sexual activity (Rodgers, Harris, & Vickers, 1991). A more random distribution of events would be expected if subjects falsified entries.

Table 5 *Average Proportion of Diary-Recorded Condom-Protected Coital Events by Questionnaire Reports of Regularity of Condom Use*

	Questionnaire Regularity of Condom Use				
	Never	Rarely	Some of the Time	Most of the Time	All of the Time
Diary Proportion of Condom-Protected Events, mean (SD)	0.4 (0.5)	0.4 (0.3)	0.5 (0.2)	0.7 (0.3)	0.9 (0.3)
Range	0.1 to 1.0	0.0 to 0.8	0.0 to 0.8	0.1 to 1.0	0.0 to 1.0
N	3	6	12	10	15

The curvilinear relationship between diary records and questionnaire reports for number of coital events deserves special comment. This finding supports the observation of others that questionnaire reports of coital frequency become unreliable as the number of events rises (Berk, Abramson, & Okami, 1995). As has been pointed out in studies of adult women, computational strategies used to estimate high-frequency events may fail to account for circumstantial interruptions in usual patterns of behavior (i.e., menses, a symptomatic sexually transmitted infection, or unavailability of a partner) that are not included in the estimate (Hornsby & Wilcox, 1989).

Diary records and questionnaire reports for number of partners were substantially concordant; even higher levels of agreement may have been obtained if the diaries had included a means of distinguishing partners with the same initials (see footnote 2). For most adolescents, the number of partners is relatively small and the identities of partners are highly salient. Thus diary records and questionnaire reports may be expected to produce very similar data.

We also found that diary records and questionnaire reports for frequency of substance-associated coitus were highly concordant among subjects who did not pair substance use and coitus. However, among subjects who did pair substance use and coitus, questionnaire reports identified a substantially greater number of substance-associated coital events. Substance-using subjects may be less thorough about diary completion and may fail to record each substance-associated coital event. However, for those subjects who reported any substance-associated coitus (either by diary or by questionnaire), their total number of diary-recorded coital events was substantially greater than those subjects reported by questionnaire. This suggests that substance users did not fail to record a significant num-

Table 6 *Concordance between Diary and Questionnaire for Regularity of Condom Use in Past Three Months*

Diary Regularity of Condom Use	Questionnaire Regularity of Condom Use				
	Never	Rarely	Some of the Time	Most of the Time	All of the Time
< 20%	2	2	2	1	1
21%–40%	–	–	2	1	–
41%–60%	–	1	5	–	–
61%–80%	–	2	3	5	1
> 81%	1	–	–	3	12

ber of coital events. Alternatively, subjects may overreport substance-associated coital events. Such overreporting of substance-use behaviors by adolescents has been noted by others (Cohen et al., 1988), although diary studies of alcohol use among adults have shown that diaries identify significantly greater amounts of alcohol use than questionnaires (Poikolainen & Karkkainen, 1983). Overreporting by adolescents may be due to desire by participants to present themselves as uninhibited or as risk takers. Such attributes may represent a self-presentation bias for behaviors valued among some adolescent groups (Dolcini & Adler, 1994; Moore & Rosenthal, 1991; Urberg, 1992).

Finally, we found that adolescent women's reports of regularity of condom use—using an ordinal scale similar to others widely used in research and clinical work—were interpretable in terms of the proportion of coital events (by diary record) that were condom-protected. Thus condom use "all of the time" was associated with a higher average proportion of condom-protected events than were "most of the time" or "some of the time" reports. It is important to note, however, that "all of the time" did not universally mean "with each coitus." The discrepancy between a pattern of highly regular condom use and event-specific condom use may explain high rates of subsequent sexually transmitted infection even among patients who report regular condom use (Zenilman et al., 1995; Orr, Langefeld, Katz, & Caine, 1996).

In summary, we found that coital diaries provide information that is consistent with that obtained by questionnaire-derived behavioral reports for the same time interval. This provides some reassurance about the validity of the unique insights about sexual behavior that can be obtained only by event records such as coital diaries.

Acknowledgments

Supported in part by grants from the National Institute of Allergy and Infectious Diseases (U19 AI31494; Robert B. Jones, M.D., Ph.D., principal investigator) and the Maternal-Child Health Bureau (MCJIN189596). We wish to thank Rochelle Marker, Patricia Brooks, Cathy Roberts, Sara Smith, and Paula Linnemaier for invaluable assistance with data collection. Special thanks to Virginia A. Caine, M.D. of the Marion County Health Department for her support. Portions of this research were presented at the International Society for Sexually Transmitted Diseases Research, New Orleans, LA, August 1995.

References

Aral, S. O., & Holmes, K. K. (1990). Epidemiology of sexual behavior and sexually transmitted diseases. In K. K. Holmes, P.-A. Mårdh, P. F. Sparling, P. J. Wiesner, W. Cates, Jr., S. M. Lemon, & W. E. Stamm (Eds.), *Sexually transmitted diseases* (pp. 19–36). New York: McGraw-Hill Information Services.

Berk, R., Abramson, P. R., & Okami, P. (1995). Sexual activities as told in surveys. In P. R. Abramson & S. O. Pinkerton (Eds.), *Sexual nature, sexual culture* (pp. 371–386). Chicago: University of Chicago Press.

Catania, J. A., Gibson, D. R., Chitwood, D. D., & Coates, T. J. (1990). Methodological problems in AIDS behavioral research: Influences on measurement error and participation bias in studies of sexual behavior. *Psychological Bulletin, 108,* 339–362.

Cates, W. J. (1990). The epidemiology and control of sexually transmitted diseases in adolescents. *Adolescent Medicine State of the Art Reviews, 1,* 409–427.

Cohen, S. J., Katz, B. P., Drook, C. A., Christen, A. G., McDonald, J. L., Olson, B. L., Cloys, L. A., & Stookey, G. K. (1988). Overreporting of smokeless tobacco use by adolescent males. *Journal of Behavioral Medicine, 11,* 383–393.

Dolcini, M. M., & Adler, N. E. (1994). Perceived competencies, peer group affiliation, and risk behavior among early adolescents. *Health Psychology, 13,* 496–506.

Fleiss, J. L. (1981). *Statistical methods for rates and proportions.* New York: John Wiley & Sons.

Forsyth, B. H., Lessler, J. T., & Hubbard, M. L. (1992). Cognitive evaluation of the questionnaire. In C. F. Turner, J. T. Lessler, & J. C. Gfroerer (Eds.), *Survey measurement of drug use: Methodological studies* (pp. 13–52). Washington, DC: U.S. Department of Health and Human Services.

Hornsby, P. P., & Wilcox, A. J. (1989). Validity of questionnaire information on frequency of coitus. *American Journal of Epidemiology, 130,* 94–99.

McLaws, M.-L., Oldenburg, B., Ross, M. W., & Cooper, D. A. (1990). Sexual behavior in AIDS-related research: Reliability and validity of recall and diary measures. *Journal of Sex Research, 27,* 265–281.

Moore, S., & Rosenthal, D. (1991). Adolescents' perceptions of friends' and parents' attitudes to sex and sexual risk-taking. *Journal of Community & Applied Social Psychology, 1,* 189–200.

Orr, D. P., Langefeld, C. D., Katz, B. P., & Caine, V. A. (1996). Behavioral intervention to increase condom use among high-risk female adolescents. *Journal of Pediatrics, 128,* 288–295.

Poikolainen, K., & Karkkainen, P. (1983). Diary gives more accurate information about alcohol consumption than questionnaire. *Drug and Alcohol Dependence, 11,* 209–216.

Rodgers, J. L., Harris, D. F., & Vickers, K. B. (1991). Seasonality of first coitus in the United States. *Social Biology, 39,* 1–14.

Turner, C. F., Miller, H. G., & Moses, L. E. (1989). *AIDS: Sexual behavior and intravenous drug use.* Washington, DC: National Academy Press.

Upchurch, D. M., Weisman, C. S., Shepherd, M., Brookmeyer, R., Fox, R., Celentano, D. D., Colletta, L., & Hook, E. W., III. (1991). Interpartner reliability of reporting of recent sexual behaviors. *American Journal of Epidemiology, 134,* 1159–1166.

Urberg, K. A. (1992). Locus of peer influence: Social crowd and best friend. *Journal of Youth and Adolescence, 21,* 439–450.

Zenilman, J. M., Weisman, C. S., Rompalo, A. M., Ellish, N., Upchurch, D. M., Hook, E. W., III, & Celentano, D. (1995). Condom use to prevent incident STDs: The validity of self-reported condom use. *Sexually Transmitted Diseases, 22,* 15–21.

Discussion

Susan Newcomer: What guarantee do you have that the kids didn't fill that diary out while they were sitting in the waiting room waiting for their appointments?

Dennis Fortenberry: I don't have an absolute guarantee. But first, they're often observed in the waiting areas, so "filling in" was never observed. Second, the diaries themselves have been individually examined to see if there was any evidence such as completing with the same writing instrument. We didn't find any evidence of that kind. Although I can't say that it didn't occur in some circumstances, I think it's unlikely that it occurred to any extent.

Joe Catania: I think the diary in comparison to other modes is interesting for studying a number of different things, but in both of your studies there's this mix of explanations for the differences; part of it could be self-presentation biases, some of it could be memory distortion. Could you speculate on what you think accounts for differences that are showing up?

Cynthia Graham: Although I didn't interview the women in Manila, the Manila researchers did, and they were of the opinion that this was something to do with being resistant to talking about sexual thoughts. Women were given instructions on both the interview and the diary, and sexual interest was defined as "apart from the times when your partner first approached you wanting to make love, how often have you found yourself thinking about sex with interest or desire?" So that was said in both interview and diary context. We did get feedback from Manila about how the women responded to the interview and they did find some of the more sensitive questions on masturbation and orgasm quite embarrassing. It's also consistent with the differences between Manila and Edinburgh in other sexuality variables. They reported very low frequency of arousal during intercourse, very low frequency of initiation and of orgasm. Sexual intercourse was the only variable on which the Manila group showed a slightly higher frequency than Edinburgh. And for sexual-intercourse frequency there was really fairly good agreement between diaries and interview for that month. I know that keeping diaries during that month probably inflated recall accuracy, by how much it's impossible to say. But when talking about sexual thoughts and their frequency, I'm sure that's much more difficult to recall over one month.

John Bancroft: But it was consistent underreporting.

Cynthia Graham: It was consistent underreporting on the questionnaire in both centers.

Dennis Fortenberry: I've never seen an adequate approach to understanding how young people respond to an item that asks how often did you do something over x period of time: retrospective recall for low-frequency events, especially highly salient low-frequency events. It may be quite easy to give a precise answer to items like that. But most people, and probably young people as well, don't keep a precise tally and don't know how to answer except by a formula where they may take some unit of time, estimate the occurrences within that and multiply. So I think that's where the errors come from, particularly when you take into account the fact that for many people sexual behavior doesn't always follow this plan for estimation. They may have menses; these young women I've studied have been infected by sexually transmitted disease, so they're symptomatic and they've been instructed not to have sex for a period of time; sex partners come and go. They may be out of town, all of those things occur.

Alex Carballo-Diéguez: I have two comments. When we were talking about the laptop system, we said that if there is an increase in the report of unsafe behavior, for example, we see that information as more valid than a self-assessment questionnaire where less risk behavior is reported. But here it seems that the criterion switches. No matter what the direction of the difference is, if it is reported in the diaries there is a tendency to attribute more validity to that information. So I think it is important to consider how we assess how good a method is. We seem to change the criteria when we like the method more. The second comment is that it should be simple to assess how much the recall was influenced by keeping the diary, by having another group that didn't have the diary. I wondered why you didn't have a control group not keeping diaries.

Cynthia Graham: The reason is that the data I reported was part of a large placebo-controlled study, comparing two different oral contraceptives in two different cultures. It was a very involved, very demanding study for the women. We were looking at three different groups. So the comparison I reported wasn't something that was a major focus of the study. It was something that became interesting, in terms of the methodology, once the study was completed. Going back to your first point, are you talking about the diary being the gold standard? Was that your point? I don't regard it as being that, but I think there is some kind of commonsense feeling that because it's closer in time that it will be probably more accurate than a retrospective one-month or three-month rating, particularly for something like sexual interest or frequency of sexual thoughts. There are likely to be biases with the diaries as well, of course. The diary we used involved 15 or 16 items concerning mood and physical change as well as sexuality. In addition to sexual interest and sexual activity, subjects also rated masturbation. They were asked to also rate lovemaking not involving intercourse, but the frequencies for that reported in the diaries were so low that we have not looked at them more closely. They were very low for the both centers. The ratings were made on one page per day. When they made the ratings, they were asked not to refer back to previous pages and they posted them back to us every week. So in response to the question about completing the diaries just before sending them back, a question which is often raised, there were a number of indicators in our study that that didn't happen. Women were quite open if they did forget the diaries. A few women did say they'd forget the diaries occasionally and fill them in the next morning, as well. We did have some missing data; we had some missing weeks. We had occasions where diaries were completed and then a child spilled a juice over it and you couldn't read them; things like that. I was also very impressed, both in this study and in an earlier study also looking at women keeping daily diaries for five months, by the motivation and the interest of the women in the topic, how important they felt it was. I sense there was a lot of commitment to the study. Women continued in the study despite a lot of breakthrough bleeding, for example, and they spent a lot of time with other questionnaires and interviews as well.

Richard Udry: We have had at least 30 years of experience of comparisons of the kind that are being discussed this morning, using many different designs and with studies of variable quality. Could the speakers address the question in a more general way? If you have to choose between one of these two methods, when should you choose one and when should you choose the other?

Dennis Fortenberry: Well, you know, as we decided yesterday, before asking a question, you should define the theoretical aspects that you wish to address, and then design the method to address it. I think that there are a number of things that are event related that are difficult to understand. We won't be able to address such issues with a questionnaire or interview-based method which tries to sum behaviors over a period of time. A specific question that we've addressed, for example, is whether substance use causally influences condom use leading to risk behavior. We've used the coital diaries to address that question. We asked ourselves, "Does the addition of substances at that particular coital event change the probability that a condom will be used?" That's not something that I think can be adequately addressed using other methods.

Cynthia Graham: I would agree with that. There are some variables, for example, more qualitative variables relating to sexual activity, that we only assessed in the interview, which we believed were more appropriate for the interviewer's method. We were also looking at premenstrual symptoms in our study, and there is a lot of evidence from previous studies of differences in the data collected between retrospective and prospective methods. So it depends on the question being asked and also the demands on the subjects. I would prefer to use daily diaries in most studies looking at sexual interest over the menstrual cycle, but I think you have to limit the number of variables that women are rating daily if you want to keep them in the study. That's important as well.

Ulrich Clement: I think both studies are interesting because they might provide data which will give us an insight into how long-term memory is working. One result is of particular interest; you found that sexual interest was reported lower in the retrospective assessment. Do you think that long-term memory effects desexualize memory? Could there be a tendency that the longer the distance in time is, the more you desexualize memory?

Cynthia Graham: I'm not sure about that, and I don't think it's a gender issue, either. The study of men by Reading found poor agreement between interview and daily diaries in ratings of sexual interest over a three-month period.

Ulrich Clement: It would be interesting if there was a recall bias.

Joe Catania: To come back to Dick Udry's original question, you can spend lots of resources getting ever better estimates with greater and greater precision, but do you really need it?

Dennis Fortenberry: I wouldn't do it this way unless I thought there were specific things that I needed from an event-level analysis. And the only reason for me then to compare methods is to have some sense when I interpret this unique data of what I don't think I can get from another method. At least on some things there is comparability from method to method. In the study we're doing now, we're using questionnaires, individual interviews, and diaries so that we can triangulate on some behaviors, but also get unique pictures on other things that you can't adequately obtain from any one of those methods alone.

Alain Giami: It seems that we are regarding sexual interest as a measurable behavior. If you read some novels and fiction, for example I'm thinking of Colin Wilson's *Sex Diary of a Metaphysician* (first published in 1963), he represents himself as thinking about sex all the time. Do you think that you can specify sexual thinking as you can specify sexual practices—with the same objectivity that is possible for a sexual practice? Maybe the difference between the diary and the report is much more interesting because it's a reconstruction. Reflecting Colin Williams's comments yesterday, the data lies in the discrepancy between the daily diary and the retrospective report.

Cynthia Graham: I don't think it's possible to measure sexual interest in the same way as specific behaviors. It will be very approximate and different, but it provides a rough measure. If someone thought about sex all the time, they would rate 5 frequently. It can't be measured in the same way as a behavior, but as for a number of other subjective variables, it's the closest we can get. Daily ratings of sexual thoughts are much better than asking how often someone thought about sex over a three-month period. I think it's about the best we can do. There are more intensive methodologies that have been developed. For example, Cynthia Hedricks uses a beeper methodology in which people are called up at random intervals through the day and asked to rate their sexual thoughts. But that can be done on only a very small number of people, a very select group as well, but it's still an interesting methodology. So to answer your question, I don't think it is possible in the same way, but I still think it's worth doing.

Colin Williams: Why can't you make your questionnaire items more like a diary instead of saying this kind of decontextualized "how often do you." Why don't you just ask, "tell me about your sex life in the last month" or "what do you do or who did you do it with." That then might allow you to connect it to whatever it is that you're trying to study, whether it be some kind of contraceptive device or whatever.

Cynthia Graham: I think you can and should do that as well. But I think that there are many studies that need some measures of frequency for various reasons—large-scale studies. But what you suggest is a useful thing to do as well. In our semistructured interviews, we asked those types of questions in order to help the woman be comfortable talking about sex. We would start the interview with "Tell me about how things have been in your sexual relations." We didn't go right in and say, "Tell me the frequency." And, by the way, for many of the questions in the interview we had the type of enhanced condition that Joe Catania talked about yesterday for items such as masturbation and orgasm; for example, we said that some women are able to reach orgasm and some are not, some only this way and some other ways, and so on before we asked a woman whether she had experienced orgasm.

John Bancroft: I've been using daily diaries for many years, not as long as Dick Udry of course, but I haven't been doing anything as long as Dick has. They are very demanding. They require a fair amount of motivation from your subjects which has to be generated by explaining to the individual how important they are. If you don't do that, they won't fill them in. But they are extremely useful for specific purposes. I think the point that Cynthia made at the beginning of the presentation was that they may be useful to validate other types of assessment. This is a relatively novel idea because it hasn't been used very much. And, as Ulrich was saying, you could extend that model back, and this has been done to a limited extent, and see how as you go further back in time the picture changes, how we conceptualize ourselves over a long period of time. We probably use very different criteria; we probably have some image of ourselves as being a certain type of person, and therefore we choose a description that fits that type of person. Whereas if we try to describe how we've been over the last month, we recall how we've responded to life's vicissitudes over the last month. So I think there are methodological issues that could be addressed by using daily ratings. I've used them in quite a number of treatment outcome studies in which we've been looking at change in specific variables. I think they are extremely valuable for that, and notwithstanding Alain's and Colin's point, just asking them how they're feeling in a general, chatty sense isn't a very good way of establishing whether a treatment is effective or not in comparison with a placebo. One of the instances where this has been consistently and robustly useful is assessing the effect of hormones given to men who are hormone deficient. I've used them for many years in the clinic for women complaining of symptom changes around their menstrual cycles and, in particular, mood changes. And although we started using them in that way as a research tool, it became incorporated into our clinical practice because it proved to be extremely helpful for both the clinician and the woman in sorting out what was happening. In that particular example, they are women who are motivated to get help, and perhaps for that reason they also have a tendency to amplify their patterns. They come with the idea of the premenstrual syndrome and they present their complaints in a way which conforms to their concept of premenstrual syndrome. If you compare their diary data that they do over a couple of months with their initial retrospective assessment, then you will consistently find that the retrospective assessments amplify the cycle-related pattern that you get in their daily ratings. And one of the things that has struck me is how rarely we get any evidence that a woman is altering her diaries to present a picture in a particular way. They do do that with their retrospective account; they recall themselves, they present themselves in a particular way. But they do not seem to do that in how they rate things on a day-by-day basis. It just seems to be more difficult to present a consistent, distorted picture with daily ratings. They do miss diaries sometimes, and I want to ask Dennis, with his particular group of adolescent, mainly African American girls with STDs, how consistent they were in their diary keeping. Most people if you motivate them and stress the importance, they'll do it well. But the uses I've referred to are restricted and time-limited. You can't expect people to do this for too long and, as Cynthia said, you can't ask people to do too much on a daily basis. And then another use is the one that Dennis is talking about when you want to look as close as you can at specific events and what is going on around those events. Am I right in saying, Dennis, that from your data you did not find any evidence of association between substance use and condom nonuse?

Dennis Fortenberry: That's right. Except in the very specific circumstance of substance use with a change of partner, since we have initials we can identify when the initials change and assume that that represents a new partner. That was a low-frequency event. So by and large, the only prediction of condom use at a specific event was their usual pattern of use.

John Bancroft: This goes against the picture that is emerging of an association between condom use and substance abuse, and therefore it's important to know whether this is a more valid picture. So here is another illustration of how diary use may be valuable. I think we should be paying attention to it, but it's not going to solve all of our problems.

Alex Carballo-Diéguez: If diary use is important but demanding on the people, I wonder if a computer-aided questionnaire like the one Charles Turner presented done by telephone would help. What's your impression?

John Bancroft: I think that filling in a little bit of paper in the bathroom before you go to bed at night on a regular basis actually is an easier and possibly more relevant sequence to involve people in than asking them to answer questions periodically on the phone. But your suggestion may be worth trying.

Leonore Tiefer: I was thinking of broadening the issue in a different way, like some of the issues we were raising at the beginning, studying only risk-related behaviors versus a broader conceptualization of sexuality. I was thinking of this as a methodology that's more intimate, more subjective, more appropriate in some ways for issues of gender construction. One might learn from a participant over the period of a month, for example, a variety of different kinds of gender-related, sexually related events that would be helpful in theory building. This would not be seeing sexual events so out of context. Could one try to identify experiences over the course of a month that made one feel more like a man, less like a man, more like a woman, less like a woman, and connect those in some ways then to feelings of sexuality and were these good experiences or bad experiences? So then these episodes of sexual interest or sexual activity would be seen more in the narrative and more related to the construction of gender in one's life. It seems that of all the methods we've been discussing this would lend itself most towards a broadening out of sexuality into life in a way that would then lead to theory building.

Stuart Michaels: There have been some attempts to use that sort of method in the sense of contextualization in interviews of various sorts, especially in retrospective interviews. The obvious example which I'm sure is familiar to most people here is, of course, Kinsey. I was in the Kinsey Institute's library yesterday and rereading Pomeroy's account of how the interview was done and the use of "pegs"—getting people to think about a number of life-course events and then using these as the organizing framework for asking about all types of sexual activity. In a similar way in our national survey, we used major life events, major relationships, which we defined in terms of cohabitation, as pegs when we asked respondents to enumerate the number of partners over their whole lifetime. They were asked about other sexual partners before, during, and between/after their major live-in/marital relationships. In that sort of structured survey it's actually very complicated, and we had some difficulty with it in terms of interviewer training and minimizing recording errors and in terms of simplicity of final data structure.

Part 6.
Participation Bias

Sampling Male Homosexuality

THEO G. M. SANDFORT

> *Because something is real, it does not mean that it cannot be a construct. Nor does its being a construct mean that it cannot be real.*
>
> —Ruse, 1995, p. 65

Homosexuality figures in social scientific investigations in a variety of research designs in which different research questions are addressed. Studies have looked at the origins, occurrence, and development of homosexual behavior and identities, at differences between homosexual and heterosexual people in the way they function, and at various aspects of homosexual lives and relationships. These studies are done to assemble knowledge which applies to more than just the group under study. The resulting findings are intended to contribute to the accumulating knowledge about (homo)sexuality.[1] What I would like to do in this paper is to show that this pretense has serious complications and that the potential for making empirically based, generalizing statements about gay men and lesbians or about homosexuality in general is limited.

In most of the studies about male homosexuality[2] it has become a platitude to say that the sample studied is not representative and that higher-educated, white, middle-class males are overrepresented. Implicit in this statement is the suggestion that, at least theoretically, it would be possible to compose representative samples of gay men and to make generalizable statements about male homosexuality. The problem with this assumption is that findings in a specific study depend heavily on the definition and operationalization of homosexuality adopted, and on the way the sample has been put together. Furthermore, it presupposes the existence of an ahistorical, universal homosexual and ignores the diverse historical, social,

---

1. This paper will not address epistemological issues. My assumption here is that intersubjective knowledge about social life is possible and can be gained via empirical research.

2. Most of the methodological arguments developed in this paper apply to female as well as male homosexuality. Since the examples which will be presented originate from studies among gay men, the focus will be on male homosexuality. It will be clear that from a constructionist perspective male and female homosexuality cannot be equated.

cultural, and legal factors which affect the expression of homosexuality and, therewith, the outcomes of social scientific studies.

Definitions

In surveying homosexuality a variety of definitions (and operationalizations) can be used. As others have frequently pointed out, homosexuality can be defined in terms of feelings of physical or emotional attraction, fantasies, actual behavior, and self-definition (encompassing a variety of labels related to homosexuality; Donovan, 1992; Klein et al., 1985; Shiveley & De Cecco, 1977). The various aspects do not necessarily overlap and may change during someone's personal development. These aspects also do not exclude the concurrent or subsequent existence of heterosexual feelings and behavior. Labeling a feeling, a behavior, or a person as homosexual by a researcher does not necessarily have to coincide with the perspective of the person involved. The broadest operationalization of homosexuality is probably being used in studies which aim at assessing the occurrence of homosexuality and for which respondents are not selected on the basis of specific sexological criteria. Kinsey's study, as well as some of the more recent general population surveys carried out in the context of HIV/AIDS, has shown that depending on the definition of homosexuality applied, the actual occurrence of homosexuality varies considerably.[3] This proportion ranges from 4% to 37%, referring respectively to (white American) men who have been exclusively homosexual throughout their lives after the onset of adolescence and to men who have had at least some overt homosexual experience to the point of orgasm between adolescence and old age (Kinsey et al., 1948).[4]

In a representative general population survey carried out in the Netherlands in 1990, we also looked at the way in which the different aspects

---

3. The inability to replicate Kinsey's high proportions in recent studies is often attributed to the selective composition of his sample. Other explanations are, however, as likely. One explanation is methodological: in the interview schedule, homosexuality was extensively covered, more so than in subsequent surveys. Comparatively, Kinsey and his co-workers were probably more skilled than the interviewers who were deployed in the recent studies, regardless of the latters' specific training and experience. These methodological factors made it more difficult for Kinsey's respondents to forget, to deny, or to hide homosexual experiences. A generational factor may play a role as well. Since Kinsey's days, homosexuality has become a more public phenomenon; people are more aware of the stigma attached to the behavior and may consequently be more reluctant to engage in it and/or to report it.

4. Cf. Laumann et al. (1994): " . . . estimating a single number for the prevalence of homosexuality is a futile exercise because it presupposes assumptions that are patently false: that homosexuality is a uniform attribute across individuals, that it is stable over time, and that it can be easily measured" (p. 283).

of homosexuality are interrelated (Zessen & Sandfort, 1991) (see fig. 1).[5] Of the 385 men interviewed, 13.5% said that at least once in their lives they had experienced feelings of physical attraction toward a person of the same sex. Of these 52 men who reported feelings of physical attraction for the same sex, 51.0% said that these feelings disappeared in a later stage of their lives. The proportion that had been in love at least once with someone of the same sex was considerably smaller than the proportion reporting same-sex attraction: 6.5% of all the men. Almost all the men (97.4%) who had felt physically attracted toward their own sex stated that at least once they had also been in love with a person of the opposite sex. All the men who had been in love with somebody of the same sex had experienced same-sex physical attraction as well. On the other hand, a substantial proportion of the men reported having experienced same-sex physical attraction without ever having been in love with someone of the same sex: 51.1% of the men.

Most of the 48 Dutch men who reported having had sex with someone of their own sex at least once (12.5% of the total sample) had experienced physical attraction and/or love for someone of the same sex (66.7%); one third of the men who reported sexual contacts with someone of the same sex also reported never having experienced same-sex attraction or love. From all the 52 men who said they had ever felt same-sex physical attraction, 61.5% had never had sexual contact with someone of the same sex. When asked whether they ever had considered whether they were homosexual, 8.3% of the men reported to have done so. All men who ever considered themselves to be homosexual reported experiencing attraction toward someone of the same sex. Most of these men reported having had sexual contacts with other men as well (78.1%).

The figure illustrates how all the different aspects are interrelated (cf. Laumann et al., 1994) as well as how they relate to the current self-labeling of the respondents. All men who, at the time of the study, self-identified as predominantly or exclusively homosexual had experienced same-sex attraction and love and contact with another man at some stage. For most of the men who identified as bisexual (threes, fours, and fives on a Kinsey-scale), the same applies, however. There were also several men who now identified as (predominantly or exclusively) heterosexual who had had various kinds of homosexual experiences.

Less elaborate definitions of homosexuality are being used in studies

5. Although the Dutch data give in-depth insights into the relationship between attraction and behavior, they should be treated with caution. The number of cases are generally rather small. Furthermore, the data presented reflect not only people's actual experiences but also what the person in his current situation is able and willing to remember. This reproductive process will, of course, also be influenced by negative associations, usually attached to homosexuality.

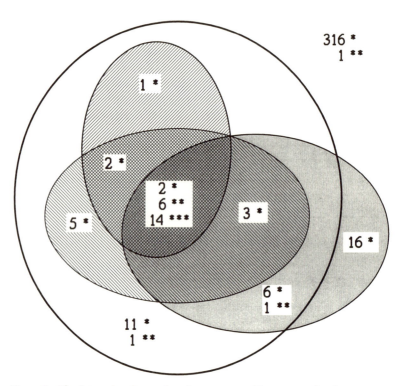

Figure 1. The interrelatedness of various aspects of homosexuality in men (n = 385)

focusing specifically on gay men. In these studies, the definition of homosexuality is quite often more or less implicit and probably completely determined by the way the sample was put together. Since having shown homosexual behavior is a criterion for inclusion of respondents in these studies, they are almost completely dependent upon the possibilities available to find these people. The channels available for recruiting men who show homosexual behavior are all part of a homosexual subculture, encompassing the directories of gay organizations, gay bars and festivities, public meeting places and so on. These channels predominantly result in samples of men who are more or less part of a gay culture and will quite likely be self-identified gay men.[6] We know very little about the homosexuality of men who are not linked, either superficially or strongly, to the gay world. What these percentages and figures show is that, at least from the perspective of individual lives and not just looking at behavior, there is a lot more homosexuality than there are homosexually identified men. Having considered oneself to be homosexual just once in one's life should of course not be equated with a gay life filled with numerous same-sex partners. The figure does show, however, that the boundaries between homosexuality and heterosexuality are less sharp than people usually assume (cf. Gagnon, 1990).

That studies among gay men offer only a limited perspective on homosexuality has become apparent in studies in the field of HIV/AIDS. Doll et al. (1992), in their study among blood donors, found that almost a quarter of the men who had had sex with another man in the preceding year did not label themselves as homosexual. This was more often so among black men and Latino men than among white men, indicating that among white men homosexual self-labeling is a more common practice (cf. Seldman, 1993). This finding, as well as findings in comparable studies, led to the introduction of the term *men who have sex with men*, criticized by some because it makes gay men less visible and takes away from the political power of the gay movement. The "discovery" of men who have sex with men (as well as with women) in the context of HIV/AIDS should also be seen as the major source for the current social and scientific interest in bisexuality (cf. Tielman et al., 1991; Weinberg et al., 1994).[7]

Various definitions and operationalizations can be chosen and applied in a specific study. Which one is chosen should of course depend on the

---

6. Humphreys' study about men visiting tearooms to find (male) sexual partners (1970) is one of the few exceptions.

7. Weinberg et al. (1994) started their project before it was clear how AIDS was going to affect the lives of bisexual people. Compared with most other recent studies, their project is, however, exceptional. AIDS also heavily influenced the design as well as the outcomes of their study. It is quite likely that without HIV/AIDS, bisexuality would still be seen predominantly as a temporal stage of transition or an unwillingness to come out as gay.

question under investigation. Even if a study exclusively focuses on self-identified gay men it will remain difficult to generalize the outcomes. As the following section will show, the outcomes of such a study are heavily dependent upon the recruitment procedures applied.

Sampling

One of the conclusions which can be drawn from the preceding is that in studies about homosexuality the population can be defined in various ways, depending on the specific aspects of homosexuality selected and the time frame taken into account.

The next step after having defined a "homosexual" population would be to draw a representative sample from that population. For practical reasons this is almost impossible, since an inventory of people fulfilling the criteria is not available. This is the case even if the population is defined as self-identified gay men. The only option is to select a large enough sample from the general population and to identify a group which fulfills the stated criteria; this approach, however, limits the questions which can be studied with regard to homosexuality specifically.

The fact that even a representative sample of self-identified gay men cannot be drawn would constitute less of an insurmountable problem if gay men were more or less alike and constituted a more or less homogenous group. If that were the case, it would not really matter so much which way of recruiting respondents was chosen. That is, however, not the case. Consequently, results of studies depend on the sample studied.

Studying the effects of recruitment procedures has become possible because of the abundant opportunities brought by the AIDS epidemic to do research among gay men. Many of these studies have focused on identifying determinants of safe and unsafe sex in order to develop effective prevention activities. Another objective of these kinds of study has been to monitor attitudinal, cognitive, and behavioral developments relevant to HIV/AIDS. Our department has carried out several studies among gay men as well as studies in the general population.

One of our studies focused on HIV risks within steady gay relationships (Sandfort et al., 1996). For this study we recruited gay men involved in steady relationships in two ways: (1) at a gay (and lesbian) household fair which was held in a city about 15 miles from Amsterdam (n = 130), and (2) in the commercial gay subculture of Amsterdam (n = 109).

In some respects these groups were comparable: they did not differ in age, the duration of their relationship did not differ, nor did the mean number of evenings a week couples in both studies spent together. Despite these agreements, both subgroups differed significantly with respect to the living arrangements: in the gay fair group, more men lived together compared with the men in the Amsterdam group (respectively 71.5% and 59.3%). The relationships of the men in the gay fair group were, according to their reports, more often monogamous than the relationships of the men in the Amsterdam group (32.6% and 9.3%). With respect to the preceding six months, the difference was slightly bigger: 37.3% versus 9.5% of the relationships in the gay fair group and the Amsterdam group had been monogamous.

In the same study, we looked at the determinants of extrarelational sex, applying Ajzen's model of planned behavior (Ajzen, 1991). The two subgroups differed significantly from one another with respect to the intention to have sex with someone outside of the relationship, the intention of the Amsterdam men to do so being stronger. Both groups also differed with respect to all the determinants of this intention: the Amsterdam group had a more positive attitude and subjective norm and a lesser degree of perceived behavioral control. The men in the Amsterdam group also assumed that their homosexual friends had a stronger intention to have sex with someone other than their steady partner.[8]

These differences between the two subgroups suggest that we are dealing with two different subpopulations of gay men who quite likely participate in different subcultures. Although conclusive statements cannot be made, it is quite likely that if we wanted to generalize to gay men in the Netherlands, the gay fair group would be more representative (at least of gay men involved in steady relationships).

Comparing the consequences of sampling strategies, already done by various researchers (Harry, 1988; Weinberg, 1970), becomes even more interesting if an unselected sample of gay men is available, one big enough to make reliable comparisons.[9] We were able to compose such an unselected group from a semiannual telephone survey which had been carried out in the Netherlands between 1987 and 1994 (Dingelstad et al., 1994a, 1994b). The aim of the study was to monitor developments in the context of safe sex among the general population. For each of the 14 waves a new representative sample was drawn from the Dutch population, in the age range of 15 to 45 years, resulting in a total of 13,911 persons. Of the 5,686 men who participated in this study, 214 (3.8%) could be classified as homosexual (Sandfort & Vroome, 1996).[10]

This unselected sample of homosexual men was compared with the

---

8. We were surprised to find that the intention of the men in the gay fair group did not differ from the intention in a sample of heterosexual men studied by Buunk and Bakker (1995). The two groups showed no difference with respect to attitude and perceived behavioral control. Compared with the heterosexual men, gay men did report, however, a more positive subjective norm; these men also assumed that their gay friends would have a more positive intention to have sex outside their relationship.

9. Harry (1990) compared 16 homosexual men and 8 bisexual men who were part of a random population sample with 627 heterosexual men and, despite small numbers, found several differences between them.

10. Men were classified as homosexual based on their sexual behavior in the preceding half year. Of the total group, 186 reported having had sex with another man in the preceding half year; 17 of them also had had sex with a woman. From the 682 men

following convenience samples: (1) Men who filled out a questionnaire which was included in a biweekly magazine for gay men and lesbians (*De Gay Krant*; Boega et al., 1994); this group will be referred to as the *readership group*. (2) Men who were randomly selected from a membership list of the main Dutch gay and lesbian organization (COC); they were approached by mail to fill out a written questionnaire about condom use (the *membership group*). (3) Men who were participating in the Amsterdam Cohort Study and who since 1984 had filled out a questionnaire related to safe sex twice a year (the *cohort group*; for this comparison, data used were collected in 1991; Wit, 1994).

Data-collection methods and specific questions posed were not completely identical in the four studies. However, by merging some of the answer categories, it was possible to compose variables for each sample that allowed for optimal comparisons. Not all variables with respect to which comparisons between samples can be made were assessed in each sample, however. Comparisons between the subgroups can be made with respect to education, urbanity, political orientation, religiosity, relationship status, relationship duration, and the partners' sexual behavior.[11]

Partially as a consequence of recruitment procedures in the random sample, there were strong differences between the samples with respect to age, the men in the convenience samples being significantly older. In the convenience sample, no restriction with respect to age had been applied. After applying an upper age limit of 45 years, the mean age in the convenience samples was still significantly higher than in the unselected sample. This suggests that in convenience samples of gay men, younger men are quite likely to be underrepresented. After introducing a lower age limit of 21 years—excluding the young men in the unselected sample—the mean age did not differ significantly. To prevent age-related differences between samples from being misattributed to other factors, comparisons of the unselected sample with the three convenience samples were made only after excluding men who were either younger than 21 years or older than 45 years. To prevent the samples from getting too small to make valid comparisons, no further matching was executed. The sample sizes after matching for age were 189, 974, 195, and 490 for the unselected, readership, membership, and cohort samples respectively.

The comparisons show several interesting differences between the unselected sample and the convenience samples. Even controlling for age, the educational level in the samples differs. The mean level of education is

---

(12.0% of the total) who reported having had no sexual contact in the preceding period, 3.1% said they preferred sex with men and 1.0% said they preferred sex with both men and women; the latter were included in the homosexual group. The rather meager operationalization of homosexuality in this study was determined by the limited data available.

11. The way these variables have been constructed will be discussed elsewhere.

lower in the unselected sample compared with the readership group and especially with the sample of COC members (having 73.3% men with a higher educational level, compared with 49.5% in the unselected sample). There is no difference between the unselected group and the cohort group.

Excluding the Amsterdam cohort group, the men come from more or less the same urban backgrounds.[12] The unselected group is more religious and politically more conservatively oriented compared with the readership group (for the other samples no data are available on these variables). Major differences emerge when we look at various relationship variables. In the unselected sample, 71.4% of the men are involved in steady relationships. In the readership group and the cohort group this percentage is significantly lower (60.8% and 61.2%), while among the higher educated membership group significantly more men report having a steady relationship (80.6%). For gay men who are in a steady relationship, the mean duration of this relationship is much higher in the unselected group compared with the membership group (respectively 8.3 and 5.4 years).

If we look at the proportion of men involved in a steady relationship who also had sex with third parties in the preceding six months, we can see that convenience samples give a very biased impression of promiscuity, or, less judgmentally, sexually open relationships among gay men. In contrast with the 24.4% of the men with a steady partner in the unselected sample, 50.2%, 65.4%, and 72.7%, respectively, in the readership group, the membership group, and the cohort group report that they had sexual contact with others in the preceding six months as well.[13]

These differences are mirrored in the behavior of the respondents' partners in the two samples where this information has been collected. In the unselected sample, 43.4% of the men with steady relationships report that their partner had or might have had[14] sex with someone else in the

---

12. In this respect, the homosexual men in the unselected group differ significantly from the heterosexual men in the unselected sample, the homosexual men living much more often in the bigger cities (53.5% versus 26.9%) and less often in rural areas (1.4% versus 9.8%). This difference, which is usually attributed to migration, can also be a consequence of living in environments with respectively less and more illicit homosexual experiences (cf. Laumann et al., 1994). At the same time, the pressures to show heterosexual behavior might be less strong (Wilkinson & Kitzinger, 1994).

13. It should be said that in the unselected sample homosexual men involved in steady relationships more often report having had sex with someone outside of the relationship compared with the heterosexual men (respectively 22.5% and 4.9%). The mean duration of the steady relationships also differs significantly (respectively 7.8 and 9.7 years). These comparisons were made after matching on age and level of education.

14. "Don't knows" were included as a positive answer, probably explaining the difference between the reports about their own behavior (24.4%) and about their partner's behavior (43.4%).

preceding six months, while in the readership sample this is reported by 69.6% of the men.

To complement the picture, men in the unselected sample significantly less often had sexual contact only with casual partners compared with the readership group and the cohort group (respectively 17.5%, 28.7%, and 33.6%). Except for the men in the cohort group, the proportion of men without any sexual contact in the preceding half year does not differ between the samples. In the cohort group this proportion is significantly smaller compared with the unselected group (respectively 5.2% and 11.1%).

The comparisons presented here are limited in scope. With respect to the men in the unselected sample, we don't know anything about their self-identification; it is quite likely that this unselected sample would contain more closeted homosexuals or fewer men who self-identify as gay. It would have been interesting to see whether the unselected group differed from the others with respect to factors such as self-esteem and general well-being, acceptance of homosexuality, sexual behavior, conceptions of homosexuality, social support systems, levels and kinds of homonegativism experienced, participation in a gay subculture and other aspects of homosexual lifestyles, identification with the gay movement, and so on.

What do the differences presented here tell us? First, the main conclusion should be that convenience samples present us with a biased image of current homosexual behavior. This bias results from two factors, which empirically are hard to disentangle. Although it is unlikely that there is no overlap at all between the four groups, different segments of the homosexual "population" will have been reached via the various recruitment methods applied. Second, each recruitment procedure will induce specific self-selection or nonresponse patterns.

Nonresponse was not looked at in any of the four studies compared. Several studies among general populations have shown that nonresponse and self-selection do affect the outcomes of sexological studies (Catania et al., 1990; Strassberg & Lowe, 1995; Wiederman, 1993). Basically what these studies show is that nonresponders have less sexual experience and more restrictive attitudes toward sexuality. As far as I know, there are no studies among gay men which extensively report on aspects of nonresponse and self-selection. Most of the time they are not mentioned at all. It is quite likely that in studies among gay men, self-selection has a serious influence on the outcomes. Men who feel less positive about their own homosexuality might be less willing to participate in studies. It is also likely that gay men cooperate in studies out of specific ideological motives. In order to get a better understanding of the results of our studies, reasons for gay men to participate or not should be considered as an important subject for investigation.

Homosexual Diversity

The fact that sampling techniques determine the outcomes of studies among homosexual men implies that within a homosexual population one could identify various segments. The notion of diversity of homosexual populations is an important one. In social scientific studies, predominantly in the field of psychology, gay men have become a universal, independent breed of people, insulated from the social world in which they live. This understanding does not acknowledge the constructive nature of homosexuality. This constructive nature is not only a prerequisite to understanding historical and cross-cultural differences in the occurrence and expression of homosexuality; it applies to contemporary homosexuality within a specific culture as well. The diversity of homosexual populations probably gets even bigger when we cross national boundaries. It is interesting to see how, as part of the still-developing internationalization of a gay subculture (cf. Altman, 1982), gay men in San Francisco and Amsterdam have come to look much alike. However, this should not distract us from the differences between them. These differences result not just from a differential impact of HIV/AIDS but from other factors as well.

If different segments of a homosexual population could be identified, what would the constituting factors be? Maybe one universal feature affecting the kind of homosexuality observed in studies is the societal rejection of homosexuality. Although countries differ in the extent to which homosexuality is negatively evaluated (Halman et al., 1994), no Western country legitimates homosexuality on a par with heterosexuality. This societal rejection often is associated with the legal situation regarding homosexually in a specific country.[15] Countries which legally acknowledge same-sex relationships or which have adopted antidiscrimination legislation are more supportive of homosexual expression and the formation of gay and lesbian lifestyles than countries where specific forms of homosexual expression are still illegal. In Britain, for example, the age of consent for heterosexual and for homosexual contacts differs.

A social climate is also related to the religious situation in a specific country. Countries where traditional religions promoting heterosexual monogamy are still dominant differ from countries where the influence of the church on the organization of social life has become weak.

The occurrence and expression of homosexuality also depend upon the

---

15. There is certainly not a perfect relationship between the social climate and the legal situation in specific countries. A good example is Ireland, which, from a legal perspective, belongs to the group of progressive countries but which still has one of the most negative social climates regarding homosexuality in Europe.

general visibility of homosexuality in a given society. This visibility is related to the existence of homosexual subcultures and the strength of a gay and lesbian movement. Subcultures are a crucial factor in the expression of homosexuality, since they offer homosexual men and women opportunities to meet each other, to find potential partners, and to develop a shared frame of reference. When a gay and lesbian subculture is strongly developed, it will independently affect the expression of homosexuality and the development of various homosexual lifestyles.

Other factors which might contribute to the diversity of homosexuality are social geographical factors such as urbanization and population density. Higher levels of urbanization create more anonymity and diminish the level of social control. In less densely populated areas it is also harder to find similarly oriented people and to develop networks.

The factors discussed, and probably a long list of other factors which have not been discussed, affect the kind of homosexuality we sample in our studies. It is to be expected that restrictive social climates will thwart and delay the process of homosexual identity formation. As a consequence, people will have their coming out at different stages in life.[16] People who eventually "turn out" to be gay might also attempt for a longer period of time to ignore their homosexual desires and to adopt a heterosexual lifestyle. A more positive climate toward homosexuality might counteract the furtive expression of homosexuality and foster the finding of intimate partners and the developing and maintaining of gay relationships. The shorter duration of gay relationships has been explained as a consequence of the lack of social support and legal recognition of these relationships. Since the various factors discussed will influence the functioning of gay men—and in more ways than I have addressed here—they cannot be ignored and should, at least on a theoretical level, be included in our studies.

Discussion and Conclusion

The way homosexuality is conceptualized and operationalized is always a matter of choice; it should, however, become a reasoned and deliberate choice. In line with the definition of homosexuality chosen, sampling and recruitment procedures have to be motivated and reasoned; inherent implications for the outcomes have to be understood and acknowledged. The impossibility of composing a representative sample does not release the

---

16. Coming out and self-acceptance have become concepts which are indissolubly tied to homosexuality in contemporary social scientific studies. It is, however, unclear to what extent we, by applying these concepts, are describing a sexual reality or actually constructing one. For various people exhibiting homosexual behavior, these dimensions might be completely irrelevant. The role gay and lesbian studies play in the construction and reproduction of (homo)sexuality would be an interesting topic for further exploration.

researcher from the obligation to carefully consider his sampling procedures. It is evident that the sampling procedures used have consequences for the external validity of the findings. Representative samples are, of course, not a prerequisite to furthering our understanding of homosexuality. For building and testing theories one might decide to sample extreme or deviant cases, critical or typical cases. Other considerations might be to compose a sample with maximal or minimal variation. All these strategies have different consequences for the external validity of a study.

To assess the meaning of research findings it is not sufficient to know that persons in a study show homosexual behavior or identify themselves as gay: self-identified homosexuals do not constitute an invariable, unified breed of people. Knowing about somebody's homosexuality (either through behavior or self-identification) becomes meaningful if the personal, social, cultural, legal, and historical contexts are taken into account, since these factors heavily influence the expression and experience of homosexuality.[17] As far as possible, elements of this context have to be integrated as variables into the research design. Otherwise this context should be taken into account in interpreting the meaning of the research findings. The way respondents effectively evaluate and cognitively conceive their own homosexual behavior and feelings, as well as homosexuality in general, should be a structural part of studies and be systematically analyzed in relation to the issue under study.

References

Ajzen, I. (1991). The theory of planned behavior. *Organizational Behavior and Human Decision Processes, 50,* 179–211.
Altman, D. (1982). *The homosexualization of America.* New York: St. Martin's Press.
Boega, M. G., Wit, J. B. F. de, Vroome, E. M. M. de, Houweling, H., Schop, W., & Sandfort, Th. G. M. (1994). Perceptie van risico op HIV-infectie onder homoseksuele mannen. *Gedrag & Gezondheid, 24*(6), 277–289.
Buunk, A. P., & Bakker, A. B. (1995). Extradyadic sex: The role of descriptive and injunctive norms. *Journal of Sex Research, 32,* 313–318.
Catania, J. A., Gibson, D. R., Chitwood, D. D., & Coates, T. J. (1990). Methodological problems in AIDS behavior research: Influences on measurement error and

---

17. It may be contended that part of the argument developed here applies to the study not only of homosexuality but of heterosexuality as well. As has been documented in recent studies, heterosexuality is not an ahistorical construct either (Katz, 1994; Wilkinson & Kitzinger, 1994). This is to a certain extent a valid argument. People involved in sexual activities with the opposite gender are too easily considered as a homogeneous group, amplifying the differences between heterosexual and homosexual people. It could well be that other taxonomies of sexuality than the one based on sexual object choice might offer more fruitful perspectives.

participation bias in studies of sexual behavior. *Psychological Bulletin, 108,* 339–362.

Dingelstad, A. A. M., Paalman, M. E. M., Vroome, E. M. M. de, Kolker, L., & Sandfort, Th. G. M. (1994a). Toename in vellig vrijen bij jongeren en niet monogamen. Kennis, houding en gedrag met betrekking tot veilig vrijen en condoomgebruik van 1987 tot en met 1992. *Tijdschrift voor Sociale Gezondheidszorg, 72,* 60–65.

Dingelstad, A. A. M., Vroome, E. M. M. de, & Sandfort, Th. G. M. (1994b). *Velig vrijen en condoomgebruik onder de aigemene Nederlandse bevolking. Resultaten 13 metingen April 1987–Mei 1993.* Homostudies/ISOR, Utrecht.

Doll, L. S., Petersen, L. R., White, C. R., Johnson, E. S., Ward, J. W., & the Blood Donor Study Group. (1992). Homosexually and nonhomosexually identified men who have sex with men: A behavioral comparison. *Journal of Sex Research, 29,* 1–14.

Donovan, J. M. (1992). Homosexual, gay, and lesbian: Defining the words and sampling the populations. *Journal of Homosexuality, 24,* 27–47.

Gagnon, J. H. (1990). Gender preference in erotic relations: The Kinsey scale and sexual scripts. In D. P. McWhirter, S. A. Sanders, & J. M. Reinisch (Eds.), *Homosexuality/heterosexuality: Concepts of sexual orientation* (pp. 177–207). New York: Oxford University Press.

Halman, P., & de Moor, R. (1994). Religion, churches and moral values. In P. Ecter, L. Halman, & R. de Moor (Eds.), *The individualizing society* (pp. 37–65). Tilburg: Tilburg University Press.

Harry, J. (1988). Sampling gay men. *Journal of Sex Research, 22,* 21–34.

Harry, J. (1990). A probability sample of gay males. *Journal of Homosexuality, 19,* 89–104.

Humphreys, L. (1970). *Tearoom trade: Impersonal sex in public places.* Chicago: Aldine.

Katz, J. N. (1994). *The invention of homosexuality.* New York: Dutton.

Kinsey, A. C., Pomeroy, W. P., & Martin, C. E. (1948). *Sexual behavior in the human male.* Philadelphia: W. B. Saunders.

Klein, F., Sepekoff, B., & Wolf, T. J. (1985). Sexual orientation: A multi-variable, dynamic process. *Journal of Homosexuality, 11,* 35–49.

Laumann, E. O., Gagnon, J. H., Michael, R. T., & Michaels, S. (1994). *The social organization of sexuality: Sexual practices in the United States.* Chicago: University of Chicago Press.

Ruse, M. (1995). Sexual identity: Reality or construction. In H. Harris (Ed.), *Identity: Essays Based on Herbert Spencer Lectures in the University of Oxford* (pp. 65–99). Oxford: Clarendon.

Sandfort, Th., Vroome, E. de, Buunk, B., & Bakker, A. (1996). Determinanten van buitenrelationele seks bij homoseksuele mannen; een replicatie en een vergelijking met heteroseksuele mannen en vrouwen.

Sandfort, Th. G. M., Vroome, E. M. M. de. (1996). Homoseksueliteit in Nederland: een vergelijking tussen aselecte groepen homoseksuele en heteroseksuele mannen. Tijdschrift voor Seksuologie.

Seldman, S. (1993). Identity and politics in a "postmodern" gay culture: Some historical and conceptual notes. In M. Warren (Ed.), *Fear of a queer planet: Queer politics and social theory* (pp. 105–142). Minneapolis: University of Minnesota Press.

Shiveley, M. G. & De Cecco, J. P. (1977). Components of sexual identity. *Journal of Homosexuality, 3*, 41–48.

Strassberg, D. S., & Lowe, K. (1995). Volunteer bias in sexuality research. *Archives of Sexual Behavior, 24*, 369–382.

Tielman, R. A. P., Hendricks, A., & Carballo, M. (Eds.). (1991). *Bisexuality and HIV/AIDS* (pp. 73–80). Buffalo: Prometheus.

Weinberg, M. S. (1970). Homosexual sample: Differences and similarities. *Journal of Sex Research, 6*, 312–325.

Weinberg, M., Williams, C. J., & Pryor, D. W. (1994). *Dual attraction.* New York: Oxford University Press.

Wiederman, M. W. (1993). Demographic and sexual characteristics of nonresponders to sexual experience items in a national survey. *Journal of Sex Research, 30*, 27–35.

Wilkinson, S., & Kitzinger, C. (1994). The social construction of heterosexuality. *Journal of Gender Studies, 3*, 307–318.

Wit, J. B. F. de (1994). *Prevention of HIV infection among homosexual men: Behavior change and behavioral determinants.* Amsterdam: Thesis.

Zessen, G. van, & Sandfort, Th. (1991). *Seksualiteit in Nederland. Seksueel godrag, risico en preventie van AIDS.* Amsterdam: Swets & Zeitlinger.

Assessing Participation Bias

ANNE M. JOHNSON AND ANDREW COPAS

Introduction

A major focus of sexual behavior surveys in recent years has been to estimate the distribution of behaviors in representative population samples, motivated by the need to inform the epidemiology and prevention of HIV and sexually transmitted diseases. Key parameters include the prevalence of infrequent and censured behaviors. The robustness of population estimates (e.g., the prevalence of homosexuality, anal intercourse, commercial sex contacts, etc.) depends upon a number of methodological concerns. These include sampling strategy, sample representativeness, response rate and participation bias, mode of interview, question validity, test-retest repeatability, respondent error, and observer error including interviewer effects. Any of these as well as other factors may influence the accuracy of key parameter estimates and have been reviewed elsewhere (Catania, Gibson, Chitwood, & Coates, 1990).

This paper focuses on particular methodological issues around survey participation and its effect on population parameter estimates. Not everyone approached in a sexual behavior survey agrees to take part, and many of those who do nevertheless refuse to answer specific questions or incorrectly assume that some questions do not apply to them. This is clearly an issue of concern, since if the nonparticipants and/or item nonresponders have different sexual behavior than the item responders, then the crude estimates derived from the item responders will be biased. There is an important distinction to be made about the nature of any difference in behavior. If nonparticipants, item responders, and item nonresponders have the same sexual behavior within demographic classes, e.g., age and marital status categories, across which we know sexual behavior varies strongly, then estimates of behavior within those demographic classes will be unbiased. Furthermore, unbiased estimates for the target population can be simply constructed through weighting procedures (see later). However, if these groups differ with respect to their sexual behavior even within demographic classes, then the situation is more complex and estimates of behavior within demographic classes will be biased. We call this second source of bias participation bias. For an example of how participation bias may arise and how it affects estimates, see our later discussion of techniques of analysis. In the following section we discuss how various factors affect overall participation; we also discuss the variation in participation and questionnaire completion by demographic class. The focus of this paper, however, is in the section on the identification of the likelihood and probable nature of any participation bias, the reasons why it matters, and how one might adjust estimates to remove the resulting bias.

Participation Rates

The Effect of Survey Design

Bias in population estimates may arise as a result of a sampling frame which systematically excludes sectors of the target population, e.g., exclusion of the homeless in house-to-house surveys and exclusion of many poor or transient groups of people in telephone surveys. Bias will also arise through differential willingness of members of the sample to participate and to answer all relevant questions, which may itself be influenced by a number of factors. We consider here the effects of various aspects of survey design on participation.

Mode of interview alone will affect participation, both the overall rate and the kinds of people who agree or refuse to take part. There have been some assessments of participation and item response rates comparing face-to-face interviews, self-administered questionnaires, and telephone interviews in surveys of varying subject matter, but results vary (Groves et al., 1988). While some studies have suggested that household surveys result in higher participation rates than telephone surveys, others have found rates to be comparable. In particular, the recent French study (ACSF Investigators, 1992) found similar participation rates using telephone and face-to-face methods but some differences in the nature of responses to questions, including item response rates. More recent approaches include exploration of computer-assisted self-completion methods for researching sensitive topics, which may influence not only participation rates but also the validity of responses (Weeks, 1992; Couper, 1996). See the paper by Turner et al. in part 2 of this volume for discussion of this new methodology. The British survey (Wellings et al., 1990) found higher rates of reported censured behaviors in self-completion than in face-to-face interviews. This relates to question validity rather than participation bias but suggests that interview mode may also influence participation. Other influences on the probability of participation by individuals may include the gender of interviewers and the nature of the approach to potential respondents. In the British survey, those approached by male interviewers were significantly less likely to participate than those approached by female interviewers. Among those addresses visited where the outcome was either the completion of an interview or a refusal by the selected eligible person, by proxy, or refusal of all information, male interviewers achieved a completed interview at 61.4% (1959/3192) of addresses and female interviewers at 67.8% (16917/24962).

Factors such as these may also affect how participation varies across population subgroups. For instance, male interviewers may particularly deter female participants; the nature of the approach may encourage some but offend others; and, more obviously, the use of self-administered questionnaires will deter those with poor literacy skills in the language used.

Variation in Participation by Demographic Class

There are two ways of determining how participation has varied by demographic variables. The first is the indirect method of comparing the demographic characteristics of the participants with those of the census or another large-scale survey thought to be representative of the target population. Under the assumption that the sample of potential participants was similar demographically to the population as a whole, an over- or underrepresentation of a group of people can be interpreted as arising from above- or below-average participation in that group. This assumption may well be reasonable where the sample of potential participants is a single-stage random sample, but in the case of a household survey, addresses will clearly be sampled in "clusters" so as to save time and money. If the sample is clustered, then those demographic variables that vary strongly geographically may be distributed differently in the sample of potential participants to the census.

In the British survey, comparison with the census data reveals an underrepresentation of men (in Britain this is true in social survey research in general). With respect to age, in the British and other surveys relatively small differences were observed, but the most marked underrepresentation is in older age groups, balanced by overrepresentation in younger age groups (see Figure 1). In the British survey, representation of the combined ethnic minorities is comparable to the census figure. Comparisons on marital status in the British survey suggested a slightly higher proportion of single men and divorced and cohabiting men and women. Differences in several surveys are also observed in participation rates by region, with lower rates of participation in large inner city populations. In the British survey, it has been shown (Johnson, Wadsworth, Wellings, & Field, 1994) that the use of entry-phones may well explain part of this phenomenon.

The second approach is the more direct approach of comparing participants with nonparticipants with respect to those variables collected for both. Typically the number of variables collected for the nonparticipants will be small and will only be available for some nonparticipants in any case. However, if one is prepared to assume that those nonparticipants for whom data were recorded are comparable to other nonparticipants, then

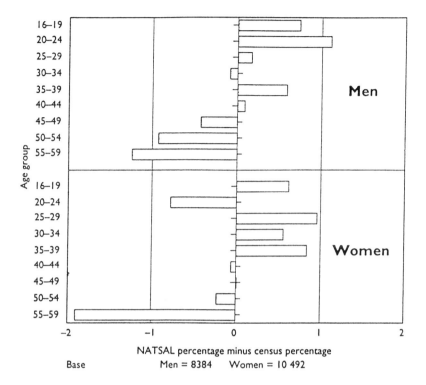

Figure 1. Age distribution of the survey (NATSAL) participants compared with the 1991 census. Adapted from Johnson et al. (1994).

one can proceed with the comparison. For example, in the British survey, the ages and sex of all those residents were collected, from households who were sufficiently cooperative, before selection of one specific individual to be interviewed (without replacement). Hence, if the selected individual refused to participate, then the age and sex of that nonparticipant will be recorded. In the British survey, comparing directly the participants with those nonparticipants for whom data were recorded, the nonparticipants were found more likely to be male, more likely to be older, and more likely to live in large urban areas (see Table 1)

Variation in Completion Rates by Demographic Class

Survey design and other factors may also affect whether participants answer all the questions expected of them. In the British survey, we have performed a regression analysis (Copas, Johnson, & Wadsworth, 1997) to assess how the completion of the self-completion booklet of the more sensitive questions varied by demographic class. Logistic regression was performed with booklet refusal as the response variable, and significant asso-

Table 1 *Participation by Age and Sex in British Survey*

Sex	Age	Number of Participants (%)
Male	16–24	1,489/1,947 (76.5)
	25–34	2,368/3,237 (73.2)
	35–44	2,143/3,069 (69.8)
	45–59	2,118/3,331 (63.6)
Female	16–24	1,888/2,392 (78.9)
	25–34	3,273/4,085 (80.1)
	35–44	2,604/3,289 (79.2)
	45–59	2,993/4,155 (72.0)

ciations with demographic variables were found. The strongest associations were lower completion among those over 45 years old, those with problems of understanding, e.g., literacy problems, and those from ethnic minorities in Britain. There were also weaker yet significant associations, indicating lower completion rates among those aged 25–44 relative to those younger, among those in large urban areas, those of unskilled or manual occupation, and those cohabiting, widowed, divorced, or separated relative to those married. This suggests that future efforts may well need to be directed at these groups in order to improve completion rates. The use of alternative booklets in languages other than English may improve matters, and it may be that older persons need special encouragement to complete questions.

Does Participation Bias Arise?

The Experimental Evidence

A number of experimental approaches have been used to assess willingness to participate in sexual behavior studies. The studies published before 1990 have been reviewed elsewhere (Catania et al., 1990). In summary, various studies have been undertaken which recruited respondents (in most cases college students) and then invited them to volunteer for either a sex survey or a nonsex survey or laboratory experiment. Some of these studies were able to collect some data on sexual behavior, even in the nonsex-survey arm. Studies of this type have in broad terms suggested that men are more likely to volunteer than women for sexual behavior surveys, a result that is surprising in the light of our previous statements. Volunteers are also likely to be more sexually liberal and permissive and, in general, tend to have higher levels of sexual activity than nonvolunteers. Two more recent studies are consistent with these general findings. In one study of college undergraduates (Strassberg & Lowe, 1995), volunteers were found to have more sexual experience, among both men and women. In the other study of genitourinary clinic attendees (James, Bignell, & Gillies, 1991), it was found that among those who agreed to an initial questionnaire, those who refused a further interview were significantly less likely to report vaginal penetration with fingers but not significantly different with respect to any of the other behavioral variables. However, the difficulty with such experimental studies is that their applicability to participation in large-scale random sample studies is unknown. All experimental studies are based on those who are willing to participate, at least in some kind of study, and who are also able to express a preference for one kind of research above another. This is a very different scenario from population-based studies that invite participation in sexual behavior surveys alone. Furthermore, the finding of different reported sexual experiences between volunteers for a sexual behavior survey and volunteers for another experiment can be interpreted as a genuine difference only if both groups have reported accurately. One has to be concerned that those who are less prepared to talk about their sexual experiences may also be more inclined to misreport these experiences, particularly any unusual experiences (see next section for further consideration of this point). The magnitude of the participation or volunteer bias in these experimental studies is seen to increase with the level of detail of the sex survey. A sexual behavior survey such as the British survey is considerably less invasive than some types of sex research, but nevertheless the broad nature of participation bias in these studies, we feel, may be suggestive of its nature in population sex surveys. Furthermore, since the sexual behavior of nonparticipants in a sexual behavior survey will never be known, this experimental evidence will always be one of the strongest reasons to suspect participation bias and to suggest its nature in broad terms.

Evidence from Sexual Behavior Surveys

By making assumptions, we may be able to construct broad hypotheses about the likelihood and probable nature of any participation bias. There are two obvious techniques. The first technique is to approach a random sample of nonparticipants (perhaps by telephone), ask why they refused to participate, and seek any other useful information. If these data do not suggest an association between these people and unusual sexual experience, then one may feel that participation bias is unlikely. However, obviously behavioral information is unlikely to be given, even if asked for, by nonparticipants, and some people will refuse all information.

The second technique used is to assume that differences in sexual behavior between reluctant and less reluctant participants (defined in some way) reflect differences between the participants and nonparticipants. For example, in the British survey, those who were embarrassed during the survey have been compared to those who were not. It is assumed that if, say, the embarrassed are more/less likely to have some homosexual experience than those not embarrassed (within demographic classes), then the nonparticipants will be more/less likely to have had some homosexual experience than the participants (within demographic classes). The best way of analyzing the data would typically be to perform a regression analysis with reluctance as the outcome variable and a variety of key demographic and behavioral variables as explanatory factors. If the behavioral variables are significant in the model, with the demographic terms also included, then this indicates that reluctance is associated with behavior within demographic classes. These analyses have been performed by ourselves and others too, and we discuss the results found below.

The assumption that underpins this method is essentially that sexual behavior (perhaps unusual behavior) has caused participants to be reluctant. It is important to consider alternative ways in which differences in reported behavior between reluctant and more keen participants may have arisen. It may be that the reluctant participants felt unable to report any unusual aspects of their behavior or experience and so misreported information. If differences have arisen by misreporting, then there is no reason to rely on the method. Under this alternative scenario, there is no reason to assume that nonparticipants are likely to have behavior closer to that reported by the reluctant participants than to that reported by those more keen.

Biggar and Melbye in a Danish postal survey (1992) took an elegant approach, using both of the methods we outlined. Participants were asked to mail back a card separate from their questionnaire to confirm their participation. Follow-up questionnaires were sent to nonresponders, and the behaviors and characteristics of late responders were compared with earlier responders. The authors clearly demonstrated that simple methods could improve the overall participation rate, although, like the British survey, they showed a deficit of older men and women. Later responders had a higher item nonresponse rate and lower educational status. After adjustment for age, the authors found no major difference in key behavior variables between early and late responders who had had some sexual experience. But they did find that late male responders were more likely to have had no sexual experience. Telephone calls to a sample of nonresponders led to the conclusion that "the reasons for non-response did not suggest the lifestyle of non-responders placed them at high risk of HIV infection." Since the reasons most frequently given for nonparticipation were related to the subject matter (36% in total) rather than a general desire not to take part in surveys and since 11% would not give a reason, the possibility of appreciable participation bias cannot be excluded. However, the authors may well be correct to suggest that participation bias, if it has arisen, is more likely to have caused an underestimation of HIV transmission risk. The evidence from the comparison of late and early responders method is inconclusive, since the regression analysis includes only those with sexual experience.

Another comparison of willing and unwilling participants in a sex survey has been performed by Laumann et al. (1994), again focusing on a regression analysis of the relationship between measures of reluctance and sexual experience and attitudes after controlling for demographic variables. As measures of reluctance, Laumann et al. take whether a large payment was required to obtain participation, whether the interviewer thought participation had been very difficult to obtain, and whether five or more visits were required to obtain participation. The sexual experience variables considered in analysis were more than one partner in the last year, oral sex in the last event, touched sexually before puberty, and masturbated in the last year. In addition, one attitudinal variable, whether the respondent thought homosexuality is always wrong, was included. Taking the measures of reluctance as response variables in logistic regression analysis and controlling for a selection of demographic variables, Laumann et al. found only one strong association between any of the behavioral or attitudinal variables and any of the measures of reluctance. There is some indication that among women, those requiring more than five visits were more likely to report performance of oral sex in the last event, but the one strong association indicates that men who reported masturbation in the last year were much more likely to have required five or more visits than those who did not. Since the association with reported masturbation in the last year among men was found with only one of the three measures of reluctance, it is unclear whether, under the assumption that nonparticipants are more similar to reluctant participants, this should be taken as an indication of participation bias. Laumann et al. conclude that "our data appear to be largely free of significant nonresponse bias."

In the British survey, again a similar approach has been taken, with two measures of reluctance and two behavioral variables. Full details are published elsewhere (Copas, Johnson, & Wadsworth, 1997). The measures of reluctance were refusal of the self-completion booklet of the more sensitive questions and embarrassment during the survey. Logistic regression analysis was performed in the same way as in the other surveys, and embarrassment and booklet refusal were associated with less varied sexual experience. Assuming that these associations reflect differences between participants and nonparticipants, we suggest that participation bias did arise and that nonparticipants are more likely than participants to have less varied sexual experience.

One of the main concerns in sexual behavior research, driven by the HIV/AIDS epidemic, has been the underreporting of censured behavior of high risk for HIV transmission. Both our own results and those of Biggar and Melbye (1992) suggest that in the British and Danish surveys, in general, nonparticipants may be at lower risk of HIV transmission than participants, and so participation bias is more likely to have led to an underestimation of high-risk behaviors than an overestimation. However, the possibility of certain small high-risk subgroups, e.g., prostitutes, being underrepresented or indeed entirely absent from the survey participants cannot be excluded, and their impact upon population estimates of risky behaviors may be large (see next section). This underrepresentation could result from low participation rates in these groups or from their exclusion from the sampling frame.

In other cultural settings, the nature of participation bias may be radically different. We would suggest that any analysis of the likelihood and probable nature of participation bias should be conducted using data from the survey in question or from other surveys in culturally similar countries at similar times.

Does Participation Bias Matter?

Even mild participation bias could be a major source of error in sexual behavior surveys, since the overall participation rate is typically in the range of 60%–75%. The issue of whether participation bias has arisen is crucial to the analysis of the survey. Where participation bias has arisen, the use of techniques based upon the assumption that it has not will not in general improve estimates (see next section). The potential importance of nonparticipation by those with unusual sexual experience has been highlighted by our own work and that of Tom Smith (1990), grappling with the problem of inconsistent reporting between men and women in the numbers of partners. Wadsworth et al. (1996) have examined the range of assumptions required to bring the ratio of the mean number of partners between men and women to unity. This includes assumptions about the nonparticipation of prostitutes (or indeed their exclusion from the sampling frame), as well as issues of reporting error.

Dealing with Participation Bias in Analysis

Where participation bias as we have defined it has not arisen but participation has varied by definable demographic class, the techniques to produce unbiased estimates of the population parameters are relatively straightforward and are reviewed elsewhere (Kalton, 1983). An example will clarify both these techniques and how participation bias may arise.

Specifically, suppose we wish to estimate the proportion of the male population with homosexual experience. In our hypothetical sex survey, the response rate among those men aged 16–39 was 80% and the proportion of the population with homosexual experience in that age group was

10%. Furthermore, suppose that among those aged 40–59 the proportion in the population with homosexual experience was 5% and the participation rate in the survey was only 40%. Suppose also that two thirds of the target population (men aged 16–59) are aged 16–39, one third aged 40–59, and this was reflected in the age distribution of those sampled for potential participation in the survey.

Suppose that participation has varied by age, but within age groups participants have broadly the same sexual behavior as nonparticipants. Then estimates of the proportion with homosexual experience in the two age groups will be unbiased, and the estimate for the total population will be a weighted sum of the two observed proportions. Specifically, here it will be two thirds multiplied by 10% plus one third multiplied by 5%, equal to 8.3%, and this is the true population proportion. The unweighted estimate is obtained by ignoring the response pattern and simply calculating the proportion among the participants. Here, since four times more participants were aged 16–39 than aged 40–59, this will be four fifths multiplied by 10% plus one fifth multiplied by 5%, which equals exactly 9%.

Now suppose that, on the other hand, participation bias has arisen and that, while men aged 16–39 decided whether to participate without reference to their sexual behavior, men aged 40–59 without homosexual experience were more inclined to take part than those with such experience, who often felt that they would be embarrassed to report this and so declined to participate. Suppose then that the true proportion with homosexual experience among the general population of men aged 40–59 is also 10% (but the measured prevalence is 5% due to participation bias), so that the proportion among men aged 16–59 is 10%, then clearly the weighted estimate (8.3%) is, in fact, more biased than the unweighted (9%). This example illustrates that the technique of weighting provides a simple way to derive unbiased estimates where participation has varied across demographic classes known to be associated with sexual behavior, but within those classes participation was independent of behavior. If, however, participation bias (as we define it) has occurred, then weighting may in fact increase the bias of estimates.

To deal with suspected participation bias, a method to generate assumptions about the sexual behavior of the nonparticipants is required. One might decide, as before, that the best assumption is that they have behavior similar to that of reluctant participants, although the assumption need not be based upon that specific survey at all. On this basis, one could then construct estimates of their behavior and hence of the population as a whole. Since any specific assumption is likely to be wrong to varying degrees, the sensitivity of estimates to the assumption made should be examined. One could, for instance, make several assumptions and see how estimates vary over these assumptions. More research is needed in how to construct such assumptions and into issues around the estimation of behavioral parameters under such assumptions. The authors have begun to address these topics (Copas & Farewell, work in progress).

Conclusions

Participation bias is a major concern in sexual behavior research. Further methodological work is required, both to assess the sensitivity of parameter estimates to potential sources of bias and to develop methods to maximize participation and reduce all sources of bias. Split experiments in sampling strategies, interview techniques, etc., are all required to assess influences on participation rates and item nonresponse. Statistical approaches can be used to assess the limits of influence of participation bias on estimates of the distribution of behaviors in populations. Qualitative work on language difficulties, comprehension, and approaches to respondents are all relevant to assessing participation bias and minimizing it. There remains an extensive research agenda in improving participation rates and the resulting quality of data from sexual behavior surveys.

References

ACSF Investigators. (1992). Analysis of sexual behaviour in France (ACSF): A comparison between two modes of investigation, telephone survey and face-to-face survey. *AIDS, 6*, 315–323.

Biggar, R. J., & Melbye, M. (1992). Responses to anonymous questionnaires concerning sexual behaviour: A method to examine potential biases. *American Journal of Public Health, 82*, 1–7.

Catania, J. A., Gibson, D. R., Chitwood, D. D., & Coates, T. J. (1990). Methodological problems in AIDS behavioural research: Influences on measurement error and participation bias in studies of sexual behaviour. *Psychological Bulletin, 108*, 339–362.

Copas, A., Johnson, A. M., & Wadsworth, J. (1997). Assessing participation bias in a sexual behavior survey: Implications for measuring HIV risk. *AIDS, 11*, 783–790.

Couper, Rowe, B. (1996). Evaluation of computer-assisted self-interview component in a computer-assisted personal interview survey. *Opinion Quarterly, 60*, 89–105.

Groves, R. M., Biemer, P. P., Lyberg, L. E., Massay, J. T., Nicholls, W. L., & Waksberg, J. (Eds.). (1988). *Telephone survey methodology.* New York: John Wiley and Sons.

James, N. I., Bignell, C. J., & Gillies, P. A. (1991). The reliability of self-reported sexual behavior. *AIDS, 5*, 333–336.

Johnson, A. M., Wadsworth, J., Wellings, K., & Field, J. (1994). *Sexual attitudes and lifestyles.* Oxford: Blackwell.

Kalton, G. (1983). *Compensating for missing survey data*. Ann Arbor: University of Michigan Press.

Laumann, E. O., Gagnon, J. H., Michael, R. T., & Michaels, S. (1994). *The social organization of sexuality: Sexual practices in the United States*. Chicago: University of Chicago Press.

Smith, T. W. (1990). Discrepancies between men and women in reporting numbers of sexual partners: A cross-national comparison. *GSS Methodological Report, 68*. Chicago: NORC.

Strassberg, D. S., & Lowe, K. (1995). Volunteer bias in sexuality research. *Archives of Sexual Behaviour, 24*, 369–382.

Wadsworth, J., Johnson, A. M., Wellings, K., & Field, J. (1996). What's in a mean? An examination of the inconsistency between men and women reporting sexual partnerships. *Journal of the Royal Statistical Society, A, 159*, 111–123.

Weeks, M. F. (1992). Computer-assisted survey information collection: A review of CASI methods and their implications for survey operations. *Journal of Official Statistics, 8*, 445–465.

Wellings, K., Field, J., Wadsworth, J., Johnson, A. M., Anderson, R. M., & Bradshaw, S. A. (1990). Sexual lifestyles under scrutiny. *Nature, 348*, 276–278.

Discussion

Charles Turner: Several investigators, including the folks who did the field test for the aborted National Household Seroprevalence Survey, adopted a strategy of taking a random subsample of nonresponders and working very hard (and paying substantial incentives) to try to get that subsample to respond in order to have actual data with which to adjust for the overall nonresponse bias. If you do that with a small subsample of nonrespondents, it can be relatively inexpensive. In the U.S. context, you might pay a $100 incentive—which is relatively small compared with the field cost of a case requiring 15 callbacks. The resultant data gives you a direct way of getting a handle on what your nonresponders really look like.

Anne Johnson: Do you have any sense of the direction of that?

Charles Turner: Dallas was special because the survey was conducted in the midst of a campaign by one of the six gay organizations in Dallas that encouraged nonresponse. So I'm not sure how the overall result would generalize to other contexts.

Anne Johnson: One of the problems we have in Britain is that there is an unchangeable ethos that we do not pay people for participation in survey research.

Charles Turner: Why not?

Anne Johnson: Well, I don't fully understand; perhaps it's something we ought to challenge.

Edward Laumann: Do you have a professional proscription against it?

Anne Johnson: In general, the research councils will not pay for costs like this.

Charles Turner: My colleagues found in the National Survey of Family Growth experiment that if you paid an incentive to your respondents (as a partial compensation for the time you're taking out of their lives), you saved money, because respondents were often willing to do the interview the first time you found them at home. So overall you wound up saving money.

John Bancroft: I agree with Anne. I think this principal in the U.K. should be challenged. The research councils, certainly the Medical Research Council, have the policy which forbids you from paying anything other than expenses that the subjects incur. But having worked in a Medical Research Council unit, if we were doing studies funded by, for example, the WHO and not the MRC, Cynthia Graham's study is an example, and if it was clear that it was going to be very difficult to recruit without some financial incentive, we were able to do that. In the current male contraception studies, it's being done. So I think it probably would be worth trying to challenge it.

Anne Johnson: Well, I am particularly interested in the data that show it saves money. That would be very helpful.

Ted Myers: In Canada, if money is used to reimburse persons for their time, it is considered unethical to pay below the minimum wage. However, one can give a gratuity. In many studies of gay men and HIV/AIDS where a reimbursement is made, most respondents are motivated regardless and donate the money to a local AIDS organization. In venue-based surveys, a small payment may attract men who would not normally respond, i.e., heterosexual men who just happen to be in the premises. The effect of payment for men with lower incomes is unknown. Another aspect to consider in terms of motivation is the anonymity with which persons can respond, their comfort with a topic, and their feeling that they are being supported and making a worthwhile contribution. Here media campaigns and advance promotional information about the survey have a major role to play. In the bisexual study currently being conducted in Ontario, I would say only a small proportion of the men who contact our study through the 1–800 telephone line have disclosed their bisexuality to any of their partners, but they are comfortable in responding, having seen the repeated series of advertisements and hearing about the confidentiality and anonymity of the study through a variety of media. I would hypothesize that if that same population was contacted by a random telephone survey, at a time which was not at their convenience, they would give quite different responses.

Joe Catania: Bob Groves and Heather Turner did a nonresponse study with the National AIDS Behavioral Survey where they followed up the nonrespondents. They found that nonrespondents tended to be white, to be older, to be more likely to go to church. They also looked at hard-to-reach respondents and found that they were a different set of people. They were young, highly sexually active, and not likely to be at home very much, which is why they were hard to reach. But these findings aside, one of their key results was that the vast majority of nonrespondents dropped out before they ever heard that this study was about sex. Now that was a phone survey and there may be mode differences, but I was wondering to what extent you had found that the dropouts were occurring during the enumeration or the interview process.

Anne Johnson: I think a high proportion of refusers are those who would refuse to participate in surveys on any subject. There are some people who just shut the door and won't talk to an interviewer at all. There were relatively few people who dropped out, I think, on the basis of the subject. And once people had agreed to participate, very few gave up halfway through. I think there's a general issue as well as a specific issue.

Alain Giami: I would like to react to Charles Turner about the incentive of money. Money is a very sensitive issue and a cultural issue which is not the same in different countries. It seems that in the U.S., whatever you do you have to pay, you have to ask money for everything. I don't have the experience of paying people for quantitative questionnaires. But in my experience with qualitative research, it seems that when people are motivated it works better. When you ask people to respond, they do it best if they have some interest and some inner motivation in doing so. Moreover, establishing what kind of motivation helps people to respond is also a matter of interest. When you pay people, you lose the possibility to understand why they agree to participate. But money is the cheapest way to pay!

Cynthia Graham: You looked at interview assessed embarrassment and problems of understanding, which could be reasons for not taking part. I wondered if any of the surveys have had time or money to ask the nonresponders why they didn't want to take part.

Anne Johnson: We don't have any data on that. But, yes, ideally I think we should have tried to go back to them.

Cynthia Graham: I didn't mean to go back to them, but asking them at the time what were their reasons for refusing?

Anne Johnson: There were some limited data on whether the interviewer thought it was the subject of the survey or not. We also reissued quite a lot of our interviews, so if at an address there had been a refusal, then the interviewer was asked to assess whether it was worth going back again. The reason for refusing might be "I'm going on holiday tomorrow morning and I'm sorry, I can't take part." And by the time they were coming back, it would have been too late. Those would have been reissued, another interviewer would be sent. So I suppose we might be able to sort that out and look at the difference in behavior between early and late responders.

Alfred Spira: I would like to give some information about an experience we had in France. Because of the reactions of our national ethical committee, we compared two letters that we sent to persons who were randomly selected to participate in the survey. The first letter was quite a positive letter. We asked the persons to participate so that we could obtain more information about health problems in order to improve public health. The other one, which was imposed by the ethical committee, was to ask persons to participate to give us more information about these terrible diseases which are going to kill everybody in the country. And it was very interesting because, I don't remember the exact figure, but approximately 70% of the persons agreed to participate with the first positive letter and less than 50% with the negative letter. The interesting thing is that the ethical committee told us, "Well if only 50% of the persons agree to participate, it's not a problem, you have just to double the number of persons in your sample." It took us months to convince them that a bias is a bias. I also completely agree with Anne about dropouts for sexual reasons; that is, when getting to sexual and very sensitive questions in our survey. I think that 0.6% of the persons stopped answering the questions when we came to the very sensitive questions. Our impression was that once you have established a good contact with the person, once they realize that it's a very serious questionnaire, even if the questions become embarrassing, they don't stop answering them.

Stuart Michaels: I want to turn this back to some of the points that Theo raised because I think they're interrelated and are of interest to some people in the room. Joe Catania is involved in trying to design a national survey that focuses on gay men and there are many, many issues that come up with that. Two aspects are: whether or not someone will agree to participate and then what they say when they do. I'm wondering if you want to comment on the usefulness of very large probability surveys, because I think there is a tradeoff. There's a whole set of economic issues that limit what's really possible, but if there wasn't a limitation on resources, if you really wanted to study the fullest range of homosexual behavior, ideation, and identity, wouldn't you want to give every man in the population a chance? I will identify a couple of further things and maybe you could then comment on them. I think that even quite closety or even nonidentified gay/homosexual men are sometimes quite responsive to the public health issues involved in these studies and I actually think there's some indication that you get higher participation and response from such persons when you're talking about a sex and AIDS survey. But then there may also be a countervailing tendency due to fear of exposure. In a sense these men may be more practiced in the art of deception, and since they are managing these things in their everyday life so as not to disclose, they will react to a survey in that same way.

Theo Sandfort: I think there's one very big difference between the nonselected sample that we had and the convenience samples and it has to do with promiscuity. Gay people have the image of being very promiscuous and all our studies in a way confirm that impression. But when you look at a nonselected sample, the level of promiscuity goes down tremendously, and that's a very important reason to sample as widely as possible.

Anne Johnson: I just wanted to comment on the differences between focused, purposive samples in Britain and the National Sex Survey. What came out of the NATSSAL survey was that we found we were picking a lot of people up who were not "out," who had had a homosexual experience (often an adolescent experience), but who had been entirely heterosexual for some time. Researchers like Tony Coxon and Graham Hart in Britain have acknowledged the importance of having a broad-based look to place their own purposive samples of gay men in context of the overall distribution of behaviors. Obviously a large, national sample cannot answer the kind of detailed questions which are relevant to understanding homosexual lifestyle, but they can point to where particular samples fit into the overall distribution. This can perhaps help to inform future sample strategies to identify more closeted behaviors, for example. I think that's their usefulness.

Ulrich Clement: In a way it seems to me that our discussion is one-eyed. One-eyed in the sense that we are so much concerned about the non-responders. Nobody has asked about the motivation of the responders. Theo, you brought up the plea for a theory-driven approach. Do you have a theoretical idea of what motivates people to respond to strangers about their intimate life and their sexual secrets? The question that should be answered is why should people participate?

Theo Sandfort: There are several reasons and I think there are a lot of general reasons like it's very nice when people pay a lot of attention to you. It's anonymous, you don't have a continuous relationship with that person, it's something you don't talk about, but you would like to talk about a lot. It can be helpful.

Ulrich Clement: It's rewarding, you mean?

Theo Sandfort: It's rewarding, it can be rewarding, depending on the quality of the interview, of course, but I think that with respect to homosexuality, there are other factors that might play a role, like promoting interest in homosexual issues in one way or another.

Joe Catania: We've been interested in the issue of respondent motivation. We've asked respondents why they participated and how it felt to them to participate. Some people started out by saying they were curious about what this was going to be about, but once they got into it, it felt so good to unload stuff they'd never been able to talk about. There are also a large group of people who participate for altruistic reasons. They just want to be helpful, at least this is what they express. But there's also a third group who end the interview or answered this question with something like "Well, there's this little problem I was hoping we might get to." They represent the help seekers who participate because they want to get information on their problem.

Leonore Tiefer: In a not unrelated question, I think we also need to look at the motivation and the response biases of the researchers. One of the things that I'm learning about during the coffee breaks are aspects of research that have not been reported. The selection bias of what aspects of the data one chooses to report versus not report seems to me a fascinating question, and it has not been limited by the confidence in the data themselves. There are other considerations being introduced, including the whole issue of disclosure by the researchers. This is a very large and complicated question, but I just offer an example. A colleague of mine, a feminist pedagogue from the University of South Florida, in her students' master's degrees and dissertations, requires them to include a section that describes the researcher comparable to the section that describes the participants in the research. She says that her students find this mind boggling. First, they have no models for this, they've read 42 million studies that have described in many ways the population being studied. They've never seen how you describe yourself as the researcher, and yet I think this is a general theme and we might think about how we would describe ourselves in terms that would somehow indicate our participation biases. What elements would we see as relevant to mention? It's to get away from the notion of the universal researcher who has no specificity.

Theo Sandfort: I think it's a very good point that you're making. My experience in teaching is that I force the students to find out why they want an answer to a certain question. When they do that, they discover that the way they had formulated the question is inappropriate. I show them that there's a background theory which makes them able to state more precisely what they want to study, and frame the question better. I don't think they have to give their full biography, but they should find out what their motivations are. What are their reasons for studying, for looking at a problem in a certain way?

Leonore Tiefer: The idea that we are looking at the problem in a complete way is an illusion. It's always a selection, so if somehow we articulate more of who we are, it becomes clearer why we're looking at the problem in the way that we're looking at it.

John Bancroft: I'd like to respond to Leonore and this issue of characteristics of the researcher. I've been confronted by this in relation to Kinsey, because Kinsey studiously avoided passing judgment on the various behaviors he encountered, and this has gotten him into all sorts of trouble. But I think his justification would be that if it was known what his views were about sex, then it might influence what people would be prepared to tell him or indeed whether they would be prepared to speak to him at all. So I think the question of the characteristics of the researcher have to be looked at on two levels. First of all, the effect on the subject in the research and then also the effect on those who are interpreting the results of the research, when the biases of the researcher need to be taken into account. I, for my sins, write in my textbook, which should be hitting its third edition before too long, a personal statement. I don't give details of my sex life, but I do talk about my sexual values, and I have had a considerable amount of very positive feedback from people about that. My justification for it is that it does give people some help to appreciate the sort of biases I might have in how I approach the data. I think it's something that is seldom done, and I'm interested in your colleague down south. In a way this ties in with a point about motivation. Thinking as much as I have about Kinsey and his interviews, it seemed to me that there were some characteristics of that particular point in history which would influence whether people were prepared to be interviewed by him or not. There were reasons to think that a lot of people really welcomed the opportunity to be able to talk about their sexuality at a time when sex just wasn't talked about. That presumably influenced his recruitment and affected the particular form of volunteer bias that he presumably had. So we need to consider how that aspect of motivation changes over time. We were talking about changes over time this morning. There will be different points in history when being prepared to answer questions about sexuality will have a different meaning, and the nonresponse is going to reflect changes of that particular kind.

Colin Williams: I think this question of researcher effect is incredible. In 1969, I think it was, when I first started studying gay organizations, this really hit me. When you go to do fieldwork and you get into the field, you are actually interacting with people who want a say in what you do. To do some of the things that we wanted to do, we found we had to be very political, we had to do certain things, we couldn't do some things, we had to watch who we talked to, we had to be sure that we weren't perceived as being on one side or another. So there was this problem with the people that you studied. Other than that, doing sex research for the first time there was trouble with our colleagues: what the hell are you doing? Sociologists were saying, "You're studying sex? We don't study things like that." So we had to be careful about what we said to them. There were also problems with our families. "Where are you going tonight?" "I'm going to this gay bar or gay bath." And so on. So the outcome was that I wrote a paper with Marty Weinberg at that time on these things (Weinberg & Williams, 1972), a kind of a sociology-of-knowledge paper on how relationships with your subjects, with your families, with your colleagues, and so on can have a very direct or even a very subtle effect on where you go, what you do, how long you stay out, who you talk to, who you let know what you're doing. I can't say I know the answer as to how it affects your research, but I'm certainly sure that it does and I'm certainly sure that we should need to do more research into what Leonore is saying.

Ann Stueve: So far we've been talking about studies where the units of analysis are adult individuals, who can decide for themselves whether or not to participate. But that leaves out a whole lot of sampling units. Certainly if we're dealing with children, parents are key players. There are a lot of questions about what role parents should be playing in allowing the participation of their youngsters in studies. What constitutes informed consent on the part of parents? Is passive consent really consent, or should we have active, written consent? And if the latter, how do we go about getting it, and what kinds of resources and costs are going to be entailed in getting it? And for those of us in the U.S., that's a pretty critical question with the Family Privacy Act still working its way through Congress, which could end up mandating written parental consent for many school studies.

We have done it. We did achieve it, but it has come at considerable cost, and it's also come with considerable benefits. But in addition to just individuals, be they young or old, there are also other units that we can sample. For example, event histories. Often the units of analysis we really care about are dyads or neighborhoods or schools or other organizations. Here there are a whole different set of factors that influence who participates and who doesn't and that serve as filters between us and the individuals we may ultimately want to be interviewing. We haven't talked about these other units that are also critical in our work.

Stuart Michaels: A point came up in Theo's paper and I'm not sure that it was highlighted as much as it could be. I'm thinking of the study that he did with, I think the COC, an organization where you actually have a random sample of the members of the organization. This is an important methodological alternative that is often not considered. There is a tendency when we study large populations to use representative samples, and when we study selected groups or organizations, we end up using convenience samples. There's no necessary reason for that to be the case. It's not always possible, but in this case you have an interesting comparison of a representative group of a membership organization which you know quite a bit about and the general population. That's good and we need more of those comparisons.

Anne Johnson: Just to respond to that. As a point of information, over the last year we've developed a sampling strategy for gay bars and gay venues in central London, on the basis that one could do this repeatedly as a form of behavioral surveillance. So far this has been highly successful, with the response rates in excess of 90% with a survey instrument that took 10 minutes and which could be filled in in that environment. We hope to do that again, but I'm interested to see that it's being developed in other places as well.

Reference

Weinberg, M. S., & Williams, C. J. (1972). Fieldwork among deviants: Social relations with subjects and others. In J. Douglas (Ed.), *Research on deviance* (pp. 165–185). New York. Random House.

Part 7.
Researching Sexual Networks

Integrating Quantitative and Qualitative Methods in the Study of Sexuality

STUART MICHAELS

As a sociologist and a member of a team of researchers based at the University of Chicago that has been working on what might well be called a set of Kinsey studies for the age of AIDS, one of the central precepts of our work has been to treat sexuality as a form of social interaction. While in many ways heirs to Kinsey's project to study sexual behavior in all its variability across whole populations, we differ from Kinsey in that we do not treat the individual organism as the fundamental unit of analysis. Working in a different era, coming from very different disciplinary backgrounds, with more developed technologies of modern survey research at our disposal, and with the immediate and pressing issues related to the spread of STDs and AIDS, we have sought to focus consistently on the sexual dyad or pair as the unit of analysis. The initial results of this effort based on a national survey of U.S. adults have been presented in *The Social Organization of Sexuality* (Laumann, Gagnon, Michael, & Michaels, 1994). What I would like to try to do in this brief document is to describe some of the key characteristics of the design of our more recent work, an attempt to advance our understanding of the social context in which sexual interaction takes place and to integrate both quantitative (survey) and qualitative (ethnographic) methods in the study of sexual interaction and sexual networks.

As we completed the National Survey of Health and Social Life Study (NHSLS) in 1994, we began the design and implementation of the Chicago Health and Social Life Study (CHSLS). While local in scope, confined as it is to metropolitan Chicago, the CHSLS is an attempt to address issues that go beyond the national study. In particular, the CHSLS focuses to a large extent on the further specification of and the addition of measures of the social context in which sexual behavior and interaction take place. The questionnaire from the national survey was thoroughly revised to include the enumeration of respondents' social as well as sexual networks, to incorporate information to locate activities—both socially and spatially—within the metropolitan area (e.g., where respondents live, work, socialize), and to gather information about contacts with key public health and social control institutions (e.g., doctors, clinics, police). In addition to a cross-section survey of adults 18–59 years old in Cook County (the county that encompasses all of the city of Chicago as well as its adjacent suburban ring), the CHSLS includes two further components focused primarily on four specially selected neighborhoods within the city. The first component is quantitative, consisting of separate representative samples of residents of these neighborhoods. The second component is qualitative, consisting of open-ended key informant interviews with community leaders in each neighborhood chosen from four separate institutional domains: health, religious, legal (e.g., police), and secular/counseling (community advocacy and counseling).

Dyads, Networks, and the Relational or Interactional Approach

There are two major advantages to the focus on the dyad or pair as the fundamental unit of analysis in research on sexual behavior. First, this approach emphasizes the interactional nature of much sexual behavior. It points to the fact that the outcomes are the product of (at least) two interacting parties and in that sense they are negotiated. It also emphasizes the importance of the bond or relationship between the actors as distinct from their individual characteristics and preferences in determining what occurs sexually. Second, the sum total of the actors and their relations describe a sexual network. The structure of this network as a whole can be used to explore a number of important questions, such as the extent and pathways of diffusion or spread (or lack thereof) of transferable quanta that depend on interaction, e.g., information or infectious agents.

It is one thing to assert the importance of the relational level of analysis; it is quite another to study it empirically. What are the implications of the emphasis on dyads and networks in work that uses survey research based on a probability sample of individuals? There is in fact some tension between the individually based survey and network concepts. For a number of pragmatic reasons it has not been possible to investigate directly either dyads or the structure of whole networks in large-scale population studies. (This may be possible in somewhat more restricted settings such as specific communities or institutions; cf. Tony Coxon's [1995] work on sex in gay networks in Glasgow and London and the work presented in this volume by Richard Udry.) In our work, instead of using direct methods for studying dyads, such as interviewing both partners in sexual relationships, or for studying networks, such as by tracing members of ramifying sexual networks and interviewing all of them, the emphasis on networks of sexual interaction is substantive. For example, the survey questionnaire focuses on the enumeration of sexual partners over given time periods and gathers detailed descriptive information on the social characteristics of the partners as well as detailed information on the nature (duration, definition, sexual content, etc.) of the relationship itself. In the subsequent analysis, the focus is on the characteristics of both partners in various types of sexual relationships and how these shape sexual practices and outcomes.

Why Study a Single Metropolitan Area?

Population-based studies that focus on individual characteristics often mask or miss key components of the environment that shape social and sexual life. Therefore we have turned to a more intensive study of a single metropolitan area to measure more directly constructs that approximate the actual social context in which persons carry on their sexual lives. There are various ways these mediating structures are conceptualized: neighborhood, community, city, institutions and organizations, networks of family and friends, etc. Traditionally qualitative methods, such as ethnographic fieldwork and convenience sample surveys, have been used to study these more socially defined and bounded systems. What we have tried to do in the CHSLS is to marry probability surveys of individuals with qualitative key informant interviews, to study a number of issues related to ways that specific social contexts affect sexual behavior.

Research methodology and design is an exercise in pragmatics, attempting to fit methods to research questions within the bounds of limited resources. In moving from a national survey to a single city, one gives up generalizability to a larger population. The advantages gained are in the realm of being able to characterize structures that have a very real impact on people's lives. In studying sexual behavior we are dealing with ongoing face-to-face interaction which therefore has an inherently local quality. We are in a better position to ask questions such as this one: from what pool of eligibles do persons select potential sexual partners and how are such persons socially defined? Significant others, especially family and friends, form an important context for the formation, content, and maintenance of sexual relationships. To a large extent these nonsexual social networks, a set of stakeholders in and an audience to sexual relationship, are local.

In fact, while cities may define the boundaries of most interactions, it seems probable that to a large extent it is neighborhoods and/or smaller-scale communities that are closer to the actual boundaries within which persons operate. Of course, this varies for different types of individuals. Cities themselves are made up of a variety of partially overlapping and sometimes completely distinct networks of interaction. Structures such as ethnic group, community, and the urban ecology of social spaces organize the boundaries between potential networks and the structures within which they are more likely to form.

It has therefore seemed important to study not just a single city but neighborhoods and/or communities within the city. A couple of examples of the contrast between what is possible in a national survey compared with a single community study may help bring these points home. Key to the formation and structure of sexual networks is the selection of sexual partners. One approach to understanding selection is in terms of similarities and differences between sexual partners along salient social distinctions, such as gender, race, ethnicity, generation, class or social status, religion, etc. In a national survey with respondents selected at random from the population of the country as a whole, the best that one is able to do is to compare individuals' sets of partners based on these relatively abstract categories. But these aggregated estimates are based on treating all such persons as if they have the same opportunity of encountering persons of another group in spite of the extremely wide variation in the heterogeneity of the different locations from which persons in a national sample are selected. On the other hand, in a more localized study such as the Chicago survey, the overall population proportions (e.g., of whites, blacks, Asians, etc.) are constant for everyone. Therefore the estimates of extent of in-group and out-group choices are much more reflective of the operative social structural barriers, such as geographic and social segregation and personal preferences. Similarly it is possible in a city like Chicago to resolve a largely artificial social science category such as "Hispanic" into its locally recognized and operative components of Mexican/Mexican American, Puerto Rican, Cuban, etc. Even a category such as African American or black, which in a race-conscious society like the United States is both highly salient and relatively undifferentiated, can be analyzed in Chicago in terms of Southside and Westside residence, and questions about the interconnections and differences between these two relatively distinct segments of the city's black population can be addressed.

Neighborhood/Community as a Context

The general form of the argument being made here is that social interactions such as sexual relationships, from the evanescent one-night stand to the long-term marriage, need to be studied in terms of the local and rather concrete structures or contexts in which they take place. The various sociodemographic variables that are used to describe the social statuses or positions of individual actors, what we have called "master statuses" such as gender, age, race, ethnicity, etc., can be thought of as indicators of characteristics of concrete social networks in which people operate and through which much of the disciplinary force of social control is exerted. The closer we come to describing these concentric zones of social structure in appropriate terms, the more we will be able to explain and account for the regularities in behavior that we observe. In the Chicago study we have attempted to study a few of these mediating structures, particularly community and institutional sector.

First, let us look at how we have approached the study of community. Rather than take community as static and given, we have tried to approach the idea of community as multidimensional and variable. The first step in doing this has been to use a comparative approach to study geographically defined neighborhoods using both a survey of residents and qualitative interviews with key informants to describe the community as a whole and key institutional sectors within each community.

The selection of neighborhoods and the reasoning behind it illustrates some of the goals of this comparative analysis. Rather than select community areas at random, given that we could afford to do surveys in at most four areas, we proceeded purposively. We were interested in neighborhoods that would help us to understand some of the culturally distinct groupings that make up a city as diverse as Chicago. At the same time we were interested in selecting neighborhoods that would be as similar as possible on certain dimensions (e.g., class) while likely to vary on other dimensions (e.g., degree of insularity). We started with a set of important culturally distinctive "communities": Mexican American, African American, Puerto Rican, and gay/lesbian. We also considered possibilities such as city versus suburban and Anglo or white enclaves defined by nationality and/or class. We decided on four neighborhoods that could be defined in terms of the predominant group living in them or that had at least a sizable minority of an important group. Our final set includes a neighborhood that is about 85% Mexican American (with the preponderance of recent immigrants), an area that is over 95% African American selected as being roughly comparable in terms of average income to the Mexican American neighborhood, the area in Chicago that is the most visible center of the gay and lesbian communities both in terms of institutions and residents, and finally an area that has the highest concentration of Puerto Rican residents (approximately one third). These neighborhoods have been intensively studied via quantitative survey methods and via qualitative, open-ended, key-informant interviews. The survey of a representative sample of approximately 300 residents is comparable to the survey of the residents of the metropolitan area as a whole, the latter providing an important baseline against which to compare the community samples.

Interviews with a representative sample of individuals within the four neighborhoods can be analyzed from different perspectives. On the one hand, they can be thought of as studies of individuals, but individuals selected from a more homogeneous population than the city as a whole and living within a more or less bounded social system. These populations can be conceived of as, for example, Mexican Americans living in a predominantly recent immigrant neighborhood rather insulated from much of the rest of the city by language and cultural differences or as persons living in a relatively recently gentrified, "yuppie" urban neighborhood with a high concentration of out gays and the highest concentration of gay and lesbian bars and organizations, etc. On the other hand, the individual-level data can be used to characterize the neighborhood itself, e.g., to describe the age, racial, ethnic, educational, marital status, and linguistic composition of the neighborhood. Rates of STDs, domestic violence, unwanted pregnancies, etc. in each neighborhood (and the city as a whole) can be computed from the survey data. Many of these rates for given populations and especially for given neighborhoods are unknown. What are sometimes available and known are service rates, e.g., the number of persons seen at STD clinics, the number of charges or arrests for domestic violence, or the number of abortions performed.

However, a survey of individuals is only one way to characterize a neighborhood or community, and it necessarily focuses on qualities of a community that are based on the summary of individual characteristics. There also are supraindividual levels of social structure made up of the institutions and agencies in a community as well as a cultural context based on social and political history, etc. There are many methods for trying to tap into this level of reality. In the Chicago study we have utilized a particular form of ethnographic fieldwork, key-informant interviews, that seemed under the circumstances (including fairly limited time and money) to serve this purpose well.

The focus of the ethnographic component, the key-informant interviews for this study, has been on the organized, institutional sectors of the four neighborhood communities. Qualitative, open-ended interviewing is often done as an adjunct to survey research, e.g., focus groups or one-on-one open-ended interviews to help in the construction of survey questionnaire items. In the CHSLS, the ethnographic work has been organized as a parallel and complementary study. Open-ended interviews, organized around a relatively stable set of issues, were conducted with key informants selected to represent a set of four broadly defined institutional sectors within each community, including health, legal, religious and secular/moral.

We used a version of "matrix management" to organize this work and to minimize several potential drawbacks to this sort of qualitative research. The "matrix" for the allocation of responsibilities for the eight fieldworkers was defined by crossing the four communities with the four institutional sectors (see Figure 1). It was used to identify potential interviewees in each community, starting by identifying a few key organizations in each community and then using initial informants within each agency to identify other important institutional and individual actors in the community. In addition, this matrix formed the basis for organizing the fieldwork. Each fieldworker was given both a primary and a secondary assignment, one from the institutional sectors and one from the neighborhoods. Most interviews were done by a pair of fieldworkers, usually selected based on their areas of responsibility but also on availability. This accomplished a number of important objectives. Two independent sets of field notes were written for each interview, providing greater completeness as well as some different emphases and perspectives. Since fieldworkers had primary responsibilities that crossed either neighborhood or sector, a comparative perspective was

	Mexican American	African American	Puerto Rican	Gay
Medical (clinics, doctors, etc.)				
Religious (ministers, social-service programs, etc.)				
Secular (mental health agencies, shelters, etc.)				
Legal (police, lawyers, prosecutors, etc.)				

Figure 1. Matrix of institutional sector by neighborhood for CHSLS ethnographic work.

consistently being developed and brought to bear in the interviews themselves and in the field notes. Initial assignments were made to maximize the skills and backgrounds that fieldworkers brought to the project, e.g., a fieldworker from divinity school was given the primary assignment for the religious sector, whereas a graduate student in history interested in lesbian and gay studies had as her primary assignment the gay community. The matrix organization helped to prevent overspecialization but also allowed for some pursuit and emphasis on areas of personal interest. It also helped to maintain a system and to bring completeness to the distribution of interviews, as we tried to get a fairly even spread of interviews across the matrix to maintain comparability across both dimensions.

The qualitative interviews had a tendency to focus on the "externalities" of sexuality, the more public consequences of sexual behaviors. While the decision to focus on the more macro structures, contexts, frameworks in which sexuality is embedded has been quite deliberate and without reservation, the focus on the public consequences of sexuality, the tendency to emphasize problematic outcomes such as STDs, AIDS, domestic violence, and homosexuality (often treated either as a "problem" itself or as involving problems such as discrimination or harassment) has not been our unalloyed intent. We were and remain interested in the ways that the social context shapes sexuality more generally, in other words sex as an outcome, a consequence itself rather than the cause of certain problems. But this is much more difficult to study, largely because of the ways that people are used to thinking and talking about sexuality. When we approached our informants about being interviewed for a study of sexuality in Chicago, the almost universal response in the interview was to talk about social problems related to sexuality, such things as AIDS, unwanted pregnancies, domestic violence, etc. Some respondents said that these were not problems in their communities or sought to marginalize them; sometimes they expressed a great concern about one or more of these issues. On the other hand, "normal" (unproblematized) sexuality was harder to talk about. The subtle ways that sexuality is organized in persons' lives in an ongoing, everyday way was much harder to specify. This may also have to do with our decisions as researchers, the people we were able to interview, the fact that we did want our interviewees to comment on a series of potential sexual problems, and the decision to interview "key informants" rather than try to do more traditional forms of ethnography. As we analyze the field notes, we are attempting to redress this balance and to elucidate the more positive, formative aspects of the context and organization of sexuality. In part this is done by synthesizing the material in a comparative way, attempting to identify the underlying, usually unstated, taken-for-granted assumptions and frameworks that our informants seem to be using in thinking about sexuality and responding to it in their communities. Sometimes this points to a more general communitywide framing of sexuality and sometimes to organizationally specific approaches.

One of the most exciting aspects of this study is the ability to compare the survey data of a representative sample of individuals from a given community with the perceptions of community leaders. We will be able to compare rates of various aspects of sexuality in these different neighborhoods, e.g., numbers and types of sexual partners, amount of various kinds of sexual activity, problems such as STDs, sexual dysfunctions, domestic violence, sexual coercion, etc. with the perceptions of agents of social control and social service and how they perceive these problems—their incidence, who is at highest risk, who is being treated or serviced.

Conclusion

This paper has briefly described one attempt to integrate quantitative and qualitative methods in the study of some of the more sociological aspects of sexuality, sexual networks, the contexts in which sexuality takes place at the local level, and the responses of local institutions to sexual behavior and problems that break out of the confines of the privacy of relationships and households. But this study involves only one possible set of decisions about integrating quantitative and qualitative research methods. I have identified three dimensions—quantitative/qualitative, micro/macro, and objective/subjective—that can be used to define a set of choices or possibilities regarding domains of study that arise when designing research on sexuality and some typical methods associated with them (see Figure 2). Most of this discussion has focused on the distinction between quantitative (primarily population-based surveys of individuals) and qualitative methods in terms of various points along a continuum from micro (individual) to macro (community) levels of analysis (with the dyadic and net-

	Quantitative (Surveys)		Qualitative (Ethnographic)	
	Objective (Behavior)	Subjective (Meaning)	Objective (Behavior)	Subjective (Meaning)
Micro	Survey (behavioral)*	Survey (attitudes)*	Observation, fieldwork	Focus Groups, open-ended interviews
Macro Dyads Networks Institutional	Surveys Network-oriented* institutions	Survey of organizations/ institutions	Observation, fieldwork, or interviews of networks or site-based	Key-informant interviews*

*Method used in the Chicago Health and Social Life Study.

Figure 2. Methods for the study of sexual behavior.

work levels between the endpoints of this latter dimension). In Figure 2, a further distinction is introduced, between the objective (behavioral) and the subjective (attitudinal or interpretive). Often it is assumed that quantitative approaches and behavioral content go together and that qualitative methods are the only ones appropriate to study more subjective issues. Figure 2 points to the fact that there are other options available that complement the more standard approaches. These distinctions may prove helpful in designing future research to advance our understanding of sexual behavior, its relational aspects and its social context.

Author Note

The research described in this paper has been developed and carried out in collaboration with my colleagues Edward O. Laumann, John H. Gagnon, Robert T. Michael, and Martha Van Haitsma as well as the contributions of many graduate students and staff members of NORC. This work has been partially funded by grants from the Ford Foundation, the National Institute on Child Health and Human Development (NICHD) and the Office of AIDS Research of NIH.

References

Coxon, A. P. M. (1995). Networks and sex: The use of social networks as method and substance in researching gay men's response to HIV/AIDS. In R. G. Parker

& J. H. Gagnon (Eds.), *Conceiving sexuality: Approaches to sex research in a postmodern world*, pp. 215–234. New York & London: Routledge.

Laumann, E. O., Gagnon, J. H., Michael, R. T., & Michaels, S. (1994). *The social organization of sexuality: Sexual practices in the United States.* Chicago: University of Chicago Press.

A Research Design for Studying Romantic Partners

J. RICHARD UDRY

The purpose of this paper is to describe some innovative methodological solutions to opening up new substantive problems in sex research. The research project involved is the National Longitudinal Study of Adolescent Health, hereafter Add Health. This research project is concerned only incidentally with the sexual behavior of adolescents. Its main object is to study contextual factors contributing to adolescent health and health behaviors broadly conceived.

I want to focus on the design features of the Add Health study that make possible the study of sexual behavior in ways mostly not possible with the usually available research designs. The main breakthrough made possible is the study of sexual networks and sex partners.

Add Health tried to approach sexual behavior as activity of a pair of individuals, not a single individual. This may be the only large survey in which such an approach has been carried out. This means that we can situate the sexual behavior of pairs of individuals into the social lives of each partner in ways never possible before. The data from Add Health are available for the use of qualified researchers under certain restricted conditions. Because the collection of data is not yet finished, I can give only preliminary results to illustrate the possibilities of the data.

The Design of Add Health

This is a study of a nationally representative sample of adolescents in grades 7 through 12 in the United States. The study is designed to help explain the causes of adolescent health and health behavior with special emphasis on the effects of the multiple contexts of adolescent life. Add Health was mandated to the National Institute of Child Health and Human Development (NICHD) by action of the U.S. Congress. This study is funded by NICHD and 18 other federal agencies, as a program project. I am the principal investigator. I have a nationwide group of adolescent health researchers as co-investigators. An important feature of the project is that the data from the study are available for varying levels of public use.

When we say this is a study of adolescent health, we mean that we tried to provide coverage of all the main health conditions and health be-

Diet and Nutrition	Eating Disorders	Depression	Violent Behavior	Intentional Injury
Unintentional Injury	Suicidal Thoughts and Suicide Attempts	Exercise and Physical Activity	Health Service Use	Health Insurance Coverage
Drug Use	Sex and Contraception	Alcohol Use	Tobacco Use	Weapon Use
Hereditary Conditions of Health	Physical Disabilities	Obesity	Mental Health	Other Health Conditions
Sleep Problems	Safe Vehicle Use	Chronic Health Problems	Viral and Bacterial Infections	Dental Health

Figure 1. What the Add Health study tries to understand.

haviors of current concern. Figure 1 gives an idea of the aspects of health that we cover. When we say we focus on the effect of context, we cover the following contexts in the study: community, neighborhood, school, peer group, family, friends, and romantic partners.

From a scientific perspective, Add Health is unusual in the degree to which the major theoretical issues of the study are articulated in the features of the research design. Figure 2 gives the layout of our sampling design. Our primary sampling frame is a list of all high schools in the United States. From this frame, we selected a stratified sample of 80 high schools, with probability proportional to size. For each high school, we selected one of its feeder schools with probability proportional to its student contribution to the high school. We then gave a self-administered op-scan questionnaire simultaneously to everyone who attended each school on a particular day of administration. Some schools did not let us do a school administration. We have administered more than 90,000 school questionnaires. The school administration of the project was completed in 1994–95.

The purposes of the school questionnaire are: (1) to measure school context variables, (2) to obtain friendship networks, (3) to measure a variety of health conditions, and (4) to obtain data on the basis of which to select special samples of individuals in rare but theoretically crucial categories. No sensitive questions were asked in the school interview. A school administrator also completed a half-hour self-administered questionnaire on characteristics of the school in 1994 and again in 1996.

A Research Design for Studying Romantic Partners | *311*

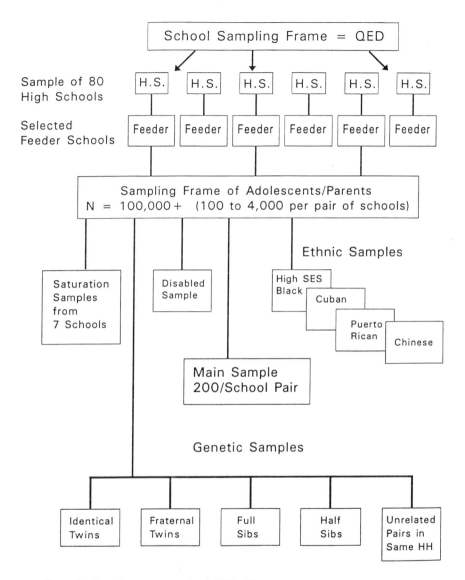

Figure 2. Sampling structure for Add Health.

We also obtained a roster of students enrolled in each school. From the rosters, we randomly selected a main sample of 16,000 for a 1.5-hour home interview. Approximately 200 students were selected from each school pair, irrespective of size. This creates a self-weighting sample. Whether or not the student was included in the school administration does not affect inclusion in the main home sample. A parent of each respondent received a half-hour interview. The adolescent home interview was administered on a laptop computer. Half of the interview was conducted by the interviewer and half was self-administered on the laptop, with an audio through earphones.

In two large schools and several small schools we attempted home interviews on all students on the roster. This allowed us to get a complete view of the effects of friend pairs on health and health behaviors.

From the school questionnaires, we selected the following special samples. In most cases, the sample exhausts those available in the school administration.

1. High SES blacks n = 1,500
2. Puerto Ricans n = 500
3. Cubans n = 500
4. Chinese n = 400
5. Physically disabled (limb disabilities) n = 500
6. Adoptees n = 500

We also selected a genetic sample using the school questionnaire information. In most categories, the sample exhausts the cases available in the school administration. The categories of pairs of adolescents in the genetic sample are as follows:

1. Identical twins
2. Fraternal twins
3. Full sib pairs
4. Half sib pairs
5. Unrelated pairs of adolescents in the same household

The genetic sample can be used for many different types of analysis. For the social scientist uninterested in genetic aspects, the sample can be used for analysis that distinguishes variance due to shared parental environment from environmental variance from other sources. It is especially useful for identifying "family effects" as usually defined by social scientists, but can provide a measure of family effects purged of genetic variance.

The first wave of home interviews was completed in 1995. In 1996, those originally in grades 7–11 were followed up with a second adolescent home interview. This will enable us to follow changes in behavior over the year. Figure 3 lists the five questionnaires used in the study and the approximate number of completes for each questionnaire.

We can now examine how design features map onto the measure of contextual effects. Figure 4 gives the sources of data used for each level of context in the design.

We have 80 communities. For each community, one of our investigators will prepare a list of attributes from public data. Neighborhoods were specified for each home respondent, and neighborhood attributes were assembled from public data. School attributes can be aggregated from school

- School Adolescent Questionnaire   N = 90,000
- School Administrator Questionnaire   N = ~140
- In-Home Adolescent Questionnaire—Wave I   N = ~20,000
- In-Home Adolescent Questionnaire—Wave II   N = ~14,000
- Parental Questionnaire—Wave I   N = ~18,000

Figure 3. Add Health questionnaires.

questionnaires, administrator questionnaires, and home questionnaires. Peer groups are constructed and friends matched from school and home questionnaires. Family characteristics are obtained from parental questionnaires. The highly clustered sample design creates the possibility of estimating these contextual effects.

Add Health sets a new standard in the protection of confidentiality. This is most important because of the highly contextualized research design. I will not try to spell out the security features of the design. The design makes it possible to match questionnaires where needed, and at the same time makes it impossible for anyone—even me—to match any respondent identity with a questionnaire response. The main feature that makes this possible is a third-party contract with a security manager.

Release of the data for public use was scheduled for early 1997. Because of the problems of deductive disclosure involved in providing contextual data, access to various types of data has different restrictions. But for the basic data sets, off-the-shelf unrestricted data sets are available from Sociometrics. Our object is to make as much data as possible available as soon as possible and with the minimum restrictions necessary to control deductive disclosure of identities.

Almost all the parts of the home questionnaire that collected information on sexual behavior were contained in the self-administered section of the laptop questionnaire, so that the respondent entered responses directly into the computer. The advantage of this is that neither the interviewer nor others in the room heard any questions asked or heard any responses. The disadvantage is that adolescent respondents didn't always follow instructions exactly. But, of course, skip patterns are all automatic, and respondents did not even see questions that were skipped. For example, if a respondent said she had never had sexual intercourse, she never even saw any questions about contraception. There was no printed questionnaire at the interview scene.

In the "relationship" section of the questionnaire, respondents were

- Schools: School Administrator Questionnarie, aggregated questionnaire data

- Neighborhoods: Census data

- Communities: Census data, other published sources

- Families: Questionnaire responses of parents and siblings

- Peer relationship: Friendship nominations and matches

Figure 4. Contextual data.

asked to identify by initials individuals with whom they had had romantic relationships in the last 18 months. They were to identify up to three. Then they identified up to three others with whom they had done all the following: kissed, held hands, told partner she loved him or liked him. This was to screen out nonerotic friendships. They then identified other components of the relationship in the order of their occurrence. Altogether our respondents identified more than 20,000 relationships, or an average of one per respondent (see Table 1). Many had none, while others reported three. When the relationship involved sexual intercourse, the use of contraception was explored. Of course, many romantic relationships did not involve intercourse. Respondents also identified many social characteristics of their romantic partners. Finally, if the partner was in the same school, a respondent looked the person up on a complete roster of students contained in each laptop and highlighted the person's name. An ID number associated with that partner was entered into the respondent's computer. Respondents were allowed to identify same-sex romantic relationships. About 2% of the relationships identified were between individuals of the same sex. (A few of these were self-nominations.) In another section, respondents identified individuals with whom they had sexual relationships that did not qualify in the previous categories. About 3,000 such partnerships were identified. Since the relationship screen was so easy to pass, these nonromantic partnerships must be an interesting group of sexual relationships.

Because of the roster identification of partners, if a partner is in the same school, there is some probability that the partner was also interviewed. Overall, more than 80% of enrolled students completed an in-school questionnaire, and more than one in six students from the school was interviewed at home. Most of their mothers were also interviewed. So there is a relatively high probability that we can find the partner's in-school questionnaire and a one-in-six probability the partner was also in-

Table 1 *Nominated Partners Who Attend the Same School as the Respondent*

Attends Same School	Male Respondent	Female Respondent	Total Relationships
Romantic relationship partners			
No	3,904	4,814	8,718
Yes	4,231	3,654	7,885
Total	8,135	8,468	16,603
% "yes"	52.01	43.15	47.49
Nonromantic relationship partners with whom respondent has held hands, kissed on lips, and told they liked or loved			
No	631	625	1,256
Yes	482	268	750
Total	1,113	893	2,006
% "yes"	43.31	30.01	37.39
Nonromantic sex partners			
No	1,202	793	1,995
Yes	633	281	914
Total	1,835	1,074	2,909
% "yes"	34.5	26.16	31.42

terviewed at home. In two large schools and eight small schools, all respondents were eligible for home interview, and about 80 percent were successfully interviewed. In these saturated schools, the probability of interviewing both respondents is quite high. Sometimes we are able to find partner questionnaires for more than one partner per respondent.

Examination of Table 1 shows some interesting patterns. In all three types of relationship, males name proportionately more same-school partners than females do. For both sexes, those relationships identified as "romantic" are more likely to be in the same school than those who met the behavior screen but whom the respondents did not identify as romantic, while the nonromantic sex partners are much less likely to be in the same school with the respondent.

If partners were not enrolled in the school, we could not interview them. But we know enough about them from respondent descriptions to know how they differ from school partners. Our list of relationships is in a general way a random sample of the romantic and sex partners of all adolescents enrolled in schools in the United States. On each pair in which both were interviewed at home, we will have a sex history of sex partners. Since most of those interviewed at home were reinterviewed in 1996, we have another batch of romantic and nonromantic relationships on the same sample, this time for about 14,000 respondents.

It is worth remembering that if an in-school partner was identified, we have not only the partner's report of sexual behavior but also a broad array of other information from the partner, including smoking, drinking, drug use, the names of friends in the school and other romantic and sex partners, the names of the friends' friends and romantic relationships, interviews of both parents in the pair in most cases, and lots of other health-relevant behavior. While these networks will be incomplete, we have so many cases that lots of patterns can be traced.

Figure 5 gives an illustration of the questionnaire matches possible and the kind of information that can therefore be obtained. We start with three in-school respondents who also completed an in-home questionnaire and for whom we have a parental questionnaire. Respondents 104 and 255 chose one another as friends. R 320 chose R 255 as a friend. R 104 named R 320 as a romantic partner. R 255 also named R 320 as a romantic partner. R 320 named R 255 as a romantic partner as well as a friend. The three parents of this triad can be grouped to determine the different types of parental control each adolescent is experiencing.

The month of beginning and end of each relationship is recorded in the laptop, so we can determine overlapping romantic relationships and the order in which they occurred. On Wave II, a year after the first wave, we can tell which relationships that were active at Wave I were still continuing and what has happened in them since the first interview.

Validity of Reports

Now it will have occurred to readers that in the case of partners both interviewed at home, we presumably have a pair in which at least one of the pair identified the other as a romantic partner. Therefore we have an interesting opportunity to validate responses about the relationships, since presumably something occurred between partners. The first validity check is this: when A identified B, and B was interviewed, in what proportion does B identify A also as a partner? If Yes, then they will be reporting on what was presumably a relationship with one another. Do they identify the same content of their joint relationship? If A says he had intercourse with B, does B say so also? What characteristics of respondents predict congruence or discrepancy of reports on the same relationship? If A says he had sex with B, but B says she had a relationship with A and didn't have sex, we know that one of these responses is invalid. While this is useful, it is much more interesting to be able to say that when A has characteristic x, he tends to deny he had sex with B, but only when B has characteristic z. Are relationships likely to be denied by the respondent of higher status? Does the good-looking girl refuse to acknowledge a relationship with an

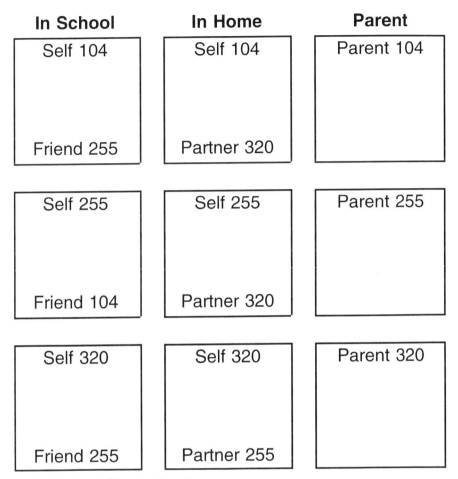

Figure 5. Matching questionnaires.

unpopular boy? So the validity checks contain much more information than just a validity check. Such validity checks are so rare in sex research that this study will give us a useful basis for evaluating responses in other studies in which such checks are not possible.

Third-Person Attributes

In many studies of sexual behavior, respondents have been asked the attributes of sex partners. For the first time (except in studies of married pairs), we will be able to evaluate these secondhand reports by comparing them with the reports of respondents themselves.

Same-Sex Relationships

A few hundred of the relationships identified are same-sex partners. We presume that respondents were less likely to report such relationships when they existed, but also were not likely to fabricate them when they did not exist. The numbers are small, so it remains to be determined what can be learned from them. Since no one has had a sample of several hundred same-sex relationships from a national representative population, every question we can answer will be answered for the first time. To what extent do those who name same-sex partners also name cross-sex partners? How do the same-sex relationships differ from cross-sex relationships in the extent of their integration into other aspects of one another's lives, such as knowing one another's parents?

Sequences of Relationships

From the depth of data on romantic pairs over time, we will be able to tell how subsequent relationships depend on prior relationships. For many respondents, we will have three or more relationships in chronological order. We can examine how the character of sexual relationships of a single individual changes with subsequent experience, and how the character of those relationships changes with subsequent partners of differing characteristics.

Predicting Behavior

Most work predicting the sexual behavior of adolescents is based on prediction of individuals. In Add Health, we have the ability to predict whether a particular couple in a relationship will have sex with one another, using the attributes of both participants. As predictors, we can use the prior sexual experience of each, their ages, IQs, physical attributes, social characteristics (popularity, network location, parental attributes), personality, etc. We can also use interaction of the attributes of the two individuals. Providing our validity analysis shows reports of partner attributes to be accurate, we can conduct this analysis on all reported partnerships whether or not the partner is in the same school, and whether or not the partner has a matched in-home questionnaire.

Discussion

The study we describe in this paper is monumental in scope and is not likely to be repeated often. But the methods we describe have broad applicability in the study of adolescent romantic and sexual partners. While Add Health is a national representative sample, for the purposes described here it can be thought of as a study of 80 separate communities of potential partnerships. It can be replicated within a single school or community. It will work best when everyone or nearly everyone in the school or community is a research respondent. Add the collection of biological specimens for STD exposure and you create not only a sexual partnership network but an actual STD transmission network. The logistics of surveys of this sort has been tested and been found fieldworthy for home interviews.

While laptop administration creates an efficient system with few errors and a privacy mechanism second to none, the method is adaptable to other administrations. Nonromantic friendship nominations for Add Health were collected in school classrooms with printed school rosters in the hands of every student, who used a self-administered op-scan questionnaire. The lucky few researchers who can find a school system that will allow a classroom study of sexual behavior can use this traditional sociometric method for romantic partners with appropriate ingenious confidentiality procedures. Of course the error rate in bubbling nomination numbers on an op-scan form is relatively high compared to the laptop technique.

One might think that our technique is a rather roundabout way of constructing adolescent partnerships. Why not interview a sample of adolescents and ask them the names, addresses, and phone numbers of their romantic partners? And then go and interview them? First, a proposal to do this would almost certainly not get Institutional Review Board approval. Second, what do you tell a mother when getting permission to interview her son? "Barbara Jackson told us your son was her romantic partner?" This kind of "contact tracing" may be OK for public health departments in combating STDs, but it is an invitation to trouble for a research design.

The partnership nominations are the most highly sensitive data in the entire Add Health data set. While no data user will ever have names or other identifiers of the participants or their nominees, the risk that a data intruder who knows some participants in the study could identify a respondent by deduction is not beyond the realm of the possible. Therefore public-use Add Health data sets do not contain the romantic nomination links. Potential users are invited to contact the project to discuss arrangements for supervised data use at the Carolina Population Center. Please check the home page for the Carolina Population Center <http://www.cpc.unc.edu/addhealth> for further information about Add Health and data availability.

Discussion

Ulrich Clement: You make a lot of causal statements in your talk and I wonder how you are going to tackle that. How are you going to decide whether this influences that?

Stuart Michaels: I think of this research in several ways: I think of it as exploratory, involving model building and development as well as hypothesis testing. Having both qualitative data and quantitative data should contribute to being able to do this. We have the individual-level data from an hour and a half interview with a representative sample of the people in the specific neighborhoods and the city as a whole and in addition we have the accounts and interpretations of institutional actors about issues related to sexuality. Many of these latter accounts involve assumptions about what is going on in various subsets of the population. We hope to formalize some of these assumptions into models and test parts of the model using the population data. I think it's important to make at least some hypothetical assertions about causal relationships, whether or not we'll be able to test all of them.

Richard Parker: The attempt to integrate these methods is really interesting to me exactly because it gets at some of the issues that we were talking about earlier, issues of the meaning and context of behaviors. You mentioned in your talk, Stuart, that you've tried to collect data on both sexual networks and social networks and at the level of analysis that you're at so far, to what extent can you hierarchize between those two different types of networks in terms of which is more important in influencing the structure of sexual values that lead to the sexual behaviors?

Stuart Michaels: Not at all. We have not begun the analysis of these data. Basically, we've collected the quantitative data so we have it and we're beginning to clean it. But there has been no analysis yet, and what happens in this kind of work is that the relational data is the most difficult so we're actually just beginning to get that data in shape to look at. But just to let people know a little bit, the basic pattern that we followed in the national study was to get people's sexual network for the last year and enumerate those people completely and to find out social background characteristics and then collect detailed sexual activity for the two most recent partnerships. We're doing the same kind of thing in this study, although we're using a longer time frame, five years. Then, in addition, we enumerate up to six social network partners defined by who respondents spend the most time with and who they discuss important issues with. We don't predefine family or friends as being in that network. Who's in the network is defined in terms of those activities, but we do treat them a little bit differently if they're family.

Joe Catania: Stuart, I was just wondering, would it be possible to do the informant interviews and contacts by telephone?

Stuart Michaels: Let me just say a little more about these key-informant interviews. These were really open-ended interviews. There was a standard protocol and the time they lasted depended on the people. Some of the people were extremely busy, so sometimes we only got 20- or 30-minute interviews. Some of them went for 2–2.5 hours. We didn't plan to do any of them on the telephone, except that some of the very short ones ended up being done on the telephone. Sometimes informants were reluctant to meet and then they actually got into a conversation on the telephone about our interests and from this field notes were written. I should say that these telephone interviews are not transcribed, they're not recorded. In fact, none of the qualitative interviews were recorded. We tried to have two fieldworkers for each of the face-to-face interviewers, so we get two sets of field notes on each interview.

Joe Catania: Why weren't they recorded?

Stuart Michaels: There were a couple of issues. One was just the cost of the transcription, which was actually quite large. And there were a variety of informants with a wide variety of interests and sometimes high visibility in the community. Getting those people to talk to us wasn't always that easy. We thought tape recording would make it even more difficult.

Dennis Fortenberry: Dr. Udry, could you describe just a little the kind of measures you have of the activities that individuals do with their romantic or sex partners, because I've been interested in particular in teenagers, what they do when they're not having sex with the people that they may be having sex with.

Richard Udry: On many of the previous studies I've done, we've looked at, what shall we call them, subcoital behaviors. On this one, we spend very little time on subcoital behaviors, although they're in there. In the first round we didn't go beyond coitus. In the second round, we go beyond coitus. Contraception history is available, but the social history of the couple is also available. For example, we asked them what is the context of their romantic relationship. Have they met the partner's parents? Have they told their friends that they're a couple? And then, many other components of the social context of their relationship. We asked them how their relationship fits into their circle of activities.

Carol Jenkins: I was just wondering if the vast array of data that will be available would answer such questions as relative power of peers versus parents versus teachers in various kinds of behaviors, substance use, initiation of sex, and so on.

Richard Udry: We certainly hope so. You can put these data together in any way you want to and you can impute whatever causal frameworks you wish to. The design itself doesn't constrain you very much.

Stephanie Sanders: In your paper, you mentioned that they were able to identify up to three romantic relationships in the last 18 months and I was wondering if any of them had more than three and then how were they to choose which ones to tell you about.

Richard Udry: They were instructed to give us the three most significant. They could have mentioned three romantic partners, but they could also mention up to three more sexual partners.

Joe Catania: Did you collect any data that could be used to identify the larger social crowds that kids might belong to in the schools?

Richard Udry: You can put the network data from this and the school together in any way that any network analyst would want to put them together. On this set of nominations, you have up to five of each sex and then if you want to trace any network property out of that, it's all there to do. I don't know whether that answers your question or not, but you can, for example, aggregate any data you want on the whole school. Some of the schools have 2,400 home interviews in the one school. Well, you can aggregate those. I feel like I'm not answering your question.

Joe Catania: Some people have felt they have identified social crowds within which there may be friendship networks, some of which don't interact.

Richard Udry: You could put that together.

Joe Catania: You could? Fully saturated?

Richard Udry: Well, for the fully saturated, you can do it, completely. For the less saturated schools, you have an incomplete network. But you can generally discover the network attributes of those schools, anyhow.

Fabio Sabogal: I think the methodology that you, Stuart, are using is very interesting and I just wonder about the interaction between these communities, for example, the Mexican American community and the Puerto Rican and the gay community. What is the interaction? And the second question is in your Figure 1, I didn't see anything about the family. For Hispanics, the family is the most important social institution. There are strong feelings of loyalty, reciprocity, and solidarity among members of the Hispanic family.

Stuart Michaels: It's true that the qualitative interviews, the open-ended interviews, are more with institutional actors, so they don't always get at the family. It is quite different when it comes to the individual survey data. Both Dick's study and ours have an interest in the dyad and the social networks around the sexual dyads. But there is an incredible opportunity when you have 20 million dollars and you can do saturation samples. Then you can actually begin to have interviews on both sides. We've not really been able to design or afford a study that would allow that, so we're always asking the individual respondent to describe these other people and we treat that as a true representation of these other people's social characteristics and sometimes attitudes. Usually it's more their social attributes and behaviors and that's where the family would come in. We have the individual interview and as part of the interview, we're asking questions about the primary social network and then we have random samples of different ethnic and social groups and we could compare to what extent the family forms the major social network. In terms of your other question about the relationship between Hispanic and gay communities, this comes mainly from the qualitative work and we're just beginning to synthesize these materials. We've collected all of the ethnographic key-informant interviews. They've all been entered into the computer in a system where you can do searches across all the field notes on topics. Some of them are pre-coded. You can also do word-based searches. And currently we have half the fieldworkers still working on synthesizing some of this information. Through that, some of these issues are beginning to emerge. You're right to point to importance of studying this kind of interaction. For example, there is no organized gay group in the Mexican American neighborhood. The presence of gayness and homosexuality and so on is not, as far as we can tell, at an organized level. Actually there are some bars where one finds transvestite prostitutes serving mainly single immigrant men. So that's an organized form. While we didn't do real fieldwork in these bars, they are discussed in some of the interviews. But if you go to the Puerto Rican neighborhood you do find Latino organizations that are AIDS-related and gay-related. They are predominantly Puerto Rican, even though that community has some Mexican population. These organizations also seem to be defined as generically Hispanic, even though they are predominantly Puerto Rican and are based in the Puerto Rican neighborhood. One of the things we're doing now is to look at how the different actors in these communities describe and respond to issues related to homosexuality. What is their description of homosexuality? Every informant interview included questions about a series of issues, including homosexuality. Many of the Latino community leaders begin by saying that there's no homosexuality or there are no gay people or no homosexuals in their neighborhood, but after a while they'll tell you about problems related to the bars I mentioned before. When asked what is going on at that bar, they are not seen as Mexican American homosexuals, they're seen as men who are having sex with men and there's a whole interpretation and explanation of how that goes on. For example, that the men who go there are single immigrants and they are looking for ready, easy sex. Other issues seemed to come up in the Puerto Rican neighborhood where there are visible homosexuals. There people raised issues related to identity, whether people are identified with or participate in their own ethnic community versus the gay community. It's quite interesting to hear Puerto Rican institutional leaders talking about having respect for certain openly gay Puerto Ricans. They're not totally happy with them, but they approve the fact that they're committed to the Puerto Rican community and remain there.

Alain Giami: You make a distinction between social networks and sexual networks, but don't you think that sexual networks are also social networks? Wouldn't it be better to construct a framework for the social networks in which some parts are sexualized? The question then should be "Does the sexual network function as a normative milieu or as a reservoir of partners, or both?" Also you seem to have a narrow conception of the social; how did you select those four institutions? For people like Goffman, for example, a bar is an institution; a sex shop, a porno shop, is an institution; and can we say that those institutions as well as the family, as Fabio Sabogal pointed out, shape the sexual life of individuals from a normative point of view? Or do they act as a reservoir of potential partners?

Stuart Michaels: I think you're pointing to a real problem. I think, theoretically, we would like to encompass all of the things you mention, in a general model of the social organization of sexuality or the social context that shapes sexuality or the sexual aspects of the social. There is this tendency, of course, to describe what we actually did and treat it as if we've covered the complete map, and in fact, what I think we've done here is we've expanded the terrain that people usually study, and we've tried to push it in a number of different directions, but it's quite incomplete in a number of ways. To respond to your specific questions. We don't do anything to disallow people being both social network members and sexual network members. In the national survey, we thought of sexual partners as forming a set of sexual relationships which ultimately are part of sexual networks, and so that's very much maintained in this recent survey. There's also lots of research about social networks, and we're also building on that, and we've generated these social networks as a separate item in the survey. But, as I said, the same people can be nominated for both, and we're using computer-assisted personal interviewing, which helped deal with some of these things because the computer actually knows where people came in and doesn't have to re-ask certain questions. There are two answers to the issue about why we chose these four institutions. It's not that we don't see the importance of many much more informally organized institutions and kinds of communities. In the population survey questionnaire we did ask socially and geographically specific questions about where and how respondents meet sexual partners. So for the individual-level data there is a sense in which we were trying to map some of these phenomena in space around the city, which often has social meaning, boundaries, and organization. But we were also faced with many practical constraints. What would be really wonderful, of course, would be to do extensive ethnographic fieldwork where we could really have explored places such as bars and parks and bathrooms and church socials. There are lots of ways that people meet partners in organized settings, both social and sexual partners. We, basically, couldn't afford to do that. The qualitative interviews were conceptualized more in terms of public policy concerns, where we tried to focus on the institutions that are often charged with dealing with many of the social problems that arise from or alongside sexuality.

Leonore Tiefer: I am unfamiliar with social network theory; I read and re-read to try to get a grasp of it, and I need some help with this. My impression is that the meaning of sexuality, with regard to this or as elaborated in social network theories/sexual network theories, is choice of partner, selection of partner; that is the beginning, the middle, and the end of this modality. I can understand that as a very elaborate and sophisticated way of studying the vectors of STDs and so on, but for understanding sexuality, any sort of subjective issue, I don't grasp what you get out of this extremely complex methodology. What are you going to learn about sexuality, what is the definition of sexuality, and what is the meaning of the construct of sexuality within your research method?

Richard Udry: For the meaning of the constructs of sexuality in our study of sexual behavior, we have attitude components that you can plug into. I gave several examples of what we are going to learn about sexual behavior in the paper. But, for further example, in our study we will be able to say what it is about this romantic pairing which leads it to become a coital relationship, whereas two others which look similar don't lead to coital relationships. We may find that it is the nature of the friendship circle within which the sexual relationship is embedded, or the relationship of the families within which it is embedded, or the relationship of the neighborhood or the community within which it is embedded or the school. We'll have all of those things to explore how these two romantic relationships come to different consummations.

Ed Laumann: To answer Leonore, it's a fairly long-winded story and I can only say so much (but see, for general introductions to social network analysis, Berkowitz, 1982; Wellman & Berkowitz, 1988; Laumann & Schumm, 1992; Burt, 1982; Wasserman & Fautz, 1994). Basically, for all current sexual partnerships, about 85% consisted of partners who were acquainted with each other for at least a month before they had sex for the first time. In fact, 45 of every 100 current partnerships comprised partners who knew each other at least a year before they had sex for the first time. The point here is that the bulk of sexual partnerships are embedded in ongoing social relationships resting on grounds other than sexual, such as being workmates, friends, or attending the same school. Moreover, about

60% of all sex partners were introduced to each other by another person who knew both of them—another clear indication of the significance of social networks in orchestrating sexual contacts.

Anne Johnson: Are you talking about the adolescents now?

Edward Laumann: I'm talking about the adults; that's what we study.

Richard Udry: But everything he's said so far applies to us.

Ed Laumann: Yes, since we come from somewhat similar points of view. So there are several types of long-term partnerships: marital partners, cohabs who live together primarily for sexual purposes, and non-coresiding, long-term dating relationships versus short-term partnerships of less than a month's duration—usually amounting to what are called one-night stands. We generally observe that partnerships which weave the network acquaintances and kin of their partners into their own personal social network tend to survive longer than those partnerships which fail to integrate each other's personal networks. Many features of a network that are being construed as aspects of partner choice are just first steps in an ongoing interweaving or segregating process of network construction of the parties to the sexual partnership. Everyone has all this baggage of social associates, and we're trying to characterize those social associates so that we can see, for example, if people in a Mexican setting have only people from the same ethnic group composing their network. Other parts of the community may not report ethnically homogeneous characteristics, and the features of their social and sexual behavior are likely to be rather different.

Leonore Tiefer: The implication is, then, that through an understanding of which people are connected to which people, one will understand the sexual experiences of those people.

Edward Laumann: Properly speaking, yes.

Ulrich Clement: A question to Stuart. I would like to understand better what you mean when you say qualitative, or qualitative interview. Could you illustrate it a bit? Is it just free talk, so to speak? Or is it standardized, half-standardized, or what? What do you do in the interview? And then a further question, do you have any systematic idea of how to connect the qualitative and the quantitative results or are you just looking on your left hand at the transcripts and on your right hand at the tables to see if a good idea emerges?

Stuart Michaels: You might call these semistructured interviews. They were based on standard protocol that set out a number of topics that were to be covered in each interview. But there were no specific detailed questions. The fieldworkers, usually in pairs, were allowed to tailor the interviews to the particular respondents and attempt to draw them out on areas that seemed important. Usually one fieldworker had a primary interest in the neighborhood and the other in the institutional sector. Separate field notes were written by each fieldworker and entered into the text data base.

Your second question had to do with how you integrate the two types of data. We have ideas about this and we're in the process of exploring how these will work, and there are several ways that it's going. One aspect is a little bit of the left hand and the right hand except that the left hand is a very specific set of interviews with a specific kind of actor. So one of the issues we're really interested in is institutions and organizations as opposed to individuals, because that seems to be where a lot of intervention and activity and policy goes on. But it isn't often studied very directly. So part of our aim is to compare the accounts that these institutional actors give of what's going on in their neighborhood with a characterization of the adults who live in that neighborhood. In Chicago, and in most places in the United States, nobody knows what the rates of STDs are. There's no public collection of that information. All we know is the number of people who go to clinics, and we don't even know if the same person goes two or three times, so we only get the rough total counts. The only way to get that information is to do a population survey. Some have been done, but what we will now have is a population survey of the people in this city and these neighborhoods and we will know the rates of their STDs and their sexual experiences with violence, forced sex, good sex, lots of sex, little sex, that kind of thing, compared to the characterizations that people in positions of power have of these things. I think there are other kinds of things that are important to try to do. Sociology is generally fairly multimethod as a discipline. Everybody has a little bit of training in qualitative methods as well as quantitative methods, and we've tried to construct a team of people with strengths on both sides. One of the things that's very interesting for me after spending a lot of time basically analyzing quantitative data from a survey is the struggle to integrate the qualitative interviews with the survey data. Of course, the qualitative interviews have lots of gaps in them; there are lots of questions that were never answered or there are specific stereotypical kinds of answers. I think it's important to ask how do people (especially in specific types of organizations) construct narratives about what the sexual problems are, and how does sex get so problematized by these kinds of actors.

Anke Ehrhardt: Both of these studies are obviously very important and very fascinating. Can I push you a little bit further? What, for each of you, is the most important question to answer? I understand from what you just said that we might get very interesting information on disease transmission, who visits what clinic. That, by itself, may be justification enough, but what in terms of sexual behavior do you hope to get from your more qualitative approach that you don't get out of your quantitative method?

Stuart Michaels: One of my problems is I'm interested in everything and that's partly a reflection of my personality. But there's also one other thing I think that's very important in this. It's illustrated more by the design of the quantitative data collection than the issue of integration of the quantitative and qualitative data. Drawing these samples from specific socially and culturally defined neighborhoods points to our attempt to characterize the role of social context in shaping individual behavior and thought. I found it frustrating to analyze data from a fairly small national sample of only 3,400 cases, where of necessity you are averaging across people drawn from many different contexts. In this second study, of course, we have much smaller samples, which is going to create lots of problems, but they are drawn from and represent much more homogeneous socially organized and comprehensible units such as a neighborhood/community, and that's what I'm the most interested in.

Anke Ehrhardt: What the sexual behavior is like in that particular neighborhood?

Stuart Michaels: That's right.

Anke Ehrhardt: And how the quantitative data relates very specifically to that kind of social structure?

Stuart Michaels: Let me give you one example. Take the issue of homosexuality. Drawing a sample in a gay neighborhood is going to give you a random sample of people who report having homosexual sex in that neighborhood. They won't necessarily define themselves as gay men or lesbians, but many of them will and many will participate in various aspects of the gay community. You will also find a much larger proportion of the men in that neighborhood who have a gay identity and/or homosexual experience than you will elsewhere. I thought it was going to be at most 25%, it seems to be more like 30% or 40%. I'd love to compare these "homosexually active" men with men who live either in the Mexican neighborhood or the Puerto Rican neighborhood and who are having sex with men. I think they will look quite different in terms of their social networks, their sexual and social identities, the kind of sex that they're having, etc.

Ed Laumann: To give a further example, we interviewed a number of church leaders in the African American community of a local neighborhood. Some of these churches had in excess of 10,000 members. How is it that the leaders knew men who were gay, but whom they would not acknowledge as such because of fear of provoking adverse "community opinion"? Will such men eventually move to a predominantly white gay area in another part of Chicago to find a more congenial environment, or will they remain in the neighborhood, maintain a "closeted" status with their neighbors although many will "know" and will act as if they don't? Church leaders were reluctant to discuss this issue with us, and it took considerable effort on our part to establish sufficient rapport to secure more candid discussion of the matter. Since over half of our national sample claimed that religion was an important guide in conducting their sex lives, we need to know much more about what religious leaders are telling their parishioners and others about these matters.

Anke Ehrhardt: Dick, to what extent did you obtain information from your adolescents about coming out, sexual identity, and homosexuality?

Richard Udry: That was never intended to be a featured element of the study. However, we have data on the romantic and sexual relationships; they could nominate partners of either sex, and for about 500 of the relationships they nominated same-sex partners. You can consider that a representative sample of same-sex relationships in adolescence.

Anke Ehrhardt: And were adolescents explicitly told it could be same-sex or opposite-sex romantic partners?

Richard Udry: They were asked which sex and they told us which sex so that's the basic information. But, in addition, everybody in the sample irrespective of their sexual behavior and before they told us anything about their sexual behavior was asked, "Have you ever had a romantic interest in a male? Have you ever had a romantic interest in a female?" Both males and females answered both questions. That gives a first grasp on selecting a group and looking at their sexual behavior.

Charles Turner: Dick, if I understand the paper correctly, the out-of-school samples were not in the Add Health survey.

Richard Udry: The out-of-school samples are not interviewed. The only information that we have on them is what the respondent gives us. To interview the out-of-school friends would have doubled the price of the study.

Charles Turner: I anticipate that at least a few policymaker types will sit back and say you've done a large-scale, congressionally mandated study to understand adolescent health and the things that shape it, but you've lost part of the population that in terms of many of the issues is quite different.

Richard Udry: "Lost" is a relative term. We didn't interview them, but every other study I know uses second-person reports on data of their partners and you will have that for all of the out-of-school partners.

Charles Turner: I was actually asking a question about high school dropouts and their importance to the study of adolescent health.

Richard Udry: Their out-of-school friends are not necessarily dropouts; they may be in some other school.

Charles Turner: If you take the segment of the population that those grades represent and your task is to come to a better appreciation of the status of adolescent health and the things that shape health and health behaviors in the adolescent population, ages 13 to 17, then it strikes me that when you're all done, somebody's going to come and say, "You left out this part of the population!"

Richard Udry: Charles, it has probably occurred to you that someone has already asked this question of us, perhaps even six years ago. And so it is a question with which we have a relatively broad range of prepared answers, and it is a matter to which we devoted considerable attention. You have these people first interviewed in 1994 and last interviewed in 1996. Now a person becomes a dropout from being in school and then not being in school. And so all of the people who are in school in 1994 and not in school in 1996 are people who are in our sample, and after they have dropped out of school they are not deleted from the sample because we don't know that they've dropped out until we go back. Now we have the behavior on whatever number of dropouts this is going to be and we know what they were like before they dropped out, and therefore you will have an adequate sample of dropouts during a two-year period and we will be interviewing and you will know about them.

John Bancroft: It seems to me that an important thrust in Stuart's paper is the combining of quantitative and qualitative methodology. The idea of taking representative samples from different communities and then looking closely at those communities to see what extent you can explain the differences makes a lot of sense to me. It reminds me of a similar thing that the Alan Guttmacher Foundation did on a national basis rather than on a community basis with teenage pregnancies. They looked in detail at the different national contexts, the family planning clinics, sex education, and made a lot of sense out of their data. I have a little bit more difficulty and share some of Leonore's problems with comprehending where we're going with the network analysis. At Richard Parker's conference in Rio, Kate Bond gave a very interesting paper on networks that she was studying in Thailand. I think they were networks of bar-inhabiting youngsters, and she presented some beautiful analyses of really quite complex networks. She could look at the relationships between the people in the networks, and she could even have some idea about the contact between the individuals on the edge of the network and going outside the network. But it was incredibly complicated, and presumably a lot of the networks will be complicated if you allow them to become so. What wasn't clear to me is how you would deal with more than half a dozen networks in this way. How are you going to compare one network with another? So that brings me to my final question. We have heard of two different methodologies for getting networks, one which is relatively easy and inexpensive in that you ask people about the other people, and the other the extraordinarily clever and mind-boggling method that Dick has, which is perhaps unique, as it would be difficult to think of how else you would do it except through school communities of that kind. Now, Dick's cost a whole lot more than Stuart's. It's not clear to me because I don't have a clear idea of how you analyze, summarize, and draw conclusions from analyzing huge numbers of networks, how much more value are you going to get for your money than he's going to get?

Richard Udry: Well, I am not a network person, but one of my closest colleagues is a network person, and so we are putting together a rather sophisticated set of measures of all of these networks, which four or five years ago would have been impossible to imagine being analyzed. When we began planning this, I wrote a little note to myself and put it in my drawer which said, "These networks will never be analyzed." But in the meantime, the sophistication of the software for analyzing networks has become so exquisite that if you can think of the question to ask, the data are now capable of being analyzed. If you haven't worked with network data, then you probably can't think of the right questions at this point, but let me give you an example. School networks have quite different properties. Some of them are very isolated into small groups which we used to call cliques, which are very little connected with one another, and therefore there's very little drift or interaction between networks. In others, the whole school constitutes a single network in which everybody knows everybody else in the school or it breaks down along ethnic lines. We have one school, for example, one of our larger schools, which is 25% each of four different ethnic groups. The way that network structure breaks down among those ethnic groups is going to have a very strong effect on the sexual behavior of the people in that school because there are very different patterns within those ethnic groups. So if networks stay within their own ethnic group, the outcome is going to be quite different than if there is complete mixing across ethnic groups, which won't happen.

John Bancroft: You wouldn't get that evidence from just breaking the data down by ethnic group?

Richard Udry: No, you'd know that the sexual behavior of each of the groups was different, but you wouldn't know what their social patterns had to do with creating them.

Ed Laumann: It is ironic that the interest in social networks actually first came out of anthropology. It was basically an effort to break down the excessive focus on static social structures like kinship systems that used to dominate structured/functional analysis in anthropology. The idea was to grab hold of an individual and have him or her describe the ramifying social ties or connections that he or she has in the course of his/her everyday life. And it turns out that there are a lot of very powerful mathematical and analytical techniques that you can use to see to what extent there is cohesiveness and connectivity in such networks. It is no longer a matter of opinion, you can actually demonstrate that a particular structure has a much quicker implosion rule about how quickly one runs out of potential choice options in comparison to another structure which allows one to ramify his or her social ties in different directions that never come back on themselves. Consider, as a simple example, the case of a person who tells us about his three best friends and then tells us which of them are also socially connected with one another. In the instance where none of the friends knows each other, you have a radial network; in the case where several or all of your three best friends know each other, you have an interlocking network. By simply knowing this formal feature of the connectedness of the network, I can make a prediction that people in radial networks will have less consistent, more ill-defined sets of attitudes than those who are embedded in interlocking networks where at least two of the friends can compare notes about ego and hold him/her to a common expectation. I found empirical support for the hypothesis in a large urban sample of white men (cf. Laumann, 1973, Chapter 4).

Alain Giami: Don't you think that there might be a confusion between what he says about his friends and the reality of this network? It seems that when you ask individuals about social networks, they report the "mental social network" they have in mind, which is an interesting topic. The French anthropologist Maurice Godelier wrote: "social relations are not only between individuals, they are within them. . . . Ideology constitutes the inner framework of social relations and this framework is found as much within the individual as within his or her relationships" (Godelier, 1996, p. 28).

Richard Udry: We really don't know how good these reports of the attributes of the other people are. We'll know eventually because I have the data, but generally we've been forced to make the assumption that what they tell us about other people is true, even though in previous studies I've done I know it isn't so.

Alain Giami: It might be true, but it might not be real. Truth and reality are not the same category, Richard.

Richard Udry: I don't understand your point. Suppose we say that my friends influence me only through my perception of their behavior, even though my perception has no relationship to their actual behavior. In that case, I don't think we are talking about a social influence, because the whole process is taking place inside me and is independent of my friends' behavior. The accuracy of interpersonal perceptions varies enormously, from zero to quite accurate. As an example, I have shown that adolescent girls have rather accurate information about the sexual behavior of their individual girl friends, but boys' information about their individual male friends' sexual behavior is close to random. As a consequence, female friends influence one another's sexual behavior, but male friends do not influence one another's sexual behavior.

John Bancroft: But, Ed, if I could just follow up on your illustration, are you saying that using Dick's data, you could identify large numbers of a certain type of network and large numbers of another type of network and you could contrast them and test your hypothesis?

Ed Laumann: Dick basically has information on what are called sociocentric or total networks (viz., for the completely enumerated schools in his sample). Most of us have been operating with egocentric networks (i.e., a focal person and the people with whom he or she has social relationships, however defined). A literature going back 30 years or more has attempted to evaluate the accuracy with which people describe the characteristics of their network members (e.g., Laumann, 1973, Chapter 2). There are clearly pitfalls to relying upon individual respondents for such reports. Sometimes respondents can describe the features of their relational partners exactly and honestly; other times they will distort the description in what appears to be systematically biased ways. But these issues about validity have been under discussion here for the past two days and are no different in kind from those pertaining to any measurement device in the social sciences. But it is worth stressing that social network analysis is a distinctive perspective that organizes the way one thinks about data and their interpretation quite differently from that of conventional survey methodology or other person-centered approaches. It pushes the investigator to focus on the nature of sexual partnerships and the fact that sex is a negotiated transaction between at least two individuals. All the sexual fantasies and sexual motivations of an individual will come to naught unless he or she can find and persuade someone else who shares at least some of these sexual interests to engage in joint sexual activity. Sexual activity is thus jointly produced; our account of it needs to take this feature explicitly into account.

Barbara Marín: What is it that we really are going to learn about sex from knowing about people's networks? One thing that I'm really interested in knowing is the effect of the age of the person's partner on their sexual behavior, because there's now a certain amount of data suggesting that young girls are at risk particularly from older partners (Males, 1993; California Vital Statistics Section, 1992; National Center for Health Statistics, 1988). The problem with the social network data that you'll have is that the most interesting partners aren't in the schools, because they aren't the same age as the kids. The most interesting partners are the 22-year-old men that are having sex with middle-school girls.

Richard Udry: Those may be the ones that you're most interested in, but they're not necessarily the ones that everyone is most interested in. But if you want to know something about the 22-year-old partner, the data that are in my study are as good as the data that anybody else is ever going to have on them because they are descriptions by the girl of the attributes of her partner whom she has identified as 22 years old if she knows his age. What you don't have is a 22-year-old in the study.

Barbara Marín: What are the attributes that you'll have?

Ed Laumann: We ask about everything that we thought she could know about her partner with some accuracy and some things that she probably does not know so well, for example, whether her partner has sex with other partners concurrently. We need to think very carefully about the differential reliabilities of reported information about partners. We find that respondents can readily be asked about their partners' demographic attributes, whether they are in another school or not in school, whether they are employed or not, what their religion is, and so on.

Stuart Michaels: One way to think about the social network approach is as emphasizing certain aspects of social reality, in particular the relational. In this sense, it's quite objective, and structuralist in lots of ways. It begins by looking at the more concrete relations between individuals. In our study, it's egocentric. So in that sense Dick's work and ours are complementary; it's not either/or. He is able to look at these much larger full-scale network examples which have, up till now, only really been studied in very special limited spaces. Tony Coxon has been able to trace out some networks in gay communities and actually conduct interviews with both partners and trace out the whole network. People have done it in monasteries and in small-scale social institutions, but to be able to do it on this large scale is quite important and a bit unusual. We cannot do that. We're thinking about the structures of larger networks, but we basically look at the individual and the immediate relations that that person has, and we don't know much more about where it goes after that. Those are what I would call fairly objective relations. However, I think we do give them a fair amount of "social flesh." In other words, it's not just behavioral; we're asking about social characteristics of these people, class, education, occupation; we ask about qualities of the relationships between people. One argument about sexuality that we're trying to make is that it's the relationship that ought to be emphasized. Often when we get very behavioral, we forget, as if every time there's vaginal intercourse it's the same act or every time there's anal intercourse it's the same act, but they can be taking place in the context of very different relations.

Alex Carballo-Diéguez: I was wondering, what do you do when you have contradictory information from two people in the network, both of whom have been interviewed? For example, someone says I have a romantic partnership with so-and-so, but so-and-so says they have a sexual partnership with so-and-so.

Richard Udry: I'm sure we will find that, and there are interesting ways to model this analytically, but that is one of our main sources of interest. One imagines that the male will say it's a sexual relationship and the female will say it's a romantic relationship or something like that. What may turn out to be just as interesting is that the male says he has a sexual relationship with a girl and the girl doesn't mention him. And so there are all kinds of contradictions that can arise out of this, and it's one of the best validity measures of reports of sexual behavior that I know of.

Alex Carballo-Diéguez: Not according to Joe Catania, who does not see the partner's report as necessarily a measurement of validity.

Richard Udry: Well, that's a matter that I don't think I want to debate right now. I think the issues there are extremely clear. If two people give you different reports about the occurrence or nonoccurrence of an item of sexual behavior, then they both cannot be valid, and so you have a contradiction.

Leonore Tiefer: This is not true; this happens all the time. The husband and wife disagree; you bring them in; they discuss it, and all of a sudden you realize that they are both right—it's the interpretation.

Richard Udry: Well, I don't think we have any disagreement. Instead of looking at this as a problem, we look at it as an opportunity. We will try to predict the attributes of the actors and their network relationships and their family characteristics that cause one of the partners to report yes and the other one to report no. So we'll take that as something to be explained, and we'll have wonderful opportunities to explain it. So I don't look at it as a problem. I'll just be delighted if somebody disagrees with someone else as to what happened.

Ann Stueve: I think it's absolutely critical that we start looking at the networks. Over dinner some of us were talking about what kinds of interventions we think would work with adolescents and saying we weren't sure that individualistically oriented interventions that target individual kids' skills and attitudes would work. We need instead to change the climate or the normative beliefs of the network. That's based on the assumption that an individual's behavior is going to be influenced by the attitudes and behaviors of other members of a peer group, and we can begin to test that assumption with some of your data. Are kids more likely to initiate sex at an early age if their friends are already sexually active than if they aren't? Are they more likely to develop positive attitudes about sex if their friends hold positive attitudes than if they don't?

Richard Udry: Yes, I have already shown that. I did it with actual pairs that were matched.

Ed Laumann: The whole issue of mapping stakeholders in social networks is really the theoretical spin that needs to be elaborated and tested. We have many examples from a variety of settings other than sex that show how orderly networks are. As Dick was saying, the computer resources for analyzing these things have advanced considerably. When I started working on these issues in the early 1970s, the ability to look at a network with more than 30 or 40 members was impossible. I mean, it just blew the computers out of the water. You just couldn't do it. Now you can do most any of these analyses on a laptop.

Richard Udry: Well, actually we've been having to use the Convex. We have networks with 2,200 people in them.

Colin Williams: I like the idea of networks, being a sociologist, but again I find network analysis tremendously complex. Can you say what the major types of networks are that you would find involved in sexual behaviors, so that the rest of us could look for those networks and not worry too much about their complexities? In other words, do you have a theory?

Ed Laumann: Two chapters in *The Social Organization of Sexuality* (Laumann et al., 1994), "Sexual Networks" and "The Epidemiology of Networks," present a clear agenda for how data from a cross-section sample can be used for this purpose. The main hypothesis presented there is the idea of "equal status contact," that is, the tendency for people to pick others for social relationships who are as similar to themselves as possible. One of the great surprises uncovered in our data is how powerful this tendency is. Before looking at the results, we were convinced that one-night stands would comprise people who were from very different social backgrounds. We were thinking of the classic story of the socially prominent, wealthy man and a prostitute from a low-ranking ethnic group. We were stunned to observe how rarely such combinations occurred. The vast majority of one-night stands involved two persons who were almost exact social replicas of one another, manifesting almost as much social similarity as that observed for marriage partners. The obvious reason for this is that if you're proposing to talk somebody into bed on the strength of a short, casual meeting, you'd better have as many things going for you as possible. You are thus likely to target people for short affairs who are preselected socially to be as like yourself as possible. When we observe people who violate the equal-status-contact rule, we can learn about the grounds for the violation and the kinds of consequences that flow from it. Certainly an interesting consequence of "bridge persons," who have sex with people from socially discrepant circumstances, is their role as a vector for the spread of sexually transmitted infection across social groups. This is just one example of the interpretations engendered by a network approach.

Joe Catania: There's another theoretical twist on the network research, concerning social crowds. Crowds are reputation-based groups that have some shared symbolism and encompass multiple friendship networks. Some people have been looking at crowds among adolescents (e.g., nerds versus dopers versus skaters). If you look at the behaviors within crowds, things like drinking, smoking or sex, they vary across crowds, and there's a body of theory looking at how those crowds develop and what sorts of things lead to particular behaviors popping up in one crowd or another. It would be great if you were able to do that kind of analysis with your data set.

References

Berkowitz, S. D. (1982). *An introduction to structural analysis: The network approach to social research.* Toronto: Butterworths.

Burt, R. S. (1982). *Toward a structural theory of action: Network models of social structure.* New York: Academic Press.

California Vital Statistics Section. (1992). *California resident live births, 1990, by age of mother, age of father, race, marital status.* Sacramento: California Department of Health Services.

Godelier, M. (1996). Sexualité et société. In J. Cournut (Ed.), *Psychanalyse et sexualité. Questions aux sciences humaines* (pp. 27–40). Paris: Dunod.

Laumann, E. O. (1973). *Bonds of pluralism: The form and substance of urban social networks.* New York: John Wiley.

Laumann, E. O., Gagnon, J. H., Michael, R. T., & Michaels, S. (1994). *The social organization of sexuality; Sexual practices in the United States.* Chicago: University of Chicago Press.

Laumann, E. O., & Schumm, L. P. (1992). *Measuring social networks using samples: Is network analysis relevant to survey research?* Paper presented at the symposium on "The Frontiers of Social Measurement," The National Opinion Research Center, Chicago, March 13.

Males, M. (1993, January). Poverty, rape, adult/teen sex: Why "pregnancy prevention" programs don't work. *Phi Delta Kappa,* pp. 407–410.

Marín, B. V. (1995). *Analysis of AIDS prevention among African American and Latinos in the United States.* Report prepared for the Office of Technology Assessment (OTA), U.S. Congress, Washington, DC.

National Center for Health Statistics. (1988). *Vital Statistics of the United States, Vol. 1, Natality.* Hyattsville, MD: Public Health Services.

Wasserman, S., & Fautz, K. (1994). *Social network analysis. Methods and applications.* New York: Cambridge University Press.

Wellman, B., & Berkowitz, S. D. (Eds.). (1988). *Social structures: A network approach.* Cambridge: Cambridge University Press.

Part 8.

Researching Sexual Interactions

Coding Interactional Sexual Scripts

ULRICH CLEMENT

Question

Sexual behavior surveys refer to (mostly) interactional behavior. However, most surveys do not conceptualize the interactional dimension. The scripting approach offers a perspective for analyzing sexual conduct as interactional behavior. Here, sexual scripts are defined as *repetitive interactional patterns*. "Repetitive" refers to the assumption that the way a person sexually interacts follows a draft on which the person improvises his/her behavior.

This version of the scripting approach presented here is based on *narratives* of a respondent. Narratives—as compared with standardized interviews—deliver a different type of data, as they provide meaningful stories of the respondent. These stories follow a "dramatic" pattern that contains suspense and resolution.

Interactional scripts include the behavior of both interacting partners. Since the script is cognitively represented in the mind of the interviewed person, who knows about his own intentions but not necessarily about the partner's intentions, the script model should include intentions of the respondent, the perceived reaction of the partner, and the respondent's behavior.

Method

To assess sexual scripts, the CCRT (Core Conflictual Relationship Theme) (Luborsky & Crits-Christoph, 1990) was modified and applied to sexual-interaction narratives. Narratives need a particular method of guiding interviews: the interviewer invites the respondent to report on sexual relationship episodes that he/she has experienced with different or the same person/s. The aim of the interviewer is to facilitate the respondent to narrate as many episodes as possible.

We used the following instruction:

> This interview is about sexual experiences you have had. Please tell me about events in your life which happened when you met a real or potential sexual partner. Each of your stories should deal with a special moment, a real situation or a scene which in some way or other was of

particular—positive or negative—importance to you. We are interested in events that happened with various potential or real partners—both in the present and in the past. For each of such episodes, please let me know: 1st when it happened and 2nd, with whom, 3rd what the partner said or did, 4th what you said or did, and 5th how the story ended. (Hilffert et al., 1995)

Within each SRE (sexual relationship episode), three components are coded:

W (wish)
RO (reaction from other)
RS (reaction from self).

For each component, specific sexual categories were developed and added to the CCRT standard category list. Example:

(female, 29 yrs.)
"B" used to be all loving and tenderness,
and this was okay at the time but now it
is no longer enough for me, just tenderness,
I *also need* something *passionate and ardent*;   W63: I want passionate sexuality
or I am actually a very self-confident woman
and actually *I am for somebody stronger than*   W65: I want a strong, attractive
I, who does not always mollycoddle and   partner, want to be controlled
adore me but *occasionally will tell me to do*
what he wants, break my will so to speak.
And he used not to be able to do this. And   RO71: he is sexually weak
then we went to J. (town) together and a
completely different side of his character
was revealed to me, well, *I had not known*   RS2: I am surprised
him to be like that, he was just that . . . totally
passionate, and *he did not ask me at all*   RO63: he is passionate
and *just overpowered me* and so on, which was
simply a totally new experience, *he just took*   RO65: he shows initiative
me, practically, yes in fact, exactly what I   RS29: I am happy
had always *longed for*, I did not have to
fumble around, seduce him or so, but it was
just as I had always wished it would be.

Data Analysis

The sexual-interactional script is defined as the dominant W-RO-RS sequence. There are two major ways of identifying the interactional-sexual script. First, the standard analysis as proposed by Luborsky et al. (1990) is to add up frequencies of the coding categories over all relationship episodes. The combination of the most frequent W, the most frequent RO, and the most frequent RS then forms the script. Second, for each relationship episode, a psychologically plausible W-RO-RS combination is stated that formulates the central message of this episode ("A-level coding," Dahlbender et al., 1993). Only the A-level coding for each relationship episode is then included in the further analysis.

For the example above, the A-level coding would be formulated:

W63:   I want passionate sexuality
RO63, 65: he is passionate and shows initiative
RS2, 29:   I am surprised and happy

The coding of one SRE does not define a script yet. Ideally, a significant W-RO-RS combination would define a script, but due to the extremely low expected frequency of such a combination, it is useful to identify significant W-RO or RO-RS combinations.

Empirical Results

Example: Study "Gender Differences in Sexual Scripts" (Clement et al., 1995)

In a sample of 24 (12 male, 12 female) heterosexual young adults, a total of 265 SREs was coded (range: 8–17 per person). For each person, the RO-RS combinations were calculated.

Result A:

A characteristic gender-specific RO-RS sequence could be identified:

RO: is abusing/exploiting	males: r = + .48 (p<.01) $\rightarrow$ females: r = − .48 (p<.01)	RS: is sexually interested

In the male SREs, abusing/exploiting RO is *positively* correlated with a sexually interested RS. In the female SREs, this correlation is negative.

Result B:

In the same study, a highly significant non-gender-specific RO-RS sequence was identified:

RO: is tender/attractive/playful	males: r = + .78 (p<.001) $\rightarrow$ females: r = + .70 (p<.001)	RS: is sexually interested

For both males and females, a tender/attractive/playful RO is highly correlated with a sexually interested RS.

Without going into a deeper substantial interpretation of the results themselves, this study gives an example of what type of data may result

344 | Researching Sexual Behavior

from a SRE-analysis: These reported correlations can be understood as interactional patterns as experienced by the respondent of a SRE-interview.

Conceptual Note: Should Interactional Scripts Be Conceptualized as Behavior Sequences or as Feedback Loops?

In the CCRT approach, scripts are conceptualized as sequences. Here, the root of the script is the wish. The reaction of the interactional partner is evaluated as a reaction to the wish (from the perspective of the respondent!). The reaction of the respondent, again, is the third step that confirms or disconfirms the wish. So, the sequential concept is this:

From a systemic perspective, that ignores the motivation of behavior, and considers exclusively consequences of behavior, one would propose a different model. The basic theoretical claim here is, that for the process of a sexual interaction, it is not important who started, but rather how the interaction is maintained and proceeded. In this perspective, the wish would be omitted. A feedback model would be more appropriate:

Applying the feedback model to the transcribed example above, result B would be spelled as:

The more passionate and initiative he is, the more I am surprised

and

The more surprised and happy I am, the more he is passionate and initiative

Both models could refer to SRE-interviews. If the research question focuses on the narrator's perspective and subjective experience, the sequential model fits better with the "dramatic" patterns of narrated stories, while the feedback model fits better with an approach that focuses on behavior regulation and interactional negotiation and balance.

Perspectives and Limitations

Perspectives

- As a qualitative method, SRE analysis is sensitive to context information and at the same time allows the identification of psychologically plausible scripts
- It may be applied to case studies

- Assuming that sexual experiences are organized in interactional schemata rather than in accounts of behavioral units, the SRE analysis is a promising method to identify these schemata

Limitations

- The representativity of the narrated SREs remains a crucial question so far. Which episodes are selected by the narrator? There is no evidence that the most frequent episodes are the most frequently narrated ones. Therefore, several selection biases are to be expected. One is that unusual experiences (for instance: first encounters) are overrepresented, whereas everyday experiences (for instance: intercourse with a long-term partner) are underrepresented.
- Interrater reliability has proved to be good for trained raters. The reliability of the wish component is somewhat lower than that of RO and RS ratings, which might be due to the fact that wishes are often implicit and depending on the interpretation of the rater.
- Coding SRE interviews is extremely time-intensive. Experienced raters need about six hours of coding for an interview of one hour.

References

Clement, U., Hilffert, S., & Schrey, C. (1995). *Gender differences in sexual scripts.* Poster presented at the 21st Meeting of the International Academy of Sex Research, Sept. 19–23, 1995, Provincetown, MA.

Dahlbender, R. W., Torres, L., Reichert, S., Stbner, S., Frevert, G., & Kchele, H. (1993). Die Praxis des Beziehungsepisoden-Interviews. *Zeitschrift für Psychosomatische Medizin und Psychoanalyse, 39,* 51–62.

Hilffert, S., Schrey, C., & Clement, U. (1995). *The assessment of sexual interactions using the CCRT.* Paper presented at the International Workshop on the Core Conflictual Relationship Theme Method (CCRT), April 22–24, 1995, Ulm, Germany.

Luborsky, L., & Crits-Christoph, P. (1990). *Understanding transference: The CCRT method.* New York: Basic Books.

Discussion

Alex Carballo-Diéguez: I have some questions about the way you deal with these scripts. In the example you presented, you said that the woman wanted passionate sex with a strong partner who controlled her. However, you said she was surprised and it sounded as though that was not her original wish, but rather that she attributed a meaning to the event after it happened. Your diagram seems quite linear: there is an observation of what the other person is doing, and therefore this is how I respond. But your own examples make it appear as a circular rather than linear process: something happened and it wasn't what I expected. I may say, "Wow! I like this!" And then after the fact, I'm saying, "You know, maybe that's what I wanted, to be dominated."

Ulrich Clement: The respondent here has a temporal order integral in what she said. She said, "First I had this wish." But you bring up an important question. Do we have causal connections or is the behavior of both interactional partners circularly interconnected? It's important to know from what perspective you are discussing this point. There's a causal logic from the respondent's perspective. As an observer, you as a researcher might say, "That's a circular kind of thing and you might have invited him to do that." But usually narratives don't have the feedback structure, "The more I did this, the more he did that." That's what the researcher would say from the external perspective. Respondents tend to have a linear understanding of behavior. Narratives are sequential things and one results from the next. The circular aspect—that's an interpretation by the external observer, the researcher.

Alex Carballo-Diéguez: Well, I'm not sure, because she can go back to the event. In the same way when we work with childhood sexual abuse, the respondents may go back to the event and give it a different meaning. They may say, "Oh, I was abused, but, at that time it didn't feel like abuse." Or they can say, "Actually, it was the initiation of my sexual life, it was great, but at the time, I hated it." So I don't know whether in the narrative you can say, "that is inherently what they are saying," because there's a going back all the time to change the meaning.

Ulrich Clement: To change the meaning, to reinterpret it. Okay, that might happen, they might reinterpret it in a way, but my first data approach was to take it as given what the respondent tells me. He might be reinterpreting or not, you never know, that was my epistemological remark in the beginning. All sexual experiences are cognitively transformed or reinterpreted in a way and I don't know how you can avoid that. So I think the best approach is to take it as given, as the respondent tells it.

Alfred Spira: I didn't understand how you calculated correlation coefficients. Do you code for responses?

Ulrich Clement: I code the responses.

Alfred Spira: So, this is a reinterpretation, isn't it?

Ulrich Clement: It's an interpretation, of course. Coding is always partly an interpretation of what the respondent means, otherwise you cannot code. Coding without interpretation simply doesn't work, so we have this category list, we translate, we code the narration and then we have a frequency distribution overall and each respondent has a certain value and then you can calculate correlations or also probabilities or conditional probabilities. But in this case I did it with correlations.

Alain Giami: When I read your transcript, I see the element that you don't include in your analysis. For example, one of the first sentences is, "I am actually a very self-confident woman." In my empirical view, the fact the woman says that she is very self-confident is a part of the explanation of why she might allow herself to be dominated. So in your model, there is no space for the self-definition and the self-representation of the person that might help to explain the construction of the script. Another question is that your model of the script appears to be too rational; there is no place for internal contradiction and ambivalence in the script. I want this and I don't want this, I want this and I want that. When we carry out an interview, we know that this occurs and we don't know which part of the contradiction to choose.

Ulrich Clement: The second question is easier to answer because we have an ambivalence category in the wish list. Very often respondents say, "I didn't know, should I/should I not." And so this is one category, ambivalent wish. And the first question, you're right, this is a coding scheme for interactional aspects, not for self-descriptions. If I were doing a case study on this person, I would include the self-description, "I'm a self-confident woman," or such like. But I was interested in the interactional pattern, and the logic is that we include self-descriptions only if they refer to interaction.

Alain Giami: Do you think this element does not refer to the interaction, the fact that the person says that I am self-confident?

Ulrich Clement: In the broader sense, yes, but the problem was to limit the things that we wanted to code; the focus was on the interaction and on the idea that each person is reacting to the other. And so "I'm a self-confident woman" is not a reactive term, it's a self-description. I understand what you mean, but we excluded this because we are exclusively interested in the actual interaction terms.

Fabio Sabogal: Do you know how the individuals select their episodes, and if they are only selecting some, is there bias in their selection process? And how do they sample the information that they are giving you? A further question is how are you comparing subjects if you are not giving some standard information? For example, it is different if you ask, "Give me the most romantic situation, or give me one situation where you were abused."

Ulrich Clement: Let me again start with the second question first. That's what we are actually trying. We are actually comparing different instructions; the one instruction that you saw, "Just tell me stories," is compared with another instruction, "Tell me the most important story or tell me the worst story," to see if this would produce a different selection of stories. The first question is essential. The question is, in other words, "Are the stories representative of what a person experiences, or is there a selection?" That's a weakness and a strength at the same time with this approach. The weakness is that these stories are definitely not representative. I have never had the idea that they would be representative. Clearly, unusual stories are overrepresented. First encounters are overrepresented. My impression also is that experiences with violence are overrepresented because they are events, so to speak. On the other hand, everyday sexuality, I mean sexuality in a long, committed relationship, is underrepresented because people would not tell about the 255th intercourse with a steady partner because it was more or less the same as the 157th. So, in a way, people select more or less unusual events. So there's clearly a bias there. So we are not getting a valid frequency distribution for experiences, but what we are getting is an understanding of the interaction patterns. These stories are a way of presenting oneself as a sexual being, and they select what is typical for them.

Richard Parker: I'm really interested in what you're doing because it seems to me that it offers a possibility of operationalizing the notion of scripts. For a lot of us who have worked in the field and who have found the metaphor of the script something interesting and exciting, it's been tough to know how to transform it into our research method. But the sense that I get in hearing you talk and reading your paper is that you're reducing the narratives more than you might want to. It might be interesting to try and look at the complexities and even the contradictions within the narratives in even more detail, because I suspect, at least in HIV-prevention work, what we often find is that those contradictions are the key points where the problems and possibilities related to intervention exist. So it might be useful, rather than just trying to get the sequence A leads to B leads to C, to find ways to look at some of those internal contradictions. The other thing that I wondered is if you've looked at the large literature on narrative, the morphology of folk narratives, that tries to look at formulaic structures in narrative. The sexual stories that people tell us are perhaps organized by cultural formulas. They may not have as much to do with what really happened as with ways that we're taught to tell about what happened.

Joe Catania: When you look at interactional patterns, do you consider other elements of this process? There's a verbal exchange and an emotional flow between folks. It seems like your emphasis is on the cognitive behavioral elements, what this person wished, what this person did, what that person did. So in a sense it's as if you've untied those things from the verbal interaction and emotional interaction that's going on. Do you feel you might want to tie those things back together at some point?

Ulrich Clement: You make a difference between emotional and cognitive?

Joe Catania: Well, I see emotional elements in these narratives that aren't being represented in your distillate remarks. There are a number of different elements in how people interact. You're representing some of those elements, but there are others. What I'm struck by is what happens when you start untying these pieces from the interaction. Is it useful to untie these things or do you need to look at all of it together?

Ulrich Clement: I don't think I left out the emotional dimension. These interactions are not behavioristic descriptions like "he did this or that." They have an emotional tone. All this behavior that she's narrating has an emotional tone.

Joe Catania: How was the tone coded?

Ulrich Clement: This is the coding list of the nonsexual responses of the self: "I understand," "I feel respected," "I oppose others," "I feel disappointed," "I feel angry," "I feel depressed," things like that, so you have all the emotional elements in there. The idea is not to identify a behavior but the emotional tone of a behavior, of a response. I don't split it, so I don't have to tie it together again.

Diane di Mauro: Do those responses need to be verbalized by the person or is this the interpretation of the coder? And are all of those other things that may not be cognitively or consciously aware lost? I'm not saying that you should be able to get at them, that would be an almost impossible task.

Ulrich Clement: It's a good question. The person doesn't have to say literally what is in their coding list, of course, but what she means. So there's an interpretative step in between. A person does not have to say "I felt disappointed" in order to get the coding, but sometimes the person will say "Oh, too bad!" simply, so then we would code: "I feel disappointed." The problem is with the interpretation: it must be explicit, it must not be between the lines, but it must be in the lines. And of the problems that we have with coding, the wishes are the most difficult thing to code. The reactions of the partner and of the self are mostly explicit, but wishes are sometimes implicit. They are sometimes not clear, and so actually I'm wondering whether the wish category should be omitted or not. One would lose something very important in terms of motivation, but on the methodological level, it would help because the interrater reliability is clearly lower for the wishes than for the other components.

Alex Carballo-Diéguez: Whenever I try to do qualitative research, I find that reality exceeds the categories I have to fit it in. When you have a sequence like "if a woman treats me bad, then I'm interested," the feeling "she treats me bad" may have many different ways of expressing itself and it may mean different things. If she treats me bad because she says "no, you're always wanting sex," maybe I'm interested. But if she treats me bad and doesn't cook, maybe I have a completely different reaction. You have one category, "she treats me bad," to group many different situations. You run the risk of losing the specificity and being unable to account for what follows.

Ulrich Clement: In this particular case, I would not agree, because we have a quite differentiated category which would apply to "he treats me bad." So in this situation, it was my verbalization of what the category said. Exploiting me, pushing me, humiliating me, there were a lot more categories for this. But generally speaking, that's a problem for all of us, that research is reduction. Research is always reduction. The seduction of qualitative research is to go very much into details, and the more you do it, the more you lose it. The risk is that you lose the global thing that you're interested in. Research is reduction and that's our destiny as researchers.

Anke Ehrhardt: This always happens when we talk about gender scripts. There's a lot of both interest and skepticism initially because, as Ulrich described it, it is a very broad approach. We have used it in a more focused way. We have just finished a study on heterosexual men: What is your most romantic situation? What is your first encounter? Describe them, etc. We found fascinating information about when men like to talk, when it is appropriate for women to bring up condoms, what gets everybody out of the mood. It's a really interesting method which can be used in different kinds of ways, and Ulrich only had a little time to introduce it. It might get at gender in terms of people's expectations of how we behave. We all have gender scripts for how we behave at a conference; we have gender scripts in terms of sexual encounters, romantic encounters, sexual behavior in a committed relationship. To know more about that in terms of HIV, etc., is a very fruitful exploration.

Alain Giami: What you say is one part of the contradiction that we have in this conference between problem-oriented and basic fundamental research. Don't you think we lose something if we reduce too early the study of scripts to the identification of messages of safer sex?

Anke Ehrhardt: I'm saying we can do the basic gender scripts and that will help us to understand how safer sex may then be integrated.

Cynthia Graham: Has this method ever been used to look at more everyday experiences, rather than the unusual?

Ulrich Clement: It could be. It depends upon the instruction. If you give just the general instruction "tell me what comes in your mind," then everyday stories usually will not come up. But you could change the instruction and say just let's talk about your long-term partner only, and tell me a typical story about the beginning of the relationship, after three years, after 10 years, if you are interested in longitudinal change. It could be used in that way.

Cynthia Graham: I thought you were suggesting that people would find it hard to tell stories about the everyday experiences.

Ulrich Clement: They would not find it hard, but it's not what they would do spontaneously. You need to invite them to do that.

John Bancroft: We used something like this many years ago in Oxford when we were studying attempted suicide to analyze the accounts that people gave about why they took an overdose. We would ask them to give a narrative of what led up to the actual taking of the overdose and we did similar, comparable narrative analysis and we made distinctions between expressive and instrumental accounts. The predominant picture that came out was that they would account for their behavior in a way which described how they were feeling rather than what they were trying to achieve, whether or not they had any particular goals. Richard raised this interesting question about the research value of scripts and I would like to ask you more about that. The distinction you made at the beginning between scripts and narratives implied that the script had some sort of organizing or causal relevance to the behavior. Richard was suggesting that the script was, if I understood him correctly, a culturally shaped way of accounting for your behavior after the event. Does it make any difference whether it's one or the other and which do you think it is?

Ulrich Clement: You might see it both ways. Scripts organize behavior and they shape the way of accounting it after it was done. The question's just, on which level do you analyze them? Gagnon differentiated between scripts at cultural, interactional, and individual levels. That's a good perspective, but it tells you nothing about how to assess them. So my question is much more to find a methodology for script analysis, and previously I haven't been able to find very much methodology. Gagnon hasn't developed a methodology for script analysis. That is lacking in the whole field and that's the reason for my endeavor.

Part 9.
Conclusions

Sex Surveys in the Context of Survey Research

JOHN M. KENNEDY

My comments focus on the themes that I heard in the papers. As a survey researcher, I conduct relatively few surveys that are related to sexual behaviors and attitudes, so my comments are intended to place the papers in two perspectives. First, I looked at the papers from the perspective of a sociologist. The second perspective I used is that of survey research in general.

To begin, I learned over the past two days that sex survey researchers are interested in the methodology of survey research as well as the content of surveys. In many instances when I work with researchers, it is very difficult to convince them that there are methodological issues that must be solved before the survey can yield good, useful data. It was satisfying to hear that most presenters acknowledge the methodological difficulties of conducting good surveys and that they recognize that a collaborative and cooperative effort between the researcher and survey specialist is required to produce good data. Survey researchers know the techniques of survey research but generally do not know the subject matter. As a group, these papers demonstrate an understanding of the methodological problems of doing high-quality surveys.

From a sociologist's perspective, in listening to the papers, I heard three contrasts that seem to describe the range of sex survey research. The first contrast is between what might be termed big science and little science, which is not the same as good and bad science. Essentially, there are big studies, such as some of the epidemiological surveys. These are generally large and expensive studies that study social problems. They contrast with smaller studies whose purpose is to try to generate an in-depth understanding of behaviors. The big studies try to understand problem behaviors. The smaller studies (for example, the study Cynthia Graham reported) focus more intensely on the understanding of sexual behavior. Each has different requirements, different goals, and different procedures that are necessary to carry them out. In some ways, I see this contrast as an extension of what Colin Williams mentioned—one researcher's error is another researcher's data. That is, some of the measurement problems in a big study are areas of interest in small studies. Measurement error in large

355

epidemiological studies indicates the types of interesting issues that can be resolved by using smaller in-depth studies.

Another contrast I noticed was the difference between applied and basic research. In sex research, in contrast with many other sciences, applied research receives the most funding, and basic research works with smaller budgets. This is neither good nor bad—just different from most other kinds of research. In sex research, it appears that the large-cost projects study problem behaviors and the small-cost projects are aimed at a more basic understanding of sex issues. (The NORC Sex in America Study does not fit this classification.)

The third contrast is between quantitative/qualitative approaches in the types of research. I need not discuss this contrast because the conference participants clearly recognize the issues. In general, the papers I heard demonstrated a clear understanding of the approaches.

Let me further discuss the papers from the perspective of a survey researcher. To do so, I can use the concept of total survey error to approach the research presented. Total survey error comprises essentially four components—sampling error, coverage error, nonresponse error, and measurement error. Personally, I add a fifth component that I call "researcher error." That is, not only are the first four components part of every survey, but the researcher also brings to the survey certain tendencies and outlooks that cause what might be considered "error." I sense that those conducting large research projects understand the idea of total survey error. For example, many papers presented data that demonstrated that certain sexual behaviors are underreported and the attempts made to understand the nature of the problem and the resulting impact on the survey data.

Despite the number of possible errors in survey research, it is relatively robust, and survey error does not necessarily invalidate the findings. For example, the Gallup studies in the 1930s and 1940s were conducted using a method that essentially amounted to interviewing people on street corners. For almost twenty years, Gallup was able to predict elections fairly well using those procedures.

There is one sampling issue that the presenters understand better than most other survey researchers, and that is the need to determine the appropriate units of measurement. What should be sampled? Individuals? Dyads? Networks? Households? Interactions? It was very interesting to hear how much more thoroughly the presenters thought about these issues than most people who do survey research. Most survey research still focuses on the individual, even though researchers are trying to understand relationships in which the individual respondent is embedded. The consideration of the appropriate research unit is one area in which sex surveys are ahead of much survey research.

In terms of coverage error, many presenters were concerned with sampling from rare populations. Overall, the papers demonstrated both an understanding of the issues and effective strategies dealing with them. Sex surveys use venue sampling and multiplicity sampling as well as any in the survey research field.

There is one area that I didn't hear discussed. I don't know if this is an area that sex researchers have discussed, forgotten about, and do not consider an issue anymore, but I did not hear any papers on surveying non-household populations, i.e., the military, students in residence halls, the prison population, the homeless, people in mental institutions. There was nothing discussed about these types of populations, which—from my perspective as an interested observer more so than as a sociologist or a survey researcher—are the areas in which it seems that many of the problem types of sexual behavior take place. I assume there is some reason there have not been any papers in these areas discussed here, but whatever the reason, it wasn't apparent to me.

The next issue I will discuss is survey participation rates. In terms of participation rates, sex surveys appear to be doing as well as, and in some cases better than, general population surveys. Much of what I heard, especially about the large surveys where researchers work hard to increase participation, indicates they are quite successful. The surveys presented in the past two days attained much better participation rates than general-population, random-digit-dialing surveys. The survey procedures are generally conceived and executed very well.

Overall, from a survey researcher's perspective, the papers presented here indicate that sex survey researchers are very concerned about and work very hard at conducting quality research. The types of people who don't cooperate with sex surveys are about the same as the noncooperative types in all types of surveys. All surveys have problems convincing older persons to cooperate. All have problems with younger people who are hard to find. None of what I heard appears to be different from most surveys.

Some consideration might also be given to whether nonparticipation is caused by the difficulty of reaching people and/or getting them to cooperate or if some assumed nonparticipation is related to measurement error. It may appear that surveys miss people who are poorly educated, but research we conducted at the Center for Survey Research indicates that, at least in terms of telephone interviews, respondents exaggerate their education. So if we say that we're missing people with less education, we may not be. Instead, some people might actually be giving us the wrong answers about their education.

Measurement error was the issue that most papers discussed. Joe Catania's paper on enhanced modes, for example, discussed an area that most of us in survey research are currently researching. The difficulties described in concept formation and concept definition in sex surveys are, I think, more difficult than those in most surveys that we conduct at our Center. For example, it is very difficult to define what homosexuality and bisexuality mean. Rarely do survey researchers have to make the difficult determination of whether a concept is an attitude, a behavior, or a combination of both that respondents must use when they self-identify in response to survey questions. I appreciated hearing how much thought the presenters gave to decision-making in these areas.

There was one research mode—cognitive interviewing—that is often used by survey researchers to understand concepts that was not mentioned in any papers. In the past five years or so, cognitive interviewing has become a commonly used procedure in developing survey questions and concepts. It's possible that the presenters may have used cognitive interviewing and found that it didn't work or felt it did not contribute significantly to the research.

Essentially, cognitive interviewing is a procedure that attempts to understand how respondents conceptualize questions and formulate responses. Often a series of questions are asked of a respondent after he or she has answered a survey-type question. The researcher might ask the respondent to recall how he or she arrived at an answer—what information he or she used to create the answer. If, for example, someone is asked how many times he or she went to the doctor in the past six months, the researcher might ask the respondent to describe the strategies he or she used to arrive at the number. Did the person count the number of times in a typical month and multiply by six? Did the person count each visit to a doctor to try and create an answer? I don't know if this method is used extensively in sex survey research or if it's not very effective for the types of issues researched. Some of the organizations I know, such as NORC and RTI, use cognitive interviewing often, so I was a little surprised that nothing was mentioned about this technique.

I would also like to discuss the issue, based on a number of papers, of the differences among interviewing modes and the coming changes in interviewing technology. The papers on audio-CASI and T-ACASI indicate that we will soon be able to use technology in many more interesting ways in telephone and in-person interviewing. Survey researchers should think about how quickly we want to proceed with these technologies.

I am personally very interested in survey research technology. Currently I am organizing a conference on survey technologies. But I think that we need to approach the use of new technology cautiously. There is something about the personal interaction between an interviewer and the respondent that helps us to understand what the respondent is telling us. Removing that interaction means that we are changing something essential about survey research. I feel that as we get closer to using these technologies, we must continually evaluate the impact of the changes. Are people being more expressive or less expressive when using technology? Maybe their reports are more accurate, but are they less willing to share their thoughts in their answers.

For example, to interrupt an interview to have a question clarified during an audio-CASI interview, the respondent must push a button and call the interviewer. Will respondents find that as easy to do as asking for clarification in a fully interactive interview? I'm fairly sure we are going to use more technology in the survey process, but we should be proceeding with both caution and forethought and with an awareness of what we already know about what an interviewer contributes in an interview.

A few times during this conference, people mentioned problems in survey research that would be more fully understood if researchers listened more often to interviews while they were being conducted. I recommend that researchers spend some time "on the floor." That is, get more involved in listening to a telephone survey or in-person interviews, and in particular listen to the respondents and interviewers more closely. I recognize that your time is constrained, but you would get a better understanding of what the interviews are measuring if you could occasionally listen to some as they are actually occurring. You can also learn more about survey processes by watching interviewers while they are conducting interviews.

For example, some papers discussed the higher rates of item nonresponse among older persons. At our Center, our interviewers are usually required to probe a "don't know" response. If a respondent said he or she didn't know if condoms could slip off, our interviewers would use a standardized probe such as "Well, we need just your best guess." When I listened to some of the problems listed in the papers presented, I wondered if our interviewers would probe the condom question as effectively with a 70-year-old woman as they would with a 25-year-old man. If researchers spent time "on the floor" listening to interviews, they could get a better understanding of the data-quality issues. They could better understand the interviewer's contribution (both good and bad) to the interview.

Many papers presented a concern that the characteristics of the interviewers make a difference—for both improving quality and causing error. I believe that the gender and age of the interviewer affect results. But our experience indicates that more mature interviewers are usually able to handle the situations demanded in difficult research projects better than even our most experienced interviewers. I would say, cautiously, that interviewer maturity is as important as gender in predicting responses to survey questions.

Finally, I would like to explain what I mean by researcher error in surveys. Each researcher brings certain approaches and values to his/her research. In some research, these values should be minimized; in others, they can be used to improve the research. The improper use of these approaches and values are a form of survey error. I noticed in the papers that sex researchers have tried to determine whether they should make themselves part of their research processes. For policy studies, I assume the researchers usually tried to distance themselves from the research. For those who do other types of studies, I believe they should include themselves in the research processes with the expectation that their projects will be improved because they are closely involved in the processes. Overall, the researchers who conducted the surveys presented here tend to minimize researcher error as I define it.

Those of us in the academy often find ourselves discussing research with those who don't accept positivist science as the only way of doing science. These criticisms about the value of surveys are often based on postmodernist theories. While I am not convinced these theories are useful for all research, I believe we should use them to help us think through what we are doing in surveys. They can serve to make us aware of how we can place ourselves in our research—into the narratives, into the processes, and into the written analysis of the data—and they can help us improve our understanding of what we are researching. Many of the researchers who presented papers appear to be more willing to consider these issues than most researchers who use survey methods for other types of research. The use of these perspectives is an important contribution to survey research. These approaches will help move survey research into important new areas.

Gender

ANKE A. EHRHARDT

In terms of gender, Anne Johnson really summed it up on the first day when she suddenly said, "Are we going to talk about gender differences?" In fact, we haven't really done so in a focused way, and this is an extraordinary contrast to Richard Parker's conference in Rio, which I have just attended. For the Rio conference, "Reconceiving Sexuality," gender was clearly prominent as a theme throughout. Another striking difference was the conclusion from the Rio meeting that you couldn't look at sexuality without a theoretical frame, and you certainly couldn't look at sexuality without looking at the power differences between men and women, between gay and straight, and between other different groups. We heard in Rio a number of papers from around the world considering sexual behavior in the context of gender, with, for example, women in certain types of power relationships with men feeling little or no sexual desire. So can you properly hold a methodology conference without some theoretical framework to it? Maybe not. I think we may have felt some frustration, some unfulfilled need, in looking at methods and contradictory findings without a theoretical context.

Gender has arisen when considering women and men as interviewers and women and men as participants, particularly in survey or interview research. We seem to be approaching consensus that women as interviewers have higher response rates and may be preferred to men. We are not yet clear whether we are talking about women in general, middle-aged women, more mature women, or better trained women. Do women interviewers get the same kind of information as men? I think we have enough evidence now that we should start to ask such questions systematically: qualitative research which asks what it is that makes people more comfortable with women interviewers and experimental studies in which we vary interviewer characteristics in some systematic way.

With women as participants, we again had some discrepant information. We heard that, for instance, women might be more compliant in certain situations. We also heard that women are less likely to give sensitive information. We heard in Joe Catania's paper that the enhanced condition will get more information from men about condoms but not from women. That kind of finding points to the lack of theoretical perspective. Condom use, for men, is something different than for women. Why we get a different response may have something to do with our conceptualizations of that gender-specific behavior. And we have discussed what goes on in the interview situation. The interviewer is not just an objective robot; there is an interaction taking place. And then there is an interaction with the computer, which we need to understand and which may be gender-specific also. So I think we urgently need, as has been mentioned more than once, a theory of the interview. If we understood the interview process better, we could formulate better the different components which might contribute to this interaction; we could clarify the relevant questions and explore them in a more detailed way.

In terms of methods, we didn't have enough on qualitative methodology and the complex issues of analyzing qualitative data. We heard about different methods such as the diary. From Cynthia Graham's and Dennis Fortenberry's papers we learned that it's generally not a problem to get women to fill out daily diaries, especially if the information sought is meaningful to them. This may also be a good method to add more qualitative components, as Leonore Tiefer suggested, asking for details about the day-to-day interaction of gender and gender roles. We haven't heard much about gender roles, either. Alex Carballo-Diéguez showed us that it is very important, when working with Latino gay men, to understand gender roles because they determine how we would sample people and how we would approach them.

Our discussion exploded, in a constructive fashion, when Lynda Doll suggested that we needed randomized samples of bisexual men and women, particularly women. In response, Colin Williams said, "What population are you talking about, what are you actually after?" We could say more about his question. Basically, the problem we are trying to solve should define which method we use. Gender may be relevant here also. Women tend to have same-sex behavior later in their life cycle than men. A good theory to account for such differences in women's and men's sexuality would lead us to the questions we should ask.

In conclusion, we have learned that different methods fulfill different goals. There is no hierarchy of methods or approaches. I think we all agree that we need to struggle to achieve objective, replicable, scientifically sound and unbiased methodology; but within that premise, there are different approaches which will give us different answers. Finally, I would again stress that we need more theory to guide our methodology as well as determine our particular research questions.

Cross-Cultural Issues

BARBARA VANOSS MARÍN

I'm always delighted when culture gets the last word, because often we are unaware of the role culture plays in our research. It could be argued that we haven't talked about anything but culture during this meeting, because one of the definitions of culture is that it is aspects of the world made by people (Triandis, 1994). Objective culture includes the things we can see and subjective culture, ideas, meanings, values, such as the culture of science. Do we, as scientists, have a culture? Of course we do. Do we have values, meanings, ideas? We're certainly not value-free. The fundamental value that I heard over the last two and a half days was the search for truth—we're looking for reliable and valid information about human sexual behavior. Our first question then becomes, "What interferes with finding the truth?" Often, in answering that question, we will be confronted by culture.

I want to highlight four ways that culture is relevant to the methodology of sex research. They are: stigmatization, embarrassment, meanings, and subcultures.

Stigmatization. A fundamental reason for difficulty in recruitment of research participants and inaccurate reporting of certain data is stigmatization of certain sexual behaviors. People don't want to say that they've engaged in certain socially stigmatized behavior. It appears from some of the work being done now that providing participants with a more anonymous way to report stigmatized behaviors, i.e., using computers to collect data, can reduce the effects of stigmatization (see the chapter by Turner, Miller, and Rogers in part 2 of this volume). Of course, what behaviors are considered socially desirable or stigmatized will vary from culture to culture, so those doing cross-cultural work must attempt to determine whether differing prevalences of behavior are due to true population differences or to differences in the levels of stigmatization of the behavior.

In a similar way, stigmatization of certain behaviors can change over time. Again, if the prevalence of a certain behavior increases over time and that behavior is also becoming less stigmatized, it is unclear whether the number of people engaging in that behavior actually changed or whether people are simply more likely to report it because it is less stigmatized. In this area, the importance of good qualitative work cannot be overemphasized.

Embarrassment. A topic related to stigmatization and specific to sexual behavior reporting is embarrassment. An interviewee was quoted here as saying that it was unnatural to speak of sex. To the extent that that's true, everything that sex researchers do becomes difficult. In the Graham and Bancroft study (see part 5 in this volume), the women in Manila are much more embarrassed about their sexuality and more uncomfortable discussing sexual issues than the women in Scotland. In addition, women in Manila are having fewer orgasms and reporting less interest in sex than those in Scotland. This discomfort and disinterest are cultural in origin.

Permission-giving introductions to sensitive questions (see Catania et al.'s chapter in part 3 of this volume) may help alleviate some of the embarrassment that respondents feel and reduce some of the stigmatization surrounding certain behaviors. This important innovation should help to reduce differences in the reported prevalence of stigmatized behaviors across cultures that are due to embarrassment.

The discussion about being a professional stranger versus establishing rapport with the respondent was fascinating. How do we create a situation in which we can reduce embarrassment but still not elicit socially desirable answers? This is a balancing act. Data collection and the interview situation are examples of the "culture of science" which may or may not ensure honest responses. No matter how much we want our interviewers to be data-collection instruments, they are involved in a human interaction which will sometimes elicit responses in participants that are other than absolute truth.

Another methodological issue with cultural meanings is whether to match gender of the interviewer and interviewee. Based on the understanding of sex in Latino culture (Burgos & Diaz-Perez, 1986; Pavich, 1986) and experience of survey research organizations, it is inappropriate to have a Latino man or any man ask Latino women questions about their sexual behavior, because it is considered disrespectful for men to talk to women about sex. In some cultures more than others, gender of interviewer may be an important factor to consider in facilitating data collection.

The next cultural issue to consider in doing sex research is that of *meanings*, meanings of words primarily, but of behaviors as well. Meanings of terms change over time, so in longitudinal studies the potential for changes in meaning can create real problems in finding truth. Another problem is that meanings are not shared across cultural groups. For example, in Latino culture, sometimes incentives may be offensive because the person feels they are participating in a research project for altruistic reasons. Another issue is the connotation of words. Condoms could be called "prophylactics" or they can be called "jimmy hats." Different audiences will prefer different words to express the same idea. Did the word *condom* take on new meanings since the AIDS epidemic? These are important issues that are cultural in nature and will require qualitative work.

There's no equivalent in some languages for certain words or behaviors—"fist fucking" doesn't exist in French, "gay" is not a word that has a translation in Spanish. This lack of translatability provides important information about these other cultures that we're attempting to study.

The importance of clear and easily understood questions becomes even greater as technology replaces the interviewer. The computer can't see a lack of understanding. Anybody using that technology must be sure that all of their respondents are going to be able to understand whatever the stimulus is. A respondent will almost always provide an answer, and that answer will go in a computer and be thought of as data (i.e., truth), but it can't be truth if the person didn't understand the question.

Subcultures. Commonly, we think of ethnic groups as having different cultures, but there are probably as many cultures as there are demographic categories. There are different linguistic subcultures within the Latino population and different levels of acculturation to U.S. mainstream culture within immigrant groups. Age cohorts clearly have major differences that might be deemed cultural. Gender is a culture, because there are so many ways in which each gender is socialized to behave in certain ways. Sexual orientation, clearly, is a subculture in its own right and creates all kinds of differences in the way we ask questions.

Language equals culture because language is the carrier of meaning. Language tells us what the meaning of sex is in each culture, so when we develop a question in a different language, we are actually changing everything about that question.

There are three things that we should consider when we think about culture and sex research that have not been extensively discussed at this conference. One is the idea of cultural scripts of sexual behavior. Sexual behavior may be highly scripted, and cultural scripts certainly contribute to that scripting and are likely to differ across cultures. Research on sexual scripts across cultures could be a promising way to understand in more detail the factors that put individuals at risk for HIV, STDs, and unwanted pregnancy.

Second, we need to ask whether we should be changing our research questions as we go across cultures. It may be that in Latino culture, the primary issues determining sexual behavior have to do with certain cultural constructs like gender roles, machismo, sexual comfort (Marín et al., in press), but that those issues are less important or nonexistent in Scandinavian countries or in some other parts of the world. Methods for effectively studying more than one culture at a time are complex (Marín & Marín, 1991) but may be essential to help us find "truth."

Finally, our research has focused too much on categories and subgroups. We tend to ask questions like "Are Latinos different from Anglos?" and "Are men different from women?" A more interesting question might be: What are the mechanisms and meanings behind the differences we find? Why is it that one group reports more risk behaviors than another? What are the underlying meanings of those behaviors for that group?

References

Burgos, N. M., & Diaz Perez, Y. I. (1986). An exploration of human sexuality in the Puerto Rican culture. *Journal of Social Work and Human Sexuality, 4,* 135–150.

Marín, B. V., Gomez, C. A., Tschann, J., & Gregorich, S. (in press). Condom use in unmarried adult Latino men: Test of a cultural model. *Health Psychology.*

Marín, G., & Marín, B. V. (1991). *Research with Hispanic populations.* Newbury Park: Sage Publications.

Pavich, E. G. (1986). A Chicano perspective on Mexican culture and sexuality. *Journal of Social Work and Human Sexuality, 4,* 47–65.

Triandis, H. C. (1994). *Culture and social behavior.* New York: McGraw-Hill.

Part 10.
Postconference Papers

Qualitative Methods in Sex Research in Papua New Guinea

CAROL JENKINS

Research designs to study sexuality are plagued with tension and compromise. Although the terms *qualitative* and *quantitative* as descriptors of methodological approaches have been used as if they were polar opposites, they are not. They are complementary and should be positioned as such. Truth is a squirmy substance and neither approach may claim hold to it. Nonetheless, the recent history of sociological inquiry into sexuality has developed methods which fall roughly into one camp or the other. Qualitative modes of inquiries typically yield rich, poignant, and insight-bearing material that is compromised by unknown and, at times, known sampling biases. Quantitative modes of inquiry may provide data with better defined and representative samples but often lack contextual depth and explanatory power. While there have been efforts to close the gap between these two approaches, at the moment no single method can supply all the information one might like in all circumstances. Therefore it is best to understand what each of these approaches, with their various inclusive techniques, can provide.

This paper will discuss the strengths and weaknesses of a few selected qualitative methods in sex research as utilized for various studies in Papua New Guinea. The term *qualitative* is used to refer to narrative material, either short or long, that emphasizes personal, usually verbal, expression, as opposed to an approach labeled *quantitative* that is set up to be easily codified and counted, as in questionnaire survey research or structured observations. Qualitative data are usually produced through interviews with individuals or groups of individuals or as observation.

Approaches to Design

Extensive poverty and illiteracy make Papua New Guinea a nation in which telephone interview surveys or self-completed, written questionnaire surveys are not options. Random samples generated through census registration lists are also impossible, as enumeration of the population has never been completed. A trial within a single large village of self-completed short survey instruments written in Melanesian Pidgin using stamped, self-addressed envelopes proved to be a dismal failure. Over 50%

were filled out with the same pen and handwriting, and nearly all choices on each question were ticked. Therefore, at the time the Papua New Guinea Institute of Medical Research (PNGIMR) began sex research, qualitative techniques appeared to be the only option.

Although no one had ever tested whether gender of interviewers mattered in sex research in Papua New Guinea, local received wisdom asserted that same-gender interviewing was necessary. During the first years of our research program, this assertion was left unquestioned. Previous experience with somewhat less sensitive issues, such as hygiene and sanitation, had revealed a few pointers, for example, that it was best to have interviewers who were of a familiar ethnic group, preferably the same as that of those being interviewed. This is especially true among the rural population, which comprises 85% of the nation, but has also proved important among commercial sex workers in urban settings. Because people are generally socialized to trust only others of their own clans, interviews concerning intimate matters are not easily conducted by strangers. It is equally true that material revealing transgression may be too sensitive to allow one's own clansmen or clanswomen to hear. In Papua New Guinea (PNG), the most successful interviewing on sexual matters was carried out in a study conducted in 1991 in which the criteria for recruitment of interviewers included formal education at least to grade 8, current residence in a town away from own villages, and the maintenance of regular contact with their home village, with at least one visit within the last five years. Persons who fit these criteria were trained and sent back to their own villages for a six-week period to interview people they had grown up with, who knew and trusted them. This quasi-ethnographic approach has proved to be the best for general sexual life history interviews in PNG (National Sex and Reproduction Research Team and C. Jenkins, 1994).

Subsequent studies of the sex lives of truckers, sailors, and dockworkers to assess risk for HIV attempted to use an ethnographic approach in a more conventional style. In this case, matching by ethnolinguistic group was not possible. There are over 860 languages in PNG and there are no specific ethnic-occupation castes. Trained interviewers were sent out to ride on long-distance trucks and commercial and passenger ships to observe the circumstances under which sex took place in these occupational groups. They also interviewed individuals about their sex lives and key informants, such as maritime union officials, about their perception of the sex lives of maritime workers. The combined sets of observations and interviews produced a fuller picture of the sex lives of these men than either approach alone could have done. This approach allowed our researchers to confirm by observation the activities reported verbally (Behavioural Risk Assessment for HIV/AIDS Among Workers in the Transport Industry, September 1994).

Other studies, such as one on youth and sexuality (Final Report on

Youth, Urbanization and Sexuality in Papua New Guinea, October 1995) and another on the acceptability of the female condom (A Study of the Acceptability of the Female Condom in Urban Papua New Guinea, May 1995), made fruitful use of the focus-group discussion. In order to assess whether the cultural patterns related to sexuality were similar among young people speaking related languages in the same language family, a rapid assessment process was used in which a team of seven persons swept through a set of villages in a period of two weeks. Focus-group discussions among males were easily formed and provided abundant information rapidly. In PNG, focus-group discussions among females, particularly in rural areas, are sometimes difficult to conduct because of the shyness and reluctance of uneducated women to speak up in front of each other. In the female condom study, special care was taken to recruit women of similar backgrounds in terms of education and occupation. In addition, these were urban women, although many had never attended any school. The discussion was carefully guided to cover specific topics and succeeded in providing a broad view of the range of women's self-assessments concerning the ability to negotiate condom use. It has become quite clear, however, that most of the material produced through focus-group discussions represented the public culture of sexuality, and in some important aspects contradicted the realities reported through other qualitative methods of research.

Public Culture and the Private Interview

In most societies, there are acceptable and unacceptable ways and settings in which people discuss sex. In a society with extensive mass media and a long history of examining its own sexuality, an interview about one's sex life may elicit a presentation which utilizes idioms made familiar by mass media. Although it has never been systematically tested, it may be that small face-to-face societies have a less extensive repertoire of sexual storytelling styles than do larger, more complex societies. Whether there are few or many options for telling sexual stories, the revelation of one's private sexual thoughts and acts in the confidential, private interview is usually an experience in which public sexual culture is constantly being weighed against the private reality. What is finally revealed or asserted as true may be interpreted to be some compromise between these two bodies of data. Public culture is embedded within the private experience. In PNG, it appears that there are really at least three levels at which people operate sexually. These may be labeled public, private and secret.

First, there is a public sexual culture which includes the proper ways in which young people should learn about sex, the proper ways in which people should engage in sex, and the proper relationships between those people. When people observe others not adhering to these proper behaviors or relationships, they may make public statements of disapproval. Occasionally, depending upon the social disruption caused by the revelation of transgression, some punitive action is taken. In PNG, this is almost always violent and/or monetary, i.e., someone is beaten and/or payment demanded. Adultery is considered a more serious crime than murder in many PNG societies.

Gathering information on a society's public sexual culture is best accomplished using focus-group interviews. In PNG, the degree to which norms described in contemporary group interviews are traditional as opposed to church-induced is an historical question and very difficult to disentangle. Nonetheless, considerable coherence and agreement exists in the way public sexual cultures are described in focus-group interviews, even across ethnolinguistic groups.

In contrast to this public culture, there is a private culture. It, too, is fairly public, in the sense that many people recognize that those around them do not always follow the proper rules, that they themselves sometimes do not, and that this is more or less the norm. Public acceptability is contingent on revelation. If the transgression is not revealed or not revealed too widely, then it is acceptable. Access to this level of revealed behavior is possible with sensitive interviewers placed in good settings. In our studies, many people report with relative ease the transgressions they regularly or occasionally engage in. While we always guarantee confidentiality and anonymity, it is the anonymity that matters most. As long as those interviewed know their names are not attached to any document, almost everyone seems able to discuss private sexual transgressions, presumably because they know that most people will be revealing the same behaviors to our interviewers. These behaviors are not the public norms but the private norms.

Face-to-face private interviews often yield abundant and rich material and, as the psychiatric case study has demonstrated, can be a source of profound theorizing. Without engaging in further worry about how much people fabricate and omit in such interviews, it is abundantly clear that the private interview provides the opportunity to link reported sexual material to contexts—social, situational, historical, cultural, economic, and, if the interviewer is appropriately skilled, psychological states as well. Collections of private interviews from a defined population can then build up a picture of a private sexual culture, a more or less shared set of attitudes, experiences, values, and emotions among a group of people.

The social and economic factors that influence these private norms are important to delineate. In particular, if the aim of research is to provide an understanding of sexual behavior as a foundation for the design of interventions to reduce the risk of acquiring sexually transmitted diseases, including HIV, then such factors are essential keys. Qualitative interview data can more clearly provide the context and reveal the meaning of most common sexual behaviors than can the usual brief responses elicited by quantitative surveys. A recent survey of sexual behavior among young people conducted on several Pacific Islands illustrates this problem clearly. In Western Samoa, only about 4% of young men stated they had bought sex with cash or gifts over the past year, but almost double that number claimed they had accepted cash or gifts for sex over the same time period (Baseline Surveys for Youth Peer Education Project, South Pacific Commission, June 1996). Because such a difference was never anticipated, no questions on the survey instrument could reveal why this was so and in what contexts these various sexual activities took place. Without well-designed qualitative studies, understanding the social context and meaning of unexpected and often contradictory findings in quantitative surveys is very difficult.

As each culture includes ways of representing oneself to others, the private interview may produce a portrait of actions that are not really those carried out. It may be important, in order to preserve face or status, either to omit or to reveal particular transgressions to an interviewer, which may have little relationship to actual events. These reported actions—for example, having high levels of multiple partners, having no sexual partners, or displaying a particular level of sexual aggression—may have real status value and, on some level, be experienced by a person, but may not have actually taken place as an interpersonal act. Qualitative observational approaches offer the opportunity to confirm self-reports and deepen understanding of private norms and the way they operate.

Secrecy and Sexuality

One might expect that the most transgressive, odd, and idiosyncratic aspects of a person's sexuality would be the most secret, but our research has revealed this is not always true. Frequently we find that the most secret aspects of sexuality are not transgressive at all to the public culture norms but are apparently the hardest to admit to oneself or to others. Gaining access to the secret levels of sexuality is particularly difficult without a device by which the interviewer can probe. Recent studies conducted at the PNGIMR utilized vignettes as projective devices. These vignettes dealt with some of the most sensitive aspects of sexual culture, including incest, group sex, rape, and love magic. By presenting the informants with a set of events and asking them to explain their experience with such events, another level of personal reality was revealed, one which contradicted to some degree what was stated in personal interviews. This qualitative technique was the only one so far which elicited material on female homosexual experiences and the reluctance of some young men to participate in rape or group sex. Used in conjunction with other qualitative methods, the vignette proved to be a productive approach to personal sexual values as well as emotions, abstractions which many people find difficult to express in the context of the usual event-oriented private interview.

Quantifying Qualitative Data

The pressure to express information in a quantitative form may be damaging to a qualitative study. Increasingly, the value of qualitative data is being appreciated, even by economists and others conventionally dependent on numbers. But there are times when it is useful to apply simple quantification, even to qualitative data. If, for example, the size of the sample is quite large, analysis may be practically impossible if counts are not taken. In some of our studies conducted in PNG, totals of between 500 and 1,000 interviews, observations and focus-group discussions were conducted. Analyzing such a body of textual data is nearly impossible without recording the frequency of certain types of responses. Even if one cannot calculate confidence intervals, distinguishing a majority from a minority response is very valuable and necessary. Several textual-analysis computer programs now make such counting relatively easy. Nonetheless, making sense of these responses still requires a type of analytic thinking that is not at all quantitative in nature but more closely related to literary interpretation. Issues and themes form the core and the frequency counts provide the surrounding flesh to the arguments constructed from the data.

Rather than quantifying qualitative data that have been collected in poorly defined sampling schemes, using qualitative data to illustrate well-documented and sound statistical statements has usually proved to be a superior approach. One fine study in the field of reproductive behavior rather than sexuality per se that demonstrates this design well was conducted about two decades ago by Reining et al. (1977). Contemporary studies of sexuality would benefit from using such an approach. Perhaps the era for well-funded studies of sexuality with a full complement of techniques is nearing.

References

Baseline Surveys for Youth Peer Education Project, South Pacific Commission. (June 1996). Report submitted to the South Pacific Commission, Suva, Fiji.

Behavioural Risk Assessment for HIV/AIDS among Workers in the Transport Industry. (September 1994). Bangkok: Papua New Guinea, AIDSCAP (FHI), 19 pp.

Final Report on Youth, Urbanization and Sexuality in Papua New Guinea. (October 1995). Report submitted to GPA/WHO.

National Sex and Reproduction Research Team and Jenkins, C. (1994). *Sexual and reproductive knowledge and behaviour in Papua New Guinea*. (Monograph No. 10). Goroka: Papua New Guinea Institute of Medical Research.

Reining, P., Camara, F., Chiñas, B., Fanale, R., Gojman de Millán, S., Lenkard, B., Sinohara, I., & Tinker, I. (1977). *Village women: Their changing lives and fertility: Studies in Kenya, Mexico and the Philippines.* Washington, DC: American Association for the Advancement of Science.

Study of the Acceptability of the Female Condom in Urban Papua New Guinea, A. (May 1995). Report submitted to UNFPA, Port Moresby, 22 pp.

Item Nonresponse to Questions about Sex, Substance Use, and School

Results from the Reach for Health Study of African American and Hispanic Young Adolescents

ANN STUEVE AND LYDIA N. O'DONNELL

Introduction

Classroom surveys have become an important epidemiological tool for investigating patterns of adolescent sexuality and evaluating school-based programs aimed at promoting positive attitudes and responsible sex. When done carefully, such surveys are a cost-effective way of collecting information from large and diverse samples of adolescents and following youth longitudinally. They provide access to reasonably representative samples, at least for those age groups and localities with high rates of school attendance (Gans & Brindis, 1995). The anonymity offered by self-administered questionnaires, as opposed to personal interviews, also may be an advantage, especially when questions ask respondents to reveal potentially embarrassing or socially undesirable behaviors and attitudes (Catania, Gibson, Chitwood, & Coates, 1990). Since studies of adolescent sexuality by definition cover sensitive material, classroom surveys may be one of the most effective ways of characterizing the sexual knowledge, attitudes, and practices of adolescents and identifying misperceptions and behaviors that place their health and well-being at risk.

Classroom surveys confer advantages, however, only if the quality of data can be assured. When the topic of inquiry includes adolescent sexuality, questions about the reliability and validity of data have been raised (Newcomer & Udry, 1988; Rodgers, Billy & Udry, 1982). For example, will adolescents respond honestly—or at all—to questions about their sexual attitudes and experiences? Will younger adolescents understand questions about such topics as intercourse and birth control, and if not, will they feel comfortable asking for clarification in front of their teachers and peers? Such questions are particularly relevant for data collected in group settings, such as classrooms, for even with well-motivated students and well-trained facilitators to oversee the process, the potential for mistakes, skipped questions, inconsistent answers, and so on is greater than with more resource-intensive, one-on-one data-collection procedures using trained interviewers. Yet the need to document patterns of adolescent health behaviors and risks, especially given the increasingly early age at which sexual experimentation begins, makes it critical that effective tools be developed to assess youth involvement in such activities.

In this paper, we focus on one form of measurement error, item nonresponse (colloquially referred to as missing data). We investigate the extent and patterns of item nonresponse to questions about sex and other health- and school-related behaviors collected from classroom surveys of economically disadvantaged African American and Hispanic middle-school students. We focus on missing data because it is readily observable, quantifiable, and consequential. High rates of missing data reduce the effective sample size available for analyses and raise questions about the generalizability of results. Insofar as youth who skip questions differ systematically from those who answer (as is likely the case), missing data may lead to biased parameter estimates, including the prevalence of high-risk behaviors (Catania et al., 1990; Kelsey, Thompson, & Evans, 1986), and result in the failure to identify important populations at risk (Catania et al., 1990). In addition to being a data analytic nuisance, patterns of missing values may be of substantive interest. For example, item nonresponse often is used as an index of content threat and sensitivity (Rodgers et al., 1982) and thus may inform work on gender and cultural differences in attitudes about sexuality and other sensitive topics. It may also inform intervention efforts by pinpointing program messages and audiences that warrant special attention.

While there is a large literature on item nonresponse and methods of imputation, relatively few studies explicitly investigate the extent and correlates of missing data in the context of sex research (see the review by Catania et al., 1990). Virtually none examines nonresponse patterns of young adolescents, much less those living in urban minority communities where the consequences of early adolescent experimentation with unprotected sex are often felt. Thus we organize our analysis around several basic but largely unexplored questions. First, what is the extent of missing data on questions pertaining to sexual attitudes and behaviors, and does it vary by the sensitivity of the questions asked? Second, what are the correlates of missing data? Here we examine several respondent characteristics, including gender, ethnicity, grade in school, and academic performance, that may influence item nonresponse. For comparative purposes, we also report correlates of missing data for questions pertaining to alcohol and drug use and school activities. Third, do missing data cluster within an identifiable subset of respondents? That is, are youth who skip one question more likely to skip others, and if so, how do nonresponders differ from their more compliant counterparts? Fourth, are missing data temporally stable? That is, are students who skip many questions at one survey administration more likely to skip many questions in subsequent surveys? And finally, does item nonresponse in a baseline survey predict behavioral reports at follow-up?

Study Design

Overview

The Reach for Health Study was funded by the National Institute of Child Health and Human Development to design, implement, and evaluate middle-school interventions that address early sexual behaviors, alcohol and drug use, and violence among economically disadvantaged African American and Hispanic youths. Reach for Health programs are based on a comprehensive framework that combines health promotion with risk reduction and explicitly addresses the context-specific risks and opportunities of young adolescents in poor urban communities. The goal is to provide such students with the information, positive attitudes, skills, and support they need to make informed and health-promoting decisions during a particularly vulnerable developmental stage.

Three middle schools located in Brooklyn, New York, were selected to participate. Two schools, designated intervention sites, are implementing Reach for Health interventions with the entire student body, including youths attending bilingual and special education classes. The third school, a control site, provides students with only the basic health instruction required by New York City school regulations. The three middle schools share the following characteristics: (1) a large, ethnically diverse student body, with over 700 primarily African American and Hispanic students per school; (2) a high-risk health profile, as indicated by high rates of teen pregnancy, HIV/STD infection, violence-related injuries, and other sources of morbidity; (3) a high-risk academic profile, based on below-grade standardized test scores, low attendance, and low high school graduation rates; and (4) limited access to resources, as indicated by an above-average Title I poverty index, limited school-based health programs, and few community youth services.

All students attending classes in one of the three schools were invited to participate in the evaluation component of the study, which entails completing classroom surveys each fall and spring. In this paper, we report baseline data collected in fall 1994 from seventh- and eighth-grade students and follow-up data collected in spring 1995. Following IRB guidelines, only students for whom we have written parental and youth consent were enrolled in the evaluation component. For the student data reported here, 88% of parents returned signed consent forms, 86% of whom agreed to their child's participation. Very few students (fewer than 1%) declined to participate once parental permission was granted, and 97% of students with appropriate permission completed a baseline survey. Thus the overall baseline survey completion rate is about 73% for data reported. This completion rate is similar to those reported for other school-based surveys that do not require written parental consent (e.g., Brener, Collins, Kann, Warren, & Williams, 1995; French, Perry, Leon, & Fulkerson, 1995; Holtzman, Lowry, Kann, Collins, & Kolbe, 1994). As we have described elsewhere (O'Donnell et al., in press), achieving these survey completion rates required substantial resources and labor on the part of research and school staff. Extensive efforts were required to obtain written consent from parents, many of whom were unfamiliar with and at times suspicious of school-based research. In addition, multiple make-up surveys had to be administered in each school (and for each round of data collection) in order to offset participation losses due to unreturned parental forms and parental refusals.

Data were collected through self-report questionnaires administered in classrooms. Each survey consisted of approximately 250 close-ended questions that cover a wide range of health and school-related activities as well as key influences on adolescents' attitudes and behaviors. In the analysis, we focus on 40 attitudinal and behavioral items pertaining to sex, alcohol and drug use, and school activities (see Table 1). Because the Reach for Health Study is part of an NICHD collaborative agreement, several of the measures discussed here were developed in collaboration with the multisite steering committee, which included eminent researchers in the field of adolescent health research. The survey content was also informed by extensive formative research involving local adolescents, parents, school personnel, health professionals, and other community leaders to ensure that the survey instrument, as well as the Reach for Health interventions, were developmentally, culturally, and gender appropriate. Questionnaires were available in both English and Spanish; a shortened version was used with students attending special education classes. The survey was administered during a two-period session and led by trained facilitators from the school communities; teachers assisted with classroom management. Both the questionnaire and data collection procedures were pretested in spring 1994 with seventh-grade students from the three participating schools.

Sample Characteristics

In fall 1994, 1,587 seventh- and eighth-grade students completed baseline surveys; 1,626 students completed surveys in spring 1995; 1,451 youths completed both baseline and follow-up questionnaires, for a retention rate of 91%. Virtually all of the attrition is due to students transferring to nonstudy middle schools between baseline and follow-up. Given the school-based nature of the study, students who transferred elsewhere were dropped from the sample, while those transferring into one of the study schools were invited to join the evaluation. Consistent with school charac-

Table 1 *Percentage of Respondents with Missing Data by Gender and Ethnicity at Baseline*

	Total	Gender		Ethnicity[a]	
		Male	Female	Black	Hispanic
School-related behaviors					
School grades	2.7	3.4	2.2	2.0	4.5[c]
How hard work in school	0.7	1.0	0.4	0.8	0
Alcohol and drug behaviors					
Ever smoked cigarettes	1.6	2.3	1.0[b]	1.4	1.4
Smoked cigarettes last month	1.8	2.7	1.0[c]	1.5	2.0
Ever drunk alcohol	1.4	1.7	1.1	1.4	1.0
Drank alcohol last month	1.2	1.9	0.6[c]	1.1	0.7
Ever used marijuana	1.8	2.5	1.1[c]	1.9	1.0
Used marijuana last year	1.4	2.3	0.6[d]	1.4	1.0
Sex behaviors					
Ever had personal talk	6.7	9.2	4.6[e]	6.9	4.9
Ever gone out alone	7.3	10.0	5.1[e]	7.7	4.9
Ever held hands	7.6	10.1	5.5[d]	8.0	4.9
Ever kissed	8.1	9.8	6.6[c]	8.3	6.0
Ever kissed long time	8.2	10.4	6.3[d]	8.1	7.5
Ever had intercourse	8.8	11.7	6.2[e]	8.6	6.8
Intercourse last 3 months	7.6	10.6	4.8[e]	7.8	5.1
Use of birth control last 3 months	10.0	14.6	5.9[e]	10.1	7.8
Use of condoms last 3 months	9.3	13.1	5.8[e]	9.3	6.8
Ever pregnant (females)	3.9	—	3.9	4.8	1.6
Ever got someone pregnant (males)	10.0	10.0	—	9.7	7.3
Ever forced someone to have sex	6.4	9.1	4.1[e]	6.5	4.9
Behavioral intentions: expect to:					
Finish high school	0.7	0.9	0.5	0.5	0.8
Drink alcohol next year	1.2	1.9	0.6[c]	1.4	0.4
Use marijuana next year	1.2	1.8	0.6[b]	1.2	0.4
Have intercourse next year	8.3	10.9	6.1[d]	8.5	6.0
Attitudes about school					
Like classes	2.0	3.5	0.7[e]	1.8	1.7
Feel part of school	3.1	4.4	1.9[d]	2.8	3.1
Care what teachers think	2.5	3.5	1.7[c]	2.3	2.4
Attitudes about sex: before having sex:					
Wait until older	8.7	12.4	5.4[e]	8.7	8.2
Consider self-respect	9.5	13.7	5.6[e]	9.0	9.5
Ensure pregnancy/disease prevention	10.5	14.3	7.1[e]	10.2	9.9

(Continued next page)

Table 1 (*Continued*)

	Total	Gender		Ethnicity[a]	
		Male	Female	Black	Hispanic
Refusal skills: can say no to:					
Smoking	5.6	7.6	3.8[d]	5.8	3.0[b]
Alcohol	5.5	7.4	3.7[d]	5.6	3.4
Sex	6.9	9.6	4.4[e]	6.8	5.1
Sex with steady	6.7	9.4	4.4[e]	6.8	5.3
Adult normative constraints: maternal (dis)approval of:					
Good grades	12.5	15.2	10.3[d]	12.6	10.2
Alcohol and drug use	12.5	14.9	10.5[c]	12.7	9.8
Sex	13.0	16.1	10.3[d]	13.2	10.2
Parent-youth communication about:					
School	3.1	4.5	1.9[d]	2.6	2.6
Alcohol use	5.0	7.0	3.1[e]	4.3	5.4
Sex	4.6	6.5	2.9[e]	3.9	4.8
Condom use	4.2	6.0	2.8[d]	3.6	3.8

(a) Excludes "other" ethnic groups. (b) $p<.10$ (c) $p<.05$ (d) $p<.01$ (e) $p<.001$

teristics reported earlier, student self-reports indicate that 18% are Hispanic and 75% are non-Hispanic blacks; the rest either declined to report their ethnicity or indicated another race/ethnic group. As expected, the sample divides about evenly with respect to gender (47% males, 53% females) and grade in school (53% seventh grade, 47% eighth grade). Approximately 8% of students attended special education classes at baseline; among general education students, 57% reported academic grades of As and Bs or higher, with the rest reporting lower grades.

Measures

Forty items are emphasized in the following analysis; their content is listed in Table 1. All used close-ended response categories and were located in the first two thirds of the questionnaire. Twenty items focus on sex-related content; 12 focus on substance use content; and 8 focus on school attachment. The items include self-reports of past behaviors, behavioral intentions, attitudes, refusal skills, and parental influences.

Several considerations influenced our selection of items for this analysis. First, we chose items that vary in their likely sensitivity and saliency for young adolescents. For example, we report on items about hand-holding and dating as well as sexual intercourse and birth control; we also report on questions about alcohol and drug use and school activities. Second, because we wanted to focus on issues that are consequential to the decisions young adolescents are making, we excluded questions about extremely rare behaviors (e.g., forced someone to have intercourse last year, use of inhalants) and focused instead on those with higher base rates. Third, we gave priority to items asked of the entire sample, including students attending special education classes, who took a briefer version of the survey instrument that excluded more cognitively challenging attitudinal items. Finally, since some students were unable to finish the survey in the time allotted, we excluded items that were located in the last third of the questionnaire.

Analysis Strategy

Each of the items listed in Table 1 was recoded into a dichotomous variable, scored "-9" for a missing value and "1" for a valid (i.e., codable) response. Item nonresponse, or missing data, is defined as the failure to provide a codable answer. In most cases, this refers to items that students skipped, intentionally or not. In a small number of cases, it also includes uncodable answers, such as multiple responses to a question or written-in responses that could not be assigned to the available categories. We recognize that codable responses are not necessarily honest or accurate answers and plan to report validity results in future publications.

The behavioral data were edited by Research Triangle Institute (RTI), the data center for the NICHD collaborative agreement. RTI's editing rules have two implications for these analyses. First, lifetime and recent behaviors pertaining to sexual activities and alcohol and drug use were checked and corrected for logical inconsistencies. Specifically, several youths who reported that they had never engaged in a given behavior (e.g., intercourse) skipped the following question asking whether they had engaged in the given behavior recently (e.g., intercourse in the last three months). Here, a score of "no" was imputed to the recent behavior to be consistent with the lifetime report. Second, students occasionally failed to circle any response category, but wrote in answers that fell within the response format. In these cases, students' written responses were recorded as valid answers. Such checks reduce the amount of missing data and maximize the number of codable responses.

Response patterns for individual items are examined using frequency distributions and bivariate cross-tabulations. Reports of statistical significance use the Yates continuity correction for 2×2 tables and the Fishers exact test for tables with small cells. We also counted the number of missing values scored for each respondent. Because these counts yield highly skewed distributions, we use nonparametric and parametric procedures to assess group differences and correlations between baseline and follow-up.

Results

Table 1 shows the extent of missing data by item. Nonresponse ranges from 3.9% to 13% for sex-related questions and from .7% to 12.7% for questions about alcohol, drugs and school. We introduced questions about intercourse and protection with items about romantic and precoital behaviors and found a small but progressive increase in nonresponse as item intimacy increased. The extent of missing values increased as follows: ever have a really private conversation with someone of the opposite sex (6.7%), go out alone (7.3%), hold hands (7.6%), kiss (8.1%), kiss and hug for a long time (8.2%), and ever have intercourse (8.8%). Nine to ten percent of the students had missing data on questions about use of birth control and condoms, and 10% of males were missing information about whether they had ever gotten a girl pregnant. Only 6.4% were missing data on the question about forcing sex on another, presumably because most students could honestly answer "no." The small amount of nonresponse for the question about pregnancy (3.9%) reflects girls' greater tendency to self-disclose (see below).

Tables 1 and 2 show the relationship between missing data and respondent characteristics, including gender, ethnicity (black/Hispanic), grade in school, and a composite measure of academic performance and special education assignment. Virtually every item had more missing data for male than female respondents. By contrast, there were few significant differences for black and Hispanic students, for seventh- and eighth-graders, and for those reporting higher versus lower academic grades. Several of the attitude items, however, elicited more missing data from special education than general education students; these items tend to be more linguistically complex than those tapping past behaviors, perhaps explaining the difference.

Item analyses also indicate more missing data on questions with sexual content than on those about substance use and school. These differences are difficult to interpret, however, because we purposely placed questions about sex later in the survey, and items located later in the survey were more subject to fatigue effects. We delayed asking about sexual matters partly out of concern that students who were uncomfortable with sexual questions might break off the survey. We were also concerned that if students were confronted with highly intimate questions early in the questionnaire they might be more motivated to skip the questions or give socially desirable answers (Bradburn, 1983; Sudman & Bradburn, 1988). We tried to disentangle order and fatigue effects from question content by comparing the extent of missing data on inventories placed before and after questions with sexual content, but results were inconclusive. We also examined inventories containing items with both sexual and nonsexual content and found few differences (e.g., see maternal approval items and

Table 2 *Percentage of Respondents with Missing Data by Grade in School and Academic Grades/Type of Class at Baseline*

	Grade in School		Academic Grades/Class Type		
	7th Grade	8th Grade	As & Bs	Lower Grades	Special Education
School-related behaviors					
School grades	3.2	2.2	—	—	—
How hard work in school	0.5	0.9	0.2	0.5	—
Alcohol and drug behaviors					
Ever smoked cigarettes	1.4	1.8	1.0	1.7	0.8
Smoked cigarettes last month	1.5	2.0	1.1	1.7	1.6
Ever drunk alcohol	1.2	1.6	0.9	1.3	1.6
Drank alcohol last month	0.9	1.5	0.7	0.8	2.3
Ever used marijuana	1.9	1.6	1.1	2.0	1.6
Used marijuana last year	1.3	1.5	0.7	1.5	0.8
Sex behaviors					
Ever had personal talk	6.7	6.7	5.2	7.6[a]	—
Ever gone out alone	7.3	7.4	6.1	7.9	—
Ever held hands	7.6	7.6	6.1	8.6[a]	—
Ever kissed	8.7	7.4	6.3	9.1[a]	—
Ever kissed long time	8.7	7.7	6.4	9.3[a]	—
Ever had intercourse	9.6	8.0	8.1	8.9	8.6
Intercourse last 3 months	8.0	7.0	6.5	8.3	7.8
Use of birth control last 3 months	10.6	9.3	8.0	11.9	10.2[b]
Use of condoms last 3 months	9.5	9.0	7.7	10.1	11.7
Ever pregnant (females)	4.3	3.5	3.8	4.0	—
Ever got someone pregnant (males)	9.3	10.8	8.8	9.7	—
Ever forced someone to have sex	6.2	6.6	5.5	6.8	—
Behavioral intentions: expect to:					
Finish high school	0.5	0.9	0.4	0.5	—
Drink alcohol next year	0.9	1.6	0.5	1.3	—
Use marijuana next year	0.9	1.5	0.7	1.0	—
Have intercourse next year	8.4	8.2	6.8	9.4[a]	—
Attitudes about school					
Like classes	1.2	3.0[b]	0.9	1.5	5.5[d]
Feel part of school	2.7	3.5	2.7	1.7	6.3[b]
Care what teachers think	2.2	2.8	2.0	1.2	6.3[d]

(Continued next page)

Table 2 (*Continued*)

	Grade in School		Academic Grades/Class Type		
	7th Grade	8th Grade	As & Bs	Lower Grades	Special Education
Attitudes about sex: before having sex:					
Wait until older	8.6	8.8	6.9	8.4	16.4(c)
Consider self-respect	9.9	8.9	7.4	8.9	18.8(d)
Ensure pregnancy/disease prevention	11.2	9.7	8.7	9.6	20.3(d)
Refusal skills: can say no to:					
Smoking	4.5	6.7(a)	4.7	6.0	—
Alcohol	4.6	6.5	4.5	5.8	6.3
Sex	6.5	7.3	6.0	6.8	7.0
Sex with steady	6.5	7.0	5.9	6.4	—
Adult normative constraints: maternal (dis)approval of:					
Good grades	13.0	12.1	10.4	14.2(b)	—
Alcohol and drug use	12.8	12.2	10.0	14.7(c)	—
Sex	13.7	12.1	10.8	14.7(b)	—
Parent-youth communication about:					
School	2.1	4.2(b)	2.2	3.5	—
Alcohol use	4.7	5.3	2.7	4.1	20.3(d)
Sex	4.0	5.3	2.7	4.6	11.7(d)
Condom use	3.9	4.7	2.9	5.0(a)	—

(a) p<.10 (b) p<.05 (c) p<.01 (d) p<.001

parent-youth communication items in Table 1), but these inventories typically focused on less threatening issues. What our results do show is that blocks of items with sexual content did not result in a groundswell of break-offs, though it is possible that large blocks of questions about sexual attitudes and behaviors may have initiated a small increase in item nonresponse.

In order to investigate the extent to which students differed in their propensity toward nonresponse, we counted the number of missing values generated by each respondent for all 40 items and for items with and without a sexual content. Sixty-six percent of youths provided codable answers to all 40 questions, and 94% answered at least three quarters of them. Ninety-one percent answered at least three quarters of the questions about sexual attitudes and behaviors (72% answered all), and 97% provided codable answers to at least three quarters of the items about alcohol, drugs, and school (78% answered all). Consistent with the item analyses, black and Hispanic youths did not differ significantly in the mean number of missing data, nor did seventh- and eighth-graders. By contrast, the mean number of missing values was significantly higher for males than females (mean = 3.01 and 1.53 respectively, p<.001) and for those reporting lower than higher academic grades (mean = 2.34 and 1.77, p<.05). Nonparametric tests yielded the same conclusions.

To address the question of temporal stability, we focused on students who completed both baseline and six-month follow-up surveys and counted the number of missing values they reported to parallel items asked at wave 2. We restricted attention to students in general education classes to maximize the number of usable items. The association between missing values at baseline and follow-up was only moderate (r = .30, p<.001; Spearman's rho = .26, p<.001), indicating temporal volatility in many students' propensity toward nonresponse. Three fourths of students with no missing data at baseline, however, also had no missing data at follow-up.

Finally, we examined the relationship between missing data at baseline and reports of health risk behaviors six months later. We were interested in whether missing data indexes students who are experimenting with, or about to experiment with, the behavior in question but who are reticent to label or think of themselves as someone who does x, y or z. We cross-tabulated four baseline behavioral questions—ever had intercourse, ever smoked cigarettes, ever used alcohol, ever used marijuana—with their follow-up counterparts. While students with missing values at baseline were more likely to have missing values at follow-up, fortunately they were no more (or less) likely to report engaging in the risk behavior at follow-up than were students providing codable baseline answers.

Discussion

The results of our analyses of item nonresponse in a classroom survey of urban young adolescents are reassuring. Despite the young ages of our respondents (most were 12 or 13), both the extent and the patterns of missing data are consistent with results found for older respondents. Catania and colleagues (1990) in their exhaustive review of the literature report nonresponse rates between 6% and 13% for items about the frequency of vaginal intercourse, between 6.7% and 19% for items about masturbation, and about 6% for questions about number of sexual partners in the last year. Although the specific content of the items examined differs, the range of missing values (3.9%–13%) we found with seventh- and eighth-grade students compares favorably with levels reported for adults.

We also found evidence of a relationship between levels of nonresponse and item sensitivity within the battery of questions about romantic and sexual behaviors, but the differences in nonresponse were small. Whereas about 6–7% of students skipped questions about having a private conversation or going out alone with someone of the opposite sex, 9–10%

skipped questions about intercourse and use of birth control and condoms. Our analyses comparing questions about sex with those about alcohol and drug use and school were inconclusive. In light of research on response effects and item sensitivity (Bradburn, 1983; Sudman & Bradburn, 1988), we purposely placed questions with a sexual content later in the questionnaire; however, questions located later in the survey, regardless of content, show more missing data than those placed earlier. Thus the higher levels of nonresponse to questions with a sexual content may have as much to do with students' fatigue as with their reticence to disclose sexual behaviors and attitudes. Since young adolescents may be less skilled and motivated test takers than older respondents, more work on the best placement of questions about sex and other sensitive topics needs to be done.

The relationship between gender and item nonresponse was pronounced in our survey. Virtually every item examined, regardless of content, showed more missing data for young males than females. Similarly, when the number of missing values was counted for each individual, the mean number was greater for males. This finding is consistent with several possible explanations. Adolescent girls may be more willing than boys to disclose personal information, more compliant with rules and adult requests, and/or better able to read and comprehend the questionnaire. Of course, codable answers are not necessarily accurate answers; these results do not address the question of whether girls' responses are more or less valid than boys'.

In contrast with gender, we did not find consistently pronounced differences in nonresponse for the other respondent characteristics examined. We found no significant differences between African American and Hispanic adolescents in their patterns of nonresponse to sexual questions and minimal differences on items about substance use and school. Catania and colleagues (1990) review studies suggesting that Hispanic respondents may experience conflicting pressures on response tendencies; for example, the cultural value of *simpatía* may result in a greater desire to please and thus fewer missing data, while greater sexual conservatism may result in less willingness to disclose sexual activities and attitudes. We also considered grade in school and self-reported academic performance. Both of these measures are gross indicators of reading comprehension and probably compliance as well. We found no significant differences in nonresponse by grade level for questions with sexual content and only two small differences for items about school. Although item-by-item analyses show little difference in nonresponse by students' self-reported academic performance, those reporting better grades tended to skip fewer questions in the survey than those reporting poorer grades. In addition, students attending special education classes had more missing data on some of the items measuring attitudes, which tended to entail more complex sentence structure and response formats. Because of the importance of disentangling the effects of reading comprehension, motivation to please, and self-presentation, we plan to refine these analyses of gender, ethnicity, and academic performance in later publications using students' scores on standardized reading and math tests, measures of social desirability, and beliefs about adult and peer group norms.

Finally, we examined the temporal stability of nonresponse by investigating the relationship between item nonresponse on the baseline survey with students' answers to questions on a follow-up survey conducted six months later. While students who skipped many questions at baseline were more likely to skip many questions at follow-up, there was considerable volatility in adolescents' propensity to nonresponse from one survey to the next. Thus the tendency to skip questions appears to be, at least in part, state-dependent, which is in keeping with conceptions of adolescence as a period of substantial change. We also investigated whether students who skipped questions about intercourse, alcohol, and drug use on the baseline survey were more likely to endorse these risk behaviors six months later than students who answered the questions initially. While missing data at baseline predicted missing data at follow-up, it did not predict subsequent risk behaviors.

In conclusion, our results clearly show that most young adolescents are able and willing to answer questions about their sexual behaviors and attitudes and that the extent of missing data in classroom surveys is not prohibitively high. Our results also show, however, that item nonresponse is clearly influenced by respondent characteristics and placement in the survey; the assumption (or hope) that data are missing at random is untenable in our survey and, we suspect, in others as well. This raises questions about the selection of statistical procedures to handle missing data and the most informative way of reporting results.

Acknowledgments

Funding for this work has been provided under grants from the National Institute for Child Health and Human Development. We would like to acknowledge Alexi San Doval, Richard Duran, Wanda Jones, Greg Juhn, Cindy Young and Michael Breslin for their many and varied contributions to the REACH for Health data collection effort.

References

Bradburn, N. M. (1983). Response effects. In P. H. Rossi, J. D. Wright, & A. B. Anderson (Eds.), *Handbook of survey research* (pp. 289–328). Orlando, FL: Academic Press.
Brener, N. D., Collins, J. L., Kann, L., Warren, C. W., & Williams, B. I. (1995).

Reliability of the Youth Risk Behavior Survey questionnaire. *American Journal of Epidemiology, 141,* 575–580.

Catania, J. A., Gibson, D. R., Chitwood, D. D., & Coates, T. J. (1990). Methodological problems in AIDS behavioral research: Influences on measurement error and participation bias in studies of sexual behavior. *Psychological Bulletin, 108,* 339–362.

French, S. A., Perry, C. L., Leon, G. R., & Fulkerson, J. A. (1995). Changes in psychological variables and health behaviors by dieting status over a three-year period in a cohort of female adolescents. *Journal of Adolescent Health, 16,* 458–464.

Gans, J. E., & Brindis, C. D. (1995). Choice of research setting in understanding adolescent health problems. *Journal of Adolescent Health, 17,* 306–313.

Holtzman, D., Lowry, R., Kann, L., Collins, J. L., & Kolbe, L. (1994). Changes in HIV-related information sources, instruction, knowledge, and behaviors among U.S. high school students, 1989 and 1990. *American Journal of Public Health, 84,* 388–393.

Kelsey, J. L., Thompson, W. D., & Evans A. S. (1986). *Methods in observational epidemiology* (1st ed.). New York: Oxford University Press.

Newcomer, S., & Udry, J. R. (1988). Adolescents' honesty in a survey of sexual behavior. *Journal of Adolescent Research, 3,* 419–423.

O'Donnell, L., Duran, R., San Doval, A., Breslin, M., Juhn, G., & Stueve, A. (in press). Obtaining written parental permission for school-based health surveys of young urban adolescents. *Journal of Adolescent Health.*

Rodgers, J. L., Billy, J. O. G., & Udry, J. R. (1982). The rescission of behaviors: Inconsistent responses in adolescent sexuality data. *Social Science Research, 11,* 280–296.

Sudman, S., & Bradburn, N. M. (1988). *Asking questions.* San Francisco: Jossey-Bass.

Measuring Social Networks Using Samples

Is Network Analysis Relevant to Survey Research?

EDWARD O. LAUMANN AND L. PHILIP SCHUMM

Introduction

The field of network analysis has become so broad in scope that we cannot possibly report on it in its entirety within the limited context of this chapter. Moreover, a large part of the network literature has been devoted solely to studying social structure within small groups and is therefore not appropriate for a discussion of social networks in large populations. For these reasons, we shall focus our comments on some of the issues involved in using survey responses from probability samples to measure social networks. This topic has received little systematic attention within the network literature, despite the increasing amount of network data being collected through large-scale surveys (e.g., Laumann, 1973; Laumann & Knoke, 1987; Heinz & Laumann, 1982; Laumann, Gagnon, Michael, & Michaels, 1994; Heinz, Laumann, Heinz, Nelson, & Salisbury, 1993; Burt, 1984, 1992; Wellman & Wortley, 1990; Fischer, 1982; Kadushin, 1982; NCES, 1981).

Two basic questions should be asked in evaluating the relevance of network analysis for survey research. The first and most important question is "Can the study of social networks inform substantive questions that survey research seeks to answer?" Research on social networks has identified two master modes of explanation by which concrete social relationships can be linked to individual behaviors and attitudes. One mode involves viewing relations as links across which information is communicated from one individual to another. Research on social diffusion (Coleman, Katz, & Menzel, 1966), job searching behavior (Granovetter, 1973, 1982; Marsden & Hurlbert, 1988; Wegener, 1991), community elites (Laumann & Pappi, 1976), national policymaking domains (Laumann & Knoke, 1987; Heinz et al., 1993), and corporate networks (Baker, 1984, 1990; Thurman, 1979; Levine, 1972; Fennema & Schijf, 1979; Krackhardt & Stern, 1988; Burt, 1992) all exemplify this orientation toward social networks as structuring access to information. A specialized biomedical application of the diffusion-of-information approach to network analysis is the transmission of infection through direct sexual contact (cf. Morris, 1993; Laumann et al.,

1994: chapter 7). A second mode of explanation views social relations as the method by which individuals secure various types of social support from each other. Social support has been the focus of analyses of intimate friendships (Laumann, 1966, 1973; Wellman, 1979; Fischer, 1982), student peer cultures (Coleman, 1961; Campbell & Alexander, 1965; Hallinan & Williams, 1990), and the exchange of support among adults (Kadushin, 1982; Wellman & Wortley, 1990).

While this academic distinction between the flow of information and social support may seem straightforward, social reality confronts us instead with innumerable types of relationships, many of which combine both informational and supportive components. This fact has fundamental consequences for the utility of network analysis for survey research. In fact, we would argue that the apparent lack of success among attempts to add social network items to conventional surveys is largely due to the failure to specify adequately a theoretical link between the specific social relations being measured and the outcomes being explained. Only after specifying this link can one determine both the types of populations and the types of social relations that are appropriate for study.

Once the substantive utility of a network approach has been established, we may then ask, "Do the technical means exist for using samples to study networks?" The answer is yes, although many existing methods could be expanded or have not yet been tested empirically. Unfortunately, many of the technical advances that have been made in methods for studying networks in small, completely enumerated populations are difficult to generalize for use with data collected from a probability sample of individuals. This fact has created a schism within network analysis between the research on small, whole networks and that on large networks measured through surveys. In this paper, we report on attempts that have been made to bridge this gap.

Though the answers to these two questions regarding the relevance of network analysis for survey research are highly interrelated, for the sake of clarity we have divided our presentation into two sections. In the first section, we identify the origins of research on social networks and discuss several methodological developments in using survey-based data collection to describe empirical networks. The second section is devoted to examining some of the substantive issues involved in applying these network methods.

Methodological Approaches

The Current "Level Problem"

In a recent introduction to the field, Wellman (1988) wrote that social network analysis has "mystified many social scientists." One reason for this is that the highly distinctive and often technical concepts and methods employed by network researchers render much of their literature inaccessible to the uninitiated. A more important reason, however, is that the logic involved in relating network structures to their many behavioral and attitudinal consequences is very different from the logic commonly employed in social survey research. Berkowitz (1988) refers to this distinction as the difference between *psychologistic* and *sociologistic* explanations of behavior. Psychologistic explanations are based solely on the characteristics embodied within an individual, whereas sociologistic explanations take into account the persistent patterns of relationships among members of society.

That these two logics are different is illustrated by the fact that many of the developments of network analysis over the past thirty years have been directed as critical responses to what has become the standard theoretical and methodological orientation underlying survey-based research. Most survey research consists in collecting individual-level data from a probability sample of independently selected respondents, then using these data to draw inferences about social process at work in the population. Yet instead of social processes, this strategy is appropriate for examining only those processes whose sole constituent elements are individual attributes, attitudes, and behaviors. Such processes, if they exist, would contradict our very raison d'être as sociologists—that the social relationships in which people are embedded are important determinants of their behaviors and of the way in which they understand the world around them (cf. Granovetter, 1985). Our response to this dilemma as researchers has generally been to view attributional variables as proxies for social positions and to speculate about the actual social relationships that exist between persons in these positions. However, this is not an easy task, and many researchers eventually succumb to psychologistic explanations.

Contextual effects analysis represents an important attempt to confront this problem of specification and thereby to "bring society back in" (Barton, 1968). In its early formulation, the goal was to measure social influence by aggregating individual attributes within groups and then use these group-level characteristics to predict the behavior of individual group members. Although several efforts were made to refine the methods of aggregation, the approach itself was fundamentally inadequate owing to its inability to identify the underlying mechanism through which social influence was occurring (Erbring & Young, 1979). Erbring and Young proposed an alternative endogenous feedback model in which only those persons who are explicitly tied to an individual are considered to be potentially influential. This model and others (e.g., Burt, 1987) offer the possibility of measuring the effects of network structure on the behaviors of individual actors. Unfortunately, they are suited to measuring processes only in whole populations and require a full enumeration of the network structure, making them unsuitable for analyzing samples from large populations.

The shortcoming of standard survey research in studying social processes is not inherent in the concept of using data on a sample of respondents to describe the population from which it is drawn. Rather, it is the statistical simplification that comes from viewing respondents as independent observations that often straitjackets researchers into focusing solely on individual-level characteristics and the numerical associations between them. In fact, it is highly ironic that so much of network analysis has developed in opposition to survey research, since much of the early survey work done at Columbia's Bureau of Applied Social Research was explicitly devoted to measuring respondents' relationships with others around them. Classic pieces of survey research such as *Voting: A Study of Opinion Formation in a Presidential Campaign* (Berelson, Lazarsfeld, & McPhee, 1954), *Personal Influence: The Part Played by People in the Flow of Mass Communications* (Katz & Lazarsfeld, 1955), and *Medical Innovation: A Diffusion Study* (Coleman, Katz, & Menzel, 1966) all represented systematic attempts to measure social networks and their impact on individual behavior. And surprisingly, despite endorsements from several influential figures regarding the potential utility of social network research (e.g., Katz, 1957; Coleman, 1958; Rossi, 1966), the agenda begun by these early Columbia researchers was not pursued (Sheingold, 1973).

Although there are several reasons why this early work was not continued, part of the explanation certainly lies in the fact that at that time the technical insights necessary for analyzing network data had not yet been made. The early Columbia researchers were ahead of their time in terms of designing studies to collect data on social networks within large groups, yet they were limited in their analyses to the available methods of that period. Several technical advances in analyzing network data came later, first from a group of social psychologists at Michigan (Cartwright & Harary, 1956; Rapoport, 1956, 1958; Rapoport & Horvath, 1961; Harary, Norman, & Cartwright, 1965) and later from a group of sociologists and formal mathematicians at Harvard (Lorrain & White, 1971; White, Boorman, & Breiger, 1976; Boorman & White, 1976). Most of the advances made by these researchers, especially the latter group, consisted of new methods for analyzing sociomatrices—square matrices containing information about the relationships between all pairs of individuals in a population. Their objectives were to extract from the data the underlying structure within the group, to relate that structure to the behavior of the group as a whole, and to use the locations of persons within that structure to explain their individual behaviors. This type of analysis involving the complete enumeration of group members and of the relationships between them, called *sociocentric* analysis, represents one of the two major methodological orientations within the network literature.

Obviously there are practical restrictions on the size of groups that can be studied using sociocentric methods. These are due to the fact that the number of possible relations in a group increases at a much greater rate than the group's size. For example, in a group of 20 individuals there are 380 potential relationships, yet in a moderately sized town of 50,000 persons the number of potential relationships swells to nearly 2.5 billion. Collecting the data necessary to do a sociocentric analysis of this town would require not only interviewing each of the 50,000 residents but also an inordinate amount of cooperation and effort on the part of each respondent. In addition, the computations required to analyze data of this magnitude would be both time-consuming and costly. For these reasons, sociocentric methods are prohibitive for any population greater than a few thousand.

The second major methodological orientation used to conduct network research consists of what are called *egocentric* analyses. Unlike sociocentric methods, egocentric analyses do not take into account the global structure of networks, but instead view each individual as the center of a unique personal network of kin, friends, coworkers, and acquaintances. The theoretical concerns that motivate egocentric analyses do not include hypotheses relating the features of whole networks to individual or group behavior. In fact, whole network features become epiphenomenal, and the individual behaviors and attitudes are explained solely in terms of the set of alters to whom the individual is directly tied.[1] Clearly, egocentric analyses are more closely related to standard survey research than are sociocentric analyses. Since they focus on independent individuals as the relevant units of analysis, they can take advantage of the more conventional statistical "muscle."

On the one hand, the egocentric mode of thinking can be used to collect relational data through surveys; these data can then be analyzed using the more conventional multivariate techniques. An example is the ongoing work by Wellman and his colleagues on the processes by which adults secure various types of social, financial, material, and emotional assistance from their direct acquaintances (Wellman, Carrington, & Hall 1988; Wellman & Hiscott, 1985; Wellman et al., 1987; Wellman & Wortley, 1990). On the other hand, there are at least two inherent weaknesses in egocentric reasoning that prohibit us from using it to draw conclusions about group structures. The first and most serious weakness is that most egocentric data cannot be used to establish a link between two respondents. The alters named by respondents are for practical purposes anonymous entities, and only their relevant characteristics are usually recorded and analyzed. This

---

1. This approach is exemplified by the analysis of the roles of various stakeholders who surround the focal respondent and his or her sex partners that is presented in the National Health and Social Life Survey (Laumann et al., 1994). These stakeholders serve, in effect, as a Greek chorus commenting on the appropriateness and content of the ongoing sexual activities of the focal actors. Stakeholders (or, in other words, members of the focal actor's social network) may act to introduce sex partners (over 60% of current sexual partners were introduced to one another by network members), support or discourage ongoing sexual activities, and so on.

feature of the data makes it impossible to reconstruct certain aspects of the whole network in which the individual respondents are embedded.

A second weakness is analogous to a familiar problem that occurs when the occupations of a sample of individuals are compared to the occupations of their fathers in order to explore patterns of intergenerational mobility. The problem is that a random sample of sons does not generate a random sample of fathers, because the fathers of large families are overrepresented. In the network case, the analogous problem is that a random sample of individuals cannot automatically generate a random sample of dyadic relations. Instead, to the extent that the total number of relations in the system are unevenly distributed among the actors in the system, conclusions based on egocentric data in which a finite limit has been imposed on the number of alters that could be reported will overrepresent those relations maintained by the "less popular" individuals. Studies of sexual partners provide a good example of this phenomenon, since people's total numbers of sexual partners in the past year vary from zero to more than 100. As a result, the egocentric networks of sexual partners generated by a random sample of respondents are not necessarily representative of the "total volume of sexual activity."

Although this weakness is a particularly fine point that may have little real consequence for interpreting a particular set of results, it illustrates a critical distinction between the sampling of independent individuals from a population and the sampling of relations from a graph. Social networks are in principle analogous to mathematical graphs. Therefore, when sampling relations from them, one must follow the methods of graph sampling, not conventional survey sampling. We will have more to say with regard to graph sampling later on. As for the inability to use egocentric data to locate respondents with respect to each other in their social networks, this weakness represents a fundamental gap between the levels of analysis at which sociocentric and egocentric methods are usually carried out, both in terms of the data they require and the types of conclusions they yield.

This gap may be understood in terms of what is commonly referred to as the micro-macro problem in sociology (Alexander et al., 1987). Typically, the micro-macro problem is identified as a theoretical disjuncture and/or void between those explanations of behavior that invoke processes occurring at the individual level and those that invoke processes occurring at the group level. Since many authors who discuss the micro-macro problem are purely theorists, the practical implications of the problem for empirical research are less often addressed (but see Coleman, 1987, for an exception). However, the theoretical gap between micro and macro explanations of behavior implies a corresponding gap between the research methods and types of data that are used to test these explanations. As Coleman (1990, pp. 1–10) has argued, neither type of research method alone is entirely adequate. This problem is particularly acute within the network literature, where an overwhelming majority of work consists either of sociocentric studies of very small and often arcane populations or egocentric analyses of large population samples with no means for comparing respondents' relative network locations in the relevant population universe.

Numerous authors have claimed to offer solutions to sociology's micro-macro problem. Among these, some have suggested that adopting network analysis as a theoretical orientation leads to a superior "solution" to the micro-macro problem. However, in our view, efforts to prove that one's theoretical orientation has "solved" the levels problem are not as productive as are efforts to determine how the levels problem can inform and motivate more accurate empirical research. As such, we will not claim that network analysis as a paradigm offers a superior solution to the lack of theoretical harmony between explanations of social structure and individual behavior. We will, however, make the more modest claim that the only way to solve network analysis' own levels problem is by directing more attention toward the issues involved in measuring group-level network structures through survey samples. Alternatively, focusing on the individual requires that the researcher theorize about how group-level network structures affect the probable interactional processes in which the individual is located.

Bridging the Gap

Several approaches to bridging the gap in network research have been proposed. The first and most widely used was developed by the senior author in his 1966 study of the social networks among male adults living in the two urban communities of Belmont and Cambridge, Massachusetts (Laumann, 1966). The author continued to refine and explore this approach in a subsequent analysis of similar data from the Detroit Area Study (Laumann, 1973) and a small German community (Laumann & Pappi, 1976), and in an analysis of the social structure of Chicago's legal profession (Heinz & Laumann, 1982). In each of these examples, the purpose of the research was first to identify and describe patterns in group-level network structures, whether among an urban community of residents or among a community of licensed professionals, and second to make inferences about the effects of these structures on the behaviors of the nodal actors (and vice versa).

The general approach seeks to develop a link between the sociometric choices made by randomly selected survey respondents and certain aspects of the global network structure in which the respondents are embedded. For this reason, it might be useful to conceive of this approach as a hybrid of both the conventional egocentric and sociocentric approaches. Specifically, it consists of "relativiz[ing] the notion of a concrete social relationship, like friendship, work partners, or marriage, into a stochastic relationship" (Laumann, 1979). This is done by focusing solely on the aggregate relations among identified population subgroups, and measuring those aggregate relationships as the probability that different groups' constituents are tied to one another by the particular relation in question. To bring this idea down to the level of an empirical example, consider the author's study of the social structure among religious and ethnoreligious groups in Detroit (Laumann, 1969, 1973). A central purpose of this research was to adjudicate between three rival hypotheses about how religious affiliation affects the formation and maintenance of friendships within an urban community. The three hypotheses were: (1) that all barriers to intimate social interaction created by religious differences are slowly disappearing, (2) that these barriers still exist but are largely restricted to the major divisions between Jews, Catholics, and Protestants (Herberg, 1955), and (3) that the occurrence of friendships is strongly affected by all religious distinctions, even those among individual Protestant denominations, due to differences in the values (Stark & Glock, 1968) and social composition of their memberships (Niebuhr, 1929; Dermerath, 1965).

The data consisted of a probability sample of 1,013 native-born white men between the ages of 21 and 64. Relational data were collected using two different types of survey questions. The first type has been called *name generators*; in this case, the specific question asked respondents to enumerate their closest friends (typically three to five persons). The second type is called *name interpreters*. These questions ask the respondent to describe each of the alters that he or she has previously enumerated according to various specified criteria, such as their religious affiliations. It is through comparing respondents' own religious affiliations with the reported affiliations of their friends that the author was able to measure the relative probabilities of friendships occurring between the different religious groups. And it is precisely this logic that has enabled the author to use survey data from a random sample of respondents to draw inferences about the network structure that exists in a larger population.

A variety of mathematical and statistical techniques can be used to examine the global network structure using this type of relational data. The author's preferred method has been first to transform the individual-level data into a set of numeric scores that describe the degree to which the friendship choices of different subgroups, such as those determined by ethnoreligious membership, differ from each other. In the specific research we have been describing, the author used an index of dissimilarity to compare the percentage distribution (by religion) of one group's choices to the distribution of choices made by another group. This index is simply the absolute difference, in percentage terms, between the distributions of the friendship choices made by two groups and may therefore be interpreted as the percentage of either group's choices that would have to be redistributed in order to make the two distributions equal (Duncan & Duncan, 1955). By using multidimensional scaling analysis to model these dissimilarity scores simultaneously, the set of ethnoreligious groups can be located in a three-dimensional Euclidean space according to the relative similarities in their friendship choices. This method revealed that the structure of intimate associations among religious groups had considerable variation, not only between Jews, Catholics, and Protestants but also between individual Protestant denominations. In addition, one dimension of this structure was strongly correlated (.449) with the median family income of each group, suggesting that religious outgroup choice was at least partially structured according to socioeconomic status.

What is important here are not the specific techniques that the author used to analyze these data but rather the structure and content of the data themselves, because these dictate the set of research questions to which the approach can be fruitfully applied. For example, the data collection procedure requires that the analyst already be informed about the specific social distinctions or characteristics that are likely to be important in structuring the social interactions among the population under study. This information can come from explicit hypotheses about the way the population is socially organized, as in the author's research on ethnoreligious groups in Detroit. Information can also come from past research on similar populations or from a qualitative understanding of the population at hand. However, without prior knowledge of the potentially important social distinctions, it is clear that appropriate name interpreter questions cannot be constructed. This means that one cannot use this approach to search blindly for relevant social distinctions from among the myriad possible ones.

In addition to this practical limitation imposed by the data collection procedure, there are important theoretical considerations that become transparent during the data collection and analysis but are critical to interpreting the results accurately. These have to do with the way the empirical network is specified, or, more precisely, with how both the population and the types of relations are selected for study. Laumann, Marsden, and Prensky (1983) have labeled this the *boundary specification problem* in network analysis and have argued that choosing a study population and selecting specific relationships to measure are highly interdependent processes. The goal is to choose both population boundaries and a set of specific relations so that the relations are of common relevance to the population of actors defined by the boundary specification principle. This criterion of common relevance ensures that the networks of relations among the population can be treated as a relatively closed system, in which the actors are mutually oriented toward each other. Laumann's studies of the patterns of friendship and social distance within urban communities, the patterns of collegial ties with a professional community, and the assortative mating of sex partners meet this criterion. Without this type of specification beforehand, the significance of patterns found in the data for the actors themselves is less clear. Moreover, as Laumann, Marsden, and Prensky have noted, failure to specify the network carefully may result in inaccurate and misleading characterizations of the network being studied.

Several other approaches to bridging the gap have been proposed.

Building on the author's approach as well as on theoretical work by Blau (1974; 1977a; 1977b), Burt (1981) suggested a method for using mass survey data to measure the "ersatz network positions" of respondents. Individuals occupy the same network position to the extent that they have similar sets of relations to other members of the network. In this way, actors occupying the same position are *structurally equivalent* and are therefore likely to share similar experiences, attitudes, and behaviors (for an introduction to the concept of structural equivalence, see Lorrain & White, 1971; for a comparison of structural equivalence to other types of analysis, see Marsden & Laumann, 1984). While network positions have conventionally been identified using sociocentric analyses, Burt's method can be used to infer positions from relational data similar to that collected in the Detroit study. By assuming that individuals who occupy the same network position also share a similar combination of socially meaningful attributes, individual respondents can be located in ersatz positions on the basis of those attributes. This can also be done with the individuals cited by respondents as sociometric alters. The relational data from all respondents can then be aggregated into a matrix of "average" relations between members of different ersatz positions. The amount of variation in the relationships among incumbents of the same ersatz position can be used to verify the degree to which respondents with similar attributes are in fact structurally equivalent.

Unlike the author's own approach, Burt's was intended as an exploratory technique for determining the set of individual attributes that are important in organizing relationships among a population. For this reason, it requires that a comprehensive set of attribute questions be asked not only of respondents but also of each of their sociometric alters—a task that may be impractical for large sets of attributes or for situations in which the number of different alters cited by individual respondents is high. In addition, although Burt does not explicitly address the problem of boundary specification, it is clear that both suitability of his technique and the interpretation of findings based on it are contingent on the nature of the population sampled and the specific relational criteria used to generate the sociometric data. Unfortunately, an attempt to measure network density between ersatz positions using data from the 1985 GSS proved unreliable (Burt, 1987).

Yet another approach can be found in the well-known work of Travers and Milgram (1969) on the "small world problem." These researchers randomly selected 160 people who lived in Nebraska and asked them to transmit a folder to a target person living in Boston. The participants did not know the target person, and instead were instructed to give the message to someone they knew who was likely to know the target. In this way, the chains were to continue until the messages finally reached the target, with each intermediary adding a specified set of personal information to the folder so that the chains could be traced once they were completed. The essential result of this study was that of the 44 chains that were finally completed, the median number of intermediaries required was only five. And the conclusion regarding the structure of acquaintances throughout the national population was that it must be much more connected than had been previously thought.

There are several grounds on which Milgram's analysis and conclusion can be criticized. However, the idea of measuring characteristics of large network structures by beginning with a group of "starters" and tracing chains of relationships outward from them is another unique strategy for measuring global network properties using samples. While Milgram's analysis was more suggestive than rigorous, others have pursued a similar approach in a more formal and precise manner. Before Milgram's study, Rapoport and his colleagues had already introduced *net theory*, a mathematical theory designed to use samples of empirical networks enumerated by *tracings* to measure the effects of various factors on the stochastic process of tie formation (Rapoport, 1958; Rapoport & Horvath, 1961). Out of this early work grew a literature on random and biased nets, empirical networks being biased to the extent that the occurrence of certain ties within them was not purely random (Fararo, 1981, 1983; Skvoretz, 1982, 1990; Fararo & Skvoretz, 1984). Notable among these was an empirical study by Fararo and Sunshine (1964) of a New York junior high school.

The advantage of net theory over Milgram's work is the ability to estimate parameters describing the effects of specific factors such as reciprocity, balance, and individual attributes on the occurrence of ties within the larger network. To date, the biased net approach has been applied only to empirical situations in which data were available on all relations in the network. This makes sense, given that a researcher cannot know ahead of time which individuals will be implicated by a given tracing. Incorporating this technique into a social survey would require interviewing a randomly chosen group of "starters," all the individuals cited by the starters as being tied to them, all the individuals cited by those who were tied to the starters, and so forth. While this process may sound unrealistic, it is very similar to snowball sampling; the only difference is in the number of links in the chain that are pursued. Therefore, although this approach was not originally developed with surveys in mind, future work should be directed toward determining whether or not it could be adapted to study large networks using samples.

Finally, our discussion would not be complete without discussing graph sampling. Earlier we mentioned that social networks can be formally represented by the mathematical concept of a graph, a fact that has allowed researchers to apply the well developed tools of graph theory to the study of social networks. The specific tools that are of interest to us here are those that involve making statistical inferences about graphs. Most of the formal work in this area has been done by Frank (1971, 1978, 1981). His work consists of derivations of several estimation results and illustrations for how they can be applied to estimate various global properties of a social network, such as the total number of ties, the number of reciprocal ties, the distribution of ties across individuals, and the number of distinct components (components are groups of actors who are tied to each other but not to those outside the group).

The formal results used to estimate these global network properties are derived for samples that correspond to either subgraphs or partial graphs. A sampled subgraph consists of both a random sample of nodes and all the relations that occur among those sampled nodes. In contrast, a sampled partial graph consists of a random sample of nodes and all the relations that involve that sample, regardless of whether they link two members of the sample or not. From this description, it is evident that it would be difficult to collect social network data in the form of either a subgraph or a partial graph, especially for large populations. For example, to generate sampled subgraphs one would need to draw a sample from the population, then present the respondents with a list of the names of each person in the sample, asking them to indicate each person to whom they are tied in a specific manner. This procedure requires that the ratio of the sample size to the population size be great enough to ensure that a tractable number of respondents are connected to each other by the relation in question. This fact, together with the existence of a finite limit on the number of names a respondent can reasonably be asked to scan through, imposes a practical constraint on the size of networks than can be sampled in this manner (for a discussion regarding the feasibility of this procedure, see Morgan & Rytina, 1977, and Granovetter, 1977; for empirical examples, see Wallace, 1966, and Erickson, Nosanchuk, & Lee, 1981).

Aside from the problems involved in data collection, much work remains to be done in applying graph statistics to substantive social network research problems. We are aware of only two such applications, both to very specific questions: estimating network density from a sampled subgraph (Granovetter, 1976; Beniger, 1976) and sampling hypernetworks of individuals linked together by their common membership in voluntary organizations (McPherson, 1982). The former procedure involves drawing a random sample of respondents from the population to be studied, then presenting a complete list of the respondents' names to each one, asking him or her to scan the list and indicate those persons whom he or she knows by name. These data can then be used to make an estimate of the density of the overall network. Network density is normally defined as the ratio of ties occurring in a network to the total number of ties that are possible, and as such represents an important formal feature of a network—its degree of connectedness. One can readily appreciate the relevance of connectedness to studies of sexual networks and disease transmission.

McPherson's hypernetwork sampling is also a solution to a highly specific research question. Hypernetwork sampling involves asking a random sample of respondents to name all the voluntary organizations to which they belong, in addition to reporting certain information about the organizations, such as their size. From these data, it is possible to estimate the total number of organizations in a population, the size distribution of those organizations, and the degree to which their membership overlaps. This last feature is especially interesting to network researchers, since common membership in a group can provide enhanced opportunities for relationship formation (Feld, 1981; Brieger, 1974).

In addition to the four general sampling approaches we have identified, the efficacy of using surveys to measure social networks is also dependent upon the ability of respondents to accurately recall their relations with others and the relevant characteristics of those individuals. Research on this subject has yielded mixed results, however, most studies suggest that although people have trouble recalling past interactions with a specific time frame, they are able to accurately recall their more typical interactions. Research by the senior author (Laumann, 1973) and others (see Marsden, 1990) on the accuracy with which respondents report on the characteristics of their alters has demonstrated that respondents report the sociodemographic attributes of alters quite accurately, while their reports of characteristics such as political party tend to be biased toward their own. In addition to studies of the accuracy of responses to network items, efforts have also been directed toward developing specific strategies for questionnaire construction that will elicit a maximum amount of accurate network information in a minimum amount of time (Neyer et al., 1991; Bien, Marbach, & Neyer, 1991; McAllister & Fischer, 1978). (For a complete review of the literature on these and related topics, see Marsden, 1990.)

The further refinement of sampling approaches will undoubtedly create more opportunities to extend the study of social networks to large populations, and to incorporate network research into current survey programs. However, as we have stated in the introduction, this is only half the problem involved in adapting survey methodology to the study of social networks. The second half has to do with selecting an appropriate population of individuals to sample and set of relations to measure. These choices are intimately connected with the substantive questions that the researcher is attempting to answer.

Substantive Applications

Identifying Socially Relevant Subgroups

There are at least two ways that the study of social networks can inform and improve survey research. The first involves identifying socially relevant subgroups within a particular population. Berkowitz (1982, 1988) has argued that the various orientations within sociology are unified by the nominalist idea that we can identify certain a priori classifications that somehow intuitively correspond to meaningful social groups in the real world. Although some qualitative researchers may not agree that this assessment accurately represents their perspectives, the focus on a priori groups has certainly informed, if not shaped, a bulk of quantitative social research. Such thinking has even routinized the social research process through an ever expanding canon of "control" or "background" variables, all of which must be considered before an analysis is "complete." This overreliance on a priori classifications, both in theory building and empirical investigation, is one of the most frequent criticisms leveled by network analysts against mainstream sociology. The primary empirical issue, network analysts argue, is not how the addition of social classification variables alters a regression model, but is instead the degree to which these conventional labels actually correspond to social reality.

One method for measuring the social significance of attributional distinctions is to estimate the probability that persons with different attributes are connected to each other by a specific relation, then compare this probability to that which would be expected if the relation occurred at random. The extent to which ties linking persons with different attributes occur less often than chance would predict indicates the degree to which the attribute(s) in question form socially relevant subgroups. This approach is evident in the work of Freeman (1978) and Hallinan and Williams (1989) on network segregation, and in Verbrugge's (1977) reanalysis of data collected by the Detroit Area Study on adult friendships. Verbrugge's work used a series of crosstabulations, one for each attributional variable, to classify the dyadic relationships reported by a sample of respondents. These tables, often referred to as aggregate "chooser by chosen" tables, are arranged so that the rows indicate the attribute of the respondents and the columns indicate the attribute of their alters. The virtue of such tables is that they can be analyzed with log linear and related techniques to measure the patterns of both in-group and out-group choices with respect to a specific attributional variable (Marsden, 1981, 1986; Yamaguchi, 1990). Such an approach has been used to analyze the clustering of sexual networks in the U.S. population (cf. Laumann et al., 1994, pp. 269–82; Laumann et al., in press).

This idea of the social "entitativity" of groups can also be extended to the study of specific subpopulations that necessarily direct certain social ties only among themselves. The Chicago bar of lawyers is a good example, as are similar groups of professionals. One important question Heinz and Laumann (1982) raised in their research on the bar was "Given that Chicago lawyers are highly likely to form collegial relations with other Chicago lawyers, are demographic and other characteristics of the lawyers themselves important in shaping the way these collegial ties are formed?" The answer was an unambiguous yes. Collegial ties were much more likely to form between lawyers with similar ethnoreligious backgrounds, those of the same race, those who attended the same caliber of law school, and those with similar political attitudes. This finding, that factors logically unrelated to the practice of law have such a marked impact on the social structure of the profession, yields valuable insight into why the bar resembles a set of competing interest groups often riddled by divisive conflicts rather than a unified body of professionals. The finding also suggests that contrary to the prophecies of the early theorists, the importance of ascriptive distinctions persists even into as seemingly meritocratic a realm as a modern, organized profession. Similar structuration of sexual networks by ascriptive and achieved social attributes (such as race, age, and education) into effectively segregated subpopulations has been demonstrated for the U.S. population with important implications for the selective group-based spread of sexually transmitted infection (cf. Laumann et al., 1994).

One advantage of the network approach is the ability to locate social groups even when they do not correspond to the conventional attributes commonly measured by social surveys. For example, the authors and their colleagues have recently explored the possibility of using survey questions that inquire about a respondent's acquaintance with persons who have experienced a rare health event to make independent estimates of the distribution of that event among the population as a whole (Laumann et al., 1989, 1993). In considering an event such as AIDS, we noted that the likelihood that a respondent knew a person with AIDS was strongly associated with the respondent's race, educational background, and geographic area of residence. These results undoubtedly reflect the different distributions of AIDS cases among the various population subgroups. However, we also noted that many more respondents reported knowing no one with AIDS than chance alone would dictate and that a very small proportion reported knowing unusually large numbers of persons with AIDS. Knowing large numbers of people with AIDS is likely indicative of having social access to either the gay or IV drug communities, since these groups have traditionally had AIDS rates much higher than those of other groups in the population.

Although aggregate chooser by chosen tables can be constructed from any set of relational data in which the respondents have been asked to describe specific alters, the ability to draw meaningful interpretations from the patterns in such tables is contingent upon accurately estimating the "base" probabilities of contact. Work by Blau (1974, 1977a, 1977b) and others (Rytina & Morgan, 1982) has explored the effects of changes in population distributions among subgroups on the relative likelihoods of contact within and between groups. While relative group size is certainly a good place to start in determining base probabilities of contact, research has demonstrated that additional factors such as residential propinquity and educational and occupational structures can significantly alter the probability that any two individuals may come into contact with each other. These "structural" effects do have real consequences on the people involved, even though they might not be consciously aware of them. However, it would be a mistake to confound such effects with the process by which individuals decide to interact with certain alters rather than others.

This mistake becomes especially acute if the network being studied is so large that there are almost nonexistent probabilities of contact between whole sets of persons. A good example of this arises in using the 1985 GSS data on respondents' recent discussion partners to measure the homogeneity based on gender, race, age, religion, and education of intimate social interaction in U.S. society (Marsden, 1988). Using log linear and log multiplicative models to describe aggregate choice tables (based on gender, race, education, and religion), Marsden estimated several different parameters that describe the differential likelihood of certain types of respondents to report certain types of discussion partners. Although each parameter accurately describes the average tendency, at the national level, for a certain type of person to be related to a certain type of discussion partner, it is not clear how many of these effects are due to conscious decisions on the part of individual respondents. Instead, it is likely that regional variations in the attitudes, behaviors, and composition of social groups yield diluted patterns that are difficult to interpret meaningfully at the national level. Marsden is careful not to overstate his conclusions; however, the apparent simplicity in these types of analyses can be quite deceiving.

In addition to the inability of relational data collected from a national sample to yield an understanding of the process by which respondents choose their alters, it is also unlikely that national averages of the probabilities of contact between two groups are significant realities for individual persons. For example, the social structure of ethnoreligious groups in Detroit is no doubt different from that in St. Louis or Philadelphia. Moreover, it is unlikely that an individual in Detroit takes into account the social structure in St. Louis when he or she selects a friend. Therefore we must issue a caution with regard to how we think about social entitativity in large networks. If all individuals in a network are not plausibly aware of each other and do not have at least some possibility for contact with each other, then the results that emerge from analyzing the data as a whole will not describe a reality that is meaningful for the persons involved.

The nature of the specific social relations used to measure group entitativity will also strongly affect the results for at least two reasons. First, the same type of relationship may have very different social meanings in different areas and among different populations. On a college campus, where the relationship of "friend" is relatively diffuse and students maintain many friendships, we would expect the network of friends to be less differentiated than a network of friends among adults. And when differentiation does occur, it is likely structured by different attributes than those that structure adult friendships. Second, the structure revealed by studying a particular type of relation can only be interpreted in light of the mechanism by which the relation is generated and maintained. The ways in which the relation structures the flow of information and/or social support has consequences for how it affects specific attitudes and behaviors of individuals. We believe that these two problems preclude the creation of a general, all-purpose network item that can be taken off the shelf when needed, and that attempts to do this will result in data that are too emulsified for use in investigating specific substantive hypotheses.

Improving the Specification of Explanatory Models

Once the effects of specific characteristics in structuring social interaction have been established, we can then begin to relate the ways in which people are embedded in this structure to their attitudes and behaviors. The frequent lack of strong associations among conventional social variables, especially when compared with those among variables in the physical sciences, has forever been a noose around the neck of empirical social scientists. In fact, they have gone to great lengths to "explain away" the problem, either by appealing to the inherent nature of the discipline (correlations in the social sciences are not as large as in the hard sciences because social reality is simply more complex) or by claiming that their variables do not adequately measure what they are supposed to. Both explanations are undoubtedly true, however the latter one suggests that there is room for improvement.

Most of the variables used by quantitative sociologists are measurements of the outcomes of various social processes (Berkowitz, 1988). Variables such as income, occupational prestige, and racial tolerance are all outcomes of multiple social processes, many of which assume distinctive characteristics in different situations. Since these variables are the outcome of multiple processes, the degree to which they reflect the dynamics of any given process will be muted. For example, consider income, one of the most frequently used independent variables in sociological research. A person's income is dependent upon his or her job and several characteristics relating to that job, such as formal title, seniority, level of education, age, previous work history, and certainly the region in which that job is located.

In contrast, variables based on social structural data can be linked more directly to the specific processes they are designed to measure. For example, consider measuring an individual's prestige in a social system as the extent to which that individual is connected to a small group of well-known and influential "notables." This network measure of prestige does not suffer from the usual pitfalls associated with measuring prestige as the aggregation of individual-level variables such as income and job title. Rather, it is a purely social measure of prestige, a quality that is highly desirable since prestige is both conferred and exercised through social interaction. The data collected by this method can also be used to explore other important facets of the system, such as the distribution of individuals' access to the locus of decision making, and the differentiation among the notables according to their constituencies (Heinz & Laumann, 1982, chap. 9; Heinz et al., 1993, chap. 9 and 10). Of course constructing an appropriate list of notables cannot be done without considerable preliminary qualitative investigation. Similarly, the boundary specification issues that we have discussed are critical in determining the accuracy of this method.

Another excellent example is the attempt to measure the effects of subgroup membership on individual attitudes. Statistical comparisons are often made between subgroup membership and the specific attitudes held, however the social processes that produce these attitude differences are often not systematically addressed. Intuitively, the specific effects of membership in a given subgroup on attitude formation are numerous; a brief but incomplete list of factors would include the physical, economic, and social characteristics of the group, as well as the mutual influence of group members on each other. This latter effect is often purported to explain group differences, even though the assumptions it makes about within-group interaction are rarely scrutinized (Erickson, 1988).

In an earlier book that used data from the Detroit Area Study to examine the friendship networks of urban men, the senior author developed an innovative research design to measure the impact of having occupationally and ethnoreligiously similar friends on respondents' attitudes (Laumann, 1973, chap. 5). Having already used the technique discussed in the first section of the paper to represent graphically the structure of associations among occupational groups within three-dimensional Euclidean space, the author measured the occupational homogeneity of each man's egocentric network as the sum of the distances between his occupational group and those of the friends that he reported. Thus a man whose friends were drawn exclusively from his own group had the maximum homogeneity (a sum of zero), while the larger the sum, the more heterogeneous the friendship network. The same technique was also used to measure the ethnoreligious homogeneity of the men's networks.

It was expected that ascription-oriented attitudes would be especially associated with ethnoreligious homogeneity and achievement-oriented attitudes with occupational homogeneity. These expectations were based on the supportive elements of close friendships—namely, that people choose and maintain similar friends who support and reinforce their own beliefs. Congruent with these expectations, the results indicated that ethnoreligious homogeneity was positively related to church attendance and devotionalism, while occupational homogeneity was associated with the preference to associate with members of the same social class and the willingness to discuss job changes with friends. These findings and others like them conform to the notion that "ethnoreligious homogeneity reflects an ascriptive orientation to the world while occupational homogeneity taps an achievement orientation" (p. 108), although these data did not seem to indicate a fundamental incompatibility between the two, as many theorists have predicted.

The main rationale behind relating the homogeneity of close friend networks to personal attitudes is that within the functionally diffuse and supportive context of close friendships, there are multiple resources that can be used to exert and maintain influence. For this reason, the homogeneity of relationships that do not share this quality, such as those of coworker, kinship, or neighbor, are likely to be less important in determining an individual's attitudes.

The flow of information is also important in considering the effects of ego-centered friendship networks on behavior. Usually, network ties that are particularly important from an informational perspective are not strong, but are instead weak ties that are often initiated inadvertently. Thus mere acquaintances who are outside an individual's immediate circle of associates are often likely to have access to new information about job openings (Granovetter, 1973), and the large number of informal contacts made by a college student who lives near the stairs in a dormitory can later on become instrumental in electing that student to a position in the student government. The flow of information is also important, however, in determining the extent to which an individual's close friends are able to bring normative sanctions to bear upon him or her. If that person's friends know each other well, then chances are that the behaviors and discussions in which he or she engages in the presence of one friend will come to be known by the others. This should make the focal individual less likely to deviate from normative expectations that are unanimously accepted by his or her friends. The author's research on Detroit men also confirmed this hypothesis.

One main rationale behind the inclusion of relational items in the 1985 GSS was the ability to link them to attitudes and behaviors. However, since the GSS is used to investigate so many different issues, it was proposed that a more broadly defined name generator question be used so that the data from it could be linked to a larger set of substantive questions and would be comparable with that collected by other general surveys (assuming that they also chose to incorporate a similar question; Burt, 1984). With this in mind, it was proposed that a criterion of intimacy in terms of "discussing personal matters" be used to elicit the names of alters, since an analysis of data from the Northern California Communities Study showed that discussing personal matters was a central quality of relationships based on friendship, work, kinship, and acquaintance (Burt & Minor, 1983, pp. 46–56).

Despite aspirations for the 1985 GSS questions to become a benchmark for the collection of survey network data (Burt, Marsden, & Rossi,

1985), little work has been done on relating the GSS network items to specific attitudes and/or behaviors. A notable exception to this is research by Knoke (1990) on the association between characteristics of respondents' discussion partners and their political participation. Knoke measured the political partisanship of respondents' discussion networks by comparing the number of Democrats to Republicans among the set of alters cited by each respondent. Those respondents who reported equal numbers of Democratic and Republican partners, or who reported Independent partners, were said to have politically neutral networks, while those who reported more or fewer Democrats than Republicans were said to have either a Democratic network or a Republican network, respectively. The results indicated that those with Democratic or Republican networks were more likely to talk about politics than those with neutral networks, and that both network partisanship and frequency of political discussions had significant partial associations with measures of national political participation such as voting, contributing time and money, and attending rallies. Though this research was unable to separate out the effects of selection versus persuasion, it does suggest that being embedded in a partisan environment and talking about political matters are important in determining political participation at the national level.

It is our belief that the GSS data on discussion partners is perhaps best suited to research such as Knoke's on political participation, and that the networks of discussion partners might prove less useful in studying other phenomena. Moreover, even the associations between network partisanship and participation are relatively weak, possibly due to the fact that "discussing personal matters" is so broadly defined. For example, people are likely to discuss personal matters with their spouse, their neighbors, their coworkers, and others. However, we would not expect these persons to have the same influence on the focal individual. Similarly certain individuals may be strongly influenced by persons who are not their most salient "discussion" partners.

Applications to Other Social Measurement Problems

The applicability of social structural thinking is by no means restricted to research questions whose primary focus is the dynamics of social relations and their consequences for behavior. In fact, the logic of social networks can inform and improve upon our efforts to measure a wide variety of social phenomena. Perhaps the easiest example of this was the introduction of multiplicity sampling for estimating features of extremely rare subgroups in the population. The idea behind multiplicity sampling is to ask respondents to report on the occurrence of a specific characteristic (e.g., veteran status) within a set of alters systematically defined by a multiplicity rule (usually their immediate neighbors or relatives). The effect of this procedure is to increase effectively the size of the sample, thereby providing information about a larger number of persons with the characteristic of interest. Along with information about those alters who possess the particular characteristic in question, respondents are also asked to enumerate the total number of alters defined by the multiplicity rule (referred to as a respondent's "multiplicity"). The alters of interest reported by all respondents can then be combined and subjected to various statistical analyses, using respondents' multiplicities as weights (Sirken, 1970; Sudman, 1972; Kalton & Anderson, 1986).

More recently, Laumann et al. (1989; 1993) used GSS data, in which respondents were asked to enumerate and describe all persons they knew who had AIDS, to make estimates of the relative prevalence of the disease in different demographic subgroups. Unlike multiplicity sampling, this procedure cannot easily be used to make statistical inferences. However, it provides a cost effective and practical strategy for collecting information about a much larger number of persons than would be possible within the multiplicity framework, due to the fact that each respondent can be expected to know between 2,000 and 6,000 individuals (Pool & Kochen, 1978). More important, because the total number of acquaintances known to a given individual is not a random set but is instead highly structured, these data can be used to determine other important facts about how the attribute in question is distributed throughout the population. The vignette we presented earlier regarding the nonrandom distribution of the likelihood of knowing a person with AIDS illustrates this line of reasoning.

A second application of network methods to a nontraditional research problem is the work by Morris (1991) on the diffusion of AIDS in the population. By altering the standard epidemiological models of disease transmission to account for the fact that sexual relationships do not occur at random, she was able to demonstrate that the in-group biases we know are present in the way people choose their sexual partners dramatically alter the spread of the disease. Once accurate estimates of these biases are made (and some of these biases can be assessed with data gathered in the National Health and Social Life Survey; cf. Laumann et al., 1994: 225–82), such models can be used to generate more accurate predictions of the future spread of the disease than are currently available. In fact, we have just completed an empirical evaluation of such a model for the epidemiological spread of sexually transmitted infections (cf. Laumann & Youm, 1997).

Conclusion

The contribution of network analysis to survey research is not simply a few relational items that can be "tacked on" to standard surveys and then included in regression models to boost explained variance. Such an expectation is doomed to be unmet. Instead, integrating network analysis into survey research forces us to reconceptualize many of the classic empirical investigations within sociology. Unfortunately, much of the current literature within network analysis relegates the theoretical reasons for studying social networks to being self-evident and, therefore, is of little help in suggesting how network items might be successfully incorporated into conventional surveys. This is a dangerous trend, especially for a sub-field that has long been criticized by mainstream sociology as being "mere methodology, which lacks due regard for substantive issues" (Wellman, 1988). Our mathematical and statistical advances have allowed us to work with ever more complex and specialized network structures; however, we must make certain not to "lose the forest for the trees."

In this chapter, we have identified several successful attempts to measure social networks using data collected from a sample of respondents. These efforts have succeeded because the researchers carefully theorized about the specific mechanisms generating the relationships that they were studying, and about the effects that these relationships might have on the people connected by them. For this reason, network analysis cannot offer a standardized set of relational questions that may be used to study the full spectrum of social processes. Rather, survey researchers who wish to utilize the advances made by network analysis must adopt a network mode of reasoning about the problem to be studied. Only then can advances be made in our understanding of substantive issues.

Author Note

This chapter is an updated and modest revision of a paper prepared for presentation at the symposium "The Frontiers of Social Measurement" in celebration of the 50th anniversary of the National Opinion Research Center, Chicago, March 13, 1992.

References

Alexander, J. C., Giesen, B., Münch, R., & Smelser, N.J. (Eds.). (1987). *The micro-macro link.* Berkeley: University of California Press.

Baker, W. E. (1984). The social structure of a national securities market. *American Journal of Sociology, 89,* 775–811.

Baker, W. E. (1990). Market networks and corporate behavior. *American Journal of Sociology, 96,* 589–625.

Barton, A. H. (1968). Bringing society back in: Survey research and macro-methodology. *American Behavioral Scientist, 12,* 1–9.

Berelson, B., Lazarsfeld, P. F., & McPhee, W. N. (1954). *Voting: A study of opinion formation in a presidential campaign.* Chicago: University of Chicago Press.

Berkowitz, S. D. (1982). *An introduction to structural analysis: The network approach to social research.* Toronto: Butterworths.

Berkowitz, S. D. (1988). Afterword: Toward a formal structural sociology. In B. Wellman & S. D. Berkowitz (Eds.), *Social structures: A network approach* (pp. 477–97). Cambridge: Cambridge University Press.

Bien, W., Marbach, J., & Neyer, F. (1991). Using egocentered networks in survey research: A methodological preview on an application of social network analysis in the area of family research. *Social Networks, 13,* 75–90.

Blau, P. M. (1974). Parameters of social structure. *American Sociological Review, 39,* 615–635.

Blau, P. M. (1977a). *Inequality and heterogeneity.* New York: Free Press.

Blau, P. M. (1977b). A microsociological theory of social structure. *American Journal of Sociology, 83,* 26–54.

Boorman, S. A., & White, H. C. (1976). Social structure from multiple networks II: Role structures. *American Journal of Sociology, 81,* 1384–1446.

Breiger, R. L. (1974). The duality of persons and groups. *Social Forces, 53,* 181–90.

Burt, R. S. (1981). Studying status/role sets as ersatz network positions in mass surveys. *Sociological Methods and Research, 9,* 313–37.

Burt, R. S. (1984). Network items and the General Social Survey. *Social Networks, 6,* 293–334.

Burt, R. S. (1987). A note on the General Social Survey's ersatz network density item. *Social Networks, 9,* 75–85.

Burt, R. S. (1987). Social contagion and innovation: Cohesion versus structural equivalence. *American Journal of Sociology, 92,* 1287–335.

Burt, R. S. (1992). *Structural holes: The social structure of competition.* Cambridge: Harvard University Press.

Burt, R. S., Marsden, P. V., & Rossi, P. H. (1985). *A research agenda for survey and network data.* Paper presented at the Sunbelt Conference of the International Network for Social Network Analysis, West Palm Beach, FL.

Burt, R. S., & Minor, M. (1983). *Applied network analysis: A methodological introduction.* London: Sage.

Campbell, E. Q., & Alexander, C. N. (1965). Structural effects and interpersonal relationships. *American Journal of Sociology, 71,* 284–89.

Cartwright, D., & Harary, F. (1956). Structural balance: A generalization of Heider's theory. *Psychological Review, 63,* 277–93.

Coleman, J. S. (1958). Relational analysis: The study of social organizations with survey methods. *Human Organization, 17,* 28–36.

Coleman, J. S. (1961). *The adolescent society.* New York: Free Press.

Coleman, J. S. (1987). Microfoundations and macrosocial behavior. In J. C. Alexander, B. Giesen, R. Münch, & N. Smelser (Eds.), *The micro-macro link* (pp. 153–173). Berkeley: University of California Press.

Coleman, J. S. (1990). *Foundations of social theory.* Cambridge: Belknap Press of Harvard University Press.

Coleman, J. S., Katz, E., & Menzel, H. (1966). *Medical innovation: A diffusion study.* New York: Bobbs-Merrill.

Dermerath, N.J., III. (1965). *Social class in American Protestantism.* Chicago: Rand McNally.

Duncan, O. D., & Duncan, B. (1955). A methodological analysis of segregation indexes. *American Sociological Review, 20,* 210–7.
Erbring, L., & Young, A. A. (1979). Individuals and social structure: Contextual effects as endogenous feedback. *Sociological Methods and Research, 7,* 396–430.
Erickson, B. H. (1988). The relational basis of attitudes. In B. Wellman & S. D. Berkowitz (Eds.), *Social structures: A network approach* (pp. 99–121). Cambridge: Cambridge University Press.
Erickson, B. H., Nosanchuk, T. A., & Lee, E. (1981). Network sampling in practice: Some second steps. *Social Networks, 3,* 127–36.
Fararo, T. J. (1981). Biased networks and social structure theorems: Part I. *Social Networks, 3,* 137–59.
Fararo, T. J. (1983). Biased networks and the strength of weak ties. *Social Networks, 5,* 1–11.
Fararo, T. J., & Skvoretz, J. (1984). Biased networks and social structure theorems: Part II. *Social Networks, 6,* 223–58.
Fararo, T. J., & Sunshine, M. H. (1964). *A study of a biased friendship net.* Syracuse, NY: Syracuse University Youth Development Center.
Feld, S. (1981). The focused organization of social ties. *American Journal of Sociology, 86,* 1015–35.
Fennema, M., & Schijf, H. (1979). Analysing interlocking directorates: Theory and methods. *Social Networks, 1,* 297–332.
Fischer, C. S. (1982). *To dwell among friends.* Chicago: University of Chicago Press.
Frank, O. (1971). *Statistical inference in graphs.* Stockholm: Research Institute of National Defense.
Frank, O. (1978). Sampling and estimation in large social networks. *Social Networks, 1,* 91–101.
Frank, O. (1981). A survey of statistical methods for graph analysis. In S. Leinhardt (Ed.), *Sociological methodology 1981* (pp. 110–55). San Francisco: Jossey-Bass.
Freeman, L. C. (1978). Segregation in social networks. *Sociological Methods and Research, 6,* 411–29.
Granovetter, M. S. (1973). The strength of weak ties. *American Journal of Sociology, 78,* 1360–80.
Granovetter, M. S. (1982). The strength of weak ties: A network theory revisited. In P. V. Marsden & N. Lin (Eds.), *Social structure and network analysis* (pp. 105–30). London: Sage.
Granovetter, M. S. (1976). Network sampling: Some first steps. *American Journal of Sociology, 83,* 727–9.
Granovetter, M. S. (1985). Economic action, social structure, and embeddedness. *American Journal of Socioloqy, 91,* 481–510.
Hallinan, M. T., & Williams, R. A. (1989). Interracial friendship choices in secondary schools. *American Sociological Review, 54,* 67–78.
Hallinan, M. T., & Williams, R. A. (1990). Students' characteristics and the peer influence process. *Sociology of Education, 63,* 122–32.
Harary, F., Norman, R. Z., & Cartwright, D. (1965). *Structural models: An introduction to the theory of directed graphs.* New York: John Wiley and Sons.
Heinz, J. P., & Laumann, E. O. (1982). *Chicago lawyers: The social structure of the bar.* Chicago: Russell Sage Foundation.

Heinz, J. P., Laumann, E. O., Heinz, J. P., Nelson, R., & Salisbury, R. (1993). *The hollow core: The structure of influence and interest representation in national policy-making.* Cambridge: Harvard University Press.

Herberg, W. (1955). *Protestant, Catholic, Jew.* New York: Doubleday.

Kadushin, C. (1982). Social density and mental health. In P. V. Marsden & N. Lin (Eds.), *Social structure and network analysis* (pp. 147–58). London: Sage.

Kalton, G., & Anderson, D. W. (1986). Sampling rare populations. *Journal of the Royal Statistical Society, 149,* 65–82.

Katz, E., & Lazarsfeld, P. F. (1955). *Personal influence: The part played by people in the flow of mass communications.* Glencoe: Free Press.

Katz, E. (1957). The two step flow of communication: An up-to-date report on an hypothesis. *Public Opinion Quarterly, 21,* 61–78.

Knoke, D. (1990). Networks of political action: Toward theory construction. *Social Forces, 68,* 1041–63.

Krackhardt, D., & Stern, R. N. (1988). Informal networks and organizational crises: An experimental simulation. *Social Psychology Quarterly, 51,* 123–40.

Laumann, E. O. (1966). *Prestige and association in an urban community: An analysis of an urban stratification system.* New York: Bobbs-Merrill.

Laumann, E. O. (1969). The social structure of religious and ethnoreligious groups in a metropolitan community. *American Sociological Review, 34,* 182–97.

Laumann, E. O. (1973). *Bonds of pluralism: The form and substance of urban social networks.* New York: John Wiley.

Laumann, E. O. (1979). Network analysis in large social systems: Some theoretical and methodological problems. In P. W. Holland & S. Leinhardt (Eds.), *Perspectives on social network research* (pp. 379–402). New York: Academic Press.

Laumann, E. O., Gagnon, J. H., Michael, R. T., & Michaels, S. (1994). *The social organization of sexuality: Sexual practices in the Untied States.* Chicago: University of Chicago Press.

Laumann, E. O., Gagnon, J. H., Michaels, S., Michael, R. T., & Schumm, L. P. (1993). Monitoring AIDS and other rare population events: A network approach. *Journal of Health and Social Behavior, 34,* 7–22.

Laumann, E. O., & Knoke, D. (1987). *The organizational state: A perspective on national energy and health domains.* Madison: University of Wisconsin Press.

Laumann, E. O., Marsden, P. V., & Prensky, D. (1983). The boundary specification problem in network analysis. In R. S. Burt & M. Minor (Eds.), *Applied network analysis* (pp. 18–34). Beverly Hills, CA: Sage.

Laumann, E. O., & Pappi, F. U. (1976). *Networks of collective action: A perspective on community influence systems.* New York: Academic Press.

Laumann, E. O. & Youm, Y. (in press). Social, attitudinal and behavioral determinants of sexually transmitted infections: In search of the core. In E. Hook & W. Cockerham (Eds.), *The social determinants of sexually transmitted diseases.* Chapel Hill: University of North Carolina Press.

Levine, J. H. (1972). The sphere of influence. *American Sociological Review, 37,* 14–27.

Lorrain, F. P., & White, H. C. (1971). Structural equivalence of individuals in social networks. *Journal of Mathematical Sociology, 1,* 49–80.

Marsden, P. V. (1981). Models and methods for characterizing the structural parameters of groups. *Social Networks, 3,* 1–27.

Marsden, P. V. (1986, April). *Heterogeneity and tie strength: An analysis of second-order association.* Paper presented at the session on Categorical Data Analysis of the Annual Meetings of the Southern Sociological Society, New Orleans, LA.

Marsden, P. V. (1986). Homogeneity in confiding relations. *Social Networks, 10,* 57–76.

Marsden, P. V. (1990). Network data and measurement. *Annual Review of Sociology, 16,* 435–63.

Marsden, P. V., & Laumann, E. O. (1984). Mathematical ideas in social structural analysis. *Journal of Mathematical Sociology, 10,* 271–94.

Marsden, P. V., & Hurlbert, J. S. (1988). Social resources and mobility outcomes: A replication and extension. *Social Forces, 66,* 1038–59.

McAllister, L., & Fischer, C. S. (1978). A procedure for surveying personal networks. *Sociological Methods and Research, 7,* 131–48.

McPherson, J. M. (1982). Hypernetwork sampling: Duality and differentiation among voluntary organizations. *Social Networks, 3,* 225–49.

Morgan, D. L., & Rytina, S. (1977). Comment on "Network sampling: Some first steps," by M. Granovetter. *American Journal of Sociology, 83,* 722–7.

Morris, M. (1991, February). *Race and ethnic boundaries in the spread of AIDS.* Paper presented at the Sunbelt Conference of the International Network for Social Network Analysis, Tampa, FL.

Morris, M. (1993). Epidemiology and social networks: Modeling structural diffusion. *Sociological Methods and Research, 22*(1): 99–126.

National Center for Education Statistics, U.S. Department of Education. (1981). *High school and beyond, 1980.* [MRDF] Ann Arbor, MI: Inter-University Consortium for Political and Social Research [distributor].

Neyer, F., Bien, J., Marbach, W., & Templeton, R. (1991). Obtaining reliable network data about family life: A methodological examination concerning reliability of egocentered networks in survey research. *Connections, 14,* 14–26.

Niebuhr, H. R. (1929). *The social sources of denominationalism.* New York: Holt.

Pool, I., & Kochen, M. (1978). Contacts and influence. *Social Networks, 1,* 5–51.

Rapoport, A., & Horvath, W. J. (1961). A study of a large sociogram. *Behavioral Science, 6,* 279–91.

Rapoport, A. (1956). The diffusion problem in mass behavior. *General Systems, 1,* 48–55.

Rapoport, A. (1958). Nets with reciprocity bias. *Bulletin of Mathematical Biophysics, 20,* 191–201.

Rossi, P. H. (1966). Research strategies in measuring peer group influence. In T. M. Newcomb & E. K. Wilson (Eds.), *College peer groups.* Chicago: Aldine.

Rytina, S., & Morgan, D. L. (1982). The arithmetic of social relations: The interplay of category and network. *American Journal of Sociology, 88,* 88–113.

Sheingold, C. A. (1973). Social networks and voting: The resurrection of a research agenda. *American Sociological Review, 38,* 712–20.

Sirken, M. G. (1970). Household surveys with multiplicity. *Journal of the American Statistical Association, 65,* 257–66.

Skvoretz, J. (1982). Comment on Fararo's "Biased networks and social structure theorems." *Social Networks, 3,* 313–5.

Skvoretz, J. (1990). Biased net theory: Approximations, simulations, and observations. *Social Networks, 12,* 217–38.

Stark, R., & Glock, C. Y. (1968). *American piety: The nature of religious commitment.* Berkeley: University of California Press.

Sudman, S. (1972). On sampling of very rare human populations. *Journal of the American Statistical Association, 67,* 335–9.

Thurman, B. (1979). In the office: Networks and coalitions. *Social Networks, 2,* 47–63.

Travers, J., & Milgram, S. (1969). An experimental study of the small world problem. *Sociometry, 32,* 425–43.

Verbrugge, L. M. (1977). The structure of adult friendship choices. *Social Forces, 56,* 576–97.

Wallace, W. L. (1966). *Student culture.* Chicago: Aldine.

Wegener, B. (1991). Job mobility and social ties: Social resources, prior job, and status attainment. *American Sociological Review, 56,* 60–71.

Wellman, B., & Hiscott, R. (1985). From social support to social network. In I. Sarason & B. Sarason (Eds.), *Social support* (pp. 205–22). The Hague: Martinus Nijhoff.

Wellman, B., & Wortley, S. (1990). Different strokes from different folks: Community ties and social support. *American Journal of Sociology, 96,* 558–88.

Wellman, B., Mosher, C., Rottenberg, C., & Espinoza, V. (1987). *The sum of the ties does not equal a network: The case of social support.* Paper presented at the annual meeting of the American Sociological Association, Chicago.

Wellman, B., Carrington, P., & Hall, A. (1988). Networks as personal communities. In B. Wellman & S. D. Berkowitz (Eds.), *Social structures: A network approach* (pp. 130–84). Cambridge: Cambridge University Press.

Wellman, B. (1979). The community question: The intimate networks of east Yorkers. *American Journal of Sociology, 84,* 1201–31.

Wellman, B. (1988). Introduction: Studying social structures. In B. Wellman & S. D. Berkowitz (Eds.), *Social structures: A network approach* (pp. 1–14). Cambridge: Cambridge University Press.

White, H. C., Boorman, S. A., & Breiger, R. L. (1976). Social structure from multiple networks I: Blockmodels of roles and positions. *American Journal of Sociology, 81,* 730–80.

Yamaguchi, K. (1990). Homophily and social distance in the choice of multiple friends: An analysis based on conditionally symmetric log-bilinear association models. *Journal of the American Statistical Association, 85,* 356–66.

A Model for Investigating Respondent-Interviewer Relationships in Sexual Surveys

JOSEPH A. CATANIA

Introduction

Among the various methods used to collect information on human sexuality, the survey offers a unique opportunity for gathering information on large numbers of representative individuals in a society. As with other research topics, surveys of sexuality have their share of problems with nonparticipation and item nonresponse (Catania, Binson, Van der Straten, & Stone, 1995; Catania, Gibson, Chitwood, & Coates, 1990).

There are statistical techniques for adjusting for item nonresponse and nonparticipation, but these techniques require a large number of assumptions. Many of these assumptions are untestable; but, lacking viable alternatives, these statistical adjustment techniques are often the best choice. Another approach is to develop new procedures that may minimize bias. However, methods for conducting surveys on human sexuality have only begun to be investigated in a systematic fashion (Catania et al., 1990; Turner, Danella, & Rogers, in press). The present paper focuses on the problem of item nonresponse in the area of sex survey research, along with theoretical ideas to guide development of new methodological procedures.

Hindering development of new survey procedures is the lack of a theoretical framework for this type of research. Although Groves, Cialdini, & Couper (1992) have recently developed a theoretical model for understanding survey participation in general, their model does not deal explicitly with the interviewer-respondent interaction. Nor is their model generalizable to "hot" topics, that is, topics that are heavily laden emotionally (e.g., sexual abuse, sexual dysfunctions).

Of theoretical relevance to the interviewer-respondent situation is Sudman's general observation that interviewer characteristics increase in their relevance to the interviewer-respondent relationship as a function of the survey topic (Sudman & Bradburn, 1974). Consequently, topics that have a large interpersonal component to them, such as sexuality, would be expected to invoke a different and highly salient set of interpersonal issues than other potentially less emotionally laden topics (e.g., consumer habits). More recently Catania et al. (1996; 1995) have presented self-disclosure and stress control models to help understand the relationship between the interviewer and the respondent, as well as the respondent and the questions that they are being asked. Self-disclosure theory (Catania, McDermott, & Pollack, 1986; Dindia & Allen, 1992; Gebhard, 1972; Pennebaker, 1995) suggests that people tend to disclose more honestly and in greater detail to people they feel emotionally comfortable with. Identifying conditions that increase self-disclosure to questions on sexual topics is a goal of methodological research in this area. In this regard, Catania et al. (1996) also considered the effects of enhancing personal control on self-disclosures. A general tenet of control theory is that in ambiguous situations that are potentially harmful, anything that enhances a person's perceptions of being in control of the situation will reduce distress (Archer, 1979; Lefcourt, 1982). Situations perceived to have unpredictable negative outcomes have a high probability of increasing distress. An interview situation has ambiguous and threatening facets including the following features: (a) uncertainty about what will happen or what will be asked, and (b) anxiety about the credibility of the interviewer, and consequently, confidentiality of responses. We expect that these worries and anxieties will be high when the survey topic concerns a sensitive issue like sexuality. Although it is always theoretically possible for respondents to terminate an interview after they have started one, it doesn't occur with a high frequency. For people who stay in an interview even after they've become distressed, "control-disclosure" theory would then predict that any procedures that increase a respondent's feelings of control may enhance comfort and consequently facilitate honest self-disclosure. Key to the self-disclosure–respondent control model are the underlying emotional conditions of the interview, and how distressed the respondent might become by the questions or the conditions under which they're being asked questions. Consequently, as I will discuss later, emotional components are a strong part of the sexological interview situation because the topic is sensitive.

Although the self-disclosure–control models are useful, they can be significantly expanded upon. Indeed, there are numerous considerations from other social psychological models relating to interpersonal activities that may help us understand the interviewer-respondent exchange. The model presented here is an attempt to bring together a variety of models and factors that may be useful to understanding the rather limited, and in many ways somewhat unusual, interpersonal relationship that exists between an interviewer and respondent.

Topic Sensitivity

As mentioned, topic sensitivity plays a key role in determining how important the interviewer is to the respondent's decision to disclose honestly. In this regard, we expect that there is a range of sensitive topics that would be pertinent to consider (e.g., from sexuality and mental health issues to physical health, political attitudes, and consumer behavior topics). If we arrayed all survey topic areas along a sensitivity dimension, we'd probably find that sexuality questions, like mental health questions, fall near the extreme end of the sensitivity distribution. However, this general picture belies the fact that there is a wide range of sensitivities even among sexual topics.

Investigators have begun to look at item-response rates for specific sexual topics (Catania et al., 1996). For instance we (see the Peterson and Catania chapter in part 3 of this volume) found that fewer than 0.1% of respondents were either unwilling to answer or said they didn't know whether or not they had ever had sex in the past five years. This increases to approximately 1% of respondents who declined to answer or answered "don't know" for an item on sexual activity for the past 12 months. Thus even the time span which the question covers may lead to a small but nonetheless significant increase in the percentage of people who fail to respond to a question. Other studies (for review, see Catania et al., 1990) have found that questions on masturbation, extramarital sex, sexual dysfunctions, and same-gender sexual activity (depending on the sample population) all elicit moderate to high levels of nonresponse.

It's important at this juncture to note that questions on income often elicit the highest levels of nonresponse; from 10% to 20% of respondents may fail to complete income questions. Peterson and Catania found that only condom attitude questions, particularly those related to hands-on experience with condoms, attained such correspondingly high levels of nonreporting. For instance, 5–8% of respondents refused to answer questions on whether or not the person believes that condoms slip off during sex, whereas a less intimate question on whether or not people are too embarrassed to buy condoms elicited a much lower level of nonresponse (1–2%). Peterson and Catania's report showed that there are significant differences in missing cases on some sexuality questions in terms of gender and age of respondents. Males and females both show instances of providing more missing data. In general, there is an increase in nonresponse to sexual questions with increasing age. Figure 1, for example, shows the missing data for an item that asks if respondents believe that condoms take all the fun out of sex. For respondents 18–29 years of age, roughly 3% refuse to answer. This percentage increases dramatically to 10–11% for people over the age of 60. These results tend to hold, with some minor variations, for both white and African American adult respondents.

Additional evidence on the range of sensitivities among sexual topics is provided by a large-scale experimental field study in which Catania et al. (1996) found that variations in question wording, gender of interviewer, and respondent control over the interview situation elicited very different levels of bias depending on the topic. Much more sensitive topics tended to

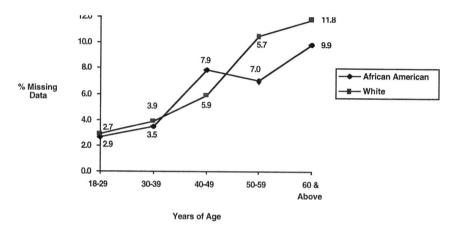

Figure 1. Missing data—condoms take all the fun out of sex.

elicit bigger effects across a wider variety of manipulations. For instance, questions on rape, extramarital sex, and sexual dysfunctions proved to be sensitive to wording, gender of interviewer, and personal-control manipulations. However, questions on numbers of sexual partners in the past year were relatively insensitive to any of these manipulations except for wording.

In a recent national methodological study of African Americans (18–49 years; Catania, Binson, Adler, & Canchola, 1996), we examined respondents' perceptions of their difficulties in answering different kinds of sexual questions. We used a method which provided both a direct and an indirect assessment of people's discomfort. We reasoned that some individuals might be less than forthright in admitting that they are uncomfortable answering particular types of questions on sexuality. Thus, although the first method asked respondents directly whether they would be comfortable with a topic, the second asked how they thought other people would respond. It was expected that respondents would be more likely to rate others as being more uncomfortable than themselves, a perspective that is consistent with the concept of projection. Thus the respondent's perceptions of how other people are going to respond may better reflect their own true feelings. For instance, 16% of women (total $n = 663$) said they would be uncomfortable answering an abortion question but thought that 58% of their friends would be uncomfortable answering this question. Similarly, 15% said they would be uncomfortable answering a question on rape but 53% thought their friends would be uncomfortable answering such a question. A slightly smaller difference is observed for a less sensitive topic, vaginal intercourse, where 18% said they would be uncomfortable answering a relevant question but thought that 32% of their female friends would be uncomfortable answering such a question. We see similar patterns among men ($n = 443$). For instance, 13% of men reported they would be uncomfortable answering questions on sexual dysfunctions but thought that 58% of their friends would be uncomfortable answering such questions. Approximately 11% of men said they would be uncomfortable answering a question on rape but reported that 52% of their male friends would be uncomfortable answering this question. Again the difference is slightly less for a question on vaginal intercourse, where about 12% of men said they would be uncomfortable answering a question on vaginal intercourse but thought that 30% of their friends would be uncomfortable. All these values can be contrasted with our question on whether or not people would be comfortable answering a question on education, where only 5–6% said they would be uncomfortable answering this item.

In general, it appears that questions on miscarriage, abortion, sexual dysfunctions, extramarital sex, and rape are questions that elicit moderate to high levels of discomfort among respondents. Questions on same-gender sex and anal intercourse, however, elicit extremely high levels of discomfort, with from 25% of respondents to approximately two thirds of their friends expected to have a great deal of discomfort answering such questions. Although these data are not definitive, they do give a sense of how even among a set of fairly sensitive sexual questions, there exists a range of sensitivities. It's also clear that asking people directly whether or not they would be comfortable answering sexuality questions provides a lower estimate of the percentage of the population who would be uncomfortable.

Understanding Respondent-Interviewer Interactions

Figure 2 provides an overview of a heuristic model developed to guide work on methodological issues in the assessment of sexual behavior in population surveys. From this perspective, the interviewer and the respondent have a dynamic, bidirectional relationship whether on a phone or in a face-to-face interview. In addition, the model specifies that the interviewer-respondent relationship is contained within a broader contextual framework that is composed of the investigator's motives for conducting the survey, the topic that's being assessed, the order in which questions are asked, the specific wording of the questions, the difficulties that are posed for the respondent by the interview (e.g., requiring respondents to recall extreme amounts of detail about distant events can be very difficult), recruitment procedures (e.g., informed consent), and respondents' motives and dispositions relating to their decision to participate. All these factors which bring the respondent and the interviewer together would be expected to influence their interaction. By the same token, it's important to note that these broader contextual variables are also framed by a larger societal context that may influence participation in the study as well as how respondents conduct themselves in the interview. For instance, as we begin to inundate people in our society with ever increasing numbers of surveys,

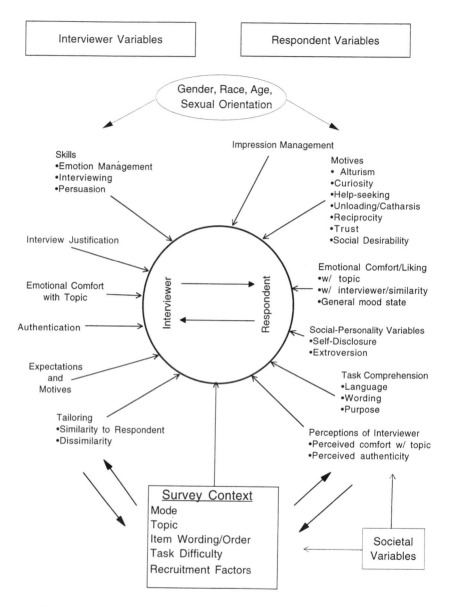

Figure 2. Respondent-interviewer model.

commercial and scientific, the whole idea of participating in a survey may become abhorrent (see Groves et al., 1992). Thus we pose a larger societal context that shapes people's perceptions of the interview process before they ever participate.

Initial motives for participation have been studied and reflect a number of issues such as altruism and help-seeking (see Groves et al., 1992). Our model assumes that these motives carry over into the interview situation. However, although they carry over, they may also change over the course of the interview as the respondent becomes more fully aware of the topics they are being asked about.

Also providing a context for the interviewer-respondent interaction is the survey topic. The interview may concern a broad array of sexual topics, or it may concern a more specific line of inquiry (e.g., childhood sexual abuse or sexual dysfunctions). Each topic shift may cause respondents' emotional states, disclosure tendencies, and motives for continuing to change. The degree of change and their influence on non-response is an important area of inquiry.

In a similar fashion, the words that are used to ask the questions and make up the response categories provide a context for the respondent and the interviewer. They stimulate emotional reactions in both individuals, reactions that may be communicated to each other through voice or non-verbal behavior. By the same token, a self-administered questionnaire also has a potential for this kind of interaction when the self-administered questionnaire is being presented by an interviewer. It's a more limited kind of social interaction, but the respondent's belief that the instrument may be examined by the interviewer provides a limited social context in which to consider the interviewer-respondent interaction.

Interviewers

Interviewers, even when well trained, come to an interview situation with a variety of skills and predispositions about the topics that they'll be asking about, as well as expectations about answers that are to be given.

A common example in the area of human sexuality surveys is the emphasis that is placed on training interviewers to quiet their nonverbal feedback to respondents when using sexual words which we don't typically use in our day-to-day interpersonal communication with others. If the interviewers blush or in some other way show embarrassment, this may cue a respondent to the idea that the interviewer actually thinks something is wrong with these behaviors. Such an interpretation could lead the respondent to inhibit the answer in some way. Consequently, a great deal of effort is used in the training of interviewers to do sexological surveys and in teaching them how to do these in a manner that displays comfort with the topic and acceptance of the answers. In a similar fashion, most investigators attempt to construct the wording of a question so that when the words are spoken by an interviewer, the words and voice reflect emotional comfort with the topic. Calm, comfortable, nonjudgmental cues are thought to enhance topic acceptance and calmness on the part of the respondent. An example is the recently published work by Catania et al. (1995; and prior work by Blair, Sudman, Bradburn, & Stocking, 1977), which showed that asking questions on sexual behavior in more emotionally supportive ways increases reports of less socially acceptable events, situations, or conditions such as noncondom use, sexual dysfunctions, rape, and extramarital sex.

In addition to experiences and training that enhance skills and shape appropriate expectations, interviewers need to learn to manage the emotional content of the interview. Respondents may become embarrassed or get upset and the interviewer needs to know how to respond to these emotional reactions and how to cope with their own feelings so as not to bias respondents' answers. Studies have been conducted on interviewing skills and persuasion strategies used in survey work in general (for example, see Groves et al., 1992), but very little research has been conducted on these issues in the context of sex interviews. The issue of emotion management skills is one that's completely untapped to our knowledge; it is an area of inquiry that deserves considerable attention.

Interviewers also need to be skilled at providing information that justifies the line of inquiry that's being followed. At the same time, they need to be skilled at authenticating the interview. Respondents will be more comfortable and therefore more disclosing when they believe that the sexuality survey is being conducted for a good purpose and it's being collected by ethical people who will honor the confidentiality of the interview. The skills and information needed to provide respondents with adequate justification and authentication of the interview is an understudied area. In some instances too much emphasis on confidentiality actually boomerangs and makes respondents more suspicious (Singer, Von Thurn, & Miller, 1995).

There's been considerable research on the effects of social demographic similarities between interviewers and respondents (Sudman & Bradburn, 1974). Gender, race, age, and sexual orientation have all been considered (Catania et al., 1990). According to Sudman et al. (1982), these demographic similarities become particularly salient when the topic at hand is one that's relevant to the social relationship between the interviewer and the respondent. With regard to sexuality and the social relationship between interviewers and respondents, there may be a host of other factors that may become important other than gender, race, age, and sexual orientation. One might also want to consider such things as the physical attractiveness of the interviewer relative to the respondent. There is certainly good reason to consider that the interview being conducted by an extremely sexually attractive interviewer, particularly when the topic interview concerns sexuality, could result in biased responses from respondents (i.e., who find the interviewer attractive). Physical attractiveness is an important issue in studies of interpersonal liking and attraction, which are important factors in the interview situation. The extent to which physical attractiveness would either increase or reduce bias is an area that would be worth further investigation.

Many of the studies that have looked specifically at the topic of sexuality and have considered characteristics of the respondent and the interviewer have not been based on systematic studies of these demographic characteristics where respondents are randomized to different types of interviewers. Most of these past studies are nonrandomized types of comparisons, where an investigator at the end of the study does a comparison between, for instance, the male and female interviewers (for review, see Catania et al., 1995; 1990). These studies are interesting but do not provide the necessary support for ruling in or out a particular characteristic.

Past studies suggest that people tend to report more sexual information or make more sexual statements in general to female interviewers and that women may be more influenced than men by interviewer gender differences (Abramson & Handschumacher, 1978; Catania et al., 1996; Darrow et al., 1986; DeLamater, 1974; DeLamater & MacCorquodale, 1975; Hansen & Schuldt, 1982; Johnson & DeLamater, 1976; Singer, Frankel, & Glassman, 1983). We recently investigated the interviewer gender issue in a study where respondents were randomized to male or female interviewer conditions and found some interesting results (Catania et al., 1990). We found that same-gender interviewers significantly decreased dropouts in the study. We also found that same-gender interviewers significantly increased responses of nonuse of condoms, extramarital sex, sexual problems, and sexual violence. Interviewer gender had no impact on reports for numbers of sexual partners for varying periods of time, same-gender sexual activity, or age of first coitus, although there was a significant trend ($p < .10$) for more people to report same-gender sex to same-gender interviewers. Overall, these results do not support the notion that people are more likely to report sexual activity or feel more comfortable with female interviewers. Furthermore, we did not find that women were more influenced by the gender of the interviewer than male respondents. In fact, there was a tendency for males to be more susceptible to gender-of-interviewer differences. However, we should note that when we gave respondents an opportunity to select the gender of their interviewer, women overwhelmingly selected female interviewers (95%), as opposed to males, who were more evenly split between selecting a male or female interviewer.

Our results (Catania et al., 1996) suggesting that same-gender interviewers elicit higher levels of reporting of many sensitive sexual activity questions, as well as results from studies on general factors affecting liking when strangers meet, support the proposition that perceived similarity may produce more liking. That is, more similarity between interviewer and respondents in terms of age, social class, gender, and so on produces more liking and consequently more self-disclosure. The more you like a person, the more comfortable you are with him/her and therefore the more likely you are to disclose to that individual. However, it's also important to consider the issue of how sexually attractive the interviewer is to the respondent and whether this factor comes into play in answering questions on sexual behavior. One might expect that increased attraction to an interviewer could produce more liking and consequently more self-disclosure. However, it could just as well produce a great deal more embarrassment and self-presentational bias. Furthermore, anecdotal evidence suggests that you can have too much similarity. For instance, in studies conducted among African Americans in San Francisco (Catania et al., 1992), we found that an African American interviewer, approximately the same age and the same gender as the respondents, elicited discomfort because respondents felt they might be disclosing to someone who might know their friends or family and therefore might break confidentiality. These obviously are difficult contingencies to plan for.

In addition to the interviewer's skills, demographic and social characteristics, and physical attributes, there are a variety of other emotional and motivational factors that may be pertinent to the interviewing situation. Certainly the interviewer's motivations and expectations are relevant areas of methodological inquiry. For example, when interviewers believe the survey questions are sensitive, they tend to achieve higher missing data rates (Singer & Kohnke-Aguirre, 1979). In addition, the added skills of being able to manage the emotional content of the interview and manage one's own emotion, as well as emotional issues that come up for the respondent, are necessary and important issues to consider in interviewer training and research on interviewer-respondent relationships. Further, the interviewer's (and respondent's) general emotional state at the time of administering the interview may also be important. An interviewer who is feeling depressed may communicate a very different tone to a respondent than an interviewer who seems more alert and interested.

Respondents

On the respondent's side of the equation, a variety of factors may influence the relationship between interviewer and respondent. For instance, as noted, respondents come to the interview with a variety of motives which may change over the course of the interview. Motives for participation may reflect altruism, curiosity, help-seeking, or a need for catharsis. Such motives may be balanced against the time and energy necessary for respondents to expend in order to complete the interview. Length of the interview and other burden factors are relevant methodological issues to consider here. In addition, the health status of the respondents, their mistrust of authority, and the perceived reciprocity in the interviewer-respondent relationship may influence willingness to answer questions thoughtfully and accurately.

Researchers sometimes attempt to elicit certain motives in respondents by offering them, for instance, financial incentives for participation. These efforts are directed at stimulating a reciprocity motive in the respondent. It's important to keep in mind, however, that motives such as those related to rules of reciprocity in social relationships can be somewhat stilted in the interview situation. The interview situation brings two strangers together to enact extremely structured roles. One person asks questions and the other person answers. When two people meet for the first time in a more normal social exchange, their reciprocity tends to be in terms of information exchange. I tell you something about myself, and you in turn tell me something about yourself. There's usually a back-and-forth in terms of the kinds of information exchanged and in the degree of intimacy that people will reveal. There are rules governing how rapidly this process takes place as well as how intimate the conversation should become. Typically, when two people meet for the first time, they don't, within 15 minutes, go directly to talking about the most detailed aspects of their sexual relationships. However, this is the circumstance in survey research. This is extremely unusual, and one might say that the social relationship between the interviewer and the respondent is unnatural. This "unnaturalness" may become acceptable when there is evidence or motivations that override the "normal" social rules governing appropriate behavior when two strangers meet. An interesting area of methodological inquiry would be to examine what motives and evidence permit detailed disclosure in this atypical social exchange. That is, what are the optimal conditions that give the respondent permission to break the normative rules for social conduct with a stranger in a fashion that meets the goals of the study?

Social desirability is also a motive that influences self-disclosure, in that some people want to please the interviewer or provide answers that will not be viewed as socially deviant. How such motives interact with other factors (e.g., trust, reciprocity rules, and need for catharsis) to elicit particular biases or general tendencies toward honest self-disclosure is an area that has not been investigated. For example, we could speculate that as the respondent becomes more comfortable with the interviewer and more trusting of that individual, the respondent's need for giving socially desirable answers would decrease. Thus one might expect that over the course of the interview, motives such as social desirability might wax and wane as other motives come to the fore. The process of "warming the respondent up" typifies procedures that attempt to reduce bias in target questions by first getting the respondent to feel good about the interviewer. The type of warm-up, its content, length, and mode of delivery, are all pertinent areas of inquiry in the context of sexological interviews.

In thinking about the interviewing situation as a process and how motives might change over the course of the interview, it is also important to consider how the mood state of the respondent might change over time. Some topics may be fairly unemotional for the respondent and very easy to answer, while other topics may elicit strong feelings that impact subsequent topics and thereby make it more difficult for the respondent to stay focused or to switch to another area of inquiry. For instance, a person may be asked a series of questions about current sexual behavior which appear on the surface to be relatively innocuous. He or she then may be asked about instances of sexual violence, abuse, or rape. The respondent who has had such experiences but has not had an opportunity to deal with them could find such questioning extremely disturbing. Responses to later questions might then be overshadowed or colored by the emotional associations of the sexual trauma.

The process by which respondents balance conflicting motives and their emotional responses to questions and at the same time gain a sense of the interviewer and his/her acceptance of the respondent's answers might be considered in terms of interpersonal impression management. For instance, an altruistic but moderately exhibitionistic respondent might shade his/her responses in an attempt to make the interviewer believe that he/she is incredibly sexually unconventional, even though this may not be a generally socially approved behavior. Studies are needed on how the multiple motivational and emotional demands on respondents help shape the "sexual personae" they project to the interviewer.

Over the course of this presentation I have emphasized self-disclosure as a key outcome, but facets of self-disclosure may also be important antecedents. People have histories of disclosing to individuals, and there may be particular tendencies or dispositions toward the amount of information that people will disclose and the situations in which they will disclose that type of information. Some individuals are extremely low self-disclosers, having a great deal of difficulty disclosing any type of personal information to others. On the other hand, there are individuals who can be very self-disclosing and may tell someone their life stories in an hour and a half and feel very comfortable about that. Other individuals may be very disclosing in some situations and to some types of people but not others. An obvious example is the kind of information adolescents may be willing to tell adolescent friends versus what they would be willing to tell their parents. Certainly the social situation, characteristics of the interviewer, and respondents' expectations about what will be done with the information are expected to influence self-disclosure tendencies. However, the tendencies themselves may also have a direct impact on the amount of disclosure in a particular situation. So knowing something about the particular disclosure history of a person might tell you a lot about what factors would make him or her a high or honest self-discloser in the sexological interview situation.

In addition to the motives, skills, and disposition of the respondent, there are some perceptions that are perhaps specific to the interviewing situation that should also be considered: (1) Do respondents believe that the survey is worthwhile? (2) Do they believe that the information will be used for a good purpose and that their confidentiality will not be violated? (3) Do the respondents' perceptions of the interviewer's comfort with the topic and their perceptions of the authenticity and importance of the survey topic influence comfort and disclosure honesty?

In terms of understanding respondents' perceptions of the interviewer, a useful theoretical guide is offered by the classic person-perception paradigm (Jones, 1979). In the person-perception framework, the interviewer's behaviors (verbal, nonverbal) are perceived by the respondent to carry social meanings which affect how the respondent evaluates and categorizes the interviewer and interview situation. These evaluations and categorizations of the interviewer can then influence how the respondent behaves toward the interviewer and how the respondent views him/herself. Thus person-perception considerations may well provide an important link to other factors, such as impression management and social-desirability motives. That is, particular judgments by the respondent of the interviewer (and the interview) may well stimulate biases that conform to the respondent's self-presentational style in the interview situation. For instance, a heterosexual Don Juan being interviewed by a beautiful female interviewer may perceive the act of asking sexual questions as hinting at a sexual invitation that, in turn, stimulates responses that are tailored to be seductive rather than truthful.

Another fundamental respondent factor to consider is whether respondents understand and comprehend the words and concepts that make up the question. Similarly, standardized response categories used in most surveys will also pose comprehension problems and difficulties that might occur as a function of unfamiliarity with standard rating scales. If respondents don't understand what is being asked of them, then even if they feel very comfortable with the topic, they are obviously going to have a difficult time in being able to respond. Comprehension issues in surveys on sexual behavior have not been widely discussed in the literature; at least empirical results are difficult to find. However, many of the large-scale surveys that have been conducted over the last 20 years in North America, Europe, and Asia have made use of numerous kinds of qualitative approaches to understanding whether people comprehend terms used to describe different kinds of sexual behaviors. This work (see Catania et al., 1995) has generally shown that most people understand terms such as vaginal or anal intercourse; however, there are segments of the population which have difficulties with these terms. Binson and Catania (under review) have shown that a sizable segment of low SES individuals, approximately 25%, report having difficulty understanding the term *anal intercourse*. In general, there is a need to examine comprehension issues in large probability surveys. The smaller, qualitative comprehension studies (e.g., focus groups, small-scale pilot studies) are useful, but obtaining adequate representation in these studies is difficult. Consequently the results achieved in current qualitative research on comprehension issues likely do not represent the extent of the problems.

In addition to language issues, difficulties for respondents also arise when investigators examine more complex topics (e.g., sexual relationships, sexual communication) that employ item concepts that are beyond respondents' observational powers or cognitive schema. Little systematic work, to my knowledge, has been conducted on the conceptual problems that respondents have with more sophisticated concepts tapped by sex-relevant interpersonal and psychological scales currently in use. My experience with this matter has been in looking at issues of translation to other languages. For instance, some sexual concepts in English pose problems for Spanish-speaking respondents because conceptual parallelism is difficult to achieve. Conceptual work across languages on sex-relevant concepts is needed. Puerto Rican, Mexican, and Cuban Spanish dialects may, for example, have subtle but important differences in expression of certain kinds of sexological concepts. It would be important to understand what those are so that investigators can build in language that is meaningful to the respondent.

Antecedents of Respondent and Interviewer Variables

Up until now we've been primarily interested in variables that have proximal impact on the interviewer-respondent relationship. I have also mentioned broader contextual factors that may affect this relationship. However, there remains a large number of antecedents to these proximal influences that would be relevant to examine. For instance, many of the demographic characteristics of the respondent and interviewer that I have discussed are relevant to consider. In terms of age, respondents in their 60s and 70s have less experience than younger respondents with survey participation and in discussing sexual matters (Catania et al., 1996; Ostrow & Kessler, 1993). That is, a historical cohort effect may be evidenced in surveys of interpersonal sexual experiences. Older respondents would be expected to come to the interview situation with a different set of motives, expectations, and emotional comfort than would persons in their 20s. Whether or not the motives and expectations are qualitatively different is a matter for research, but a conservative expectation would be that the differences are a matter of degree rather than a matter of type. Consideration of historical differences in experience with sexual matters and with interviews also brings to the fore the general issue of experience with surveys. Even among younger respondents there will be differential experience with surveys, with the kinds of questions that are asked, and with the kinds of response formats used. People have recognized for some time, for example, that well-educated people have a great deal more ease and comfort with the more structured types of survey formats than less-educated respondents. People's survey experience may, of course, be a mixed bag of positive and negative events. Understanding how these experiences influence people's motives for participation and for answering honestly is an interesting research question. It would be correspondingly important to test methods that would rectify the negative experiences that people have in participating in surveys. The success of our work in the future depends on having a population of people who feel good about surveys and about contributing to the general welfare of human beings. The declining cooperation rates observed over the last 40 years in the United States certainly describe a population that is becoming less tolerant of survey intrusions regardless of the topic.

Developmental and gender issues may also be important to consider. For instance, among questions on numbers of sexual partners, biases sometimes differ depending on whether we are asking adult respondents about adult sexual behavior or adolescent sexual behavior (Catania et al., 1996; also see Catania et al., 1995). These types of biases may also differ by gender. In this regard, men and women have been found to have opposite responses to the same experimental manipulations (Catania et al., 1996; also see Catania et al., 1995). For instance, we've found, with respect to age of coital onset during adolescence, that supportive wording manipulations were associated with an increase in the percentage of men reporting being virgins during adolescence but a decrease in the percentage of women reporting being virgins during adolescence. Consequently, men overstated and women understated their sexual activity during adolescence. What's amazing is that these results are found with adult respondents reporting on their sexual behavior during adolescence. The results conform to expectations about response bias patterns that might arise for men wishing to demonstrate their virility in sexual experiences and for women tending to downplay their sexual experiences so as not to seem sexually promiscuous. This particular pattern of findings may reflect the influence of a sexual double standard in the area of response bias. That is, with standard, less-supportive survey questions, the form of the bias for reports of adolescent sexual activity conforms to the view that sex is OK for men but not for women. Questions that are more supportive appear to break down the need to adhere to a sexual double standard. These speculations are limited to reports concerning adolescence because this pattern of male-female convergence was not observed for reports of numbers of partners in adulthood. In reports of adult behavior, we found that more supportive items were associated with decreased reports of numbers of adult sexual partners for both men and women. That is, we found increased reports in the number of people reporting zero partners and decreases in the percentage of people reporting extreme high values (five or more partners in the past year). Consequently, it would appear in the interviewing situation that particular types of topics may elicit some very different forms of response bias, depending on the developmental importance of the behaviors. Apparently the importance of self-image concerns in adolescence carries forward into adulthood so that even in the interviewer-respondent relationship the respondent still tries to maintain a semblance of the image that they wanted to project as an adolescent (i.e., in terms of males being sexual or females being nonsexual). Further, the findings suggest that a profitable area for inquiry into the antecedents of response bias would be an examination of the gender-role stereotypes that males and females adhere to with respect to sexual behavior. We would add to this that historical context would round out such an inquiry, as one would expect that the gender-role requirements for males and females have changed over the years and are quantitatively if not qualitatively different today for men and women in their 20s than they were sixty years ago.

In thinking about other antecedents of the proximal factors influencing the respondent-interviewer relationship, we would do well to consider research conducted in the broader area of survey methods. For instance, Groves et al. (1992) have identified two general issues that seem to be useful in eliciting high levels of response from respondents. The first is interviewer tailoring, which involves the use of different dress styles, physical behaviors, words, and persuasion strategies for different types of respondents. Second are strategies involved with reducing the likelihood of the respondent terminating the discussion prematurely. These two general strategies are important in getting respondents to participate in surveys and to be helpful in augmenting the degree of perceived similarity and consequently the liking the respondents might have for the interviewers. Might there be tailoring or "maintaining" procedures that are particularly salient for sex surveys?

Summary

We presented a model of the interviewer-respondent interaction relevant to sex surveys as a guide for research in this methodological area. The model is heuristic and no attempt was made to provide a definitive review of the literature. Relevant reviews can be found elsewhere (Catania et al., 1990; 1995). Not discussed here, for instance, is how the degree of sexual guilt experienced by both the interviewer and the respondent around the topic of sex might influence their general emotional comfort in asking and answering questions. Other types of personality characteristics also may be important in terms of the degree of self-disclosure that respondents will evidence. In many regards, the breadth of research needed in this area is somewhat daunting. Empirical literature on such fundamental issues as respondent comprehension of sexual terms and concepts does not exist in the abundance that one would typically like in planning a survey in this area. There is a seat-of-the-pants quality to even some of the most recent sophisticated studies in this area where both respondents and interviewers may often be left wondering just what a particular question was asking about. Despite this somewhat negative perception of the methodological world in the field of sexological surveys, work does continue and is continuing in this area at a pace that is somewhat unprecedented historically. Research on mode effects, on ways of combining different modes of collecting data, different ways of asking questions, interviewer variables, and respondent variables continues and has led to interesting and consistent results regarding the direction of biases (see Catania et al., 1995). There is great need for research on procedures for providing respondents with anonymity and sufficient emotional support during the interview. Although people are very willing to talk about their sexual lives, the fact that they haven't had a lot of opportunities for doing so in an in-depth, systematic way often leaves these people with the uncomfortable feeling that what they are about to tell is something that's rather extreme and strange and no one could possibly have thought of this before. This is not an unusual sentiment among respondents, and even to be simply told that other people have expressed a variety of views and practices will set some respondents at ease. Such tactics can quickly be put into effect in sexological surveys. However, there is a general conservative impulse in this field, as in many other fields of science, that requires replication studies be conducted before investigators change their time-honored methods. I would generally agree with this principle, but I also would contend that there is a consistency between the results of many of the recent studies in this area that would lead one to adopt some of these strategies without extensive replication of the results, although it certainly would be important to look at the differential impact of new methods across all the varied populations available in the United States and elsewhere. In our multicultural heritage, there remains potentially significant cultural differences in how ethnically different people perceive our survey procedures.

Acknowledgment

This work is funded in part by NIMH/NIA grants MH52022, MH/AG51523, and MH54320.

References

Abramson, P., & Handschumacher, I. (1978). Experimenter effects on responses to double-entendre words. *Journal of Personality Assessment, 42,* 592–596.
Archer, R. (1979). Relationships between locus of control and anxiety. *Journal of Personality Assessment, 43,* 617–626.
Binson, D., & Catania, J. A. (under review). Respondents' understanding of the words used in sexual behavior questions. *Public Opinion Quarterly.*
Blair, E., Sudman, S., Bradburn, N., & Stocking, C. (1977). How to ask questions about drinking and sex: Response effects in measuring consumer behavior. *Journal of Marketing Research, 14,* 316–321.

Catania, J. A., Binson, D., Adler, N., & Canchola, J. (1996). Unpublished data from the National AIDS Behavioral Methodology Study—Minority Expansion.

Catania, J. A., Binson, D., Canchola, J., Pollack, L. M., Hauck, W., & Coates, T. (1996). Effects of interviewer gender, interviewer choice, and item context on responses to questions concerning sexual behavior. *Public Opinion Quarterly.*

Catania, J. A., Binson, D., Van der Straten, A., & Stone, V. (1995). Methodological research on sexual behavior in the AIDS era. *Annual Review of Sex Research, 6,* 77–125.

Catania, J. A., Coates, T. J., Kegeles, S., Thompson-Fullilove, M., Peterson, J., Marín, B., Siegel, D., & Hulley, S. (1992). Condom use in multi-ethnic neighborhoods of San Francisco: The population-based AMEN (AIDS in Multi-Ethnic Neighborhoods) study. *American Journal of Public Health, 82,* 284–287.

Catania, J. A., Gibson, D., Chitwood, D., & Coates, T. J. (1990). Methodological problems in AIDS behavioral research: Influences on measurement error and participation bias in studies of sexual behavior. *Psychological Bulletin, 108*(3), 339–362.

Catania, J. A., McDermott, L., & Pollack, L. (1986). Questionnaire response bias and face-to-face interview sample bias in sexuality research. *Journal of Sex Research, 22,* 52–72.

Darrow, W., Jaffe, H., Thomas, P., Haverkos, H., Rogers, M., Guinan, M., Auerbach, D., Spira, T., & Curran, J. (1986). Sex of interviewer, place of interview, and responses of homosexual men to sensitive questions. *Archives of Sexual Behavior, 15,* 79–88.

DeLamater, J. (1974). Methodological issues in the study of premarital sexuality. *Sociological Methods and Research, 3*(1), 30–61.

DeLamater, J., & MacCorquodale, P. (1975). The effects of interview schedule variations on reported sexual behavior. *Sociological Methods and Research, 4,* 215–236.

Dindia, K., & Allen, M. (1992). Sex differences in self-disclosure: A meta-analysis. *Psychological Bulletin, 112,* 106–124.

Gebhard, P. (1972). Incidence of overt homosexuality in the United States and Western Europe. In L. M. Livingwood (Ed.), *National Institute of Mental Health Task Force on Homosexuality.* Washington DC: National Institute of Mental Health.

Groves, R. M., Cialdini, R. B., & Couper, M. P. (1992). Understanding the decision to participate in a survey. *Public Opinion Quarterly, 56*(4), 475–495.

Hansen, J. E., & Schuldt, W. J. (1982). Physical distance, sex, and intimacy in self-disclosure. *Psychological Reports, 51,* 3–6.

Johnson, W., & DeLamater, J. (1976). Response effects in sex surveys. *Public Opinion Quarterly, 40,* 165–181.

Jones, E. E. (1979). The rocky road from acts to dispositions. *American Psychologist, 343,* 107–117.

Lefcourt, H. (1982). *Locus of control: Current trends in theory and research.* Hillsdale, NJ: Lawrence Erlbaum Associates.

Ostrow, D. G., & Kessler, R. C. (Eds.). (1993). *Methodological issues in AIDS behavioral research.* New York: Plenum Press.

Pennebaker, J. W. E. (1995). *Emotion, disclosure, and health.* Washington, DC: American Psychological Association.

Singer, E., Frankel, M., & Glassman, M. (1983). The effect of interviewer characteristics and expectations on response. *Public Opinion Quarterly, 47,* 68–83.

Singer, E., & Kohnke-Aguirre, L. (1979). Interviewer expectation effects: A replication and extension. *Public Opinion Quarterly, 43*(2), 245–260.

Singer, E., Von Thurn, D., & Miller, E. (1995). Confidentiality assurances and response. *Public Opinion Quarterly, 59,* 66–77.

Sudman, S., & Bradburn, N. (1974). *Response effects in surveys.* Chicago: Aldine.

Sudman, S., & Bradburn, N. (1982). *Asking questions: A practical guide to questionnaire design.* San Francisco: Jossey-Bass.

Turner, C. F., Danella, R. D., & Rogers, S. M. (in press). Sexual behavior in the United States, 1930–1990: Trends and methodological problems. *Sexually Transmitted Diseases.*

Contributors

John Bancroft, M.D., was trained in medicine at Cambridge University and in psychiatry at the Institute of Psychiatry, London. He has been Director of the Kinsey Institute for Research in Sex, Gender, and Reproduction, and professor of psychiatry at Indiana University since May 1995. For the previous 19 years he was Clinical Scientist at the Medical Research Council's Reproductive Biology Unit in Edinburgh, Scotland. He has extensive research and clinical experience in the relationship of reproductive hormones to sexuality and well-being, psychophysiology and pharmacology of sexual response, and the management of sexual problems. He is author of *Human Sexuality and Its Problems* (2nd edition, 1989) and was until recently editor of *Annual Review of Sex Research*. He is currently President of the International Academy of Sex Research.

Alex Carballo-Diéguez, Ph.D., was born in Argentina and migrated to the United States in 1982. He received his Ph.D. in Clinical Psychology from the New School for Social Research in 1986. During his initial years in New York, Dr. Carballo-Diéguez provided psychotherapeutic services to individuals afflicted with AIDS and HIV. In 1988 he joined the HIV Center for Clinical and Behavioral Studies at New York State Psychiatric Institute and Columbia University, and his professional activity progressively switched to a full-time involvement in research. His area of inquiry is sexual risk behavior among men who have sex with men, particularly those of Latin American background. His work, published in peer-reviewed journals, discusses issues of sexual identity, childhood sexual abuse and its association with adult HIV-risk behavior, perceived barriers to condom use, and cultural issues to be considered in HIV prevention.

Joseph A. Catania, Ph.D., is an Associate Professor in the Department of Medicine at the University of California at San Francisco, where his central focus has been on the social epidemiology of AIDS. He is currently Principal Investigator for the Gay Urban Men's Survey (GUMS), which will obtain a random sample of 5,800 gay and bisexual men, constituting the first large-scale national study of this population. Dr. Catania is also Principal Investigator of several other national surveys of sexual behavior, including the National AIDS Behavioral Survey, the Family of AIDS Behavioral Survey, and the Sex and AIDS Methodology Surveys. He is the author and co-author of over 70 scientific journal articles and nine book chapters, and a member of the editorial board for the journal *Sexually Transmitted Diseases* and the *Journal of Sex Research*.

Ulrich Clement, Ph.D., Prin.-Doz. Dr.phil. Dipl.-Psych, is senior research psychologist at the Psychosomatic Hospital, University of Heidelberg, Germany; Research Associate at the HIV Center of Clinical and Behavioral Studies, Columbia

University; licensed psychotherapist and supervisor; and editorial board member of several journals. He has done active research since 1978 on different fields of sex research (sex therapy, survey research, HIV/AIDS-related sex research, transsexualism) and other fields of clinical psychology (body image research, treatment of social phobias, psychotherapy research).

Diane di Mauro, Ph.D., has worked over 15 years in the field of human sexuality, specializing in the areas of sexuality education and sexuality research. She is currently the Program Director of the Sexuality Research Fellowship Program at the Social Science Research Council, which provides dissertation and postdoctorate support for sexuality research in the social and behavioral sciences. Dr. di Mauro is the author of *Sexuality Research in the United States: An Assessment of the Social and Behavioral Sciences* and the co-author of *Winning the Battle: Developing Support for Sexuality and HIV Education* and *Communication Strategies for HIV/AIDS and Sexuality*.

Lynda S. Doll, Ph.D., is Chief of the Behavioral Intervention Research Branch in the Division of HIV/AIDS Prevention at the Centers for Disease Control. In this role, she funds and supervises research designed to develop and evaluate the effectiveness of HIV-related behavioral interventions. Dr. Doll's degree is in educational/developmental psychology. She has been at CDC for 10 years. Her research focus during this period has been on determinants of risk behaviors among gay and, more recently, bisexual men and HIV seropositive blood donors.

Françoise Dubois-Arber, M.D., M.S., received her doctorate in internal medicine, followed by a master's in public health. She has done work on implementation of primary health care programs in South America (Peru and Nicaragua, 1983–86). Since 1987, she has specialized in evaluation research. She is Head of the Prevention Programs Evaluation Unit at the University Institute for Social and Preventive Medicine in Lausanne, Switzerland, and is in charge of the evaluation of the national AIDS prevention strategy. In this context, she directed several trend surveys and qualitative research on sexual behavior in the general population and various other groups.

Anke A. Ehrhardt, Ph.D., is a Research Chief at the New York State Psychiatric Institute and a Professor of Medical Psychology in the Department of Psychiatry at Columbia University. She is an internationally known researcher in the field of sexual and gender development of children, adolescents, and adults. In 1981, she was the President of the International Academy of Sex Research. In addition, Dr. Ehrhardt has received a number of prestigious awards for her research accomplishments. Dr. Ehrhardt's research in the area of sex and gender over the last 30 years has covered the interaction between sex hormones, social/environmental factors, sexual behavior, and mental health, including the long-term effects of prenatal diethylstilbestrol (DES) exposure on gender, sexuality, and mental health in female and male offspring, the psychosexual development of adolescents with early puberty, sex hormones and sexual orientation in lesbians and heterosexual women, and the effects of antidepressants on sexual functioning. Dr. Ehrhardt is currently the Principal Investigator and Director of the HIV Center for Clinical and Behavioral Studies at the New York State Psychiatric Institute and Columbia University, College of Physicians and Surgeons.

J. Dennis Fortenberry, M.D., M.S., is Associate Professor of Pediatrics at Indiana University. He specializes in adolescent medicine, with specific research interests in adolescents' sexual behavior and sexually transmitted diseases. His earlier research includes factors related to the timing of first intercourse among adolescents, the influence of alcohol and drugs on adolescent women's sexual behavior, and the validity of adolescent women's self-reports of sexual activity.

Alain Giami obtained a Ph.D. from University Paris 7 in Social Psychology (1978). He worked on the history of sex education and attitudes and representations of educators toward the sexual behavior of mentally retarded persons. He participated in the ACSF, the French National Survey on Sexual Behavior. He is currently working on the representations of sexuality and partnership in the time of AIDS. He is the main co-author of *Des Infirmières face au Sida* (Paris: INSERM, 1994).

Cynthia A. Graham, Ph.D., is Adjunct Assistant Professor in the Department of Psychology and Assistant Professor in the Department of Psychiatry at Indiana University. She obtained a MAppSci in clinical psychology from the University of Glasgow, Scotland, and her Ph.D. in clinical psychology from McGill University, Canada. Her research interests include menstrual synchrony, premenstrual changes, and the behavioral effects of oral contraceptives.

Michel Hubert,* Ph.D., is Professor at the Facultés Universitaires Saint-Louis in Brussels, where he teaches methodology of social sciences research and is in charge of the AIDS research program of the Centre d'Etudes Sociologiques. After working in the field of urban sociology, he has been involved in several research projects, both qualitative and quantitative, on sexual behavior and HIV risk and was one of the principal investigators in the Belgian national survey on sexual behavior and attitudes toward HIV/AIDS. He was also the project leader of the European Union Concerted Action on Sexual Behavior and Risks of HIV Infection within the Biomedical and Health Research Program (BIOMED). He is coeditor with Nathalie Bajos and Theo Sandfort of *Sexual Behaviour and HIV/AIDS in Europe: Comparisons of National Surveys*, which will be published in 1997 by Taylor & Francis (London) as one of the outcomes of Concerted Action.

Carol Jenkins, Ph.D., joined the staff of the Papua New Guinea Institute of Medical Research (PNGIMR) in 1982 and is presently Principal Research Fellow in Medical Anthropology. For many years her work focused on the sociocultural aspects of malnutrition. By 1987, most of her work had shifted to the social and behavioral aspects of infectious diseases. When AIDS became an issue in Papua New Guinea in 1990, her work on sexuality began. She conducted a national qualitative study of sexual behavior whose results were published as a PNGIMR monograph, *Sexual and Reproductive Knowledge and Behaviour in Papua New Guinea* (1994). Her work in sexuality continued with studies on sex workers and their clients and one on the effects of urbanization on the sexuality of youth. Her most recent publication is "The Homosexual Context of Heterosexual Practice in Papua New Guinea," in P. Aggleton (Ed.), *Bisexualities and AIDS: International Perspectives*, Social Aspects of AIDS Series, London: Taylor & Francis (1996).

Anne M. Johnson, M.D., is Professor of Epidemiology in the Department of Sexually Transmitted Diseases, University College London Medical School. She is also Director of the United Kingdom's MRC Co-Ordinating Centre for HIV/AIDS Epidemiology. She is honorary consultant in Public Health Medicine in London. She has worked on the epidemiology of HIV and STDs since 1985. She was one of the principal investigators on the British National Survey of Sexual Attitudes and Lifestyles involving nearly 19,000 randomly sampled adults. The study was carried out in

1990 and published as *Sexual Attitudes and Lifestyles* (Blackwells, 1994) by A. M. Johnson, J. Wadsworth, K. Wellings, and J. Field. She has published many scientific articles in the field of sexual behavior research and HIV and STD epidemiology.

John M. Kennedy, Ph.D., is Director of the Indiana University Center for Survey Research and adjunct associate professor of sociology at Indiana University. He received his Ph.D. in sociology from Pennsylvania State University in 1986. Dr. Kennedy recently completed a book, *Knowledge Diffusion in the U.S. Aerospace Industry*, with a colleague at NASA (Ablex Press, 1997).

Leighton Ku, Ph.D., MPH, is a Senior Research Associate at the Urban Institute, a policy research organization in Washington, D.C. He is one of the core investigators for the National Survey of Adolescent Males, a series of nationally representative surveys of young American men concerning AIDS and fertility-related behaviors among teenagers. He has co-authored about 50 papers on these topics. Another area of interest is Medicaid, the U.S. health care program for low-income, disabled, and elderly people. He was a co-author of *Medicaid Since 1980: Costs, Coverage and the Shifting Alliance Between the Federal Government and the States*. He is also an Associate Professorial Lecturer in Public Policy at George Washington University and teaches research methods to doctoral students.

Edward O. Laumann, Ph.D., is the George Herbert Mead Distinguished Service Professor in the Department of Sociology and the College at the University of Chicago, Director of the Ogburn Stouffer Center for Population and Social Organization, and Editor of the *American Journal of Sociology*. Previously he was Chairman of the Department of Sociology, Dean of the Social Sciences Division, and Provost (Chief Academic Officer) at the university. Before coming to Chicago, he taught at the University of Michigan. Laumann's research interests include social stratification; the sociology of the professions, occupations, and formal organizations; social network analysis; the analysis of elite groups; and national policymaking and the sociology of human sexuality. Among his eleven books are two volumes on human sexuality published in the fall of 1994: *The Social Organization of Sexuality* (University of Chicago Press) and *Sex in America* (Little, Brown).

Barbara VanOss Marín, Ph.D., is Associate Adjunct Professor of Epidemiology and Biostatistics at the University of California at San Francisco. She holds undergraduate and graduate degrees from Loyola University of Chicago in Applied Social Psychology and did a postdoctoral fellowship at UCSF in Health Psychology. Her primary interest over the past 15 years has been research and intervention to promote healthy behaviors among Hispanics/Latinos, in culturally appropriate ways. Her current interests include identifying the cultural issues related to AIDS prevention among Latinos, including a study on condom use in unmarried Latino adults. She has just been funded by the National Institute of Mental Health to develop, implement, and evaluate a culturally appropriate sex education program for sixth, seventh, and eighth graders in predominantly Latino schools. She will be directing a project to train ethnic minority scholars in HIV prevention research. Dr. VanOss Marín was born in Green Bay, Wisconsin, and during her twenties lived in Bogotá, Colombia, for four years, where she developed her strong attachment to Latino culture.

Stuart Michaels, Ph.D., is a Researcher at the University of Chicago and a co-author of *The Social Organization of Sexuality: Sexual Practices in the United States*. He was Project Director of the National Health and Social Life Survey and is currently directing the Chicago Health and Social Life Study.

Ted Myers,* Ph.D., a sociobehavioral epidemiologist, is an Associate Professor in the Department of Health Administration, Faculty of Medicine, University of Toronto, and a Research Consultant to the City of Toronto, Department of Public Health. He has worked and studied extensively in the field of addictions and mental and community health, and is involved with a variety of community-based AIDS/HIV research projects. Projects for which he has been principal investigator include the Talking Sex Project, the National Survey of Gay and Bisexual Men and HIV, the Ontario First Nations AIDS and Healthy Lifestyle Survey, and a National Survey of Community Pharmacies and HIV/AIDS Prevention. In addition, he is a co-investigator on the WHO Collaborating Study of Injecting Drug Users and the Ontario HIV in Prisons Study. He has published numerous articles and presented papers at international conferences in the areas of health education, health promotion, and health policy. Currently he is a National Health Scholar for AIDS Research.

Susan Newcomer* holds a 1983 Ph.D. in Population Studies and Sociology from the University of North Carolina, an M.A. in educational administration from Iowa State University, and a B.A. in psychology and Chinese from Barnard College. Since 1988 she has been a statistician/demographer in the Demographic and Behavioral Sciences Branch of the Center for Population Research at the U.S. National Institutes of Health, where she is responsible for a portfolio of extramural research on adolescent health, contraception, and other fertility-related behaviors. From 1984 to 1988 she was the national Director of Education for the Planned Parenthood Federation of America. Her own research and writing have been on adolescent fertility, and she has done consulting work for international organizations on intervention program design and evaluation.

Richard G. Parker, Ph.D., is in the HIV Center for Clinical and Behavioral Studies at the New York State Psychiatric Institute and Columbia University. Prior to 1997 he was Professor of Medical Anthropology and Human Sexuality and Chair of the Department of Health Policy and Institutions in the Institute of Social Medicine (IMS) at the State University of Rio de Janeiro (UERJ). He also served as Secretary General for the Brazilian Interdisciplinary AIDS Association (ABIA) and as a member of the Board of Directors for the Commission on Citizenship and Reproduction (CCR) in Brazil. He was born in the United States and educated at the University of California at Berkeley, where he received his doctorate in social and cultural anthropology in 1988. His research has focused on the social and cultural construction of gender and sexuality and, for more than a decade now, the social aspects of HIV/AIDS. He has conducted long-term field research in Brazil since the early 1980s and has lived in Rio de Janeiro since 1988. Parker's major publications in English include *Bodies, Pleasures and Passions: Sexual Culture in Contemporary Brazil* (Boston: Beacon Press, 1991), *Sexuality, Politics and AIDS in Brazil* (with Herbert Daniel; London: Falmer Press, 1993), and *Conceiving Sexuality: Approaches to Sex Research in a Postmodern World* (edited, with John H. Gagnon; New York and London: Routledge, 1995).

John Peterson, Ph.D., is Associate Professor of Psychology at Georgia State University. His publications include basic and applied research on interventions to prevent high-risk sexual behavior among African American gay/bisexual men, sexual surveys of African American heterosexual adults, and studies on stress and coping processes among African American men.

Fabio Sabogal, Ph.D., is an Associate Adjunct Professor in the Division of General Internal Medicine, the Center for AIDS Prevention Studies, and the Medical Effectiveness Research for Diverse Populations at the University of California at San Francisco. He is a Hispanic health psychologist who has conducted various research studies on factors involving health behavior and behavioral change in the Hispanic community, including sexuality, HIV, cancer, smoking, tuberculosis, diabetes, and nutrition. He has done extensive cross-cultural research in Colombia, Guatemala, and the United States involving Hispanic health services.

Theo G. M. Sandfort, Ph.D., is Director of the Department of Gay and Lesbian Studies at Utrecht University and Research Coordinator at the Netherlands Institute of Social Sexological Research, Utrecht. As a social psychologist, he has done research on pedophilia, sexual abuse, and sexual development. He currently studies sexual behavior in the context of AIDS and STDs, among gay men as well as in the general population. Furthermore, he studies aspects of contemporary gay and lesbian lives. He is co-editor of *Sexual Behavior and HIV/AIDS in Europe: Comparisons of National Surveys* (Taylor & Francis), and *Gay and Lesbian Studies, an Interdisciplinary Perspective* (Sage).

Freya L. Sonenstein, Ph.D., is Director of the Population Studies Center, one of the seven operational divisions of the Urban Institute, Washington, D.C. She has over 20 years of experience conducting applied and behavioral research related to family and children's policy. Dr. Sonenstein has designed and conducted a number of major national studies which have informed the adolescent pregnancy field. She is currently preparing materials for the California Wellness Foundation Teen Pregnancy Prevention Campaign and conducting an assessment of women's reproductive health needs in the District of Columbia. She also directs the longitudinal National Survey of Adolescent Males, which has been funded by grants from the National Institute for Child Health and Human Development to study fertility and STD risk behaviors among a national sample of young men ages 15–19. Her research has included the first successful national survey of sex education provided by school districts in 1982, the national evaluation of the Office of Adolescent Pregnancy Programs Demonstration Projects completed in 1984 with Martha Burt, the Survey of Absent Parents, the Child Care and Self Sufficiency Study, the National Survey of Paternity Establishment, and the National Examination of Publicly Funded Family Planning, a study commissioned by the Kaiser Family Foundation.

Alfred Spira, M.D., Ph.D., is Professor of Epidemiology and Public Health at the University of Paris XI and Director of the Unit of Public Health Research of the French National Institute for Health and Medical Research (INSERM). He was the coordinator for the French National Behavioral Surveys undertaken from 1989 to 1994.

Ann Stueve, Ph.D., is an Assistant Professor (Clinical) of Public Health in the Division of Epidemiology at Columbia University School of Public Health. Her major work has been in the area of psychiatric epidemiology, especially on the relationship between stress and serious mental illness and on the impact of mental illness on family relationships. She is currently senior methodologist for the Reach for Health Study, an NICHD-funded evaluation of school-based programs aimed at reducing African American and Hispanic young adolescents' involvement in risky behaviors associated with early and unprotected sex, alcohol and drug use, and violence. She is also senior methodologist on a CDC study of young men at high risk of contracting HIV infections.

*Leonore Tiefer,** Ph.D., 1969, University of California at Berkeley, is a born-again social constructionist sexologist who originally trained as a physiological and comparative psychologist with Frank A. Beach. Her recent empirical publications have followed up men and couples utilizing new medical erectile dysfunction treatments. Most of her theoretical works are included in a 1995 volume, *Sex Is Not a Natural Act, and Other Essays* (Westview).

Charles F. Turner, Ph.D., is director of the Program in Health and Behavior Measurement at the Research Triangle Institute, a nonprofit research organization established in 1958 by Duke University, North Carolina State University, and the University of North Carolina. Prior to joining RTI, Dr. Turner was a scholar-in-residence at the U.S. National Academy of Sciences (NAS) and served from 1987 to 1991 as director of the NAS Committee on AIDS Research and the Behavioral, Social, and Statistical Sciences. Among his publications, Dr. Turner is co-author and co-editor of three recent books on AIDS research and policy: *AIDS, Sexual Behavior, and IV Drug Use*, *AIDS: The Second Decade*, and *Evaluating AIDS Prevention Programs*. Outside of the AIDS arena, he is co-editor of a two-volume reference work on survey measurement, *Surveying Subjective Phenomena*, and of the monograph *Survey Measurement of Drug Use: Methodological Issues*.

J. Richard Udry is Kenan Professor of Maternal and Child Health and Kenan Professor of Sociology at the University of North Carolina at Chapel Hill. He received a Ph.D. in sociology from the University of Southern California in 1960. His first foray into research on sexual behavior appeared in *Nature* in 1970. Partly based on archival data from the Kinsey Institute, this article demonstrated that the frequency of women's sexual intercourse is distributed in the menstrual cycle with a peak at midcycle and a trough in the luteal phase. More recently, his research has focused primarily on the sexual behavior of adolescents. He was the first to actually document the effects of hormones on the development of sexual behavior during puberty and to show the interaction of hormonal and sociological factors in shaping adolescent behavior.

*Colin Williams,** Ph.D., is a Sociologist at Indiana University and was formerly a Senior Sociologist at the Kinsey Institute. He most recently co-authored *Dual Attraction: Understanding Bisexuality* (Oxford University Press, 1994).

*Was a participant at the conference, but did not contribute a paper for this volume.

Index

Abortion: self-administered questionnaires and biases in data on, 42; and nonresponse to questions on sensitive topics, 420

Academic performance: and nonresponse in Reach for Health Study of African American and Hispanic adolescents, 384–85, 387

Acculturation: and ethnic self-identification among Hispanic Americans, 117; and nonresponse bias for Hispanic Americans, 126–27; of Latino men who have sex with men to gay culture, 142; and sexual attitudes and behaviors among Hispanic Americans, 165–66; and class differences among Hispanic Americans, 169

Adolescence and adolescents: international studies of sexual cultures of, 12; and self-administered questionnaires on alcohol use, 42n.5, 43; measurement of sexual behavior among males, 87–103; availability of data on bisexuality and female homosexuality, 146; trends over time in sexual behavior of in Switzerland, 208, 210; self-questionnaires versus daily diaries in study of sexual behavior in females with STDs, 237–47; and design of study on romantic partners of, 309–19; older sexual partners of female, 333; nonresponse to questions about sex, substance use, and school in study of African American and Hispanic, 376–88; reports of adult respondents on sexual behavior during, 431–32

Adorno, T. W., 62n.2

African Americans: self-administered versus telephone surveys and data on drug use, 44; and nonresponse in National AIDS Behavioral Survey, 106–109; and effects of question wording in National AIDS Behavioral Survey, 110–13; and issues of culture, 161; nonresponse in study of sex, substance use, and school among adolescents, 376–88; and nonresponse to questions on sensitive topics, 420–21; as interviewers in sex research, 426

Age: T-ACASI interviews and, 50n.15, 51; of interviewer and interviewer-respondent relationship, 73, 430; and response bias in National AIDS Behavioral Survey, 106–109; at first sexual intercourse and effect of question wording, 111–12; and sampling procedures in study of male homosexuality in the Netherlands, 268; and participation rates in British survey, 280; and participation bias in hypothetical survey of homosexuality, 285; and older sexual partners of adolescent girls, 333. *See also* Adolescence and adolescents

Aggleton, Peter, 155

AIDS (acquired human immunodeficiency virus): and recent increase in survey research on sexual behavior, ix, xvi; and international research on sexuality, 10–13; policy goals of research on sexual behavior in Brazil, 18–19; and issue of values in sexuality research, 27–28; evidence of biases in survey measurement of sexual behavior and, 37–56; T-ACASI technology and survey on, 50–53; survey of sexual behavior and AIDS in France, 61–76; race and nonresponse in National AIDS Behavior Survey, 106–109; rate of among Hispanic Americans, 115, 137; repeated population surveys and evaluation of efficacy of prevention campaigns, 185–95; trend analysis of prevention program in Switzerland, 197–210; and ethics of randomized controlled trials, 219–21; limited perspective on homosexuality in studies of, 265; and social network analysis, 404, 410. *See also* HIV

AIDS and Reproductive Health Network (ARHN), 13–15

AIDSCAP Project, 12

AIDSCOM Project, 12

AIDSTECH Project, 12

Ajzen, I., 267

Alcohol use: self-administered questionnaires

445

and adolescents, 42n.5, 43; and study of sexual behavior in adolescent females with STDs, 243, 245, 246–47. *See also* Substance use
Altruism: and help-seeking behavior in interviewer-respondent relationship, 423
Ambivalence: and dynamics of interviewer motivation, 71; and interactional sexual scripts, 347
Amsterdam Cohort Study, 268–70
Anal intercourse: T-ACASI and survey data on, 52, 54; and nonresponse patterns on sensitive topics, 421; respondent difficulty in understanding term, 429
Analysis of Sexual Behavior in France (ACSF), 61–76
Anthropology: and Sexuality Research Fellowship, 6; and concept of social networks, 331
Applied research, and basic research in studies of sexuality, 356
Aquilino, W., 44
Argentina: and national variations in use of Spanish, 138
Asian Americans, and gay community, 168
Assessment report, on sexuality research in U.S., 3–8
Audio computer-assisted self-interviewing (audio-CASI): and biases in measurements of sexual behavior, 46–48; future research and, 53, 56, 102; discussion of methodological issues related to, 78–80, 83; and survey of sexual behavior among adolescent males, 95; and sexuality research among Hispanic populations, 120; impact of on survey research, 359
Austria: survey of gay and bisexual behavior in, 11n.3
The Authoritarian Personality (Adorno et al., 1950), 62n.2

Back-translation: research instruments and process of, 121
Bakker, A. B., 267n.8
Bancroft, John: on policy issues in sexuality research, 23, 27, 33; on methodology issues related to interviews and interviewers, 78, 80, 81; on methodology issues related to specific contexts, 160, 164, 167, 168, 171, 175, 177, 179, 180–81; on measurement of changes in sexual behavior over time, 214, 217–18, 221, 222, 223; on participation bias in sexual behavior surveys, 254–55, 256, 288–89, 293–94; on sexual network analysis, 330, 331, 332; on interactional sexual scripts, 351
Beeper methodology, for daily ratings of sexual interest, 254
Behavior: sequences of and interactional sexual scripts, 344; sociologistic and psychologistic explanations of as issue in social network analysis, 392. *See also* Sexual behavior
Berkowitz, S. D., 392, 402
Berlin, B., 87
Bias: evidence of in survey measurement of sexual behavior, 37–56; Hispanic populations and selection of study participants, 123–24; and HIV-focused research on bisexual men, bisexual women, and lesbians, 155–56; assessment of in trend analysis of AIDS prevention program in Switzerland, 199; of self-presentation in study of sexual behavior in adolescent females with STDs, 247; and interactional sexual scripts, 348; and gender-role stereotypes, 431–32. *See also* Participation bias
Biggar, R. J., 282, 283–84
Billy, J., 87, 96n.2
Binson, Diane, 161, 429
Bisexualities and AIDS (Aggleton, 1996), 155
Bisexuality: and national surveys on sexual behavior, 11n.3; and concepts of sexual orientation in Latin American cultures, 135–36; qualitative assessment of recent studies of sexual behavior with bisexual men and women, 145–56; context and definition of, 174–76; and self-identification of sexual orientation, 263; and recruitment of study participants in Canada, 289; gender and studies of, 362
Blau, P. M., 399, 404
Blumstein, P. W., 156, 177
Bond, Kate, 330
Boundary specification problem, in network analysis, 398
Bradburn, N., 63, 112, 161
Brazil: sexuality research on AIDS in, 11n.2, 12; survey on gay and bisexual behavior in, 11n.3; study of sex work in, 11n.4; intervention study on women and AIDS in, 13n.6; policy goals of research on AIDS and sexual behavior in, 18–19; gay and lesbian community of, 169

British National Survey of Sexual Attitudes and Lifestyles, 38n.1
Bureau of Labor Statistics, 48n.13
Burt, R. S., 399
Burundi: national survey on AIDS, 11n.2
Buunk, A. P., 267n.8

Canada: and gay Latino-Hispanic community, 168; and incentives for research participants, 289
Carballo-Diéguez, Alex: on methodology issues related to interviews and interviewers, 81; on methodology issues related to specific contexts, 159, 162, 170, 171, 172, 174; on measurement of changes in sexual behavior over time, 213–14; on participation bias in sexual behavior surveys, 251, 256; on sexual network analysis, 334; on interactional sexual scripts, 346, 350, 362
Carolina Population Center, 319
Cash incentives. *See* Incentives
Catania, Joe: on methodology issues related to specific contexts, 159–64, 171; and National AIDS Behavioral Surveys, 194; on participation bias in sexual behavior surveys, 250, 253, 254, 289, 292; on sexual network analysis, 321, 322, 336; on interactional sexual scripts, 349; and review of literature on nonresponse rates, 386, 387; and interviewer-respondent relationship, 417–18, 423; on comprehension issues in sex research, 429
Catholic Church: influence of on sexual behavior of Hispanic subgroups, 165. *See also* Religion
Celentano, David, 45n.8
Census: Hispanics and self-categorization of race, 116
Centers for Disease Control, 31, 91
Center for Survey Research, 357
Central African Republic: national survey on AIDS, 11n.2
Central Americans, and diversity among Hispanic subgroups, 115, 165
Chicago Health and Social Life Study (CHSLS), 299–307
Childhood sexual abuse: reinterpretation of meaning of by respondents, 346–47
Cigarette smoking: and collection of saliva specimens by researchers, 101; underreporting of by Hispanic Americans, 166

Class, socioeconomic: and numbers of sexual partners in Great Britain, 24; correlation of to race, 159; Hispanic Americans and acculturation, 169; income and ethnoreligious groups in Detroit study, 398. *See also* Demographic class
Classroom surveys as epidemiological tool, 376. *See also* Schools
Clement, Ulrich: on methodology issues related to interviews and interviewers, 78–79, 82; on methodology issues related to specific contexts, 159, 160, 162; on measurement of changes in sexual behavior over time, 218; on retrospective interviews versus daily diaries for assessment of sexual behavior, 253; on participation bias in sexual behavior surveys, 292; on analysis of sexual networks, 320, 326; on interactional sexual scripts, 346–51
Cocaine: modes of survey administration and bias in data on, 41–42. *See also* Drug use; Substance use
Coding of interactional sexual scripts, 341–45
Cognitive interviewing, applications of in survey research, 358
Coital diaries. *See* Daily diaries
Colombian Americans: and diversity among Hispanic subgroups, 137; and national variations in use of Spanish, 139
Columbia University, Bureau of Applied Social Research, 393
Coming out: homosexuality and concept of in social science research, 272n.16
Communication about sexuality: and gender of interviewer, 73; perception of difficulties in interviewer-respondent relationship, 73–74; complexity of in professional context, 75–76. *See also* Language; Terminology
Community: as context for study of sexual networks, 302–306; and design of study of romantic partners of adolescents, 312
Conceiving Sexuality: Approaches to Sex Research in a Postmodern World (Parker & Gagnon, 1995), 14
Condoms: T-ACASI and data on use of, 53, 54; and survey of sexual behavior among adolescent males, 100–101; and demographic variables in nonresponse rates, 107–109; and effect of question wording, 111, 419; changes in sexual behavior in France and, 191; changes in sexual behav-

ior in Switzerland and, 199–205; use of terms for in Germany, 218; and study of sexual behavior in adolescent females with STDs, 244, 246, 247. *See also* Female condom

Confidentiality: and telephone audio-CASI technology, 79; and adolescent males as survey respondents, 91; of diary material in study of adolescent females with STDs, 238; in study of romantic partners of adolescents, 313

Conflict, and neutrality of interviewers, 69

Context: sexuality research in social and behavioral sciences and historical, 4; and concepts of sexuality in developing world, 13–16; communication about sexuality in professional, 75–76; discussion of issues related to methodology and, 159–81; and definition of bisexuality, 174–76; neighborhood or community as focus of studies of sexual networks, 302–306; and studies of romantic relationships of adolescents, 321; and private sexual culture in Papua New Guinea, 372–73

Contextual effects analysis, and social networks, 392

Contraceptives: validation and alternative measures of use in survey of sexual behavior in adolescent males, 100–101; and assessment of sexual behavior of women in Scotland and the Philippines, 227–36. *See also* Condoms

Control: question wording and psychological theory of, 110; and respondent-interviewer relationship, 418

Copas, Andrew, xiv–xv

Core Conflictual Relationship Theme (CCRT), 341

Cost-benefit relationship, of changes in surveys, 206, 208

Côte d'Ivoire: national survey on AIDS, 11n.2

Countertransference, and interviewer-respondent relationship, 64

Coverage error, in survey research, 357

Cox, B., 45–46

Coxon, Tony, 291–92, 300, 334

Cross-checks: for validity and reliability of indicators of sexual behavior in trend analysis of AIDS prevention program in Switzerland, 198–99

Cross-cultural issues. *See* Culture

Crowds, social networks and sexual behavior within, 336

Cuban Americans: and diversity among Hispanic subgroups, 114–15, 165; and self-identification of ethnicity, 117

Culture: and developmental framework for research on sexuality, 4–5; cross-cultural initiatives of AIDS and Reproductive Health Network/Working Group on Sexual Behavior Research, 14; and values of Hispanic populations, 119–21; and black community, 161; and differences in Hispanic national traditions, 164–65; language and issues of meaning, 166–70; and measurement of changes in sexual behavior over time, 213–14; diversity of among homosexual men, 271–72; overview of cross-cultural issues in sex research, 363–66; sex research in Papua New Guinea and public versus private, 371–73. *See also* Acculturation

Current Employment Survey, 48n.13

Daily diaries: versus retrospective interviews in assessment of sexual behavior of women in Scotland and the Philippines, 227–36; versus self-questionnaires in study of sexual behavior of adolescent females with STDs, 237–47

Decentering, and translation of research instruments, 121

Definitions. *See* Language; Terminology

Delamater, J., 62

Demographic class: variation in participation rates by, 278–79; variation in completion rates by, 279–80. *See also* Age; Class, socioeconomic; Ethnicity; Race

Demographic and Health Surveys, 10

Denmark: participation bias in postal survey of sexual behavior in, 282–83, 284

Design of survey research: effect of participation rates on, 277–78; of study of romantic partners of adolescents, 309–19; of study of sexuality in Papua New Guinea, 369–71; of Reach for Health Study among African American and Hispanic adolescents, 378–79

Detroit, Michigan: study of social structure of religious and ethnoreligious groups in, 397–98, 407–408

Development: and theoretical framework for research on sexuality, 4–5; and respondent-interviewer relationship, 431

Devereux, G., 64

Díaz, T., 137

Di Mauro, Diane, x–xi, 9, 30, 32, 349
Discussions of topics in sexuality research: of policy issues in, 23–33; of methodology issues related to interviews and interviewers, 78–83; of methodology issues related to specific contexts, 159–81; of measurement of changes in sexual behavior over time, 213–23; of retrospective interviews versus daily diaries for assessment of sexual behavior, 250–57; of participation bias in sexual behavior surveys, 288–95; of research on sexual networks, 320–36; of interactional sexual scripts, 346–51
Dissemination, sexuality research and mechanisms for, 7–8, 24
Diversity: and ethnicity among Hispanic population, 114–15, 118; among homosexual men, 271–72
Doll, Lynda: on methodology issues related to specific contexts, 173, 174, 176–78; on gender as issue in studies of bisexuality, 362
Dominican Americans, and diversity among Hispanic subgroups, 137
Dominican Republic: study of sex work in, 11n.4
Double-bind situation, and interviewer-respondent relationship, 70
Drug use: evidence of bias in data from personal visit surveys, 41–42; evidence of bias in data from telephone surveys, 42–44; and study of sexual behavior in adolescent women with STDs, 243, 245, 246–47. *See also* Cocaine; Substance use
Dubois-Arber, Françoise, xiii–xiv, 32–33, 213, 216
Dyads, as unit of analysis in relational approach to sexual behavior research, 300

Education: interview process as, 82; and sexuality research among Hispanic populations, 123; Latino men who have sex with men, and language used for data collection, 141; and sampling procedures in study of male homosexuality in the Netherlands, 268–69. *See also* Literacy; Sex education; Training of interviewers
Egocentric analysis, and social networks, 332–33, 394–95, 396, 407
Ehrhardt, Anke: on policy issues in sexuality research, 27, 33; on methodology issues related to interviews and interviewers, 78; on methodology issues related to specific contexts, 171, 177; on measurement of changes in sexual behavior over time, 218, 220; on sexual network analysis, 327–29; on interactional sexual scripts, 350
Elias, Norbert, 215
Embarrassment of interviewer during interview process, 70–71; of interviewer and wording of questions on sensitive behavior, 73–74; and participation bias in sexual behavior surveys, 282; as cross-cultural issue, 364
Emotion management, and skills of interviewers, 424
Epidemiology: and measurement of efficacy of prevention programs, 185; and classroom surveys, 376
Erbring, L., 392
Eroticism, and interviewer-respondent relationship, 75, 76
Error: participation bias as source of in sexual behavior studies, 284; sex research and concept of total survey, 356–60. *See also* Bias
Ethics, and randomized controlled trials, 219
Ethnicity: self-identification of among Hispanic populations, 116–18, 136–38; of interviewers and Latino men who have sex with men as study participants, 143; and differences in Hispanic cultural traditions, 164–65; and neighborhood as context for study of sexual networks, 303; of interviewers and sex research in Papua New Guinea, 370; and nonresponse in Reach for Health Study of adolescents, 380–81; and study of social structures of religious groups in Detroit, 397–98. *See also* Hispanic Americans
Ethnography, and studies of sexual networks, 304
Experimental evidence for participation bias in sexual behavior studies, 280–81
Extramarital sex, questions on and respondent discomfort or nonresponse, 420, 421

Family of AIDS Behavioral Survey (FABS), 116
Family Privacy Act, 294
Fantasies and interviewers, 71–72
Feedback loops, and interactional sexual scripts, 334
Female condom, international studies of social acceptability of, 12
Fertility, and surveys of sexual behavior, 88,

89. *See also* Reproductive health, and international research on sexuality
Flandrin, Jean-Louis, 215
Focus-group discussions, and sex research in Papua New Guinea, 371
Food and Drug Administration, 42
Ford Foundation, 6, 12
Forrest, J. D., 42
Fortenberry, Dennis: on retrospective interviews versus daily diaries for assessment of sexual behavior, 250–53, 255–56, 362; on sexual network analysis, 321
Fotoplatica: research instrument for use in sexuality research among Hispanic populations, 123
France: influence of policy on sexuality research in, 29–30, 31–32; survey on sex behavior and AIDS in, 61–76, 191–93; comparative study of sexual behavior and AIDS in Great Britain and, 193–94; and participation bias in sexual behavior surveys, 290–91
Frank, O., 400–401
Freeman, L. C., 403
Furstenburg, F., 87

Gagnon, J., 63, 351
Gatekeepers, to reach Latino men who have sex with men as study participants, 143
Gay: Latino men and definition of, 135. *See also* Homosexuality
Gender: and analysis of sexuality in context of developing world, 16; of interviewer and interviewer-respondent relationship, 73, 425, 431; and response bias in National AIDS Behavioral Survey, 106–109; and effect of question wording in National AIDS Behavioral Survey, 110–13; of interviewer and sexuality research among Hispanic populations, 118; traditional Hispanic culture and multiple sex partners, 120; and nonresponse bias for Hispanic Americans, 126–27; and participation rates in British survey, 280; differences of in interactional sexual scripts, 343–44; overview of impact on sexuality research, 361–62; of interviewers and sex research in Papua New Guinea, 370; and focus-group discussions in Papua New Guinea, 371, 372; and nonresponse in Reach for Health Study of African American and Hispanic adolescents, 380–81, 387; and patterns of nonresponse, 420–21. *See also* Males; Sex roles; Women
General Accounting Office, 38
General population surveys, and recent studies on bisexual behavior and female homosexuality, 146–47
General Social Surveys, 46, 146
Genetic sample, applications of in sexuality research, 312
Germany: AIDS and changes in use of terms for *condom*, 218
Gfroerer, J. C., 43n.b, 44
Ghana: study of sex work in, 11n.4
Giami, Alain: on methodology issues related to interviews and interviewers, 78, 80–81, 82; on methodology issues related to specific contexts, 170–71, 179, 180; on measurement of changes in sexual behavior over time, 215–16, 218–19; on retrospective interviews versus daily diaries for assessment of sexual behavior, 253; on participation bias in sexual behavior surveys, 290; on sexual network analysis, 324, 332; on interactional sexual scripts, 347, 350
Global Program on AIDS (World Health Organization), 11
Godelier, Maurice, 65, 332
Graham, Cynthia: on retrospective interviews versus daily diaries for assessment of sexual behavior, 250–54, 362; on participation bias in sexual behavior studies, 289, 290; on interactional sexual scripts, 351
Graph sampling, and analysis of social networks, 400–401
Great Britain: survey on gay and bisexual behavior in, 11n.3; study of sex work in, 11n.4; socioeconomic class and number of sexual partners, 24; influence of politics on sexuality research in, 28; comparative study of sexual behavior and AIDS in France and, 193–94; participation rates in studies of sexual behavior, 278–80, 283, 284; and incentives for research participants, 288–89
Greece: survey on gay and bisexual behavior in, 11n.3
Groves, R. M., 289, 432
Guatemala: intervention study on women and AIDS in, 13n.6
Guinea Bissau: national survey on AIDS, 11n.2
Guttmacher Foundation, 330

Hallinan, M. T., 403
Harry, J., 267n.9
Hart, Graham, 291–92
Harvard University, 393
Health, sexual: sexuality research and developmental models of, 3–4; focus on questions of in international sexuality research, 13. *See also* Public health; Reproductive health, and international research on sexuality
Health Education Quarterly, 168
Hedricks, Cynthia, 254
Heeren, T., 87
Heinz, J. P., 403–404
Help-seeking, and respondent-interviewer relationship, 423
Heterosexuality: and self-identification of sexual orientation, 263; and taxonomies of sexuality, 273n.17
Heuristic model for understanding of respondent-interviewer interactions, 421–30
High School and Beyond study, 87
Hingson, R., 87
Hispanic Americans: and methodological issues for research on sexual behavior among, 114–28; and sexual research with men who have sex with men (MSMs), 134–43; differences in national cultural traditions of, 164–65; nonresponse to questions about sex, substance use, and school in study of adolescents, 376–88
HIV (human immunodeficiency virus): and sexuality research on bisexual men, bisexual women, and lesbians, 149–50, 154; studies of programs for prevention of mother-to-child transmission of, 188–89; frequency of testing in Switzerland, 203; study of transmission risks within steady gay relationships in the Netherlands, 266–67. *See also* AIDS
HIV Prevention for the Family (Sabogal & Otero-Sabogal, 1990), 167
Homophobia: in Latin American environments, 142; and diversity among homosexual men, 271–72
Homosexuality: and national surveys on sexual behavior, 11n.2; adolescents and data collection via self-administered questionnaire versus audio-CASI, 48, 49; sexual research with Latino men who have sex with men (MSMs), 134–43; disaggregation of data on bisexuality and, 154–55;

culture and models of gay sexuality, 172; participation bias in studies of, 261–73, 284–85; and study of romantic relationships of adolescents, 314, 318; and social networks in Latino neighborhoods, 323–24; respondent discomfort or nonresponse to survey questions on, 421
Hormone therapy for premenstrual syndrome, 255
Hughes, A. L., 43n.b, 44
Humphreys, L., 265n.6

Identity: Hispanic populations and ethnic, 116–18. *See also* Sexual orientation
Incentives: and participation of adolescent males in survey, 92–93; and Latino men who have sex with men as study respondents, 143; and participation bias in sexual behavior surveys, 288–90; and respondent-interviewer relationship, 426
India: intervention study on women and AIDS in, 13n.6
Indianapolis: study of sexually transmitted disease prevention among adolescent females, 238–47
Information, social network analysis and flow of, 390–91, 408
Informed consent, and adolescents as study respondents, 91
Institute of Medicine, 37
Institute of Sex Research (Hamburg), 171
Institute for Survey Research, 90
Interactional approach, and research on sexual behavior, 300
Interactional behavior: sexual behavior surveys and coding of sexual scripts, 341–45
International Center for Research on Women, 13, 28
Interviewer, and survey research on sexuality: attitudes and representations of in survey on sexuality and AIDS in France, 61–76; discussion of methodology issues related to, 78–83; selection and training of for survey of adolescent males, 93; gender of and effect of question wording, 110, 113; and sexuality research with Latino men who have sex with men, 143; impact of characteristics of on survey research, 359; effectiveness of women as, 361; sex research in Papua New Guinea and characteristics of, 370; and model for

investigation of relationship with respondent, 417–33
Interviewer-administered questionnaires (IAQs): and data on drug use, 41–42
Interviewer ratings of sexual functioning (IRSF): in study of sexual behavior of women in Scotland and the Philippines, 228–30
Interviews: and training program for interviewers, 68; interviewers and experience of process, 70–72; discussion of methodology issues related to, 78–83; impact of changes in technology on survey research, 358–59
Ireland: negative social climate regarding homosexuality, 271n.15
Israel: survey on gay and bisexual behavior in, 11n.3

Jamaica: intervention study on women and AIDS in, 13n.6
Jenkins, Carol: on policy issues in sexuality research, 28–29; on methodology issues related to interviews and interviewers, 81–82; on measurement of changes in sexual behavior over time, 214–15, 220–23; on sexual network analysis, 321–22
Jessor, S. L., and R. Jessor, 87
Johnson, Anne: on policy issues in sexuality research, 24, 28; on methodology issues related to interviews and interviewers, 79; on methodology issues related to specific contexts, 162, 163, 172–73, 178, 179, 181; on measurement of change in sexual behavior over time, 214, 219; on participation bias in sexual behavior surveys, 288–91, 295
Johnson, W., 62
Jones, E. F., 42

Kantner, J. F., 87, 88, 94, 95
Kennedy, John, xv
Kenya: national survey on AIDS, 11n.2
Kinsey, Alfred, ix–x, xii, 27, 61–62, 146, 262, 293
Knoke, D., 409
Ku, Leighton C., 87, 166, 215, 217

Language: and audio-CASI technology, 46–47; and sexuality research among Hispanic populations, 118, 121–22, 138–41, 166, 168; culture and issues of meaning, 166–70, 364–65; and validity of indicators of sexual behavior in trend analysis of AIDS prevention program in Switzerland, 198; and changes in meaning over time, 200, 218; and measurement of changes in sexual behavior over time, 213; and definition of *homosexuality*, 262–63, 265, 272; and sex research in Papua New Guinea, 370; and respondent-interviewer relationship, 429–30. *See also* Question wording; Terminology; Translation
Latino: use of term, 114, 136. *See also* Hispanic Americans
Latino National Political Survey, 136
Laumann, Ed: on policy issues in sexuality research, 23, 26–27, 31; and data on anal intercourse, 52n.17; and interviewer training for National Health and Social Life Survey, 63; on methodology issues related to research in specific contexts, 161, 178; on measurement of changes in sexual behavior over time, 221–22; on estimates of prevalence of homosexuality, 262n.4; on participation bias in sexual behavior surveys, 283, 288; on sexual network research, 325–26, 328, 331–33, 335; and study of social structure among religious and ethnoreligious groups in Detroit, 397; on boundary specification problem in network analysis, 398; and methodology of social network analysis, 402; and study of Chicago bar of lawyers, 403–404; and study of social networks and AIDS, 410
Leitsch, Richard, 134
Lesbianism: qualitative assessment of recent studies of sexual behavior and, 145–56; subcultures and expression of, 272. *See also* Homosexuality
Lesotho: national survey on AIDS, 11n.2
Literacy: and limitations of self-administered questionnaires, 45; and audio-CASI, 47; and sexuality research among Hispanic populations, 123
Long-term trend, and reliability as methodological issue in trend analysis, 208–209
Luborsky, L., 342

MacArthur Foundation, 13
Males: study measuring sexual behavior among adolescent, 87–103; participation bias in samples of homosexuality, 261–73
Malgady, R. G., 139
Marín, Barbara: on methodology issues related to interviews and interviewers,

79–80; on methodology issues related to specific contexts, 159, 166–67; on measurement of changes in sexual behavior over time, 213, 221; on sexual network analysis, 333

Marsden, P. V., 398, 405

Matrix management, and research on sexual networks, 304–305

Maturity of interviewers in survey research, 359. *See also* Age

Mauritius: national survey on AIDS, 11n.2; intervention study on women and AIDS in, 13n.6

McKeown, T., 208

McPherson, J. M., 401–402

Measurement: discussion of changes in sexual behavior over time and, 213–23; determination of appropriate units of in survey research, 356; and error in survey research, 357–58

Media: and interaction between sexuality research and policy, 23–24; and recruitment of study participants, 289

Medical Innovation: A Diffusion Study (Coleman, Katz, & Menzel, 1966), 393

Medical Research Council (U.K.), 288–89

MEDLINE database, 145

Melbye, M., 282–83, 284

Memory: sexual interest and long-term, 253

Menstrual cycle: and daily diaries to assess sexual interest over, 253; and hormone therapy, 255

Men who have sex with men (MSMs): and sexual research with Hispanic populations, 134–43; introduction of term, 265

Methodology: and assessment report on status of research on sexuality, 5–8; and evidence of biases in measurements of sexual behavior, 37–56; interviewer attitudes and representations in survey of sexuality and AIDS in France, 61–76; discussion of issues related to interviews and interviewers, 78–83; and study measuring sexual behavior in male adolescents, 87–103; race and nonresponse rates in National AIDS Behavioral Survey, 106–109; effects of question wording in National AIDS Behavioral Survey, 110–13; issues of in sexual behavior research among Hispanics, 114–28; and sexual research with Latino men who have sex with men (MSMs), 134–43; qualitative assessment of recent studies of bisexual men, bisexual women, and lesbians, 145–56; discussion of issues related to specific research contexts, 159–81; problems in trend analysis of sexual behavior, 196–210; and participation bias, 276–86; overview of sex surveys in context of survey research, 355–60; and cross-cultural issues in sex research, 363–66; samples and measurement of social networks, 390–411

Mexican Americans: and diversity among Hispanic subgroups, 114, 137–38, 165; homosexuality and social networks, 323

Michaels, Stuart: on policy issues in sexuality research, 24–25, 27–28; on methodology issues related to interviews and interviewers, 82–83; on methodology issues related to specific contexts, 161, 167, 171–72, 175–76; on retrospective interviews versus daily diaries for assessment of sexual behavior, 256–57; on participation bias in sexual behavior surveys, 291, 295; on sexual network analysis, 320–28, 334

Milgram, S., 399–400

Miller, P. Y., 87

Moore, K., 87

Morris, M., 410

Mosher, W. D., 87

Motivations: of interviewers in survey of sexuality and AIDS in France, 68–69; ambivalence and dynamics of interviewer, 71; and incentives for research participation, 290, 292; disclosure of by researchers, 292–94; and respondent-interviewer relationship, 426–27

Multidisciplinary approach: and Sexuality Research Fellowship Program, 6–7; and theory as issue in sex research projects, 222–23

Multiplicity sampling, and social network analysis, 409–10

Myers, Ted, 168–69, 216, 222, 288

Narratives: and interactional sexual scripts, 341; morphology of folk and formulaic structures in, 348–49; and study of attempted suicide, 351

National Academy of Sciences, 37, 39, 41

National AIDS Behavioral Survey (NABS), 38–39, 50–53, 106–109, 110–13, 116, 146, 164, 194–95

National Center for Education Statistics, 45

National Commission on AIDS, 38

National Health and Social Life Survey, 38n.1, 63, 118, 146, 394n.1
National Household Seroprevalence Survey, 146, 288
National Household Survey on Drug Abuse (NHSDA), 41, 42–44
National Institute of Child Health and Human Development, 309
National Institutes of Health, 38
National Longitudinal Study of Adolescent Health (Add Health), 309–19
National Longitudinal Survey of Labor Market Experience, Youth Cohort (NLS-Y), 42
National Longitudinal Survey of Youth, 87
National and Maternal Infant Health Survey, 100
National Opinion Research Center (NORC), University of Chicago, 63
National Research Council, 4
National Survey of Adolescent Males (NSAM), 47–49, 87–103
National Survey of Family Growth (NSFG), 42, 47, 88, 89, 95, 100, 288
National Survey of Health and Social Life Study (NHSLS), 299
National Survey of Men, 38n.1
National surveys, on partner relations and AIDS, 11n.2
National Surveys of Young Women, 88, 94
Nature (journal), 74n.6
Neighborhood: as context for study of sexual networks, 302–306; and design of study of romantic partners of adolescents, 312; homosexuality and social networks in Latino, 323–24
The Netherlands: survey on gay and bisexual behavior in, 11n.3; study of interrelation of different aspects of homosexuality, 262–64; study of HIV risks within steady gay relationships, 266–67, 268–70
Network analysis: relevancy of to survey research, 390–411. *See also* Sexual networks; Social networks
Newcomer, Susan, 250
New York: and Reach for Health Study of African American and Hispanic adolescents, 378
Nonresponse in survey research: and limitations of self-administered questionnaires, 45; and race in National AIDS Behavioral Survey, 106–109, 163–64; and bias in sexuality research among Hispanic populations, 124–27; changes in over time, and trend analysis of AIDS prevention program in Switzerland, 204–205; and sex surveys in context of survey research, 359; in study of sex, substance use, and school among African American and Hispanic adolescents, 376–88; and topic sensitivity, 419. *See also* Zero response
Northern California Communities Study, 408

Objective culture: definition of culture and concept of, 363
Occupation, and sex research in Papua New Guinea, 370
O'Donnell, Lydia, xvi
Oral sex: telephone audio-CASI (ACASI) and data on, 54; terminology and interviewer embarrassment, 73–74
Organizations: Latino gay and recruitment of study subjects, 142; gay and lesbian in the Netherlands and recruitment of study subjects, 268, 295; donations to as form of incentive, 289; social networks and Latino gay, 323

Papua New Guinea: intervention study on women and AIDS in, 13n.6, 28–29; AIDS prevention programs and sex education in, 220–21; qualitative methods in sex research in, 369–74
Papua New Guinea Institute of Medical Research (PNGIMR), 370
Parental consent, and surveys with adolescent respondents, 90–92, 378–79
Parker, Richard: on policy issues in sexuality research, 23–26; on sexual self-identity, 135–36; on methodology issues related to specific contexts, 161, 164, 169–70, 171, 176–77; on sexual network analysis, 320; on interactional sexual scripts, 348–49
Participation bias: and studies of male homosexuality, 261–73; assessment of as methodological issue, 276–86; discussion on methodological issues related to, 288–95; sex surveys in context of survey research, 357; in Reach for Health Study of African American and Hispanic adolescents, 378–79
Peer-reviewed literature: and studies of bisexual men, bisexual women, and lesbians, 147–56
Personal Influence: The Part Played by People in the Flow of Mass Communications (Katz & Lazarfeld, 1955), 393

Personal visit surveys: evidence of bias in measurements of sexual behavior from, 41–42
Person-perception paradigm: and respondent-interviewer relationship, 429
Peterson, John, xiii, 87
Philippines: urban center survey on AIDS in, 11n.2; study of sexual interest and activity in women, 227–36
Physical attraction: aspects of homosexuality and same-sex, 263
Planned Parenthood Poll, 94
Pleck, J. H., 87
Policy: influence of recent international sex research on formation of, 16–19; discussion of issues of in sexuality research and, 23–33
Politics: and historical context of sexuality research, 4; and funding for sexuality research, 24–25; and government withdrawal of support for surveys of sexual behavior, 87; and general population sexuality surveys, 146; social network analysis and study of party affiliation, 409
Pomeroy, W., 62
Porto, M. D., 137
Postal survey of sexual behavior in Denmark, 282–83
Postmodernism, and criticism of value of surveys, 360
Prediction of sexual behavior of adolescents, 318
Pregnancy: concern about teenage as motivation for studies of sexual behavior, 88, 89; and data on contraceptive use in survey of sexual behavior among adolescent males, 100–101
Premenstrual syndrome: hormone therapy for, 255
Prensky, D., 398
Presidential Commission on the HIV Epidemic, 38
Pretesting, and translation of research instruments, 121–22, 167
Prevention programs: repeated population surveys and evaluation of efficacy of for AIDS, 185–95; trend analysis of AIDS program in Switzerland, 197–210; study of sexually transmitted disease among adolescent females, 238–47
Private culture, and sex research in Papua New Guinea, 371–73
Process analysis: and causal relationship between action and observed modification, 186
Project HOPE Survey of AIDS-Risk Behaviors, 146
Prostitutes and prostitution: and trend analysis of AIDS prevention program in Switzerland, 206
Pryor, D. W., 156
PSYCHLIT database, 145
Psychology, and Sexuality Research Fellowship, 6
Public culture, and sex research in Papua New Guinea, 371–73
Public health: and studies of sexual behavior of adolescents, 88; short-term and long-term trends in, 208
Public opinion: influence of media on, 24; on HIV blood testing in France, 194
Puerto Ricans: and diversity among Hispanic subgroups, 114, 137, 165; and national variations in use of Spanish, 138, 139; homosexuality and social networks, 323–24

Qualitative research: integration with quantitative methods in research on sexuality, 5–6, 356; and Sexuality Research Fellowship Program, 6–7; and studies of bisexual men, bisexual women, and lesbians, 151–52, 153, 156; integration with quantitative methods in studies of sexual networks, 299–307; and sex research in Papua New Guinea, 369–74
Quality: issues and concerns related to survey data on sexual behavior, 39, 41
Quantitative research: integration with qualitative methods in research on sexuality, 5–6, 356; and studies of bisexual men, bisexual women, and lesbians, 151–52, 153, 156; integration with qualitative methods in studies of sexual networks, 299–307; and qualitative data from sex research in Papua New Guinea, 374
Questionnaire: problems in construction of, 83; and survey of sexual behavior among adolescent males, 93–95. *See also* Language
Questionnaire-based surveys: interviewer attitudes and representations in study of sexuality and AIDS in France, 61–76
Question wording: and interviewer embarrassment, 73–74; and survey of sexual behavior among adolescent males, 95–97; effect of in National AIDS Behavioral Sur-

vey, 110–13; and sensitive behaviors, 162–63. *See also* Language; Terminology

Race: and item nonresponse in National AIDS Behavior Survey, 106–109; Hispanics and self-categorization of, 116–18; and diversity of Hispanic population, 118; and social class, 159; and study of prevention of sexually transmitted disease in adolescent women, 240, 241. *See also* African Americans; Ethnicity
Randomized controlled trials (RCTs): ethics of, 219
Randomized design: and studies of efficacy of AIDS prevention campaigns, 187–88
Rape: factors in nonresponse to questions on, 420, 421
Rapoport, A., 400
Reach for Health Study, 378–88
"Reconceiving Sexuality: International Approaches to Gender, Sexuality and Health" (conference, 1996), 15, 361
Recruitment, of Latino men who have sex with men as research participants, 141–43
Reining, P., 374
Reisman, Judith, 33
Relational approach: and research on sexual behavior and sexual networks, 300; and study of social structure of religious and ethnoreligious groups in Detroit, 397, 399, 405, 408
Relationships. *See* Interviewer; Respondents; Sexual partners; Sexual relationships; Social networks
Reliability: of reports of sexual experience in survey of sexual behavior among adolescent males, 98–100; of indicators of sexual behavior in trend analysis of AIDS prevention program in Switzerland, 198–99, 205–10
Religion: and homophobia, 271; and study of social networks and ethnicity in Detroit, 397–98. *See also* Catholic Church
Repeated surveys, and evaluation of efficacy of AIDS prevention campaigns, 185–95
Representation of sexuality by interviewer, 72–74. *See also* Self-representation
Reproductive health, and international research on sexuality, 10–13
Research. *See* Methodology; Sexuality research; Survey research

Researcher error: as issue in survey research, 359–60
Research Triangle Institute (RTI), 46, 90, 94, 382
Respeto: and cultural values of Hispanic Americans, 119, 120
Response rates: survey research and adolescent males, 89, 90. *See also* Nonresponse in survey research
Respondents to surveys on sexual behavior: preferences for T-ACASI to telephone interviews using human interviewer, 52; establishment of interviewer-respondent relationship, 64–65, 69–70; and model for investigation of interviewer-respondent relationship, 417–33
Retrospective interviews: versus daily diaries in assessment of sexual behavior of women in Scotland and the Philippines, 227–36
Risman, B., 152, 155
Rockefeller Foundation, 4, 12
Rodriguez, O., 139
Roger, L. H., 139
Romantic partners, research design for study on, 309–19. *See also* Sexual partners

Sabogal, Fabio: on methodology issues related to specific contexts, 164–69; on sexual network analysis, 322; on interactional sexual scripts, 348
Samoa: survey of sexual behavior in Western, 373
Sampling and sample size: and specific context of research, 178–80; as technical problem in trend analysis of AIDS prevention program in Switzerland, 205–208; studies of homosexuality and definition of study population, 266–70; and Reach for Health Study of African American and Hispanic adolescents, 379–81
Sanders, Stephanie, 322
Sandfort, Theo: on policy issues in sexuality research, 30, 31, 33; on methodology issues related to interviews and interviewers, 79; on methodology issues related to specific contexts, 160, 163; on measurement of changes in sexual behavior over time, 222; on participation bias in sexual behavior surveys, 291–93
Schmidt, Gunter, 171, 218
Schools: and study of romantic partners of adolescents, 310–13; African American

Index | 457

and Hispanic adolescents and study of sex, substance use, and, 376–88
Schwartz, P., 152, 155–57
Science: data collection and culture of, 364
Scotland: study of sexual interest and activity in women, 227–36
Seasonality of adolescent sexual activity, 245
Secrecy and sexuality in Papua New Guinea, 373–74
Self-acceptance: concept of and social science studies on homosexuality, 272n.16
Self-administered questionnaires (SAQs): and data on prevalence of illicit drug use, 41; limitations on use of, 44–46; and sensitive behaviors in survey of sexual behavior among adolescent males, 94–95; versus daily diaries in study of sexual behavior in adolescent females with STDs, 237–47; adolescents and anonymity of, 376
Self-disclosure: question wording and theory of, 110; Hispanic cultural characteristics and, 119, 120; and respondent-interviewer relationship, 418, 428
Self-identity: and sexual orientation of Latino men who have sex with men, 135–36; and sexual orientation of male homosexuals, 263. *See also* Identity
Self-presentation: as source of bias in study of sexual behavior in adolescent females with STDs, 247. *See also* Social acceptability/desirability
Self-representation: in interactional sexual scripts, 347. *See also* Representation of sexuality by interviewer
Sensitive behaviors: and T-ACASI technology, 52–55; and survey of sexual behavior among adolescent males, 94–95; and question wording, 162–63; and participation bias, 291; respondent-interviewer relationship and disclosure of, 418–21. *See also* Anal intercourse; Condoms
Sex and AIDS Methodology Survey, 124
Sex Diary of a Metaphysician (Wilson, 1963), 253
Sex education: AIDS and ethics of randomized controlled trials, 219–21
Sex roles: among Hispanic subgroups, 115; and gender stereotypes as source of bias in sexual behavior surveys, 431–32
Sexual behavior: evidence of biases in survey measurement of, 37–56; measurement of among adolescent males, 87–103; future research and development of explanations of, 102; methodological issues for research among Hispanics, 114–28; qualitative assessment of recent studies of bisexual men, bisexual women, and lesbians, 145–56; retrospective versus daily assessment in study of women in Scotland and the Philippines, 227–36; evidence for participation bias in surveys of, 281–84; prediction of in adolescents, 318; influence of interpersonal perceptions on, 332; and crowds, 336; in context of gender, 361; cultural scripts of, 365
—change in over time: repeated population surveys and evaluation of efficacy of AIDS prevention programs, 185–95; problems of methodology in trend analysis of, 196–210; discussion of issues related to measurement of, 213–23
Sexual dysfunction: respondent discomfort or nonresponse to questions on, 420, 421
Sexual experience: measuring levels of in survey of sexual behavior among adolescent males, 97–98; reliability of reports of in survey of sexual behavior among male adolescents, 98–100
Sexual interactions: and coding of sexual scripts, 341–45; discussion of, 346–51
Sexual intercourse: problems with definition of in survey of sexual behavior among adolescent males, 95–97, 99; frequency of in study of sexual behavior in adolescent females with STDs, 240–42
Sexuality: reconception of in context of developing world, 13–16; complexity of communication about in professional context, 75–76; culture and models of gay, 172; differences in concepts of across time and societies, 200, 202–203; need for interdisciplinary theoretical model of, 223; need for expanded taxonomies of, 273n.17; as form of sexual interaction, 299; sexual behavior in context of, 361; and secrecy in Papua New Guinea, 373–74
Sexuality research: recent increase in, ix; overview of methodological issues in, ix–xi; influence of AIDS crisis on, xvi; assessment report on, 3–8; review of recent international initiatives, 9–20; evidence of biases in measurements of sexual behavior, 37–56; interviewer attitudes and representations in survey of sexuality and AIDS in

France, 61–76; discussion of issues related to interviews and interviewers, 78–83; measurement of sexual behavior among adolescent males, 87–103; race and nonresponse in National AIDS Behavioral Survey, 106–109; effect of question wording in National AIDS Behavioral Survey, 110–13; sexual research with Latino men who have sex with men, 134–43; qualitative assessment of recent studies of sexual behavior of bisexual men, bisexual women, and lesbians, 145–56; repeated population surveys and efficacy of AIDS prevention campaigns, 185–95; methodological problems in trend analysis of changes in sexual behavior, 196–210; retrospective interviews versus daily diaries in assessment of sexual behavior of women in Scotland and the Philippines, 227–36; self-questionnaires versus daily diaries in study of sexual behavior in adolescent females with STDs, 237–47; participation bias in samples of male homosexuality, 261–73; and assessment of participation bias as methodological issue, 276–86; quantitative and qualitative methods in studies of sexual networks, 299–307; design for study of romantic partners, 309–19; coding of interactional sexual scripts, 341–45; overview of in context of survey research, 355–60; gender as issue in, 361–62; cross-cultural issues in, 363–66; and qualitative methods and study in Papua New Guinea, 369–74; nonresponse to questions about sex, substance use, and school by African American and Hispanic adolescents, 376–88; measurement of social networks by samples, 390–411; and interviewer-respondent relationship, 417–33
—Discussions: on policy and, 23–33; on methodology issues related to interviews and interviewers, 78–83; on methodology issues related to specific contexts, 159–81; on measurements of changes in sexual behavior over time, 213–23; on retrospective interviews versus daily diaries in assessment of sexual behavior, 250–57; on participation bias in sexual behavior surveys, 288–95; on sexual behavior research on sexual networks, 320–36; on interactional sexual scripts, 346–51
Sexuality Research Assessment Project, 30–31

Sexuality Research Fellowship Program, 3–8, 32
Sexuality Research in the United States (di Mauro, 1995), 3–8
Sexually transmitted diseases (STDs): concern about in adolescents as motivation for studies of sexual behavior, 88; and survey of sexual behavior among adolescent males, 101; rate of among Hispanic Americans, 115; study of prevention program in Tanzania, 189, 190; self-questionnaires versus daily diaries in study of sexual behavior in adolescent females with, 237–47; and analysis of social networks, 410
Sexual negotiation, international studies of, 12
Sexual networks: integration of quantitative and qualitative methods in study of, 299–307; design of study on romantic partners, 309–19. *See also* Social networks
Sexual orientation: and effect of question wording, 112; and sexual self-identity of Latino men who have sex with men (MSMs), 135–36. *See also* Homosexuality; Lesbianism
Sexual partners: numbers of and socioeconomic class in Great Britain, 24; partner-by-partner accounts of sexual behavior in survey of adolescent males, 97–98; future research and problem of getting information about, 102–103; and Hispanic culture and gender, 120; and study of sexual behavior and AIDS in France, 191–92; and changes in meanings of terms over time, 200; and trend analysis of AIDS prevention program in Switzerland, 207; and study of sexual behavior in adolescent females with STDs, 242–43, 244, 246; design of study on romantic partners, 309–19; social networks and study of, 325–26; egocentric networks of, 395; in-group biases and STDs, 410. *See also* Sexual relationships
Sexual relationships: telephone audio-CASI (T-ACASI) and data on stability and quality of, 54–55; interviewer-respondent relationship as, 72; and changes in meanings of terms over time, 200; study on HIV risks within steady gay relationships in the Netherlands, 266–67; explanations for shorter average duration of gay, 272. *See also* Sexual partners

Sexual scripts: coding of interactional, 341–45; discussion of research on sexual interactions and, 346–51
Sex work, national studies on, 11n.4
Short-term trend, and reliability as methodological issue in trend analysis, 208–209
Simon, P., 63, 202, 215
Simon, W., 87
Simpatía: and cultural values of Hispanic Americans, 119, 120, 387
Singapore: national survey on AIDS, 11n.2
Smith, T. W., 46, 284
Social acceptability/desirability: as source of bias in sexual behavior surveys, 186–87; and validity as problem in trend analysis of AIDS prevention program in Switzerland, 203–204; and respondent-interviewer relationship, 427
Social and Behavioral Research Unit (WHO/GPA/SBR), 11
Social and Behavioral Studies and Support Unit (WHO/GPA/SSB), 11–12
Social construction of sexuality: and reconceptualization of sexuality in context of developing world, 15–16, 23
Social desirability. *See* Social acceptability/desirability
Social interaction, sexuality as form of, 299
Social movement, and issue of values in sexuality research, 26–28
Social networks: and research on sexual networks, 323–26; anthropology and concept of, 331; and egocentric networks, 332–33; and relational aspects of social reality, 334; sexual behavior and "equal status contact," 336; samples and measurement of, 390–411. *See also* Sexual networks
The Social Organization of Sexuality (Laumann et al., 1994), 299, 325–26
Social Science Research Council, 3, 5–8
Social sciences: current status of sexuality research in, 3–4; and policy implications of sexuality research, 17–18
Social support, and social network analysis, 391
Society: and developmental framework for research on sexuality, 4–5. *See also* Social networks
Sociocentric analysis: and social networks, 393–94, 395, 396
Sociology: and Sexuality Research Fellowship, 6; micro-macro problem in, 395–96

Sonenstein, Freya L., xii–xiii, 87, 215
Sorensen, R., 87
South Africa: intervention study on women and AIDS in, 13n.6
South Americans, and diversity among Hispanic subgroups, 115, 165
Spain: survey on gay and bisexual behavior in, 11n.3
Special education, and classroom surveys of sexual behavior, 379, 382, 383, 387
Special Program of Research, Development, and Research Training in Human Reproduction (WHO/HRP), 12
Spira, Alfred: on policy issues in sexuality research, 29–33; on methodology issues related to interviews and interviewers, 81; on methodology issues related to specific contexts, 179–81; on measurement of changes in sexual behavior over time, 213, 216–18; on participation bias in sexual behavior surveys, 290–91; on interactional sexual scripts, 347
Sri Lanka: national survey on AIDS, 11n.2
Stakeholders: roles of and analysis of social networks, 394n.1
State University of Rio de Janeiro, Program on Gender, Sexuality and Health in Institute of Social Medicine, 14–15
Stigmatization: as cross-cultural concept, 363–64
Stigmatized behavior. *See* Sensitive behaviors
Strunin, L., 87
Stueve, Ann: on methodology issues related to specific contexts, 160–61; on measurement of changes in sexual behavior over time, 217; on participation bias in sexual behavior surveys, 294; on sexual network analysis, 335
Subcoital behaviors, and studies of romantic relationships, 321
Subculture: recruitment of study subjects and homosexual, 265; developing internationalization of gay, 271; as crucial factor in expression of homosexuality, 272; and cross-cultural issues in sex research, 365
Subgraphs, and analysis of social networks, 401
Subgroups: social network analysis and identification of socially relevant, 402–406
Subjective culture: definition of culture and concept of, 363

Subjectivity: and representations of sexuality and AIDS by interviewers, 64–65
Substance use: nonresponse in study of sex, school, and among African American and Hispanic adolescents, 376–88. *See also* Alcohol use; Cocaine; Drug use
Sudman, S., 63, 112, 161, 417, 424
Suicide: narrative analysis and study of attempted, 351
Sumaya, C. V., 137
Sundet, J., 62
Survey research: recent increase in sexual behavior studies, ix; evidence of biases in measurements of sexual behavior, 37–56; and sampling size, 178–80; repeated population surveys and evaluation of change over time, 185–95; effect of participation rates on study design, 277–78; overview of sex surveys in context of, 355–60; relevancy of network analysis to, 390–411; and model for investigation of respondent-interviewer relationship in sex research, 417–33
Switzerland: trend analysis and evaluation of AIDS prevention program, 197–210

Talking Posters, and sexuality research among Hispanic populations, 123
Tanfer, K., 38n.1
Tanzania: national survey on AIDS, 11n.2; study on efficacy of STD prevention program, 189, 190
Telephone audio-CASI technology (T-ACASI): and bias in survey measurements of sexual behavior, 48–53; future research and, 53, 56; discussion of impact on sex research, 79
Telephone surveys: NIH-funded on AIDS-related behavior, 38–40; evidence of bias in measurements of sexual behavior from, 42–44; of sexual behavior among Hispanic populations, 115–16, 120, 127; and daily diaries, 256. *See also* Telephone audio-CASI technology
Temple University, 90, 92
Terminology: survey of sexual behavior among adolescent males and use of informal, 95–97; and ethnic self-identification among Hispanics, 117; sexual slang and national variations in use of Spanish, 138–40, 430; and surveys of homosexuality, 262–63, 265; and respondent-interviewer relationship, 429–30. *See also* Language; Question wording
Thailand: national survey on AIDS, 11n.2; study of sex work in, 11n.4; intervention study on women and AIDS in, 13n.6; study of sexual networks in, 330
Thatcher, Margaret, 28
Theory: and multidisciplinary approaches to sexuality research, 222–23; survey research and postmodernist, 360; and micro-macro problem in sociology, 395–96; model for understanding survey participation, 417; heuristic model for understanding respondent-interviewer interactions, 421–30
Third-person attributes, of sexual partners in study of adolescents, 317
Tiefer, Leonore: on policy issues in sexuality research, 25; on methodology issues related to interviews and interviewers, 79, 82; on methodology issues related to specific contexts, 168, 179; on measurement of changes in sexual behavior over time, 214, 223; on retrospective interviews versus daily diaries for assessment of sexual behavior, 256; on participation bias in sexual behavior surveys, 292–93; on sexual network analysis, 325, 326, 335; on gender issues in sexuality research, 362
Time: Hispanic culture and attitude toward, 120; and temporal stability in Reach for Health Study of African American and Hispanic adolescents, 388
Togo: national survey on AIDS, 11n.2
Training of interviewers: need for comprehensive in sexuality research, 7, 23; and qualitative survey of interviewers, 65; and survey of sexuality and AIDS in France, 66–68; and interviewer-respondent relationship, 80, 423–26; and sexual behavior survey of adolescent males, 93. *See also* Education
Translation: sexuality research among Hispanic populations and procedures of, 121–22. *See also* Language
Travers, J., 399
Trend analysis of sexual behavior and methodological problems, 196–210
Turner, Charles, ix, xi, xii, xiv: on policy issues in sexuality research, 23; and National Survey of Adolescent Males, 47n.12, 50n.14; on methodology issues related to interviews and interviewers, 78, 79, 89;

on methodology issues related to specific contexts, 173, 178; on measurement of changes in sexual behavior over time, 214, 215, 220; on participation bias in sexual behavior surveys, 277, 288; on sexual network analysis, 329
Turner, Heather, 289

Udry, Richard: and research on sexual behavior of adolescents, 87, 96n.2; on methodology issues related to specific contexts, 162, 178–79, 180; on retrospective interviews versus daily diaries for assessment of sexual behavior, 252; on sexual network analysis, 321, 322, 325, 329–35
University of Chicago, sex and gender faculty seminar, 23. *See also* National Opinion Research Center
University of Michigan, 46n.9, 393
Urban Men's Health Survey, 53
Urban environments and urbanization: and diversity of homosexuality, 272; metropolitan areas as focus of research on sexual networks, 301–302. *See also* Neighborhood
Urine specimens, and survey of sexual behavior among adolescent males, 101
USAID: funding of international research on sexuality, 10; support for initiatives related to women and AIDS, 12–13

Validation: and alternative measures of sexual or contraceptive behaviors among adolescent males, 100–101
Validity: and trend analysis of AIDS prevention program in Switzerland, 197–98, 199–205; and participation bias in survey research, 277; and study of romantic partners of adolescents, 316–17
Values: issue of in research on sexuality, xi–xii; and policy implications of sexuality research, 17–18; and linkages between social movements and sexuality research, 26–28; interviewers and conflict during interview, 69; and culture of Hispanic Americans, 119–21; and biases of researcher, 293–94

Verbrugge, L. M., 403
Violence, sexual: data collection and question wording, 162–63. *See also* Rape
Voting: A Study of Opinion Formation in a Presidential Campaign (Berelson, Lazarsfeld, & McPhee, 1954), 393

Wadsworth, J., 284
Weinberg, M. S., 156, 265n.7, 294
Wellcome Trust, 28
Wellman, B., 391, 394
Williams, Colin: on methodology issues related to interviews and interviewers, 78; on methodology issues related to specific contexts, 156, 159, 165, 174, 175, 176, 177; on retrospective interviews versus daily diaries for assessment of sexual behavior, 254; on participation bias in sexual behavior surveys, 294; on sexual network analysis, 335; on randomized samples of bisexual men and women, 362
Williams, R. A., 403
Wilson, Colin, 253
Women: retrospective interviews versus daily diaries in assessment of sexual behavior in Scotland and the Philippines, 227–36; and hormone therapy for premenstrual syndrome, 255; as interviewers in sexuality research, 361, 425; as participants in sexuality research, 361–62. *See also* Gender
Working Group on Sexual Behavior Research (WGSB), 13–15
World Fertility Surveys (WFS), 10
World Health Organization (WHO), 10–12

Young, A. A., 392
Youth Risk Behavior Survey (CDC), 87, 91

Zambia: urban center survey on AIDS, 11n.2
Zelnik, M., 87, 88, 94, 95
Zero response: and differential responses among Hispanics, 125–27. *See also* Nonresponse in survey research
Zimbabwe: intervention study on women and AIDS in, 13n.6